Public Broadcasting and European Law

A Comparative Examination of
Public Service Obligations in Six Member States

KLUWER LAW INTERNATIONAL

Public Broadcasting and European Law

A Comparative Examination of Public Service Obligations in Six Member States

Irini Katsirea

Wolters Kluwer
Law & Business

AUSTIN BOSTON CHICAGO NEW YORK THE NETHERLANDS

Published by:
Kluwer Law International
PO Box 316
2400 AH Alphen aan den Rijn
The Netherlands
Website: www.kluwerlaw.com

Sold and distributed in North, Central and South America by:
Aspen Publishers, Inc.
7201 McKinney Circle
Frederick, MD 21704
United States of America
Email: customer.care@aspenpubl.com

Sold and distributed in all other countries by:
Turpin Distribution Services Ltd.
Stratton Business Park
Pegasus Drive, Biggleswade
Bedfordshire SG18 8TQ
United Kingdom
Email: kluwerlaw@turpin-distribution.com

ISBN 978-90-411-2500-2

Information Law Series

Volume 17

General Editor

Prof. P. Bernt Hugenholtz

Institute for Information Law, University of Amsterdam

The titles published in this series are listed at the back of this volume.

For Katerina

Acknowledgments

Many scholars have helped me in various ways since I started working on European broadcasting law almost ten years ago, and I wish to express my gratitude to all of them. Special thanks are due to Alan A. Dashwood for his guidance and support throughout my research. I would like to thank Malcolm Ross for having awakened my interest in the cultural dimension of European Union law. For comments on the European law part of this book I am also grateful to Philip Allott, Rachael Craufurd-Smith, Michael Dougan, Meinhard Hilf, Joanne Scott and Bruno de Witte.

For suggestions on specific points and chapters of the comparative part of the book I am indebted to Eric Barendt, Georgina Born, Egbert Dommering, Nico van Eijk, Thomas Gibbons, Bernd Holznagel, Ioanna Kiki, Karl-Nikolaus Peifer and Zenon Zencovich. They, as well as Bernt Hugenholtz and Tarlach McGonagle, have contributed to this book with their incisive comments. I wish to thank my research assistants, Rosa Maria Ballardini, Rosa Hamming and Alexander Juechser whose dedication and thorough research have been invaluable; many thanks to the Leverhulme Trust for funding their work. I am grateful to my colleague Brenda Barrett for reading a first draft and commenting on the substance and style. Finally, I wish to acknowledge my first teachers – Detlef Leenen, Martin Nettesheim and Albert Randelzhofer – who remain inspiring models.

A number of officials at the broadcasting authorities also offered advice and assistance, for which I am deeply grateful: Georgios Anagnostaras of the Greek National Council of Radio and Television; Monica Arino of Ofcom; François David, Nicole Gendry and Caroline Grinberg-Labourdette of the *Conseil Superieur de l'Audiovisuel*; Marcel Betzel and Edmund Lauf of the *Commissariaat voor de Media*; Lisa Feliciantonio, Mirelle Lefosse, Andrea Stazi and their colleagues of the AGCOM. Among the officials in the Commission and the Council who willingly gave their time to answer my questions, special thanks to Anna Herold.

I have benefited from generous financial support from the following organizations, to which I am indebted: the Cambridge European Trust, Magdalene College, Cambridge, and foremost the Leverhulme Trust. A research fellowship at Middlesex University that lightened my lectureship duties for a period of three years is also gratefully acknowledged.

I would like to record my warm appreciation to the staff in the following libraries in Belgium, Britain, France, Germany, Greece, Italy and the Netherlands: the Libraries of the Council and of the Commission of the European Union; Bodleian Library; British Library; Cambridge University Library and Squire Law Library; Institute of Advanced Legal Studies, London; Bibliothèque Nationale, Paris; Abteilung Europäisches Gemeinschaftsrecht, Hamburg; Institute for Information-, Telecommunications-, and Media Law, Münster; Institute of Media and Communications Law, Cologne; Max-Planck-Institute for Intellectual Property, Competition and Tax Law, Munich; Bar Association, Athens; European University Institute, Florence; Institute for Information Law, Amsterdam.

On a more personal note, I wish to thank my parents for their unfailing support and my husband, Stefan, who has not only encouraged me but also accompanied me in my research trips and provided meticulous editorial assistance. I also owe many thanks to Maria Papadopoulou for selflessly assisting me in my research. Finally, this book is dedicated to my young daughter, Katerina, for all the hours she had to spend without me while I was researching and writing.

Table of Contents

Table of Abbreviations

AfP	*Archiv für Presserecht*
AmJCompL	*American Journal of Comparative Law*
AöR	*Archiv des öffentlichen Rechts*
AVMS	*Audiovisual Media Services*
BayVwBl	*Bayerisches Verwaltungsblatt*
BFI	British Film Institute
BGBl	*Bundesgesetzblatt*
CardozoArts&EntLJ	*Cardozo Arts and Entertainment Law Journal*
CDE	*Cahiers de Droit Européen*
CMLRev	*Common Market Law Review*
ColumJEurL	*Columbia Journal of European Law*
CR	*Computer und Recht*
ΔEE	*Dikaio Epixeireseon kai Etaireion*
ΔιMEE	*Dikaio Meson Enemeroses kai Epikoinonias*
DÖV	*Die Öffentliche Verwaltung*
DVBl	*Deutsches Verwaltungsblatt*
ECLR	*European Competition Law Review*
EΔΔΔ	*Epitheorese Demosiou Dikaiou kai Dioiketikou Dikaiou*
EIPR	*European Intellectual Property Review*
ELJ	*European Law Journal*
EλλΔ	*Ellenike Dikaiosine*
ELRev	*European Law Review*
EMLR	*Entertainment and Media Law Reports*
ENT L R	*Entertainment Law Review*
EPL	*European Public Law*
EPRA	European Platform of Regulatory Authorities
EStAL	*European State Aid Law Quarterly*

ETS	*European Treaty Series*
EuR	*Europarecht*
EuZW	*Europäische Zeitschrift für Wirtschaftsrecht*
EWS	*Europäisches Wirtschafts- und Steuerrecht*
Fordham Int'l L J	*Fordham International Law Journal*
GG	*Grundgesetz*
GRUR Int.	*Gewerblicher Rechtsschutz und Urheberrecht International*
GV. NRW	*Gesetz- und Verordnungsblatt für das Land Nordrhein-Westfalen*
GVOBl. M-V	*Gesetz- und Verordnungsblatt für Mecklenburg-Vorpommern*
Hastings Int'l&CompLRev.	*Hastings International and Comparative Law Review*
ICLQ	*International and Comparative Law Quarterly*
IJCLP	*International Journal of Communications Law and Policy*
ILM	*International Legal Materials*
Int'l&CompLRev	*International and Comparative Law Review*
JCMS	*Journal of Common Market Studies*
JuS	*Juristische Schulung*
JZ	*Juristenzeitung*
K&R	*Kommunikation & Recht*
LIEI	*Legal Issues of Economic Integration*
LJN	*Landelijk Jurisprudentie Nummer*
Media L&P	*Media Law & Practice*
MJ	*Maastricht Journal of European and Comparative Law*
MLR	*Modern Law Review*
MMR	*Multimedia und Recht*
MP	*Media Perspektiven*
NJ	*Nederlandse Jurisprudentie*
NJW	*Neue Juristische Wochenschrift*
NVwZ	*Neue Zeitschrift für Verwaltungsrecht*
OxJLS	*Oxford Journal of Legal Studies*
RAE	*Revue des affaires européennes*
RdJB	*Recht der Jugend und des Bildungswesens*
Riv dir europeo	*Rivista di diritto europeo*
RMC	*Revue du Marché Commun*
RMUE	*Revue du Marché Unique Européen*
RTDE	*Revue Trimestrielle de Droit Européen*
ToΣ	*To Syntagma*
TwF	*Television without Frontiers*
U of Pa L Rev	*University of Pennsylvania Law Review*

ULR	*Utilities Law Review*
VandJTransnat'lL	*Vanderbilt Journal of Transnational Law*
YEL	*Yearbook of European Law*
YLJ	*Yale Law Journal*
YMEL	*Yearbook of Media and Entertainment Law*
ZeuP	*Zeitschrift für Europäisches Privatrecht*
ZHR	*Zeitschrift für Handelsrecht*
ZRP	*Zeitschrift für Rechtspolitik*
ZUM	*Zeitschrift für Urheber- und Medienrecht*

General Introduction

The suggestion that European Union law might have an impact on the legal frameworks for public broadcasting in the Member States, and consequently, a share of responsibility for the future of these once trusted and now contested guardians of quality, innovation and moral purpose, is puzzling at first sight.[1] The Amsterdam Protocol on Public Broadcasting, by stating

> [t]hat the system of public broadcasting in the Member States is directly related to the democratic, social and cultural needs of each society and to the need to preserve media pluralism

and that

> The provisions of the Treaty establishing the European Community shall be without prejudice to the competence of Member States to provide for the funding of public service broadcasting insofar as such funding is granted to broadcasting organizations for the fulfilment of the public service remit as conferred, defined and organized by each Member State,

expresses the deference of the European Union to the Member States' competence to define the main parameters of their public broadcasting systems, namely their funding and remit.

Also, the Television without Frontiers (TwF) Directive, the most important regulatory instrument for the audiovisual sector in Europe, was adopted in 1989 as a single market initiative to establish a legal framework for the cross-border transmission of television programmes. This framework was deemed to be mainly of interest to the newly emerged commercial broadcasters that would be able to profit of economies of scale in a large European market. By contrast, public broadcasters

1. This book uses mostly the term 'European Union' rather than 'European Community' in view of the Union's planned succession to the European Community under the Draft Reform Treaty.

were not expected to have a significant presence in the nascent European audio-visual area in view of their national mission and remit and of their lacking commercial motivation.[2] The European market proved more resistant to transnationalization than originally predicted, largely due to deeply entrenched cultural and linguistic fault lines. The commercial broadcasters internationalized their ownership structures and had some success in reaping the benefits of scale by broadcasting across borders, mostly in their linguistic spheres. Public broadcasters remained, as expected, tied to their national remits.[3]

These observations do not reveal, however, the whole truth about the relationship between national public broadcasting orders and European Union law. First, the Amsterdam Protocol does not remove the Damocles sword of competition law hanging over public broadcasters, but goes on to stress that funding granted to them must 'not affect trading conditions and competition in the Community to an extent which would be contrary to the common interest'. As a result, the Protocol could not quell the unceasing waves of complaints by commercial broadcasters against the anticompetitive nature of the licence fee received by their public service counterparts. The requirements imposed by the Commission on the national systems for funding public broadcasting risk subordinating the latter to the logic of the marketplace. They are also ill fitted with the constitutional traditions of some of the Member States and constitute an important source of friction with the European Union.

Secondly, the TwF Directive, preoccupied though it might be with the commercial sector in the main, its provisions apply equally to public broadcasting. So as to facilitate the mutual recognition of national broadcasting laws, the Directive harmonizes key areas that are particularly likely to hamper the free movement of television broadcasts across borders. Even though the Directive's foremost objective is the opening up of national markets, some of its rules, such as the advertising restrictions and the rules on the protection of minors, coincidentally also protect the public interest. Others, such as the European broadcasting quota, purport to protect the public interest.

All of these rules have in common that they are set at a minimum level, the Directive being a minimum harmonization Directive. Member States are free to impose higher standards on their broadcasting industry if they so wish. In reality, this freedom is a double-edged sword. As a commentator characteristically notes:

> [n]ational governments face a central dilemma. They wish to retain the traditional controls over television, as a politically and culturally sensitive sector, yet fear the consequences of international competition if neighbouring

2. D. Krebber, *Europeanisation of Regulatory Television Policy. The Decision-making Process of the Television without Frontiers Directives from 1989 & 1997* (Baden-Baden, Nomos, 2002), p. 82.
3. *Ibid.*, pp. 49 et seq., 53; D. Ward, *The European Union Democratic Deficit and the Public Sphere. An Evaluation of EU Media Policy* (Amsterdam, IOS Press, 2004), p. 130.

> countries introduce a more relaxed regulatory regime, which is more attractive to the big media companies.[4]

Public broadcasters are less likely to relocate to neighbouring countries.[5] The deregulatory pressure exercised by the TwF Directive does, however, also affect them. Not all Member States have different rules in place for the public and the commercial sector. A lowering of standards as regards the latter would also extend to the former. In Member States where a distinct legal framework exists for public television, certain aspects of broadcasting law, such as the rules for the protection of minors, are shared with the commercial sector. Also, a balance needs to be maintained overall between the regulatory burdens imposed on the two sectors. If programme requirements are relaxed to prevent commercial operators from moving across the border, this might translate into a more liberal regime also for the public broadcasters. What is more, even if a Member State braves the threat of delocalization and opts for a high level of protection of vulnerable values, this will be of little use if foreign channels, some specifically targeting its territory, take a more relaxed stance.

The EU state aid regime and the TwF Directive are the main sources of friction between the public broadcasting orders of the Member States and European Union law. The general assumption is that the Directive's impact on public broadcasting is not very dramatic, while the EU state aid rules are likely to have far-reaching consequences for the future development of public broadcasting in the European Union.[6] This work will demonstrate that both of these forces have the potential to transform public broadcasting values in unprecedented ways.

The Commission is well aware of these problems but does not have a satisfactory answer to them. It failed to grasp the opportunity to afford a more prominent role to public interest considerations in the course of the negotiations for the 1997 revision of the TwF Directive. The European Parliament proposed 44 amendments that were linked *inter alia* to the content of programming, the protection of minors, the tightening of the advertising rules. All of these amendments were rejected by the Council.[7]

Now that the process of modernization of the TwF Directive and of its transformation to the AVMS Directive is complete, the Commission admires complacently the excellent equilibrium it has achieved 'between the deepening of the

4. D. A. L. Levy, *Europe's Digital Revolution. Broadcasting Regulation, the EU and the Nation State* (London, Routledge, 1999), p. xi.
5. *See, however*, T. McGonagle, A. van Loon, *Iris Special: Jurisdiction over Broadcasters in Europe - Report on a Round-table Discussion and Selection of Background Materials* (Strasbourg, European Audiovisual Observatory, 2002), p. 15 who argue that even public broadcasters might relocate abroad if foreign owners acquire the company.
6. C. Nissen, *Public Service Media in the Information Society. Report prepared by the Council of Europe's Group of Specialists on Public Service Broadcasting in the Information Society (MS-S-PSB)* (Strasbourg, Council of Europe, 2006), p. 45.
7. A. Harcourt, *The European Union and the Regulation of Media Markets* (Manchester, Manchester University Press, 2005), p. 81.

internal market and the guarantee of fundamental values'[8]. At the same time it invites national legislators not to 'overload the boat' by adding too many additional national rules. It tries to dissuade Member States from adopting stricter rules and argues that a 'light touch' transposition of the new Directive will solve the problems caused by the lack of cooperation between Member States and their regulatory authorities.[9] This argumentation lays bare the Commission's fundamentally economic approach and its indifference, even hostility, to national public interest concerns. It is also slightly disingenuous given that enhanced cooperation between regulators could fly in the face of the country of origin principle, the Directive's very backbone.

The discussion of the European Union media policies so far has demonstrated that public broadcasting is by no means insulated from the market opening mechanisms of the TwF Directive or from the rigours of state aid law. However, the European Union's relationship with public broadcasting has not always been cast in these narrow economic terms. In 1980, when the European Union first became seriously involved in communications policy, the European Parliament proposed the creation of a pan-European channel. The European Parliament's Hahn Report, often considered to be the cornerstone of EU broadcasting policy, stated that 'information is a decisive, perhaps the most decisive factor in European integration'.[10] The assumption was that the transmission of a programme in the whole of Europe would foster European consciousness and lend support to the goal of European unification.

The proposed channel, Europa, was to be established as a joint venture between existing public broadcasters from the Member States with the backing of the European Broadcasting Union.[11] It was modelled after the generalist national channels and was meant to broadcast a full range of programmes provided by the participating broadcasters as well as news programmes with a European outlook. Europa started broadcasting in October 1985, but only stayed operational for one year. It closed down as a result of financial difficulties linked to its failure to attract a large enough audience.

With the demise of Europa, the idea of constructing a pan-European public service channel to bring the European Union closer to the public was also put aside. Faith was placed in the commercial sector to bring about a European audiovisual area by means of the cross-border transmission of television programmes. Hahn's

---

8. V. Reding, 'Le nouveau contexte des médias audiovisuals – tendances et enjeux publics. Colloque international pour les 10 ans du Conseil supérieur de l'audiovisuel de la Communauté française de Belgique' (Brussels, 21 September 2007) <www.europa.eu/rapid/pressReleasesAction.do?reference=SPEECH/07/560&format=HTML&aged=0&language=FR&guiLanguage=en>, 28 October 2007, 3: 'Je suis convaincue que nous avons établi, dans la nouvelle directive, un excellent équilibre entre aprofondissement du marché intérieur et garantie des valeurs fondamentales'.
9. *Ibid*
10. Hahn Report I, 23 February 1982-DOK1-1013/81; European Parliament, Report on radio and television broadcasting in the European Community, Doc. 1-1013/81, OJ C 87/110, 1982; European Parliament, Resolution on a policy commensurate with new trends in European television OJ C 117/201, 1984.
11. Ward, *European Union Democratic Deficit*, p. 45.

reasoning resurfaced in the 1984 Green Paper to bolster argumentatively the establishment of a single broadcasting market:

> European unification will only be achieved if Europeans want it. Europeans will only want it if there is such a thing as a European identity. A European identity will only develop if Europeans are adequately informed. At present, information via the mass media is controlled at national level.[12]

The emphasis on the utilization of television as a medium for the promotion of a European identity that prevailed during the early 1980s subsided later on. It was replaced by the slogan of safeguarding cultural and linguistic diversity.[13] This turn of the tide is attributed by Collins to the failure of all-European television channels Europa and Eurikon, Super-channel and Sky Television in the 1980s, which demonstrated that European audiovisual markets are divided along cultural and linguistic lines.[14] Also, the theme of diversity was designed to allay fears that the single market in broadcasting would be predominantly exploited by English language producers.[15] It appears that the prevailing view in the Commission continues to be that European unity can only be constructed in diversity whereby multiple, overlapping identities interact in a European multi-level polity.[16] Whether one agrees with this post-nationalist *fata morgana* or not, it is important to bear in mind that the Union is not one organic body so that differences in approach between the Commission and the European Parliament and even between various Directorates-General are likely.[17]

In recent years, the European institutions have taken a renewed interest in the media, not as a means of instilling a European identity of sorts but as a way of closing the so-called 'communication gap' between the European Union and its citizens. This gap is largely attributed to the fact that there is no genuine dialogue between the two sides. Communication is Brussels-based, one-way, and citizens have limited means of putting their views across. Also, citizens learn about Europe through their national education systems and via their national media. The Commission proposed that in order for public debate to improve in Europe, communication needs to become an EU policy in its own right.[18] Faith has been placed in the internet to open up new channels of dialogue on European issues. Interestingly, the European

---

12. OJ C 28, 1984.
13. *See* COM (94) 96 final, 4; Principles and guidelines for the Community's audiovisual policy in the digital age, 14 December 1999, COM (99) 657 final, 2, 7.
14. R. Collins, 'Unity in Diversity? The European Single Market in Broadcasting and the Audiovisual, 1982–92' (1994) 32 JCMS, 89, 96.
15. *Ibid.*
16. On the theme of 'unity in diversity' *see* M. Pantel, 'Unity in Diversity: Cultural Policy and EU Legitimacy' in *Legitimacy and the European Union: The Contested Polity*, T. Banchoff and M. P. Smith (eds) (London, Routledge, 1999), p. 46.
17. J. Harrison and L. Woods, 'European Citizenship: Can Audio-Visual Policy Make a Difference?' (2000) 38 JCMS, 486.
18. European Commission, White Paper on a European Communication Policy, 1 February 2006, COM (2006) 35 final, 4.

Parliament is planning once again to launch a television channel. This time it is not a generalist channel. It is planned to provide live coverage of full sessions of Parliament and Committee meetings as well as educational and historical documentaries, and it will only be available online. It is hoped that this and other concerted initiatives of all EU institutions will help Europe reach out to the citizen and develop its place in the public sphere.

This brings us to the question as to whether the European audiovisual policy is really conducive to the emergence of a European demos and of a European public sphere. The public sphere is a mediating link between the power of the individual (the market) and public power. In Habermas' model it is 'a contested participatory site in which actors with overlapping identities as legal subjects, citizens, economic actors, and family and community members (i.e. civil societies) form a public body and engage in negotiations and contestation over political and social life'.[19] The existence of a public sphere is generally considered to be a prerequisite of democracy.[20]

It is beyond question that an EU public sphere or civil society hardly exists for the time being. A web of autonomous associations that are independent of the state and have an effect on public policy is missing in the supranational realm.[21] There are no European media, no developed European party system or interest groups. More significantly, there is no common language that would allow political communication to transcend national frontiers.[22] Nor does a demos, a group of people who identify sufficiently with each other to be willing to engage in democratic discourse and decision-making, exist at European level.

Some argue that the absence of a demos capable of recognizing the European Union as the appropriate political forum is the essence of the 'democratic deficit' of the European Union.[23] The perception that the European Communities suffer from a 'democratic deficit' has been a matter of concern since the earliest days of European integration. The problem of the democratic legitimacy of the European Union and the idea that it should be brought closer to its citizens have been the subject of intense discussion for academics and politicians throughout the 1990s.

---

19. Reformulation of Habermas' concept by M. Somers, 'What's Political or Cultural about Political Culture or the Public Sphere? Toward a Historical Sociology of Concept Formation' (1995) 23 *Sociological Theory*, 124.
20. Closa, 'Supranational Citizenship and Democracy', p. 422 *et seq.*
21. C. Taylor, 'Invoking Civil Society' in C. Taylor, *Philosophical Arguments* (Cambridge, MA, Harvard University Press, 1995), p. 206.
22. C. Closa, 'Supranational Citizenship and Democracy: Normative and Empirical Dimensions' in *European Citizenship: An Institutional Challenge*, M. La Torre (ed.) (The Hague, Kluwer, 1998), p. 423; D. Grimm, 'Does Europe Need a Constitution?' (1995) 1 ELJ, 294–296.
23. J. H. H. Weiler, 'The Transformation of Europe' in J. H. H. Weiler, *The Constitution of Europe: 'Do the New Clothes Have an Emperor?' and Other Essays on European Integration* (Cambridge, Cambridge University Press, 1999), p. 85; *see* K. H. Ladeur, 'Towards a Legal Theory of Supranationality – The Viability of the Network Concept' (1997) 3 ELJ, 33, 40–41; A. von Bogdandy, 'The Contours of Integrated Europe: The Origin, Status and Prospects of European Integration' in *European Legal Cultures*, V. Gessner, A. Hoeland and C. Varga (eds) (Aldershot, Dartmouth, 1996), pp. 506, 508–509.

Whereas previously, EU political elites were mainly concerned about the effectiveness, not the legitimacy of the system, the 1992 Maastricht Treaty sparked off a discussion about a legitimacy crisis of the European Union, attributed partly to the abovementioned 'communication gap'.[24] Recently, the initial Irish no vote on the Nice Treaty, and the defeat of the EU Constitution after the negative French and Dutch referenda, confirmed the belief that a further development of the system may be shackled by the lack of public support.

Even though the European Union's ailment is beyond doubt, its causes are quite uncertain. The question whether national identity is a founding element of democracy and whether its absence is a hurdle for democratic governance at the European level is very controversial. A brief excursus will be made into three theories of nationalism so as to illustrate the contrasting views. Ethno-nationalists, with Anthony D. Smith as their most prominent representative, argue that political identities derive directly from cultural identities.[25] For them, the nation-state will always be the only meaningful political entity, while the European Union will remain a cipher.

Post-nationalists, on the other hand, take a constructivist approach to identity-formation. In their view, it is false to assume that political identities automatically spring from pre-existing ethnic cores. Far greater importance has to be attached to political and intellectual elites who deliberately mobilize or silence cultural schisms.[26] The connection between nationalism and republicanism is, in this line of thought, historically contingent. Given that nations are artificial constructs, symptoms of the 'age of nationalism',[27] it is expected that it will be possible to deconstruct them and separate politics from culture.

At the intersection of these two contrasting approaches to identity-formation lies a third theory of nationalism that has been termed by Cederman the theory of bounded integration.[28] This theory shares the scepticism of ethno-nationalists with regard to the prospects for the supersession of national identities by some kind of supranational identity. Yet, it does not consider cultural continuity to be the motor that keeps identities going. Not unlike the post-nationalists, it places emphasis on explicit mechanisms of identity-formation.

One of these mechanisms is, in accordance with Ernest Gellner's theory of nationalism, the mass media. Gellner, obviously influenced by McLuhan's formula

24. B. Laffan, R. O'Donnell and M. Smith, *Europe's Experimental Union: Rethinking Integration* (London, Routledge, 2000), p. 201.
25. *See* A. Smith, 'National Identity and the Idea of European Unity' (1992) 68 *International Affairs*, 55; J. Habermas, 'Citizenship and National Identity: Some Reflections on the Future of Europe' (1992/93) 12 *Praxis International*, 7. The essentialist or ethno-nationalist line of thinking was endorsed by the German Constitutional Court in its famous 'Maastricht decision', BVerfGE 89, 155.
26. Cederman, L.-E., *Nationalism and Bounded Integration: What It Would Take to Construct a European Demos*, European Forum Series RSC, no. 2000/34 (Florence, European University Institute, 2000), p. 11 *et seq.*
27. E. Gellner, *Nations and Nationalism* (Oxford, Blackwell, 1983).
28. Cederman, *Nationalism and Bounded Integration*, p. 14 *et seq.*

that 'the medium is the message', claimed that 'it is the media themselves, the pervasiveness and importance of abstract, centralised, one to many communication, which itself automatically engenders the core idea of nationalism'.[29] The content of the transmitted message matters little in his view. Expectedly, Gellner's interpretation of the role of the media has not remained uncontested. Schlesinger showed that a national media structure can hardly contribute to the reproduction of national identity if the broadcast programmes were predominantly imported.[30] Other authors such as Deutsch and Mackenzie stressed the importance of communication for the construction of national identity. Deutsch considered the 'complementarity or relative efficiency of communication among individuals'[31] to be the quintessence of nationality, of the unity of a people. For Mackenzie, those who share a network occupy the same 'social space' and even share an identity.[32]

It follows from the foregoing that the mass media are key identity-building and legitimization factors. Accordingly, one potentially productive line of enquiry is whether a European communications system has emerged that produces citizens who recognize the European Union as the appropriate political forum. It is important to note that the comparison between European integration and historical processes of national community formation does not suggest that the two are identical. Patterns that are grounded on the model of the nation-state only apply to the European Union polity *mutatis mutandis*. Nonetheless, this approach is methodologically fruitful to the extent that the European Union is an *aliud* compared to traditional international organizations, requiring a legitimacy of its own alongside its recognition by the Member States and their political elites.[33]

In keeping with the insights of the theory of bounded integration, one could take the view that only radical measures of Europeanization of television programming would allow the Union to gain control of these crucial identity-building processes. However, the creation of a fully-fledged European television programme as envisaged by the European Parliament failed.[34] Plans to increase the powers of the European Union in these sensitive areas are double-edged. If they are not rejected in the first place, they risk worsening the legitimacy problem. This will be the case if the limitations of the Union's legitimacy base are not respected.[35]

---

29. Gellner, *Nations and Nationalism*, p. 127.
30. Schlesinger, *Media, State and Nation*, pp. 161–162.
31. K. W. Deutsch, *Nationalism and Social Communication: An Inquiry into the Foundations of Nationality* (2nd edn, Cambridge, MA, MIT Press, 1966), p. 188.
32. W. J. M. Mackenzie, *Political Identity* (Manchester, Manchester University Press, 1978).
33. T. Theiler, 'The European Union and the "European Dimension" in Schools: Theory and Evidence' (1998) 21 *Journal of European Integration*, 313; Beetham and Lord, 'Legitimacy and the European Union', pp. 17–18; contra T. Kostakopoulou, 'European Union Citizenship as a Model of Citizenship beyond the Nation State: Possibilities and Limits' in *Political Theory and the European Union: Legitimacy, Constitutional Choice and Citizenship*, A. Weale and M. Nentwich (eds) (London, Routledge, 1998), pp. 158–159.
34. M. Meckel, *Fernsehen ohne Grenzen? Europas Fernsehen zwischen Integration und Segmentierung*, Studien zur Kommunikationswissenschaft, vol. 3 (Opladen, Westdeutscher Verlag, 1994), p. 89.
35. Cederman, *Nationalism and Bounded Integration*, p. 26.

In accordance with the neo-functionalist notion of 'authority-legitimacy transfers', the pace of integration has to be commensurate with its legitimization. In other words, there has to be a balance between the Europeanization of a given area and the extent to which it can be legitimized.[36] This book will therefore evaluate the Union's policies on the basis of two criteria: first, their encroachment upon the sovereignty of the Member States and second, their aptness to increase the legitimacy of the integration project.

The European Union policy in the audiovisual sector is guided by the alleged existence of a 'European audiovisual model'.[37] At the heart of this model lies the recognition that the production and distribution of audiovisual media services are not only economic, but also cultural activities calling for the protection of a range of objectives of general interest: cultural diversity, protection of minors, consumer protection, particularly in the field of advertising, media pluralism, and the fight against racial and religious hatred.[38] It is considered essential, in the interests of the maintenance of these values, that the 'European audiovisual model' be founded on 'a balance between a strong and independent public service sector and a dynamic commercial sector'.[39]

If a dual broadcasting order, regulated in view of general interest goals, is the hallmark of the 'European audiovisual model', the European Union would arguably gain in legitimacy by nurturing this model, by promoting what national policies have in common. This book assesses whether the presumed 'European audiovisual model' really exists, whether cultural values still matter in national broadcasting policy. Its emphasis is on public broadcasting and on the values that have informed it since its inception. Only occasional references are made to the rules applicable to commercial broadcasting. Cultural values to some extent also inform the latter. The prevailing tendency is, however, for public broadcasters to carry the lion's share of public service obligations. Even though public service broadcasting can also be delivered by private enterprises, the reality is that most countries have entrusted public companies with the delivery of the public service mission.[40]

---

36. Theiler, 'European Union', 311.
37. A. Herold, 'Country of Origin Principle in the EU Market for Audiovisual Media Services: Consumer's Friend of Foe?', unpublished paper, 3 October 2007, 1.
38. *See* recitals 3 and 5 to European Parliament and Council Directive 2007/65/EC of 11 December 2007 amending Council Directive 89/552/EEC on the coordination of certain provisions laid down by law, regulation and administrative action in Member States concerning the pursuit of television broadcasting activities OJ L 332/27, 2007.
39. H. Weber, *Report on the application of Articles 4 and 5 of Directive 89/552/EEC (the 'TV without Frontiers' Directive), as amended by Directive 97/36/EC, for the period 2001–2002 (2004/2236(INI))*, A6-0202/200521, June 2005, p. 7.
40. S. Nicoltchev, 'European Backing for Public Service Broadcasting: Council of Europe Rules and Standards' in *Iris Special: The Public Service Broadcasting Culture*, European Audiovisual Observatory (ed.) (Strasbourg, European Audiovisual Observatory, 2007), pp. 7, 10. The Netherlands and the United Kingdom are exceptions to this rule.

Even though Member States share a tradition of regulating public broadcasting for the public interest, such regulation has been in demise in recent times. It has been challenged by the emergence of commercial television sworn to the market logic. The growth of satellite services, and more recently the internet, outpacing the power of governments to control the content of broadcast schedules, has put further strain on regulation for the public interest.

Public broadcasting values represent the dirigiste model of social order according to which public interventions are necessary so as maintain the well-being of society and a certain quality of life. At the other end of the spectrum stands the liberal idea that cultural standards are no longer appropriate and that the viewers as consumers should have the last word.[41] The faith in viewer sovereignty and the aversion to the so-called 'paternalistic role' of public broadcasting are indicative of a general ideological shift across Europe towards private and market-based answers.

In Part One of this book we examine the extent to which, despite these trends, the legal frameworks for public broadcasting in six European countries regulate for the public interest. The six countries under examination are France, Germany, Greece, Italy, the Netherlands and the United Kingdom. Four of these countries – France, Germany, Italy and the United Kingdom – have the four most important audiovisual industries in Europe, while Greece and the Netherlands are smaller countries with less powerful audiovisual industries. The choice of countries is influenced by the fact that they represent widely different public broadcasting models. Public broadcasters in France, Italy and Greece are thought of as being particularly vulnerable to political pressures, while the German, Dutch and British public broadcasters are considered to be more independent.[42]

In Part Two of this book, we turn to the audiovisual policy of the European Union. We explain how the forces unleashed by the creation of the internal market in broadcasting services have put public broadcasting values under threat. This section shows that the Television without Frontiers Directive and the case-law of the European Court of Justice in tandem have given priority to economic considerations. They have encouraged deregulation at national level without offering adequate safeguards at the supranational level in exchange.

Part Three focuses on the uneasy relationship between the national licence fee based systems for financing public broadcasting and the European Union state aid law. It demonstrates that – notwithstanding the 'hands-off' attitude of the Amsterdam Protocol – the Commission and the European Courts have not shied away from demanding a radical overhaul of the national systems for funding public television and for defining its remit.

In the concluding section, the discussion of the overarching theme of this work is resumed, seeking to answer the question whether the examined EU policies can be legitimized and engender further 'legitimacy transfers' to the European Union.

---

41. M. Tracey, *The Decline and Fall of Public Service Broadcasting* (Oxford, Oxford University Press, 1998), pp. 20, 51.
42. Harcourt, *Regulation of Media Markets*, p. 159.

Part 1

Public Service Obligations in Six Member States

Chapter 1
Introduction

Before embarking on an examination of the broadcasting law and policy of the European Union and of its impact on the broadcasting orders of the Member States, it is necessary to gain a better understanding of the basic tenets of these broadcasting orders. All of the countries scrutinized in this book have included a similar catalogue of public service obligations in their legislation.[1] The similarity in the formulation of these obligations can be attributed to the harmonizing effect of European Union broadcasting regulation, mainly the TwF Directive.[2]

The Directive was initially adopted in 1989 and was subsequently amended in 1997. A second revision has now been completed. The TwF Directive only covered the simultaneous transmission of a predetermined schedule of programmes to more than one recipient, but not on-demand services such as video-on-demand. After a lengthy consultation process that began in 2003 and was concluded in 2005 and a legislative process of two years, a new Audiovisual Media Services without Frontiers (AVMS) Directive was agreed upon between the European Parliament and the Council.[3] The new Directive covers all audiovisual media services, both scheduled and on-demand ones, whose principal purpose is the provision of programmes. It also includes more flexible rules on television advertising.

---

1. The terms 'public service obligations', 'programme requirements' and 'broadcasting standards' are used in this work. Since the term 'broadcasting standards' has qualitative connotations, the first two terms seem preferable in the case of obligations that are less concerned with quality such as quotas.
2. European Parliament and Council Directive 97/36/EC of 30 June 1997 amending Council Directive 89/552/EEC on the coordination of certain provisions laid down by law, regulation and administrative action in Member States concerning the pursuit of television broadcasting activities OJ L 202/60, 1997.
3. European Parliament and Council Directive 2007/65/EC of 11 December 2007 amending Council Directive 89/552/EEC on the coordination of certain provisions laid down by law, regulation and administrative action in Member States concerning the pursuit of television broadcasting activities OJ L 332/27, 2007 (hereafter referred to as the AVMS Directive).

The existence of a floor of minimum broadcasting standards at Union level cannot detract from the fact that there are considerable differences between the broadcasting laws of the Member States. The countries under examination protect broadcasting standards with different intensity and employ diverse means to this end. This is not surprising given that these standards have grown with the public broadcasting systems of the Member States, and are hence greatly informed by the historical, social and political context in which these were born. The diversity of these broadcasting systems also accounts for the different forms and methods each Member State has chosen in order to implement European Union rules. In some respects national legislation exceeds the standards set by the TwF Directive; in others it still lags behind. The range of countries examined enables drawing of firm conclusions as to whether the presumed 'European audiovisual model' exists and whether public service obligations are still prominent in the broadcasting laws and policy of the Member States. If so, the next question to be asked is whether these obligations have been furthered or jeopardized by the involvement of the European Union in this area.

The public service obligations, which will be analysed in the following chapters, are: pluralism and impartiality, particularly in political and election broadcasting; the cultural obligations of public broadcasters; the principle of separation of advertising from editorial content; the protection of minors, also in the field of advertising; the right of reply. It is not claimed that this is an exhaustive list of public service obligations. Restrictions on the content of advertisements have been left out with the exception of the rules on the protection of minors in the field of advertising. Restrictions on the frequency of advertising messages are not covered by this work either.

A conscious choice has been made to neglect these aspects and focus on the principle of separation of advertising instead. This principle marks the dividing line not only between advertising and editorial content but also between the conception of television as a cultural experience from its conception as an economic good like any other. As will be seen in the following, the liberalization of product placement in the framework of the revised TwF Directive means that this principle is now in the firing line. The rules on the protection of minors in the field of advertising have also been covered not only because of their affinity with the restrictions on indecent and violent programming, but also because the protection of minors is arguably the foremost reason why broadcasting content is being regulated.

Some of the obligations examined in this part of the book have been harmonized by the TwF Directive: the European broadcasting and independent quotas, the principle of separation, the protection of minors and the right of reply. The European broadcasting quota and the rules on the protection of minors, except in the field of advertising, will be considered in detail in the second Part of this book. It suffices to make a few introductory remarks at this stage.

The European broadcasting quota, laid down in Article 4 of the TwF (now AVMS) Directive, obliges Member States to ensure, where practical and by appropriate means, that broadcasters reserve for European works a majority proportion of their transmission time, excluding the time appointed to news, sports events, games, advertising, teletext services, and teleshopping. European works are defined in a rather complex way in Article 6 of the same Directive.

The independent quota, laid down in Article 5 of the TwF (now AVMS) Directive, obliges Member States to ensure, where practicable and by appropriate means, that broadcasters reserve at least 10 per cent of their transmission time, excluding the time appointed to news, sports events, games, advertising, teletext services, and teleshopping, or alternatively, at least 10 per cent of their programming budget, for European producers who are independent of broadcasters. Furthermore, Member States are enjoined to earmark an adequate proportion for recent works, that is to say works transmitted within five years of their production.

As far as the protection of minors from offensive content is concerned, the relevant norm is Article 22 of the same Directive. This provision absolutely bans programmes which might *seriously* impair the physical, mental or moral development of minors, in particular those that involve pornography or gratuitous violence. This prohibition extends to programmes which are likely to impair the physical, mental or moral development of minors, except where it is ensured, by selecting the time of the broadcast or by any technical measure, that minors will not normally hear or see such broadcasts. Closely related is Article 22a (now Article 3b of the AVMS Directive) on the protection of public order, which enjoins Member States to ensure that broadcasts do not contain any incitement to hatred on grounds of race, sex, religion or nationality.

The extent to which the six Member States covered by this comparative analysis endorse the principle of separation of advertising from editorial content, protect minors in the field of advertising and confer a right of reply has also been shaped by relevant provisions in the TwF Directive. So as to better understand theses aspects of their broadcasting laws, it is useful to briefly outline the relevant rules contained in the TwF Directive.

1.1 The Principle of Separation

The principle of separation of advertising and programme elements is grounded in at least three distinct rationales: first, the protection of viewers from misleading representations, secondly, the editorial independence of broadcasters, and, finally, the protection of author's rights. It ensures audiences are not misled about the nature of content-programming or advertising they are consuming. It also ensures that broadcasters retain full responsibility and control for their programmes without further interference from advertisers, thus safeguarding the independence and credibility of mass media.[4] However, the principle of separation – as other areas of content regulation – has been watered down over time to respond to

4. Ofcom, 'Product placement. A consultation on issues related to product placement' <www.ofcom.org.uk/consult/condocs/product_placement/product.pdf>, 4 September 2007.

commercial developments. Sponsorship, split screens, virtual advertising and increased opportunities for interactivity obfuscate the distinction between editorial content and commercial communication. A prominent advertising technique that breaches the principle of separation is product placement.[5]

The principle of separation of advertising from editorial content was laid down in Article 10 (1) of the TwF Directive, which stipulated that 'television advertising and teleshopping shall be readily recognisable as such and kept quite separate from other parts of the programme service by optical and/or acoustic means.' Also, Article 10 (4) of the TwF Directive prohibited surreptitious advertising, which was defined in Article 1 (d) as 'the representation in words or pictures of goods, services, the name, the trade mark or the activities of a producer of goods or a provider of services in programmes when such representation is intended by the broadcaster to serve advertising and might mislead the public as to its nature. Such representation is considered to be intentional in particular if it is done in return for payment or for similar consideration.'

Under the AVMS Directive, Article 3e (1) (a) maintains the prohibition of surreptitious advertising, albeit replacing advertising with the concept of 'audio-visual commercial communication', which includes sponsorship, teleshopping and product placement next to advertising. Surreptitious advertising is distinguished from product placement, which is exceptionally allowed subject to a number of conditions. Product placement is defined in Article 1 (m) as 'any form of audio-visual commercial communication consisting of the inclusion of or reference to a product, a service or the trade mark thereof so that it is featured within audiovisual media services, normally in return for payment or for similar consideration.'

The original Commission proposal allowed product placement in principle, but subjected it to certain requirements that also applied to sponsorship.[6] The updated Commission proposal, after the Council and the European Parliament first reading, divorced the regulation of product placement from that of sponsorship. Sponsorship is dealt with under Article 3f and product placement under Article 3g of the AVMS Directive. Product placement is prohibited in principle. It is only allowed by way of derogation for certain types/genres of programmes, namely cinematographic works, films and series made for audiovisual media services, light entertainment and sports programmes, or in cases where no payment is made but certain goods or services are merely provided free of charge. Children programmes are specifically excluded from this derogation.

---

5. This work only looks at the European and national legal frameworks for product placement. Sponsorship is touched upon only incidentally, while new advertising techniques are beyond its scope. As regards these new techniques, *see* Commission interpretative communication on certain aspects of the provisions on televised advertising in the 'Television without frontiers' Directive, 28 April 2004, COM (2004) 1450 final, paras 37 *et seq.*; McGonagle, van Loon, *Jurisdiction over Broadcasters in Europe*, p. 15 *et seq.*
6. Proposal for a Directive of the European Parliament and of the Council amending Council Directive 89/552/EEC on the coordination of certain provisions laid down by law, regulation or administrative action in Member States concerning the pursuit of television broadcasting activities, 13 December 2005, COM (2005) 646 final, Art. 3h.

It is worth noting that the original Commission proposal only banned product placement for certain types/genres of programmes, namely news and current affairs, audiovisual media services for children and documentaries. In response to calls for a less permissive regime on product placement, the Council replaced the negative list of programme types for which product placement is forbidden with a positive list of programme types for which it is allowed. This is a welcome move as it restricts the scope of product placement: it is now outlawed in consumer information programmes for instance. Doubts still remain as to the proper treatment of hybrid forms of programmes such as docu-soaps or infotainment.

Member States may decide to opt out from the derogation mechanism and to outlaw product placement completely. This 'opt out' mechanism was introduced by the European Parliament and replaces the 'opt in 'mechanism suggested by the Council, which asked Member States to explicitly permit product placement by way of derogation. Obviously, this reversal waters down the principle of the prohibition of product placement and means that it will be the norm in most Member States.

Programmes that contain product placement must meet the following requirements.[7] First, the content, and, in the case of television broadcasting, the scheduling of programmes must not be influenced in such a way as to affect the responsibility and independence of the media service provider. Secondly, programmes containing product placement must not directly encourage the purchase or rental of goods or services, in particular by making special promotional references to those goods or services. Thirdly, they must not give undue prominence to the product in question, i.e. prominence which is not justified by the editorial requirements of the programme, or the need to lend verisimilitude.[8] Finally, programmes containing product placement must be appropriately identified at the start and the end of the programme, and when a programme resumes after an advertising break, in order to avoid any confusion on the part of the viewer. These conditions seek to protect, on the one hand, viewers from being misled about the advertising intention behind the product placement and, on the other hand, the editorial independence of broadcasters.

It is questionable whether identification at the start of the programme, at the end and after each advertising break serves sufficiently the interests of viewers for transparency or merely reinforces the advertising effect of product placement. In any case, dangers lurk for the editorial integrity of programmes. Once the Pandora's Box of product placement has been opened, the content and scheduling of programmes will easily fall prey to external manipulation. The prohibition of undue prominence is a weak bastion against the excessive commercialization of

7. AVMS Directive, Art. 3g (2).
8. Amended proposal for a Directive of the European Parliament and of the Council amending Council Directive 89/552/EEC on the coordination of certain provisions laid down by law, regulation or administrative action in Member States concerning the pursuit of television broadcasting activities ('Audiovisual media services without frontiers'), 29 March 2007, COM (2007) 170 final, recital 46.

programmes given that advertisers are inclined to go to great lengths to ensure that the costly integration of products into storylines yields satisfactory results in terms of audience recognition.[9]

The explanation given in recital 46 of the AVMS Directive for the liberalization of product placement is that it is 'a reality in cinematographic works and in audiovisual works made for television, but Member States regulate this practice differently. In order to ensure a level playing field, and thus enhance the competitiveness of the European media industry, it is necessary to adopt rules for product placement.'[10] Indeed, it is not entirely clear whether product placement was incompatible with the TwF Directive.

In its 2004 interpretative Communication on the Directive, the Commission stated that product placement must meet three cumulative conditions to be considered surreptitious advertising: 'it must be intended by the broadcaster, it must be done to serve advertising and it must be capable of misleading the public as to its nature'.[11] It follows from this definition that product placement could not constitute surreptitious advertising if viewers were made aware of it, for example by explicitly referring to it in the credits. However, the Commission recently argued for the first time that product placement was outlawed under the TwF Directive. In its Issue Paper on 'Commercial Communications' for the Liverpool Audiovisual Conference it pronounced that: 'The dual requirement of identification and separation implicitly has the effect of not authorising, within the current legal framework, recourse to product placement in programmes produced by broadcasters covered by the TWF Directive.'[12] In other words, even if product placement was disclosed and hence compatible with the prohibition of surreptitious advertising, it still violated the separation principle.

Nonetheless, this damning finding was not unqualified. For one, in the Commission's view, product placement only fell foul of the TwF Directive if it was done by the broadcaster in return for payment or other similar consideration. Indeed, product placement in independently produced works is common practice. For another, the Commission seemed to hold that product placement was only outlawed if it was unduly prominent.[13] In other words, the mere representation of

---

9. J. Grant, 'Ofcom Buys into Product Placement: Consultation on Issues Related to Product Placement' (2006) 4 ENT L R, 118, 120.
10. Common Position of 24 May 2007, recital 46.
11. Commission interpretative communication on certain aspects of the provisions on televised advertising in the 'Television without frontiers' Directive, 28 April 2004, COM (2004) 1450 final, para. 31.
12. European Commission, Issues Paper for the Liverpool Audiovisual Conference: Commercial Communications, July 2005, 4.
13. *See* W. Schultz, 'Stellungnahme zur Anhörung des Ausschusses für Kultur und Medien zur geplanneten Novellierung der EU-Fernsehrichtlinie', 4 <www.hans-bredow-institut.de/forschung/recht/StellungnahmeFSRL-WS060510.pdf>, 15 May 2007; T. McGonagle, 'Workshop Report' in *Iris Special:Audiovisual Media Services without Frontiers: Implementing the Rules*, European Audiovisual Observatory (ed.) (Strasbourg, European Audiovisual Observatory, 2007), p. 56.

goods in a programme without actually promoting them would have been permissible. This is the case for instance when a character eating breakfast is seen handling the packet of a particular brand of cereal without a close up of the packet featuring in the programme.

As a result of the lack of clear rules on product placement, its treatment in the Member States varies considerably. It is only allowed in Austria under certain conditions. Few Member States explicitly ban it, while others rely on the prohibition of surreptitious advertising. We will consider the position taken by France, Germany, Greece, Italy, the Netherlands and the United Kingdom in the following chapters.

The Commission also made much of the argument that product placement is allowed in the United States. Even though it still only accounts for a small percentage of the total advertising revenues of free-to-air broadcasters, it is growing at a very fast rate. It is thus a common feature of films and other programmes imported from the United States. The Commission is obviously keen to boost the European television industry whose revenues from spot advertising are dwindling as a result of the impact of personal video recorders (PVRs) and changes in the market and in viewer behaviour. However, these financial gains need to be carefully balanced against the serious threats for the principle of separation and the editorial integrity of programmes. The fact that product placement is allowed in the United States is not sufficient in itself to justify its deregulation in Europe, the more so given that an attempt is made in the States to turn the tide. American scriptwriters have considered adopting a voluntary code of conduct to prevent programme content from being tailored to suit advertising needs.[14] Such a degradation of television programming is also likely to take place in Europe. The interest of broadcasters to keep tight editorial control so as not to alienate their viewers is not an adequate safeguard against the exaggerations of product placement. It is expected that there will be a greater diversification of programme quality. A demand for high quality feature films and series will still exist, but low budget productions infiltrated with advertising will also be increasingly on offer.[15]

1.2 Advertising and Minors

Turning now to the protection of minors in the field of advertising, the relevant TwF Directive provision was Article 16. It required that television advertising should not cause moral or physical detriment to minors and laid down certain criteria for their protection:

> Advertising shall not directly exhort minors to buy a product or service by exploiting their inexperience or credulity; it shall not directly encourage minors to persuade their parents or others to purchase the goods or services being

14. Schultz, 'Stellungnahme', 6.
15. *Ibid.*

> advertised; it shall not exploit the special trust minors place in parents, teachers or other persons; it shall not unreasonably show minors in dangerous situations.

Dir. 97/36 added a second paragraph on teleshopping, subjecting it to the above-mentioned requirements and stipulating that it 'shall not exhort minors to contract for the sale or rental of goods and services'.

Under the AVMS Directive, the requirements of Article 16 (1) have been placed *in toto* in Article 3e (1) (g) as part of Chapter II A, which contains provisions applicable to all audiovisual media services. Their application has been extended to all audiovisual commercial communications. Therefore, teleshopping is also subject to these general rules, and in particular to the requirement that it shall not directly exhort minors to buy or hire a product or service by exploiting their inexperience and credulity. This requirement is somewhat laxer than the one contained in Article 16 (2), which has been removed under the AVMS Directive. Article 16 (2) proscribed any form of exhortation, not only a direct one, and did not contain the clause 'by exploiting their inexperience and credulity'.[16]

1.3 The Right of Reply

Finally, the right of reply in television broadcasting is laid down in Article 23 of the AVMS Directive.
Article 23 (1) stipulates that:

> Without prejudice to other provisions adopted by the Member States under civil, administrative or criminal law, any natural or legal person, regardless of nationality, whose legitimate interests, in particular reputation and good name, have been damaged by an assertion of incorrect facts in a television programme must have a right of reply or equivalent remedies. Member States shall ensure that the actual exercise of the right of reply or equivalent remedies is not hindered by the imposition of unreasonable terms or conditions. The reply shall be transmitted within a reasonable time subsequent to the request being substantiated and at a time and in a manner appropriate to the broadcast to which the request refers.

The European Parliament and the Council, together with the public broadcasters, have been in favour of extending the right of reply or equivalent remedies to the

16. *See also* A. Scheuer, 'Implementation and Monitoring: Upholding General Interest in View of Commercial Communications' in *Iris Special:Audiovisual Media Services without Frontiers: Implementing the Rules*, European Audiovisual Observatory (ed.) (Strasbourg, European Audiovisual Observatory, 2007), pp. 23, 31; T. Kleist and A. Scheuer, 'Neue Regelungen für audiovisuelle Mediendienste: Vorschriften zu Werbung und Jugendschutz und ihre Anwendung in den Mitgliedstaaten' (2006) 4 MMR, 208, who argue that European Parliament and Council Directive 2005/29/EC of 11 June 2005 on unfair commercial practices OJ L 149/22, 2005 should also be considered to establish the future level of protection.

online media.[17] The European Parliament proposed to introduce a right of reply for all audiovisual media services, which are covered by the AVMS Directive.[18] This right would have a more extended scope than the current right of reply for traditional broadcasting services. It would be granted to every natural or legal person whose legitimate interests have been affected by an assertion of facts in a transmission regardless of whether these facts were incorrect or not.

This proposal has been vigorously opposed by the United Kingdom, the commercial broadcasters, the written press and most telecom operators and internet service providers (ISPs) with the argument that it would stifle the development of the European internet and other digital platform industries and restrict their ability to compete with non-European operators.[19] Besides, so the argument goes, the internet automatically embodies a right of reply, given that persons considering themselves harmed by an on-line entry can easily rebut it by setting up for instance their own websites or blogs. The European Parliament's proposal has not been accepted by the Commission. The argument that the internet offers plenty of opportunities for direct reply in blogs, forums, chat rooms etc is not wholly convincing in regard to those television-like services available on the web that are covered by the modernized TwF Directive. A compromising assertion made in a programme transmitted online arguably has a much greater capacity to reach the public than a reply given in a private website or forum.

In the following chapters we will consider the extent to which the legal systems under examination provide natural and legal persons with a right of reply to allegations made on television and possibly the internet. All other aforementioned standards will also be analysed against a brief historical overview of the broadcasting systems of each of the six countries under examination, followed by a discussion of their broadcasting authorities, and of their methods for financing public broadcasting and for defining its mission.

---

17. *See* Recommendation of the European Parliament and of the Council of 20 December 2006 on the protection of minors and human dignity and on the right of reply in relation to the competitiveness of the European audiovisual and on-line information services industry OJ L378/72, 2006, recital 15.
18. European Parliament legislative resolution on the proposal for a Directive amending Council Directive 89/552/EEC on the coordination of certain provisions laid down by law, regulation or administrative action in Member States concerning the pursuit of television broadcasting activities, 13 December 2006, A6-0399/2006, Amendment 136.
19. *See* DCMS, 'Protection of Minors and Human Dignity: Right of Reply' <www.culture.gov.uk/what_we_do/Broadcasting/international_broadcasting/>, 15 May 2007; Liverpool final report of the Working Group 6, 'Protection of Minors and Human Dignity: Right of Reply', 20–22 September 2005.

Chapter 2
France

1. BACKGROUND

During most of its post-war existence public broadcasting in France has been dominated by the State. Until 1982 broadcasting was a state monopoly that was vested in a sole body, initially the *Radiodiffusion télévision française*, and from 1964 onwards the *Office de la radiodiffusion télévision française* (ORTF). ORTF was tightly controlled by the Minister of Information, and then of Culture, and the government often manipulated its programmes, especially its news content, for its own ends.[1] ORTF was entirely financed by licence fees until 1968 when advertisements were permitted.

In 1974, following the election of Giscard d'Estaing, ORTF was broken up into seven separate institutions with the aim of rationalizing costs and enhancing its political independence as well as the variety of its programming by allowing the three public channels, TF1, A2 and FR3, to compete. This was a failed reform. The government continued to supervise all seven broadcasting organizations (*tutelle*), which therefore enjoyed limited autonomy. It laid down their programme obligations in terms of reference (*cahiers de charges*), appointed the company presidents and determined the amount of the licence fee. What is more, the competition between different providers led to a ratings battle and to a deterioration of programme standards.[2]

The government only loosened its grip on public broadcasting somewhat in 1981 when Mitterand was elected. A law adopted in 1982 abolished the state

1. Barendt, *Broadcasting Law*, p. 14; T. Vedel, 'France' in *Television across Europe: Regulation, Policy and Independence*, Open Society Institute (ed.) (New York, Open Society Institute, 2005), p. 644.
2. B. Holznagel, *Rundfunkrecht in Europa: Auf dem Weg zu einem Gemeinrecht europäischer Rundfunkordnung*, Jus publicum, vol. 18 (Tübingen, J. C. B. Mohr, 1996), p. 35.

monopoly on broadcasting and established an independent authority, the *Haute autorité de l'audiovisuel*, to appoint the presidents of public channels and to guarantee their political independence.[3] Despite these groundbreaking reforms the government retained a significant amount of influence through the release of the *cahiers de charges* and the method of selection of the nine members of the High Authority. As in the case of the *Conseil Superieur de l'Audiovisuel* (CSA), the current regulatory authority for broadcasting, the President of the Republic, the President of the Assembly and the President of the Senate chose three members each.

The Chirac government that came to power in 1986 liberalized French broadcasting further. A new law was adopted in 1986, which replaced the High Authority with the *Commission Nationale de la Communication et des Libertés* (CNCL), a thirteen-man body with enhanced powers.[4] The CNCL failed to elicit the support of the public and the parliamentary opposition and was heavily criticized for political bias. In 1987, in a very controversial move, the government privatized TF1, the biggest and most favourite broadcaster in France. To assuage public anger, the government was forced to impose special cultural obligations on TF1.[5]

In 1989, a new broadcasting law was adopted by the recently elected Rocard government. However, it did not change the broadcasting landscape to any significant extent. Its main aim was the dissolution of the CNCL and its replacement by the *Conseil Superieur de l'Audiovisuel* (CSA). CSA's regulatory powers differed only slightly from those of its predecessor. However, it established the reputation of an impartial regulator, not least due to the selection of its members on objective rather than party-political grounds.[6]

Since 1989, Law 86-1067 has been modified and supplemented many times. Law 94-88 of 1 February 1994 deserves special mention. It laid the foundation for the creation of a channel devoted to education, training and employment – originally La Cinquième, now France 5 – and extended the sanctioning powers of the CSA to the public channels.[7] Also, Law 2000-719 of 1 August 2000 modified the 1986 Law in many ways, *inter alia* by reorganizing the public broadcasting sector and by introducing so-called 'contracts of objectives and means' (*contrats d'objectifs et de moyens*) between the state and the public broadcasters.[8] These contracts fix the framework of development and the financial means to be allocated by the state to public broadcasters for a period of three to five years, and specify their public service missions. A new contract was concluded between the government and *France Télévisions* for the period 2007–2010 on 24 April 2007.[9]

---

3. Law 82-652 of 29 July 1982.
4. Law 86-1067 of 30 September 1986 on freedom of communication, also known as *Law Léotard.*
5. Holznagel, *Rundfunkrecht in Europa*, p. 44.
6. *Ibid.*, p. 45.
7. C. Debbasch, X. Agostinelli *et al.*, *Droit des médias* (Paris, Dalloz, 2002), para. 655.
8. Law 86-1067 of 30 September 1986, Art. 53, as modified by Law 2000-719 of 1 August 2000, Art. 15.
9. Contract of Objectives and Means-Synthesis <www.francetelevisions.fr/data/doc/synthese_com.pdf>, 29 November 2007.

The main French public broadcasters, France 2, France 3, France 4, France 5, Arte and RFO, have been assembled in 2000 into a holding company called France Télévisions, entirely owned by the state.[10] France 2 is a 'generalist' channel. It offers a variety of programmes, stimulating social cohesion and preserving the French cultural identity. France 3, another general interest channel, operates both at national and at regional level, providing programmes and news on French regions. France 4 is the most recent addition to the France Télévisions channel holdings. Created in 2005 following the introduction of digital television, it is considered as complementary to the other channels. Its aim is to promote cultural and artistic programmes with particular emphasis on French and European productions.[11] France 5 focuses on education and knowledge. It used to share a frequency with the Franco-German channel Arte, but acquired its own channel in 2005.

Arte, a European cultural channel, is unique in the public broadcasting system. It was established by agreement between the French and German governments in 1990. It offers quality documentaries and high brow cultural programmes. Arte is the only channel that is not controlled by the CSA. It is supervised exclusively by the owners of the company.[12] Finally, the Société Réseau France Outre-mer (RFO) broadcasts French television and radio programmes overseas. It controls nine regional stations with two television and two radio channels. The first channel offers the programmes of the national channels TF1 and France 3, while the second channel offers the majority of the France 2 programmes.

The public broadcasting system also includes Chaîne parlementaire. Established in 1999, it broadcasts parliamentary and civic programmes.[13] The same frequency is shared between two channels: one for the National Assembly (*Assemblée National*) and one for the Senate (*Sénat*).[14] The Chaîne parlementaire is not supervised by the CSA, but by the two chambers.

France Télévisions is managed by an Administrative Board of fourteen members serving a five-year term. The Board is composed as follows: two members of Parliament, one appointed by the National Assembly and one by the Senate; five state representatives appointed by the government; five qualified personalities appointed by the CSA, at least one of which must come from a non-governmental organization, one from the television or film industry and another from the French overseas territories; and two personnel representatives.[15] The Administrative Board's President is elected for five years by the CSA from the personalities appointed by it. The Administrative Board is entrusted with the task of defining the strategic orientation of the society, of supervising its services and of ensuring the observance of its programming commitments. In practice, the Board is barely involved in day to day management and the role of its members is very limited.[16]

---

10. Law 86-1067 of 30 September 1986, Art. 44.
11. *See Cahiers des missions et des charges de France 4.*
12. Arte's Act of Constitution, Art. 1.
13. Law 99-1174 of 30 December 1999.
14. Law 86-1067 of 30 September 1986, Arts 45-1 and 45-2.
15. Law 86-1067 of 30 September 1986, Art. 47-1.
16. Vedel, 'France', pp. 673–674.

Each of the broadcasting companies of France Télévisions is managed by similar Boards.

2. BROADCASTING AUTHORITIES

2.1 *Conseil Superieur de l'Audiovisuel*

The CSA, created by Law 89-25 of 17 January 1989, is the most important broadcasting authority in France. It is an independent, administrative body whose aim is to safeguard the observance of the broadcasting principles laid down by law.

The CSA is composed of nine Counsellors (*conseillers*), one of whom is the President, nominated by Presidential Decree for a non-renewable period of six years. Mandates are staggered so that one third of the Council is replaced every two years.[17] Three of these members (including the President) are appointed by the President of the Republic, three by the President of the Senate and three by the President of the National Assembly. This appointment method is modelled after the one applicable to the French *Conseil Constitutionnel.*[18] The functions of the Counsellors are incompatible with any other term of office, employment in the civil service or any other professional activity. Breach of these rules may result in the dismissal from the function or even criminal prosecution.[19]

The CSA is vested with a number of powers. First, it issues broadcasting licences to private radio and television companies, but not to public broadcasters that are established by law. Second, it appoints five members of the administrative board, including the President of France Télévisions, Radio France and Radio France Internationale for a five-year period. Even though the CSA enjoys overall a better reputation than its predecessor, the CNCL, it has often been accused of 'rubber-stamping' the government's choices when appointing the heads of public broadcasters.[20] Third, the CSA monitors and enforces compliance with the broadcasting principles established by law, particularly pluralism, advertising, the protection of minors, market competition and the relation between mass media and politics.[21] To this end, it monitors all terrestrial television programmes on a daily basis, and broadcasters need to report every year to the CSA on the fulfilment of their commitments. It does not have censorship powers, and never intervenes before a programme has been broadcast.

In cases of violation, the CSA has a panoply of sanctions at its disposal, ranging from an initial warning through the imposition of fines to the revocation of a licence. It can require the broadcasting of a communiqué related to a transgression, impose a licence suspension or reduce the term of a licence. In reality, the

17. Law 86-1067 of 30 September 1986, Art. 4 (5).
18. Debbasch *et al.*, *Droit des médias*, para. 549.
19. Law 86-1067 of 30 September 1986, Art. 5 (3), (4).
20. T. Vedel, 'France', p. 661.
21. Law 86-1067 of 30 September 1986, Arts 13-17.

CSA has never suspended, reduced or withdrawn a national television or radio licence.[22] It refrains from taking such drastic steps in view of their grave economic repercussions, and contents itself with warnings and fines. This also reflects, perhaps, a change in the regulatory style of the CSA. Between 1989 and 1995, under its first chair Jacques Boutet, a senior civil servant, the CSA was narrowly focused on issuing formal warnings and on imposing sanctions. Under its second chair, Hervé Bourges, the CSA adopted a more inclusive and far-sighted approach, negotiating agreements with the broadcasters instead.[23] However, the CSA is now often accused of dealing with problems too slowly, partly due to insufficient staff means and partly due to complicated procedures.[24]

Finally, the CSA has regulatory powers that are more limited than those of its predecessor, the CNCL.[25] It can only set general rules in relation to: election campaigns; the right of reply to governmental announcements; and access rights of political and professional organizations or trade unions.[26] It is required to give published opinions to the government on the *cahiers des charges* for the public broadcasters.[27] Further, it may also be requested by the government, the Parliament or the Competition Council to comment on other matters within its competence. It is worth noting that the CSA does not have any powers as regards the financing of public broadcasters. It only publishes the financial statements of the national public and private television stations as well as of local metropolitan companies broadcasting in the overseas territories.

2.2 Institut National de l'Audiovisuel

The INA is a public body of industrial and commercial character created by the Law of 6th January 1975. INA's main function is to preserve and to promote France's audiovisual patrimony by managing the country's television and radio archives and by contributing to professional training and research on new technologies. INA's administrative board is composed of 12 members with a 5-year mandate. The CSA designates four members of the board, while the President is appointed by the government.

3. FINANCING

Public television is financed by licence fees paid by each household and by advertising. In addition, it receives from the state funding that is earmarked for specific

22. T. Vedel, 'France', p. 660.
23. *Ibid.*, p. 661.
24. *Ibid.*
25. Barendt, *Broadcasting Law*, p. 66.
26. Law 86-1067 of 30 September 1986, Arts 16, 54, 55.
27. *Ibid.*, Art. 48.

purposes such as the dissemination of French television abroad, the development of new technologies or the compensation of financial shortfalls suffered, for instance, as a result of licence fee exemptions.[28] Advertising is a limited source of income for French public television. It only represented 29.3 per cent of its total revenues in 2004. This is largely due to two factors. First, no advertising is permitted during feature films on public television. Second, public broadcasters' advertising rights were drastically reduced in 2000 to 8 minutes per hour in peak time, as opposed to 12 minutes previously.[29] This measure aimed to reduce the dependence of France 2 and France 3 on commercial revenues. The receipts diminution was entirely covered through the state budget.

The level of the licence fee, currently set at 116 euros (EUR) per year, is considerably lower than in many other European countries. Since 2005, the licence fee has been attached to the domicile tax so as to avoid problems of collection and licence fee evasion. It is linked to the possession of a television set or a similar appliance that is capable of receiving television, such as a DVD player, a video projector equipped with a tuner or a PC that can receive television via the internet, regardless of its actual use. Exemptions from the licence fee exist for the same categories of people as are exempted from the domicile tax such as senior citizens over 65 years of age with low income and people with disabilities.

The amount of the licence fee is set yearly by Parliament together with the entire budget of public broadcasters, including their advertising revenue and expenditures. First, the budget is drafted by the Ministry of Communication in tandem with the Ministry of Finance. Then it goes for approval to the Prime Minister and finally to the Parliament. This means that public broadcasters have little influence on their financing and spending.[30] A move towards greater control by public broadcasters over their financial affairs was made in 2000 by means of the introduction of the abovementioned *contrats d'objectifs et de moyens*.[31] These contracts allocate funding over a three to five-year period in exchange for the commitment of public broadcasters to fulfilling certain public service obligations. However, the duty to have their budgets approved by Parliament on a yearly basis remains. Also, the promises made in the *contrats d'objectifs et de moyens* are not always honoured. The government of Prime Minister Raffarin refused to fund new digital France Télévisions channels out of the state budget in 2002, even though the previous government had included the grant in the *contrats d'objectifs et de moyens*.[32]

---

28. Vedel, 'France', pp. 669–670.
29. The commercial broadcasters TF1 and M6 also broadcast six minutes of advertising per hour on a daily average. However, they are allowed to transmit up to 12 minutes of advertising per hour.
30. Vedel, 'France', p. 670.
31. *See* Part 1, Ch. 2.1, p. 14 *above*.
32. Council of Europe, Parliamentary Assembly, *Report of the Committee on Culture, Science and Education: Public Service Broadcasting*, Doc. 10029 (Strasbourg, Council of Europe, 2004), para. 73.

4. THE FRENCH CONSTITUTION

Neither freedom of expression nor broadcasting freedom is laid down in the French Constitution of 4 October 1958. However, Article 11 of the Declaration of the Rights of Man of 1789 proclaims that all citizens can talk, write and print freely, notwithstanding their responsibility to abstain from the abuse of this freedom in the circumstances determined by the law. This provision is considered to be binding on all branches of government since it is mentioned in the Preamble to the Constitution.[33] The French Constitutional Court (*Conseil Constitutionnel*) has interpreted this fundamental freedom as including the freedom of dissemination of thought and opinion by audiovisual means.[34]

The *Conseil Constitutionnel*'s role in the broadcasting field was marginal during the first two decades of its existence, not least due to a peculiar feature of French judicial revue precluding an examination of the constitutionality of legislation after its final adoption.[35] It was only in the eighties that the *Conseil Constitutionnel* emerged as a powerful player in this area. In 1982, it upheld the constitutionality of the Law of 29 July 1982 that made the establishment of private television stations dependent on prior authorization. It considered that freedom of expression needed to be reconciled with existing technical constraints – presumably the shortage of frequencies – as well as other constitutional values such as the pluralism of socio-cultural currents.[36] In academic writing, 'socio-cultural currents' have been interpreted as views expressed by social groupings as opposed to individual views.[37]

In later judgments the *Conseil Constitutionnel* has consistently recognized pluralism as a principle of constitutional value, indispensable for the functioning of democracy.[38] When the proposed 1986 legislation, that paved the way for the privatization of TF1, was referred to it, the *Conseil Constitutionnel* stroke down its anti-concentration provisions as unconstitutional for failing to guarantee pluralism. Interestingly, the *Conseil* raised no objections to the decision to privatize TF1 and to subject it to a system of administrative authorization – as opposed to a state concession – that would oblige it to comply with public service requirements. It held that it was within the legislator's discretion to choose the way in which

33. Barendt, *Broadcasting Law*, p. 13; Holznagel, *Rundfunkrecht in Europa*, p. 105. The Conseil cleared doubts as to the constitutional status of the Preamble in its seminal decision 71-44 of 16 July 1971 on freedom of assembly. M. Schellenberg, 'Pluralismus: Zu einem medienrechtlichen Leitmotiv in Deutschland, Frankreich und Italien' (1994) 119 AöR, 427, 429; R. Craufurd Smith, *Broadcasting Law and Fundamental Rights* (Oxford, Clarendon, 1997), p. 87.
34. Decision 82-141 of 27 July 1982; Decision 86-217 of 18 September 1986.
35. E. M. Barendt, *Freedom of Speech* (2nd edn, Oxford, Oxford University Press, 2005), p. 68; Craufurd Smith, *Broadcasting Law*, p. 86.
36. Decision 82-141 of 27 July 1982.
37. Schellenberg, 'Pluralismus', 430.
38. Decision 86-217 of 18 September 1986; *See also* Decision 84-181 of 10/11 October 1984 concerning the press; L. Franceschini, *Télévision et Droit de la Communication* (Paris, Ellipses, 2003), p. 140.

broadcasting was organized. The *Conseil* appeared therefore to be more interested in the constitutional imperatives to which broadcasting needs to adhere than in establishing a specific broadcasting model.

5. LEGAL FRAMEWORK

The main law regulating public broadcasting in France is Law 86-1067 of 30 September 1986 on freedom of communication. This law has been modified many times. A host of other laws and decrees from all legal branches, such as Law of 4 August 1994 on the use of the French language or the Consumer Law of 26 July 1993, regulate specific aspects of broadcasting. Law 2004-669 of 9 July 2004 attempts to draw a clear division of responsibilities between the CSA and the Telecommunications Regulator (*Agence de regulation des telecommunications* – ART).

6. PUBLIC BROADCASTING MISSION AND STANDARDS

The missions of public broadcasting and the principles with which it needs to comply are laid down in Article 43-11 of Law 86-1067 of 30 September 1986. This is the first provision under Title III of the 1986 Law that is entirely dedicated to the discipline of public broadcasting. It contains a detailed list of the wide range of obligations of public broadcasters. It has been introduced by Law 719-2000 of 1 August 2000 and contrasts sharply with earlier broadcasting laws that were quite vague on this point.[39] It is therefore worth reciting this provision in its entirety:

> The public broadcasters must serve the public interest and are in charge of fulfilling public service missions. They must provide the public, taken in all its components, with a set of programmes and services characterized by diversity and pluralism, quality and innovation, respect for peoples' rights and democratic principles as defined by the constitution.
>
> They must supply a wide range and diversity of programmes, covering the areas of news, culture, knowledge, entertainment and sports. They must contribute to the democratic debate within French society as well as to the social inclusion of citizens. They must ensure the promotion of the French language and reflect the diversity of cultural heritage in its regional and local dimensions. They must contribute to the development and the diffusion of ideas and arts. They must also spread civic, economic, social and scientific knowledge and contribute to media literacy.
>
> They have to ensure that the deaf and people who are hard of hearing can access their programmes.

39. Debbasch *et al.*, *Droit des médias*, para. 638.

Public broadcasters must provide honest, independent and pluralist news and contribute to the pluralist expression of social and political forces on an equal basis and according to the recommendations issued by the CSA.

Finally, public broadcasters must take part in French external audiovisual policies and contribute to the diffusion of French language and culture abroad. They must develop new technologies and services in order to continuously enrich their programmes.[40]

Even though this provision applies specifically to public broadcasting, some of the obligations contained therein such as pluralism and the promotion of the French language are not unique to it. The public service mission is specified further in the *cahiers des charges* of the public broadcasters, which are adopted by the Prime Minister or by the Minister in charge of audiovisual communication and formalized by means of decrees. These documents define the programming obligations of each of the public broadcasters, notably those related to their educational, cultural and social mission.[41] The CSA monitors public broadcasters' compliance with the *cahiers des charges*, which are not, however, the only source of public broadcasters' obligations.

The *contrats d'objectifs et de moyens* that were concluded for the first time between the government and France Télévisions in 2001 also define the mission of France Télévisions more clearly in line with the requirements of the 2001 Broadcasting Communication.[42] However, whereas the 2001 Communication required an effective supervision of public service obligations by an authority that is independent from the entrusted undertakings, the objective and means contracts escape CSA's control.[43] The President of France Télévisions only has to present the Cultural Affairs Commissions of the Parliament and Senate with a report on the execution of the contracts.[44]

7. POLITICAL AND ELECTION BROADCASTING

We have seen that the *Conseil constitutionnel* has recognized the principle of pluralism as a principle of constitutional value. Also, Article 1 of Law 86-1067 of 30 September 1986 lays down the freedom of communication by electronic means. Exceptions from this fundamental right can only be made on specific grounds listed in the same article, *inter alia* for the respect of the pluralist character of currents of thought and opinions. Strictly related to the principle of internal pluralism is the representation of political ideas in the mass media, particularly

40. Translation by Vedel, 'France', p. 666.
41. Law 86-1067 of 30 September 1986, Art. 48.
42. Communication from the Commission on the application of State aid rules to public service broadcasting, OJ C 320, 2001.
43. CSA, 'Avis du 26 mars 2002 sur les cahiers des missions et des charges des chaînes de France Télévision' <www.csa.fr/infos/textes/textes_detail.php?id=5943>, 19 April 2007.
44. Debbasch *et al., Droit des médias*, para. 655.

during electoral periods.[45] Article 13 (1) of Law 86-1067 provides that the CSA shall assure the respect of the pluralist expression of currents of thought and opinion in radio and television programmes, particularly as far as general and political information programmes are concerned. In this section we will consider, first, the application of the principle of pluralism to political broadcasts, and, secondly, to election broadcasts before turning to the obligation to transmit messages of general interest and governmental announcements.

7.1 Election Broadcasts

As far as political broadcasts other than election broadcasts are concerned, both during and outside of electoral periods, it is established that each chain shall ensure both equal time and equal conditions of access to the members of the government, the representatives of the parliamentary majority and the representatives of the opposition. Until 2000, a purely quantitative approach was taken to the allocation of airtime. The so-called rule of three thirds (*règle des trois tiers*), established in 1969 in an internal ORTF[46] directive, required that one third of the speaking time should be accorded to the government, one third to the parliamentary majority and one third to the opposition. However, this practice did not apply to the President of the Republic who represents the whole nation, not a particular party or political group.[47]

The rule of three thirds was criticized for a long time, for favouring the parliamentary majority which is also represented in government, for neglecting extra-parliamentarian parties and for measuring speaking time accorded to politicians regardless of the content of the intervention.[48] In 2000, the CSA decided that speaking time should not be allocated on the basis of strict arithmetics.[49] The qualitative dimension of pluralism should also be taken into account. Its new formula, the principle of reference (*principe de reference*) required that the period of time given to the members of the Parliamentary opposition could not be less than half of the total time assigned to the government and the members of the Parliamentary majority altogether.[50] Moreover, the CSA also included political parties not represented in Parliament.

---

45. *See* P. J. Humphreys, *Mass Media and Media Policy in Western Europe* (Manchester, Manchester University Press, 1996), pp. 144–149.
46. *Office de Radiodiffusion Télévision Française.*
47. CSA, 'Réflexions sur les modalités du pluralisme', 18 July 2006 <www.csa.fr/actualite/dossiers/dossiers_detail.php?id=118335&chap=2855>, 7 September 2006; Holznagel, *Rundfunkrecht in Europa*, p. 254.
48. Franceschini, *Télévision et Droit de la Communication*, p. 142.
49. CSA, 'Le principe de référence adopté par le CSA pour l'évaluation du respect du pluralisme dans les médias', 8 February 2000 <www.csa.fr/infos/textes/textes_detail.php?id=8546>, 6 September 2006.
50. More time is accorded to the Government at times of international crisis such as the war in Lebanon in July 2006.

The principle of reference did not simply revamp the rule of three thirds. It took a more qualitative approach to pluralism and established a series of new indicators. Instead of focusing on speaking time only, the entire airtime devoted to political, economic and social subjects was considered so as to enable the CSA to appreciate the importance of a subject in the general context of political broadcasts. Also, attention was paid not only to the volume of broadcasting time but also to the time slot allotted. Finally, the application of the principle of reference was monitored on a monthly basis as before, but a sliding three month period was taken into consideration at the same time.

A recent evaluation of the principle of reference showed, however, that the use of these indicators has complicated data collection without necessarily enhancing pluralism.[51] The principle of reference was not sufficiently refined so as to differentiate between individual positions within the same political formation or within the government. Nor did it solve the problem of how to qualify purely editorial broadcasts such as chronicles and commentaries. What is more, the emergence of a plethora of thematic news channels on digital terrestrial television raised doubts as to the need to maintain constraining quantitative rules. The CSA therefore came to the conclusion that the principle of reference was in need of modernization. It decided that it would be preferable to abandon the quantitative evaluation of political broadcasts in favour of a more qualitative approach such as was applied by Ofcom. Until October 2006, a team of nine CSA observers systematically monitored the application of the principle of reference in all programmes accommodating political personalities.[52] Now the television stations compile the data themselves. The CSA only looks at samples. This new system of occasional as opposed to systematic observation allows the CSA to monitor a greater number of channels, including the digital terrestrial ones.

As far as broadcasts which are directly linked to the election are concerned, the control of pluralism exercised by the CSA is more rigorous. The principles applied differ depending on the type of election as well as on the time of transmission. The nearer the date of the election, the stricter the requirement of pluralism.[53] The last and most decisive stage of the election is the so-called 'official campaign' period (*campagne officielle*). The election broadcasts that are transmitted during this period are produced exclusively by the CSA.[54] As a result, an *a priori* control of their content takes place, which is not the case in earlier election stages. In these earlier stages parties are free to express themselves as long as they do not undermine public order or public security, do not incite to hatred or violate the law in any other especially grave manner, do not make use of the national flag or anthem and do not pose in front of public buildings. During the official campaign period, the airtime allotted to candidates is measured on a weekly basis so as to be able to

51. CSA, 'Réflexions sur les modalités du pluralisme'.
52. CSA, 'Chaînes hertziennes nationales: une observation systématique' <www.csa.fr/infos/controle/controle_chaines.php>, 18 July 2007.
53. Franceschini, *Télévision et Droit de la Communication*, p. 146.
54. Law 86-1067 of 30 September 1986, Art. 16 (1).

rectify violations forthwith.[55] Notably, only public broadcasters are obliged to make free time available to parties and candidates for official campaign broadcasts.[56]

During legislative or European Parliament elections the CSA requires that each party or political formation must have equitable access to airtime. The principle of equity is interpreted in a flexible way. It does not entail that candidates should enjoy equal broadcasting opportunities.[57] It can be understood as an obligation to allocate broadcasting time that is commensurate with the presumed influence of candidates. The channels have a margin of appreciation provided that the sincerity of the ballot is not affected.[58] However, presidential elections are treated differently: equal access must be granted to all candidates.

More specific rules for the time and conditions of intervention are established by the CSA by means of recommendations addressed to all broadcasters.[59] These rules are set anew for each electoral period. The latest recommendation issued by the CSA concerns the presidential election 2007. The CSA defines the electoral period, the concept of a 'candidate', the speaking time and airtime accorded to candidates and the principles applicable to each of the campaign stages.[60] The CSA monitors the application of these rules. If it notices a violation, it can impose sanctions but it cannot invite a candidate or allocate airtime to candidates that were treated unfairly.[61] The judiciary is not competent to issue injunctions against television channels either. Only the election judge is able to act *à posteriori* by annulling the elections in case of a manifest disequilibrium.[62] Under French law, any paid political advertising is prohibited.[63] A EUR 75,000 fine applies to any violation of this rule.[64]

The Electoral Code also contains a number of rules concerning the transmission of the election campaign.[65] Notably, all electoral propaganda is prohibited on the eve of the election.[66] Also, no opinion polls can be published in the week

55. *Ibid.*
56. Electoral Code, modified by Law 2004-575 of 21 June 2004, Art. L. 167-1.
57. EPRA, 'Political Communication on Television. Matters for debate' (EPRA/2000/02).
58. Franceschini, *Télévision et Droit de la Communication*, p. 147.
59. Law 86-1067 of 30 September 1986, Art. 13 (for the public broadcasters), Art. 16 (for the private broadcasters); CSA, 'Campagnes électorales' <www.csa.fr/infos/controle/television_elections_archives.php>, 12 January 2007; R. Negrine, *Parliament and the Media: A Study of Britain, Germany and France* (London, Royal Institute of International Affairs, 1998), pp. 113–119.
60. Recommendation 2006–7 of 7 November 2006 <www.csa.fr/infos/controle/television_elections_detail.php?id=120454, 12 January 2007. For an analysis of the recommendation *see* CSA, 'Election présidentielle 2007: le CSA publie sa recommandation' (2006) 200 *La lettre du CSA*, 1.
61. Franceschini, *Télévision et Droit de la Communication*, p. 148; E. Mauboussin, 'Le CSA et les élections: entre loi et jurisprudence, une competence sous haute surveillance' (1997) 143 (2) *Légipresse*.
62. Franceschini, *Télévision et Droit de la Communication*, p. 148.
63. Law 86-1067 of 30 September 1986, Art. 14.
64. Electoral Code, modified by Law 2004-575 of 21 June 2004, Art. L 90-1.
65. Electoral Code, modified by Law 2004-575 of 21 June 2004, Art. L 167-1.
66. *Ibid.*, Art. L 49.

preceding the election.[67] The effectiveness of this statutory ban is, however, doubtful in view of the plethora of other means of communication. During the 1997 legislative elections, the election poll results were published on the Internet through the website of the Tribune de Genève in Switzerland.

7.2 Broadcasts of General Interest

Public broadcasters are required to transmit general interest messages such as programmes on consumer rights (ten minutes per week in primetime on France 2 and four minutes per week in prime time on France 3) and programmes aimed at integrating foreign nationals.[68] They are also obliged to grant free airtime to organizations selected by the government to promote a national cause such as the action against AIDS or the integration of people with disabilities.[69] Moreover, they are required to broadcast at any time governmental announcements, giving a right of reply to the opposition (*droit de réplique*).[70] The Prime Minister traditionally airs a message to the nation on New Year's Eve, and occasionally before election days or other important occasions. However, ministerial broadcasts are in general less popular than interviews in political talk shows, which are considered a more efficient way of putting ideas across and do not attract an immediate right of reply.[71]

8. CULTURAL OBLIGATIONS

8.1 Language Policy

All broadcasters in France are obliged to use the French language in their programmes and in all commercials included therein.[72] The law only makes certain exceptions for cinematographic or audiovisual works in their original version, for musical works in a foreign language, for programmes that are intended to be transmitted exclusively in a foreign language, for religious services and foreign language programmes. When programmes other than the exempted ones include foreign words, a translation in French needs to be provided that is as legible and comprehensible as the foreign language version. It is the task of the CSA to 'ensure the defence and demonstration of the French language and culture'.[73] In order to

67. Law 77-808 of 19 July 1977, modified by Law 2002-214 of 19 February 2002, Art. 11.
68. Vedel, 'France', p. 675.
69. *Ibid.*
70. Law 86-1067 of 30 September 1986, Art. 54. The reply of the opposition has usually the same duration and the same format as the governmental announcement. The concept of 'governmental announcement' is very formal, depending on whether the broadcast was initiated by the government rather than by the channel. Franceschini, *Télévision et Droit de la Communication*, p. 152.
71. Vedel, 'France', p. 675.
72. Law 86-1067 of 30 September 1986, Art. 3 (1).
73. *Ibid.*, Art. 3-1.

disseminate French language and culture abroad, France Télévisions participates in channels with a European and international vocation such as Arte, TV5 and the programme bank Canal France International (CFI). The latter supplies its programmes to partner channels in developing countries at no cost.[74]

8.2 High Culture

The *cahiers des charges* of the public broadcasters include specific obligations concerning the transmission of 'cultural programmes' in a narrow sense, i.e. classical arts, theatre etc. France 2 and France 3 must each air fifteen musical, dance or drama performances per year.[75] They also need to broadcast at least two hours per month of musical programmes and at least sixteen hours per year of concerts.[76] Public broadcasters usually broadcast more cultural programmes than required by these quotas. [77] However, the creation of the cultural European channel Arte has meant that the generalist public channels have been increasingly inclined to marginalize culture, for instance by scheduling it late at night.[78] There are no such cultural requirements for private broadcasters except for TF1.[79]

8.3 Regional Programmes

We have seen that Article 43-11 (2) of Law 86-1067 obliges public broadcasters to reflect the diversity of cultural heritage in its regional and local dimensions.[80] Regional and local identity is mainly fostered in France by the national public broadcaster France 3. France 3 is required to contribute to the expression of the principal regional languages spoken in the metropolitan territory, to offer programmes of a regional and local character and to develop the provision of information on regional and local issues.[81] It may also diffuse the main debates of the regional Assemblies.[82] In practice, France 3 airs regional and local news bulletins and programmes produced by thirteen regional directorates and thirty-seven local bureaus on a daily basis.[83] However, France 3 regional channels only cover large

74. P. Marcangeo-Leos, 'France' in *Iris Special: The Public Service Broadcasting Culture* (Strasbourg, European Audiovisual Observatory, 2007), pp. 89, 97.
75. *Cahiers des missions des charges de France 2 et France 3*, Art. 24.
76. *Ibid.*, Art. 26.
77. T. Vedel, 'France', p. 679.
78. Marcangeo-Leos, 'France', p. 96.
79. T. Ader, 'Der kulturelle Auftrag und der Aspekt "Regionalität" im Pflichtenprogramm der Rundfunkveranstalter', (2006) 8 *IRIS plus*, 1.
80. *See* Part 1, Ch. 2.6, p. 20 *above*.
81. *Cahiers des missions des charges de France 2 et France 3*, Arts 16, 22, 24.
82. *Ibid.*, Art. 14.
83. Vedel, 'France', p. 667.

regions while the few existing local channels only reach a small percentage of the population.[84]

8.4 Education

Educational programming is mainly provided by France 5, which is also known as '*la télévision du savoir, de la formation et de l'emploi*' ('the broadcaster of knowledge, training and employment'). It is obliged to promote knowledge transfer in all areas, to improve understanding of the employment market and of trends in employment and life within a company, to raise awareness of social and economic issues and of civic life, to pay particular attention to children and youth programming.[85] All France Télévisions channels are obliged to transmit programmes on science and technology. The Chaîne parlementaire also has a 'mission of public service, information and training in public life for citizens, by means of parliamentary, educational and civic programmes'.[86]

8.5 Religious Programmes

France 2 is obliged to broadcast every Sunday morning religious programmes dedicated to the main religious associations that are active in France.[87] These programmes cover religious services and other topics of religious interest. The associations have editorial control, but need to obtain the opinion of the Ministry with responsibility for religious observance prior to production. Also, when these programmes are not retransmissions, France 2 may view the programmes in advance and refuse to transmit them.[88] Transmission costs are born by the channel, subject to a limit fixed by the *cahiers des charges.*

8.6 Cultural Quotas

Quotas are a favoured instrument for protecting cultural identity and for stimulating programme-making in France. Programming quotas go beyond the requirements of the TwF Directive. Broadcasters are required to reserve at least 60 per cent of their yearly audiovisual and cinematographic productions for European creations and at least 40 per cent for French language productions.[89] Interestingly,

---

84. M.Bourreau, 'Digital Terrestrial Television in France: An Attempt to Enhance Competition in an Oligopolistic Market' <ses.enst.fr/bourreau/Recherche/DTV.pdf>, 20 April 2007.
85. *Cahiers des missions des charges de France 5*, Art. 11 *et seq.*
86. Law 86-1067 of 30 September 1986, Art. 45 (2).
87. Law 86-1067 of 30 September 1986, Art. 56.
88. Marcangeo-Leos, 'France', p. 99.
89. Law 86-1067 of 30 September 1986, Art. 27 and Decree 90-66 of 17 January 1990, Arts 7, 13, 14. For the distinction between audiovisual and cinematographic productions, a number of criteria are laid down in Arts 2, 3, 4 of Decree 90-66. French language productions are defined

the French language quota was lowered from an initial percentage of 50 per cent as a result of an agreement reached with the Commission in the beginning of the nineties, so as to allow a wider 'corridor' for European works. The European and French language quotas apply to the entire schedule and especially at primetime (between 8.30 P.M. and 10.30 P.M. for cinematographic works, between 6 P.M. and 11 P.M. for audiovisual works).[90] For cable and satellite channels and for digital terrestrial television (TNT) the thresholds can be reached incrementally within a greater time span. Moreover, the satellite and cable channels may see their European quotas lowered (although never below the threshold of 50 per cent fixed by the TwF Directive) provided that they invest more into independent French language productions.[91]

Moreover, broadcasters are obliged to invest in the production of European and French language audiovisual and cinematographic works. Investment quotas are also more far-reaching than is required by the TwF Directive. As far as audiovisual works are concerned, broadcasters have to invest at least 16 per cent of their turnover from the previous year in the production of French language audiovisual works (and to diffuse 120 hours of original European and French language works). Two thirds of the investments must be devoted to independent productions.[92] As far as cinematographic works are concerned, all channels, whatever their support (terrestrial, cable or satellite), whose principal object is not the diffusion of cinematographic works and that diffuse at least 52 cinematographic works of long duration per annum must invest a minimum of 3.2 per cent of their turnover from the previous year in European films and 2.5 per cent in French language films.[93] Again, three quarters of these investments must be devoted to independent productions.

9. ADVERTISING

9.1 BACKGROUND

France was one of the last European countries to introduce the use of television advertising. The United Kingdom was the first European country to adopt the use of adverts in the private channel ITV in 1955, followed by Italy who has been using adverts since 1957 and Germany who started to authorize the use of adverts in the public channels since 1959.[94] In France the use of advertising on television was not

in Art. 5 of Decree 90-66, European productions in Art. 6 of the same Decree that implements Art. 6 of the TwF Directive.

90. Decree 90-66 of 17 January 1990, Arts 7, 14.
91. *Ibid.*, Art. 13.
92. Decree 2001-609 of 9 July 2001.
93. CSA, 'Les obligations de production d'oeuvres audiovisuelles et cinématographiques à la télévision', <www.csa.fr/infos/controle/television_quotas_production.php>, 18 July 2007.
94. CSA, *Publicité, parrainage, et téléachat à la télévision et á la radio* (Paris, CSA, 2006).

authorized by the ORTF until 1968, with an initial limit of 2 minutes a day, progressively increased during the following years.

The discipline of advertising and teleshopping is nowadays enshrined in Decree 92-280 of 27 March 1992.[95] It is established that advertising and teleshopping spots must be clearly recognizable as such and be kept separate from other parts of the programmes by the use of optical or acoustic means. Furthermore, the use of adverts must always be considered as exceptional and be included between programmes. The insertion of advertising during programmes is acceptable only under the condition that the integrity and value of the programmes is preserved.[96]

The CSA monitors adherence to broadcasting principles in advertising, both in the private and in the public sector. It only exercises its monitoring activities ex post, after the broadcast of a message.[97] Ex ante control is exercised by the Advertising Verification Bureau *(Bureau de verification de la publicité*, BVP), a non-state body. The BVP drafts the rules that apply to the entire advertising industry in the form of a Charter. It also gives advice during the production of the messages on their conformity with existing regulations and compiles a list of all new advertising messages. Advertisers are obliged to obtain advance clearance of their television advertising from the BVP.[98]

9.2 The Principle of Separation

One of the main reasons for intervention by the CSA and for the imposition of numerous sanctions is surreptitious advertising (*publicité clandestine*).[99] Article 9 of Decree 92-280 defines surreptitious advertising as: 'any verbal or visual representation of goods, services, name, trade mark or activities of a producer of goods or a provider of services in programmes when such representation is intended to serve advertising'. These kinds of advertisements are prohibited.

This rule transposes into French Law the provisions of the TwF Directive.[100] However, the definition of Article 9 is stricter than the one laid down in the Directive. According to Article 1 (d) the representation of goods, services etc. constitutes 'surreptitious advertising' if it 'is intended by the broadcaster to serve advertising and might mislead the public as to its nature. Such representation is considered to be intentional in particular if it done in return for payment or for similar consideration'. Article 9 does not make any reference to a quid pro quo.

95. Decree 92-280 of 27 March 1992 modified by Decree of 28 December 2001.
96. *Ibid.*, Arts 3 and 4.
97. Law 86-1067 of 30 September 1986, Art. 14.
98. Hans-Bredow-Institut, 'Final Report: Study on Co-Regulation Measures in the Media Sector', June 2006 <www.ec.europa.eu/avpolicy/docs/library/studies/coregul/coregul-final-report_en.pdf>, 18 July 2007, p. 47.
99. CSA, 'Chaînes hertziennes nationales: une observation systématique' <www.csa.fr/infos/controle/controle_chaines.php>, 18 July 2007; Debbasch, *Droit des médias*, para. 1454.
100. Dir. 97/36 of 30 June 1997, Arts 1 (d), 10 (4).

Indeed, the CSA has declined to prove the existence of remuneration in order to establish its surreptitious nature. Even if a television station has only been incautious, but has not drawn any financial or other advantage, the surreptitious character of advertising cannot be excluded.[101]

The crucial distinction is between promotion and information. The reference to goods or services in programmes is not prohibited as long as it aims to inform the viewers without promoting the products in question. Other criteria utilized by the CSA to identify the existence of surreptitious advertising are the absence of pluralism in the presentation of goods, services or trade marks; the frequency of the citation or visualization of a product or a mark; the indication of the address or telephone number of the trader; the lack of a critical approach.[102] For example, the practice of reviewing critically cultural products such as cinema films or literary works is widespread and is wholly legitimate in so far as it aims to keep viewers informed.[103] This contrasts sharply with the forceful and repeated reference to a cinematographic work as in the programme *C'est mon choix* of 15 April 2004 on France 3. The CSA accepted that showing five extracts as well as the trailer of the film '*Treize à la douzaine*' in the framework of the mentioned programme to coincide with the release of the film amounted to surreptitious advertising.[104] The CSA asked France 3 to comply with the law, the more so since cinema is one of the sectors for which advertising is prohibited in France.[105] The CSA also pays attention to the acknowledgements and thanks to certain undertakings that habitually appear at the end of a programme. Such acknowledgements risk being classified as surreptitious advertising if they are particularly pronounced (large characters, close-ups) or if they use a logo.[106]

As far as surreptitious advertising in films is concerned, also known as product placement, the CSA differentiates between cinematographic and audiovisual works. As far as the former are concerned, the CSA does not criticize the editor of a television service for programming a film that was intended to be primarily shown on the big screen and that contains persistent product placement, not even if the distributor had contributed to the financing of the work. This approach is consistent with that of the Community authorities. The CSA's approach is stricter in relation to product placement in films that are aimed to be programmed exclusively on television. Editors of television services must be vigilant not to transmit audiovisual works that contain an excessive visual or verbal display of goods, services or marks. This is even more so in the case of works whose scenario is influenced by a certain product or which take place in an identified or identifiable undertaking. In other words, the CSA uses the criterion of 'undue prominence' adopted by the Commission in its interpretative Communication of April 2004.[107]

101. Debbasch, *Droit des médias*, para. 1454.
102. CSA, *Publicité*, p. 31.
103. *Ibid.*, p. 29.
104. *Ibid.*, p. 30.
105. Decree 92-280 of 27 March 1992, Art. 8.
106. CSA, *Publicité*, p. 37.
107. Commission interpretative communication on certain aspects of the provisions on televised advertising in the 'Television without frontiers' Directive, 28 April 2004, COM (2004) 1450 final.

The CSA pays particular attention that programmes aimed at minors do not contain any product placement. In a recent recommendation the CSA laid down the ground rules for the diffusion of works directed at minors whose protagonists are commercially exploited.[108] Without putting into question the well-established practice of 'derived products', i.e. products or services that are the upshots of other pre-existing products or services, the CSA seeks to prevent a confusion in the minds of young viewers between advertising and fiction caused by the commercial exploitation of film characters. The CSA draws a distinction between programmes that have given birth to derived products or services such as educational products or toys and programmes that include characters directly emanating from the world of toys such as dolls, soft toys etc. In the first case, the CSA requires a clear chronological separation between the programme and the advertising message promoting the derived products. In the second case, the CSA requires that the first run of the programme does not coincide with the launching of the product or service in the national territory. Also, a period of at least 45 minutes needs to elapse between the transmission of the programme and the advertising message.

9.3 Advertising and Minors

The requirements of Article 16 of the TwF Directive have been verbatim transposed in Article 7 of Decree 92-280 of 27 March 1992. Decree 87-37 of 26 January 1987 prohibits the use of minors as principal actors in advertisements for products not designed for them, i.e. not intended for family consumption or not consumed mainly by them. Scheduling restrictions exist for the transmission of advertising messages for videos, DVDs, Audiotel or Télétel services, internet sites and video games.[109]

10. PROTECTION OF MINORS

The protection of minors is a fundamental concern of the French broadcasting order. Article 15 of Law 86-1067, which is largely identical to Articles 22, 22a of the TwF Directive, entrusted to the CSA the important mission of regulating on the matter.[110] On 5 May 1989 the CSA adopted a directive establishing precise family viewing hours. Broadcasters were required to refrain from transmitting programmes of an erotic nature or which encouraged violence between 6 A.M. and 10.30 P.M., and from broadcasting trailers for such programmes before 8.30 P.M.

108. Recommendation of 7 June 2006.
109. CSA, *La Protection de l'Enfance et de l'Adolescence à la télévision et à la radio. Bilan de l'Action du CSA*, (Paris, CSA, 2006), pp. 23–24.
110. CSA, *The Protection of Children and Adolescents on French Television* (Paris, CSA, 2005), p. 7; CSA, *Protection de l'Enfance*, p. 17.

However, the unsatisfactory results obtained in practice led the CSA to further strengthen the protection of minors by adopting a system of classification and certificate rating of programmes: the youth certificate rating. The youth certificate rating was introduced on 18 November 1996 with the aim of creating a system of classification into five categories of cinematographic and audiovisual works and of selecting appropriate broadcasting times according to the classification of each programme. At the beginning the youth certificate rating only applied to terrestrial hertzian channels, but since 2000 it has been extended to all channels, including cable and satellite channels.

In 2000 and 2001, the *Médiamétrie* institute conducted two surveys to assess the effectiveness of the youth certificate rating. The surveys showed that the public was not sufficiently familiar with the pictograms and did not properly understand their meaning. So as to render the system more legible, the CSA conducted a broad consultation in 2002 that led to the system's adaptation. Since November 2002, youth certificate ratings have been based on a system of classification according to age.[111]

Category I programmes are suitable for all audiences. Category II, -10 programmes include some scenes liable to harm minors under ten. The scheduling of these programmes is left to the discretion of the broadcaster as long as they are kept separate from children's programmes. Category III, -12 programmes are cinematographic works prohibited for children under 12 and other programmes that may disturb minors under 12, especially due to the systematic use of physical or psychological violence.[112] Such programmes may not be broadcast before 10 P.M. on channels other than cinema channels. Exceptionally, programmes of this category may be broadcast after 8.30 P.M. except on certain days and on school holiday periods when children are likely to stay up late. On cinema channels, these programmes must not be broadcast on Wednesdays before 8.30 P.M. Category IV, -16 programmes are cinematographic works prohibited for minors under 16, and programmes of an erotic or extremely violent character. These programmes may only be broadcast after 10.30 P.M. on channels other than cinema channels, and after 8.30 P.M. on cinema channels. Finally, category V, -18 programmes are cinematographic works prohibited for minors under 18, and pornographic or extremely violent programmes. Such programmes may only be broadcast on authorized channels subject to a specific dual access lock between 12 midnight and 5 A.M.[113] A recent CSA recommendation allows extracts and trailers for such programmes to be broadcast after 10 pm provided that they do not have pornographic character or display extreme violence.[114]

The fact that pornographic and extremely violent programmes are allowed on French television indicates that France has implemented Article 22 of the TwF Directive on paper only. As a result of the Directive's imperfect transposition,

111. *CSA*, *Protection de l'Enfance*, pp. 15–16; CSA Recommendation of 7 June 2005.
112. Cinematographic works are classified by the Minister of Culture after obtaining the opinion of a classification commission. *See* Decree 90-174 of 23 February 1990.
113. Such channels need to enter into a contract with the CSA, which specifies the maximum number of broadcasts allowed per year, and obliges the channels to invest in film production. Vedel, 'France', p. 698.
114. CSA Recommendation of 4 July 2006.

Canal Plus and certain cable channels are allowed to transmit pornographic programmes in the small hours.[115] CSA proposals to modify Article 15 of the Broadcasting Law of 30 September 1986 so as to explicitly ban pornographic and extremely violent programmes were dropped as a result of allegations that the CSA President at the time, Dominique Baudis, was involved in sadomasochistic orgies.[116]

The public is informed of the certificate ratings at the beginning of each programme. Also, pictograms, with the exception of the -10 pictogram, have to be displayed throughout the entire duration of the programme and in the trailers. The -10 pictogram has to be present on the screen at the start of the programme and/or after each advertising break depending on the duration of the programme and on whether it includes such breaks.[117]

The youth certificate rating system prescribes that each channel should set up a viewing committee responsible for proposing a programme classification system. The composition of the committee is left to the discretion of the companies; the CSA only wishes to be kept informed in the interests of transparency. Some channels, such as France 2 and France 3, have appointed internal committees while others choose their committee members among external experts or television viewers.[118] Public channels have also included a public channel mediator in their self-regulatory system. Mediators are independent agents, appointed by and responsible to the President of France Télévisions. Their role consists in working alongside the teams of France 2, France 3 and France 5, in representing the television viewers and reporting their views.

The CSA monitors the coherence of the classifications and the programming hours decided by the channels. It examines all complaints from the public, but may only take action after a programme has been broadcast. In cases of violation, the CSA normally sends a letter of warning to the respective channel or, more rarely, a letter of formal notice. The Authority is circumspect about the application of sanctions so as not to unduly restrict freedom of communication. Only in cases of particularly serious or repeated breaches would the CSA apply financial penalties.

There have been frequent complaints by viewers concerning the transmission of films with shocking scenes on Arte in the early evening without prior notice. Arte does not apply the youth certificate rating system. It takes the view that it does not need to respect this system nor the French laws implementing the TwF Directive as a result of its status as a Franco-German channel conferred on it by its constitutive international Treaty of 2 October 1990. Notwithstanding these objections, Arte argues that it complies with the Directive by using an acoustic warning and a visual symbol for programmes liable to harm minors. The CSA's view is that Arte falls under the French jurisdiction in accordance with Article 2 (2), (3) (a) TwF Directive given that its head office is located in Strasbourg and the editorial decisions about programme schedules are also taken there. Even though it does not exercise control

115. Franceschini, *Télévision et Droit de la Communication*, p. 136.
116. Harcourt, *Regulation of Media Markets*, p. 191.
117. Decision 2003-443 of 17 June 2003, Art. 4.
118. CSA, *Protection of Children*, p. 17.

over this channel, the CSA asked the French Prime Minister in June 2006 to raise the question of the law applicable to Arte with the *Conseil d'État.*

11. RIGHT OF REPLY

Any natural or legal person has the right of reply if allegations have been made in a television programme that are likely to affect his or her name or reputation.[119] The reply shall be transmitted at a time and in a manner appropriate to the broadcast to which the request refers. The right of reply has to be exercised within three months from the time of the broadcast. If the broadcast is related to criminal proceedings this limit restarts on the day when the decision acquitting the aggrieved party becomes final. If the broadcaster refuses to transmit the reply within eight days – or 24 hours in the case where an election candidate has been offended – the right can be enforced through the civil courts. All broadcasters are obliged to designate a person in charge of the enforcement of the right of reply. Detailed rules about the modalities of the exercise of this right are laid down in Decree 87-246 of 6 April 1987.

Law 2004-575 of 21 June 2004 on confidence in the digital economy introduced a right of reply that is applicable to online communication services.[120] The modalities for the exercise of this right have recently been fixed in Decree 2007-1527 of 24 October 2007.[121] The right of reply is granted to any natural or legal person that is directly or indirectly named in an online communication service. The named person has a right of reply on the same service regardless of whether the assertion made has been inaccurate or whether his/her legitimate interests have been damaged. The right of reply is only granted provided there is no possibility of direct reply on the respective site. The request for the right of reply has to be addressed in writing to the webmaster of the site within three months from the publication of the initial article. The webmaster has to place the reply on the site within three days from the receipt of the request. The reply must be available at the same section of the site and under similar conditions as the article that gave rise to the reply. A simple hypertext link to a new page containing the reply would not be sufficient.[122] It must be accessible on line for as long as the contentious article is and in any event for at least 24 hours. Two questionable provisions of the decree are, first, that the person exercising the right of reply can refrain from using it if the webmaster agrees to modify or remove the contentious entry and, second, that the reply cannot exceed 200 lines.[123] This vaguely defined maximum length makes it clear that the right of reply envisaged by the Decree is not tailored to websites whose principal purpose is the distribution of audiovisual content, but to ones containing mainly text.

---

119. Law 82-652 of 29 July 1982, Art. 6.
120. Law 2004-575 of 21 June 2004, Art. 6 (4).
121. Decree 2007-1527 of 24 October 2007.
122. T. Verbiest and P. Reynaud, 'Le régime juridique du droit de réponse sur internet' (2006) 236 *Légipresse*, 133, 138.
123. Decree 2007-1527 of 24 October 2007, Arts. 3, 5.

Chapter 3
Germany

1. BACKGROUND

The structure of the German broadcasting system has been shaped to a great extent by the experience of the role played by the German media in the first half of the twentieth century. In the Weimar Republic of the 1920s and early 1930s, conservative elements in the German press strove to undermine democratic institutions. Later, the Third Reich exploited all media for propaganda purposes. After the Second World War, when the allied occupational forces established public broadcasting in Germany, they sought to make sure that such phenomena could not be repeated. For one, they entrusted broadcasting to the states (*Länder*), not to the federation (*Bund*). For another, they tried to model broadcasting in their areas of influence after their own preferences.

The British preferred a public service system modelled after the British Broadcasting Corporation (BBC). Indeed, the Nordwestdeutscher Rundfunk (NWDR), instituted in Hamburg with the guidance of Hugh Carleton Greene, former senior manager of the BBC, was greatly influenced by the British ideals. It is often said that the Americans favoured their system of deregulated commercial broadcasting, but this is doubtful.[1] In fact, the Americans did not really trust a purely commercial system. They also favoured a public service system which would be better placed to re-educate Germany after the war.[2] In any case, it was not conceivable that the totally impoverished Germany would be able to bring up the necessary resources to fund television from advertising revenues.[3]

1. R. Woldt, 'Germany' in *Television across Europe: Regulation, Policy and Independence*, (New York, Open Society Institute, 2005), p. 735.
2. I am grateful to Professor Karl-Nikolaus Peifer for this comment.
3. H. Bausch, *Rundfunk in Deutschland: Rundfunkpolitik nach 1945*, vol. I, part 1 (Munich, Deutscher Taschenbuch Verlag, 1980), p. 18.

Nine regional public broadcasting organizations were set up in different *Länder*, some covering one state only, such as the Bavarian Broadcasting Corporation (Bayerischer Rundfunk), others covering jointly several states, such as the NWDR. In 1950, these public broadcasters formed an association, the ARD (Arbeitsgemeinschaft der öffentlichrechtlichen Rundfunkanstalten Deutschlands – Association of Public Service Broadcasters in Germany). Members of the ARD are currently nine regional public broadcasting organizations, Deutsche Welle (DW), Germany's international channel, and DeutschlandRadio, the national public radio broadcaster.[4] The ARD established the first public channel (Erstes Deutsches Fernsehen) to which the regional broadcasting organizations contribute programmes for common distribution according to specified percentages. Besides the nationwide 'First programme', the ARD corporations also broadcast seven nationwide programmes with a regional accent, the so-called 'Third programmes'.[5] A second public television channel, the ZDF (Zweites Deutsches Fernsehen), was established in 1961 by a treaty (*Staatsvertrag*) between all West German *Länder*. ZDF's mission is the transmission of a national television service. Programming changes, especially as regards the news, need to be coordinated with the ARD.[6]

ARD and ZDF are involved in a number of joint ventures. They transmit a satellite, German language cultural programme, 3sat, together with Austrian and Swiss television.[7] They are also involved in the European cultural channel Arte along with the French company Arte France.[8] Further, they transmit together two thematic channels: Ki.KA, a children's channel without commercials, and Phoenix, a current affairs and documentary channel.[9] Finally, they are involved since 2002 together with Deutsche Welle in an international digital channel, German TV.[10]

2. BROADCASTING AUTHORITIES

German public broadcasters are supervised directly by the governments of the *Länder*, but only to a limited extent due to the constitutional principle of freedom of broadcasting from state control (*Staatsfreiheit*).[11] The Constitutional Court has

4. Bayerischer Rundfunk (BR), Hessischer Rundfunk (HR), Mitteldeutscher Rundfunk (MDR), Norddeutscher Rundfunk (NDR), Radio Bremen (RB), Rundfunk Berlin Brandenburg (RBB), Saarländischer Rundfunk (SR), Südwestrundfunk (SWR), Westdeutscher Rundfunk Köln (WDR).
5. Bayerisches Fernsehen, hr Fernsehen, MDR Fernsehen, NDR Fernsehen, rbb Fernsehen, SWR-/SR-Fernsehen, WDR Fernsehen.
6. ZDF-Staatsvertrag (ZDF-StV) modified by the 9th Rundfunkänderungsstaatsvertrag of 1 March 2007, § 2 (2).
7. Rundfunkstaatsvertrag (RStV) of 31 August 1991, last modified by the 9th Rundfunkänderungsstaatsvertrag of 1 March 2007, § 19 (2) a).
8. *Ibid.*, § 19 (2) second para.
9. *Ibid.*, § 19 (2) b).
10. German TV ceased to exist in its former shape by the end of 2005. It is now run by Deutsche Welle alone but there is still a cooperation with ARD and ZDF.
11. BVerfGE 12, 205 (1961); BVerfGE 73, 118 (1986).

ruled that public broadcasters can only be subjected to a limited control as regards the legality as opposed to the expediency of their actions.[12] In cases of violation of the law, the *Länder* governments have to notify the broadcasters first and give them adequate time to take remedial action before passing any formal orders.[13] Also, in some of the *Länder*, there is an explicit legal provision stating that directions cannot be given with regard to programming matters.[14] In view of these constraints, state supervision of public broadcasters has been rare.

Internal supervision of German public broadcasters is exercised by three authorities: the Director General (*Intendant*), the Broadcasting Council (*Rundfunkrat*; ZDF: *Fernsehrat*) and the Administrative Council (*Verwaltungsrat*). The Director General runs and represents the institution in public. The Broadcasting Council is the largest collegiate body having as its main function the representation of the interests of the public. The Broadcasting Council elects the Director General and members of the Administrative Council. It approves the budget, lays down programme guidelines, advises the Director General on programming questions and supervises the programme to ensure that it complies with legal requirements.[15] The Administrative Council is a smaller collegiate body, with 7 to 15 members, that watches over the management of the institution and advises the Director General on financial and personnel questions.

The Broadcasting Council is arguably the most important of these authorities. Not only is it instrumental in the election of the other two bodies. Moreover, the broadcasting laws of the *Länder* require – in line with the case-law of the Constitutional Court – that all significant social forces (‘*gesellschaftlich relevante Gruppen*) are represented in the Broadcasting Council.[16] This is to ensure the balanced composition and accountability of broadcasting organizations and to prevent their domination by the state or by private interests. Naturally, it is impracticable to require the representation of all social groups. The legislator has wide discretion in selecting the groups that should be represented.[17] The *Länder* statutes contain detailed catalogues of the organizations that have a seat in their Council. The big churches, employers and trade unions, youth and sport organizations, cultural organizations, universities, the media sector and local government are represented in most Broadcasting Councils.[18] Some statutes also include members of the parliaments and/or of the *Länder* governments in the Council.[19] The size of

---

12. BVerfGE 12, 205, 261; 57, 295, 326. However, according to § 1 (1) 2 HR-Gesetz, the public broadcaster of Hessen (Hessischer Rundfunk) is self-regulated and not subject to state supervision.
13. MDR-StV, § 37 (4); NDR-StV, § 37 (4); WDR-G, § 54 (4).
14. MDR-StV, § 37 (3) 2; NDR-StV, § 37 (3) 2; WDR-G, § 54 (5).
15. This supervisory power only exists in some of the *Länder*. *See* for instance MDR-StV, § 20 (1); WDR-G, § 16 (4); ZDF-StV, § 20 (1) 2.
16. BVerfGE 12, 205, 261 *et seq.* (1961); 83, 238, 332 *et seq.* (1991).
17. BVerfGE 83, 238, 334 (1991).
18. M. Kühn, *Meinungsvielfalt im Rundfunk: Die Sicherung von Pluralismus in den Rundfunksystemen Deutschlands und der USA* (Munich, C. H. Beck, 2003), p. 65.
19. *See* for instance MDR-StV, § 19 (1) 1, 2.

the Broadcasting Councils varies between 18 and 77 members, the ZDF Council having the highest number of members.

The influence of the state and of political parties on the administration of public broadcasting in Germany is often criticized as antithetical to the constitutional imperative of *Staatsfreiheit*. The Constitutional Court has sanctioned a certain state representation in the broadcasting authorities as long as it does not amount to direct or indirect state control.[20] However, in practice Broadcasting Councils are often dominated by political parties. Given the close ties between the state and political parties, it seems justified to treat them as one power block.[21] State control of public broadcasting may be either direct by means of the representation of parties and governments in the Councils or indirect by selecting the representative of a non-state organization, for instance, of an environmental or cultural organization.[22] Also, regardless of whether they have been nominated by the state, representatives of social groups tend to align themselves with political parties: the trade unions support the Social Democrats, the employers associations the Christian Democrats.[23]

The representation of the state and of political parties in the Broadcasting Council is generally considered to be acceptable when it does not exceed one third of its members.[24] This limit may not be required by the *Grundgesetz* but was imposed on the previously strongly politicized Councils of the NDR and WDR in 1980 and was included in the Bavarian Constitution after a referendum in 1972.[25] As a result of the politicization of the Broadcasting Councils, public broadcasters within the ARD association often align themselves with the ruling party in their area.[26] Doubts have also been expressed as to the constitutionality of the ZDF Council where state control is most pronounced. Of the 77 seats in the ZDF Council, 16 are reserved for the governments of the federal states, three for the federal government and 12 for the parties that are represented in the *Bundestag*.[27] Moreover, the state exerts indirect influence by appointing 16 representatives from the areas of education and culture and by selecting another 25 members from among the nominees of certain non-political associations.[28] This means that only five of the 77 members of the ZDF Council are nominally independent of the state.[29]

20. BVerfGE 12, 205, 263 (1961).
21. H. Möller, 'Die Stellung der "Gesellschaftlich relevanten Gruppen" im öffentlich-rechtlichen Rundfunk' (2001) 4 AfP, 275, 277.
22. *Ibid.*
23. Woldt, 'Germany', p. 751.
24. Möller, 'Stellung der "gesellschaftlich relevanten Gruppen" ', 276.
25. Barendt, *Broadcasting Law*, p. 62.
26. D. A. L. Levy, *Europe's Digital Revolution. Broadcasting Regulation, the EU and the Nation State* (London, Routledge, 1999), 28.
27. ZDF-StV, § 21 (1) (a), (b), (c).
28. ZDF-StV, § 21 (1) (r), (g)–(q), (3), (4).
29. Möller, 'Stellung der "gesellschaftlich relevanten Gruppen" ', 278.

Even if the 'one third rule' is not cast in stone, evidence of such excessive state representation calls the very principle of *Staatsfreiheit* into question. The counter-argument has always been that public broadcasting belongs to the people and has to be controlled by the people as represented by the parties. This argument is, however, flawed as it is tantamount to saying that there are no other significant social forces (*gesellschaftlich relevante Gruppen*) that deserve to have a say. State control over public broadcasting in Germany is only mitigated by the country's federal structure. Given that different parties are in power in each of the *Länder*, it is quite impossible for a single party to exercise control over the entire public broadcasting system.[30]

3. FINANCING

Public broadcasting in Germany is financed by means of the licence fee, advertising revenues and other revenues from programme sales, sponsoring, merchandising etc. Its main source of income is the licence fee.[31] In 2005, the licence fee accounted for 83.1 per cent of ARD's total income, advertising revenues for about 2.1 per cent and other revenues for 14.8 per cent.[32] The current level of the licence fee is set at 17.03 euros (EUR) per month for both radio and television, consisting of a basic fee of EUR 5.52 and of a television fee of EUR 11.51.[33] The licence fee is linked to the possession of a television set regardless of its actual use.[34] A series of exemptions from the need for a licence exists for persons receiving welfare benefits, persons with disabilities etc.[35]

The obligation to pay the basic fee of EUR 5.52 per month has been extended since January 2007 to computers and mobile phones that can receive television services via the internet. However, this obligation is waived if the same household already pays the licence fee for a radio or television set. Therefore, the 'PC licence fee' is likely to affect businesses more than private households that are usually equipped with radio and television sets. Also, if more then one computer is kept in the same premises the licence fee only needs to be paid once.[36] The licence fee for computers has met with considerable resistance from the industry and has been challenged before the Constitutional Court. The German Chamber of Industry and Commerce rightly argues that computers and mobile phones are often indispensable work instruments, which are not normally used to receive television

30. Levy, *Europe's Digital Revolution*, p. 28.
31. RStV, § 13 (1) 1.
32. *See* ARD, 'The Broadcasting System 2007' <www.ard.de/-/id=161952/property=download/kvilfq/index.pdf>, 18 July 2007.
33. Rundfunkfinanzierungsstaatsvertrag (RFinStV) of 31 August 1991, last modified by the 9th Rundfunkänderungsstaatsvertrag of 1 March 2007, § 8.
34. Rundfunkgebührenstaatsvertrag (RGebStV) of 31 August 1991, last modified by the 9th Rundfunkänderungsstaatsvertrag of 1 March 2007, § 4 (1).
35. *Ibid.*, § 6.
36. RGebStV, § 5 (3).

services. A reform of the licence fee system is currently under consideration. It is claimed that linking the licence fee to the possession of a single appliance seems anachronistic in view of the convergence of television, computer and telephone. The introduction of a fee for every household is a possible alternative model.

The amount of the licence fee is decided in Germany by means of a unique system that aims to shield public broadcasters from political influence. A Commission made up of 16 independent experts, the Independent Commission for the Assessment of Financial Requirements of German Public Broadcasting (*Kommission zur Überprüfung und Ermittlung des Finanzbedarfs der Rundfunkanstalten*, KEF) fixes licence fees at three stages. First, public broadcasters notify KEF of their financial requirements every two years. Second, KEF examines whether the notified financial requirements are appropriately estimated and whether they are in accordance with the principles of business efficiency and thrift.[37] KEF then recommends to the *Länder* a certain amount for the licence fee in the next period. This proposal must be approved by the *Länder* governments and parliaments. Finally, the licence fee is determined on the basis of this recommendation by an Interstate Treaty of the *Länder*.[38]

According to the *Eighth Broadcasting* case of the BVerfG, political authorities can only depart from KEF's recommendation on grounds that are consistent with the freedom of broadcasting, essentially grounds related to access to information and the appropriate burdening of viewers and listeners.[39] The pursuit of goals related to programming or to media policy is excluded as it would open the gate for political influence on public broadcasting. KEF's recommendation is hence of a virtually binding nature. However, in 2004 the *Länder* governments deviated for the first time since the *Eighth Broadcasting* case from the original KEF proposal. KEF had suggested an increase of EUR 1.09, but they only approved an increase of EUR 0.88 from 1 April 2005.

The deviation from KEF's proposal and the fact that the discussions on the increase of the licence fee were used by some *Länder* to negotiate for structural reforms of public broadcasters, notably the restriction of the number of their programmes,[40] was criticized as unconstitutional.[41] As the Constitutional Court has stated succinctly 'programming decisions have funding prerequisites, and

37. RFinStV, § 3 (1).
38. RStV, § 14 (4).
39. BVerfGE 90, 60 (1994).
40. According to § 19 RStV, ARD and ZDF are allowed to broadcast one general-interest channel each as well as one joint cultural channel (in addition to their participation in Arte) and two joint thematic channels. They can also transmit three more digital channels in the areas of culture, education and information. The ARD broadcasting corporations are not allowed to broadcast more programmes than those in existence on 1 April 2004. New ARD and ZDF programmes can only be offered in exchange for existing ones provided the public service mission is fulfilled and no additional costs ensue as a result.
41. F. Ossenbühl, 'Spielräume des Gesetzgebers bei der Gebührenfestsetzung' (2004) 3 MP, 129; contra C. Degenhart, 'Öffentlich-rechtlicher Rundfunkauftrag und Rundfunkgebühr nach dem siebten und achten Rundfunkänderungsstaatsvertrag' (2005) 7 K&R, 295–296.

funding decisions have programming consequences'.[42] The multistage assessment of the financial needs of public broadcasters by KEF is designed to ward off the restriction of public broadcasters programming autonomy (*Programmautonomie*) by means of a politically loaded allocation of resources. Even though the *Länder* are clearly allowed, and indeed obliged, to define media policy, tinkering with the KEF proposal to push structural reforms goes against the grain of the *Eighth Broadcasting* case. ARD and ZDF have brought an action against the *Länder* before the Constitutional Court.

The Constitutional Court reached its verdict on 11 September 2007. It held that the decision of the *Länder* infringed public broadcasters in their basic rights under Article 5(1) 2 of the German Constitution (*Grundgeszetz,* GG). It argued that the *Länder* had not substantiated on the basis of verifiable facts that it was necessary to deviate from KEF's proposal so as not to unduly burden viewers nor to impede their access to information.[43] Instead, they justified their decision on the grounds of, first, a general reference to the tight financial situation in 2004, secondly, the existence of further saving potentials, and finally, the exigencies of the dual broadcasting order and the competition between public and private media.

The Constitutional Court criticized the first ground for being very open ended but did not examine it in great detail given that the *Länder* did not intend to base their decision on this ground alone.[44] The Court struck down the second ground since the supposed further saving potentials had not been adequately fleshed out or had been based on complex, ill-founded prognoses.[45] Finally, it ruled that the third ground embodied unconstitutional decision-making *par excellence* given that it confounded media policy considerations with the setting of the licence fee.[46]

The Constitutional Court's verdict – the first one since the nineties related to the role of public broadcasters – also went beyond the relatively narrow question of the violation of the procedure for the setting of the licence fee. The Court confirmed that the requirements on the dual broadcasting order in Germany, as they have been formulated in its jurisprudence, are still valid. Their authority has not been diminished by recent technological progress or by the concomitant expansion of transmission capacities nor by developments in the media markets. The need to subject broadcasting to a special regulatory oversight is still justified by its unique potential to influence the public. This potential has even gained in weight by the enhancement and greater differentiation of programme offers as a result of new technologies.[47]

The Court, in line with its previous case-law, acknowledged further that the financing of public broadcasting by way of advertising revenues is apt to

---

42. BVerfGE 90, 60, 102.
43. BVerfG, 1 BvR 2270/05 of 11 September 2007 <www.bverfg.de/entscheidungen/rs20070911_1bvr227005.html>, 21 September 2007, paras 158 *et seq.*
44. *Ibid.*, para. 166.
45. *Ibid.*, paras 168 *et seq.*
46. *Ibid.*, paras 193, 194.
47. *Ibid.*, paras 115, 116.

strengthen its independence from the state. It stressed, however, that it is necessary to continuously assess whether the benefits of this form of financing still outweigh the risks it poses in terms of the alignment of public television with the interests of the advertising industry, its increased reliance on mass attractive programming as well as the erosion of its distinctiveness.[48] It is not likely that the Court, by saying this, intends to cut the ground from under the feet of public television by altogether depriving it from advertising revenues. Its statement is to be understood rather as a word of caution against the public broadcasting sector's excessive commercial orientation of recent times.

The Court held further that an increase of the licence fee *ex tunc* would not be apt to compensate for a possible deterioration of public service programming that has already taken place due to the lack of sufficient resources.[49] In the coming months, KEF will ask public broadcasters to report their financial requirements for the period beginning 1 January 2009. It is likely that they will request an increase of the licence fee. The Court ruled that the new settlement will need to include a compensation for public broadcasters if the unconstitutional determination of the licence fee for the current period deprived them of resources needed for the accomplishment of their mission.[50]

4. THE GERMAN CONSTITUTION

The constitutional basis for the regulation of the German broadcasting system is Article 5 (1) GG which provides:

> 'Everyone shall have the right freely to express and disseminate his opinion by speech, writing, and pictures and freely to inform himself from generally accessible sources. Freedom of the press and freedom of reporting by means of broadcasts and films are guaranteed. There shall be no censorship.'

Article 5 (1) GG only refers to 'freedom of reporting by means of broadcasts', not to 'freedom of broadcasting' in parallel to the 'freedom of the press'. However, it is not possible to draw a clear line between reporting and opinion nor would it make sense to reduce Article 5 (1) GG to a guarantee of the freedom of news reporting.[51] The German Federal Constitutional Court (*Bundesverfassungsgericht*, BVerfG), that has had a lasting effect on the development of broadcasting in Germany, has also interpreted Article 5 (1) GG expansively. In its so called '*First Broadcasting Case*' it declared that broadcasting is not just a 'medium' but a 'factor' in the formation of public opinion.[52] Its participation in the formation

48. *Ibid.*, para. 127.
49. *Ibid.*, para. 198.
50. *Ibid.*, para. 199.
51. H. von Mangoldt, F. Klein and C. Starck, *Das Bonner Grundgesetz: Kommentar*, vol. I: *Präambel, Artikel 1 bis 19* (4th edn, Munich, Franz Vahlen, 1999), Art. 5 I, II para. 100.
52. BVerfGE 12, 205 (1961).

of public opinion is by no means limited to news programmes, political commentary, or series of political programmes of the present, past or future. The formation of opinion takes place equally in dramas, musical presentations, and broadcasts of comedy programmes. The contours of broadcasting freedom remain vague in the Constitution and have only been concretized further in a series of landmark judgments of the German Constitutional Court.[53]

In the conception of the Constitutional Court, broadcasting freedom is instrumental (*dienende Freiheit*), assisting the freedom of formation of opinion. From this starting point two conclusions are drawn. Freedom of broadcasting requires first of all that broadcasting be free of state dominance and influence. This 'warding-off' effect is typical of classical civil rights. The principle of freedom from state control (*Staatsfreiheit*) is central to the German broadcasting order. It prohibits state control of broadcasting corporations and also the state supervision of programme content.[54] However, broadcasting freedom is more than just a subjective right of non-interference. It is also an objective guarantee obliging the lawmaker to create a positive order, which ensures that the variety of existing opinion is expressed in broadcasting as widely and completely as possible and that in this way, comprehensive information is offered. In order to achieve this, substantive, organizational and procedural rules are necessary. The prerequisites of guaranteeing broadcasting freedom must be determined by Parliament itself and cannot be left for the executive to decide nor can they be delegated to the broadcaster's charter or contractual rules.[55]

The Constitutional Court distinguishes between two possible structures to ensure that broadcasting will not be put at the mercy of one or several societal groups and that relevant forces are able to have their say. The first is an 'internally pluralistic' structure of broadcasters. Under this model, broadcasters are organized in such a way that the influence of the relevant forces is dealt with internally by their organs. The second is an 'externally pluralistic' structure where the variety of opinion is expressed in the overall offering of domestic programming. In Germany's dual broadcasting system, public broadcasters are modelled on the principle of internal pluralism, while private broadcasters are modelled on the principle of external pluralism in most but not in all *Länder*.[56] The Constitutional

53. BVerfGE 12, 205 (1961) – *First Broadcasting* Case (*Deutschland-Fernsehen*); BVerfGE 31, 314 (1971) – *Second Broadcasting* Case (*Umsatzsteuer*); BVerfGE 57, 295 (1981) – *Third Broadcasting* Case (*FRAG*); BVerfGE 73, 118 (1986) – *Fourth Broadcasting* Case (*Niedersachsen-Urteil*); BVerfGE 74, 297 (1987) – *Fifth Broadcasting* Case (*Baden-Württemberg-Urteil*); BVerfGE 83, 238 (1991) – *Sixth Broadcasting* Case (*Nordrhein-Westfalen-Urteil*); BVerfGE 87, 181 (1992) – *Seventh Broadcasting* Case (*Rundfunkfinanzierung*); BVerfGE 90, 60 (1994) – *Eighth Broadcasting* Case (*Rundfunkgebühren*).
54. BVerfGE 12, 205 (1961); BVerfGE 73, 118 (1986).
55. BVerfGE 57, 295 (1981).
56. The fiction in § 20 (2) RStV and in some of the *Länder* used to be that balanced variety is automatically achieved when there are at least three nationally transmitted private programmes. § 20 (2) RStV has been replaced by § 25 (2) RStV, which requires that no single programme should imbalance public opinion to a great extent. The media laws of the *Länder* stipulate a range of different pluralism requirements. Some *Länder* prescribe an internal pluralistic model

Court entrusts public broadcasters with the mission of guaranteeing the essential basic provision for all (*Grundversorgung*).[57] Public broadcasters are in other words responsible to inform, educate and entertain, to offer a range of programmes for the whole population that are comprehensive in their content. The *Grundversorgung* doctrine does not, however, share tasks between public and private broadcasters in the sense that the former should be responsible for serious programming while light entertainment should be the domain of the latter. Public broadcasters are asked to cover the full spectrum of programming.[58] As long as public broadcasters discharge their responsibilities effectively, programme requirements imposed on private broadcasters as to the ensuring of balanced pluralism can be relaxed somewhat. This is justified in view of the consequences that financing through advertising has for the programming of private broadcasters. To be sure, setting less stringent requirements for private than for public broadcasting regarding the breadth of program offerings and the securing of balanced diversity is permissible but not mandatory. Also, by no means would it be constitutionally permissible completely to release private broadcasters from the requirement of balanced diversity as the resulting bias would imbalance the total programme offering available on television.[59]

The *Grundversorgung* doctrine guarantees, firstly, the maintenance of existing public service programmes. In its *Sixth Broadcasting* case, the Constitutional Court held that the German Constitution does not prescribe a certain broadcasting model. It is therefore up to the legislature to choose a model that fulfils the constitutional requirements of balanced diversity.[60] However, so long as private broadcasting is limited in its reception, programming diversity and scope, the legislature needs to guarantee the requisite technical, organizational, human-resource, and financial conditions for public broadcasting.[61] Secondly, the *Grundversorgung* doctrine also guarantees the development of public broadcasting. The Constitutional Court decided that public broadcasters must be able to provide new services through new technologies that in the future can take on certain of broadcasting's traditional functions. The Court found therefore the North Rhine-Westphalian Broadcasting Act of January 1988 constitutional,

---

also for private broadcasters, which is especially strict as far as local television is concerned. *See* G. Herrmann and M. Lausen, *Rundfunkrecht* (2nd edn, Munich, C. H. Beck, 2004), p. 497.

57. BVerfGE 73, 118 (1986).
58. BVerfGE 74, 297 (1987); BVerfGE 83, 238 (1991).
59. BVerfGE 83, 238 (1991).
60. H. Schulze-Fielitz, 'Art. 5 I, II', in *Grundgesetz: Kommentar*, vol. I: *Präambel, Artikel 1-19*, H. Dreier (ed.) (2nd edn, Tübingen, J. C. B. Mohr, 2004), para. 253 argues that the legislature is free to choose a model on a scale ranging from strong faith in market competition to an orientation towards a generalist programme.
61. *Ibid.*, para. 297; contra R. Herzog, 'Art. 5 I, II' in T. Maunz and G. Dürig, *Grundgesetz: Kommentar*, vol. I: *GG Text – Artikel 11* (Munich, C. H. Beck, 2002), para. 237b (commentary from 1992) who interprets the *Fifth Broadcasting Case* in the sense that the dual broadcasting system is only a transitory system justified by the enormous costs associated with setting up a private channel, costs that are, however, bound to decline in future.

which allowed Westdeutscher Rundfunk (WDR) to develop the transmission by cable and satellite and to engage in commercial activities such as the publishing of programme magazines. In view of rapid technological changes, the Court intimated that the essential basic provision might also encompass new media services such as on demand services in the future.[62] The argument raised by commercial broadcasters that their public service counterparts exceeded their duty to provide a 'basic service' by launching *inter alia* thematic channels was therefore ill-founded.[63] Furthermore, so that public broadcasters are able to fulfil their mission, the Court ruled that the financing of their activity must be adequately assured.[64] The Constitution does not prescribe a particular form of financing. We have noted earlier that it is permissible in the Court's view for public broadcasters to be also funded by advertising and that this may even strengthen their independence from the state.[65] However, the primary funding method should be the licence fee in view of the inherent tendencies of advertising revenue to limit programme range.[66]

5. LEGAL FRAMEWORK

Legislative competence in the area of broadcasting is shared in Germany between the *Bund* and the *Länder.* The *Länder* are competent to regulate broadcast programmes, whereas the *Bund* has authority to legislate for postal and telecommunications services.[67] The *Bund* also has exclusive competence under Article 73 (1) Nr. 1 GG for 'foreign affairs'. This explains why Deutsche Welle which only broadcasts abroad is organized as a federal channel.[68] The intricacies of the division of competence between the *Bund* and the *Länder* become evident when looking at the elusive distinction between 'teleservices' (*Teledienste*) and 'mediaservices' (*Mediendienste*). The former include telebanking, data services such as traffic, weather, environmental and stock exchange data, services offering access to the internet or to telegames, and also teleshopping.[69] The latter concern services with greater emphasis on editorial arrangements to form public opinion such as periodicals and newspapers that can be accessed online, but also teleshopping.[70] Teleservices and mediaservices have been brought together under the common heading of 'telemedia' (*Telemedien*) in March

62. BVerfGE 83, 238 (1991).
63. *See* Levy, *Europe's Digital Revolution*, p. 32.
64. BVerfGE 74, 297 (1987); 83, 238 (1991); 87, 181 (1991); 90, 60 (1994).
65. BVerfGE 90, 60 (1994).
66. BVerfGE 87, 181 (1991); 90, 60 (1994).
67. Grundgesetz, Art. 73 (1) Nr. 7. The Federal Networks Agency (*Bundesnetzagentur*) is responsible for the telecommunications sector.
68. *See* Herrmann and Lausen, *Rundfunkrecht*, para. 6.24.
69. Mediendienste-Staatsvertrag of 28 January/12 February 1997, last amended by the 8. RfÄndStV of 8/15 October 2004, § 2 (2). The Mediendienste-Staatsvertrag was abolished on 1 March 2007.
70. Teledienstegesetz contained in Art. 1 of the Informations- und Kommunikationsdienstegesetz (IuKDG) of 22 July 1997, § 2 (2). The Teledienstegetz was abolished on 1 March 2007.

2007.[71] However, the regulatory bifurcation remains as the Bund only regulates questions of a commercial nature such as jurisdiction and the transmission state principle in the new *Telemediengesetz*, while the *Länder* are responsible for content related provisions such as editorial standards and the right of reply.

Each of the 16 German *Länder* has adopted broadcasting laws that define the task and competences of the regional public (and private) broadcasters.[72] The broadcasting laws of the *Länder* are nowadays fairly similar as far as organizational principles and broadcasting standards are concerned.[73] In the case of broadcasters whose activities span more than one *Länder*, such as the Norddeutscher Rundfunk (NDR), the framework for their activities is set in Interstate Treaties concluded by the governments of the *Länder*.[74] Interstate Treaties also regulate the ARD, the ZDF, the funding of these two national public broadcasters as well as the procedure by which their financial requirements and the amount of the licence fee are defined.[75] Fundamental rules concerning nationally distributed public and private television are included in the Interstate Treaty on Broadcasting (*Rundfunkstaatsvertrag*).[76] Crucially, the *Rundfunkstaatsvertrag* guarantees the funding of public broadcasters by means of licence fees and advertising. It ranks higher than the broadcasting laws of the *Länder* that apply only if the *Rundfunkstaatsvertrag* does not contain any rules to the contrary.[77] Interstate Treaties are frequently revised in the midst of hard-fought negotiations between the *Länder*. They constitute important instruments of German broadcasting policy, providing 'a national framework for an otherwise regionally fragmented market'.[78]

6. PUBLIC BROADCASTING MISSION AND STANDARDS

The mission of public broadcasting is laid down in § 11 RStV.[79] This provision, echoing the jurisprudence of the Constitutional Court, stipulates that public radio and television have to act as 'medium and factor' in the public debate by producing

---

71. Telemediengesetz (TMG) contained in Art.1 of the Elektronischer-Geschäftsverkehr-Vereinheitlichungsgesetz (ElGVG) of 1 March 2007. The TMG forms the core part of the ElGVG.
72. *See* Herrmann and Lausen, *Rundfunkrecht*, para. 3.43 *et seq.*
73. Woldt, 'Germany', p. 744.
74. For instance Staatsvertrag über den Norddeutschen Rundfunk (NDR) of 17/18 December 1991.
75. ARD Staatsvertrag of 31 August 1991, last modified by the 9th Rundfunkänderungsstaatsvertrag of 1 March 2007; ZDF Staatsvertrag of 31 August 1991, last modified the 9th Rundfunkänderungsstaatsvertrag of 1 March 2007; Rundfunkgebührenstaatsvertrag (RGebStV) of 31 August 1991, last modified by the 9th Rundfunkänderungsstaatsvertrag of 1 March 2007; Rundfunkfinanzierungsstaatsvertrag (RFinStV) of 31 August 1991, last modified by the 9th Rundfunkänderungsstaatsvertrag of 1 March 2007.
76. RStV, § 19 (2) a).
77. RStV, § 1 (2).
78. Woldt, 'Germany', p. 744.
79. § 11 RStV was introduced by the 7. Rundfunkänderungsstaatsvertrag (RfÄndStV) that entered into force on 1 April 2004. This move was partly motivated by the European Commission's calls for a precise definition of the public service remit. Previously, diverse descriptions of the

and distributing programmes. They have to provide a comprehensive overview of international, European, national and regional developments and to contribute to international understanding, European integration and social cohesion in the *Bund* and the *Länder*. Its programmes need to provide information, education, advice and entertainment and to include contributions especially to culture. They need to comply with requirements of objectivity, impartiality and balanced pluralism. Similar provisions can be found in the broadcasting laws of the *Länder*.[80] In response to pressure by the European Commission to define their public service remit more clearly, ARD and ZDF have been obliged since 2004 to publish a report every two years on the ways in which they fulfil their mission, the quality and quantity of their programmes as well as their future plans.[81] This obligation was modelled after the BBC's 'Statements of programme policy', which are published every year.[82]

General programme standards for the public broadcasters as well as for all private broadcasters that transmit programmes nationwide are laid down in § 3 RStV. They are asked to respect and protect human dignity. They should also strengthen the protection of life and freedom, the protection from bodily harm and of the beliefs and opinions of others. They shall also respect the moral and religious convictions of the population. Similar programme standards are laid down in § 41 RStV. However, § 41 RStV only applies to private broadcasters. Both provisions stress the importance of human dignity, which is inalienable in accordance with Article 1 of the German Constitution.

In Germany, serious concerns about violations of human dignity have been recently expressed in relation to reality TV shows such as 'The Big Brother'. The question has been raised whether the commercialization of human beings made possible by such TV formats infringes human dignity. This is especially the case when the contestants in the show are systematically degraded to mere objects, when they are placed in an inescapable situation where they are denounced, exposed or made a laughing stock for profit.[83] However, a violation of the participants' human dignity has to be denied if they have given their consent after having been informed about all relevant facts. Indeed, the players in 'Big Brother' voluntarily surrender their privacy after the rules of the game have been

---

mission of public broadcasters only existed in the broadcasting laws of some of the *Länder*. *See* R. H. Weber, A. Roßnagel, S. Osterwalder, A. Scheuer and S. Wüst, *Kulturquoten im Rundfunk* (Baden-Baden, Nomos, 2006), p. 260.

80. For instance Bayerisches Rundfunkgesetz (BayRG) of 22 October 2003, § 4; Gesetz zu dem Staatsvertrag über die Errichtung einer gemeinsamen Rundfunkanastalt der Länder Berlin und Brandenburg (RBB) of 25 June 2002, § 4; Gesetz über den Westdeutschen Rundfunk Köln (WDR-Gesetz) of 23 March 1985, as modified on 30 November 2004, § 4.
81. RStV, § 11 (4).
82. *See* Part 1, Ch. 7.2.2, p. 129.
83. D. Dörr, *Big Brother und die Menschenwürde: Die Menschenwürde und die Programmfreiheit am Beispiel eines neuen Sendeformats* (Frankfurt am Main, Peter Lang, 2000), p. 89; R. Hartstein, W.-D. Ring, J. Kreile, D. Dörr and R. Stettner, *Rundfunkstaatsvertrag Kommentar*, vol. I (Munich, Jehle-Rehm, 2003), § 3 RStV para. 11.

communicated to them in every detail. Also, the housemates can leave the house at any time without any explanation. In these circumstances, respect for human dignity mandates that their free decision should be respected. Still, it is conceivable that even under these conditions the dignity of the viewers or the social order (*Gesellschaftliche Werteordnung*) have been infringed. This is the case when the overall presentation of a programme denotes contempt for the individual, when a perception of the human being that is offensive to human dignity is put across systematically.[84] A programme that regularly discriminates against minorities, encourages violent behaviour or hatred would infringe the dignity of the audience as well as the social order. The reality show 'Big Brother' is not likely to transmit content of this sort. A violation of § 3 RStV can therefore not be substantiated.

Further broadcasting principles are stipulated in § 4 RStV (prohibited programmes, youth protection), in § 7 RStV (advertising and teleshopping), in § 8 RStV (sponsoring), in § 10 RStV (reporting, news, opinion polls). §§ 15-18 RStV contain detailed programme standards concerning advertisements. Also, the broadcasting laws of the *Länder* lay down detailed programme standards for the public service broadcasters.[85] Finally, programme standards are contained in §§ 5-11 of the ZDF-Staatsvertrag and in guidelines and other self-regulatory instruments issued by the ARD and the ZDF. We will examine the standards contained in this complex regulatory framework in the following.

7. POLITICAL AND ELECTION BROADCASTING

According to § 11 (3) RStV, public broadcasters have to consider the principles of objectivity and impartiality of reporting as well as the balanced pluralism of programmes when fulfilling their mission. This provision incorporates fundamental obligations of the public broadcasters that are also laid down in the broadcasting laws of the *Länder* and that have emerged from the case-law of the German Constitutional Court. Adherence to the principles of impartiality and balanced pluralism is particularly important as regards the allocation of airtime to political parties, especially during election campaigns.

7.1 Election Broadcasts

In general, political parties do not have a right of access to television outside of electoral periods. Only few *Länder* provide in their broadcasting laws that airtime is to be granted to political parties for the presentation of their views. These rights

84. *Ibid.*
85. *See* for instance Bayerisches Rundfunkgesetz (BayRG) of 22 October 2002, § 4; Gesetz zu dem Staatsvertrag über die Errichtung einer gemeinsamen Rundfunkanstalt der Länder Berlin und Brandenburg (RBB-StV) of 7 November 2002, §§ 4, 6-7; Gesetz über den Westdeutschen Rundfunk Köln (WDR-Gesetz) of 30 November 2004, §§ 4–6b.

are hardly ever used in practice.[86] The German Constitution does not confer a right of political parties to access to television during electoral periods either.[87] However, some of the broadcasting laws of the *Länder* explicitly provide that public broadcasters have to grant free airtime to political parties during election campaigns.[88] As a rule, public broadcasters transmit election broadcasts even if they are not obliged to do so by law.[89] The principles of fairness and equal opportunity require that public broadcasters grant free access to the airwaves to all political parties or to none of them. Granting airtime to some of the parties only and excluding others would go against the principle of democracy. This is also the reason why paid political advertising is forbidden in Germany.[90] Otherwise, well-established, affluent parties would be able to afford more advertising time than new or minority parties.

The principles of fairness and equal opportunity do not mandate, however, that all political parties should be allocated equal time to present their case regardless of their importance. Since elections aim at the formation of a government, it is deemed legitimate to grant more airtime to parties that are capable of forming a government. Otherwise, the task of the legislature would be hampered by the representation of a big number of small parties. The Constitutional Court held in a seminal ruling that public broadcasters are entitled to take account of the respective strengths of the political parties in allocating broadcasting opportunities.[91] Their latest results are an important criterion. However, other factors such as the length and continuity of the parties' existence, their membership, the extent and strength of their organization and their representation in Parliament and government also need to be taken into account if more recent political developments are not to be ignored.

The broadcasting laws of the Länder do not determine the way in which airtime is to be divided between the different parties. They often only require the allocation of adequate broadcasting time.[92] It is established practice for the broadcasting organizations to allocate airtime according to a combined system whereby every party or political group that is admitted to the elections and that fulfils certain formal requirements can transmit two spots of one and a half minutes each. Bigger parties are granted additional airtime in accordance with their importance. This system has been approved of by the Constitutional Court and is consistent with § 5 of the Law on Political Parties (Parteiengesetz).[93]

Editorial control of the content of election broadcasts rests with the originating political party. The Constitutional Court has ruled that broadcasters are not entitled to refuse to broadcast such messages on the ground of their alleged

---

86. Holznagel, *Rundfunkrecht in Europa*, p. 284.
87. BVerfGE 47, 198, 236 *et seq.* (1978).
88. For instance BayRG, Art. 4 (2) Nr. 2; WDR-Gesetz, § 8 (2).
89. Herrmann and Lausen, *Rundfunkrecht*, p. 302.
90. RStV, § 7(8).
91. BVerfGE 14, 121 (1962).
92. For instance WDR-Gesetz, § 8 (2).
93. BVerfGE 7, 99 (1958); Parteiengesetz of 24 July 1967, as amended by the Law of 22 December 2004.

unconstitutionality.[94] It is the prerogative of the Constitutional Court itself to declare a party and its political expression unconstitutional. Nevertheless, broadcasters are responsible for ensuring that the available airtime is used for the purposes of election broadcasting only and that nothing transmitted breaches obviously and gravely the general norms of criminal law. This light-handed control of election broadcasts enabled extreme right wing parties to transmit nationalist messages much to the indignation of the viewers, as was notably the case before the elections of 18 January 1989. Broadcasters often transmit after and/or before the election broadcasts an insert in which they point out that the political parties are solely responsible for their content. Recently, it has been argued that election broadcasts should be banned altogether so as to curb xenophobic propaganda.[95]

As far as editorial broadcasts during election time are concerned, there are no specific rules. Broadcasters are allowed to select their participants in a discussion according to whether they have a realistic chance of being elected. In an interesting case concerning a 'TV-Duel' between the presidents of the Social Democratic Party (SPD) and the Christian Democrats (CSU) prior to the elections of 22 September 2002, the public broadcasters ARD and ZDF refused to invite the president of the Free Democratic Party (FDP). The Constitutional Court held that it was legitimate to invite only those party leaders who were likely to win the election as long as the opportunities of other candidates were not marred as a result.[96] It considered that this was not to be feared in the present case since the FDP had already participated and was to take part in the remaining two weeks before the election in other editorial programmes according to its strength.

7.2 Broadcasts of General Interest

The federal government and the governments of the Länder are obliged to make airtime available for the transmission of governmental announcements, especially in cases of urgency such as natural catastrophes or epidemics.[97] Such announcements have no political content as a rule. In the case of politically controversial broadcasts, the ARD and ZDF used to grant a right of reply to the opposition on the basis of an agreement from 1962. This agreement is, however, not being applied anymore.[98] The obligation to broadcast governmental announcements does not cover other statements on important political occasions or special celebrations such as Christmas and New Year's Eve. Nor does it include the transmission of traffic and transport information that falls within the broadcasters' editorial discretion.[99]

94. BVerfGE 47, 198 (1978).
95. Herrmann and Lausen, *Rundfunkrecht*, p. 306.
96. BVerfGE of 30 August 2002, published in (2003) JZ, 365.
97. *See* for instance BayRG, Art. 4 (2) Nr. 5; WDR-G, § 8.
98. Herrmann and Lausen, *Rundfunkrecht*, p. 301.
99. *Ibid.*

8. CULTURAL OBLIGATIONS

8.1 High Culture

The cultural mission of German public broadcasters is laid down in § 11 (2) 4 RStV. This provision emphasizes the obligation of public broadcasters to broadcast cultural contributions. It becomes evident from the *travaux preparatoires* that culture is understood in a wide sense, encompassing both popular and more high-brow programme genres.[100] The ARD also sees itself obliged to cater by means of its cultural programming not only for a small elite, but for broad segments of the population.[101] Its participation in 3sat and Arte represents clearly the more intellectual and ambitious end of the spectrum. The German Constitutional Court has also developed the idea of a special cultural responsibility (*kulturelle Verantwortung*) of public broadcasting that has become particularly important with the extension of broadcasting on offer to privately produced and European programmes.[102] However, public broadcasters are often criticized for not adequately fulfilling their cultural mission. The low quality of cultural programming as well as its relegation to the late night hours or to thematic channels are denounced. It has been suggested that the Broadcasting Councils should entrust external bodies with the task of overseeing the quality of programming or that soft quotas for cultural programmes should be introduced.[103] Both proposals risk being contrary to the constitutional requirement of programming autonomy (*Programmautonomie*).

8.2 Regional Programmes

The main legal obligation of public broadcasters to broadcast regional programmes is contained in § 11 (2) 1 RStV, which obliges them to 'provide a comprehensive overview of international, European, national and *regional* developments'. In its report on the obligation of its public service mission the ARD also assumes the obligation to commission together with Degeto (the film acquisition and production arm of the ARD) around 70 per cent of its productions from independent companies so as to strengthen the German film industry.[104] Given that ARD is a cooperation of nine regional broadcasters, this commitment benefits directly regional production.[105] Moreover, seven out of nine ARD broadcasters have committed themselves to substantially supporting the film industry of the *Länder*.

100. Weber *et al.*, *Kulturquoten im Rundfunk*, p. 262.
101. ARD, *Die Programmgestaltung der ARD 2005/2006: Bericht der ARD über die Erfüllung ihres Auftrages, über die Qualität und Quantität ihrer Angebote und Programme sowie über die geplannten Schwerpunkte (§ 11 (4) 3 RStV)*, p. 27.
102. BVerfGE 73, 118, 158 (1986); BVerfGE 94, 297, 324 (1996).
103. T. Kleist and A. Scheuer, 'Kultur und Quoten' (2006) ZUM 96.
104. ARD, *Programmgestaltung*, p. 31.
105. Ader, 'Der kulturelle Auftrag', 5.

ARD's structure also guarantees that its programming, especially its Third Programmes, takes regional interests sufficiently into account. According to Article 5 (2) ZDF-StV, ZDF is also obliged to give appropriate coverage to events in the individual *Länder* and to Germany's cultural diversity.

8.3 Education

Education is part of the public service mission in accordance with § 11 (2) 3 RStV. The contribution of public broadcasters to education is exemplified in historical documentaries and science programmes as well as in dedicated education channels such as BR-alpha, the education channel of the Bayerischer Rundfunk. Next to the classical television formats, ARD is increasingly trying to combine education with entertainment by means of the so-called living history format, a type of reality TV, in which volunteers re-enact historical events.

8.4 Religious Programmes

Religious programmes are an important component of public broadcasters' cultural mission. Public broadcasters – and to a lesser extent private ones – are obliged to grant appropriate access rights to the Protestant and the Catholic Churches as well as to the Jewish Communities for the transmission of their services and other religious programmes.[106] Other religious groups are also considered provided that they are present in the whole of the country.[107] Access rights are granted at no cost and the religious groups are responsible for these programmes as opposed to general discussion programmes where the broadcasters have editorial control.[108]

Such access rights only exist for television programmes, not for online services. Recently, ARD's plan to make available on its internet site two and a half to three minute long expressions of Muslim faith in German language on a monthly basis has met with strong criticism. The fear was expressed that the 'Islamic Word' (*Islamisches Wort*) project would lead to the segregation as opposed to the integration of Muslim communities in Germany. It was also argued that it would be incompatible with public broadcasting's basic provision (*Grundversorgung*). This is a tenuous argument given that *Grundversorgung* encompasses the provision of a range of services for the whole population, including the three and a half million Muslims living in Germany. ARD has declared the theme of integration and migration as its main programme focus for 2007. It plans to go ahead with this project and ZDF is set to follow with a similar offering, 'Forum on Friday'. ARD and ZDF will retain full control over these forums.

---

106. *See* for instance ZDF-StV, § 11 (3); ARD, *Programmgestaltung*, p. 35.
107. *Ibid.*
108. Barendt, *Broadcasting Law*, p. 154.

8.5 Cultural Quotas

The law does not contain any precise cultural quotas. This is hardly surprising if one takes the traditional German hostility against quotas into account. Fixed quotas would also be problematic from the point of view of the programming autonomy of German broadcasters.[109] Article 4 of the TwF Directive, the European quota rule, has been implemented in § 6 (2) RStV, which requires broadcasters to reserve the main part of their broadcasting time for European works. Instead of listing types of programmes that do not count towards this obligation, § 6 (2) RStV explicitly mentions those genres that count towards the relevant broadcasting time, namely feature films, television plays, series, documentaries and similar productions. This provision is thus framed in narrower terms than Article 4 (1) of the TwF Directive.

As far as the independent quota is concerned, Germany has implemented it rather liberally in § 6 (3) RStV. According to this provision, general interest channels are obliged to devote a substantial part to in-house as well as commissioned and joint productions. There is neither a reference to independent producers nor a fixed quota or a requirement to earmark an adequate proportion for recent works as in Article 5 of the Directive. Therefore, § 6 (3) RStV can only achieve the result envisaged by the TwF Directive by means of its harmonious interpretation in the light of the Directive.[110] The Federal Government has expressed a preference for the promotion of independent production by means of commitments freely entered into by the public broadcasters as opposed to binding legal rules.[111] Indeed, we have seen that ARD has committed itself to commissioning together with Degeto around 70 per cent of its production from independent companies. ZDF's commitments to support the German film industry are less concrete.[112]

9. ADVERTISING

9.1 Background

Rules governing advertising in German television are laid down in the *Rundfunkstaatsvertrag* as well as in laws on specific issues. The annual average for the total duration of advertising that can be transmitted on the ARD First Programme and on ZDF is limited in each case to 20 minutes on working days.[113] Advertising time which has not been completely used up may be made up for up to a maximum of five minutes on working days. Advertisements shall not be broadcast after 8.00 P.M. nor on Sundays or on public holidays which are

109. Ader, 'Der kulturelle Auftrag', 5.
110. Weber *et al.*, *Kulturquote im Rundfunk*, p. 281.
111. *Ibid.*
112. *See* ZDF, 'Programm-Perspektiven 2007 – 2008' <www.unternehmen.zdf.de/fileadmin/files/Download_Dokumente/DD_Das_ZDF/Programm-Perspektiven__SVE_2007–2008_2.pdf>, 17 April 2007, 10.
113. RStV, § 16 (1).

observed throughout the country.[114] Also, no advertising is permitted on other nationwide television programmes of the ARD and the ZDF or on the Third programmes.[115] Most of the other advertising rules in the *Rundfunkstaatsvertrag* transpose verbatim the relevant provisions of the TwF Directive.

9.2 The Principle of Separation

The *Rundfunkstaatsvertrag* requires that advertising has to be readily recognizable as such and be kept quite separate from other parts of the programme by optical means.[116] Also, advertising and advertisers are not allowed to influence the rest of the programme neither in content nor editorially.[117] The principle of separation of programme and advertisement dictates that surreptitious advertising is not allowed.[118] Surreptitious advertising is defined as 'the reference to or representation of goods, services, names or activities of a producer of goods or a provider of services in programmes when such reference or representation is intended by the broadcaster to serve advertising and might mislead the public as to its nature. Such reference or representation is considered to be intentional in particular if it is done in return for payment or for similar consideration.'[119] Equally prohibited is 'product placement' – a term that is used synonymously with surreptitious advertising. Product placement is only allowed if it is indispensable on editorial or artistic grounds, especially so as to depict the real world.[120] If products are referred to or appear in a programme, their representation should not promote commercial interests if possible (e.g. market studies instead of representations of a single product, no shots targeted at branded products, change of products especially in series).[121] A reportage on the 100th anniversary of the Barbie doll was found to contain product placement in view of the unnecessarily frequent and uncritically positive representations and references to the doll.[122]

Germany has incorporated the tight definition in Article 1 (d) of Directive 97/36 and requires a proof of intentional acting by the broadcaster. As well as the existence of payment the following are deemed to be strong indications of such intentional acting: contractual arrangements for the representation of goods, services etc; the production of a programme with a view to including such promotional references; the discounting of programme rights in return for product placement.[123] It goes without saying that all these factors are very hard to

114. *Ibid.* Sponsoring is only allowed after 8.00 P.M.
115. RStV, § 16 (2).
116. RStV, § 7 (3).
117. RStV, § 7 (2).
118. RStV, § 7 (6) 1.
119. RStV, § 2 (6).
120. ARD Advertising Guidelines, 6 June 2000, Nr. 8.3.
121. *Ibid.*
122. OVG Niedersachsen, judgment of 15 December 1999, ZUM 1999, 347.
123. Hartstein *et al.*, *Rundfunkstaatsvertrag Kommentar*, vol. I, § 7 RStV para. 48.

prove. The case of surreptitious advertising is especially hard to make as regards acquisitions as opposed to in-house productions, co-productions or commissions. When broadcasters transmit previously acquired programmes they cannot influence their content nor is it always possible to remove references to branded products. It is necessary to strike a balance between their programme mission and the separation principle.[124] The public interest in watching these programmes and the amount of advertising are relevant considerations.[125] The interpretation given to the definition of surreptitious advertising in § 2 (6) RStV by the German authorities even falls behind the Directive's standard in some respects. The existence of similar consideration is disputed where goods are provided free of charge. Infringement proceedings are currently pending against Germany on this issue.

A more lenient approach is taken to cinema films. The German Federal Supreme Court (*Bundesgerichtshof*) has confirmed in two seminal judgments (*Feuer, Eis und Dynamit I* and *II*) that the principle of separation of programme and advertisement also applies to those.[126] However, undertakings are allowed to pay substantial sums of money in exchange for the representation of their products. The viewers of cinema films would in general not be misled by the editorially justified appearance of props that have been put at the disposal of the filmmaker at no cost. If, however, an undertaking's financial contribution covers 20 per cent of the film costs, the audience must be notified in advance.[127] Product placement is also allowed in cinema films that are broadcast on television.[128]

A special form of surreptitious advertising, the so called 'theme placement' ('*Themen placement*') has attracted a lot of attention in recent times. Theme placement is about the integration of themes or ideas into programmes. It benefits the producers of a certain type of products (such as dairy products, cars etc.) as opposed to specific brands.[129] A prominent case of theme placement is the promotion of fitted carpets and of last minute travel in the popular ARD 'Marienhof' series. An interest group representing the producers of fitted carpets paid substantial sums of money for the insertion into one episode of a dialogue praising the advantages of fitted carpets compared to parquet flooring. Also, the concept of 'last minute travel' was extolled in a number of episodes. It is generally held that the prohibition of surreptitious advertising also covers generic placement since it is equally detrimental to editorial independence and to fairness in competition and in commercial transactions.[130] Editorial independence is undoubtedly undermined when certain branches of the industry are able to influence the scenario of a programme. Nor can theme placement be justified on the basis of the provisions

124. ARD Advertising Guidelines, 6 June 2000, Nr. 8.6.
125. Hartstein *et al.*, *Rundfunkstaatsvertrag Kommentar*, vol. I, § 7 RStV para. 50.
126. BGH, judgment of 6 July 1995, AfP 1995, 966 and AfP 1996, 63.
127. Hartstein, *Rundfunkstaatsvertrag Kommentar*, vol. I, § 7 RStV para. 50.
128. VG Berlin, judgment of 15 April 1999, ZUM 1999, 742.
129. Hartstein *et al.*, *Rundfunkstaatsvertrag Kommentar*, vol. I, § 7 RStV para. 47.
130. O. Castendyk, 'Werbeintegration im TV-Programm – wann sind Themen Placements Schleichwerbung oder Sponsoring?' (2005) 12 ZUM, 857, 860.

on sponsoring.[131] In accordance with § 8 (2) RStV, the content and scheduling of a sponsored programme shall not be influenced by the sponsor in such a way as to prejudice the broadcaster's responsibility and editorial independence. Also, § 8 (3) RStV clarifies that sponsored programmes shall not encourage the sale, purchase, rental or lease of products or services of the sponsor or a third party, in particular by making special promotional references to them.

9.3 Advertising and Minors

The Interstate Treaty for the protection of human dignity and the protection of minors in the media (*Jugendmedienschutz-Staatsvertrag*) that entered into force on 1 April 2003 contains rules for the protection of minors in all electronic media: broadcasting contents as well as services provided over the internet.[132] Its provisions have to be read together with those of the Youth Protection Act (*Jugendschutzgesetz*) that entered into force at the same time.[133] On the subject of advertising and minors, the *Jugendmedienschutz-Staatsvertrag* has incorporated verbatim Article 16 of the TwF Directive.[134] Furthermore, it stipulates that advertising that might impair the development of minors to independent and social-minded personalities has to be separated from programmes directed at them.[135] Advertising that also targets or features minors should not harm them or exploit their inexperience.[136] Finally, advertising for alcoholic drinks or tobacco products should not target minors, appeal to them or show minors consuming them.[137]

10. PROTECTION OF MINORS

The *Jugendmedienschutz-Staatsvertrag* contains in § 4 a list of programmes that are absolutely prohibited, namely programmes that pose a threat to the liberal democratic constitutional order, programmes that glorify cruelty against human beings or the war, that offend human dignity, that portray minors in a sexually provocative manner, that are pornographic and depict cruelty or the sexual abuse of minors or are listed in parts B and D of the list compiled by the Federal body for the

---

131. *Ibid.*, 865; contra, L. Bülow, 'Themen-Sponsoring im Fernsehen' (1999) no. 2 CR, 112.
132. Staatsvertrag über den Schutz der Menschenwürde und den Jugendschutz in Rundfunk und Telemedien (Jugendmedienschutz-Staatsvertrag, JMStV) of 10–27 September 2002 last modified by the 9. Rundfunkänderungsstaatsvertrag. For a detailed discussion of the Jugendmedienschutz-Staatsvertrag, *see* J. Kreile and M. Diesbach, 'Der neue Jugendmedienschutz-Staatsvertrag – was ändert sich für den Rundfunk?' (2002) 12 ZUM, 849.
133. Law on the Protection of Minors (Jugendschutzgesetz, JuSchG) of 23 July 2002, last modified by Law of 23 July 2004.
134. JMStV, § 6.
135. JMStV, § 6 (3).
136. JMStV, § 6 (4).
137. JMStV, § 6 (5).

assessment of offline media (*Bundesprüfstelle für jugendgefährdende Medien*, BPjM).[138] The same applies to programmes that are pornographic in any other way; that are listed in parts A and C of the BPjM list[139]; or that are *likely* to *seriously* impair the development of minors unless they are only made accessible to an adult audience by means of 'telemedia' (*Telemedien*), i.e. the internet and other online media.[140]

On the other hand, programmes that might impair the development of minors into independent and social-minded personalities can be transmitted provided that the broadcaster ensures by technical or other means or by selecting the time of transmission that children of particular ages will not watch them.[141] Programmes with the classification 'FSK 18' can only be transmitted between 11 P.M. and 6 A.M. and programmes classified 'FSK 16' can only be transmitted between 10 P.M. and 6 A.M. These two types of programmes have to be preceded by acoustic means or identified by visual means throughout their duration.[142] In the case of programmes classified 'FSK 12', the interests of younger children have to be taken into account.[143] These classifications are carried out by the Voluntary Self-regulation of the Film Industry (*Freiwillige Selbstkontrolle der Filmwirtschaft*, FSK). The timing restrictions do not apply to news and current affairs programmes insofar as this particular form of presentation is in the public interest.[144] Exceptions can also be made when a programme has been classified more than 15 years ago.[145] In such cases, the broadcasters carry out their own assessment of the programme.[146]

All national broadcasters are obliged to appoint a Commissioner for Youth Protection (*Jugendschutzbeauftragter*) who consults them on questions of youth protection and acts as a contact point for the viewers.[147] The Commissioner for Youth Protection complements the Broadcasting Councils by safeguarding the interests of young viewers prior to the transmission of the programmes. While the protection of minors is entrusted to the self-regulation of public broadcasters, private broadcasters are supervised by the State Media Authorities (*Landesmedienanstalten*) and by the Commission for the Protection of Minors (*Kommission für Jugendmedienschutz*, KJM) that was introduced by the

---

138. JMStV, § 4 (1) Nr. 11; JuSchG, § 18 (2). These are programmes that infringe criminal law according to the judgment of the BPjM.
139. JMStV, § 4 (2) Nr. 2; JuSchG, § 18 (2). These are programmes that are likely to impair the development of minors.
140. JMStV, § 4 (2).
141. JMStV, § 5.
142. JMStV, § 10 (2).
143. JMStV, § 5 (4); JuSchG, § 14 (2) Nr. 3–5, (6). *See also* the ARD Criteria for the Protection of Minors (ARD-Kriterien zur Sicherung des Jugenschutzes bei der Beurteilung von Fernsehsendungen) of 4 February 1997, last modified on 9 September 2003.
144. JMStV, § 5 (6).
145. JMStV, § 9 (1).
146. ARD Guidelines for the Protection of Minors (ARD-Richtlinien zur Sicherung des Jugendschutzes) of 22 June 1988, last modified on 16 June 2003.
147. JMStV, § 7.

Jugendmedienschutz-Staatsvertrag.[148] In recent times, calls have been voiced to improve the protection of minors in public broadcasting by extending the supervisory role of the State Media Authorities to them. However, public broadcasters argue that a unification of the regulatory framework would not be advisable in view of the different programme profiles and risk potentials in public and private television.[149] Clearly, public broadcasters resist such plans as they would greatly reduce their programming autonomy.

11. RIGHT OF REPLY

The right of reply is laid down in the broadcasting laws of the *Länder*. These laws sometimes differ in the conditions they impose for the exercise of this right. As it is impossible to describe every detail in this context, it will only be attempted to outline the main contours of the right of reply as it is incorporated in § 9 ZDF-StV, a provision rather typical of the German rules.[150]

Broadcasters are obliged to grant a right of reply to every person or body that has been affected by a factual allegation in a television programme. There is no express requirement that this assertion of facts has to be incorrect. Therefore, a mere allegation that the broadcast was inaccurate is sufficient to trigger the right.[151] Obviously, the broadcaster has the right to turn down the request if its content is obviously untrue.[152]

The reply should not be disproportionate in its extent compared to the criticized part of the programme and should not have an illegal content. There is no right of reply in relation to accurate reports of public hearings of the European Parliament, of the legislative organs at federal, *Länder* or municipal level and of court proceedings nor in relation to official government announcements or election broadcasts. Also, so as to avoid the proliferation of replies, the law states there is no right of reply to a former reply.

The right of reply must be asserted without delay and at latest within two months of the broadcast. The reply must also be transmitted without delay within the same programme or programme type to which the request refers and at the same or an equivalent time of day. The reply is broadcast at no cost except if it is directed against a factual assertion in an advertisement. If the broadcasting authority refuses to transmit a reply, it is possible to obtain interim relief from the civil courts.

---

148. For the regulation of the protection of minors in private broadcasting *see* Hans-Bredow-Institut, 'Final Report: Study on Co-Regulation Measures in the Media Sector', June 2006 <ec.europa.eu/avpolicy/docs/library/studies/coregul/coregul-final-report_en.pdf>, 18 July 2007, p. 48.
149. I. Mohr, 'Standards gesetzt: Jugendmedienschutz in der ARD' (2005) *ARD-Jahrbuch*, 49, 50.
150. Barendt, *Broadcasting Law*, p. 162.
151. *Ibid.*, p. 163.
152. Herrmann and Lausen, *Rundfunkrecht*, p. 603.

Chapter 4
Greece

1. BACKGROUND

The beginnings of Greek television coincide with a bleak period in the history of Greece, the brutal military junta that ruled the country between 1967 and 1974. Naturally, this unfortunate historical conjuncture undermined the creation of a democratic forum for freedom of expression.[1] The first public television stations were established in 1970: the National Foundation for Radio and Television (EIRT) and the Information Service of the Armed Forces (YENED). EIRT was subject to the unlimited control of the military government, especially the Minister of the Presidency.[2] YENED, that was set up with the purpose of enlightening, educating and entertaining the armed forces, was directly controlled by the General Staff of National Defence.

In 1975, one year after the restoration of democratic government, Greek public television was restructured and ERT (Ellenike Radioteleorasis) was established as a public enterprise.[3] The Constitution of 1975 defined for the first time the public service mission of Greek broadcasting, endowing it with guarantees of objectivity, impartiality and pluralism, while at the same time subjecting it to direct state control. The state was meant to be the guardian of public service standards, but abused its powers by utilizing television as the mouthpiece of the government. The ensuing decline in the television's credibility with the public and severe criticisms

---

1. S. Kaitatzi-Whitlock, 'Greece' <www.eavi.org/reports.htm>, 18 July 2007, p. 129; IOM, *O Optikoakoustikos Tomeas sten Ellada* (Athens, European Commission in Greece Representation, 2003), p. 85.
2. P. Dagtoglou, *Atomika dikaiomata*, vol. 2 (2nd edn, Athens, Ant. N. Sakkoulas, 2005), p. 662.
3. P. Dagtoglou, *Radioteleorase kai Syntagma* (Athens, Ant. N. Sakkoulas, 1989), p. 69; N. Alivizatos, *Kratos kai Radioteleorase* (Athens, Ant. N. Sakkoulas, 1986), p. 42; Kaitatzi-Whitlock, 'Greece', p. 129.

of the state monopoly of television broadcasting paved the way for the liberalization of the market in the late eighties.[4] Private television presented itself as the champion of democracy and the public interest, winning the favour of the public and the fight for ratings.[5]

In 1982, YENED gave up its links with the armed forces and was renamed ERT 2. In 1987, Law 1730/87 set up the uniform radio and television body ERT – comprising ET-1, ET-2 and the Greek public radio ERA – as a *Societé Anonyme* (S.A.). A year later, the third ERT channel, ET-3, was established in Thessaloniki. During the following decade, the two public channels, ET-1 and ET-2, were *de facto* independent to a great extent despite their constitutional subjection to the tutelage of the state. There were certain overlaps in organizational terms as well as in their programme offerings. In 1997, their programmes were differentiated and ET-2 was renamed NET. So as to respond to the continuous expansion of private television, ERT S.A. revamped itself as a modern, pluralistic and democratic broadcaster. However, the audience share of private channels still far outstrips that of ERT S.A.[6] The dependence of ERT S.A. on the government remains given that its governing body is appointed by the competent Secretary General. All other appointments at ERT S.A. are also mainly politically motivated with little regard for merit.[7]

Five public channels exist in Greece at the moment, namely ET-1, NET, ET-3, ERT-SAT and ERT Digital. ET-1 defines itself as the first multi-collective entertainment channel, whereas NET is the main information and news channel. ET-3 is the largest regional channel in Greece that broadcasts from Thessaloniki for the entire national audience, and ERT-SAT is an internationally broadcast Greek language channel. ERT Digital consists of three pilot digital channels whose broadcast commenced in the first semester of 2006. ERT S.A., ERT S.A., the Hellenic Broadcasting Corporation, comprises ET-1, NET, ERA (the Greek public radio) and the 'Company for the production and distribution of radio and television programmes'.

2. BROADCASTING AUTHORITIES

2.1 National Council for Radio and Television

The National Council for Radio and Television (NCRTV) exercises the constitutionally prescribed direct state control over television. NCRTV is not responsible for the telecommunications sector, which is regulated by the National

4. 'The Greek Media Landscape' <www.ejc.nl/jr/emland/greece.html>, 18 July 2007, p. 4; IOM, *Optikoakoustikos Tomeas*, p. 86.
5. 'The Greek Media Landscape', p. 4.
6. *Ibid.*, p. 6; European Commission, *Commission Staff Working Paper: Media Pluralism in the Member States of the European Union*, SEC (2006), 42.
7. P. Seri, 'Das Mediensystem Griechenlands' in *Internationales Handbuch Medien 2004/2005*, Hans-Bredow Institut (ed.) (Baden-Baden, Nomos, 2004), p. 319; T. Zaxaropoulos and M. Parasxos, *Mass Media in Greece* (London, Praeger, 1993); I. Kiki, 'Greek Broadcasting Law: Past and Present' (1989) 10 (1) *Journal of Media Law and Practice*, 24.

Telecommunications and Post Commission (EETT). NCRTV is an independent authority and its members are both personally and functionally independent in the execution of their tasks.[8] This means, first, that they normally cannot be removed during their term of office and, second, that they are not subject to administrative control when exercising their functions. NCRTV is only answerable to the Minister of the Presidency, allowing the exercise of parliamentary control, i.e. control of the legality of its actions only.[9]

Until the 2001 constitutional revision the NCRTV members were elected by the political parties. This rendered them very vulnerable to political pressure. In 1999, the Fifth Division of the Greek Council of State found the nomination of the NCRTV members by political parties unconstitutional.[10] However, its Plenary Session reached the opposite conclusion provided that the selection criteria were appropriate and that the personal and functional independence of its members was guaranteed.[11] Repeated protests from academics and politicians against the method of appointment of NCRTV members led to its modification. Under the new Constitution, the members of all independent authorities, including the NCRTV, are appointed by the unanimous decision of the Conference of Presidents of Parliament. If unanimity is not feasible, they are appointed by a qualified majority of four fifths of its members.[12] The qualified majority of four fifths was chosen so that all political parties, not only the ones in power, are involved. However, scepticism has been expressed as to whether it can really guarantee the neutrality of the independent authorities given that the Conference of the Presidents of Parliament reflects in its majority the views of the government.[13]

The NCRTV is currently headed by a board of seven members, consisting of a president, a vice-president and five members, nominated by the parliamentary parties and appointed by the Committee of Chairs of the Parliament.[14] Their term of office lasts four years and it can only be renewed once.[15] The criteria for selecting the members of the NCRTV have to do with eminence, scientific distinction and professional experience, especially in areas that are directly or indirectly related to the Council's work.[16] The president and the vice-president are fully and exclusively employed by the NCRTV, while the other five members

8. Law 2863/2000, Arts 1, 3 as amended by Law 3051/2002.
9. Dagtoglou, *Atomika dikaiomata*, p. 694.
10. Council of State 944/1999, [1999] ΤοΣ, 614.
11. Council of State 656/2000, [2000] ΤοΣ, 192; *ibid.*, 553/2003.
12. Greek Constitution, Art. 101 A (2) 3.
13. I. Kiki, *E Eleutheria ton Optikoakoustikon Meson (Ypo to prisma tes Syntagmatikes anatheoreses tou 2001)* (Athens, Ekdoseis Sakkoula, 2003), pp. 157, 163 n. 272.
14. Greek Constitution, Art. 101 A.
15. Law 3051/2002, Art. 3 (2).
16. Law 2863/2000, Art. 2 (3). This provision has been criticized for not safeguarding sufficiently the specialization of the NCRTV members in the field of mass media. A. Oikonomou, 'Ethniko Symvoulio Radioteleorases: treis anekplerotes proupotheseis gia ten apotelesmatike leitourgia tou os anexartetes arxes' (2004) 2 ΔιΜΕΕ, 185.

are fully but not exclusively employed, which may raise concerns about possible conflicts of interests.[17]

The NCRTV's independence has been jeopardized in the past in manifold ways. It lacked regulatory powers given that, under Laws 2328/95 and 2644/98, licences were granted by the Minister of Press and Mass Media with only consultation with NCRTV.[18] Its decisions were subject to a scrutiny of their legality by the same Minister who frequently vetoed them.[19] Thus, in several cases fines against major television channels for contraventions of the law were indirectly wavered, not least so as to bargain for better terms of political coverage on television.[20] The constitution and powers of this authority have often been changed, making it plain that its independence was very subject to the whims of the administration.[21] The same scepticism was expressed from the start by the Greek Council of State. Notably, it annulled NCRTV's regulation for the coverage of the election campaign prior to the general elections of 8 April 1990 as unconstitutional, displaying a deep distrust towards the not democratically legitimized independent authorities.[22]

Law 2863/2000 upgraded the role of the NCRTV significantly by rendering it solely responsible for radio and television matters, including the granting of licences, and by abolishing the control of legality exercised hitherto by the Minister of Press and Mass Media.[23] Still, this law also denied NCRTV such fully-fledged regulatory powers as would befit an independent authority. The regulation of the wider field of mass media was declared as being within the purview of the Ministry of Press and Mass Media.[24] The revision of the Greek Constitution in 2001 consolidated NCRTV's independence and removed any doubts as to its democratic legitimacy, rendering it the only independent authority

---

17. *Ibid.*, 187.
18. *See also* the Council of State's ruling 930/1992 that denied NCRTV regulatory powers on the ground that it was not an administrative body nor did it regulate matters of a 'particular or detailed nature' in accordance with Art. 43 (2) of the Greek Constitution. After the 2001 constitutional revision these objections are not valid anymore. The NCRTV is part of the administration and has to exercise its regulatory powers in accordance with Art. 43 (2) of the Greek Constitution. *See* K. Chrysogonos, *Mia vevaiotike anatheorese: E anatheorese ton diataxeon tou Syntagmatos gia ta atomika kai koinonika dikaiomata* (2nd edn, Athens, Ant. A. Sakkoulas, 2002), p. 299.
19. Law 2328/95, Art. 14 (25); Law 2644/98, Art. 20 (4).
20. F. Papatheodorou and D. Machin, 'The Umbilical Cord that was Never Cut: The Post-Dictatorial Intimacy between the Political Elite and the Mass Media in Greece and Spain' (2003) 18 (1) *European Journal of Communication*, 50; Kaitatzi-Whitlock, 'Greece'' p. 124.
21. Oikonomou, 'Ethniko Symvoulio Radioteleorases', 185.
22. Council of State 930/90, [1990] ToΣ, 68, 69 annotated by N. Alivizatos, 'E "trite" apofase tou Symvouliou tes Epikrateias gia ten radioteleorase: Sxolio sten StE 930/1990 Ol.' (1990) 16 ToΣ, E. Venizelos, 'E radioteleoptike periodos se anazetese kanonistikou plaisiou' (1990) 31 ΕλλΔ, 1362; I. Kiki, 'Bouleutikes Ekloges 2000 kai 2004: Pros exomalynse ton kanonon radioteleoptikes provoles ton kommaton' (2007) 1 *Efemerida Dioiketikou Dikaiou*, 92.
23. Law 2863/2000, Art. 4; I. Kiki, *Eleutheria ton Optikoakoustikon Meson*, p. 166; Chrysogonos, *Vevaiotike anatheorese*, p. 299.
24. Law 2863/2000, Art. 10.

that is expressly mentioned in the Constitution.[25] The legislator added flesh to this constitutional imperative by adopting Law 3051/2002 on the independent authorities, especially Articles 2 (7) and 19 (1), enabling NCRTV to publish its own internal regulation and to announce the allocation of licences to private stations.[26] This allocation has yet to take place. Licences are awarded on the basis of piecemeal legislation that is constantly being revised. Effectively, the private stations operate without licences.

Despite the fact that the NCRTV is the oldest and most prominent independent authority, it is still considered by many to be 'the weakest and most depreciated of all the independent authorities of the country'.[27] Demands have been raised for further legislative reform to repeal provisions reserving powers to the Ministry of Press and Mass Media such as Article 10 of Law 2863/2000.[28] This provision states that the Ministry of Press and Mass Media shapes the state's policy and takes the necessary legislative and regulatory initiatives for the regulation of the wider field of mass media.

The Council itself tends to blame its lack of decentralization and its erratic technical and staff means for its failure to fulfil its tasks.[29] As true as this may be, what is needed most of all is a fundamental rethinking on its part. It is considered that the Council understands itself as a policing authority, imposing monetary fines to penalize transgressions instead of trying to open up a dialogue with all the stakeholders.[30] The fines imposed by the NCRTV have been excessively heavy in some cases but not in others. As a result of this irrational, discriminatory enforcement of the law, broadcasters constantly challenge the regulator's decisions before the Council of State in an attempt to avoid paying the fines. Moreover, NCRTV has failed to take its regulatory role seriously. It has missed the opportunity of devising

25. Oikonomou, 'Ethniko Symvoulio Radioteleorases', 188; I. K. Karakostas, *To Dikaio ton MME* (Athens, Ant. N. Sakkoulas, 2003), p. 91. For criticisms as to the need for revising Art. 15 of the Constitution *see* Dagtoglou, *Atomika dikaiomata*, p. 702; Kiki, *Eleutheria ton Optikoakoustikon Meson*, p. 95 *et seq.*
26. Oikonomou, 'Ethniko Symvoulio Radioteleorases', 189.
27. Kaitatzi-Whitlock, 'Greece', p. 124.
28. Karakostas, *To Dikaio ton MME*, p. 91. As of 2004 the Ministry of Press and Mass Media was dissolved and two General Secreteriats under the aegis of the Minister of State, the Secretariat General of Information and the Secretariat General of Communication, incorporated the functions of the defunct Ministry.
29. I. Kamtsidou, 'E ekthese pepragmenon tou ESR gia to etos 2004: E anexartete arxe se diarke apostase apo te rythmistike apostole tes' (2005) 3 ΔιΜΕΕ, 388, 390.
30. Oikonomou, 'Ethniko Symvoulio Radioteleorases', 191; Kamtsidou, 'E ekthese pepragmenon tou ESR', 390; Kaitatzi-Whitlock, 'Greece', p. 124. According to Law 2863/2000, Art. 4 (1) (e) in connection with Law 2328/95, Art. 4 (1) the NCRTV can penalize violations of national, European Community and international media and intellectual property law and of the deontological rules with fines between 5.000.000 and 500.000.000 Greek drachmas; with the temporary suspension of a specific programme for a period of up to three months or even with its permanent suspension; with the temporary suspension of all television programmes for up to three months; with the revocation of the broadcaster's licence; with fines of a moral nature (such as the obligation to inform the public about one of the abovementioned fines). Its sanctioning powers against subscription services are laid down in Law 2644/1998, Arts 12, 15 (3).

generally accepted rules to protect vulnerable values such as the constitutionally guaranteed rights and freedoms, especially when conflicts between interests of equal value take place.[31] As has pointedly been remarked, as long as the Council continues to lack a dynamic and inclusive role, public communication in Greece will be caught between the pressures of the governmental Scylla and the market-minded Charybdis.[32]

2.2 Hellenic Audiovisual Institute

The Hellenic Audiovisual Institute (IOM) was established in 1994 as the official institution of applied research in the field of audiovisual communication.[33] It is a state funded semi-autonomous legal body, supervised by the Secretariat General of Communication and Information and adjunct to the Ministry of State. It conducts research with the aim of supporting the Greek audiovisual public and private sector. It also represents Greece at European organizations and in relation to programmes such as MEDIA Plus, the European Audiovisual Observatory and the EuroMed Partnership.

3. FINANCING

ERT S.A. is financed from a combination of the licence fee, levied on electricity consumption, as well as from advertising revenue, ad hoc subsidies from the state budget and any other revenue.[34] The amount of the licence fee has been set at EUR 50.88 per year per electricity consumption reader and is integrated in the electricity bill.[35] All natural or legal persons residing in Greece or having their seat there and possessing an electricity consumption reader are obliged to pay the licence fee. The law provides certain exemptions from this obligation for the state, public entities, local authorities, churches etc.[36] The characterization of the licence fee as a 'retributive charge' is inaccurate as it is imposed as a surcharge on all electricity bills regardless of whether the debtor owns a television set.[37] The licence fee constitutes a tax. The determination of its amount by ministerial decision is contrary to Article 78 (4) of the Greek Constitution that does not allow taxation rates to be determined by the administration.[38]

---

31. Kamtsidou, 'E ekthese pepragmenon tou ESR', 390.
32. *Ibid.*
33. *See* IOM, Hellenic Audiovisual Institute <www.iom.gr/default.aspx?lang=en-US&page=139>, 18 July 2006.
34. Law 1730/87, Art. 14 (1).
35. *Ibid.*
36. *Ibid.*, Art. 14 (3), (4).
37. *Ibid.*; Law 2644/1998, Art. 21.
38. Dagtoglou, *Atomika dikaiomata*, p. 688.

4. THE GREEK CONSTITUTION

The Greek Constitution, as revised in 2001, states that 'the protective provisions for the press are not applicable to films, sound recordings, radio, television or any other similar medium for the transmission of speech or images. Radio and television shall be under the direct control of the state. The control and imposition of administrative sanctions are under the exclusive authority of the National Council for Radio and Television, which is an independent authority as specified by law. The direct control of the state, which also takes the form of the prior permission status, shall aim at the objective transmission, on equal terms, of information and of news reports, as well as of works of literature and art, at ensuring the qualitative standard of programmes in consideration of the social mission of radio and television and of the cultural development of the country, and at the respect for the value of the human being and the protection of childhood and youth.'[39] Interestingly, the Constitution only prescribes four types of programmes: information, news reports, works of literature and of art. Television can by no means neglect these genres or, even worse, leave them out. This does not, however, mean that other programme genres of educational, religious or entertainment nature are not equally indispensable.[40]

The protective provisions for the press mentioned in Article 15 (1) are contained in Article 14 of the Constitution. They include the freedom of the press from censorship and all other means of prior control.[41] The revision of 2001 has only punctually changed the constitutional framework of broadcasting in Greece. The Commission entrusted with the constitutional revision had originally proposed to extend the protective provisions for the press to all other media including broadcasting. However, in the end no political consensus could be reached on this proposal.[42] This means that broadcasting in Greece does not enjoy the higher constitutional guarantees that have been afforded to the press. Measures of prior control are allowed provided that they are necessary for the protection of other values of constitutional rank, such as the protection of childhood, and that they do not impinge upon the very essence of freedom of expression. Article 14 (1) of the Constitution states that everyone can express and disseminate orally, in writing and via the press one's thoughts while respecting the laws of the State. It only mentions the press by way of example, but is by no means limited to it. Freedom of expression equally applies to broadcasting and all other media and puts a limit to censorship.

The 2001 revision left the paternalistic elements of the Greek Constitution, notably the principle of direct state control over broadcasting, untouched. The direct control by the state aimed already under the previous Constitution 1975/86 to guarantee the triptych of objectivity, impartiality and good quality of

39. Constitution 1975/1986/2001, Art. 15 (hereafter referred to as the Greek Constitution).
40. Dagtoglou, *Atomika dikaiomata*, p. 671.
41. Greek Constitution, Art. 14 (2).
42. Kiki, *Eleutheria ton Optikoakoustikon Meson*, p. 118 *et seq.*

programmes.[43] The last of these objectives is the most elusive one and the least attained in practice. It is only insufficiently specified by means of the reference to 'the social mission of radio and television and the cultural development of the country'. The enforcement of the good quality of programmes ultimately rests with the courts when they are called either to review relevant NCRTV decisions or to decide on a possible collective action brought by a consumer association.[44]

The direct state control has been exercised since 1989 via the National Council for Radio and Television (NCRTV). It is a full control that covers not only the legality but also the expediency of programme related decisions, yet falling short of a complete, asphyxiating tutelage of television by the state.[45] It goes far beyond a mere oversight of broadcasting activities and allows the state to go to great lengths interfering with the functioning of broadcasting stations.[46] Even though mentioning state control and impartiality in one breadth appears to be an oxymoron, the Greek Constitution conceives of the former as an important factor for the achievement of the latter. State control means, first of all, that control by non-state actors such as political parties or interest groups is not allowed.[47] Secondly, it means that control by state authorities in a wide sense that cannot be traced back to the government and, hence, escapes parliamentary scrutiny is not permitted either.[48] The control of television by an independent authority still constitutes state control as the supervising minister is subject to parliamentary scrutiny.[49] It would have been preferable if the revised Constitution simply referred to the supervision of broadcasting by the NCRTV instead of repeating the outdated and obscure concept of direct state control.[50]

The changes brought about by the 2001 revision include the express mentioning of two objectives and two obligations of Greek television, both public and private. The objectives are the respect for the value of the human being and the protection of childhood and youth. The first of these objectives has been dictated by the assaults on human dignity by reality TV – especially the proliferating recreation of high profile trials on television with little regard to privacy, family life or the presumption of innocence – as well as by the frequent use of hidden cameras in investigative journalism.[51] The protection of childhood and youth is not really a new objective, as it has been the *raison être* of regulating Greek television

43. Alivizatos, *Kratos kai Radioteleorase*, p. 76.
44. Kiki, *Eleutheria ton Optikoakoustikon Meson*, p. 76; Chrysogonos, *Vevaiotike anatheorese*, p. 301.
45. B. Karakostas, *To Syntagma, Ermeneutika sxolia, Nomologia* (Athens, Nomikie Vivliotheke, 2006), p. 363; Dagtoglou, *Atomika dikaiomata*, p. 669.
46. Council of State 5040/87; 2544/1999; 554/2003; 152/2004.
47. Alivizatos, *Kratos kai Radioteleorase*, p. 17 *et seq.*; I. Kiki, *E Kalodiake Teleorase* (Athens, Ant. A. Sakkoulas, 1993), p. 204.
48. Dagtoglou, *Atomika dikaiomata*, p. 667.
49. *Ibid.*
50. *See* Kiki, *Eleutheria ton Optikoakoustikon Meson*, p. 134 *et seq.*, for the vehement criticisms expressed in academic writing against the direct control of the state over broadcasting.
51. Chrysogonos, *Vevaiotike anatheorese*, p. 301.

since its very beginnings. Its elevation to constitutional status is merely of a symbolic nature. It does not grant viewers rights that they can claim in court.[52] The two public duties introduced by the 2001 revision – the obligation to cover free of charge the sessions of Parliament and of its committees, as well as the electoral addresses of the political parties – will be looked at more closely below.

5. LEGAL FRAMEWORK

Public television is regulated by Law 1730/87. However, many provisions of Law 2328/95 concerning private radio and television are applicable as well. Hence, the laws governing public and private television in Greece do not differ to a great extent. These laws are supplemented by numerous Presidential Decrees, Ministerial Decisions, Regulations and Guidelines of the NCRTV, giving rise to an overregulated and extremely detailed normative framework.[53] Laws are as frequently amended as they are defied by most players in the broadcasting system.[54] The ensuing complexity of the legal framework, particularly of Law 2328/95, it renders virtually unenforceable.

6. PUBLIC BROADCASTING MISSION AND STANDARDS

The public-service mission of ERT S.A. is to provide radio and television services that contribute towards informing, educating and entertaining the Greek people, both in Greece and overseas.[55] It has been assigned the task of fulfilling the aims of the public service, of meeting the democratic, social and cultural needs of society and of safeguarding pluralism. ERT S.A. is obliged to reach the whole of the Greek population by using appropriate technical means. Its programmes are aimed at all segments of society, catering for the needs of special social groups, regardless of ratings.

According to Article 3 (2) of Law 1730/87 television programmes need to comply with the following principles: objectivity, comprehensiveness and timeliness of information; pluralism; good quality; protection of the quality of the Greek language; respect of the personality and privacy of the person; protection, promotion and dissemination of the Greek civilization and tradition.

Broadcasting standards are also contained in NCRTV Regulation 1/1991 on journalistic deontology on radio and television (Code of Journalistic Deontology). This Code requires that news has to be clearly distinguishable from commentaries, be objective and comprehensive and not present speculation as fact.[56] Reasonable efforts have to be made to present different views on contentious issues, for as long

52. Kiki, *Eleutheria ton Optikoakoustikon Meson*, p. 145.
53. *Ibid.*, p. 681; Kaitatzi-Whitlock, 'Greece', p. 123.
54. *Ibid.*
55. Law 1730/87, Art. 2 (1).
56. NCRTV, Code of Journalistic Deontology, Art. 3.

as the interest of the public lasts.[57] Persons should not be presented in ways that encourage their humiliation, their social exclusion or the discrimination against segments of the public.[58] Further rules concern respect for private life, the tactful handling of human grief or suffering, the non-disclosure of confidential sources of information, as well as standards related to the criminal trial.[59]

Further broadcasting standards are laid down in NCRTV Regulation 2/1991 on Radio and Television Programmes (Code of Radio and Television Programmes). Persons appearing in programmes must be treated fairly, correctly and with dignity; their views must not be distorted.[60] Criminal acts must not be presented in a way that encourages their imitation. The live transmission of acts of terrorism and interviews with terrorists must not further their aims.[61] Further provisions concern the reporting of riots, the conduct of competitions, a ban on the use of hypnosis and of subliminal techniques, the accuracy of news reporting, the protection of minors and the presentation of violence.[62] Finally, detailed standards concerning news and other political programmes are laid down in Presidential Decree 77/2003 incorporating the 'Code of Conduct for News and other Political Programmes'.[63] Regrettably, many of these principles are frequently violated by Greek television.[64] Complaints for violations of these principles are dealt with in the first instance by the Director-General of the broadcasting station and in the second instance by the NCRTV.[65]

7. POLITICAL AND ELECTION BROADCASTING

7.1 ELECTION BROADCASTS

According to Article 15 (2) of the Greek Constitution, matters relating to the mandatory and free transmission of the sessions of Parliament and of its committees, as well as of electoral addresses of the political parties by broadcasting media, shall be specified by law. The second section of Article 15 of the Greek Constitution was added in the course of the constitutional revision of 2001, leading to an obligation of public and private broadcasters to transmit electoral messages and to a corresponding right of political parties to deliver them.[66] Before 2001,

57. *Ibid.*, Art. 4.
58. *Ibid.*, Art. 5.
59. *Ibid.*, Arts 7–10.
60. NCRTV, Code for Radio and Television Programmes, Art. 3.
61. *Ibid.*, Art. 4.
62. *Ibid.*, Arts 5–10.
63. Presidential Decree 77/2003 (hereafter referred to as P.D. 77/2003). *See* M. Kostopoulou, 'New Code of Conduct for News and Other Political Programmes' <www.merlin.obs.coe.int/iris/2003/7/Art.20.en.html>, 12 September 2006.
64. Dagtoglou, *Atomika dikaiomata*, p. 689.
65. NCRTV, Code of Journalistic Deontology, Art.11; NCRTV, Code for Radio and Television Programmes, Art. 11; NCRTV, Reg. 4/1991 on the Submission and Examination of Complaints.
66. Dagtoglou, *Atomika dikaiomata*, p. 725.

broadcasters were under no clear legal obligation to grant political parties access to television.[67] Nonetheless, the Greek Council of State inferred from the principle of objectivity in the transmission of information and news reports under Article 15 (2) of the Constitution that the state was obliged to put at the disposal of political parties a minimum yet sufficient time for them to put across their main points.[68] This case-law has been criticized in academic writing for failing to explain how an obligation of the state translates into an obligation of the broadcasters given that all television channels, including ERT, are in the hands of private organizations.[69]

In accordance with the constitutional requirement of Article 15 (2), Law 2328/95 stipulates that television channels need to ensure political pluralism and to present the views of all political parties that are represented in the national and the European Parliament on every matter of political controversy. This obligation has to be fulfilled across the programme as a whole, especially in the framework of news and of political programmes.[70] The need to respect pluralism in political programmes during the election campaign is also stressed in Presidential Decree 77/2003.[71] The body entrusted with the oversight of political and cultural pluralism in the mass media is the NCRTV.[72]

As far as the allocation of broadcasting time is concerned, Law 1730/87 provides that it is to be divided among the parties according to the percentage of their representation in Parliament.[73] The presentation of the election campaign needs to be objective and comprehensive.[74] Airtime is therefore allocated to the parties in accordance with their performance at the previous elections.[75] This is known as the principle of 'proportional equality'. Performance at the previous elections is, however, not the only criterion. Following the jurisprudence of the German Constitutional Court, the Greek Council of State ruled that other objective factors, not related to the ideology but to the political importance of parties and to their historic role, can also be taken into account.[76] Therefore, the televisual exclusion of political parties that were not represented in the previous Parliament and which did not field candidates in at least half of the constituencies of the country is not contrary to the Constitution.[77] Statements made by persons exercising public power in this capacity do not count towards the airtime granted to their party unless if they are utilized to inform about the election campaign.

---

67. *Ibid.*, p. 724; contra Chrysogonos, *Vevaiotike anatheorese*, p. 302, who argues that this obligation could already be inferred before 2001 from the combination of Arts 5 (1), 14 (1), 15 (2), 29 (1) and 51 of the Greek Constitution.
68. Council of State 930/90, (1990) ToΣ, 68.
69. Dagtoglou, *Atomika dikaiomata*, p. 727.
70. Law 2328/95, Art. 3 (22).
71. P.D. 77/2003, Art. 16 (2).
72. Law 2863/2000, Art. 4 (1) (γ).
73. Law 1730/87, as amended by Laws 1866/89 and 2173/93, Art.3 (4).
74. Law 1730/1987, Art. 3 (5).
75. Law 1730/1987, Art. 3 (5); Law 3023/2002, Art.10; P.D. 351 of 29/31 December 2003, Art. 45 (1.a.).
76. Council of State 930/90, (1990) ToΣ, 68, 69.
77. Council of State 2423/84, (1986) ToΣ 77.

During electoral periods broadcasters are not allowed to broadcast any advertising messages nor messages of a social nature that promote political parties or groupings of such parties with the only exception of the abovementioned electoral addresses.[78] The political advertisement of candidates is also prohibited during election time.[79] However, candidates are allowed to give interviews or to take part in discussions once during election time in programmes of national broadcasters, at most twice in programmes of local broadcasters.[80] Party leaders and presidency candidates are not subject to these limitations and can appear more often in such programmes.[81]

Before the general elections of 7 March 2004 the Ministers of Interior, Public Administration and Decentralization and of the Press and Mass Media were allocated broadcasting time as follows.[82] ERT was obliged to broadcast a 60 minutes long interview and a Press conference of equal duration with every party leader. Both ERT and the private broadcasters were obliged to organize at least four round table discussions with representatives of the political parties that would be transmitted between 18:00 and 1:30. ERT also had to broadcast one pre-election rally of their choice for each of the parties. Both ERT and the private channels had to grant each of the parties ten minutes per week free of charge for them to present their political programme or for other activities of their choice. A maximum of one third of these ten minute slots could be used for advertising purposes. Finally, both ERT and the private channels had to use one third of their news programmes for the presentation of the election campaign. All journalists were obliged to give detailed account of the time allocated to each party. No opinion polls could be broadcast in the last fifteen days prior to the election. On the eve of the election and on the following day until 19:00 all electoral propaganda was prohibited with the exception of statements of party leaders made in the course of the election process.[83]

The principle of 'proportional equality' only applies to the election campaign. Do parties have a right of access to television during other periods that are not covered by Article 15 (2) of the Greek Constitution? This question has been answered in the affirmative by the Greek Council of State.[84] Outside the election campaign, the principles of political pluralism and objectivity require the allocation of minimum but sufficient airtime of at least five minutes weekly to all political parties so that they can inform the public about their political programmes and ideas.[85] The latest results of the political parties are taken into account in allocating broadcasting opportunities.[86] This is known as the principle of equity

78. Law 3023 of 21/25 June 2002, Art. 11 (1) (β).
79. Law 3023 of 21/25 June 2002, Art. 12 (1) (γ) and Common Ministerial Decree (K.Y.A.) 6140 of 16 March 2000.
80. Law 3023 of 21/25 June 2002, Art. 12 (2).
81. *Ibid.*, Art. 12 (3).
82. Common Ministerial Decree (K.Y.A.) 2846/E of 10 February 2004.
83. *See also* Law 3023 of 21/25 June 2002, Art. 10 (3).
84. *Ibid.*
85. NCRTV internal document 385EΣ of 30 March 2005.
86. NCRTV, Directive 1 of 21 February 2006.

and it applies again to all programme genres (news reports, information and entertainment programmes).[87] The airtime or speaking time that is accorded to political persons (party leaders, candidates for Parliament, ministers) or to persons supporting specific parties – regardless of whether they are party members or not – is taken into consideration.[88] National broadcasters are asked to notify the NCRTV on a daily basis of the appearance of the abovementioned political persons on television, including in news reports, and of the speaking time accorded to them. Local and regional broadcasters need to communicate this information on a weekly basis.[89] The Council monitors the application of the principle of equity at the end of each month on the basis of the average airtime allotted to each party. The Council recently found considerable violations of political pluralism regarding news reports and other political programmes, especially in the private channels.[90]

Paid political advertising is allowed in Greece, both during and outside the election time.[91] So as not to discriminate against smaller parties the law stipulates that the maximum election expenditure of each party or party grouping taking part in the general or in the European Parliament elections cannot exceed 20 per cent of the ordinary funding granted to all the parties.[92] The maximum election expenditure for every candidate is also specified by law.[93]

7.2 Broadcasts of General Interest

ERT S.A. is obliged to broadcast the sessions of the Greek Parliament, dividing airtime between the parties in accordance with their representation in Parliament.[94] Obviously, ERT S.A. is not obliged to cover the totality of the sessions of the Parliament, but only their main points. ERT-S.A. is also obliged to present matters related to the local government, productive classes and social bodies.[95] All broadcasters have to transmit messages of a social nature lasting three minutes per day without charge. The duration of each message cannot exceed 40 seconds.[96] These

87. P.D. 77/2003.
88. NCRTV, Directive 6 of 16 February 2004.
89. NCRTV, Directive 6 of 16 February 2004.
90. NCRTV, Directive 1 of 21 February 2006. *See also* Decision 7 of 27 January 2004 where the NCRTV imposed a fine of EUR 70,000 on a television station that failed to present the views of smaller parties in news and current affairs programmes.
91. Law 3023 of 21/25 June 2002, Art. 11 (1) (β); K.Y.A. 2846/E of 10 February 2004, Art. 13; EPRA, Background Paper – Plenary, Political Advertising: Case Studies and Monitoring, 23rd EPRA Meeting, Elsinore, 17–19 May 2006.
92. Law 3023 of 21/25 June 2002, Art. 13.
93. *Ibid.*, Art. 14.
94. Greek Constitution, Art. 15 (2); Law 1730/87, Art. 3 (4). The fact that this obligation also extends to the private stations has been criticized in academic writing. *See* Kiki, *Eleutheria ton Optikoakoustikon Meson*, p. 147 *et seq.*
95. Law 1730/87, Art. 3 (6).
96. Common Ministerial Decree (K.Y.A.) A.P. 24/1 of 2 January 1997, Art. 4 (1).

messages concern especially health matters, the protection of persons with disabilities as well as education programmes and other activities organized by the Greek Parliament of a national, political, cultural or social nature.[97] The State, public entities and private non-profitable organizations are entitled to such messages.[98]

8. CULTURAL OBLIGATIONS

8.1 Language Policy

ERT S.A. is subject to specific cultural obligations related to the protection of the quality of the Greek language and the defence, promotion and dissemination of the Greek civilization and tradition.[99] ERT S.A. as well as the private channels are obliged to take all necessary steps, such as recruitment of specialists and of text editors, and organization of seminars, to ensure the correct use of the Greek language in information, education and entertainment programmes as well as in the dubbing or subtitling of foreign programmes.[100] The editing, presentation and subtitling of programmes need to follow the generally accepted rules of grammar and syntax of the Greek language.[101] The same care needs to be taken in the use of foreign languages in the framework of Greek or foreign language programmes. Foreign language programmes need to be presented, if possible, by native language speakers.[102] Furthermore, ERT S.A. and the private channels have to reserve at least 25 per cent of their transmission time, excluding news, sports events, games, advertising or teletext services, for works produced in the Greek language.[103] Finally, both ERT S.A. and the private channels are obliged to organize a series of at least fifteen seminars every six months, lasting at least thirty minutes each, on the correct use of the Greek language or on its learning by foreigners or by illiterates.[104]

8.2 High Culture and Educational Programmes

The fulfilment of the cultural needs of society and the education of Greek people, both in Greece and overseas, are part of ERT S.A.'s public service mission.[105] Its programming displays a traditional public service profile, encompassing educational and

---

97. Law 2328/95, Art. 3 (21).
98. Common Ministerial Decree (K.Y.A.) A.P. 24/1 of 2 January 1997, Art.2.
99. *Ibid.*, Art. 14 (2) (δ), (στ).
100. Law 2328/95, Art. 3 (18).
101. Code 2/1991 for Radio and Television Programmes, Art.2 (4); P.D. 77/2003, Art. 2 (4).
102. Code 2/1991 for Radio and Television Programmes, Art. 2 (4).
103. Law 2328/95, Art. 3 (18).
104. *Ibid.*, Art. 3 (19).
105. Law 1730/87, Art. 2 (1).

children programmes, news and current affairs, Greek and foreign serials and feature films, music, sport and documentaries.[106] The duration of educational or cultural programmes is not specified.[107]

8.3 Regional Programmes

Regional programming is provided by the regional television station, ET3, which is located in Thessaloniki.

8.4 Cultural Quotas

Greece has implemented the 'European quota' and the 'independent quota' of the TwF Directive. Broadcasters need to reserve at least 51 per cent of their transmission time, except for news, sport events, games, advertisements, teleshopping and teletext services, to European origin programmes.[108] They also need to reserve at least 10 per cent of their transmission time, excluding the time appointed to news, sport events, advertising and teleshopping, for independent productions.[109] The Greek legislator has included the time devoted to games and teletext services into the time on the basis of which the independent quota is to be calculated in contravention of Article 5 of the TwF Directive. Also, broadcasters have to devote 1.5 per cent of their yearly bruto income – after deduction of taxes and other charges in favour of the public sector, public bodies and local authorities – for the production or co-production of cinematographic movies (with a duration of 70 to 150 minutes) that are aimed to be shown on the big screen.[110]

9. ADVERTISING

9.1 Background

ERT-S.A. can refuse to transmit any advertising messages and is not allowed to transmit advertisements that are incompatible with its general principles, with the respect for the personality of women, with the protection of the interests and the sensitivity of youth and with the respect for cultural heritage and tradition; that contain violence and can harm the personality of the individual; that are misleading; that are of poor quality or tasteless.[111] ERT-S.A. also needs to respect the rules of the Presidential Decree (P.D.) 100/2000 that has implemented the TwF Directive. Article 5 of P.D. 100/2000 has transposed mostly verbatim the advertising rules of the Directive.

---

106. Seri, 'Mediensystem Griechenlands', p. 324.
107. Oikonomou, 'Ethniko Symvoulio Radioteleorases', 191.
108. P.D. 100/2000, Art. 10 (1).
109. *Ibid.*, Art. 10 (7).
110. Law 1866/1989, Art. 7 (1).
111. Law 1730/87, Art. 3 (8).

Besides the state regulation of advertising, free-to-air broadcasters together with the Hellenic Association of Advertising and Communication Agencies (EDEE) and the Hellenic Advertisers Association (SDE) have drawn up the Hellenic Advertising and Communication Code governing the content, presentation and promotion of advertisements.[112] The Code is enforced by a non-state body, the Advertising Self-Regulation Council (SEE), which is a member of the European Advertising Standards Alliance. Responsibility for the overall supervision of the system lies with the NCRTV.

9.2 The Principle of Separation

Advertising has to be distinct from the rest of the programme. Surreptitious advertising and techniques directed at the subconscious are not allowed.[113] Greece has incorporated the TwF Directive's definition of surreptitious advertising in Article 2 (d) of P.D. 100/2000. It is therefore necessary to prove the intentional wrongdoing of the broadcaster. While the Directive states that 'such representation is considered to be intentional *in particular* if it is done in return for payment or for similar consideration', the provision in the Greek law omits the phrase 'in particular'. This creates the impression that proof of payment or of other similar consideration is indispensable so to establish intentional wrongdoing. However, the Council of State ruled that consideration does not need to be ascertained if the general circumstances of the broadcast leave no doubt that there was advertising intention. In the case of a programme whose presenter displayed the cover and parts of the content of a magazine and also discussed extensively the effective treatments offered by a slimming centre with one of the centre's customers, the Council of State found advertising intention even in the absence of a proof of payment.[114] A further indication of intentional wrongdoing is the inclusion in a programme of the telephone number of the company supplying the represented goods or services. The majority of the NCRTV held that the public broadcaster NET breached the prohibition of surreptitious advertising by mentioning the name of a fashion designer in a fashion show for beachwear and accessories, while the telephone number of the supplier appeared at the bottom of the screen.[115]

112. Hans-Bredow-Institut, 'Final Report: Study on Co-Regulation Measures in the Media Sector', June 2006 <www.ec.europa.eu/avpolicy/docs/library/studies/coregul/coregul-final-report_en.pdf>, 18 July 2007, pp. 60 *et seq.*
113. P.D. 100/2000, Art. 5 (1); NCRTV Reg. 3/1991 containing the Deontology Code for Television Advertising, Art. 3 (1), (4a). *See* P. D. Selekos, *O Kanonas tou Diaxorismou ton Diafemiseon apo to Programma ste Radioteleorase* (*To zetema tes 'synkekalymmenes' diafemises*) (Athens, Ant. N. Sakkoulas, 1997).
114. Council of State 2647/2006.
115. NCRTV, Decision 229 of 20 July 2004. The dissenting opinion argued that the appearance of these products was justified on artistic grounds.

9.3 ADVERTISING AND MINORS

The criteria of the TwF Directive for the protection of minors from advertising have been incorporated verbatim in Article 5 (10) of P.D. 100/2000. A rule unique to Greek legislation is that advertising for children's toys is prohibited between 7 A.M. and 10 P.M.[116] The Athens Court of First Instance interpreted the rationale behind this restriction as follows. In Greece, children usually watch television on their own between 7 A.M. and 10 P.M., while the whole family is more likely to be gathered in front of the television set after 10 P.M. It is hence only after this time that adults can actually prevent the undesirable effects of advertising aimed at children.[117] This reasoning is clearly informed by viewing habits in Greece that differ considerably from those in Central and Northern Europe. Interestingly, advertisements for toys shops can be transmitted at any time of the day provided that they do not contravene the spirit of the advertising restriction for children's toys.[118]

The Hellenic Advertising and Communication Code also contains a section on advertising directed at children, i.e. persons under 14 years of age. It bans advertisements that exhort minors to buy goods over the phone or in the post office. Indirect forms of advertising (advertorials-editorials) must make the advertising intention clear.[119] Special care must be taken so that the size, qualities and functions of advertised products can easily be appreciated. Advertisements must not mislead as to the price of a certain product by using words such as 'only' or by implying that the product can easily be obtained by anyone.[120] When children take part in advertisements, they must be well-behaved and the advertisements must not undermine the authority and sense of responsibility of parents nor doubt their judgment.[121]

10. PROTECTION OF MINORS

The provisions on the protection of minors of the TwF Directive, Arts 22 and 22a, have been implemented in Greece by means of Article 8 of Presidential Decree

116. Law 2251/94, Art. 14 (8). This is the latest of a series of restrictions on the advertising of children's toys. Initially, Law 1730/1989, Art. 3 (9) completely banned the advertising of children's toys. NCRTV Regulation 3/1991, Art. 9 (1) cut back this total ban to one concerning only the advertising of war games. Law 1961/1991, Art. 21 (4) introduced a restriction for children's toys adverts before 11 P.M., that was subsequently lifted by Law 2000/1991, Art. 53. Athens Court of First Instance 523/2000, *see* note by A. Delikostopoulou (2000) 11 ΔΕΕ, 1138. The European Commission started proceedings against Greece on the basis of the incompatibility of this restriction with the free movement of services, but suspended them with a decision of 28 July 1999.
117. Athens Court of First Instance 523/2000, (2000) 11 ΔΕΕ, 1136.
118. NCRTV Directive 7/2002 of 3 December 2002 on the transmission of advertisements for children's toys in the Christmas period.
119. Hellenic Advertising and Communication Code, Appendix I, Art. 2.
120. *Ibid.*, Art. 4.
121. *Ibid.*, Art. 3.
122. *See also* NCRTV Reg. 2/1991 containing the Code for Radio and Television Programmes, Art. 9.

100/2000.[122] Broadcasters are not allowed to transmit programmes which might seriously harm the physical, mental or moral development of minors. Next to programmes involving pornographic scenes or scenes of gratuitous violence, the law prohibits the display of violence in news broadcasts unless if it is necessary so as to inform the public about a certain event. The re-staging of events in news and other information programmes is absolutely prohibited.[123]

All television programmes – with the exception of advertising and teleshopping spots – are classified in five categories in accordance with the degree of their unfavourable influence on the personality and the moral and mental development of minors. These categories have been laid down in a Ministerial Decree by the Minister of Press and Mass Media.[124] The classification of programmes is the task of internal committees to be set up by every broadcaster by 15 May every year at the latest. These committees consist of scientists – mainly psychologists, pedagogues and lawyers – as well as members of the editorial team.[125] The Ministerial Decree also provides that programmes may be classified by the committees, which are entrusted with the control of cinema movies by the Ministry of Press and Mass Media.[126] This possibility has not, however, been used in practice.[127]

Category I programmes are suitable for all audiences. Their scheduling lies within the broadcaster's discretion. Parental consent is desirable for category II programmes that cannot be broadcast either during the children viewing zone or thirty minutes before or after it. Parental consent is essential for category III programmes that can only be broadcast between 9 P.M. and 6 A.M. On Fridays, Saturdays and on the eve of public holidays, these programmes may only be scheduled after 10 P.M. Category IV programmes are only suitable for minors above the age of 15. They may only be broadcast between 10.30 P.M. and 6 A.M. On Fridays, Saturdays and on the eve of public holidays, these programmes may only be scheduled after 11 P.M. Finally, category V programmes are only suitable for adults. They may only be broadcast between 12.30 A.M. and 6 A.M.

Pictograms correspond to each of these categories. The display of the category I pictogram lies in the broadcaster's discretion. The pictograms for categories 2–4 have to be displayed for specified amounts of time at the beginning of the programme and after each advertising break, while the pictogram for category 5 programmes has to be displayed throughout the entire duration of the programme. Also, trailers have to be accompanied by the appropriate pictogram throughout their entire duration. It is interesting to note that different pictograms can be used for different parts or scenes of news, information and entertainment programmes.[128] Also, programmes within a series can be classified differently regardless of whether they are editorially linked.[129]

---

123. P.D. 100/2000, Art. 8 (1).
124. Ministerial Decree 6138/E of 17 March 2000.
125. *Ibid.*, Art. 2 (1).
126. *Ibid.*, Art. 2 (2).
127. Council of State 2631/2006, (2006) 4 ΔιΜΕΕ, 565, 566 n. 9.
128. P.D. 100/2000, Art. 4 (1).
129. P.D. 100/2000, Art. 4 (2).

The five categories used in Greece for the classification of programmes are modelled upon the French youth certificate rating system. However, the Greek classification system has not benefited from the broad public consultation that took place in France so as to ensure its responsiveness to the needs of the public. Even though the Ministerial Decree explicitly requires the conduct of such a public consultation, this has not materialized up to now. Also, the Greek categories II and III are not clearly age related, which renders their application more difficult. Nor are there any obvious criteria for the classification of programmes in each category. As a result, the application of this system to news and current affairs programmes has been cumbersome in the past. Moreover, programmes have often been rated according to their time of transmission rather than the other way round.[130]

So as to address these problems, the NCRTV has issued guidelines on the protection of minors from harmful content in news and information programmes.[131] These guidelines prohibit the transmission of scenes of an erotic or pornographic character in news and information programmes during the children viewing zone, especially when these are not directly related to the subject matter of the programme. Furthermore, they oblige broadcasters to display the relevant pictogram and to verbally inform the public three minutes before the transmission of the harmful content.

These guidelines indicate willingness on the part of the NCRTV to enter into a substantive dialogue with the broadcasters and to guide them in the application of the youth protection legislation. This is a positive step back from the often criticized narrow understanding of its role as a policing organ, which is the more lamentable if it comes with a disregard for the law.

Such an understanding was recently displayed in a case in which the NCRTV recommended the rescheduling of a chat show from 2 P.M. to 11 P.M. because of the insulting and indecent comments made in two instances. This decision was challenged before the Council of State with the argument that the unsuitable content of two programmes of the series did not justify the *a priori* assumption that the whole series was unsuitable for minors and had to be rescheduled. The Council of State rather disingenuously interpreted the challenged decision in the sense that it did not require the rescheduling of the chat show but only warned broadcasters that future programmes with similar content would have to be scheduled at 11 P.M. so as not to be punishable.[132] When the broadcaster continued transmitting the said series at 2 P.M., after having renamed it, the NCRTV imposed a fine of EUR 5,000,000 as well as the provisional suspension of the series for a month. The Council of State, seized with this case for a second time, annulled NCRTV's decision given that the NCRTV penalized the disregard of its previous order without submitting that a specific programme of the series had been unsuitable for minors.[133]

---

130. Council of State 2631/2006, *see* note by M. Kostopoulou (2006) 4 ΔιΜΕΕ, 565, 567.
131. NCRTV, Directive 1/2001 of 20 March 2001; *ibid.*, Directive 2/2003 of 14 April 2003.
132. Council of State 4348/2005, (2006) 1 ΕΔΔΔ, 98.
133. Council of State 2631/2006, (2006) 4 ΔιΜΕΕ, 564.

Indeed, the rescheduling of programmes before their actual transmission comes close to censorship and violates the power of broadcasters independently to classify and schedule their programmes within the constraints of the law, taking particularly into account the possibility of separately classifying each part of a series. No such objections can be raised when a programme is rescheduled because its subject-matter is considered to be offensive to minors in general. For instance, the NCRTV rescheduled the reality show 'Big Brother' from 10.45 P.M. – a time when minors are very likely to watch television in Greece – to 12.30 A.M. and this measure was enforced by the Court of First Instance by way of interim measures.[134] This programme was considered to be harmful to minors as it propagates a voyeuristic attitude, cultivates negative role models for minors and establishes publicity at all cost as means of easy professional advancement.[135]

11. RIGHT OF REPLY

The right of reply is granted under Article 14 (5) of the Greek Constitution to anyone who is affected by an inaccurate publication or programme. A corresponding obligation of complete and immediate rectification is imposed on the offending mass medium. The right of reply is also granted to anyone who is affected by an insulting or defamatory publication or programme. The offending mass medium is obliged to publish or transmit a reply immediately. The procedure for the exercise of the right of reply or for the complete and immediate rectification is established in the law. The last revision of the Greek Constitution that took place in 2001 extended the right of reply to all mass media, not just the press as was the case before. However, Article 14 (5) is problematic in two respects. First, it actively legitimizes only those who are directly affected by a publication or broadcast, excluding others whose legitimate interests may have been damaged in a more indirect way. Secondly, the distinction between rectification and reply is obscure and requires further clarification.[136]

In response to this constitutional imperative, P.D. 100/2000 establishes the right of reply in relation to offending broadcasts.[137] It stipulates that broadcasters are obliged to grant a right of reply to every natural person or to the legal representative of a legal person whose legitimate interests have been affected by the content of a television or radio broadcast. This right is also afforded to the spouse and relatives up to the fourth degree of kinship of a deceased person whose memory is damaged in the same way. Political parties, trade unions, social or other collective entities as well as their members also have the right of reply

134. NCRTV, Decision 205 of 2 April 2002; Athens Court of First Instance 4701/2002.
135. Antenna, the private broadcaster that transmits 'Big Brother', has been repeatedly fined for contraventions of the broadcasting legislation in this programme. *See* NCRTV, Decision 92 of 21 February 2006; 144 of 27 March 2006.
136. Kiki, *Eleutheria ton Optikoakoustikon Meson*, p. 237.
137. P.D. 100/2000, Art. 9 (1).

when their views on a matter related to their activities are distorted or kept back in a way that misinforms the viewers. The law contains a non-exhaustive list of legitimate interests. In the case of natural persons, it is their personality, their honour or reputation or their private and family life or their professional, social, scientific, artistic, political or other related activity. In the case of legal persons, it is their reputation or their business interests. The right of reply has to be exercised within 20 days from the day of the transmission or retransmission of the broadcast.[138] If the affected person lives abroad, this deadline is extended by another 20 days.

The application for the exercise of the right of reply must contain the applicant's details; the date and time of the contentious broadcast; the grounds for the complaint; and the text containing the reply or the request for an appearance in the same or an equivalent programme or for the recording and broadcast of the reply. The Council of State has interpreted this last requirement in a broad way. The applicant who was secretary of a society against the illegal establishment of brothels in Greece had sent two letters to public authorities enquiring about the areas of Athens in which the operation of such establishments was allowed. He was also motivated by a personal interest as he intended to buy or rent property in these areas so as to exchange it with brothels that were located elsewhere in Athens in close proximity to his own property resulting in its devaluation. He complained about a broadcast concerning prostitution in Athens in which it was implied that he was interested in operating such establishments himself. In his application to the broadcaster he did not include the text of his reply but only asked for his letters to the public authorities to be read out. Both the broadcaster and the NCRTV rejected the application on this ground. The Council of State overturned the NCRTV's decision. It found that the application for the exercise of the right of reply was specific enough.[139] It follows from this judgment that neither the broadcaster nor the NCRTV have a right to examine the content of the reply and to substitute the affected person's view with their own view as to whether it is suitable to rectify the erroneous broadcast.[140]

Obviously, the application may not involve a punishable act, render the broadcaster liable to civil law proceedings or transgress standards of public decency.[141] The reply has to be of a similar duration to the offending statement and to be broadcast in the next programme – if the offending broadcast was part of a series – or in an equivalent programme. The broadcaster has to take a decision on the application within two days.[142] If it rejects the application, it has to transmit it within 24 hours together with its decision to the NCRTV. The NCRTV decides within three days. Its decision is binding on the broadcaster.[143] The right of reply

138. Compare BVerfGE 63, 131 in which the German Constitutional Court held that a time-limit of two weeks for the exercise of the right of reply was too short. The broadcasting laws of the German *Länder* often stipulate time-limits of two months. *See* for instance WDR-Gesetz, § 9 (3); ZDF-StV, § 9 (3) 3.
139. Council of State 926/2006, (2006) 4 ΔιΜΕΕ, 573.
140. *Ibid.*, *see* note by A. Oikonomou (2006) 4 ΔιΜΕΕ, 573.
141. P.D. 100/2000, Art. 9 (3).
142. P.D. 100/2000, Art. 9 (4).
143. *Ibid.*, Art. 9 (5).

exists without prejudice to other civil or criminal law remedies.[144] In Greece, such remedies are more popular than the right of reply, not least due to the formality of the administrative procedure and the perceived insufficiency of a verbal redress.[145]

144. *Ibid.*, Art. 9 (3).
145. Council of State 926/2006, (2006) 4 ΔιΜΕΕ, 573, *see* note by A. Oikonomou (2006) 4 ΔιΜΕΕ, 572.

Chapter 5
Italy

1. BACKGROUND

Similarly to Greece, the beginnings of public broadcasting in Italy were bound up with Mussolini's Fascist government that stayed in power from 1922 until 1943. Successively, a number of private companies were granted exclusive licences to broadcast, but the government kept a tight grip on the programmes and abused them for its propaganda purposes.[1] After the end of the war, no radical overhaul of the broadcasting system took place. In 1947, the first attempt at regulating the Italian media landscape was made by means of a statute that established the monopoly of the independent public broadcaster Radio Audizioni Italia (RAI). This statute also set up a Parliamentary Commission to secure RAI's political independence. However, this Commission lacked effective powers. In 1954, RAI, that had in the meantime been renamed Radiotelevisione Italiana, began regularly transmitting its television programmes.

Since its inception, RAI has never been truly independent as it was always dominated by the major political parties. Ironically, the subjugation of public television by politics was countersigned for the first time by the RAI Law of 1975, which intended to increase RAI's independence by freeing it from the executive branch.[2] This law increased the powers of the Parliamentary Commission by allowing it to appoint ten out of the sixteen members of RAI's Administrative Council. The governing coalition, fearful of a diminution of its powers, entered into a 'secret' agreement on the sharing of control over television and radio channels, the so-called *lottizazione*. Originally an agricultural term for the 'parcelling out' of land, *lottizazione* came to stand for the convention of

---

1. Barendt, *Broadcasting Law*, p. 24; Holznagel, *Rundfunkrecht in Europa*, p. 71.
2. Law 103 of 14 April 1975.

awarding seats on the RAI Board of Directors on party-political criteria. RAI-1 has since been traditionally controlled by the Christian Democrats, RAI-2 by the Socialist Party and RAI-3 by the Communist Party.

In 1976, a landmark ruling of the Italian Constitutional Court opened up the Italian market to private broadcasters at the local level, while upholding RAI's exclusive right to broadcast on a national basis.[3] Immediately, a large number of local stations emerged, which soon coordinated their activities by transmitting the same programmes nationwide, setting up *de facto* chains. During the eighties, a number of commercial television stations appeared on the scene, infringing RAI's national monopoly. The remarkable figure of Silvio Berlusconi who gradually became the owner of three major commercial networks, Canale 5, Italia 1 and Rete 4, stood out. A law introduced by Bettino Craxi, the then Socialist Prime Minister and a close friend of Berlusconi, prevented the closure of these stations by the magistrates.[4]

This unsatisfactory state of affairs lasted for almost a decade until, in 1990, the *Mammì Law* legalized the presence of both public and private broadcasters.[5] However, this law contained very controversial anti-trust quotas allowing Berlusconi to keep all his television channels. It was dubbed 'the photocopy law' and was heavily accused of legitimizing the duopoly of RAI and Berlusconi's Mediaset Group and of killing pluralism.[6] In 1994, the Italian Constitutional Court declared the antitrust provisions of the *Mammì Law* unconstitutional and requested the Parliament to end the duopoly by setting a 20 per cent limit on television market concentration.[7]

The *Mammì Law* was substituted by a more pluralistic regime with the *Maccanico Law* of 1997.[8] This law required the partial privatization of RAI, the restructuring of RAI-3 into an advertising free station and the dissolution of one of the private channels, Rete4. However, sustained resistance to the *Maccanico Law* by the opposition and parts of the coalition government meant that it could yield no results in the years to come.[9] In 2002, the Constitutional Court again declared some of this law's provisions unconstitutional and imposed a detailed timetable for Parliament to comply with pluralism.

Following the victory of the Central-Right coalition in 2001 and the appointment of Berlusconi as Prime Minister, the enactment of any legislation in the media field has been a matter of political controversy. The *Gasparri Law* of 2004, named after the Minister of Communication of the time, deserves special mention.[10] This

3. Decision 202/1976, [1976] *Giur. Cost.* 1267.
4. Law 10 of 4 February 1985 known as the 'Berlusconi Decree'.
5. Law 223 of 6 August 1990.
6. G. Mazzoleni and G. Vigevani, 'Italy' in *Television across Europe: Regulation, Policy and Independence* (New York, Open Society Institute, 2005), p. 876.
7. Decision 420/1994, [1995] *Il Foro Italiano*, Part I, 4.
8. Law 249 of 31 July 1997.
9. G. Mazzoleni, 'Medienpluralismus in Italien zwischen Politik und Marktwettbewerb' (2003) 11 MP, 517.
10. Law 112 of 3 May 2004.

law introduced new anti-trust rules and widened the market by including the entire communications sector ('integrated communications system'). It increased the number of RAI Board members and upheld their nomination by Parliament and Government, thus keeping RAI politically managed. Finally, the *Gasparri Law* envisioned the progressive privatization of RAI, objective to be reached in twelve years time. It provided that, initially, the RAI- Radiotelevisione Italiana Spa would be incorporated into a holding called RAI-Holding Spa. Soon after that the company's State shares would be marketed through a public offer. The entire process was to be completed by 2016.[11] Effectively, it is very unlikely that RAI will be privatized in the near future due to lack of political consensus.

The Organization for Security and Cooperation in Europe Representative on Freedom of the Media considered that the *Gasparri Law* is not likely to remedy the so-called 'Italian television anomaly', i.e. the duopoly domination in the nationwide television market and the quasi-monopoly in its private sector.[12] He reasoned that this law perpetuates or even enhances the existing media concentration while placing undue faith in the potential of universal digitization to deliver media pluralism.

With its three television channels, RAI-Radiotelevisione Italiana Spa, a joint-stock company, is currently the only public broadcaster in Italy. The public service is assigned to RAI by means of a national contract stipulated every three years between RAI and the Ministry of Communication, according to guidelines adopted by the Ministry and the Italian Communication Authority (AGCOM), and by means of two regional contracts stipulated between the Ministry and the two independent provinces of Trento and Bolzano.[13] RAI's programmes cater evenly for the genres of information, culture and entertainment.[14] While the commercial channels have relied strongly on imports of foreign programmes, RAI has consistently had a high level of in-house production.[15]

2. BROADCASTING AUTHORITIES

2.1 Communication Authority

The Italian Communication Authority, *Autoritá per le Garanzie nelle Comunicazioni* (AGCOM), is the most important and powerful body in the communications sector. It is an independent body created by Law 249 of 31 July 1997.

11. Law 112 of 3 May 2004, Art. 21.
12. M. Haraszti, 'Visit to Italy: The Gasparri Law: Observations and Recommendations' <www.osce.org/documents/rfm/2005/06/15459_en.pdf>, 20 November 2006.
13. Legislative Decree 177 of 31 July 2005, Art. 45.
14. RAI-1 transmits information, culture, entertainment and fiction programmes for a mass audience. RAI-2 offers mainly entertainment programmes and programmes for younger audiences. RAI-3 is a culture and education channel.
15. *See* R. Zaccaria, *Televisione: dal monopolio al monopolio* (Milan, Baldini Castoldi Dalai, 2003).

AGCOM is accountable to the Parliament that has established its competence, enacted its constitution and that nominates its members. It constitutes a 'convergent authority' given that it controls the entire communications sector, i.e. press, electronic media and telecommunications.

AGCOM is a collegial body with a President, a Council of eight members and two Commissions, i.e. the Commission for networks and infrastructures and the Commission for services and products. All in all, AGCOM has nine members. The President of the Authority is nominated by Parliamentary Decree, upon proposal of the Prime Minister and the Minister of Telecommunications, and appointed by the government. Each Commission is a collegiate body, composed of the President and four members nominated by the Parliament. The eight members of the two Commissions are appointed by the Chamber of Deputies and the Senate, each of which chooses four members. The Council is composed of the President plus all the members of the two Commissions. AGCOM's independence has come under critical scrutiny given that its membership replicates the two power blocks in the Italian Parliament. As a result, the government-nominated AGCOM President has the last say.[16]

AGCOM enforces the broadcasting principles established by law. It is the guarantor of the market competition rules in the communication sector. It issues the plan for the allocation of frequencies, monitors the creation of dominant positions and ensures the correct application of the antitrust laws. It also oversees the services offered by the broadcasters to ensure their quality and the respect of the rules related to advertising, politics and the protection of minors. To this end, a 24-hour monitoring system has been set up allowing the Authority to observe all national television programmes and to intervene immediately in case of violation. The sanctions applied by AGCOM are in proportion to the gravity of the violation and range from administrative sanctions of a pecuniary nature to more severe sanctions such as the withdrawal of the licence for up to ten days.[17] Every year, AGCOM submits a report to the Parliament on activities carried out.

2.2 Parliamentary Commission for the Communication Services

The Parliamentary Commission for the Communication Services, created by Law 103 of 14 April 1975, is a 'political' authority composed of 20 members from each of the Parliamentary Chambers, i.e. Deputies and Senate. The President of the Commission is selected by the parliamentary minority.[18] The Commission has numerous competences. It only has control powers over the activity of RAI.

16. 'Overview' in *Television across Europe: Regulation, Policy and Independence*, Open Society Institute (ed.) (New York, Open Society Institute, 2005), p. 51.
17. Legislative Decree 177 of 31 July 2005, Art. 51.
18. OSCE/ODIHR, 'Election Assessment Mission Report, Parliamentary Elections, 9–10 April 2006, Italy' <www.osce.org/documents/odihr/2006/06/19409_en.pdf>, 14 November 2006, p. 16.

It oversees the public broadcaster to ensure that it respects public broadcasting principles such as pluralism and fairness. It has regulatory powers allowing it to develop policies concerning the access to the broadcasting system. It also has administrative/political powers: it nominates seven of the members of the Council of administration of RAI and has a strong influence in the choice of its President.[19] It is consulted on the programmes of television and radio. Finally, it has the power to invite the President, the administrators and all the managers of RAI to express their opinion on certain matters.

2.3 The Government

The Ministry of Treasury is RAI's controlling shareholder and has the right to appoint two out of the nine members of the RAI's Board of Directors, including its Chairman.[20] Among the various other governmental organs that have regulatory powers in the broadcasting sector, the Ministry of Communications is without any doubt the most influential. Although the Minister shares most competences with AGCOM, some of them, such as the allocation of frequencies, belong to him/her individually. Both the Code of Communications and the Broadcasting Act 2005 define the Minister's competences.

The Minister has the power to approve the service contract with RAI and the licence convention between the State and RAI. The service contract specifies RAI's public service mission and is renewed every three years. The licence convention is concluded for 20 years and contains the conditions for using the licence for public radio and television broadcasting. The latest one was signed on 5 April 2007.[21]

The current Minister of Communications, Paolo Gentiloni, has proposed a reform of RAI with the aim of rendering it more autonomous from the government and the political parties. The shareholder's role would not be exercised by the government but by a Foundation controlled by various public entities that would represent the interests of the viewers along the lines of the BBC Trust. Its duties would be strictly separate from management or operational matters. Moreover, the Minister proposes the creation of three different companies within the framework of RAI: a network equipment company, a predominately public funded company with reduced dependence on advertising, and a company funded by advertising alone.[22] It is uncertain whether the government will be able to adopt the Gentiloni Reform Bill given that the last bill on the subject of RAI reform dates back to 1975, despite many other attempts.

---

19. Law 112 of 3 May 2004, Art. 20 (9).
20. Law 112 of 3 May 2004, Art. 21.
21. Licence Convention between the Ministry of Communications and RAI-Radiotelevisione Italiana S.p.a, approved by Presidential Decree of 5 April 2007 (hereafter referred to as RAI Service Contract 2007–2009).
22. P. Gentiloni, 'Guidelines for the Reform of the RAI' <www.comunicazioni.it/en/index.php?Arc=1&IdNews=125>, 21 March 2007, p. 8.

2.4 Other Authorities

Other Authorities also have competences in the broadcasting sector. The National Council of Consumers and the Regional Committees for Communications (Co.re.com) are AGCOM's main auxiliary bodies. The National Council of Consumers is composed of a minimum of 11 experts, chosen from a range of people who have distinguished themselves in supporting human rights and, in particular, the rights of minors. It represents an intermediary between consumers and broadcasting operators. The Regional Committees for Communications[23] have been set up to decentralize AGCOM's powers. An important role is also exercised by the Regions to which the State has reserved a series of competences on complementary matters, mainly administrative competences and specific powers for the protection of minority languages.

3. FINANCING

In Italy, public television is financed partly by a yearly surcharge of about EUR 104 for each household, partly by advertising revenues and partly by earnings from contracts or agreements with public administrations to render specific services (*convenzioni*). The relation between licence fee and advertising revenue is about 45 per cent to 55 per cent, while funding from the *convenzioni* makes up about ten per cent of RAI's total revenues. It becomes apparent that the two main sources of funding, public funds and advertising, carry approximately the same weight in Italy. The law caps RAI's advertising income to 12 per cent per hour and four per cent per day – a stricter limit than that provided by the TwF Directive – so as to protect commercial competitors. Nonetheless, advertising volumes in public channels are high.

The licence fee is a tax levied on the ownership of a television set. Each year RAI presents its budget to the Parliamentary Commission. The Ministry of Communications establishes the level of the licence fee. Compared to other Western European countries, such as France, Germany and the United Kingdom, the licence fee in Italy is relatively modest. It has either been left unchanged or has only been slightly increased in recent years so as to avoid public disquiet.[24] It has been argued that RAI's low public funding contradicts an important 2002 judgment of the Constitutional Court in which it affirmed the constitutionality of the licence fee and its significance for the overall function of public broadcasting.[25] On the other hand, the fact that the licence fee cannot cover RAI's operating expenses is also due to its excessive number of employees, nearly double than those employed by Mediaset.

23. Law 249 of 31 July 1997.
24. Mazzoleni and Vigevani, 'Italy', p. 905.
25. *Ibid.*, p. 906; Decision 284/2002, *Gazzetta Ufficiale* Nr. 26, 3 July 2002.

4. THE ITALIAN CONSTITUTION

Even though the Italian Constitution of 27 December 1947 does not specifically refer to broadcasting, it contains a number of provisions that bear upon its regulation. According to Article 21 (1) 'All have the right to express freely their own thought by word, in writing and by all other means of communication.' Although this article explicitly refers only to the press, the Italian Constitutional Court has confirmed the application of Article 21 to the entire broadcasting sector.[26] Article 41 stipulates that private economic enterprise is open to all, while Article 43 allows undertakings operating essential services to be reserved to the state. These norms have been relied upon by private enterprises and by RAI respectively to attack or defend the latter's monopoly.

The Italian Constitutional Court has been active in developing general guidelines for the regulation of the Italian audiovisual landscape. Much of its early case-law on broadcasting revolves around the constitutionality of RAI's monopoly. In one of its first decisions, the Constitutional Court declared RAI's public service monopoly legal on the ground of the scarcity of frequencies available for broadcasting.[27] It held that private broadcasting would be dominated by a few powerful media moguls, while public television was best placed to guarantee access of all important social and political groups.

The Constitutional Court was again called upon in 1974 to rule on the legality of RAI's monopoly. The Court upheld its earlier ruling, but at the same time pronounced its famous 'seven commandments' that required the legislator to create an internally pluralistic public broadcasting system.[28] It held that broadcasting was an essential service in a democratic society that should be controlled by the parliament, not the executive. Rules should be put in place to guarantee the objectivity and impartiality of the service and to ensure that all important social and political groups would gain access to the airwaves.

The Constitutional Court changed its jurisprudence in the early eighties against the backdrop of a private television sector that had expanded phenomenally, albeit outside the realm of the law. The Court considered that private national networks could be admitted provided the legislator would enact suitable anti-trust laws to prevent the emergence of oligopolies. The Court indicated that a comprehensive new law was needed, securing pluralism through the interplay between an internally pluralistic public sector and an externally pluralistic private sector.[29]

26. Decision 59/1960, [1960] *Giur. Cost.* 759; S. Reinemann, 'Die Auswirkungen des Legge Gasparri auf die Meinungsmacht von Silvio Berlusconi in Italien' (2004) 12 ZUM, 904, 907.
27. Decision 59/1960, [1960] *Giur. Cost.* 759
28. Decision 225/1974, [1974] *Giur. Cost.* 1775.
29. Decision 148/1981, [1981] *Giur. Cost.* 1379. In later judgments the Court developed its approach to the principle of pluralism and the dual broadcasting order further in a manner reminiscent of the German Constitutional Court's *Fourth Television* case. Moreover, it obliged the legislator to equip public broadcasting with the necessary frequencies and financial resources. *See* Decision 153/1987, [1987] *Giur. Cost.* 1141; Decision 826/1988, [1988] *Giur. Cost.* 3893.

The defiant response of the legislator was the adoption of the abovementioned '*Berlusconi Decree*' legalizing all existing private stations and links between them, but introducing no anti-trust laws of the kind required by the Constitutional Court. This mismatch between an activist Court and a weak legislature, embroiled in political controversies, has haunted Italian broadcasting throughout its existence.[30]

In two landmark decisions in 2002 the Constitutional Court stressed the importance of public broadcasting for the protection of freedom of expression and the representation of the entire political spectrum of opinions,[31] while urging RAI at the same time to 'adapt its programming schedule and quality to the specific goals of such a public service, without sacrificing it to the audience and advertising demands, and without following the same agenda as that pursued by the private networks [. . .]'.[32] These decisions affirmed that public broadcasting is indispensable for the attainment of pluralism, a position that has been consistently taken by the Constitutional Court throughout its jurisprudence.[33] It has been argued that a total privatization of RAI along the lines contemplated by the *Gasparri Law* is not only unrealistic but would also go against the grain of this case-law and be unconstitutional.[34] However, there is nothing in the Italian constitution, if interpreted in accordance with European Community law, which would prevent a public service from being rendered by a private company.[35]

5. LEGAL FRAMEWORK

The 2004 *Gasparri Law*[36] and the Broadcasting Act 2005[37] together with the Italian Code of Communications[38] are the main legal sources regulating the Italian broadcasting sector.

6. PUBLIC BROADCASTING MISSION AND STANDARDS

The Broadcasting Act 2005 identifies as the objectives of public broadcasting the promotion of education, civil growth and social development, and of the Italian

30. Barendt, *Freedom of Speech*, p. 71; E. M. Barendt, 'The Influence of the German and Italian Constitutional Courts on their National Broadcasting Systems' [1991] *Public Law* 93, 114; Craufurd Smith, *Broadcasting Law*, p. 78 *et seq.*
31. Decision 155/2002, *Gazzetta Ufficiale* Nr. 19, 15 May 2002.
32. Decision 284/2002, *Gazzetta Ufficiale* Nr. 26, 3 July 2002, as translated by Mazzoleni and Vigevani, 'Italy', p. 906.
33. Schellenberg, 'Pluralismus', 442.
34. Mazzoleni and Vigevani, 'Italy', p. 908.
35. I am grateful to Professor Vincenzo Zeno-Zencovich for this comment.
36. Law 112 of 3 May 2004.
37. Legislative Decree 177 of 31 July 2005.
38. Legislative Decree 259 of 1 August 2003.

culture and language as well as the preservation of national identity.[39] These objectives are specified further in Articles 45 and 46 of the same Act according to which public broadcasting includes: broadcasting on the whole national territory of programmes of public interest; an appropriate number of hours, including during prime time, devoted to education, information, cultural promotion through cinema, theatre and musical works; access to programming for political parties, trade unions, religious groups and other associations of social interest; programming destined to be broadcast abroad to promote the knowledge of the Italian language and culture; protection of historical archives of radio and television programmes; broadcasting in minority languages; measures to protect disabled people; long distance teaching; realization of interactive digital services.[40]

The new national service contract between the Ministry of Communications and the RAI, which covers the three year period between 1 January 2007 and 31 December 2009, sets out the details of the public service remit. It provides that RAI has the following priority duties: to guarantee the freedom, plurality, objectivity, completeness, and correctness of the information; to safeguard national identity, and the identity of local and linguistic minorities; to keep track of political and economic developments in the country, the problems related to modernization, European and international relations; to promote the country's culture, history, traditions and artistic heritage; to respect environmental heritage; to represent the realities of everyday life in the country; to promote work and working conditions; to deal with issues concerning civil rights, solidarity, equal opportunities, integration and the condition of women; to provide information on citizen security, and denounce violence, crime, social marginalization and disintegration; to deal with issues concerning the family, the protection of children, the elderly and the weakest members of the population.[41]

To attain these goals, RAI must respect its public service duties under Article 45 of the Broadcasting Act 2005 in terms of territorial coverage and programme access and characteristics, ensuring balanced editorial content; promotion and distribution of the advantages generated by new technologies; support to Italian and European audiovisual production.[42] The national service contract obliges RAI, on the one hand, to transmit in all times slots, including prime time, and on all television and radio channels, programmes of the public-service type, i.e. news, social communication, education and training, cultural promotion, children's programmes.[43] On the other hand, it pays special attention to the need to improve the quality of public broadcasting in all hour brackets, also in the context of the most popular genres of programmes.

---

39. Legislative Decree 177 of 31 July 2005, Art. 7 (4).
40. M. Cappello and R. Mastroianni, 'Italy' in *Iris Special: The Public Service Broadcasting Culture*, European Audiovisual Observatory (ed.) (Strasbourg, European Audiovisual Observatory, 2007), pp. 125–126.
41. RAI Service Contract 2007–2009, Art. 2 (3).
42. *Ibid.*, Art. 2 (4).
43. *Ibid.*, Art. 2 (5).

To this end, a new way of assessing RAI's public service duties is introduced that is no longer based solely on viewing figures but incorporates a new parameter of programme quality and public value. The following three indicators are used to assess the quality of RAI programmes: a market performance index, which includes inter alia product approval and perceived quality; a macro public value index, which takes into account personal, cultural and civil enrichment, respect for viewer sensibilities, innovation, impartiality, pluralism, independence, objectivity, entertainment capacity and originality; a macro corporate reputation index taking into account RAI's perceived image and market positioning.[44] These new criteria aim to ensure that public value will permeate all types of programmes and all platforms instead of being measured just in terms of the inclusion of certain types of programmes within the schedule.[45] AGCOM is required to take these service quality standards and user satisfaction ratings into account so as to control whether the public service is actually provided in accordance with the law and the service contract.

7. POLITICAL AND ELECTION BROADCASTING

7.1 Pluralism

The principle of pluralism is guaranteed by Articles 21 and 41 of the Italian Constitution and is enshrined in all the laws related to broadcasting.[46] The Italian Constitutional Court has often stressed the importance of the '*principio pluralistico*', a fundamental value of any democratic society.[47] We have seen, however, that, historically, RAI has been heavily politicized because of the traditional policy of '*lottizzazione*'.

During the period of leadership of Silvio Berlusconi, the already scarce impartiality of the RAI chain went trough a degenerative process that has left the public broadcaster financially in crisis and remarkably compromised its independence from the government. In many instances, RAI's employees and journalists have been put under pressure and even been removed from television for criticizing the ruling coalition.[48] Still, political pluralism has always been lively in RAI with each of the three channels canvassing for its preferred party. Naturally, the politically controlled appointment procedures mean that majority parties, especially the ruling ones, exercise a predominant influence on the

44. *Ibid.*, Art. 3 (4).
45. P. Gentiloni, 'Guidelines for the Reform of the RAI' <www.comunicazioni.it/en/index.php?Arc=1&IdNews=125>, 21 March 2007.
46. Legislative Decree 177 of 31 July 2005, Arts 3, 4, 57; Law 223 of 6 August 1990, Art. 11.
47. Decision 153/1987, [1987] *Giur. Cost.* 1141; Decision 826/1988, [1988] *Giur. Cost.* 3893; Decision 420/1994, [1994] *Giur. Cost.* 3716; Decision 155/2002, [2002] *Giur. Cost.* 1310; Decision 466/2002, <www.giurcost.org/decisioni/2002/0466s-02.html>, 18 July 2007.
48. Mazzoleni and Vigevani, 'Italy', p. 900.

content of news and current affairs programmes, while the views of minority parties often go unnoticed.[49] Directly related to the principle of pluralism is the principle of 'equal time' for political parties during election campaigns, in Italy called '*par condicio*'.[50]

7.2 Election Broadcasts

The '*par condicio*' law was adopted in 2000 to establish equal access of political parties to the broadcast media during election periods.[51] Its provisions are effective during the official campaign period that begins with the dissolution of the Parliament. Between the dissolution of the Parliament and the deadline for the presentation of the candidate lists, the law prescribes equal quantitative and qualitative coverage to all political parties represented in Parliament. From the deadline for the presentation of the candidate lists until the beginning of the campaign silence period, equal treatment of all parties competing in the elections is required.[52] AGCOM and the Parliamentary Commission draft further rules for each election.

National public television stations are obliged to allocate free airtime to political parties.[53] Local ones only allocate free airtime during the electoral period, but receive remuneration during the non-electoral period. Commercial broadcasters are under no obligation to broadcast political messages during the election period. Paid political advertising on national television is forbidden in Italy.

During non-electoral periods, public and most private broadcasters must offer 'self-managed political communication spaces', so-called *messaggi autogestiti*, with equal opportunity of access to all the political parties.[54] Specific limits on the duration of the *messaggi autogestiti* are prescribed. In order to guarantee their integrity and value, the messages must last for at least one minute, but not more than three. They must allow a motivated exposition of the political programme of the interested party. They cannot be inserted during a commercial advertising break and may not interrupt any programme, but have to be included in specific slots (*contenitori*) together with other messages. The messages must be readily distinguishable from any other programme or part of programme. They are not calculated within the daily/hourly time allowance for advertising.[55] Each operator

49. Cappello and Mastroianni, 'Italy', pp. 125, 129.
50. *See* AGCOM, Decision 200/00/CSP of 22 June 2000, *Provisions for the implementation of the rules relating to political communication and equal access to the media in non-electoral periods*, Gazzetta Ufficiale Nr. 152 of 1 July 2000.
51. Law 28 of 22 February 2000, as modified by Law 313 of 6 November 2003.
52. OSCE/ODIHR, 'Election Assessment Mission Report'.
53. Law 28 of 22 February 2000, Art. 3.
54. Law 28 of 22 February 2000, Art. 2; Parliamentary Commission for the Communication Services, Decision of 21 June 2000, *Political communication and self-managed communication spaces in the programming of the concessionary society for public service broadcasting* <www.camera.it>, 13 November 2007.
55. EPRA, Background Paper – Plenary, Political Advertising: Case Studies and Monitoring, 23rd EPRA Meeting, Elsinore, 17–19 May 2006, p. 14.

notifies their scheduling to the Parliamentary Commission and AGCOM at least fifteen days in advance.[56]

The 'self-managed spaces' cannot be in excess of 25 per cent of the total airtime of political communication programmes during the same week and during the same hour. A maximum of two broadcasts can be scheduled every day. The airtime in each programme is allocated by random selection. The airtime allocated to a political party and not used by it cannot be transferred to another party. Each spot can only be transmitted once in any given programme. Outside the electoral period, the principle of 'three-thirds' applies. One third is accorded to the parliamentary majority, one third to the government and one third to the opposition.[57]

As far as editorial programmes are concerned, such as debates, thematic round tables and press conferences, public broadcasters have to share time equally between all political parties present in Parliament. Commercial broadcasters share time according to the percentage in the previous elections. Violations of these rules are rare in editorial programmes. The situation is less clear-cut as far as news and current affairs programmes are concerned to which a generic principle of the respect of access of all political parties and of balanced debate applies.

The Parliamentary Commission for the Communication Services is responsible for monitoring and enforcing the application of these rules in relation to public broadcasters only, while AGCOM is also responsible for the private ones. During the recent general elections the public channels covered the campaign in a largely balanced way in quantitative terms, even though the tone of coverage of RAI-1 and RAI-2 favoured the centre-right coalition, while RAI-3 favoured the centre-left one. Several sanctions were imposed by AGCOM on private television channels for violations of impartiality.[58]

7.3 Broadcasts of General Interest

RAI is required to run a channel devoted to the broadcasting of parliamentary proceedings.[59] It is also obliged to provide information on public utility services, especially traffic and transport, the supply and distribution of energy, water, telecommunications, and any events, natural and manmade, that may compromise the normal life of the population.[60] The commercial broadcasters have no such obligations.

---

56. CSA, 'Annexe 9: Dispositifs de Contrôle du Pluralisme Politique à la télévision et à la radio dans les démocraties occidentales. Eléments de Comparaison Internationale' <www.csa.fr/upload/dossier/pluralisme_annexes_sept06.pdf>, 14 November 2006, p. 8.
57. *Ibid.*
58. OSCE/ODIHR, 'Election Assessment Mission Report'.
59. Law 223 of 6 August 1990, Art. 24; RAI Service Contract 2007–2009, Art. 12 (1).
60. RAI Service Contract 2007–2009, Art. 13 (1).

8. CULTURAL OBLIGATIONS

8.1 Language Policy

There are no specific obligations on RAI to watch over the use of the Italian language. RAI is only asked to promote and spread the knowledge of the Italian language as well as of the Italian culture and economy in the world, with the aim of guaranteeing Italian communities living abroad a suitable level of information on developments in Italian society.[61]

8.2 High Culture

Culture and entertainment, especially live performances such as theatre, dance, opera, drama, and classical and light music feature among the genres to which RAI has to assign a large percentage of its annual programming schedule according to the RAI service contract.[62]

8.3 Regional Programmes

The Broadcasting Act 2005 requires RAI to have an office in each region and in each of the Autonomous Provinces of Trento and Bolzano, which shall operate under a regime of financial and accounting autonomy, and to promote decentralized production centres.[63] Further, it provides that each region shall approve a regional law laying down obligations for public broadcasting and shall conclude specific regional service contracts with RAI.[64] The new RAI service contract also states that RAI may conclude agreements with the regions and autonomous provinces so as to promote regional and local culture.[65] However, no regional laws exist yet. At the moment, only a very small part of RAI 3's programme is dedicated to the regions. Probably more attention will be paid to regional and local issues once regional laws have been adopted. As far as regional languages are concerned, RAI is obliged to broadcast in German and Ladin in the Autonomous Province of Bolzano, in French in the Autonomous Region Valle d'Aosta and in Slovene in the Province of Trieste, Gorizia and Udine.[66] To this end, specific conventions have been concluded between RAI and the Italian Presidency of the Council of Ministers.[67]

61. RAI Service Contract 2007–2009, Art. 9 (1).
62. RAI Service Contract 2007–2009, Art. 4 (1) (f).
63. Legislative Decree 177 of 31 July 2005, Art. 45 (2) (p), (r), (3).
64. Legislative Decree 177 of 31 July 2005, Art. 46.
65. RAI Service Contract 2007–2009, Art. 11 (1).
66. *Ibid.*, Art. 11 (2); Legislative Decree 177 of 31 July 2005, Art. 45 (2) (f).
67. Cappello and Mastroianni, 'Italy', pp. 125, 130.

8.4 Education

The new RAI service contract provides that RAI shall assign a quota of no less than 65 per cent of its annual programming schedule and of 80 per cent on its third channel to a number of specified genres. These programmes must be evenly distributed throughout the year and also during prime time. Among the specified issues is the promotion of culture, school education and training.[68] RAI has to transmit broadcasts aimed at promoting the knowledge of the country's history and traditions, broadcasts on literary and scientific subjects, on computer literacy and multimedia interaction, programmes on developments in the school system and on the issue of choosing a school, university and professional career, broadcasts on social phenomena linked to the youth and the elderly. RAI also needs to broadcast programmes devoted to children, adolescents and young people.[69] The provision of distant learning is also part of RAI's public service mission.[70] Finally, RAI Educational is a RAI directorship, which produces a diverse range of educational programmes related to history, science, arts and culture. These programmes are broadcast both on the three RAI analogue channels as well as on two free-to-air satellite channels dedicated to education (RAI Edu 1 and RAI Edu 2).[71]

8.5 Religious Programmes

Religion and the Catholic Church have a strong influence on RAI's programming.[72] The Broadcasting Act 2005 states that respect for different faiths is a general principle of the broadcasting system,[73] and requires RAI to reserve broadcasting time for, *inter alia*, religious associations.[74] In practice, RAI transmits a number of religious programmes, such as '*A Sua immagine*', a weekly talk show on religious issues, which also broadcasts Sunday Mass and the Pope's *Angelus.*[75]

8.6 Cultural Quotas

The Broadcasting Act 2005 establishes that the quotas reserved to domestic and European productions should be determined by the AGCOM on the basis of the dispositions of the TwF Directive.

---

68. RAI Service Contract 2007–2009, Arts 2 (5) (c), 4 (1) (d), (2).
69. *Ibid.*, Art. 4 (1) (h).
70. Legislative Decree 177 of 31 July 2005, Art. 45.
71. RAI recently committed itself to buying satellite dishes for all Italian schools in order for them to receive its satellite channels.
72. Cappello and Mastroianni, 'Italy', p. 133.
73. Legislative Decree 177 of 31 July 2005, Art. 3 (1).
74. *Ibid.*, Art. 45 (2) (d).
75. Cappello and Mastroianni, 'Italy', p. 133.

The European works quota has been transposed without reference to a specific percentage. Television content providers are required to reserve most national transmission time on terrestrial frequencies for European works with the exception of news, sport events, television games shows, advertising, TV forums and tele-shopping.[76] Half of the total broadcasting time reserved to all European works has to be allocated to recent works, i.e. works produced in the last five years. This obligation is broader than the one contained in Article 5 of the TwF Directive according to which half of the independent producers' works have to be recent.[77] The Commission is unhappy with this Italian practice as it renders a cross-European comparison or an EU average of recent works more difficult.[78] Moreover, the public broadcaster has to reserve an unspecified percentage of broadcasting time on its satellite channels for European works.[79]

As far as works are concerned that are created by independent producers, private operators must devote a minimum of 10 per cent, while for the public broadcasters the quota is increased to 20 per cent.[80] Public broadcasters also have to reserve a quota of no less than 15 per cent of their annual turnover for the production of European works, including those made by independent producers, while private operators only need to invest at least 10 per cent of their annual turnover.[81] Thematic channels can apply to AGCOM for a total or partial derogation from these investment and broadcasting obligations.[82]

Moreover, RAI is required to stimulate cinematographic production and specific types of programmes by setting aside a quota of no less than 15 per cent of overall annual earnings for investment in cinematographic products, fiction, cartoons, documentaries, broadcasts promoting the cinema and audiovisual products in general, cultural broadcasts of live shows. Within this quota no less than 20 per cent has to be devoted to films primarily aimed at cinema screening, and a percentage of no less than five per cent to cartoons and/or films produced specifically for children.[83]

9. ADVERTISING

9.1 BACKGROUND

Originally, advertising regulation was intended exclusively to protect entrepreneurs against unfair competition, while consumers were provided with no legal

76. *Ibid.*, Art. 6.
77. AGCOM, *Annual Report on Activities Carried Out and Work Programme*, 30 June 2006, p. 178.
78. Seventh Commission communication on the application of Articles 4 and 5 of Directive 89/552/EEC 'Television without Frontiers', as amended by Directive 97/36/EC, for the period 2003–2004, 14 August 2006, COM (2006) 459 final, 4 n. 10.
79. Cappello and Mastroianni, 'Italy', p. 132.
80. Legislative Decree 177 of 31 July 2005, Art. 44 (3).
81. Law 112 of 3 May 2004, Art. 17 (2) (l).
82. Legislative Decree 177 of 31 July 2005, Art. 6; Resolution 9 of 16 March 2006, Art. 5.
83. RAI Service Contract 2007–2009, Art. 10 (2).

protection. For that reason, the advertising agencies decided to ratify a self-regulatory Code that would be enforced and monitored by a private Authority, the *Istituto dell'Autodisciplina Pubblicitaria.*[84] The Code was binding for all the signatory members. This represented the only regulation of advertising until 1992, when the Parliament finally issued a formal law.[85] The advertising rules of the TwF Directive have been transposed in the Broadcasting Act 2005.[86] The principal difference between the Act and the Directive is the already mentioned strict limit on the quantity of advertising in public broadcasting.

9.2 The Principle of Separation

Advertising has to be clearly identifiable as such, by inserting acoustic or optical means such as theme songs and written texts at the beginning and at the end of the message.[87] Surreptitious advertising (*pubblicità non transparente*) is prohibited. So as to decide whether there is intention to advertise, AGCOM examines the content, presentation and form of a message. It also asks whether the broadcaster has drawn any economic gain. However, its approach towards surreptitious advertising has not always been consistent. AGCOM denied, for instance, surreptitious advertising in the case of the programme 'Controcampo' where the presenter pronounced the phrase 'tomorrow all in the kiosks' ('*domani tutto in edicola*'), referring to the title of the homonymous magazine published by himself. AGCOM held that the intention behind this statement was to inform and not to advertise.[88] Inexplicably, the opposite conclusion was reached in another very similar case concerning the same programme.[89]

On the contrary, AGCOM found intention to advertise in a case where the presenters of a programme about a famous personality emphasized the fact that this personality had appeared on the cover of a journal and talked about the qualities of this journal.[90] AGCOM also found that the extensive praise of the services offered by a certain cruise liner accompanied by a close-up of the colours of the liner constituted surreptitious advertising.[91] Surprisingly, it reached the opposite

84. Code of advertising self-regulation of 12 May 1966. The first version of the Code was published in 1966 and it has been constantly updated since then. The latest edition is the 43rd of 5 September 2007.
85. Legislative Decree 74 of 25 January 1992.
86. Legislative Decree 177 of 31 July 2005, Art. 37 *et seq.*
87. AGCOM, 'The Regulation of the Media in Italy' <www.agcom.it/eng/reports_docs/resp_reg.htm#20>, 1 May 2007; Legislative Decree 177 of 31 July 2005, Art. 4 (1) (c); Legislative Decree 206 of 6 September 2005 on the Consumer Code, Art. 23 (1). AGCOM enforces Art. 4 of Legislative Decree 177 of 31 July 2005, while the Authority for Competition and Trade (AGCM) is in charge of the Consumer Code.
88. M. Di Prima, 'Publicità ingannevole e comparative' (2005–6) 13/14 *Concorrenza e mercato*, 199.
89. *Controcampo speciale Champions League*, PI 4420, Provv. N. 13317/2004, in Boll. 26/2004.
90. *Settimanale S.T.A.R. + TV*, PI 4833, Provv. N. 14700/2005, in Boll. 35/2005.
91. *MSC Crociere/Trasmissioni Mediaset*, PI 4643, Provv. N. 14100/2005, in Boll. 8/2005; *MSC Crociere/Trasmissioni Mediaset*, PI 4643B, Provv. N. 14149/2005, in Boll. 11/2005.

conclusion as regards the reference in a news programme to a pre-paid card for the reception of a digital television service. It held that this reference only aimed to inform viewers about a new way of receiving sports events rather than to advertise.[92]

Product placement is considered a form of surreptitious advertising and is, therefore, prohibited by law. The use of product placement in Italian movies was regulated for the first time by the legislative Decree 28 of 22 January 2004. Before 2004 there was no normative restriction on the so called 'cinesponsoring' in Italy. Cinesponsoring is a particular technique of sponsoring, by means of product placement, based on an agreement between the producer of a cinematographic work and a company that wants to promote its own products, services or its image by inserting into the sequences of a film representations of products, brands or other symbols of trade. Before 2004, this practice was regulated by the general rules that apply to surreptitious advertising.

The legislative Decree 28 of 22 January 2004 did not significantly change the previous legal position. It only clarified the limitations to the use of product placement in films. First, in order to show representations of products, services or brands of a certain company, it is essential to clearly and correctly inform the viewers about the cinesponsoring agreement. The cinematographic work must contain a warning in the end credits informing the public of the presence of product placement during the film and specifically mentioning the companies involved. Second, the advert shall be well integrated in the context of the story.

A different way of blending advertising and fiction is by including characters from cartoons in commercial breaks before and after these cartoons. In an effort to prevent the resulting confusion in the minds of young viewers, the new RAI service contract, following the example of the CSA, prohibits such practices.[93]

9.3 Advertising and Minors

The impact of advertising on children attracts a lot of attention in Italy. The law regulates the content of advertisements aimed at minors. It also tries to protect them from an excess of advertising spots.

As far as the content-based regulation is concerned, broadcasters are obliged to comply with a self-regulatory instrument, the Code TV and Minors (*Codice di Autoregolamentazione TV e Minori*). The Code TV and Minors provides a comprehensive framework concerning both the passive consumption by children of television programmes and advertising as well as their participation in them. Correct application of the Code TV and Minors is ensured by a Surveillance Committee (*Comitato TV e Minori*). Serious breaches of the Code are referred to the AGCOM. The Code has been formally incorporated in Law 112/2004. As a

92. *Mediaset Premium*, PI 4786, Provv n. 14536/2005, in Boll. 29/2005.
93. RAI Service Contract 2007–2009, Art. 7 (4); *see also* CSA recommendation of 7 June 2006, discussed in Part 1, Ch. 2.9.2, p. 31 *above*.

result, its requirements are binding on all broadcasters regardless of whether they have actually signed it.[94]

The Code provides three different stages of protection according to the time slots of transmission. The first level of general protection is valid for all time slots.[95] It stipulates that advertising shall not show minors in situations that are dangerous for themselves or for others; that it shall not depict minors consuming alcohol, tobacco products or drugs; that it shall not exhort minors to buy a product, either on their own or with the help of others, by exploiting their inexperience or credulity; that it shall not mislead minors as to the nature, functioning or dimensions of a toy, the necessary skills for using it, the accessories included in the packaging, its price or the need to buy complementary products.

The second level of enhanced protection is valid for the time slots between 7 A.M. and 4 P.M. and between 7 P.M. and 10.30 P.M.[96] On top of the abovementioned general level of protection, advertisements during this time slot shall not contain situations that can cause mental or moral detriment to minors, by suggesting for instance that the lack of possession of the advertised product signifies either inferiority or failure by their parents to fulfil their duties; by violating socially acceptable norms of behaviour; by decrying the authority, responsibility and judgement of parents, teachers and of other persons; by exploiting the special trust minors place in parents, teachers and other persons etc.

Finally, the third level of specific protection applies for the time slot between 4 P.M. and 7 P.M.[97] On top of all the abovementioned provisions, all advertising, promotion or other commercial communication specifically aimed at minors during this period must be preceded and followed by elements that make it easily recognizable as such even for persons that are unable to read or disabled. Moreover, advertisements for alcoholic beverages, for telephone services for entertainment purposes and for contraceptives (with the exception of social campaigns) shall not be broadcast during this time slot.

The Italian rules incorporate the requirements of Article 16 of the TwF Directive, but set even more precise conditions.[98] They are stricter in so far as they require that advertising shall not exhort minors to buy a product or encourage them to persuade their parents to do so but omit the word 'directly'. In other words, advertising that only indirectly motivates minors to behave in these ways is caught by the Italian rules.

As far as the use of children in advertisements is concerned, the *Gasparri Law* introduced a prohibition on employing minors less than 14 years of age in advertising.[99] This prohibition was, however, repealed by Article 1 of Law 37 of

94. Hans-Bredow-Institut, 'Final Report: Study on Co-Regulation Measures in the Media Sector', June 2006 <www.ec.europa.eu/avpolicy/docs/library/studies/coregul/coregul-final-report_en.pdf>, 18 July 2007, p. 62.
95. Code TV and Minors of 29 November 2002, Art. 4.2.
96. *Ibid.*, Art. 4.3.
97. *Ibid.*, Art. 4.4.
98. Law 177 of 31 July 2005, Arts 4 (1) (b), (c).
99. Law 112 of 3 May 2004, Art. 10.

6 February 2006. Turning to the content-neutral regulation, the Italian law establishes limits that are even stricter than the European Community ones. While the TwF Directive prescribes that advertisements can only be included in children's programmes if their programmed duration is 30 minutes or longer, the Italian legislator completely bans advertising from cartoons.[100]

10. PROTECTION OF MINORS

The protection of minors is an imperative of the Italian Constitution. Article 31 (2) of the Constitution proclaims that 'The Italian Republic protects children and young people and, to this end, creates appropriate institutions and associations'.

In addition, there are various laws that specifically refer to the issue of minors and the mass media. Article 10 of the *Gasparri Law*, Arts 34 and 35 of the Broadcasting Act 2005 as well as the Code TV and Minors discipline on the protection of minors in the broadcasting sector. The Code contains general obligations on the portrayal of children as perpetrators, witnesses or victims of crime as well as rules applicable to specific time frames.

Before 2004 the broadcasting of programmes that were likely to cause moral or physical detriment to minors, i.e. programmes containing gratuitous violence or pornographic scenes was completely prohibited.[101] The *Gasparri Law* 2004 and the Broadcasting Act 2005 introduced two exceptions to this ban. First, the ban applies only to a limited period of the day, and secondly, exceptions can be made for pay-TV channels. The law draws a distinction between films made for the cinema and for television. The broadcasting of cinematographic productions whose viewing is forbidden to under-14s is prohibited in the period between 7 A.M. and 10.30 P.M.[102] Cinematographic productions that contain vulgar expressions, erotic or violent scenes, surgical operations, use of drugs and that instigate feelings of hate and revenge cannot be transmitted at any time. The broadcasting of television productions containing images of sex or violence is absolutely forbidden between 7 A.M. and 11 P.M.[103]

The Broadcasting Act 2005 also introduced stricter rules that apply during the 'protected period' between 4 P.M. and 7 P.M., when it is considered more likely for children and adolescents to be exposed to risks. Specific attention is also called for when commenting on sports events – in particular football matches – so as to promote values of fair and honest competition in sports.

An AGCOM Committee, the AGCOM Committee for Services and Products (*Commissione per i servizi ed I prodotti dell' Autoritá*), together with the Surveillance Committee that is responsible for the application of the Code TV and Minors monitor over the compliance with the law and apply administrative sanctions in cases of

100. Dir. 97/36, Art. 11 (5); RAI Service Contract, Art. 7 (4).
101. Law 223 of 6 August 1990, Art. 15.10.
102. Code TV and Minors of 29 November 2002, Art. 15.
103. Law 203 of 30 May 1995, Art. 3 (4).

violation. The *Gasparri Law* heightened the range of sanctions by setting it between EUR 25,000.00 and EUR 350,000.00. This was confirmed by the Broadcasting Act 2005, which also reduced the time allowed for the broadcaster to submit any justifications for the breach of the children protection rules from thirty to fifteen days, while abolishing the possibility of a cash settlement.[104] AGCOM also submits a yearly report to the Parliament on its activities and interventions on the matter of media and minors.

11. RIGHT OF REPLY

In Italy, a natural or legal person whose legitimate interests, i.e. good name or reputation, have been damaged by an assertion of incorrect facts in a television programme, the radio or the press has the right to ask for the public cancellation or amendment of such declaration.[105] Within 48 hours from the receipt of the request, the public or private broadcaster must enforce the rectification. If the proof provided by the claimant is not sufficient to justify the request made, AGCOM can be asked to pass a verdict within the subsequent 24 hours. The rectification has to be made at the same time and to be of the same relevance as the harmful declaration.

104. Legislative Decree 177 of 31 July 2005, Art. 35; *see* AGCOM, *Annual Report on Activities Carried Out and Work Programme*, 30 June 2006, p. 187.
105. Legislative Decree 177 of 31 July 2005, Art. 32.

Chapter 6
The Netherlands

1. BACKGROUND

Broadcasting in the Netherlands was originally based on the principle of separate outlets for different groups. Until the 1960s, Dutch society had been vertically divided in several segments according to different religions and ideologies. This phenomenon, known as 'pillarization' (*verzuiling*), describes the way the Dutch dealt with their socio-cultural diversity.[1] The main groups in Dutch society were the Catholics, the Protestants and the Social-democrats, each with its own political party, schools, newspapers and broadcasting companies. The Catholic Radio Broadcasting Organization (KRO) had strong ties with the Catholics, the Netherlands Christian Radio Association (NCRV) and the Liberal Protestant Radio Broadcasting Organization (VPRO) with the Protestants, and the Association of Workers Radio Amateurs (VARA) with the socialists. The General Radio Broadcasting Association (AVRO) represented the view of the free-minded liberals.

During the 1960s, people became more independent and religious ties began to loosen. In 1969, the Broadcasting Act was introduced and new broadcasting licensees were allowed as long as they produced programmes that aimed at satisfying perceived cultural, religious or spiritual needs among the population. This system still reflected remnants of 'pillarization'. The time and money allocated to every broadcasting company depended on the number of members they were able to recruit. Until 1997, subscribing to a broadcasters' magazine automatically made you a member of this broadcaster. The Broadcasting Foundation of the Netherlands (*Nederlandse Omroep Stichting*, NOS), was set up to coordinate the broadcasting companies and to provide news and sports programmes. In 1995, the government

1. Euromedia Research Group/M. Kelly, G. Mazzoleni and D. McQuail, *The Media in Europe* (London, Sage, 2004), p. 145.

decided that some programme activities related to art, culture, youth and minorities should be transferred to an independent foundation, the Netherlands Programme Service Foundation (*Nederlandse Programma Stichting*, NPS).

Although a special non-profit foundation, the Radio and Television Advertising Foundation (*Stichting Etherreclame*), was set up to handle advertising in the public broadcasting system, commercial television companies were still not permitted in the Netherlands. The Luxembourg based CLT/RTL seized the opportunity to start a Dutch-language channel in 1989 named RTL4. The trend could not be stopped and in 1992, commercial broadcasting officially entered the media market. Today, commercial broadcasting is provided by seven main broadcasting companies, of which SBS6, Net5, Veronica and Talpa are based in the Netherlands while RTL4, RTL5 and RTL7 broadcast from Luxembourg. Although the Luxembourg channels provide for the Dutch audience, they are officially based in the neighbouring country, for the law in Luxembourg is more lenient toward commercial television broadcasting.

In 2001, the Council of State of the Netherlands (*Afdeling Bestuursrechtspraak van de Raad van State*) stated that the Dutch Media Authority had the right to claim jurisdiction over these Luxembourg based channels. Even though the Council of State materially agreed with the Media Authority, it annulled its decision with the argument that a situation of double jurisdiction would violate the goals, system and aims of the TwF Directive.[2] For the time being, the CLT/RTL-group is supervised by the Luxembourg media authority (*Conseil National des Programmes*) so that double jurisdiction is avoided.

Today, public broadcasting is provided by eight large member-based national broadcasting companies in addition to the NOS and NPS. These eight largest private but non-profit membership organizations are the KRO; the NCRV; the VPRO that was set up as the Liberal Protestant Radio Broadcasting Organization but has abandoned Protestantism and appeals to a more intellectual audience; AVRO, members of which are liberals; the Television and Radio Broadcasting Corporation (TROS), the broadcaster of choice for liberal, non-religious and non-political 'ordinary people'; VARA, a progressive broadcaster that targets a broad, general audience; the Evangelical Broadcasting Organization (EO) whose members come predominantly from Protestant churches; and the Barts News Network (BNN) that attracts young people by transmitting original and controversial programmes.[3]

Under former legislation, broadcasting companies needed 50,000 members to obtain a provisional licence to broadcast and 300,000 members to obtain a permanent licence. Today, applicants qualify for a permanent licence when they have 150,000 members. The rules were modified in 2004 to allow for BNN which only had little over 220,000 members and would have lost its licence otherwise. In addition to this formal threshold, broadcasting companies can only obtain a licence if they contribute to the diversity and realization of the main tasks of the public

2. Council of State, 8 August 2003, LJN AI0788.
3. J. Daalmeijer, 'Public Service Broadcasting in the Netherlands' (2004) 12 (1) *Trends in Communication*, 34 *et seq.*

broadcasting system. The allocation of the time and money still depends on the number of members. Airtime is also given to several small non-member-based religious broadcasting companies or educational programmes.

The national public broadcasting companies air their programmes on three national television channels and five national public radio channels. In September 2006, the system was remodelled and now every channel has its own image and target group: *Nederland 1* offers entertainment for the whole family, *Nederland 2* focuses on news and current affairs and *Nederland 3* is aimed at a young audience. Together they are meant to provide a comprehensive programme that caters for the entire social spectrum. The new system marks a shift in power from the membership organizations to the channel managers. Membership organizations do no longer have their own slot in the schedule and thus cannot profile themselves in a given channel. This is a positive development as it forces membership organizations to cooperate with each-other and gives rise to a more mixed programme.

In addition to the national broadcasting companies, airtime is also allocated to regional and local broadcasting companies. Until recently public broadcasting was transmitted by analogue as well as digital signals. However, on 11 December 2006 the analogue television signal was put to an end. Since then public television can only be received by cable, satellite, internet or through a decoder for the digital signal. Yet, almost 74,000 households not covered by the cable system are still completely dependent on the analogue signal. These households are effectively forced to switch to satellite or to purchase a digital decoder.

2. BROADCASTING AUTHORITIES

2.1 Dutch Media Authority

Supervision of the enforcement of the Media Act and of the Media Decree has been delegated to an independent body, the Dutch Media Authority (*Commissariaat voor de Media*, CvdM). The Media Authority is responsible for the broadcasting sector, while telecommunications are regulated by the Dutch regulator for telecoms and posts (*Onafhankelijke Post en Telecommunicatie Autoriteit*, OPTA). At CvdM's helm are three commissioners, appointed by Royal Decree on recommendation of the Minister of Education, Culture and Science. Appointments are made for a tenure of five years, with the possibility of reappointment for another term.[4]

The Media Authority is independent from the media sector and also from government and parliament. Its independence is guaranteed by means of incompatibilities of its membership with employment in a ministry, membership of Parliament or employment in the media sector.[5] However, its decisions can be suspended and overturned by the Ministry if they are incompatible with the general

4. Dutch Media Act, Art. 10 (2).
5. *Ibid.*

interest or the law. In practice, only five decisions of the CvdM were suspended in the past, but none was eventually overturned.[6]

One of the Media Authority's most important tasks is to monitor whether public and commercial broadcasting companies comply with the rules which are formulated in the Media Act as well as in the regulations based on this Act. It is allowed to interpret these regulations by means of policy guidelines but does not have a regulatory role as such given that democratic legitimization only resides in the Parliament. It exercises its supervisory function a *posteriori* since the Media Act prohibits any kind of prior control of programme content.[7] In case of violations, it can issue fines, reduce the amount of airtime granted or withdraw a licence.[8] However, the last two types of sanctions have only rarely been applied by the CvdM in cases of very serious or repeated violations.[9]

Another responsibility of the Media Authority is the allocation of broadcasting time to public broadcasters. Every year the Minister establishes how much national broadcasting time is available for educational, religious and spiritual broadcasters, political parties and for government information. The Media Authority allocates the national broadcasting time for these categories of public broadcasting organizations as well as for regional and local public broadcasters.[10] Broadcasting time for NOS, NPS and the other public broadcasting organizations is directly allocated on the basis of the Media Act by means of a 5-years concession.

Finally, the Media Authority is responsible for the financial control of public broadcasting companies. Every year a budget for public broadcasting is established by the Minister and the Media Authority is responsible for the actual payment of these funds to the public broadcasting companies.[11]

3. FINANCING

The costs of the public broadcasting companies are mainly born by government funding. In 2000, the licence fee was abolished and now the financing comes from a levy on income tax. The national, regional and local authorities decide how much of the levy goes to public broadcasting. So as to safeguard the independence of public broadcasting from the government, the budget that is available for public broadcasters is fixed by law.[12] This is, however, not an absolute guarantee as the law can be changed.

6. M. Betzel, 'Media System of the Netherlands' in Hans-Bredow-Institut, *Study on Co-Regulation Measures in the Media Sector* <www.hans-bredow-institut.de/forschung/recht/co-reg/reports/1/index.html>, 27 February 2007, p. 9.
7. Dutch Media Act, Art. 134 (2).
8. Dutch Media Act, Arts 45(1) and 135.
9. Betzel, 'Media System of the Netherlands', p. 7.
10. Dutch Media Act, Art. 42.
11. Dutch Media Act, Art. 101; S. Robillard and J. Libby, *Television in Europe: Regulatory Bodies* (London, European Institute for the Media, 1995), p. 161.
12. H. Zeinstra, 'De financiering van de publieke omroep in Europa' [2003–5] *Mediaforum*, 166.

Since public broadcasting is financed by the state, commercialization is restricted and the publicly funded broadcasting companies cannot service profit making for third parties. As they are not allowed to distribute advertising messages, the Radio and Television Advertising Foundation (*Stichting Etherreclame*, STER) has been given exclusive authorization to advertise. This foundation sells broadcasting time for advertising messages and the profits are reinvested in the public broadcasting system. Almost 25 per cent of the costs of public broadcasting are covered by this practice.

In 2005, the total budget for public broadcasting services was EUR 850 million. Public funding and advertising revenues have to be spent towards public television's primary objective: the provision of pluralism and quality for the whole society, and activities directly connected to this task. All other activities, the so-called sideline activities, are only permitted under strict circumstances so as not to lead to unfair competition. Whether or not a specific activity gives rise to unfair competition is sometimes debatable. Recently, an ongoing discussion on the broadcasting of radio programme 'Colourful Radio' by the NOS came to an end. The commercial radio broadcasting companies filed a complaint, requesting prohibition of this activity, because the urban-music aired by 'Colourful Radio' would not be distinctive enough to justify the use of government money. The Court of Appeal rejected the request. The Dutch Supreme Court confirmed this decision without any further motivation.[13]

In June 2006, the European Commission ordered the Dutch authorities to recover EUR 76.3 million, along with an additional EUR 10.2 million interest, from the NOS. The Commission decided to open a formal investigation into the *ad hoc* financing of the public broadcasters after several commercial broadcasting companies had raised concerns on the state aid measures in accordance with Article 86 (2) EC. The investigation showed that the *ad hoc* payments went beyond the financial needs of the broadcasters for the performance of their public service tasks. The Dutch authorities disagreed and filed an appeal against this decision.

4. THE DUTCH CONSTITUTION

Freedom of communication is guaranteed by Article 7 of the Dutch Constitution of 1983. The first paragraph of this Article offers very wide protection to the printed media by stating that 'no one shall require prior permission to publish thoughts or opinions through the press, without prejudice to the responsibility of every person under the law'. This standard has not been altered since 1815. It took until 1983 before the broadcasting media was covered by the constitutional protection. After a long debate the Dutch legislator just made a textual variation on the old formula and added in the second paragraph of Article 7 that prior supervision on the content of a radio or television broadcast shall be prohibited.

13. Dutch Supreme Court, 14 July 2006, LJN AX5380 (*NVCR v. NPS*).

The same Article also requires that rules on radio and television broadcasting be laid down in an Act of Parliament.[14] The Dutch Media Act and the Dutch Media Decree have been adopted following this constitutional imperative. The third paragraph of Article 7 covers all other media and states that 'no one shall be required to submit thoughts or opinions for prior approval in order to disseminate them by means other than those mentioned in the preceding paragraphs, without prejudice to the responsibility of every person under the law. The holding of performances open to persons younger than sixteen years of age may be regulated by Act of Parliament in order to protect good morals'.[15]

The scope of the protection of freedom of expression depends on the medium being used. Radio broadcasting was traditionally the most restricted medium because of the scarcity of frequencies. Television was also extensively regulated with the argument that it projected information directly into the living room.[16] Today this leaves us with the undesirable situation that the same content which is being broadcast on television can be subjected to more restrictions than if it were displayed on the internet. The Constitution is not ready for the convergence of different kinds of media.

A noteworthy element of this constitutional Article is that it ends by stating that commercial advertising is excluded from protection of freedom of expression as mentioned in this Article.[17] The Dutch constitutional standard seems in conflict with Article 10 of the European Convention on Human Rights (ECHR) given that the European standard covers commercial advertising. According to the Dutch constitution, statutory rules in force in the Kingdom shall not be applicable if such application is in conflict with Treaty provisions that are binding on all persons.[18] Article 10 ECHR is such a provision and the Dutch Supreme Court has aligned its jurisprudence with it. It now directly applies the 'three-step-test' so that the gap between the European and the Dutch practice is closing.[19]

An important difference, however, between the European and the Dutch constitutional standard is that censorship can be permitted under the European Convention if it meets the criteria under Article 10 (2) ECHR. The Dutch Constitution, on the contrary, explicitly prohibits prior supervision of the content of radio or television broadcasting regardless of the circumstances of the case. So, while the Dutch constitution limits freedom of expression in respect of commercial advertising, it affords it complete protection from government censorship.

Finally, it is worth pointing out that the Dutch Constitution does not guarantee the existence of public broadcasting. Nor is there a constitutional guarantee of

---

14. Dutch Constitution, Art. 7 (2).
15. *Ibid.*, Art. 7 (3).
16. J. M. de Meij, *Uitingsvrijheid: De vrije informatiestroom in grondwettelijk perspectief* (Amsterdam, Otto Cramwinckel, 2000), p. 153.
17. Dutch Constitution, Art. 7 (4).
18. Dutch Constitution, Art. 94.
19. An interference with the applicant's freedom of expression satisfies the 'three-step-test' if it is prescribed by law, has the intention to serve one of the goals mentioned in 10 (2) ECHR and is necessary in a democratic society.

pluralism. The proposal of the 'Franken Commission' to reformulate Article 7 of the Dutch Constitution in the sense that 'pluralism in thoughts and other information is to be ensured by the Government' was never adopted.

5. LEGAL FRAMEWORK

The Dutch Media Act of 1987 (*Mediawet*) is the most important source for the Dutch law of broadcasting. The Media Decree (*Media Besluit*) of 1988 is a so-called delegated general policy measure that contains more detailed provisions.[20] The *Commissariaat voor de Media* has also adopted a number of policy guidelines interpreting the provisions of these two legal instruments.[21] Most rules of the TwF Directive have been implemented in the Netherlands by means of the Media Act and the Media Decree.

6. PUBLIC BROADCASTING MISSION AND STANDARDS

The mission of public broadcasting and the principles with which it needs to comply are set out in Article 13c of the Media Act. The central task of public broadcasters is the provision of varied and high-quality programmes for general broadcasting purposes at national, regional and local level in the fields of information, culture, education and entertainment. Programmes shall also be transmitted, which are intended for countries and regions outside the Netherlands and for Dutch people residing outside the territory of the Netherlands.[22] Furthermore, public broadcasting programmes are expected to provide a balanced picture of society and of people's current interests and views on society, culture, religion and belief. They shall be accessible to the entire population, shall contribute to the socio-cultural diversity in the Netherlands, shall be independent of commercial and government influences and shall be aimed at a broad audience and at various population and age groups.[23]

In a 2005 report, the Netherlands Scientific Council for Government Policy (WRR), proposed a functional approach to media policymaking and discerned six functions that have to be fulfilled by the media in a democratic society: news and current affairs; opinion and debate; special information, for instance for consumers; culture, arts and education; entertainment; advertisements, persuasive information and communication.[24] It proposed that public broadcasters should not

20. M. Betzel, 'Media System of the Netherlands'.
21. For example Guidelines on Sanctions (*Beleidslijn Sanctiemaatregelen*) adopted in 1999 and adjusted in 2007. These guidelines are based on Dutch Media Act, Arts 46, 46a, 71c, 109c and 135. They introduce specific categories of fines that can be imposed on broadcasters for infringements based on these provisions.
22. Dutch Media Act, Art. 13 c (1).
23. Dutch Media Act, Art. 13 c (2).
24. Scientific Council for Government Policy (WRR), *Media Policy for the Digital Age* (Amsterdam, Amsterdam University Press, 2005), p. 67 *et seq.*

provide a broad and comprehensive programme offering, but should instead focus on their information and cultural functions, leaving functions such as general entertainment, sports and advertising to their commercial counterparts.[25] The proposal for a law that embodied the Scientific Council's narrow vision of public broadcasting was unsustainable and has been withdrawn by the new government that came into power after the November 2006 general elections. It is unlikely that the mission or structure of public broadcasting in the Netherlands will change to any significant extent during the new government's term of office.

7. POLITICAL AND ELECTION BROADCASTING

7.1 Pluralism

Broadcasting in the Netherlands began in 1920 by commercial companies which were also selling radios. In the early 1930's the Dutch government intervened due to the scarcity of radio frequencies but also so as to comply with international agreements. The government allocated the broadcasting frequencies according to the 'pillars' which characterized Dutch society. As a result, only the main pillars had access to the public broadcasting system. Later, the system that had prevailed in radio broadcasting ever since the early 1930's, was extended to television broadcasting. The government's liberal opposition was not strong enough to prevent this from happening. Although the pillars were represented by their own programmes, viewing habits undermined pillarization, because viewers adopted a pick and mix approach. The viewers who did not belong to any of the recognized pillars were not represented within the public broadcasting system.

The first legislation on pluralism can be found in the Dutch Broadcasting Law of 1967 (*Omroepwet*). Pluralism in Dutch public broadcasting was meant to be the outcome of the interplay of several broadcasting companies within the public broadcasting system. The traditional view of the Dutch government has been that if each broadcasting company provided its own programmes the overall picture would be one of pluralism. Thus the broadcasting organizations are not obliged to be impartial but can provide opinionated programming under the assumption that the system is able to balance itself. This model is rooted in the history of Dutch pillarization and differs from the model chosen in most other European countries where only one public broadcaster is responsible for guaranteeing pluralism. At the same time, the NOS was set up so as to provide an independent and neutral news programme as well as additional programmes catering for trends in society that were not yet represented by the other broadcasting companies.

As pluralism became increasingly important, the government felt it needed to strictly supervise access to the broadcasting system. In 1975, the highest administrative court of the Netherlands, the Council of State, ruled that the broadcaster 'Veronica' could no longer be denied access to the public broadcasting system.

25. *Ibid.*, p. 77.

Veronica was a pirate broadcaster until 1974 when it was declared illegal on the basis of the Treaty of Strasbourg of 1965, which prohibited radio broadcasting from open waters. Following the Council of State's ruling, Veronica had to be admitted into the public broadcasting system. The Dutch government then tried to further control admission to the system by tightening the law. From then on, newly interested parties needed to show upfront that they would increase pluralism. In 1985 these requirements were expanded by requiring the fulfilment of content quotas for admission to the public broadcasting system.

The importance of social, cultural and religious pluralism in Dutch broadcasting is reflected in Article 13c of the Dutch Media Act. In addition, Article 40 of the Dutch Media Act requires each public channel to offer programmes that are recognizable and distinguishable in terms of content. In 2000, the provisional recognition for a new broadcasting company, *De Nieuwe Omroep*, was rejected because it failed to prove its contribution to diversity. The broadcasting company raised the argument that Article 7 of the Dutch Constitution prohibits preliminary testing of the content of radio and television broadcasting. However, the Council of State ruled that there is a small margin of appreciation and an obligation for the government to investigate whether the new public broadcasting company contributes to pluralism.[26]

As far as regional and local public broadcasting is concerned, the government did not adhere to the idea of pluralism on the basis of pillarization. Each regional or local broadcasting company is required to provide a complete programme satisfying the social, cultural, religious and spiritual needs of the region or locality. It is debated whether a similar regime should apply to the national broadcasting system as a whole. It has become a challenging task for the eight large broadcasting companies to represent all groups within an increasingly diverse society. Especially immigrants and young people are not adequately reached by public broadcasting. The admission of new broadcasters to the public system has met with resistance from established broadcasters fearful of losing airtime and government funding.[27] The future of the membership organizations and the question whether they should be forced out of the public broadcasting structure are perennial problems of Dutch media policy. The Dutch government is in search of ways to modernize the public broadcasting system. This might lead to the rise of one national broadcasting company providing neutral, plural, and independent information. Other smaller broadcasting companies would then function as public forums for the discussion of the same contents from alternative perspectives.

7.2 Election Broadcasts

The safeguarding of pluralism is especially important as regards the access of political parties to the media through election and other political broadcasts. In

26. Council of State, 24 July 2002, LJN AE5780.
27. WRR, *Media Policy for the Digital Age*, p. 55.

the Netherlands, political parties have been allocated broadcasting time outside the election period since 1957. Every year, the Minister of Education, Culture and Science establishes how much national broadcasting time on the radio and television is to be made available to political parties.[28] Smaller parties receive the same amount of time as larger ones. The broadcasting time is allocated by the Dutch Media Authority to those political parties which have one or more seats in the House of Representatives or in the Senate.[29]

In the run up to the election, new parties can also apply for airtime. Time is allocated to parties that stand in all constituencies in elections for the House of Representatives and to parties that participate in elections for the European Parliament. Two weeks before election day, the 'regular' allocation is temporarily suspended and replaced by a 'special' allocation. Free airtime is distributed according to a system of proportional access, taking the latest results of the political parties into account.[30] Airtime allocated in that way is to be used only to provide a programme service dealing with political matters.[31] This system guarantees that political parties have at least a few minutes of access to the media to present themselves to the public. Parties can also buy additional airtime given that paid political advertising is allowed in the Netherlands.[32]

Far more important than election broadcasts per se are the news programmes and organized public debates that are broadcast during the election campaign. During the election campaign of November 2006 NOS was criticized for focusing almost entirely on the six largest political parties while new parties were hardly given any attention. In response to these criticisms, the Minister of Education, Culture and Science stated that NOS was responsible for its programmes and that the government would not interfere with this freedom. During this election campaign it also became clear that the internet was a very important source for attracting voters, especially young ones. Almost all parties were active on popular websites like Hyves.nl and YouTube.com to gain some free publicity. A lot of money was also spent on internet games and short films. Furthermore, paid political advertising is allowed in the Netherlands.[33]

Broadcasting companies determine the form and content of the programme service and are responsible for everything broadcast, including the election broadcasts.[34] The Dutch Media Authority does not scrutinize the content of such broadcasts in advance as this would violate the broadcasting companies' programme autonomy.[35] However, no broadcasting time is allocated to political parties which abuse the freedom of speech to undermine democratic freedoms. The broadcasting time allocated to a political party is revoked if the party becomes convicted for

28. Dutch Media Act, Art. 39 (c).
29. Dutch Media Act, Art. 39 (g).
30. EPRA, 'Background Paper – Plenary, Political Advertising: Case Studies and Monitoring', 23rd EPRA Meeting, Elsinore, 17–19 May 2006, p. 8.
31. Dutch Media Act, Art. 50 (7).
32. EPRA, Background Paper, p. 4.
33. *Ibid.*
34. *See* Dutch Media Act, Art. 48.
35. *See* Dutch Media Act, Art. 134.

discrimination.[36] In 1996, the leader of the far-right *Centrumpartij* was convicted for discrimination and hate speech.[37] As a consequence, no broadcasting time has been allocated to this party since its leader's conviction.

7.3 Broadcasts of General Interest

The Dutch Media Authority allocates national broadcasting time for the purpose of disseminating government information in accordance with an Order in Council. The Order in Council may also stipulate that part of the broadcasting time of the national teletext programme service may be allocated for this purpose.[38] Furthermore, the NOS is obliged to include in its programme service coverage of the Dutch and European parliaments, of national holidays and commemorations as well as of other national and international events of a special nature, including State visits.[39] The obligation to provide information on shipping, fisheries, agriculture, horticulture and traffic, along with morning exercises, is reserved for the radio programme service of the Foundation.[40]

8. CULTURAL OBLIGATIONS

8.1 Language Policy

The regulation of language use in public broadcasting mostly aims at the promotion of Dutch and of Frisian which is recognized as the second national language in the Netherlands. Public broadcasters are obliged to broadcast at least 50 per cent of their television broadcasting time to programmes originally produced in Dutch or Frisian.[41] Notably, there are no specified percentages for each of the two languages.[42] The NPS is not bound by any express commitments concerning language, but is obliged to ensure that at least 20 per cent of its television programme service consists of programmes for or relating to ethnic and cultural minorities.[43] *Omrop Fryslân*, a regional public broadcaster, broadcasts one hour of television programming daily in the Frisian language, while *Nederland 1* transmits on its national network a subtitled documentary produced by *Omrop Fryslân* once a week.[44]

36. Dutch Media Act, Art. 39 (g) (3).
37. Dutch Supreme Court, 16 April 1996, NJ 1996, 527.
38. Dutch Media Act, Art. 39 (h) (1).
39. Dutch Media Decree, Art. 16 (1).
40. Dutch Media Decree, Art. 16 (3).
41. Dutch Media Act, Art. 54 (a) (1).
42. N. van Eijk, 'The Netherlands' in *Iris Special: The Public Service Broadcasting Culture*, European Audiovisual Observatory (ed.) (Strasbourg, European Audiovisual Observatory, 2007), pp. 149, 157.
43. Dutch Media Decree, Art. 15 (2) (a).
44. T. MacGonagle, 'Regulating Minority-Language Use in Broadcasting: International Law and the Dutch National Experience' (2004) 16 *Mediaforum*, 155.

8.2 High Culture and Educational Programmes

The provision of a variety of programme services in the fields of information, culture, education and entertainment forms the core of the public service remit in the Netherlands. The total television broadcasting time for all national broadcasting companies is to be used to provide such a complete programme.[45] Minimum amounts for information, education and culture are set out in Article 50 of the Media Act. At least 35 per cent of the broadcasting time is reserved for information and education and 25 percent per cent for cultural programmes of which 12.5 per cent is set aside for the arts.[46] A programme is considered 'cultural' when at least more than half of the content is of cultural nature. No more than 25 per cent of the total broadcasting time may be devoted to entertainment. In respect of the NPS a different regime applies since its task is to satisfy social, cultural and religious or spiritual needs among the public. At least 40 per cent of its programme consists of, or relates to, the arts.[47]

To stimulate the production of cultural programmes, the Minister of Education, Culture and Science established the Dutch Cultural Broadcasting Fund in 1988 (*Stichting Stimuleringsfonds Nederlandse Culturele Omroepproducties*). Its aim is to provide funding to encourage the development and production of programmes of cultural nature that cover, *inter alia*, art, cabaret, theatre and music. Entertainment shows and quiz programmes are not eligible for financial support.

Educational programming is not only part of the general mission of public broadcasters but is also provided by an independent foundation, the Educational Broadcast Combination (*Educatieve Omroep Combinatie*, EDUCOM).

8.3 Regional Programmes

The Dutch Media Authority can allocate broadcasting time for a five year period to regional and local broadcasters that are independent from national broadcasting. Only one local or regional broadcasting organization may be allocated broadcasting time in each municipality or province. The Media Authority grants the licenses in consultation with the local or regional authorities. There are currently 296 local broadcasting organizations and 13 regional ones. The Regional Broadcast Foundation for Consultation and Cooperation (*Stichting Regionale Omroep Overleg en Samenwerking* ROOS) coordinates the regional public broadcasters.[48] Regional channels are not allowed to broadcast their programmes outside the borders of their region. Half of their broadcasting time must consist of programmes of an informative, cultural and educational nature which have particular relevance to the region for which the programme is intended.[49] The representative bodies of

45. Dutch Media Act, Art. 50 (1).
46. Dutch Media Act, Art. 50 (2).
47. Dutch Media Act, Art. 51 (b) (3).
48. Van Eijk, 'The Netherlands', p. 152.
49. Dutch Media Act, Art. 51 (e).

the local and regional broadcasters, which are entrusted with programme policy, consist of members representing the main social, cultural, religious and other movements within the municipality or province.[50]

8.4 Religious Programmes

Religious programming is not only provided by the large member-based broadcasting organizations, but also by a number of smaller non member-based foundations, such as the Netherlands Hindi Organization or the Humanist Broadcasting Foundation. These foundations are allocated a small amount of broadcasting time outside of prime time provided that they have achieved sufficient visibility as a minority in the Dutch society. The allocations remain effective for a period of five years, after which the right to broadcasting time lapses.[51] Recently, the *Commissariaat* allocated airtime to two rival Islamic groups that would not cooperate with each other. This decision was overturned by the Council of State for the *Commissariaat* is only entitled to give one authorization to every religious movement.[52]

8.5 Cultural Quotas

In addition to the abovementioned language quotas, national and regional broadcasters are obliged to devote at least 50 per cent of their broadcasting time to European works.[53] Moreover, public broadcasters are obliged to devote at least 25 per cent of their broadcasting time to works by independent producers,[54] at least one third of which must not be more than five years old.[55] The concepts of 'independent production' and 'independent producers' are defined in Policy Rules laid down by the Dutch Media Authority.[56]

9. ADVERTISING

9.1 Background

Public broadcasters are not allowed to distribute advertising messages. With respect to advertising an exclusive authorization has been given to STER.

50. Van Eijk, 'The Netherlands', p. 152.
51. Dutch Media Act, Art. 39f.
52. Highest Administrative Court of the Netherlands, 10 January 2005, AZ5851 (*Dutch Media Authority* v. *Islamic Broadcasting Organisations*). A summary of the judgment has been published in (2007) 2 *Mediaforum*, 49.
53. Dutch Media Act, Art. 54 (1).
54. Dutch Media Act, Art. 54 (2).
55. Dutch Media Decree, Art. 16a.
56. CvdM, Policy Rules for Programme Quotas, 18 December 2001.

Several rules can be found in the Dutch Media Act on the insertion of advertising messages. Most notably, public broadcasters are only allowed to insert advertising between programmes with the only exception of programmes lasting longer than one hour and a half where an interruption can take place during natural breaks or between separate parts.[57]

The content of advertising in the Netherlands is subject to a system of self-regulation.[58] In 1963 the Advertising Code Foundation (*Stichting Reclame Code*) was set up to formulate rules of conduct with which advertising messages have to comply. These rules can be found in the Dutch Advertising Code (*Nederlandse Reclame Code*) which consists of a general section and several special codes that apply to specific branches. This code applies to both commercial and ideological advertising, regardless of the medium used, and it is directed to the advertiser.

The Advertising Code Foundation monitors compliance with these rules and anyone who holds that an advertising message is in breach of these rules can file a complaint with the Advertising Code Commission (*Reclame Code Commissie*).[59] This is an independent body. It can recommend to an advertiser to discontinue an advertisement or even impose a fine. If advertisers disagree with the Commission's decision they can lodge an appeal with the Board of Appeal. The distribution of an advertising message which is to be found in conflict with the Advertising Code is prevented by both public and commercial broadcasting companies. In compliance with the Dutch Media Act, all broadcasting companies that transmit advertising messages are compulsorily affiliated with the Advertising Code Foundation and they are obliged to reject advertisements against which a negative recommendation has been issued.[60]

9.2 The Principle of Separation

STER uses its broadcasting time to distribute advertising messages supplied by third parties. In accordance with the Dutch Media Act, advertising messages must be recognizable as such and clearly distinguishable from the main programme. The viewers should be able to recognize advertisements by an optical or acoustic warning.

The Dutch Media Act does not explicitly mention surreptitious advertising. Nonetheless, the Dutch approach to it is especially severe as far as programmes are concerned that have been produced by the public broadcasting company itself. Such programmes should not contain any avoidable advertising, unless it is

57. Dutch Media Act, Art. 41a (1) (d).
58. Rules in respect of deceptive and comparative advertising can be found in Arts 194, 195 and 196 of part 6 of the Dutch Civil Code.
59. The Advertising Code Commission consists of one member appointed by the organizations of Advertisers, one member appointed by the Consumers Association, one member appointed by the Association of Communication Consultancies, one member appointed by the media organizations and one member appointed by the Advertising Code Foundation.
60. Dutch Media Act, Arts 61a and 71r.

explicitly permitted.[61] Under the Dutch rules, advertising can be surreptitious when the broadcasting company has mentioned or shown products or company names with the intention to serve advertising. It is immaterial whether the representation of these products might mislead the public.[62] In principle, product placement is also prohibited on the basis of Article 52 of the Dutch Media Act. There are, however, a number of exceptions to this rule.

First, Article 28 (1) of the Media Decree allows avoidable advertising that involves displays of or references to a product or service provided that: such display or reference is in keeping with the context of the programme service; does not affect the editorial integrity of the programme service; is not exaggerated or excessive; the product or service is not specifically recommended. This provision applies mainly to programmes of an educational or informative nature. It applies mutatis mutandis to other programmes, except for programmes predominantly targeted at minors under the age of 12.[63] However, Art. 28 of the Media Decree does not apply and product placement is outlawed if the broadcaster has received remuneration of some kind.[64]

This exception from the prohibition of avoidable advertising was introduced in November 1996. The law was changed so as to facilitate the use of products as props. The appearance of props, such as a telephone booth, in programmes was problematic prior to the law reform.[65] This excessively strict approach to product placement is evident in the early *Wokkels* case. A Dutch public broadcasting company was fined for showing the trademarks on a bottle of Coca Cola and a bag of Wokkels potato chips in a satirical sketch on fast food in a children's programme. The commercial depicted the growing addiction of young people to fast food. The producers did not act intentionally and the product placement was certainly not in the interest of Coca Cola or Wokkels. Nevertheless, the Dutch Media Authority stated that the advertising expressions were avoidable. The European Commission of Human Rights held that fining the broadcasting company for this type of product placement did not breach Article 10 ECHR as it did not go beyond the State's margin of appreciation.[66]

61. Dutch Media Act, Art. 52.
62. In the course of the consultations for the modernization of the Directive, the Netherlands suggested that the requirement of 'misleading the public' ought to be removed from the definition of surreptitious advertising. In its view, the present definition is impracticable as advertising is not surreptitious once the viewer realizes that a programme is commercially biased. It considers that the broadcaster's intention to serve advertising is sufficient. *See* Dutch Government, 'Response to the Television without Frontiers Directive' <www.ec.europa.eu/comm/avpolicy/docs/reg/modernisation/2003_review/contributions/wc_nederland_en.pdf>, 16 April 2007.
63. Dutch Media Decree, Art. 28 (2).
64. O. Schaar, *Programmintegrierte Fernsehwerbung in Europa: Zum Stand der kommunikationsrechtlichen Regulierung in Europa* (Baden-Baden, Nomos, 2001), p. 228.
65. *Ibid.*, p. 227 n. 298.
66. The European Commission of Human Rights, 13 October 1993, appl.no. 16844/90 (*NOS v. The Netherlands*).

Secondly, a more lenient approach is taken to acquired audiovisual material and films that have been released in the cinema. Such material is exempted from the rules on product placement given that the broadcaster has hardly any influence on their content.[67] The rules are also more lenient as far as commercial broadcasters are concerned.[68] Their programmes may contain avoidable advertising and they are allowed to show some sponsored products or to mention the name of the sponsoring company.[69]

Nonetheless, the broadcasting companies which fall under Dutch jurisdiction complain that they are being subjected to a much stricter regime than the Luxembourg based companies. In 2005, the Dutch rules were somewhat relaxed to create a level playing field, but even so, advertising laws in Luxembourg are much more liberal. The latter can, for example, contain techniques like splitscreen and overlay advertising by which advertising content and other content is shown on screen at the same time. There are plans to modernize the Dutch regime as far as commercial broadcasting is concerned to withstand unfair competition. It is proposed that splitscreen advertising be allowed and commercial broadcasters be able to display the contact details and slogans of sponsors.

9.3 Advertising and Minors

The Dutch Media Act requires that programmes transmitted by public broadcasters and aimed at minors under the age of 12 must not be interrupted by a commercial break.[70] Programmes broadcast by a commercial broadcasting company can be interrupted, but only if the programme has a minimum length of 30 minutes.[71]

Rules that concern the content of advertising can be found in self-regulatory codes of conduct. Some general standards on the protection of minors are laid down in the Code for Advertising Directed at Children and Young People.[72] This Code is part of the Dutch Advertising Code and divides minors into two categories: children aged 12 or younger, and adolescents between the age of 13 and 18 years old. Advertising aimed at children should not present the characteristics of a product in a way that might mislead a child. It should not cause moral or physical detriment to minors and, for that reason, it should meet the criteria mentioned in the TwF Directive.[73]

---

67. Dutch Media Decree, Art. 32 (1), (2).
68. Dutch Media Act, Arts 50.8 and 71f.
69. Dutch Media Act, Arts 71k and 71m.
70. Dutch Media Act, Art. 41a (3).
71. Dutch Media Act, Art. 71h (3).
72. Dutch Advertising Code Authority, 'The Dutch Advertising Code' <www.reclamecode.nl/bijlagen/dutch_advertising_code.pdf>, 16 July 2007.
73. The criteria which are mentioned in the Code for Advertising Directed at Children and Young People are almost an exact copy of the criteria mentioned in Art. 16 of the Television without Frontiers Directive.

The self-regulatory Code adds that advertising aimed at children should not suggest that the possession of a certain product confers on them a physical or social advantage *vis-à-vis* other children, nor should advertising be in any way demeaning of a child.[74] If an advertisement is made visible on the internet in a banner or a pop-up, it should clearly bear the word 'advertising message'. Finally, a rule that applies to all audiovisual media is that persons starring in audiovisual programmes, who are for that reason held to have an influence on children and enjoy their confidence, are not allowed to feature in audiovisual advertising.[75]

Other special Codes contain advertising standards for specific products and services. One of these is the Advertising Code for Alcoholic Beverages. The criteria mentioned in Article 15 of the TwF Directive have been implemented in this Code. In addition to these rules, the Code also prohibits the depiction of people under the age of 25 in alcohol advertising. Moreover, alcohol advertising should not reach a public that consists of over 25 percent of people which are younger than 18 years old. Other special Codes containing advertising standards for specific products or services mainly stipulate that advertising should not be specifically directed at minors or show people under a certain age.[76] Advertising should not encourage young persons to start gambling and smoking or adopt other undesirable habits. The advertising industry is also bound by similar self-regulatory standards.

10. PROTECTION OF MINORS

Television programme services which have obtained broadcasting time should not contain any programmes that might seriously impair the physical, mental or moral development of persons under the age of 16.[77] It follows that programmes containing hardcore pornography or gratuitous violence are prohibited in line with Article 22 (1) of the TwF Directive. Programmes that may impair the physical, mental or moral development of persons under the age of 16 can only be broadcast if the operators are members of an authorized organization that provides regulation concerning classification.[78] The Dutch government has accredited the Netherlands Institute for the Classification of Audio-visual Media (NICAM) to provide regulations and supervise them. NICAM was created in 1999 and is responsible for the entire audiovisual sector. Broadcasters who do not join NICAM can only broadcast programmes that are suitable for all age groups; they cannot broadcast programmes only suitable for people older than 12 years old.[79]

---

74. Code for Advertising Directed at Children and Young People, Art. 3.
75. Code for Advertising Directed at Children and Young People, Art. 11.
76. Advertising Code for Games of Chance offered by Licensees, by virtue of the Games of Chance Act, Arts III.1 and III.2; Advertising Code for Tobacco Products, Arts 8.2 and 8.3; Telemarketing Code, Art. 9; Advertising Code for Food Products, Art. 8.
77. Dutch Media Act, Art. 52d (1).
78. Dutch Media Act, Arts 52d (2) and 53.
79. Betzel, 'Media System of the Netherlands', p. 11.

In 2001 a rating system called Watch More Knowingly (*Kijkwijzer*) was introduced to provide viewers of audiovisual productions with information on possible harmful effects on children. Today all cinema and television is covered by this system. The *Kijkwijzer* warns parents by providing age-based recommendations for the categories all ages, 6, 12 and 16 years old.[80] Programmes with the classification '12 years' may not be broadcast before 8 P.M. and anything classified '16 years' may not be aired before 10 P.M. The reasons for a certain recommendation are clarified with additional pictograms indicating the categories: violence, fear, sex, discrimination, drug and/or alcohol abuse, and gross language. These pictograms are shown at the beginning of a television programme and can be found on television information page (*Teletext*) 282, television-listings, advertising posters, film websites, DVD packaging and in cinemas.

Any person who believes that these rules have been infringed can submit a complaint to NICAM which then, if necessary, will be forwarded to the independent NICAM Complaints Committee.[81] A number of options are open to the Complaints Committee. It may order that the classification be amended or the broadcasting time changed, but it can also impose sanctions. An affiliated company that breaches the rules risks a fine up to EUR 135,000.[82] The supervision of this system of self-regulation has been entrusted to the Dutch Media Authority. In respect of the functioning of the system, the Committee on Youth, Violence and Media concluded in their 2005 report '*Wijzer Kijken*' that the system is operating well.[83] Other research has indicated that today nine out of ten parents follow the *Kijkwijzer* recommendations.[84] Although the internet is not yet covered by the *Kijkwijzer*, NICAM claims to be following the developments in this area with interest.

11. RIGHT OF REPLY

When implementing the TwF Directive the Dutch government considered that the introduction of an explicit right of reply would constitute too much of an interference with broadcasting freedom. The Netherlands' reserved attitude in respect of such legislation was one of the reasons for not ratifying the European

80. In two cases a fourth category, '9 years old', was applied ad hoc to the movie *Harry Potter and the Prisoner of Azkaban* and the movie *Kruistocht in Spijkerbroek*. The NICAM considers formally introducing this category, because the gap between the category '6 years old' and '12 years old' appears too wide.
81. The losing party can appeal to the Appeals Committee.
82. Such a steep fine has never been imposed until now. Fines in the area of EUR 12,000 are the norm.
83. The Commission on Youth, Violence and Media was established in 2005 by the Minister of Education, Culture and Science to provide recommendations in respect of media and young people and the system of self-regulation. In November 2005 the Commission published the report *Wijzer Kijken*.
84. 'Kijkwijzer' <www.kijkwijzer.nl/pagina.php?id=34>, 16 July 2007.

Convention on Transfrontier Television. Although in the Netherlands it is generally considered good practice for journalists to hear both sides of a story before they publish it, there is no legal obligation to do so.[85]

Remedies equivalent to the right of reply are guaranteed by both judicial and non-judicial bodies. If inaccurate and damaging facts have been broadcast, the injured party can in the first instance file a lawsuit with the civil court. The right of rectification is codified in Article 6 (167) of the Civil Code. On the basis of this provision courts can ask a company that has broadcast inaccurate facts to publish a rectification. Lawsuits are usually based on the law of tort that enables the judge to assign financial compensation.

A different, non-judicial remedy is to file a complaint with a self-regulatory body, the Netherlands Press Council (*Raad voor de Journalistiek*). The procedure for filing a complaint with the Council is straightforward and free of charge. However, the broadcaster needs to be a member of the Council. The Council cannot impose binding sanctions, but can only give its opinion on the complaint. The opinion is then published on the website of the Council and is equivalent to a sanction. Moreover, around two third of the Council members publish valid or partially valid complaints in their own media. There is no possibility of appeal against a verdict of the Council. Although no sanctions can be imposed, such a verdict can have extensive consequences. The Court of Appeal in Amsterdam has in the past incorporated verdicts in its own rulings.[86] The Supreme Court ruled in the *Van Gasteren* case that there was no objection to the Court of Appeal following the Council's verdict.[87]

A third, more indirect avenue for being heard when one's interests have been damaged is provided by the television programme 'The Lie Rules' (*De Leugen Regeert*). The lack of a right to reply led to the development of a new television format by one of the public broadcasters. The programme's title comes from a quote by Queen Beatrix and covers lies and semi-truths in journalism. Both complainant and defendant are invited to discuss the way journalism was conducted in a given case. However, it is not possible to apply to participate in the programme; participation is by invitation only.

In reaction to the international discussion on the right of reply, the government is searching for ways to balance more effectively the power of the media and the rights of the injured party. Whether or not the current system is providing enough protection from inaccurate broadcasts, is an ongoing debate. Although the freedom of broadcasting is highly valued, the government considers improving judicial sanctions and establishing non-judicial dispute committees that could grant small reimbursements and force a rectification.

---

85. Code of Conduct issued by the Dutch Society of Chief Editors, Art. 4 <www.villamedia.nl/genootschap>, 18 July 2007.
86. Amsterdam Court of Appeal, 29 October 1988 (*Jagt v. Vrij Nederland*).
87. Dutch Supreme Court, 6 January 1995, NJ 1995, 422.

Chapter 7
United Kingdom

1. BACKGROUND

The beginnings of public broadcasting in the United Kingdom go back to 1922 when the British Broadcasting Company was granted the first licence to operate eight radio stations. The British Broadcasting Company was a private company owned by the British wireless manufacturers.[1] The transmission of radio programmes was motivated by the wish to increase the sale of radio equipment.[2] Following recommendations by the Sykes and the Crawford Committees in the 1920s that broadcasting was too important to be left in the hands of a commercial monopoly, the British Broadcasting Corporation (BBC) was established by Royal Charter in 1927.[3]

The fact that the BBC was not set up by statute was meant to express its special position and its independence of the House of Commons. The suggestion has been made in the past to set the BBC on a statutory footing, but it was turned down by the National Heritage Committee in 1993 with the argument that regulation under the Royal Prerogative gave the BBC flexibility and independence.[4] The House of Commons Select Committee on Culture, Media and Sport argued in 2004 that placing the BBC on a permanent statutory basis 'would provide for long term certainty, and transparency over the Corporation's basic terms of reference' and would render its governance more open and democratic.[5] Also, the House of Lords

---

1. E. M. Barendt and L. Hitchens, *Media Law: Cases and Materials* (Harlow, Longman, 2000), p. 70.
2. Holznagel, *Rundfunkrecht in Europa*, p. 52.
3. Barendt, *Broadcasting Law*, pp. 10–11.
4. A. W. Bradley and K. D. Ewing, *Constitutional and Administrative Law* (14th edn, Harlow, Longman, 2006), p. 547.
5. House of Commons Culture, Media and Sport Committee, *A Public BBC. First Report of Session 2004-05*, vol. I, HC 82-I (London, TSO, 2004), paras 238 *et seq.*, 244.

Select Committee on BBC Charter Renewal criticized that the process of renewal did not sufficiently involve Parliament.[6] The Government argued rather unconvincingly that an Act of Parliament would risk 'making the BBC more open to ad hoc Government and Parliamentary intervention while removing the flexibility that exists to negotiate changes to the accompanying Agreement during the life of the Charter'.[7] The new BBC Charter came into effect on 1 January 2007 for a term of ten years and is unlikely to be replaced by statute during that period.[8]

The Royal Charter defines the BBC's purpose and remit, lays down the responsibilities of the BBC and its Governors and provides for the licence fee. More practical matters such as programming and supervision are governed by the BBC Licence and Agreement that are concluded between the BBC and the Secretary of State (currently, the Secretary of State for Culture, Media and Sport).[9] The Charter has been renewed periodically since 1927. The 1996 Charter stated that the government could revoke it if it thought that the BBC had failed to observe any provisions prescribed therein.[10] The government gave up this power under the new Charter so as to strengthen the independence of the BBC. The new BBC Charter explicitly endorses the key principle of the Corporation's independence from the State 'in all matters concerning the content of its output, the times and manner in which this is supplied, and in the management of its affairs'.[11] However, the renewal of the Licence depends on the goodwill of the government, limiting severely the BBC's freedom from state control.

The government not only has the power to determine the future of the BBC. It can also 'censor' BBC broadcasting by directing the corporation not 'to broadcast or otherwise distribute any matter, or class of matter, specified in the direction, whether at a time or times so specified or at any time' in a notice given by the Secretary of State.[12] This power was used in 1988 to impose a ban on the broadcasting of words spoken by representatives of organizations proscribed in Northern Ireland, of Sinn Fein and of the Ulster Defence Association.[13] Recently the BBC was banned from broadcasting a report about the cash for honours inquiry. The ban was issued with an injunction by the Attorney General in cooperation with the police because of their concern that disclosure of certain information would

---

6. House of Lords Select Committee on the BBC Charter Review, *The Review of the BBC's Royal Charter*, 1st Report of Session 2005–06, HL 50-1 (London, TSO, 2005), para. 33 *et seq.*
7. DCMS, *Government Response to the Lords Committee Report on Charter Review* (Cm 6739, 2006), p. 2.
8. *Royal Charter for the Continuance of the British Broadcasting Corporation* (Cm 6925, 2006) (hereafter referred to as the BBC Charter).
9. *Agreement Dated July 2006 Between Her Majesty's Secretary of State for Culture, Media and Sport and the British Broadcasting Corporation* (Cm 6872, 2006) (hereafter referred to as the BBC Agreement).
10. *Royal Charter for the Continuance of the British Broadcasting Corporation* (Cm 3248, 1996), Art. 20 (2) (hereafter referred to as the 1996 Charter).
11. BBC Charter, Art. 6 (1).
12. BBC Agreement, s. 81 (4).
13. H. Fenwick and G. Phillipson, *Media Freedom under the Human Rights Act* (Oxford, Oxford University Press, 2006), p. 1037.

impede police inquiries. However, banning the BBC from broadcasting a programme on these grounds was criticized as an unprecedented action whose political motivation could not be discounted.[14] Under the 1996 Agreement, the Secretary of State could also interfere with the day to day affairs of broadcasting by giving directions as to the maximum and/or minimum time to be given to transmissions in the Home Services and as to the hours of the day in which the broadcasts are to be transmitted.[15] The new Agreement does not contain a similar provision, again with the aim of enhancing the BBC's programme autonomy.

The government influence on the BBC would appear to be at odds with the ideals of broadcasting freedom and independence from state control. It can, however, be explained in terms of the United Kingdom's unique constitutional position. Unlike the other European countries considered in this study, the United Kingdom does not have a written constitution. Historically, 'media freedom' did not exist as a constitutional concept in English law.[16] The traditional English idea of media freedom was that of a negative liberty, a freedom from censorship. Other than that, it was a residual liberty consisting of whatever remained once numerous statutory and common law restrictions had been applied.[17]

As a result of the principle of parliamentary sovereignty, the judiciary could not afford media freedom any entrenched status either.[18] Parliamentary sovereignty has a positive and a negative aspect. The positive aspect is that Parliament has the power to pass any law whatsoever and the negative that there is no competing authority having the right to override or set aside an Act of Parliament.[19] The principle of parliamentary sovereignty entails that statutory provisions override non-statutory provisions and that later statutes override earlier ones. It follows that media freedom and other civil liberties are not cast in stone but are at the disposal of the legislature. This was at least the position before the introduction of the Human Rights Act in 1998. Britain ratified the European Convention of Human Rights (ECHR) already in 1951 but it was only in 1998 that the Convention was fully incorporated into the UK legal system. The free speech guarantee laid down in Article 10 ECHR is now part of British law and has helped transform media freedom from a residual liberty to a positive right.[20]

The BBC's constitutional documents, its Charter and Agreement, were last renewed in 1996 when they replaced the previous ones that had been granted in

---

14. *See* N. Goswami, 'Cash for Honours Media Row Rumbles On' <www.thelawyer.com/cgi-bin/item.cgi?id=124640&d=122&h=24&f=46> 16 July 2007.
15. Copy of the Amendment dated 4 December 2003 to the Agreement of 25 January 1996 (as amended) Between Her Majesty's Secretary of State for Culture, Media and Sport and the British Broadcasting Corporation (Cm 6075, 2003), s. 5E (hereafter referred to as the 1996 Agreement), s. 6.1.
16. Fenwick and Phillipson, *Media Freedom*, p. 4.
17. *Ibid.*, p. 5; Barendt, *Freedom of Speech*, p. 40.
18. Craufurd Smith, *Broadcasting Law*, p. 70; Holznagel, *Rundfunkrecht in Euorpa*, pp. 109–110.
19. Bradley and Ewing, *Constitutional and Administrative Law*, p. 55.
20. *See however* the problems outlined by Fenwick and Phillipson, *Media Freedom*, p. 6 *et seq.* associated with the protection of media freedom in an instrument short of a Constitution.

1981. The 1996 Charter and Agreement were granted for a term of ten years and are currently under review. The Charter review was launched in 2003 with a public consultation. After two years of further consultation and debate the Government issued its White Paper in March 2006. The White Paper confirmed the Government's intention to renew the BBC's Charter and to continue licence fee funding of the Corporation until 2016. At the same time it introduced new governance arrangements that we will consider in more detail later on. The decisions contained in the White Paper have been implemented in the new Charter and Agreement that took full effect on 1 January 2007 (subject only to some very limited transitional provisions which continue to apply after that date).

The Charter review process has to be seen against the backdrop of a fierce dispute between the BBC and the government over the broadcast of an unscripted interview with a BBC journalist on the flagship *Today* Radio 4 news programme shortly after 6 A.M. on 29 May 2003.[21] The journalist, Andrew Gilligan, alleged that the government had 'sexed up' the evidence contained in a dossier to make a strong case for the war against Iraq. The interview was based on notes from a secret source, an unnamed senior official, who was later revealed to be Dr David Kelly, a senior adviser on chemical weapons to the Ministry of Defence. Dr Kelly was relied on as the source for claiming that government ministers had instructed the intelligence services to exaggerate the threat posed by Iraqi weapons of mass destruction. The government argued that these allegations were untrue and that the BBC was biased.

When Dr Kelly was subsequently found dead, the Prime Minister ordered a public inquiry into the circumstances of his death. Chaired by Lord Hutton, the inquiry concluded on 28 January 2004 that the government's dossier was not deliberately misleading and that the BBC had breached its editorial standards. Lord Hutton found that the most serious of Mr Gilligan's allegations in relation to a subject of great public importance were not fully supported by his notes. He characterized the BBC's editorial system as 'defective' in that Mr Gilligan was allowed to broadcast his report without editors having seen a script of what he was going to say and having considered whether it should be approved.[22] Moreover, he found that the corporation's management was at fault in failing to investigate properly the government's complaints that the broadcast made false claims and in failing to make an examination of Mr Gilligan's notes on his personal organizer of his meeting with Dr Kelly to see if they supported his allegations.[23]

On publication of this damning report, both the Chairman of the BBC's Board of Governors, Gavyn Davies, and its Director General, Greg Dyke, resigned. The

21. The BBC disputed Lord Hutton's finding that the interview was unscripted. It argued that a core script was properly prepared and cleared in line with normal production practices in place at the time, but was then not followed by Andrew Gilligan. *See* BBC, 'The Neil Report' <www.bbc.co.uk/info/policies/neil_report.shtml>, 16 July 2007, Appendix 2.
22. Lord Hutton, *Report of the Inquiry into the Circumstances Surrounding the Death of Dr. David Kelly C.M.G* (London, HMSO, 2004), Chapter 8, para. 291 (2) <www.the-hutton-inquiry.org.uk/content/report>, 13 October 2006 (hereafter referred to as the Hutton Report).
23. *Ibid.*, Chapter 8, para. 291 (3).

resignations coincided with the preparation of the first major BBC submission to the government in the course of the Charter review process. The BBC reacted to 'the most serious indictment [. . .] in its history since the Corporation was founded in 1927'[24] by forming a review team that would consider editorial changes to be put in place. The report was published in June 2004 and recommended a tightening of journalistic standards in relation to note-taking, reliance on third-parties, anonymity of sources and fairness.[25] It confirmed that accuracy, impartiality and diversity of opinion, independence and accountability are the corporation's core values. It recommended that BBC reporting should be strengthened and that editorial lawyers should be consulted in programming matters, especially in the coverage of the main news areas.

The need to improve the accuracy of BBC reporting should not mask another fundamental issue raised by Lord Hutton's inquiry: the frailty of the BBC's political independence. In the course of the inquiry, the perception was widely held both outside as well as within the BBC that its established funding and governance arrangements were not sufficiently robust to shield it from government pressure.[26] The enhancement of the BBC's independence became the motto of the government's Green Paper of March 2005 and is certainly a touchstone for the new Charter's success.[27]

BBC comprises the following public channels: the analogue channels BBC1, a general entertainment channel, and BBC2, a mixed-genres channel, and the digital channels BBC3, a channel aimed at younger audiences; BBC4, a more intellectual channel; the children's channels CBBC and CBeebies; BBC News24, a digital channel dedicated to news coverage and BBC Parliament dedicated to the coverage of politics. BBC World is the commercially funded, international counterpart of BBC News24. Other commercial thematic channels run by the BBC include BBC Prime (entertainment) and BBC America (drama, news and entertainment).

BBC is the leading public broadcaster in the United Kingdom and the only one to receive public funding. However, it is not the only public broadcaster. Channel 4 is also a public company, but it is funded through advertising. Both the BBC and Channel 4 receive frequencies for free in exchange for their public service obligations. Channel 4 was instituted by the Broadcasting Act 1980 to provide distinctive programming missing from the other commercial channels and began broadcasting in 1982. Unlike the other broadcasters it was established as a publisher of programmes that were commissioned from independent producers.[28] It is only under the Broadcasting Act 1990 that Channel 4 was turned to a statutory corporation, licensed by the ITC (now by Ofcom). A unique feature of the English

24. Fenwick and Phillipson, *Media Freedom*, p. 1006.
25. BBC, 'The Neil Report'.
26. *The Review of the BBC's Royal Charter*, 1st Report of Session 2005–06, HL 50-1, paras 22 *et seq.*
27. DCMS, *Review of the BBC's Royal Charter: A Strong BBC, Independent of Government* (Green Paper), March 2005.
28. Barendt, *Broadcasting Law*, p. 12.

broadcasting landscape is that all terrestrial free-to-air broadcasters, not only the public ones, have public service obligations to fulfil. The extent of these obligations varies, with the BBC having the lion's share, followed by Channel 4.[29] Much lighter requirements apply to the main private broadcasters, Channel 3 and Channel 5, concerning regional programming, news and current affairs and independent programmes.[30] Finally, one should also mention S4C, a Welsh channel that transmits analogue programming in Welsh in the peak time and a wholly Welsh channel on digital television. S4C does not produce programmes of its own but commissions them from the BBC and independent producers.

Commercial broadcasters challenge BBC's privileges and seek to free themselves of their public service obligations.[31] It will be even more difficult to sustain public service obligations for the commercial broadcasters, except perhaps for Channel 4, in the future in view of the dissipation of advertising revenues as a result of digitalization.[32] So as to preserve public service broadcasting, Ofcom proposed the creation of a Public Service Publisher, a new television channel broadcasting public service content on digital television and the new media and commissioning programmes in competition with the BBC. This chapter is primarily concerned with the regulatory regime for the BBC with only occasional references to the commercial public service broadcasters.

2. BROADCASTING AUTHORITIES

This section will discuss, first, the unique system of administration of the BBC by two new bodies that were instituted by the new Charter: the BBC Trust and the Executive Board. Secondly, it will consider Ofcom's role in relation to the public service broadcasters.

2.1 BBC Trust and Executive Board

So as to assess the significance of the changes introduced by the new Charter, it is necessary to outline first the previous governance arrangements for the BBC. Under the old Charter, the Corporation was controlled by twelve Governors, including one Chairman, one Vice-Chairman and three National Governors for Scotland, Wales and Northern Ireland. All Governors were part-time and were appointed by the Queen on the advice of the Government, which means that they were actually selected by the Prime Minister. However, after the Hutton

29. D. Ward, 'United Kingdom' in *Television across Europe: Regulation, Policy and Independence*, Open Society Institute (ed.) (New York, Open Society Institute, 2005), p. 1614.
30. *Ibid.*; P. Carey and J. Sanders, *Media Law* (3rd edn, London, Sweet & Maxwell, 2004), p. 237.
31. D. W. Vick, 'Regulatory convergence?' (2006) 26 Legal Studies, 26, 31.
32. T. Prosser, 'United Kingdom' in *Iris Special: The Public Service Broadcasting Culture* (Strasbourg, European Audiovisual Observatory, 2007), pp. 103, 111.

Report, Michael Grade, the Chairman of the BBC who replaced Gavyn Davies after his resignation, was appointed under the scrutiny of a panel of Privy Counsellors from the main political parties to refute allegations of bias.

The Governors' task was to oversee the BBC and to represent the public interest, while the day to day management of the Corporation was in the hands of an Executive Committee consisting of the Director General and ten other members. The Governors were acting as strategic directors in setting key objectives for the Corporation and as regulators in monitoring compliance with standards and in addressing complaints. Despite the inherent tension in this dual role, the Governors did not tend to get involved in management or programming decisions. They could impose their vision of the BBC by appointing or even replacing the Director – General and other key managers.[33] However, the Gilligan affair demonstrated that the two roles of the Governors were bound to come into conflict. Instead of investigating the government's complaints, the Governors immediately aligned themselves with the management so as to defend the Corporation's independence against the government.[34]

After lengthy consultations, the new Charter and Agreement introduced important changes on the governance of the BBC. The Board of Governors has been replaced by the BBC Trust and a formally constituted Executive Board has taken responsibility for the management and delivery of the BBC's activities. The Trust is the body responsible for the strategic direction of the BBC, embodies the public interest and represents the views of the licence fee payers. It has broadly the same responsibilities as the Governors but has assumed the significant power to approve new services that was previously held by the government.

The Trust consists of 12 Trustees, including a Chair and a Vice-Chair, appointed in the same way as the Governors. The Executive Board includes mainly senior Executives, but also a significant minority of non-executive Directors, nominated by the Board and approved by the Trust. At least a third of the Executive Board, and no fewer than four, will be non-Executive. The role of the non-Executives is to support the Executive Board as 'critical friends' and to bring an external perspective to its work.[35] The Board will be chaired by the Director General or, at the discretion of the Trust, by a non-Executive.

Various criticisms had been levelled at these arrangements in the course of the consultations leading up to the new Charter, most notably from the House of Lords Select Committee on the BBC's Charter Review.[36] In its Report it criticized the role of non-executive members on the BBC Executive Board and especially the possibility of the Board being chaired by a non-Executive. It found that the appointment of future chairmen of the BBC by the Government compromised its independence and

33. 1996 Charter, Art. 14 (1); T. Gibbons, *Regulating the Media* (London, Sweet & Maxwell, 1998), pp. 249–250.
34. Ward, 'United Kingdom', p. 1630.
35. BBC, *Annual Report and Accounts 2005/2006*, p. 8.
36. *The Review of the BBC's Royal Charter*, 1st Report of Session 2005–06, HL 50-1.

maintained that appointments should be made on the basis of a recommendation by an independent panel. Its most sustained criticism was that the new model did not adequately separate between governance and regulation of the BBC and that it maintained the confusing overlap between the BBC and Ofcom as regards standards complaints. Its preferred model was that the BBC should deal with complaints in the first instance, while there should be the possibility of a final appeal to Ofcom.

The Government did not agree with the Committee's proposals on governance of the BBC except perhaps on the range of skills that the Trust members need to possess.[37] BBC Trust members may bring knowledge or experience of broadcasting, communications and new media; competition, legal, corporate or regulatory aspects of running large corporations; any area covered by the BBC's public purposes; delivering accountability to stakeholders.[38] However, the fact that the Trustees do not necessarily need to have experience of broadcasting and communications poses a certain risk that they may be over reliant on the BBC Executive for guidance.

As far as the BBC's regulatory regime is concerned, it is clear that the reforms introduced by the new Charter are only a half measure, leaving many pressing issues untouched. The question whether the BBC should be brought fully under Ofcom has been a very controversial one. The opponents of this solution argue that the BBC is not like other broadcasters, that Ofcom is an essentially economic regulator and that there is a need for a plurality of regulators to match the plurality of content providers.[39] Its proponents retort that Ofcom is not solely an economic regulator and that this solution would draw a clear line between the BBC's regulation and governance, increase consistency across the sector and satisfy the public's expectations for accountability.[40] Undoubtedly, the aim of clarity and consistency in content regulation by a fully independent body is laudable. Is Ofcom the right body to perform this task? In order to form a view on this question, it is necessary to consider Ofcom's regulatory powers and style.

2.2 Office of Communications

Ofcom is the new 'super regulator' set up under the Office of Communications Act 2002 and with the powers and duties laid down in the Communications Act 2003. It

---

37. DCMS, *Government Response to the Lords Committee Report on Charter Review* (Cm 6739, 2006), p. 3.
38. BBC Trust, 'How Trust Members are Appointed' <www.bbc.co.uk/bbctrust/about/bbc_trust_members/how_members_are_appointed.html>, 16 July 2007.
39. J. Cowling and D. Tambini, 'Conclusions and Recommendations' in *From Public Service Broadcasting to Public Service Communications*, D. Tambini, J. Cowling (eds) (London, IPPR, 2004), p. 178; *see The Review of the BBC's Royal Charter*, 1st Report of Session 2005–06, HL 50-1, 1 November 2005, para. 102.
40. R. Collins, 'Public Service Broadcasting: Too Much of a Good Thing?' in *From Public Service Broadcasting to Public Service Communications*, D. Tambini and J. Cowling (eds) (London, IPPR, 2004), p. 139; M. Feintuck and M. Varney, *Media Regulation, Public Interest and the Law* (Edinburgh, Edinburgh University Press, 2006), p. 54; *The Review of the BBC's Royal Charter*, 1st Report of Session 2005–06, HL 50-1, para. 103.

has been entrusted with the licensing and regulation of media and telecommunications. It absorbed the roles and functions of the Independent Television Commission (ITC), Broadcasting Standards Commission, the Radio Authority, Oftel, the former telecommunications regulator, and the Radio Communications Agency, responsible for spectrum management. It is responsible both for independent and for public sector television, but has a more limited role as regards the BBC.[41] The Communications Act 2003 introduced a system of tiers for the regulation of broadcasting content and subjected BBC to much of Ofcom's Code. The first tier regulations concern negative content regulation, covering the avoidance of harm and offence, accuracy and impartiality, subliminal messages and fairness and privacy. The second tier concerns quotas for certain types of programmes – such as news and current affairs – and types of production such as original and regional production. The third tier concerns the monitoring of the public service remit of public service broadcasters.[42] The three tiers apply in their totality to the commercially funded public service broadcasters. The situation is more complicated as regards the BBC.

There is a regulatory overlap between the BBC and Ofcom as regards tier one matters given that complaints can be addressed by BBC, by Ofcom or by both. However, the BBC Trust is exclusively and finally responsible for accuracy and impartiality.[43] As regards tier two matters, the BBC needs to obtain Ofcom's agreement for their original production and regional production quotas, while it sets all other quotas after consulting Ofcom. As regards tier three matters the BBC Trust approves statements of programme policy that are drawn yearly for every BBC service.[44] The Trust is also responsible for monitoring performance in carrying out the promises contained in these statements.[45] It only needs to take Ofcom's guidance and the reports published by it into account to so as to decide how far they contain 'anything of relevance to the circumstances of the BBC'.[46] Also, Ofcom conducts a review of the effectiveness of public service broadcasting every five years in which it includes the BBC.

It is important to note that while the BSC did not have the power to impose financial penalties on the BBC, Ofcom may impose such penalties for contravention of the provisions of Part 3 of the Communications Act 2003 or of the Charter and Agreement.[47] Moreover, Ofcom may impose penalties on the BBC if it contravenes 'a relevant enforceable requirement'.[48] The Ofcom Code constitutes such

41. Also, S4C is not regulated by Ofcom but by the Welsh Broadcasting Authority.
42. *The Review of the BBC's Royal Charter*, 1st Report of Session 2005–06, HL 50-1, para. 54.
43. BBC Agreement, s. 44 (5), 46 (2) (b).
44. BBC Agreement, s. 21 (1). The statements of programme policy were introduced in 2003/2004 in replacement of the BBC's 'Statement of promises' which had been published in the 'Annual Report and Accounts' of the BBC since 1996.
45. *Ibid.*, s. 21 (5).
46. *Ibid.*, s. 21 (3) (b).
47. Communications Act 2003, s. 198 (3).
48. BBC Agreement, s. 94 (1).

a requirement. The power to impose financial penalties marks a significant departure from the previous regime since it restricts the BBC's autonomy and aligns it more with the private broadcasters.[49]

In terms of competition law, Ofcom regulates the BBC like any other broadcaster together with the Office of Fair Trading and the European Commission. It conducts Market Impact Assessments as part of the Public Value tests that have to be applied by the BBC Trust when the BBC management plans to introduce new services or to make significant changes to existing ones. However, the final decision as to whether the proposed change should be made lies with the BBC Trust.[50] The introduction of public value tests in the new Charter is thus likely to quell Government intervention into the BBC. Recently, the BBC Trust reached a favourable decision on the BBC iPlayer. It considered that the proposed services would deliver significant public value as they would strongly fit with the BBC's public purposes and play a significant role in maintaining BBC's reach in the future.[51]

Even though Ofcom is independent of the Government, Secretaries of State have to answer questions about it in Parliament. Moreover, Ofcom is accountable to Parliament by means of Select Committees and the Parliamentary Audit Committee.[52] Ofcom's complex structure differs from that of other UK utilities sectors and of the previous regulators that Ofcom has replaced.[53] Its main decision making body is its Board that provides strategic direction for Ofcom. It comprises a mix of executive members including the Chief Executive Officer, and non-executive members including a Chairman, in a manner that is modelled after the boards of companies regulated by Ofcom. The Chairman and the non-executive members of the Board are appointed by ministers in accordance with the 'Nolan principles' laid down by the Committee on Standards in Public Life. Despite these safeguards such appointments open up a potential avenue of informal ministerial influence on Ofcom.

A number of other committees and advisory bodies, most notably the Content Board and the Consumer Panel, assist the main Board in fulfilling its tasks. The Content Board is a sub-committee of the main Board. It constitutes the main forum for the regulation of broadcasting standards in television and radio. The Consumer Panel is independent of Ofcom and is responsible for 'understanding consumer issues and concerns related to the communications sector' other than those falling within the remit of the Content Board.[54]

The establishment of the Content Board and of the Consumer Panel mirrors Ofcom's twin-track 'principal duty' under Article 3 (1) of the Communications Act

49. Fenwick and Phillipson, *Media Freedom*, p. 595.
50. BBC Agreement, s. 26 (6).
51. BBC Trust, *BBC on demand proposals: Public Value Test final conclusions*, April 2007.
52. Ward, 'United Kingdom', p. 1611.
53. Feintuck and Varney, *Media Regulation*, p. 177.
54. Ofcom, 'The Consumer Panel: Functions and Role' <www.ofcom.org.uk/about/csg/consumer_panel>, 16 July 2007.

2003 to 'further the interests of citizens in relation to communications matters' and to 'further the interests of consumers in relevant markets, where appropriate by promoting competition'. The inherent tension in the janus-faced definition of Ofcom's duties is obvious. Is Ofcom a regulator that is genuinely concerned about the promotion of public service values and citizens' interests or is it a commercially oriented regulator? The indiscriminate listing in Article 3 (2), (3) and (4) of another six objectives that Ofcom has to attain and of 15 factors to which it needs to have regard does little to clarify the situation.

The reluctance of Parliament to establish a clear hierarchy between these conflicting duties has been denounced by the Puttnam Committee as an abdication of responsibility and has been forcefully criticized in academic writing.[55] The lack of support for public service values in the statutory framework has not been compensated by the exercise of Ofcom's discretion and regulatory powers either. Its conception of public service broadcasting as a 'large-scale public policy intervention in the television market' that can only be justified on the grounds of market failure, the definition of public service broadcasting on the basis of broad characteristics rather than institutions that are well-equipped to provide it and its preference for the contestability and divisibility of existing funding reveal Ofcom's pronounced market ideology.[56] It is doubtful that strengthening the Ofcom Content Board by means of its endowment with an independent budget or staff, as suggested by the House of Lords Select Committee, would suffice to shed Ofcom's consumerist image.[57] On a more positive note, it is necessary to add that Ofcom has established a relatively good record of accountability by entering into a dialogue with stakeholders, by conducting extensive consultations before taking any measures and by giving reasons for its decisions.[58]

3. FINANCING

The BBC is the only public service broadcaster that is funded by the licence fee, paid to it by the Secretary of State out of money provided by the Parliament.[59] BBC's public funding is complemented with a modest amount of revenue from commercial sources. The Secretary of State for Culture, Media and Sport

---

55. Joint Committee on the Draft Communications Bill, *Report of the Joint Committee on the Draft Communications Bill (Puttnam Report),* HL Paper 169-1: HC 876-1 (London, TSO, 2002), p. 12; Feintuck and Varney, *Media Regulation,* pp. 114 *et seq.,* 168.
56. Ofcom, *Ofcom Review of Public Service Television Broadcasting: Phase 1: Is Television Special?* (London, Ofcom, 2004).
57. *The Review of the BBC's Royal Charter*, 1st Report of Session 2005–06, HL 50-1, para. 108.
58. Feintuck and Varney, *Media Regulation*, pp. 171, 173.
59. BBC Agreement, s. 75 (1). S4C is directly financed by the Department for Culture, Media and Sports. The other public service broadcasters do not receive public funding but they are given radio spectrum in exchange for their public service obligations.

sets the amount of the licence fee.[60] The setting of the licence fee by the government could put the BBC's independence in jeopardy if it was used to influence programming or appointments. This is why the licence fee was linked in 1987 to the Retail Price Index, the method used by the government to measure inflation.[61] The annual fee for a licence is currently £135.50 for a colour television and £45.50 for a black-and-white set. Blind people are granted a 50 per cent concession to the full rate of the licence fee, while the 75 and above are exempted from the need for a licence. The BBC has been collecting the licence fee itself since 1990.[62] Previously it was the responsibility of the Post Office.[63]

The latest funding settlement that came into force in April 2007 broke the traditional link between the licence fee and the Retail Price Index. The government set the cost of the licence for the next six years as part of the new Charter. The licence fee is set to rise by 3 per cent over each of the following two years, then by smaller amounts up to a maximum price of 151.20 pounds (GBP) in 2012. The 3 per cent licence fee rise is at the level of inflation, but below the Retail Price Index of 4.4 per cent, and certainly below BBC's expectations. For the first time in the history of the Royal Charter, the BBC sought publicly an annual licence fee rise of 2.3 per cent above inflation, which was later lowered to 1.8 per cent above inflation. Such negotiations have traditionally been conducted behind closed doors.[64] The Government has called on the BBC to cover the shortfall by means of savings, commercial revenue and improvements in licence fee collection.

The current funding settlement only secured the future of the licence fee for the next ten years, i.e. for the lifetime of the current Charter. The need for alternative funding mechanisms, such as subscription or advertising will be considered after the end of this Charter in 2016.[65]

4. LEGAL FRAMEWORK

The main law regulating broadcasting in the United Kingdom is the Communications Act 2003. It was passed with the aim of introducing a lighter touch regulation for the electronic media and communications industries. It introduced sweeping changes in the UK television landscape by completely overhauling the law in almost every respect, from media ownership to technical aspects, licensing and standards.[66] It also prepared the ground for the formation of Ofcom. However,

---

60. A proposal that the licence fee be set by an independent body made by the BBC's ex Chairman of the Board of Governors, Michael Grade, during the Charter review process has not been taken up by the government.
61. Holznagel, *Rundfunkrecht in Europa*, p. 217.
62. Broadcasting Act 1990, s. 173 (3). TV Licensing is contracted by the BBC to administer the collection and to enforce the licensing system.
63. Barendt, *Broadcasting Law*, p. 71; Holznagel, *Rundfunkrecht in Europa*, p. 216.
64. R. Woldt, 'Neue Royal Charter für die BBC: Der Wert des öffentlichen Rundfunks in der digitalen Ära' (2006) 12 *Media Perspektiven*, 599, 601.
65. DCMS, *A Public Service for All: The BBC in the Digital Age* (Cm 6763, 2006).
66. Carey and Sanders, *Media Law*, p. 235.

the Communications Act is not a closed system. There are frequent references to the previous regulatory regime under the Broadcasting Acts 1990 and 1996. In addition, detailed provisions are contained in statutory instruments adopted under the Broadcasting Acts, and under the European Communities Acts 1972 as far as the implementation of EC law is concerned.[67]

5. PUBLIC BROADCASTING MISSION AND STANDARDS

BBC's objectives have traditionally been the provision of sound and television broadcasting services as public services and the provision of programmes of information, education and entertainment.[68] The triptych of 'information, education and entertainment' has been taken up in the new Charter.[69] However, for the first time, the new Charter includes a detailed definition of the BBC's mission that consists of six public purposes: sustaining citizenship and civil society; promoting education and learning; stimulating creativity and cultural excellence; representing the UK, its nations, regions and communities; bringing the UK to the world and the world to the UK; and finally, in promoting its other purposes, helping to deliver to the public the benefit of emerging communications technologies and services and, in addition, taking a leading role in the switchover to digital television.[70] The Trust is responsible for adopting a purpose remit for each of the six public purposes of the BBC set out in the new Charter and Agreement. The Purpose Remits define the Trust's priorities for the Executive Board and specify how it will assess the Board's performance against them.[71]

Moreover, the Trust is required to have regard to the purposes of public service television broadcasting set out in 264 (4) of the Communications Act 2003 and to the fulfilment of these purposes in line with s. 264 (6) of that Act.[72] The Communications Act 2003 lists as the purposes of public service broadcasting in the United Kingdom the provision of relevant television services which deal with a wide range of subject-matters, which meet the needs of as many different audiences as practicable, which (taken together and having regard to the same matters) are properly balanced and which (taken together) maintain high general standards. The Communications Act goes on to list ten factors that need to be taken account of by all public service broadcasters taken together.[73] By 'thinly parcelling

67. L.Woods, 'Media System of the United Kingdom' in Hans-Bredow-Institut, 'Final Report: Study on Co-Regulation Measures in the Media Sector', June 2006 <www.ec.europa.eu/avpolicy/docs/library/studies/coregul/coregul-final-report_en.pdf>, 12 July 2007.
68. 1996 Charter, Art. 3 (a).
69. BBC Charter, Art. 5 (1).
70. *Ibid.*, Art. 4.
71. BBC Agreement, s. 5.
72. BBC Agreement, s. 15.
73. Communications Act 2003, s. 264 (6).

out its functions among different providers', the Communications Act has arguably diluted the very concept of public service broadcasting.[74]

Broadcasting regulation in the United Kingdom is traditionally divided between regulation related to standards and regulation related to fairness and privacy.[75] Standards requirements are concerned with the portrayal of violence, of sexual conduct, of matters of taste and decency and of the accuracy and impartiality of programmes. Fairness requirements seek to ensure that programme-makers treat contributors to programmes fairly, and that they obtain their informed consent after having enlightened them about the nature and purpose of the programme. Privacy provisions are concerned with techniques employed by programme-makers that impinge on privacy and the fine balance between the public's right to information and the citizen's right to privacy.

Until 2005 broadcasting standards governing public service broadcasting were laid down in two Codes drawn up by the Broadcasting Standards Commission (BSC) under sections 107 and 108 of the Broadcasting Act 1996: the Code on Fairness and Privacy and the Code on Standards. This Commission was established under s. 106 of the Broadcasting Act 1996 after two previously existing bodies, the Broadcasting Standards Council and the Broadcasting Complaints Commission, were merged. The merger took place so as to reduce administrative costs and to tackle confusion in the minds of the public as to the respective roles of these two bodies. The BSC was under a duty to monitor programmes in relation to the portrayal of violence or sexual conduct, standards of taste and decency, and fairness and privacy.[76]

At the same time, the commercial broadcasters were also responsible to the Independent Television Commission (ITC). The ITC published its Programme Code under section 6 (3) of the Broadcasting Act 1990. The ITC Programme Code was mainly giving guidance as to family viewing policy, taste and decency and the portrayal of violence; fairness and privacy; impartiality; political broadcasting; terrorism, crime and antisocial behaviour; the conduct of charitable appeals and the portrayal of religion. The regulatory overlap between the ITC and the BSC meant that a programme might fall foul of one regulatory body, but not the other.[77]

The roles of the Independent Television Commission and of the Broadcasting Standards Commission were taken over in 2003 by Ofcom. Ofcom applied the ITC and BSC Codes to public broadcasting until 2005 when they were superseded by its own Code.[78] Ofcom would have the option of merely adopting the ITC and BSC Codes, with some amendments due to its wider remit.[79] However, it decided

74. G. Born, *Uncertain Vision: Birt, Dyke and the Reinvention of the BBC* (London, Vintage, 2005), p. 515.
75. Carey and Sanders, *Media Law*, p. 244 *et seq.*; Bradley and Ewing, *Constitutional and Administrative Law*, p. 549; Barendt and Hitchens, *Media Law*, p. 144 *et seq.*
76. Broadcasting Act 1996, s. 109, 110.
77. Barendt and Hitchens, *Media Law*, p. 116.
78. Ofcom, Broadcasting Code, 2005.
79. Fenwick and Phillipson, *Media Freedom*, p. 600.

to make a fresh start and to introduce a new Code. The 2003 Act required Ofcom to review and revise standards for the content of television programmes so as to secure a number of objectives.[80] Among these standards objectives are the protection of persons under the age of 18; the exclusion of material likely to lead to the commission of crime or to disorder; the due accuracy and impartiality of news programmes; the exercise of responsibility with respect to the content of religious programmes; the protection of the public from offensive and harmful material; the prohibition on political advertising and on advertising that is misleading, harmful or offensive; the ban on the use of subliminal techniques.[81] The BBC must observe these standards with the exception of accuracy and impartiality, and of the advertising restrictions which do not apply to the non-commercial BBC services.[82] The BBC is also required to comply with Ofcom's Fairness Code for the time being in force under s. 107 of the Broadcasting Act 1996.[83]

Detailed guidance concerning editorial standards is included in the BBC editorial guidelines to which all content producers working for the BBC are expected to adhere. These guidelines were entitled 'The BBC Producers' Guidelines' until July 2005 when the BBC introduced a new Code for its editorial staff. Under the new BBC Agreement, the Trust must approve guidelines – including a Code on accuracy and impartiality – designed to secure appropriate standards in the content of the UK Public Services.[84] The Executive Board is responsible for drafting these guidelines and for ensuring compliance with them, and is required to submit an editorial compliance report to the Trust twice a year.[85]

Complaints from the public about contravention of programme standards need to be made within 12 weeks from the transmission of the event. Within the BBC there is an Editorial Complaints Unit that examines such complaints independently. Its rulings can be appealed within eight weeks to the Editorial Standards Committee. Complaints about contraventions of programme standards – with the exception of impartiality – can be made to the BBC instead of Ofcom or to both of them cumulatively. This overlapping system of complaints is not satisfactory as it gives rise to legal uncertainty.

Allowing the BBC to be self-regulatory as regards due impartiality is a way of safeguarding its diminishing independence.[86] However, the bifurcation of complaint mechanisms for offensive broadcasts and for accuracy and impartiality complaints is prone to give rise to confusion and even to conflicting standards.[87] Moreover, the Hutton Inquiry called into question the BBC's capacity to deal with allegations of bias. Nevertheless, the government in its White Paper shied away from subjecting the BBC to Ofcom's Code in its entirety, including standards of

80. Communications Act 2003, s. 319 (1).
81. *Ibid.*, s. 319 (2).
82. BBC Agreement, s. 46.
83. *Ibid.*, s. 45. The Standards and Fairness Codes make up together Ofcom's Broadcasting Code.
84. *Ibid.*, s. 43 (1), 44 (5).
85. BBC Trust, *BBC Protocol: D4-Editorial Standards*, January 2007.
86. Fenwick and Phillipson, *Media Freedom*, p. 1003.
87. *Ibid.*, pp. 596, 1009.

accuracy and impartiality. It announced that it would not reconsider the distribution of responsibilities for the regulation of standards before the new governance arrangements for the BBC have operated for at least five years.[88]

6. POLITICAL AND ELECTION BROADCASTING

6.1 PLURALISM

So as to secure pluralism, both independent television and the BBC are subject to obligations of due impartiality and accuracy. Accuracy is a necessary but not sufficient precondition of due impartiality.[89] According to Gibbons, impartiality has its roots in politicians' anxieties about the power of the BBC. By obliging it to treat news and controversial material in an impartial manner, and by effectively banning editorial comment, they sought to stem the 'concentration of power in a single, powerful means of communication.'[90] The impartiality requirement, whose explicit and absolute formulation in Britain has no parallel in continental Europe, is 'the most striking restriction of broadcasters' freedom of speech'.[91] Impartiality is also closely connected with balanced pluralism. However, the two are not synonymous as a channel may present a range of views and yet have a particular slant.[92] Balanced pluralism requires public broadcasters to present a diversity of opinions in all areas of programming, i.e. education, information, entertainment and culture, but not necessarily in every single programme. Inevitably, programmes will display certain tendencies in their selection of topics and in their presentation.[93] Therefore, balanced plurality can be attained over a series of programmes.

The Broadcasting Act 1990 prescribed for the first time detailed impartiality rules that had to be addressed by the ITC in its Code.[94] This tightening up of impartiality was somewhat ironic in view of the government's intention to lighten the regulatory burden, but it has to be attributed to pressure from the House of Lords during the passage of the Bill.[95] The ITC Programme Code's section on impartiality was one of the most complex of the Code, but it did not raise any serious regulatory problems.[96] Complaints from the public about breaches of the impartiality rules were relatively few.[97] This may mean that the too precise

88. DCMS, *A Public Service for All*, p. 52.
89. Fenwick and Phillipson, *Media Freedom*, p. 995.
90. Gibbons, *Regulating the Media*, p. 96.
91. Barendt, *Broadcasting Law*, p. 100.
92. *Ibid.*, p. 101.
93. Gibbons, *Regulating the Media*, p. 103 with regard to news and current affairs.
94. Broadcasting Act 1990, s. 6 (1).
95. Barendt, *Broadcasting Law*, p. 101; Barendt and Hitchens, *Media Law*, p. 127.
96. For a detailed account of the ITC impartiality rules, *see* Barendt and Hitchens, *Media Law*, p. 126 *et seq.*; Fenwick and Phillipson, *Media Freedom*, pp. 996–997.
97. Barendt and Hitchens, *Media Law*, p. 127.

impartiality requirements under the ITC Code stifled broadcasting freedom and put the broadcasters off the production of more politically controversial programmes.[98]

The Communications Act 2003 has not changed the previous regime to any significant extent as far as impartiality is concerned. It requires that news is presented with due impartiality and with due accuracy.[99] However, impartiality does not only apply to news programmes but also to other programmes dealing with matters of political and industrial controversy or relating to current public policy.[100] Persons providing the programme service are required to refrain from expressing their opinion on any of these matters.[101] The need to preserve due impartiality can, however, be satisfied in relation to a series of programmes taken as a whole.[102] News programmes are thus treated differently from other current affairs programmes. Every single news item needs to be reported with due impartiality, while it is sufficient that other programmes achieve impartiality over a series.[103]

The requirement of due impartiality is set out in more detail in s. 5 of the Ofcom Code. This section does not apply to the licence fee funded BBC services, which are regulated on this matter by the BBC Governors. However, the commercial public service broadcasters need to comply with it. The Ofcom Code clarifies that 'due' is an important qualification to the concept of impartiality. It defines impartiality as follows:

> 'Impartiality itself means not favouring one side over another. 'Due' means adequate and appropriate to the subject and nature of the programme. So 'due impartiality' does not mean an equal division of time has to be given to every view, or that every argument or every facet of every argument has to be represented [. . .] Context [. . .] is important.'

As far as news programmes are concerned, the Code specifies that significant mistakes should normally be acknowledged and corrected on air quickly and that no politician may be used as a newsreader, interviewer or reporter in any news programmes unless, exceptionally, it is editorially justified.[104] As far as other programmes on matters of political and industrial controversy and matters relating to current public policy are concerned, the Code fleshes out the meaning of a 'series of programmes taken as a whole'.[105] It requires that where there are editorially linked programmes dealing with the same subject matter this should normally be made clear to the audience on air[106]; that there should be no misrepresentation of views and facts; that due weight must be accorded to views over

98. Fenwick and Phillipson, *Media Freedom*, p. 997.
99. Communications Act 2003, s. 319 (2) (c), (d).
100. *Ibid.*, s. 320 (2).
101. *Ibid.*, s. 320 (1) (a).
102. *Ibid.*, s. 320 (4) (a).
103. Fenwick and Phillipson, *Media Freedom*, p. 998.
104. Ofcom Code, s. 5.2, 5.3.
105. *Ibid.*, s. 5.5.
106. *Ibid.*, s. 5.6.

appropriate timeframes[107]; and that personal interest of presenters or reporters must be made clear to the audience.[108] Presenters of 'authored programmes' may express their views on matters of political or industrial controversy or matters relating to current public policy provided that additional viewpoints are adequately represented either in the programme, or in a series of programmes taken as a whole.[109] Presenting with a particular slant is thus allowed, but not in news programmes.

Finally, the Code tightens the impartiality rule as far as matters of *major* political or industrial controversy and *major* matters relating to current public policy are concerned. If impartiality is achieved over a series of programmes, these need to be clearly linked and timely.[110] Otherwise every single programme has to be impartial. An appropriately wide range of significant views must be included and given due weight and no misrepresentation should take place.[111]

As far as the BBC is concerned, the rules on impartiality are laid down in Article 44 of the BBC Agreement and they are broadly similar to the ones applying to independent television. The BBC must do all it can to ensure that controversial subjects are treated with due accuracy and impartiality in all relevant output. The UK Public Services must not contain any output which expresses the opinion of the BBC or of its Trust or Executive Board on current affairs or matters of public policy.[112] The BBC can, however, express its views about broadcasting and about proceedings in either House of Parliament, proceedings in the Scottish Parliament, the Welsh Assembly or the Northern Ireland Assembly or proceedings of a local authority or a committee of two or more local authorities.[113] The BBC is also allowed to express its opinion on the provision of online services.[114] In applying Article 44 (1) a series of programmes may be considered as a whole.[115] The BBC Agreement is more prescriptive than the Ofcom Code as to the announcement to the public of the dates and times of subsequent balancing programmes.[116]

Detailed guidance concerning impartiality is included in the BBC Editorial Guidelines. They distinguish between programmes within a series dealing with the same or related issues and programmes dealing with widely disparate issues.[117] While the former can achieve impartiality across the series, the latter are required to achieve impartiality within individual programmes or across two or three editorially linked programmes. Impartiality cannot, however, be achieved by ensuring other views will be heard on other services.

---

107. *Ibid.*, s. 5.7.
108. *Ibid.*, s. 5.8.
109. *Ibid.*, s. 5.9.
110. *Ibid.*, s. 5.11.
111. *Ibid.*, s. 5.12.
112. BBC Agreement, s. 44 (3).
113. *Ibid.*, s. 44 (4).
114. *Ibid.*, s. 44 (3).
115. *Ibid.*, s. 44 (2); 1996 Agreement, s. 5.2.
116. BBC Agreement, s. 44 (7) (d); 1996 Agreement, s. 5.5 (d).
117. BBC, 'Editorial Guidelines in Full: Impartiality and Diversity of Opinion' <www.bbc.co.uk/guidelines/editorialguidelines/edguide/impariality/impartialityins.shtml>, 18 July 2007.

Even though the requirement of impartiality of the BBC output is not externally monitored by Ofcom, the BBC strives to comply with it, *inter alia* by commissioning independent reviews. The first independent review was published in January 2005 and it was about the BBC's coverage of European issues.[118] The Governors asked an independent panel to consider criticisms that the BBC is systematically Europhile, that it covers the EU through a Westminster prism and that it has failed to increase public understanding of EU issues. The Panel found no evidence of deliberate bias, yet symptoms of cultural and unintentional bias. It criticized that the BBC has no reliable system to monitor standards of impartiality, that it presents different attitudes on Europe in a simplified, black and white manner, that it reports EU events through the prism of domestic politics, that journalists are often ill-informed about EU matters and that EU affairs are seriously underrepresented in the BBC News agenda. As a result, large sections of the public are ignorant about the workings of the EU. The Panel recommended that an EU editor should be appointed, that there should be more advance journalistic planning on EU issues coming up and that programme makers should be trained so that they better understand the EU.

The second review about the BBC's coverage of the Israeli-Palestinian conflict was published in April 2006.[119] The independent panel found that there was no deliberate or systematic bias and that there was evidence of high quality reporting. At the same time, it identified significant shortcomings, mainly gaps and imbalances in coverage, analysis and context and imprecision and inconsistency in the use of sensitive language and terminology. More precisely, the panel found that the BBC does not provide sufficient historical background and other contexts so as to communicate the conflict to the public in an intelligible manner. Also, it criticized inconsistencies in the use of the term 'terrorism'. The BBC Editorial Guidelines recommend that this term should be avoided as it is a barrier more than an aid to understanding.[120] The panel criticized that this term was readily used in respect of the London bombings while being avoided in the coverage of the Israeli-Palestinian conflict. It recommended that the BBC should fill in the gaps in respect of context and history, that there should be more secure editorial planning and that the BBC should be consistent in the use of language.

6.2 Election Broadcasts

The requirements of due impartiality and balanced pluralism are particularly relevant for the allocation of airtime to political parties, both during and outside

118. Independent Panel, 'BBC News Coverage of the European Union. Independent Panel Report of January 2005' <www.bbcgovernorsarchive.co.uk/docs/reviews/independentpanelreport.pdf>, 16 January 2008.
119. Independent Panel, 'Report of the Independent Panel for the BBC Governors on Impartiality of BBC Coverage of the Israeli-Palestinian Conflict' <www.bbcgovernorsarchive.co.uk/docs/reviews/panel_report_final.pdf>, 16 January 2008.
120. BBC, 'Editorial Guidelines in Full: War, Terror and Emergencies' <www.bbc.co.uk/guidelines/editorialguidelines/edguide/war/mandatoryreferr.shtml#4>, 16 July 2007.

of election campaigns. Until 2003, the BBC Charter and Agreement did not include a formal obligation for the BBC to make airtime available for party political broadcasts (PPBs). Nonetheless, the BBC transmitted such broadcasts as part of its public service mission.[121] The Amendment to the BBC Agreement that accompanied the Communications Act 2003 placed the BBC for the first time under a formal obligation to include party political broadcasts and referendum campaign broadcasts.[122] This obligation is now laid down in Article 48 (1) of the new BBC Agreement. The political parties on whose behalf party political broadcasts may be made and the length and frequency of such broadcasts are to be decided by the BBC Trust.[123] The discretion in the hands of the Governors is constrained by the requirement of impartiality and by s. 37 and 127 of the Political Parties, Elections and Referendums Act 2000 which provide that only registered parties or designated organizations are entitled to party political broadcasts and referendum campaign broadcasts.[124] In practice, the allocation of broadcasts emerges from the Broadcasters' Liaison Group, which is a forum for the BBC, S4C and the commercial broadcasters to coordinate policy and practice on party political broadcasting.[125]

The BBC Editorial Guidelines flesh out these rules further. They provide that accuracy and impartiality between parties may be achieved in various ways. They may be achieved in a single item, a single programme, a series of programmes or over the course of the campaign as a whole.[126] They explain that parties are responsible for the content of political broadcasts, yet they have to abide by the BBC and Ofcom rules on libel, incitement to racial hatred and violence, harm and offence. The resulting interference with the freedom of speech of political parties can be quite far-reaching as became apparent in the *Pro-Life Alliance* case. Pro-Life Alliance, a registered political party opposed to abortion, asked to present a party election broadcast (PEB) at the 2001 General Election describing different forms of abortion and showing aborted foetuses in a mutilated state. The BBC in consultation with Channel 3, 4 and 5 refused to transmit the PEB with the argument that it would cause widespread offence.[127] The Alliance's application for judicial review was turned down, so it was only able to broadcast a soundtrack describing the banned images before the General Election.

The Court of Appeal upheld the Alliance's appeal, finding that the freedom of speech of political parties at election time had to prevail over considerations of taste and decency.[128] However, the majority in the House of Lords reversed this decision, finding that it was tantamount to saying that the taste and decency rule

121. Barendt and Hitchens, *Media Law*, p. 151.
122. 1996 Agreement, s. 5E.
123. BBC Agreement, s. 48 (2).
124. *Ibid.*, s. 48 (3).
125. Electoral Commission, *Party Political Broadcasting: Report and Recommendations* (London, The Electoral Commission, 2003), p. 20.
126. BBC Editorial Guidelines, Ch. 10, 'Politics and Public Policy'.
127. *See* BBC Agreement, s. 5(1) (d).
128. *R v. British Broadcasting Corporation, ex p. Prolife Alliance* [2002] EWCA Civ. 297; [2002] 3 WLR 1080.

could not be applied to party election broadcasts (PEBs).[129] This ruling has been strongly criticized in academic writing for failing to strike the right balance between the taste and decency rules and the freedom of political expression.[130] Instead of interpreting the 1990 Broadcasting Act in a way so as to render it compatible with freedom of speech in accordance with s. 3 of the Human Rights Act, the Law Lords dismissed the Alliance's case as an attempt to disregard the statute.[131] Lord Hoffman went so far as to dispute that political speech was at stake, given that the Alliance's broadcast was not a genuine PEB.[132] The *Pro-Life Alliance* case sets an unfortunate precedent for an unduly close scrutiny of political speech and bodes ill for minority parties wishing to make their point by confronting the viewers with uncomfortable realities.

As far as the licensed public service broadcasters are concerned, the Communications Act 2003 requires them to include PPBs (including PEBs) and referendum campaign broadcasts.[133] The political parties and designated organizations on whose behalf PPBs and referendum campaign broadcasts may be made respectively as well as the length and frequency of these broadcasts are to be determined by Ofcom.[134] The Ofcom rules on party political and referendum broadcasts specify that major parties will normally be offered a series of broadcasts before each election.[135] Other registered parties may only qualify for a broadcast if they contest one sixth or more of the seats up for election.[136] The Ofcom rules specify that there are three options for the length of broadcasts available: two minutes and forty seconds, three minutes and forty seconds or four minutes and forty seconds.[137] TV election broadcasts by the major parties must be carried in peak time (6 P.M. – 10.30 P.M.). Editorial control of broadcasts normally rests with the parties or designated referendum organizations. However, broadcasters must ensure that broadcasts comply with Ofcom's Code, for example with the provisions regarding harm and offence.[138]

The Ofcom Code provides further that discussion and analysis of election and referendum issues must terminate when the poll opens and that broadcasters may not publish the results of any opinion poll on the polling day itself until the

129. *R v. British Broadcasting Corporation, ex p. Prolife Alliance* [2003] UKHL 23.
130. Barendt, *Freedom of Speech*, pp. 46–47, 486.
131. Fenwick and Phillipson, *Media Freedom*, p. 587; E. M. Barendt, 'Free Speech and Abortion' [2003] *Public Law*, 580–581.
132. Fenwick and Phillipson, *Media Freedom*, p. 589 *see* some merit in this argument, while Barendt, 'Free Speech', 584 rightly condemns it as a 'very bad one'.
133. Communications Act 2003, s. 333 (1).
134. *Ibid.*, s. 333 (2).
135. Ofcom Rules on Party Political and Referendum Broadcasts, 14 October 2004, cl. 10; According to Ofcom Code, s. 6.2, major parties in the UK are the Conservative Party, the Labour Party and the Liberal Democrats. In addition, major parties in Scotland and Wales are the Scottish Nationalist Party and Plaid Cymru. The major parties in Northern Ireland are the Democratic Unionist Party, Sinn Fein, Social Democratic and Labour Party, and the Ulster Unionist Party.
136. Ofcom Rules, cl. 11.
137. *Ibid.*, cl. 14.
138. Ofcom Code, s. 6; Ofcom Rules, cl. 3.

election and referendum poll closes.[139] Election candidates and participants in UK referendums must not act as news presenters, interviewers or presenters of any type of programme during the election period.[140] They may only appear in non-political programmes that were planned or scheduled before the election or referendum period.[141] Due impartiality must be strictly maintained in reports about particular constituencies or electoral areas. All or none of the candidates of the major parties and of parties with previous significant electoral support or with evidence of current support must be offered the opportunity to take part in such reports.[142]

As digital switchover approaches and the number of channels proliferates, questions have been posed about the capacity of party political broadcasts to reach the electorate. The Electoral Commission published a Report on party political broadcasting in January 2003, in which it suggested that the range of broadcasters required to carry PPBs should be increased.[143] Another possible way of extending the reach of political parties is by means of paid political advertising. However, paid political advertising is currently banned under 319 (2) (g) and 321 (2) of Communications Act 2003. The ban enjoys widespread support and it is not likely that it would be lifted. The main concern is again that the political process would otherwise be hijacked by the wealthier parties.[144] As the BBC does not carry paid advertising, the ban is not very relevant in its case.

6.3 Broadcasts of General Interest

The BBC is required to promote understanding of the UK political system, including through dedicated coverage of Parliamentary matters, and to transmit an impartial account day by day of the proceedings in both Houses of Parliament.[145] The BBC may be required to broadcast announcements by Government Ministers in exceptional circumstances, such as an emergency or a decision to go to war. The BBC must meet the cost of doing so itself and may disclose that it is broadcasting the announcement pursuant to such a request.[146] Weather and traffic information are an implicit part of the BBC's general information remit.

139. Ofcom Code, s. 6.4, 6.5.
140. *Ibid.*, s. 6.6.
141. *Ibid.*, s. 6.7.
142. *Ibid.*, s. 6.9, 6.10. This also applies to the BBC.
143. Electoral Commission, *Party Political Broadcasting: Report and Recommendations* (London, The Electoral Commission, 2003).
144. DCMS, *Party Political Broadcasting: Public Consultation*, July 2004, p. 5; contra Fenwick and Phillipson, *Media Freedom*, pp. 1012–1014.
145. BBC Agreement, s. 6 (2) (a).
146. BBC Agreement, s. 81 (3).

7. CULTURAL OBLIGATIONS

7.1 High Culture

The stimulation of creativity and cultural excellence is one of the BBC's newly acquired public purposes. The BBC is asked to enrich the cultural life of the UK through creative excellence in distinctive and original content; to foster creativity and nurture talent; and to promote interest, engagement and participation in cultural activity among new audiences. In doing so, the Trust must have regard amongst other things to the need for the BBC to have a film strategy; and the need for appropriate coverage of sport, including sport of minority interest.[147] This public purpose is not specific to cultural programmes in a narrow sense but applies across a wide range of genres and output including entertainment programmes that remain a key priority for the BBC.[148] However, the BBC has committed itself to providing a minimum of 45 hours of arts and music in 2006/2007.[149]

7.2 Regional Programmes

Representing the UK, its nations, regions and communities is another BBC public purpose. The BBC is asked to reflect and strengthen cultural identities through original content at local, regional and national level, on occasion bringing audiences together for shared experiences; and to promote awareness of different cultures and alternative viewpoints, through content that reflects the lives of different people and different communities within the UK. In doing so, the Trust must have regard amongst other things to the importance of reflecting different religious and other beliefs; and the importance of appropriate provision in minority languages.[150] The BBC is committed to the promotion of minority languages. There is a regular Thursday evening slot for Gaelic broadcasting on BBC Two. Also, the BBC has a longstanding commitment to provide 520 hours free of charge to the Welsh-language television channel S4C.[151] The latter has been very successful, giving a boost to the Welsh language and producing outstanding films.[152] The BBC also has a Gaelic Language Service for Scotland.

The importance given to the regional dimension in the United Kingdom is reflected in the governance of the BBC. Four ordinary members of the Trust are designated the Trust member for England, for Scotland, for Wales and for Northern Ireland respectively.[153] They are assisted by four Audience Councils covering the

147. BBC Agreement, s. 8.
148. BBC Trust, *BBC Public Purpose Remit: Stimulating creativity and cultural excellence*, January 2007, p. 2.
149. BBC, *BBC Statements of Programme Policy 2006/2007*, p. 6.
150. BBC Agreement, s. 9.
151. BBC, *BBC Annual Report and Accounts*, p. 57.
152. Prosser, 'United Kingdom', pp. 103, 111.
153. BBC Charter, Art. 14.

same regions. Their role is 'to bring the diverse perspectives of licence fee payers to bear on the work of the Trust'.[154] The Council of England is the largest one because it is supported by a network of regional Audience Councils, one for every broadcasting region in England. The BBC's current target for the provision of regional programming amounts to 6580 hours per year. Moreover, the BBC is obliged to secure that a suitable proportion of its programmes is made outside the so-called M25 area, i.e. outside London.[155] The target is currently one third of its programmes. The commissioning and production across the UK will increase over the coming years as significant parts of the BBC production base are set to be relocated to Greater Manchester.

7.3 Education

The BBC is required to promote education and learning by stimulating interest in, and knowledge of, a full range of subjects and issues through content that is accessible and can encourage either formal or informal learning; and by providing specialist educational content and accompanying material to facilitate learning at all levels and for all ages.[156] Education and learning have always been at the heart of the BBC's mission and they play a central role in the delivery of all its public purposes.[157] The BBC has a vast range of resources at its disposal, and in particular departments dedicated to education, its renowned Open University production centre at Milton Keynes, the BBC's own archive as well as a website devoted to online learning.[158]

On the one hand, it sees its current role in supplying a wide array of digital material to support formal and informal learning. Its particular public service contribution consists in helping audiences navigate the sheer quantity of information available on demand and in providing authoritative, trustworthy and accurate material via a range of platforms.[159] On the other hand, the BBC is aware of the 'digital divide' and seeks to meet the learning needs of those with restricted access, or no access, to digital technologies. So as to pre-empt the likely reactions of competitors, the BBC stresses that its main role is to be complementary to the market by meeting education needs that cannot be adequately catered for by others in the market in terms of quality, reach or quantity and by providing services directly to the learner.[160]

154. BBC Charter, Art. 39.
155. BBC Agreement, s. 51.The M25 London Orbital Motorway is used as a geographical boundary for London.
156. BBC Agreement, s. 7.
157. BBC Trust, *BBC Public Purpose Remit:Promoting Education and Learning*, January 2007, p. 5.
158. BBC, 'Online Learning, Support and Advice' <www.bbc.co.uk/learning>, 20 February 2007.
159. BBC Trust, *BBC Public Purpose Remit:Promoting Education and Learning*, January 2007, p. 6.
160. *Ibid.*, p. 8.

7.4 Religious Programmes

Religious broadcasting was characterized by the BBC Director General in January 2006 as the most controversial subject of his tenure at the BBC due to 'a post-9/11 sensitivity to religious belief'.[161] Ofcom considers religious programming to be 'core PSB territory' even though its review of public service broadcasting suggested that it is not particularly valued by viewers.[162] The House of Lords Select Committee suggested that the BBC must find innovative ways of tackling issues of religion across all programme genres so as to engage audiences.[163] Criticisms have also been voiced that the BBC does not provide sufficient background knowledge when news stories touch on religious issues and that it does not portray all religions fairly. The new Agreement does not specifically stress that religious programming needs to be objective. However, the accuracy and high quality of broadcasting are standards against which the BBC is measured in religious as in other output.[164]

7.5 Cultural Quotas

The BBC must allocate in agreement with Ofcom a certain proportion of time to the broadcasting of original productions, split between peak viewing times and other times.[165] BBC One for instance committed itself to dedicating a 70 per cent of hours, and 90 per cent of hours in peak, to originations (first shows and repeats) in 2006/2007.[166] The BBC is also obliged to use its best endeavours to ensure that 50 per cent of its airtime is reserved for programmes made by the BBC through its in-house production facility.[167] Conversely, it must secure that at least 25 per cent of the total broadcasting time allocated to qualifying programmes in BBC One and in BBC Two is devoted to the broadcasting of a range and diversity of independent productions.[168] This quota exceeds the independent quota under Article 5 of the TwF Directive. The United Kingdom has not adopted any quota as regards the broadcasting of programmes of European origin. The Broadcasting Act 1990 only refers to a 'proper proportion' of programmes of European origin.[169] However, the BBC agrees targets with Ofcom regarding the programming of European output each calendar year.

---

161. House of Lords Select Committee on BBC Charter Review, *Further Issues for BBC Charter Review*, 2nd Report of Session 2005–06, HL 128-1 (London, HMSO, 2006), para. 142.
162. Ofcom, *Ofcom Review of Public Service Television Broadcasting: Phase 1: Is Television Special?* (London, Ofcom, 2004) Figure 33.
163. *Further Issues for BBC Charter Review*, 2nd Report of Session 2005–06, HL 128-1, para.150.
164. BBC Agreement, s. 14 (1), 44 (1); Communications Act 2003, s. 319 (2) (e), 319 (6); *See* DCMS, *Government Response to the Lords Select Committee Report 'Further Issues for BBC Charter review'* (Cm 6787, 2006), p. 9.
165. BBC Agreement, s. 49.
166. BBC, *BBC Statements of Programme Policy 2006/2007*, p. 10.
167. BBC Agreement, s. 56.
168. BBC Agreement, s. 52; Para. 1 (1) of Schedule 12 to the Communications Act 2003.
169. For instance, Broadcasting Act 1990, s. 25 (2) (e) for Channel 4.

These targets are monitored by Ofcom and by the Trust.[170] BBC Three and BBC Four committed themselves to broadcasting at least 90 per cent and 70 per cent of programme hours of EU/EEA origin respectively in 2006/2007.[171]

8. ADVERTISING

8.1 Background

Ofcom has contracted out its responsibility for advertising content regulation to two independent bodies: the Broadcast Committee of Advertising Practice (BCAP) and the Advertising Standards Authority Broadcast (ASA (B)). However under this co-regulatory scheme, ultimate responsibility remains with Ofcom. In particular, Ofcom is directly responsible for advertising scheduling policy as well as sponsorship. BCAP is responsible for code-making, while ASA (B) is responsible for enforcing the codes. BCAP has adopted the codes of the former ITC, *inter alia* the Television Advertising Standards Code and the BCAP Rules on Scheduling of Television Advertisements comprising s. 4 of the former ITC Rules on the amount and Scheduling of Advertising. Advertisements are not reviewed prior to broadcast. ASA (B) exercises its monitoring powers afterwards, even though most television advertisements are cleared in advance by the Broadcast Advertising Clearance Centre (BACC) pursuant to a voluntary procedure.[172]

8.2 The Principle of Separation

The BBC is not allowed to carry advertising on its public television programmes.[173] According to the BBC Editorial guidelines, product placement is also illegal.[174] At the same time, the BBC Editorial Guidelines acknowledge that the Corporation needs to reflect the real world and that this will involve referring to commercial products, organizations and services in its output. However, such references must be clearly editorially justified. Also, when products are used as props in drama, comedy or entertainment, a range must be used over time to avoid undue prominence, especially if the props are accepted free or at a reduced cost. Where free or discounted props are accepted, it is essential not to guarantee that any product or service will be featured and if featured that it will be

---

170. Ofcom and BBC Trust, *Memorandum of Understanding between the Office of Communications (Ofcom) and the BBC Trust* (London, Ofcom, 2007) p. 5.
171. BBC, *BBC Statements of Programme Policy 2006/2007*, p. 20.
172. Hans-Bredow-Institut, 'Final Report: Study on Co-Regulation Measures in the Media Sector', June 2006 <www.ec.europa.eu/avpolicy/docs/library/studies/coregul/coregul-final-report_en.pdf>, 18 July 2007, pp. 90–91.
173. BBC Agreement, s. 76 (1) (a).
174. BBC, 'Editorial Guidelines' <www.extdev.bbc.co.uk/guidelines/editorialguidelines/edguide/editorial/index.shtml>, 26 January 2007.

in a favourable light. In September 2005 allegations of product placement on BBC programmes were made by the Sunday Times. The investigation carried out by the BBC rebutted many of these allegations but found that there were indeed instances of not fully editorially justified product prominence in some of its programmes.[175]

Section Ten of the Ofcom Broadcasting Code, entitled 'Commercial references and Other Matters' introduces the principle of separation between the advertising and programme elements of a service.[176] This Section does not, however, apply to BBC services funded by the licence fee or grant in aid. The following examination therefore concerns the commercial public service broadcasters. Rule 10.4 of the Broadcasting Code prohibits the giving of any undue prominence to a product or service in a programme. Undue prominence may result from the lack of editorial justification for a commercial reference or from the manner in which the reference is made. Ofcom found, for instance, that Channel 4 gave undue prominence to the energy drink Red Bull in its Richard and Judy show, both in the number of direct references to this product and also in the use of an 'expert' and sporting personalities linked to the product and extolling the benefits of caffeine and Red Bull.[177]

Under Rule 10.5 of the Broadcasting Code, product placement is prohibited. Product placement is defined as 'the inclusion of, or a reference to, a product or service within a programme in return for payment or other valuable consideration to the programme maker or broadcaster (or any representative or associate of either)'. References to products or services acquired at no, or less than full cost, are not considered to be product placement where their inclusion within the programme is justified editorially.[178] A further exception from the prohibition of product placement applies to the inclusion of products or services in programmes acquired from outside the UK and films made for cinema, provided that the broadcaster does not directly benefit from the arrangement.[179]

The Guidance Notes acknowledge that there cannot be an absolute prohibition on the appearance of branded products or services within programmes given that they are an integral part of modern society. Editorial justification will therefore depend on the nature of the programme, and there may be certain types of programme, such as sports and music coverage in television programmes, where there is a general acceptance that brands will feature.[180]

The Code also makes special reference to programme-related material, i.e. products and services that are both directly derived from a specific programme and intended to allow listeners and viewers to benefit fully from, or to interact with, that

---

175. BBC, 'Press Releases: BBC Statement on Product Placement Allegations', 24 October 2005 <www.bbc.co.uk/pressoffice/pressreleases/stories/2005/10_october/24/product.shtml>, 26 January 2007.
176. *See also* the BCAP Television Advertising Standards Code, s. 2.1.1.
177. Ofcom Content Sanctions Committee, 19 July 2004.
178. Ofcom Code, s. 10.5.
179. *Ibid.*
180. Ofcom, Guidance Notes, Section 10: Commercial References and Other Matters (London, Ofcom, 2006).

programme. Such material may only be promoted in programmes where it is editorially justified.[181] In a case concerning a lifestyle magazine launched by Channel 4, Ofcom found that it did not satisfy the Code's criteria for product-related material. The magazine was very similar to other homes and interiors magazines on the market and contained very few references to Channel 4 programmes in any of the features. Ofcom clarified that similarity, in terms of genre or theme, between a programme and product or service is not in itself sufficient to establish that the product or service is 'directly derived' from the programme.[182] The broadcaster would need to demonstrate that the material in question is directly derived *to a significant extent* from each of the programmes and that it is editorially based.[183]

Finally, as far as advertisements for merchandise based on children's programmes are concerned, the BCAP Rules on the Scheduling of Television Advertisements require that they must not be broadcast in any of the two hours proceeding or succeeding the relevant programme.[184] The ASA reserves, however, the right to require a wider separation in the case of some programmes, or even a prohibition of any advertising while a particular series is running. Also, advertisements in which characters from children television programmes (including puppets etc.) present or positively endorse products or services of special interest to children must not be broadcast before 9 P.M.[185] This restriction does not apply to public service announcements or to characters specially created for advertisements.

Ofcom launched a consultation in December 2005 on a possible relaxation of the separation principle and of the rules on product placement in line with the debate taking place at European level in the framework of the TwF Directive review.[186] In this consultation Ofcom tested the water for a limited and controlled introduction of product placement into certain genres of programmes. Eager to tap this potentially 'rich revenue stream for broadcasters and independent production companies',[187] Ofcom argued that UK viewers are already familiar with product placement in other media, including feature films and imported US drama. The thrust of the consultation was in carefully circumscribing the genres of programmes that could be allowed to carry product placement. Also, Ofcom discussed regulatory measures to effect a smooth transition from principles of separation to viewer transparency, expressing a preference for upfront disclosure. However, the responses received to this consultation led Ofcom to conclude that there is no consensus on the deregulation of product placement at the moment and that predicted economic benefits appear to remain modest. It kept the option

181. Ofcom Code, s. 10.6.
182. This has also been clarified in the Ofcom Guidance Notes, s. 10.
183. *Ibid.*
184. BCAP Rules on the Scheduling of Television Advertisements, s. 4.2.2.
185. *Ibid.*, s. 4.2.4 (a); 4.2.7 (c).
186. Ofcom, *Product Placement: A Consultation on Issues Related to Product Placement* (London, Ofcom, 2005).
187. Grant, 'Ofcom Buys into Product Placement', 118.

open to introduce changes once the review of the TwF Directive has been concluded.[188]

8.3 Advertising and Minors

.Detailed rules concerning the content of advertising directed at minors are laid down in Section Seven of the Television Advertising Standards Code. The rules concern the topics of misleading advertising, pressure to purchase and harm and distress. Advertisements must not take advantage of children's inexperience or credulity, for example by arousing unrealistic expectations or by referring to product characteristics which are not easy for children of the appropriate age to judge.[189] Advertisements for expensive toys whose retail price is above a figure specified by ASA and BCAP must include an indication of their price.[190] The rules on pressure to purchase not only outlaw direct exhortation in line with Article 16 (1) (a) of the TwF Directive but also unfair pressure to children by implying that they will be 'inferior to others, disloyal, or will have let someone down, if they or their family do not use a particular product or service'.[191] The Code includes extensive rules aimed at the avoidance not just of physical but also of mental harm that could be inflicted on children by advertisements condoning criminal activities and aggression, disparaging education, high personal standards and caring qualities and encouraging boorish, greedy or anti-social behaviour.[192] The Code recommends appropriate timing restrictions for advertisements that may harm or distress children of particular ages.[193] Further, the BCAP Rules on the Scheduling of Television Advertisements contain mandatory scheduling restrictions for advertising of certain categories of products such as alcoholic drinks and lotteries.[194]

9. PROTECTION OF MINORS

In contrast to the position in other European countries, the law in Great Britain is not only concerned with the protection of minors but also of adults from violent or sexually explicit programmes. The Communications Act 2003 requires Ofcom to set standards that protect persons under the age of 18 and other members of the public from the inclusion in television services of offensive and harmful material.[195] By including for the first time a specific obligation to protect those

188. Ofcom, *Product Placement: Summary of Responses to Consultation on Issues Related to Product Placement* (London, Ofcom, 2006).
189. BCAP, Television Advertising Standards Code, s. 7.1
190. *Ibid.*, s. 7.1.4.
191. *Ibid.*, s. 7.2.2.
192. *Ibid.*, s. 7.3.1.
193. *Ibid.*, s. 7.3.7.
194. BCAP Rules on the Scheduling of Television Advertisements, s. 4.2.1.
195. Communications Act 2003, s. 319 (1), (2) (a), (f).

under 18, the Communications Act 2003 put greater emphasis on the protection of the young. The 1990 Act only required that broadcasters should not offend against 'good taste or decency' regardless of the age of the audience.[196]

Section 319 (4) of the 2003 Act contains a non-exhaustive list of factors to be taken into account by Ofcom in setting or revising any standards. These include the degree of harm or offence likely to be caused by the inclusion of any particular sort of material in programmes; the likely size and composition of the potential audience and likely expectation of the audience; the extent to which the nature of a programme's content can be brought to the attention of the potential audience; the effect of the material on viewers and listeners who may come across it unawares; the identification of changes affecting the nature of a service.

This provision stresses the importance of context in scheduling material. In other words, offensive material should only be cut if it is not justified by the composition and likely expectations of the audience. Appropriate information about a programme should be broadcast so as to avoid inadvertent viewing of offensive material. Ofcom is asked not to regulate in a too heavy-handed manner but to take into account the desirability of maintaining the independence of editorial control over programme-content.[197] Standards should be set in a way that best protects freedom of expression for adults.

Indeed, Ofcom has adopted a less intrusive regulatory approach to material intended for adult audiences. With this aim in mind, the Ofcom Code distinguishes more clearly than its predecessor, the ITC Code, between provisions protecting those under 18 and provisions for the protection of adults. Section One of the Code seeks to ensure that people under 18 are protected. Section Two states that it is designed not only to protect adults but also people under 18. It is, however, fair to assume that its provisions apply mainly to adults.[198]

Material that might seriously impair the physical, mental or moral development of people under 18 must not be broadcast.[199] This provision mirrors Article 22 (1) of the TwF Directive. The Code is less precise as far as material is concerned that might merely impair the development of minors. It obliges broadcasters to take all reasonable steps to protect people under 18, even to a greater extent than is required by the Directive.[200] It does not, however, give further guidance as to the steps that need to be taken.

As far as children are concerned, i.e. people under the age of 15 years, they are to be protected by appropriate scheduling from material that is unsuitable for them.[201] The reference to unsuitable material is vaguer than the language used in Article 22 (1) 2 of the Directive. Appropriate scheduling consists in observing the watershed and in taking into account the likely number and age of children in

196. Broadcasting Act 1990, s. 6 (1) (a).
197. Communications Act 2003, s. 319 (4) (f).
198. Fenwick and Phillipson, *Media Freedom*, p. 601.
199. Ofcom Broadcasting Code, s. 1.1.
200. *Ibid.*, s. 1.2.
201. *Ibid.*, s. 1.3.

the audience as well as the nature of the channel and of the particular programme.[202]

The watershed for free-to-air television is at 9 P.M. More adult material should appear later in the schedule and the transition to it should not be unduly abrupt at the watershed.[203] The Ofcom Content Board found that the BBC had contravened the Ofcom Code in its scheduling of *Pulp Fiction* soon after the watershed, at 21.10 on a Saturday night, on the basis that the film contained seriously offensive material from the start.[204] Even before the watershed broadcasters are asked to give, if appropriate, clear information about content that may distress some children taking the context into account. Greater latitude is afforded premium subscription film services where the watershed is at 8 P.M. There is no watershed for premium subscription film services or pay per view services that are protected by a mandatory PIN or other equivalent devices, although 'R18' material is banned.[205] The relaxation of the rules for subscription services is questionable in view of the doubtful effectiveness of PIN protection systems.[206]

The Ofcom Code contains further guidance on the depiction of issues such as drugs, smoking, solvents and alcohol; violence; offensive language; exorcism, the occult and the paranormal, which are either prohibited before the watershed or are only allowed if there is editorial justification. Some of these issues are also taken up in Section Two on Harm and Offence where the emphasis is on whether they are justified by the context. The meaning of context, explained in s. 2.3 of the Code, largely mirrors s. 319 (4) of the Communications Act. The Code makes the point that giving information to bring the nature of the content to the attention of the potential audience may be an important factor in avoiding offence.

The importance of giving clear warnings also became evident from Ofcom's treatment of complaints by viewers against the use in various television news bulletins of CCTV footage depicting an unprovoked knife attack on two students.[207] The BBC used the disturbing pictures in an early evening news bulletin. However, the complaint was not upheld given that the BBC warned the viewers of the 'appalling' nature of the pictures to come and froze the images before the actual stabbing could be seen. Ofcom also accepted the existence of a public interest justification in alerting the public to the problem of violent crime. Warnings may

---

202. *Ibid.*, s. 1.3, 1.4.
203. *Ibid.*, s. 1.6.
204. Ofcom, 'Standards Cases: Pulp Fiction, 7 August 2004' <www.ofcom.org.uk/tv/obb/prog_cb/pcb49/>, 16 July 2007.
205. Ofcom Broadcasting Code, s. 1.4, 1.22, 1.23. The British Board of Film Classification (BBFC) reserves the R18 rating for films that are sexually explicit to a degree that exceeds the adult – 18-category. Such films can only be viewed on segregated premises. The BBFC is an independent body that classifies and censors films and videos on the basis of published Guidelines, taking criminal law and the Obscene Publications Act 1959 into account.
206. Ofcom, *Research into the Effectiveness of PIN protection systems in the UK: A Report of the Key Findings of Research among Schoolchildren Aged 11–17, and a Separate Study of Parents* (London, Ofcom, 2005).
207. Ofcom, 'In Breach: News, 23 June 2006' <www.ofcom.org.uk/tv/obb/prog_cb/obb68/>, 16 July 2007.

therefore not be sufficient in themselves if the material is not handled in an appropriate manner and if there is no editorial justification.

10. RIGHT OF REPLY

In British law there is no right of reply to an assertion of incorrect facts in a television programme. The only remedy that vaguely resembles the right of reply under Article 23 of the TwF Directive is the right of complaint to Ofcom. Any individual, association or corporate body that has been affected by a television programme may make such a complaint. The 'person affected' is someone who was either a participant in the programme and may have been the subject of the alleged unfair treatment or, whether a participant or not, had a sufficiently direct interest in the subject matter.[208] The term 'direct interest' has often been the subject of judicial interpretation in the past. Standing of potential applicants has been interpreted in a very narrow sense.[209] Ofcom may refuse to entertain a fairness complaint if it has not been made within a reasonable time after the broadcast of the programme: 50 calendar days for satellite and cable programmes and 80 calendar days for terrestrial television programmes.

Before Ofcom can entertain a fairness complaint, a number of criteria need to be satisfied. First, the complainant must be 'the person affected' or someone properly authorized to act on behalf of 'the person affected'. Secondly, the matters complained of must not be the subject of legal proceedings in the UK or more appropriately resolved by legal proceedings in the UK. Thirdly, the complaint must not be frivolous, and, finally, it must not be inappropriate to entertain or proceed with consideration of the complaint for any other reason.[210] These statutory requirements leave no doubt that the right of complaint to Ofcom is not an equivalent remedy to the right of reply. Its subsidiary nature compared to the avenue of judicial review is incompatible with the qualification in Article 23 of the TwF Directive that the right of reply must be granted 'without prejudice to other provisions adopted by the Member States under civil, administrative or criminal law'.[211]

Fairness cases are decided either by the Executive Fairness Group or by the Fairness Committee. The Executive Fairness Group, which is made up of members from Ofcom's executive, deals with straightforward cases. More complex cases are referred to the Fairness Committee, which consists of a minimum of three members

---

208. Broadcasting Act 1996, s. 130 (1) (a); Ofcom, 'Outline Procedures for Handling Fairness and Privacy Complaints' (London, Ofcom, 2006).
209. *See R v. Broadcasting Complaints Commission, ex p. British Broadcasting Corporation* [1994] EMLR 497; *R v. Broadcasting Complaints Commission, ex p. British Broadcasting Corporation* [1995] EMLR 241. A wider interpretation of 'direct interest' was given in *R v. Broadcasting Complaints Commission ex p. Channel 4 Television Limited* [1995] EMLR 170.
210. Broadcasting Act 1996, Art. 114 (2).
211. Barendt, *Broadcasting Law*, p. 164.

drawn from the Content Board. It is also responsible for reviewing decisions made by the Executive Fairness Group.

Ofcom normally publishes a copy of its decision on fairness complaints in the Ofcom broadcast bulletin on its website. If a complaint is upheld or partly upheld, Ofcom may also direct the broadcaster to transmit a summary of its decision, which can be commented upon by both parties. This is normally the case when the complainant's legitimate interests have been seriously damaged so that a remedy in addition to the publication in the Ofcom broadcast bulletin is required. Statutory sanctions may also be imposed on the broadcaster.[212] It becomes apparent once again that the right of complaint to Ofcom is not a right of reply. The transmission of the summary of Ofcom's decision is not tantamount to the broadcast of the complainant's answer.

212. Ofcom, 'Outline Procedures for Handling Fairness and Privacy Complaints', p. 9.

Chapter 8
Conclusion

Having examined the systems of public broadcasting in France, Germany, Greece, Italy, the Netherlands and the United Kingdom, it is possible to discern considerable commonalities among them, which arguably amount to a 'European audiovisual model', a 'common law of European broadcasting systems'.[1] All of the countries under examination subscribe to the principle of balanced pluralism, to the need for public broadcasters to reflect a diversity of views in all areas of programming, and to allocate airtime to political parties in election periods in accordance with the principles of fairness, equal opportunity and proportionate representation. They all require public broadcasters to transmit governmental announcements and other messages of general interest. All six broadcasting systems impose cultural obligations on their public broadcasters next to the European and independent quotas of the TwF Directive. They all subscribe to the principle of separation of advertising from editorial content, to the need to protect minors and to grant a right of reply against offending broadcasts. Some of these commonalities can be attributed to the TwF Directive's harmonization impetus, leading to a certain convergence in national broadcasting regulation across Europe.[2]

However, the considerable commonalities in the canon of public broadcasting standards adhered to by these countries cannot mask the diversity of their public broadcasting systems. Which are, broadly speaking, the unique features of these broadcasting systems?

The French broadcasting system is mainly characterised by the view of television as a cultural asset that needs to be protected from an onslaught of bland, uniform American or other international productions. To this end, programming and investment quotas are imposed that go beyond the requirements of the TwF Directive, and the mandatory use of the French language is rigorously overseen.

1. Holznagel, *Rundfunkrecht in Europa*, p. 355: 'Gemeinrecht europäischer Rundfunkordnungen'.
2. Harcourt, *Regulation of Media Markets*, p. 158 *et seq.*, 194.

The German broadcasting system places less emphasis on cultural protection and quotas than on pluralism. Public broadcasters are asked to ensure that their internally pluralistic organs bring a diversity of viewpoints to bear on their programming. Quotas are viewed with suspicion in Germany since they fit uneasily with the fundamental constitutional principle that broadcasting should be free from state control. The same uneasiness is displayed towards the recent calls by the European Commission for a clearer definition of the public service remit.

The Greek broadcasting system is marked by the domination of television by the state. The constitutional principle of direct state control over broadcasting– an outdated remainder of the old glorified ideal of national television – does little to guarantee the respect for programme standards that are enshrined in the law or to support the chronically under-funded and relatively unpopular public television.

The Italian and Greek broadcasting systems share their well-known subjugation to political interests. In Italy, the public broadcaster RAI is notoriously dominated by the government and the political parties while external pluralism suffers from the quasi monopoly of the private Mediaset. Nonetheless, the Italian television industry is of the most dynamic ones in Europe and RAI enjoys great popularity, its audience shares exceeding those of Mediaset.

The Dutch public broadcasting system, a collection of independent member-based and non-member-based broadcasting organizations, represents a unique solution to the problem of how to represent all currents of thought in a multicultural society. However, the responsiveness of the pillars of Dutch public broadcasting to the needs of the different groups within society, especially of the immigrants and young people, has been dwindling in recent times. The modernization of public broadcasting is a perennial issue in Dutch media policy, but reform is not forthcoming.

On the other hand, the governance of the BBC, the foremost English public broadcaster, has been significantly reformed under the new Charter and Agreement. The BBC Governors were replaced by a Trust, and an Executive Board was established with the aim of overcoming the dark legacy of the Hutton Inquiry. Still, the reform has left many pressing issues untouched, not least BBC's tenuous relationship with the super-regulator Ofcom. On the European front, the detailed definition of BBC's public purposes in the new Charter together with the rigorous accountability mechanisms to which the BBC is subject meet the European Commission's expectations to a great extent.

The structures of public broadcasting in the countries under examination also differ considerably.[3] Greece, Italy and the United Kingdom possess integrated structures where ERT, RAI and the BBC control every aspect of public broadcasting activity. Germany has a federated structure, which is made up of regional public broadcasting organisations in line with the country's political organization.

---

3. *See* Council of Europe, *Report of the Committee on Culture, Science and Education: Public Service Broadcasting*, Doc. 10029 (Strasbourg, Council of Europe, 2004), para. 27.

France and the Netherlands have fragmented structures where separate public operators control the different segments of the audiovisual sector.

A standard to which all countries examined in this comparative study adhere is the ideal of independence of public broadcasting from the state. This ideal is only imperfectly realized to differing degrees depending on each country's idiosyncrasy, its broadcasting history and its political culture. It is tempting to distinguish between the so-called 'Anglo-Saxon model' present in Germany, the Netherlands and the United Kingdom and the 'Latin model' present in France, Italy and Greece in accordance with the criteria developed by the *Conseil Superieur de' l Audiovisuel* (CSA) in a 1998 report on public broadcasting in Europe.[4] Countries following the Anglo-Saxon model grant public broadcasters considerable independence from the state as well as sufficient funding. In countries following the 'Latin model' the state and the political parties are actively involved in public broadcasting, and the public funding afforded to it is insufficient.

Indeed, the level of the licence fee is low in France, even lower in Italy and minimal in Greece. Political influence is notorious in Italy and institutionalized in Greece. In France, the state also holds a firm grip over public broadcasting by releasing the *cahiers des charges*, by deciding on its financing and by selecting the members of the CSA. Nonetheless, in the three 'Anglo-Saxon countries' the state has not kept aloof from public broadcasting either. In Germany, the administration of public broadcasting is dominated by the political parties. In the Netherlands, the licence fee was replaced in 2000 by a levy on income tax, enabling state authorities to decide on the amount of funding for public broadcasting. In the United Kingdom, the renewal of the BBC's licence depends on the goodwill of the government, which is also allowed to 'censor' it by directing it not to air certain broadcasts. The licence fee is also set by the government.

The range of approaches towards the principle of independence of public broadcasting from state control is also characteristic of the other standards examined in this study. In France, all broadcasters are obliged to allocate free airtime for election and political broadcasts, but only the public broadcasters transmit the official campaign broadcasts. France has been applying the principle of pluralism to political and election broadcasts in very exacting ways, minutely measuring the time allocated to the government, the parliamentary majority and the opposition. Only very recently, did it give up the quantitative evaluation of political broadcasts in favour of a more qualitative approach. In Germany, political parties have rights of access to public television only in some of the *Länder* and only during the electoral period. Airtime is allocated according to the latest results and other factors related to the parties' importance. A similar method of distributing broadcasting time during the electoral period, based on the principle of 'proportional equality', is followed in Greece. Outside the election period, airtime is allocated according to the principle of equity.

4. H. Bourges, 'La télévision publique en Europe' (1998) 111 *La lettre du CSA*, 3.

In Italy, a quantitative approach is applied similar to the one used in France until recently. During the official campaign period, airtime is allocated according to the *par condicio* law. Outside this period, *messagi autogestiti* are offered according to the principle of three-thirds: one third for the government, one third for the parliamentary majority and one third for the opposition. In the Netherlands, outside the election period, all parties which have gained one or more seats in the House of Representatives or in the Senate in the previous election receive the same broadcasting time regardless of their size or importance. During the election period, new parties can also apply for broadcasting time. In the last phase of the election campaign, airtime is distributed according to a system of proportional access, taking the latest results of the political parties into account. Finally, in the United Kingdom, both the BBC and the licensed public service broadcasters are obliged to make airtime available to registered parties and designated organizations for party political broadcasts, including party election broadcasts, and referendum campaign broadcasts. In practice, the allocation of broadcasts emerges from the Broadcasters' Liaison Group where broadcasters work together with the Electoral Commission and Ofcom to ensure a consistent approach.

As has already been noted, cultural obligations are most pronounced in France, which jealously guards over the French language. Public and private broadcasters alike have far-reaching obligations to broadcast and produce audiovisual and cinematographic works made originally in French. German public broadcasters have been entrusted with a special cultural responsibility by the German Constitutional Court, and consider culture to be one of the most important aspects of their programming.[5] As in France, however, cultural programming is often relegated to the late hours of the day or to thematic channels. In Germany, there are no precise cultural quotas as they would go against the grain of the highly valued programming autonomy of broadcasters. The quota rules of the TwF Directive have been rather loosely transposed into German law.

The main cultural concern of the Greek broadcasting system is the protection of the quality of the Greek language and the promotion and dissemination of the Greek civilization and tradition. Besides certain obligations related to the editing, presentation and subtitling of programmes, Greek broadcasters need to transmit a fixed percentage of works produced in the Greek language. The Italian public broadcaster RAI does not have particular obligations as far as the use of the Italian language is concerned, but is specifically obliged to broadcast in the languages of the Autonomous Regions and Provinces. Education and religion are important aspects of RAI's programming.

In the Netherlands, language policy centres on the promotion of the two official languages, Dutch and Friesian. The cultural diversity of the country is also catered for by the establishment of a great number of local and regional broadcasting organisations. Besides the European quotas, specific quotas exist for informational, educational and cultural programming. In the United Kingdom, the cultural obligations of

---

5. C. Palzer, 'Germany' in *Iris Special: The Public Service Broadcasting Culture*, European Audiovisual Observatory (ed.) (Strasbourg, European Audiovisual Observatory, 2007), pp. 39, 47.

the BBC have been streamlined by means of its new public purposes. Great importance has always been accorded to the regional dimension of public broadcasting, as becomes evident from the BBC's organisational structure. Education and learning are also at the heart of the BBC's mission. While the law specifies the percentage to be reserved for independent productions, there is no set quota as regards the broadcasting of European works. The programming of European output is agreed between the BBC and Ofcom each calendar year. Specific targets exist also for original and in-house productions.

As far as the principle of separation of advertising from editorial content is concerned, France has adopted a definition of surreptitious advertising that is stricter than the one contained in the TwF Directive. The promotional reference to goods or services in programmes is prohibited regardless of whether the television station has drawn any financial or other advantage. The CSA is particularly concerned that programmes aimed at minors do not contain any product placement. A more lenient approach is taken only as regards surreptitious advertising in cinematographic works. Germany also allows product placement in cinema films that are broadcast on television. As for the rest, Germany has incorporated the Directive's tight definition of surreptitious advertising and requires proof of intentional acting by the broadcaster, evidenced in particular by the existence of remuneration. Obviously, such a proof is very hard to furnish, especially since an unduly narrow view is taken of the concept of remuneration. Nonetheless, certain instances of 'theme placement' have recently been uncovered in public broadcasting. 'Theme placement', the integration of themes or ideas in programmes, is prohibited *par excellence* as it interferes with the editorial integrity of programmes.

Greece has incorporated the Directive's definition of surreptitious advertising. The existence of proof of payment or of other similar consideration is only one factor to be taken into account when establishing the existence of advertising intention. Even in the absence of such payment, the general circumstances of the broadcast may leave no doubt that advertising was intended. Surreptitious advertising is also prohibited in Italy. In order to decide whether there is any advertising intention, AGCOM asks whether the broadcaster has drawn any economic gain but also examines the content, presentation and form of a message. AGCOM's approach has, however, not always been consistent. Product placement is prohibited as a form of surreptitious advertising. Its existence is, however, tolerated in cinematographic works under certain conditions, which were codified in 2004.

The Netherlands have adopted a stricter definition of surreptitious advertising than the one contained in the Directive. Under the Dutch rules, advertising can be surreptitious when the broadcasting company has mentioned or shown products or company names with the intention to serve advertising regardless of whether the public might be misled as a result. Product placement is prohibited in principle, but there are exceptions to this rule. Product placement is allowed if it is editorially justified, the products or services are neither specifically promoted nor presented in an exaggerated manner, and there is no remuneration. As in the other countries, a more lenient approach is taken with regard to acquired material and cinematographic works. The United Kingdom prohibits 'undue prominence' rather than surreptitious advertising. The criterion of 'undue prominence' is more manageable in that it is sufficient to prove the lack of editorial justification for a commercial reference regardless of its capacity to mislead the public or the existence of remuneration. Product placement is also explicitly prohibited. An exception from the prohibition of product placement is made, first, for references to products or services acquired at no or less than full cost where their inclusion within the programme is justified editorially and, second, for programmes acquired from outside the UK and films made for cinema, provided that the broadcaster does not directly benefit from the arrangement.

It follows that, while all of the examined Member States endorse the principle of separation of advertising from editorial content, some interpret the Directive's prohibition of surreptitious advertising more narrowly than others. Also, product placement is explicitly outlawed in the United Kingdom only, whereas the other countries subject it to their rules on surreptitious advertising. All countries have more lenient rules in place for cinematographic works. The Commission takes this regulatory mosaic as its starting point for the liberalization of product placement. However, it is not clearly spelled out why it is imperative to extend to the audiovisual works the more permissive regime which applies to the cinematographic ones. It seems that the expected economic benefits of this initiative, i.e. the creation of new revenue streams and of a level playing field, have weighed more in the Commission's judgment than the serious but less tangible threats for the trustworthiness and editorial integrity of programmes. This is yet another instance of the Commission's conception of television as an economic more than a cultural phenomenon.

Turning now to the protection of minors, France has only partially transposed the TwF Directive's requirements since it allows pornographic and extremely violent programmes on authorized channels. Such programmes fall under the highest category of the French youth certificate rating system, which is based on a classification according to age. Each channel has a viewing committee that is responsible for the classification of programmes. The CSA monitors the coherence of the classifications and the programming hours decided by the channels. It may only take action after a programme has been broadcast. In Germany, the *Jugendmedienschutz-Staatsvertrag* and the broadcasting laws of the *Länder*, which are closely modelled on it, contain two types of rules in accordance with Article 22 of the TwF Directive. First, they absolutely prohibit a range of particularly harmful programmes. Secondly, they allow the transmission of other programmes that might impair the development of minors provided that the broadcaster ensures by technical or other means or by selecting the time of transmission that children of particular ages will not watch them. Classifications of programmes into three categories are carried out by the *Freiwillige Selbstkontrolle der Filmwirtschaft* (FSK). Compliance with this system relies on the social responsibility of public broadcasters which, together with all other national broadcasters, are obliged to appoint Commissioners for Youth Protection.

In Greece, programmes that might seriously impair the development of minors are prohibited. All other programmes are classified by internal committees into five categories that are modelled after the French youth certificate rating system, whose contours are however much more hazy. The NCRTV watches over the implementation of this system. It may only reschedule programmes after their transmission, not beforehand. In Italy, broadcasters have to abide by the provisions of the law and by a self-regulatory instrument, the Code TV and Minors. Until recently, Italian law imposed an absolute prohibition of gratuitously violent and pornographic programmes. This ban was lifted in 2004. It only applies now to a limited period of the day, and exceptions may be made for pay-TV channels. This relaxation of the Italian rules is out of step with the requirements of Article 22 (1) of the TwF Directive. Strangely, cinema films transmitted on television are subject to greater restrictions than television productions. An AGCOM Committee together with the Surveillance Committee of the Code TV and Minors monitor compliance with the law and apply administrative sanctions in cases of violation.

In the Netherlands, regulation concerning classification is provided by the Netherlands Institute for the Classification of Audiovisual Media (NICAM). Only broadcasters that are members of this Institute are allowed to air programmes suitable for viewers older than 12 years of age. Programmes containing hardcore pornography or gratuitous violence are absolutely prohibited in line with Article 22 (1) of the TwF Directive. Since 2001, programmes have been classified into four categories according to the rating system *Kijkwijzer*. Complaints for violations of these rules are dealt with by NICAM in the first instance. The Dutch Media Authority supervises this self-regulatory system. In Great Britain, the law is unique in that it seeks to protect not only minors but also adults from violent or sexually explicit programmes. The Ofcom Code distinguishes more clearly than its predecessor, the ITC Code, between provisions protecting those under the age of 18 and provisions for the protection of adults. Material that might seriously impair the physical, mental or moral development of people under 18 is prohibited. Other material that is unsuitable for minors has to observe the watershed and to be scheduled appropriately. There is no classification system. In accordance with the Communications Act 2003, appropriate scheduling depends on the context, i.e. the composition and likely expectations of the audience.

Finally, as regards the right of reply, it is triggered in France by allegations in a television programme that are likely to affect a person's name or reputation. These allegations do not need to be factual ones nor do they need to be incorrect. The conditions for the exercise of the right of reply in France are therefore less stringent than under Article 23 of the TwF Directive. An even wider right of reply has recently been adopted for the online media. In Germany, the right of reply is granted to every person that has been affected by a factual allegation in a television programme. Again, there is no express requirement that the allegation has to be incorrect.

In Greece, the Constitution requires that the right of reply be granted to anyone affected by an incorrect, defamatory or insulting broadcast. In response to this constitutional imperative, P.D. 100/2000 establishes the right of reply in relation to offending, not necessarily incorrect, broadcasts. It is questionable whether the time span of 20 days allowed for the exercise of this right is sufficient as required by Article 23 (3) of the TwF Directive. In Italy, the right of reply can only be claimed if a person's legitimate interests have been damaged by an assertion of incorrect facts.

The Netherlands have failed to implement Article 23 of the TwF Directive so far. Dutch law does not provide a formal right of reply for fear of excessively restricting broadcasting freedom. Besides the civil remedies available, an injured party can only file a complaint with the Netherlands Press Council. However, not all broadcasters are members of the Council. Moreover, the Council cannot impose binding sanctions, but will only give its opinion on the complaint that will then be published on the Council's website. In the United Kingdom, there is no right of reply either. The right of complaint to Ofcom does not constitute an equivalent remedy to the right of reply given that it is subsidiary to the avenue of judicial review. Also, the only redress offered is the publication on Ofcom's website or the transmission by the broadcaster of a summary of Ofcom's decision.

The overall picture that has resulted from the examination of broadcasting standards in six European countries is one of great diversity. To name but two examples, pluralism requirements in political and election broadcasting have recently been relaxed in France, but not in Italy where airtime is still being allocated on the basis of quantitative criteria. The United Kingdom explicitly bans product placement. The other Member States subject product placement to rules on surreptitious advertising that are of varying rigour. The diversity of the broadcasting standards in these Member States can be put down to their different constitutional traditions and socio-cultural characteristics and to the resulting variable geometry in the implementation of the TwF Directive.

In some respects the six Member States examined in this work exceed the minimum standard set by the Directive, while in others they fall behind it. France, for instance, imposes cultural obligations that are more far-reaching than the quotas set by the TwF Directive, and defines surreptitious advertising more widely than prescribed by the Directive. On the other hand, it has not implemented adequately the Directive's requirements on the protection of minors. The Netherlands have high standards as regards the protection of minors, and NICAM is considered a role model for non-state regulation in this field.[6] However, a formal right of reply has yet to be introduced in this country. Germany has correctly transposed the Directive's provisions on the protection of minors. However, it has implemented the European quota rule in narrow terms, and the independent quota rule inadequately, while defining surreptitious advertising in an unduly restrictive manner.

6. Hans-Bredow-Institut, 'Final Report: Study on Co-Regulation Measures in the Media Sector', June 2006, <www.ec.europa.eu/avpolicy/docs/library/studies/coregul/coregul-final-report_en.pdf>, 12 July 2007, p. 188.

The fact that Member States impose standards on their own broadcasters that are in some respects higher than required by the TwF Directive is not surprising. The method of minimum harmonization has been expressly chosen in an area that is so close to Member States' cultural sensibilities so as to accommodate national diversity above the minimum standards set in the Directive. What is perhaps more surprising is the fact that national laws to some extent still lag behind the Directive's requirements. Obviously, even the minimum standards adopted at EU level are sometimes hard to reconcile with basic tenets of the national broadcasting orders.

The analysis of public service obligations in six jurisdictions has clearly shown that such obligations are at the interface between conflicting constitutional rights and freedoms.[7] Setting broadcasting obligations involves a fine balancing exercise between interests of equal value. Member States hold on to their power to resolve these tensions in accordance with their own constitutional traditions, even in defiance of the imperatives of European Union law. Germany values its constitutional principle of freedom from state control over the quota requirements of the TwF Directive. The Netherlands resist the introduction of a right of reply so as not jeopardize broadcasting freedom. The uneasy relationship between EU law and national constitutional orders, ostensibly settled by the principle of supremacy, might well resurface in the field of broadcasting law.

These questions will be taken up again in the second Part of this book. First, it will be considered whether the Directive's minimum standards sufficiently protect vulnerable values, foremost the development of minors. Secondly, it will be asked whether Member States are in the position to enforce broadcasting standards above and beyond the areas harmonized by the Directive, in view of the constraints imposed by the country of origin principle and by primary EU law. Thirdly, the legality and legitimacy of the divisive European quota rule will be explored. Finally, the third Part of this book will look at an area where the tension between EU law and national constitutional orders looms large: the compatibility of the licence fee for public broadcasting with the EU state aid regime.

---

7. *See* A. Leidinger, 'Programmverantwortung im Spannungsfeld von Programmgrundsätzen und Rundfunkfreiheit' [1989] DVBl, 230.

Part 2

Public Service Obligations between Culture and Commerce

Chapter 9
Introduction

From the very beginning of its involvement in broadcasting, the European Union has been aware of the importance of this area for the problem of striking a balance between the sovereignty of the Member States and the development of a collective European consciousness.[1] The continued existence of national broadcasting systems attests to the close link between television and nationhood. In its first half century, broadcasting was firmly anchored in the sheltered harbour of the nation state. Its beginnings were inspired by the national awareness that arose in the aftermath of the First World War.[2] During this entire period, state regulation of broadcasting was politically necessary in order to capture the public mind and to reinforce allegiance by means of communal symbols. When the need for national reconstruction subsided, after the first two decades of the post-Second World War period, the foundations of national television began to crumble.[3]

It is possible to distinguish between two types of integrative properties of the media: cultural policy and constitutional policy ones.[4] The former category describes the role of television in catering for the society's cultural needs by

---

1. *See* Television without Frontiers: Green Paper on the Establishment of the Common Market for Broadcasting, especially by Satellite and Cable, Summary, 14 June 1984, COM (84) 300 final, 2, 5.
2. M. E. Price, *Television, the Public Sphere and National Identity* (Oxford, Oxford University Press, 1995), p. 5.
3. M. Meckel, *Fernsehen ohne Grenzen? Europas Fernsehen zwischen Integration und Segmentierung*, Studien zur Kommunikationswissenschaft, vol. 3 (Opladen, Westdeutscher Verlag, 1994), p. 73.
4. M. Seidel, 'Europa und die Medien' in *Fernsehen ohne Grenzen: Die Errichtung des Gemeinsamen Marktes für den Rundfunk, insbesondere über Satellit und Kabel*, J. Schwarze (ed.) (Baden-Baden, Nomos, 1985), pp. 121, 123; W. Hoffmann-Riem, 'Europäisierung des Rundfunks – aber ohne Kommunikationsverfassung?' in *Rundfunk im Wettbewerbsrecht: Der öffentlich-rechtliche Rundfunk im Spannungsfeld zwischen Wirtschaftsrecht und Rundfunkrecht*, W. Hoffmann-Riem (ed.), Symposien des Hans-Bredow-Instituts, vol. 10 (Baden-Baden, Nomos, 1988), pp. 201, 203.

providing a programme of high quality, covering national developments, cultivating the language, serving the interests of cultural and other minorities.[5] The latter refers to its capacity as a societally integrative factor through a pluralistic programme that allows the segments of society to approach each other,[6] promotes the public sphere and 'allows a nation to speak to itself'.[7] The distinction between cultural and constitutional policy features of television is rather formalistic since both categories likewise inform the specific relation of television to the nation as identity and as community. These features of television have been traditionally encapsulated in public service obligations such as those examined in the first Part of this book.

The second Part will investigate the influence of European law on the definition and enforcement of programme requirements. It is pertinent to outline briefly the developments that elevated the European Union to a major actor in the field of broadcasting. The introduction of a European dimension in the media laws of the Member States emerged as a necessity in the wake of technological innovations in the 1980s that overcame national borders and opened up public service monopolies.[8] The increased deregulation at the national level called for a framework for the circulation of audiovisual programmes at the European level.

Two organizations grasped the regulatory nettle in Europe: the Council of Europe and the European Community. The Council of Europe opened its Convention on Transfrontier Television for signature on 5 May 1989. The Convention entered into force on 1 May 1993 after its ratification by seven states. The TwF Directive was adopted on 3 October 1989 by the Council of Ministers of the European Community.[9] It was amended by the European Parliament and the Council in 1997.[10] On 1 October 1998, one year after the adoption of the amending Directive, a Protocol amending the Convention on Transfrontier Television was adopted.[11] The Protocol entered into force on 1 March 2002 after having been ratified by all Parties.

---

5. *See* J. G. Blumler and W. Hoffmann-Riem, 'New Roles for Public Service Television' in *Television and the Public Interest: Vulnerable Values in West European Broadcasting*, J. G. Blumler (ed.) (London, Sage, 1992), pp. 202, 211.
6. J. G. Blumler, 'Public Service Broadcasting before the Commercial Deluge' in *Television and the Public Interest: Vulnerable Values in West European Broadcasting*, J. G. Blumler (ed.) (London, Sage, 1992), pp. 7, 11.
7. R. Hoggart, 'The Public Service Idea' in *British Broadcasting: Main Principles* (London, Broadcasting Research Unit, 1983), p. 5.
8. F. Hondius, 'Regulating Transfrontier Television – The Strasbourg Option' (1988) 8 YEL, 146.
9. Council Directive of 3 October 1989 on the coordination of certain provisions laid down by law, regulation or administrative action in Member States concerning the pursuit of television broadcasting activities OJ L 298/23, 1989.
10. European Parliament and Council Directive 97/36/EC of 30 June 1997 amending Council Directive 89/552/EEC on the coordination of certain provisions laid down by law, regulation and administrative action in Member States concerning the pursuit of television broadcasting activities OJ L 202/60, 1997.
11. ETS Nr. 171.

The 1997/98 amendments were punctual. The main changes were the introduction of precise jurisdiction criteria, some amendments in the advertising rules including the regulation of teleshopping, and the establishment of new rules on the exercise of exclusive rights for events of major importance for society. As we have seen, a more radical overhaul of the TwF Directive has recently been completed with the aim of bringing it in line with technological and market developments. A modernized AVMS Directive covering traditional broadcasts and on-demand audiovisual media services entered into force on 11 December 2007. Member States have 24 months to implement the new Directive into national law. The Convention will also need to be aligned with the new Directive so as to avoid a situation where EU Member States which are also parties to the Convention have to comply with two different sets of rules.

Prior to the Directive's modernization, the two instruments – the TwF Directive and the European Convention on Transfrontier Television – were very similar. Nevertheless, their adoption called forth different reactions and a heated controversy as to the forum that would be more apt to regulate media policy. The Convention received a more favourable response. This was partly due to its non-binding nature. Even though all parties to the Convention are obliged to adhere to the Convention's standards, the Standing Committee, which is entrusted with monitoring and ensuring compliance, has no real means of enforcement.[12]

More importantly, the two instruments pursue disparate objectives. The Convention is embedded in the cultural policy tradition of the Council of Europe and seeks to encourage the free flow of information.[13] The Directive is inspired by the Union's free market orientation and aims at the free movement of services in the internal market. While national broadcasting structures deserve respect under the Convention's regime, the Directive's position is that they have to be streamlined. Admittedly, the draft Convention's cultural input has been more pronounced than that of its final version.[14] Still, these differences reflect the basic tendencies of the two instruments.

The dilemma over whether EU audiovisual policy should exclusively aim at the furtherance of economic integration or should also take account of the cultural dimension of television lies at the heart of the Europeanization of this area. We have seen that the beginnings of the EU media policy were marked by the idea that a European television programme should be created that would promote the construction of a European identity. The Green Book 'Television without Frontiers' put an end to this ambitious project and cast the dice in favour of the creation of the internal market by conceptualizing broadcasting as a service.[15] The very

12. P. Goerens, 'Interplay between Relevant European Legal Instruments: ECTT and TVwF Directive: Competition or Complementarity?' in *Iris Special: Audiovisual Media Services without Frontiers: Implementing the Rules*, European Audiovisual Observatory (ed.) (Strasbourg, European Audiovisual Observatory, 2007), pp. 1, 7.
13. K. Dicke, 'Eine europäische Rundfunkordnung für welches Europa?' (1989) 4 MP, 197; *see* Meckel, *Fernsehen ohne Grenzen*, p. 89.
14. Meckel, *Fernsehen ohne Grenzen*, p. 89.
15. COM (84) 300 final.

controversial question as to whether the European Union is competent at all to regulate broadcasting has long been decided *de facto* in its favour.

The economic emphasis of EU audiovisual policy has attracted criticism on two accounts. On the one hand, the European Union has been blamed for treating television like any other commodity despite its cultural significance. On the other hand, it has been criticized for interfering with programming issues, thus going beyond its predominantly economic mandate. This schizophrenic argumentation has led the discussion about the future of European broadcasting to a stalemate.[16]

Two measures of the TwF Directive, the European quota provision and the country of origin principle, best exemplify the real predicament in which EU media policy finds itself, caught between culture and commerce. The focus of the analysis will therefore be on these two aspects of the Directive. At the same time, these measures are of interest, because they touch in diametrically opposed ways upon the power of the Member States to maintain and assert their public broadcasting standards.

As we have already explained, the TwF Directive applies to public and commercial television alike. The observations in this Part of the book are therefore relevant for both branches of the industry. However, our main concern is over the Directive's impact on the capacity of public broadcasters to act as a much needed reference point. It is not expected that the need for such a reference point will diminish in the digital world. High quality, socially beneficial content is still likely to be underprovided by the market.[17] Also, viewers' access to such content on free-to-air television is likely to be increasingly foreclosed by the expansion of pay-TV.

The first of the abovementioned measures, the European quota, by obliging broadcasters to transmit a majority proportion of European works, constitutes a first attempt to regulate the cultural dimension of broadcasting at the European level. It partially supersedes national quotas and partially covers them in a multicultural veneer. It stands for the dirigiste approach to audiovisual policy and was devised as a 'cultural safety-net' to redress the harmful effects of the single broadcasting market.[18] The European quota has been solidly resisted by some Member States since it affected their responsibility with regard to programme content. By contrast, the country of origin principle is the very instrument of liberalization of national broadcasting markets. It views standards as restrictions on retransmission that fall potentially within the fields coordinated by the Directive. It has therefore been condemned for its indiscriminate treatment of the idiosyncratic features of national broadcasting orders.

16. I. Schwartz, 'Rundfunk, EG-Kompetenzen und ihre Ausübung' (1991) 4 ZUM, 165; I. Schwartz, 'EG-Rechtsetzunsbefugnis für das Fernsehen' (1989) 2 ZUM, 389.
17. M. Armstrong and H. Weeds, 'Public Service Broadcasting in the Digital World' in *The Economic Regulation of Broadcasting Markets: Evolving Technology and Challenges for Policy*; P. Seabright and J. von Hagen (eds) (Cambridge, Cambridge University Press, 2007), pp. 81, 116.
18. J. D. Donaldson, ' "Television without Frontiers": The Continuing Tension between Liberal Free Trade and European Cultural Integrity' (1996) 20 Fordham Int'l L J, 143.

The purpose of the present analysis is to explore the extent to which these contradictory impulses in EU media policy have encroached upon the power of the Member States to maintain the national character of their broadcasting orders by means of public service obligations as a distinct type of cultural objectives. This part of the book will look at the constraints imposed on national broadcasting regulation by the country of origin principle and by the rulings of the European Court of Justice on the free movement of services. It will then turn to the intricate legal, cultural, and industrial policy questions raised by the European quota. First of all, it is, however, pertinent to consider whether the Title on Culture in the EC Treaty could present an alternative to the hitherto market-driven approach of the European Union to the media. A more coherent development of a common broadcasting policy that would pay tribute to both economic and social/cultural features of television ultimately depends on the attainment of a higher level of cultural consensus in Europe. This work will attempt to answer the question whether such a comprehensive EU broadcasting policy is, firstly, necessary and, secondly, feasible.

Chapter 10

The Competence of the European Union in the Area of Culture under Article 151 EC

1. POWERS OF THE EUROPEAN UNION UNDER ARTICLE 151 EC

Article 151 EC is the only provision falling under the Title XI on culture. It displays many similarities to the provisions on education and vocational training in terms of its structure and content. It begins with a general declaration of intent in the '*chapeau*' of the provision followed by the concrete objectives and areas of Union action, the promise of closer cooperation with third countries and international organizations, the policy integration principle and, lastly, the legal instruments and procedural requirements. The focus of the present section will be the '*chapeau*', and the objectives of Union action in the field of culture. The aim is to assess the extent to which there is potential for the development of a European cultural policy or, alternatively, for the elevation of the Union to the role of a key player with decisive influence on the cultural policies of the Member States.

The incorporation of the Title on Culture into the Treaty has rightly been considered as a highly symbolic act, in that it poses a central question for the institutional future of the European Union: will it remain a community of nation states or develop into a federation?[1] Article 151 (1) EC cannot conceal a certain perplexity in view of this dilemma, which it fails to resolve. The long-term objective of Union action in the area of culture is to 'contribute to the flowering of the cultures of the Member States, while respecting their national and regional diversity and at the same time bringing the common cultural heritage to the fore'.

---

1. A. J. Liehm, 'Aider la création pour sauver les identities: La culture, mal-aimée de l'Europe', *Le Monde Diplomatique*, September 1999, p. 27.

It unites thus both options in an uneasy symbiosis.[2] The same indecision besets the Draft Reform Treaty, which pronounces in Article I- 3 (3) that the Union 'shall respect its rich cultural and linguistic diversity, and shall ensure that Europe's cultural heritage is safeguarded and enhanced.'[3]

1.1 The Programmatic Statement in Article 151 (1) EC

No attempt has been made in Article 151 EC to define the notion of culture in its variety in view of the uncertainties involved.[4] Instead the pragmatic solution of referring to the 'cultures of the Member States' and to the 'common cultural heritage' has been chosen.[5] The use of the plural form of 'culture' stresses the multiplicity of cultures in the Member States.[6] It is not clear whether this plural encompasses the regional in addition to the national cultures.[7] This question is of small importance anyhow given that the Union promises to respect regional cultural diversity.

The Union has also committed itself to respecting cultural as well as religious and linguistic diversity in Article 22 of the Charter of Fundamental Rights that was proclaimed by the European Parliament, the Council and the Commission on 7 December 2000.[8] The Explanatory Memorandum to the Charter refers to Article 151 (1), (4) together with Article 6 TEU as the basis for this provision.[9] Article 22 is drafted as a principle rather than a freestanding right.[10] It is

---

2. *Ibid.*
3. Draft Treaty amending the Treaty on European Union and the Treaty establishing the European Community, 5 October 2007 <www.consilium.europa.eu/uedocs/cmsUpload/cg00001re01en.pdf>, 12 October 2007.
4. Cohesion Policy and Culture. A contribution to employment, 20 November 1996, COM (96) 52 final, 3; *see* M. Ross, 'Cultural Protection: A Matter for Union Citizenship or Human Rights?' in *The European Union and Human Rights*, N. A. Neuwahl and A. Rosas (eds) (The Hague, Martinus Nijhoff, 1995), pp. 235–236.
5. F. Fechner, 'Kommentar zum Artikel 128' in *Handbuch des Europäischen Rechts: Systematische Sammlung mit Erläuterungen*, 335th instalment, H. von der Groeben, J. Thiesing, C. D. Ehlermann (eds) (Baden-Baden, Nomos, 1995), Vorbem., para. 15; I. Berggreen-Merkel, *Die rechtlichen Aspekte der Kulturpolitik nach dem Maastrichter Vertrag*, Vorträge, Reden und Berichte aus dem Europa-Institut der Universität des Saarlandes, no. 329 (Saarbrücken, Europa-Institut, 1995), p. 11.
6. L. Bekemans and A. Ballodimos, 'Le traité de Maastricht et l'education, la formation professionelle et la culture' (1993) 2 RMUE, 99, 106.
7. *See* Ross, 'Cultural Protection', p. 243; M. A. Martín Estebanez, 'The Protection of National or Ethnic, Religious or Linguistic Minorities' in *The European Union and Human Rights*, N. A. Neuwahl and A. Rosas (eds) (The Hague, Martinus Nijhoff, 1995), pp. 133, 137.
8. Charter of Fundamental Rights of the European Union of 7 December 2000, OJ C 364/01, 2000 (hereafter referred to as Charter of Fundamental Rights).
9. CONV 828/1/03 REV 1 of 18 July 2003, Updated Explanations relating to the text of the Charter of Fundamental Rights.
10. On the distinction between rights and principles in the Charter, *see* D. Ashiagbor, 'Economic and Social Rights in the European Charter of Fundamental Rights' (2004) 1 EHRL, 62; A. McColgan, 'Editorial: The EU Charter of Fundamental Rights' (2004) 1 EHRL 2.

questionable whether the aspirational character of this provision allows for its meaningful enforcement. In the European Parliament's assessment, Article 22 is liable to strengthen other Treaty rights such as the guarantee of non-discrimination, the freedom of conscience and religion, the right to education, the freedom of expression and information and the freedom of assembly and of association.[11]

The engagement of the Union in the flowering of the cultures of the Member States under Article 151 (1) EC is problematic from the subsidiarity point of view.[12] It is not evident why the Union's intervention is necessary for European cultures to thrive and why this task cannot satisfactorily be accomplished by the Member States themselves. The conclusion has been drawn from this formulation that the Union has no competence to conduct a cultural policy of its own, but has to model its action after the cultural concepts of its Member States.[13] It is submitted that this approach is incorrect insofar as it does not distinguish clearly between the cultural policies of the Member States and the cultural action of the Union that is embedded in the European project.[14] Union action is not designed to replace national policies, but to pursue its own aims without going further than the creation of a 'European added value'.[15]

As far as the 'common cultural heritage' is concerned, it is a notion frequently encountered in constitutions of developing countries.[16] This term has been preferred to the less tangible notion of a European culture.[17] It follows from its juxtaposition to 'the cultures of the Member States' that it does not merely constitute their sum. Nor is it a reference to an artificial Euro-culture, but to the common elements of European cultures, which create a shared cultural foundation in Europe.[18] The Union is not, however, confined to the demonstration of already existing cultural roots and currents common to European cultures, but can also enhance them and develop new common grounds.[19]

---

11. Charter of Fundamental Rights, Arts. 21, 10, 14, 11, 12. *See* European Parliament, 'Charter of Fundamental Rights of the European Union' <www.europarl.europa.eu/comparl/libe/elsj/charter/art22/default_en.htm>, 26 October 2007.
12. K. Bohr and H. Albert, 'Die Europäische Union – das Ende der eigenständigen Kulturpolitik der deutschen Bundesländer?' (1993) 2 ZRP, 61, 65.
13. S. Astheimer and K. Moosmayer, 'Europäische Rundfunkordnung – Chance oder Risiko?' (1994) 7 ZUM, 396 *et seq.*; Bekemans and Ballodimos, 'Le traité de Maastricht', 105; S. Schmahl, *Die Kulturkompetenz der Europäischen Gemeinschaft* (Baden-Baden, Nomos, 1996), p. 201.
14. *See* 1st Report on the Consideration of Cultural Aspects in European Community Action, 17 April 1996, COM (96) 160 final, part V, 2.
15. H.-J. Blanke, *Europa auf dem Weg zu einer Bildungs- und Kulturgemeinschaft*, Kölner Schriften zum Europarecht, vol. 41 (Cologne, Carl Heymanns, 1994), p. 101.
16. P. Häberle, *Verfassungslehre als Kulturwissenschaft* (2nd edn, Berlin, Duncker & Humblot, 1998), p. 1007.
17. Blanke, *Europa auf dem Weg*, p. 101; Schmahl, *Kulturkompetenz der Europäischen Gemeinschaft*, p. 201; G. Ress, 'Die neue Kulturkompetenz der EG' (1992) 22 DÖV, 944.
18. Bekemans and Ballodimos, 'Le traité de Maastricht', 105.
19. Fechner, 'Kommentar zum Artikel 128', para. 10; COM (96) 160 final, part V, 2.

1.2 The Objectives and Areas of Union Cultural Action

The more immediate aims of Union cultural action are described in Article 151 (2) EC as 'encouraging cooperation between Member States and, if necessary, supporting and supplementing their action'. This formulation is identical to the one coined in the area of education. It is contentious whether the Union can develop its own cultural activities independently from those of the Member States.[20] The word 'supplement' suggests that there is scope for independent Union action.[21] This action is, however, conditioned upon the existence of earlier activities of the Member States to which a European dimension has been added. Consequently, the role of the Union is purely complementary.[22]

The tight wording of Article 151 (2) EC has been widely interpreted as an expression of the principle of subsidiarity in the area of culture.[23] It has even been propounded that the restraints contained in this provision, especially the 'if necessary' clause, are more specific than the subsidiarity principle. Therefore, the subsidiarity principle could not apply to the cultural field in accordance with the maxim '*lex specialis derogat legi generali*'.[24] This thesis is, however, not sustainable since a special norm has to include *per definitionem* at least one more element in addition to those contained in the general norm. This is evidently not true of Article 151 (2) EC in relation to Article 5 (2) EC.

The clause 'if necessary' constitutes an independent condition of Article 151 (2) EC, not a mere reference to the subsidiarity principle. Support for this position can be derived from Article 130 R (4) EEC. This provision, which contained the principle of subsidiarity in the area of environmental policy, became obsolete and was removed after the insertion of Article 5 EC. It follows a *contrario* that the phrase 'if necessary' in Article 151 (2) EC is not merely a specific expression of Article 5 EC. The fact that the subsidiarity principle is not obsolete also becomes clear from the justification of Union cultural action in terms of this principle in Decision 1855/2006 establishing the Culture Programme (2007–2013).[25] Recital 30 to this Decision states that

> Since the objectives of this Decision, namely to enhance the European cultural area based on common cultural heritage [. . .] cannot be sufficiently achieved by the Member States owing to their transnational character, and can therefore, by reason of the scales or effects of the action, be better achieved at

20. Fechner, 'Kommentar zum Artikel 128', para. 12.
21. *Ibid.*; Ress, 'Neue Kulturkompetenz', 947.
22. J. M. E. Loman, K. J. M. Mortelmans, H. H. G. Post and J. S. Watson, *Culture and Community Law Before and after Maastricht* (The Hague, Kluwer, 1992), p. 208.
23. M. Niedobitek, *The Cultural Dimension in EC Law* (The Hague, Kluwer, 1997), p. 12; Schmahl, *Kulturkompetenz der Europäischen Gemeinschaft*, pp. 221–222.
24. Bekemans and Ballodimos, 'Le traité de Maastricht', 108.
25. European Parliament and Council Decision 1855/2006/EC of 12 December 2006 establishing the Culture Programme (2007–2013) OJ L 372/1, 2006, Art. 3 (2) (hereafter referred to as the Culture 2007 Programme).

Union level, the Union may adopt measures, in accordance with the principle of subsidiarity as set out in Article 5 of the Treaty.

It is contentious whether the list of areas of EU cultural action is exhaustive.[26] The wording of Article 151 (2) EC suggests that this is the case. In any event, this question is of minor importance given that these areas are phrased in an extremely open-ended manner. This applies especially to the first indent (improvement of the knowledge and dissemination of the culture and history of the European peoples) and the last (artistic and literary creation, including in the audiovisual sector).

Even though the reference to the 'cultural heritage of European significance' and to 'artistic and literary creation' might suggest otherwise, it is submitted that a broad definition of culture underlies this provision as opposed to a 'highbrow' one. No attempt is made here to assess the quality of the culture deserving promotion as in the case of education ('quality education'). The notion of 'cultural heritage' has been widely interpreted by the European Court so as to include European languages.[27] Their protection is not absent from Article 151 EC even though the European Parliament's proposal to amend this provision so as to include an express reference to language did not find fertile ground.[28] A definition of culture in the anthropological sense has also been advocated by the Commission in a Communication concerning the Culture 2000 programme. It held that 'this broadening of the definition is a consequence of the fact that culture is no longer considered a subsidiary activity, but a driving force in society, making for creativity, dialogue and cohesion'.[29]

From the four areas of EU cultural action under Article 151 (2) EC the reference to the audiovisual sector in the last indent is of particular interest since it may mean that there is a legal basis for the development of this sector along the lines of the Union's cultural policy. Some have argued that support measures for the media can be based on this norm.[30] A distinction has occasionally been drawn between the definition of programme content that has been deemed to fall within the scope of Article 151 EC, and the institutional support for a news channel that has been held to be beyond the ambit of this provision.[31]

This approach is disputable on at least two grounds. The reference to the audiovisual sector is limited to artistic and literary creation. Therefore, it cannot

---

26. Loman *et al., Culture and Community Law*, p. 194; Schmahl, *Kulturkompetenz der Europäischen Gemeinschaft*, p. 202; contra Fechner, 'Kommentar zum Artikel 128', para. 15.
27. Case 42/97, *European Parliament v Council of the European Union* [1999] ECR I-869.
28. José Escudero, 'Report on Culture: Consideration of Cultural Aspects in the European Community Action COS/1996/2075'.
29. First European Community Framework Programme in Support of Culture (2000–2004), 6 May 1998, COM (98) 266 final, 3.
30. I. Berggreen and I. Hochbaum, 'Bildung, Ausbildung und Kultur' in *Die deutschen Länder in Europa: Politische Union und Wirtschafts-und Währungsunion*, H. F. U. Borkenhagen et al. (eds) (Baden-Baden, Nomos, 1992), p. 58; Schmahl, *Kulturkompetenz der Europäischen Gemeinschaft*, p. 205.
31. Schmahl, *Kulturkompetenz der Europäischen Gemeinschaft*, p. 205.

be assumed that it was intended to include this sector in its totality under Article 151 EC.[32] It is not likely that Member States' responsibility for programme content, which is a particularly sensitive issue, has been affected by the adoption of Article 151 EC. Moreover, the inclusion of the media within the Union's cultural policy would be difficult to reconcile with the exclusion of harmonization under Article 151 (4) EC given that a certain level of harmonization has already been attained in this area on the basis of Articles 47 and 55 EC.

Most areas of Union action under Article 151 (2) EC have an evident transnational element. This might seem doubtful at first sight as regards artistic and literary creation since there is no clear link to the Union or to its twenty-seven Member States. However, the Culture 2000 programme, which simplified and consolidated the Union's cultural endeavours under the earlier Kaleidoscope, Ariane and Raphael programmes, already promoted exchanges, cultural cooperation and the circulation of artists and their works as well as of those working in the books and reading field.[33] Its successor, the Culture programme (2007–2013) aims to promote the transnational mobility of cultural players and to encourage the transnational circulation of works and cultural and artistic products. These objectives are considered essential '[I]n order to make this common cultural area for the peoples of Europe a reality'.[34] It follows that the area of artistic and literary creation also displays a transnational element.

A further conclusion that can be drawn when looking back at the Culture 2000 programme is that the second paragraph of Article 151 EC names under some headings distinct cultural fields, while under others, actions applying to several fields are listed. More precisely, 'artistic creation', 'literary creation' and the 'cultural heritage of European importance' are the three cultural fields that were incorporated into the Culture 2000 programme. On the contrary, the 'improvement of the knowledge and dissemination of the culture and history of the European peoples' as well as 'cultural exchanges' are objectives underlying most EU cultural actions.[35] They were pursued in the field of books and reading and also in the framework of so-called cultural Cooperation Agreements.[36] This mixture between areas and objectives of EU cultural action obscures the interpretation of Article 151 EC.

The Culture 2000 programme did not succeed in drawing the exact boundaries of EC activity in the field of cultural policy either. Three types of action were envisaged in this programme: firstly, cultural Cooperation Agreements that paved the way for cultural networks with a view to realizing cultural projects with a European dimension; secondly, specific innovative and/or experimental actions that mainly aimed to facilitate and widen access to culture by people of all social

32. C. E. Eberle, 'Das europäische Recht und die Medien am Beispiel des Rundfunkrechts' (1993) 1 AfP, 425; Fechner, 'Kommentar zum Artikel 128', para. 20.
33. European Parliament and Council Decision 508/2000/EC of 14 February 2000 establishing the Culture 2000 Programme OJ L 63/1, 2000, Annex II, paras I (a), (b) (hereafter referred to as the Culture 2000 Programme).
34. Culture 2007 Programme, recital 10.
35. *See ibid.*, Art. 1 (a).
36. *Ibid.*, Annex I, 1.2 (vii); II, para. I (b) (ii).

and cultural backgrounds, especially by means of the new technologies; lastly, special cultural events with a European or international dimension, including the 'European Capitals of Culture', European prizes and other emblematic activities. All three types of action were meant to follow a vertical (concerning one cultural field) or horizontal approach (associating several cultural fields). The opaque distinction between actions and cultural fields and the overblown display of aims both under the vertical and under the horizontal approach complicated EU cultural policy. Also, two main actions, namely support for European cultural organizations and the 'European Capitals of Culture', were weakly linked, if at all, with the Culture 2000 framework programme.

The Culture programme (2007–2013) has been adopted with the aim of streamlining European cultural action and of overcoming the compartmentalization between the various cultural disciplines within Culture 2000. Next to the abovementioned two objectives – the promotion of the tansnational mobility of cultural players and the encouragement of the transnational circulation of works and cultural and artistic products – it pursues a third, less specific objective: the encouragement of intercultural dialogue.

So that the projects supported are on a sufficient scale and offer maximum added value at European level, each project will have to pursue at least two of these objectives.[37] This proviso seems redundant given that projects supporting the transnational mobility of people working in the cultural sector and the transnational circulation of works of art inevitably encourage intercultural dialogue of some sort. The emphasis of the current Culture (2007–2013) programme and of the Culture 2000 programme on large scale projects offering maximum added value at the European level is problematic.[38] As the Committee of the Regions suggested, large is not tantamount to high in quality, creativity and innovation. The emphasis on big projects might militate against the participation of smaller operators and against projects that are 'small in scale but high in quality'.[39]

The abovementioned objectives are pursued in the framework of three fields of action. The first strand includes support for cultural actions through multiannual cooperation projects involving at least six operators from six different countries, cooperation measures involving at least three operators from three different countries, and special actions such as the 'European Capitals of Culture', European prizes and cooperation with third countries and international organizations. The second strand focuses on support for bodies active at European level in the field of culture. The final one aims to support analyses and the collection and dissemination of information and to maximize the impact of projects in

37. *See* Proposal for a Decision of the European Parliament and of the Council establishing the Culture 2007 Programme (2007–2013), 14 July 2004, COM (2004) 469 final, 4; Culture 2007 Programme, Annex 1.1, 1.3.
38. R. Craufurd Smith, 'Article 151 EC and European Identity' in *Culture and European Union Law*, R. Craufurd Smith (ed.) (Oxford, Oxford University Press, 2004), p. 277, 296.
39. Opinion of the Committee of the Regions on the 'Proposal for a decision of the European Parliament and of the Council establishing the Culture 2007 Programme (2007–2013)', (2005/C 164/08), para. 1.8.

the field of European cultural cooperation. It contains three complementary actions seeking to promote the production of conceptual tools and of an internet tool as well as the creation of supporting 'culture contact points'.

The Culture (2007–2013) programme pursues fewer objectives than its predecessor and has integrated support for European cultural organizations so as to increase the coherence of Union action. As far as the motives for the Union's involvement in the field of culture are concerned, the Culture 2000 programme stated bluntly that culture is appreciated in the Union context both as an economic factor and as a factor in social integration and citizenship.[40] It is entrusted with providing an answer to the challenges of globalization, the information society, social cohesion and the creation of employment.

The linkage between culture and European citizenship has been taken up with increased vigour in the new Culture 2007 programme, which views linguistic and cultural cooperation and cultural exchanges as a means of 'encouraging direct participation by European citizens in the integration process.'[41] At the same time, Decision 1855/2006 states rather circumspectly that '[I]t is essential that the cultural sector contribute to, and play a role in, broader European political developments.'[42] It then explains in no uncertain terms that cultural policies at regional, national and European level should be reinforced in view of the clear link between investment in culture and economic development and the increasingly large contribution of the cultural industries to the European economy.[43] It is thus possible to discern two separate strands in the Union approach to culture: a pragmatic one, appreciating its potential to generate jobs and to reintegrate marginalized people into society, and an ideological one, seeking to enhance the allegiance of citizens to the European project through emphasis on their common cultural values and roots.[44]

As far as the first strand is concerned, serious misgivings have been expressed about the linkage of culture with cohesion policy for fear that it could lead to an unprecedented expansion of EU activities in areas not included in Article 151 EC.[45] Funding from the Structural Funds could lure national activities into aligning themselves to the terms and conditions set by the Union. The 'capitalization of cultural assets' and the 'valorization of cultural heritage', notions commonly utilized in this context, could provide the stepping stone for the Union to conduct cultural policy in a big way.[46] The Union tries to allay these fears by stressing

40. Culture 2000 Programme, recital 2.
41. *Ibid.*, recital 1.
42. *Ibid.*, recital 4.
43. *Ibid. See also* the recent Commission Communication on a European agenda for culture in a globalizing world, 10 May 2007, COM (2007) 242 final, 8, which stresses the role of culture as a catalyst for creativity in the framework of the Lisbon Strategy for growth and jobs.
44. Culture 2000 Programme, recital 5.
45. *See* Schmahl, *Kulturkompetenz der Europäischen Gemeinschaft*, p. 202 n. 1244; I. Hochbaum, 'Kohäsion und Subsidiarität – Maastricht und die Länderkulturhoheit' (1992) 7 DÖV, 285.
46. *See* COM (96) 512 final, 8, 9.

that its approach to culture is bottom-up, that its assistance is inspired by the strategies of the Member States and by the regions' endogenous potential.[47]

On the condition that the respective spheres of competence are indeed respected, it is submitted that EU cultural activities have greater potential to underpin allegiance if they are guided by such pragmatic goals.[48] The manifestation of solid advantages of European integration connected with the raising of the standard of living and quality of life is more likely to attract support than the invocation of 'partially shared historical traditions and cultural heritages'.[49] As has pointedly been remarked, the gap between the Middle Latin unity of European literature and the European Union of the future is too wide to bridge by means of cultural policy.[50] If cultural identity is about the sense of a shared continuity, shared memories and the collective belief in a common destiny, neither a national nor a European cultural policy is in the position to convey these unifying elements.

Therefore, instead of embalming the past, it is more fruitful to search for common reference points in the present. Such reference points are the increasing convergence of political cultures in Europe and the common development towards an industrial society with all its social problems.[51] A more central role should hence be assigned to the social and political parameters of cultural policy by improving the employment perspectives of artists and by resolving the financial and creativity crisis plaguing the European market for culture.[52] This is not to say that the conservation of our cultural heritage should be neglected. On the contrary, it should be carried out with zeal, as our duty to the coming generations rather than to the integration process.

2. LIMITATIONS ON THE UNION POWERS

The main safeguards for the national sovereignty in the cultural domain in addition to the circumspect wording of Article 151 EC are the exclusion of harmonization and the procedural requirement of unanimity. We will now consider these safeguards and the ensuing limitations on the Union powers.

---

47. *Ibid.*, 10, 13.
48. H. Lübbe, 'Für eine europäische Kulturpolitik' in W. Weidenfeld, H. Lübbe, W. Maihofer and J. Rovan, *Europäische Kultur: Das Zukunftsgut des Kontinents: Vorschläge für eine europäische Kulturpolitik* (Gütersloh, Bertelsmann Stiftung, 1990), pp. 19, 47 et seq.
49. A. Smith, 'National Identity and the Idea of European Unity' (1992) 68 *International Affairs*, 55, 70.
50. Lübbe, 'Für eine europäische Kulturpolitik', p. 45.
51. W. Maihofer, 'Culture politique et identité européenne' in *Structure and Dimensions of European Community Policy*, J. Schwartze and H. G. Schermers (eds) (Baden-Baden, Nomos, 1988), pp. 215, 218.
52. Craufurd Smith, 'Article 151 EC and European Identity', p. 295; H. Brugmans, 'Five Starting Points' in *Europe from a Cultural Perspective: Historiography and Perceptions*, A. Rijksbaron, W. H. Roobol and M. Weisglas (eds) (The Hague, Nijgh & Van Ditmar, 1987), pp. 3, 17.

2.1 Exclusion of Harmonization

As in the areas of education and vocational training, the harmonization of laws and regulations of the Member States in the area of culture is prohibited. As a result, measures with a specifically cultural objective cannot be based on the general provisions of Articles 94, 95 or 308 EC.[53] On the contrary, harmonization measures pursuing primarily other objectives such as the elimination of obstacles to the freedoms of movement, while also having a cultural dimension, are by no means affected by Article 151 EC.[54] Therefore, to name but one example, legislation on the export and return of cultural property that is justified in the interests of the internal market has not been rendered illegal by the exclusion of harmonization under Article 151 EC.[55] However, such measures with a 'dual nature' have to respect the cultural diversity of the Member States in accordance with the policy integration principle in Article 151 (4) EC.

2.2 Unanimity

The procedural section of Article 151 (5) EC makes available to the Council the legal instruments of incentive measures and recommendations so that it can contribute to the achievement of the objectives referred to in his Article. Incentive measures are adopted under the co-decision procedure of Article 251 EC after consulting the Committee of the Regions. Recommendations are adopted on a proposal from the Commission without any role being assigned to the European Parliament or the Committee of the Regions.

Article 151 EC requires decision-making by unanimity for the adoption not only of incentive measures but also of recommendations despite their lacking binding force. This hurdle that has to be overcome prior to the adoption of a cultural policy measure is significant. It has been inserted in the Treaty on the European Union at the insistence of the German *Länder* so as to counterbalance the wide scope for Union action under Article 151 (2) EC.[56] The requirement of unanimity is alien to the co-decision procedure where qualified-majority voting applies as a rule. It is indicative of the hesitancy of the Member States to loosen control over cultural matters. Nonetheless, it is not always feasible for a Member State to raise a voice of dissent against a generally accepted measure. This is what

---

53. Berggreen-Merkel, *Die rechtlichen Aspekte der Kulturpolitik*, p. 17; Blanke, *Europa auf dem Weg*, p. 102; Fechner, 'Kommentar zum Art. 128', Vorbem., para. 12; Schmahl, *Kulturkompetenz der Europäischen Gemeinschaft*, p. 212; Bekemans and Ballodimos, 'Le traité de Maastricht', 132; contra Bohr and Albert, 'Die Europäische Union', 65 in respect of Art. 308 EC.
54. COM (96) 160 final, 2; COM (94) 356 final, 2; Berggreen-Merkel, *Die rechtlichen Aspekte der Kulturpolitik*, p. 17.
55. Regulation 3911/92, OJ L 395/1, 1992 on the export and Directive 93/7, OJ L 74/74, 1993 on the return of cultural property exported illegally.
56. Berggreen and Hochbaum, 'Bildung, Ausbildung und Kultur', p. 51; Niedobitek, *Cultural Dimension in EC Law*, p. 25.

the experience with Article 308 EC has demonstrated. Also, the unanimity requirement may encourage the recourse to legal bases other than Article 151 EC.

It is interesting to note that the unanimity requirement was to be abolished in the framework of the foundered draft European Constitution.[57] The draft reform Treaty that has taken the place of the draft Constitution also proposes the deletion of the unanimity requirement. It remains to be seen whether it will be possible to agree on this proposal in the current Intergovernmental Conference. In any event, the Commission is intent to overcome the procedural constraints of Article 151 (5) EC by using the open method of coordination (OMC), a non-binding intergovernmental framework for policy exchange and concerted action. In view of the fact that competence in the cultural field remains very much at national level, the Commission views OMC as the right method to deepen cooperation between Member States. The Commission's role would be limited to the setting of general objectives and engaging in a light regular reporting system together with Member States representatives.[58]

3. THE POLICY INTEGRATION PRINCIPLE

The policy integration principle, also referred to as the transverse clause, is contained in Article 151 (4) EC. It states that 'the Community shall take cultural aspects into account in its action under other provisions of this Treaty, in particular in order to respect and to promote the diversity of its cultures'. The last clause, which clarifies the aim of the policy integration principle, has been inserted into this provision by the Amsterdam Treaty.

Similar requirements of integration exist in the Titles on public health under Article 152 (1) EC, on consumer protection under Article 153 (2) EC, and on the environment under Article 6 EC. It is interesting to note that of all these clauses the Amsterdam Treaty only moved the environmental integration principle from Article 174 (2) EC to Part One of the EC Treaty, entitled 'Principles'. This move was evidently meant to underline the significance attached to the integration of environmental considerations in other Union policies.[59] Even though the culture integration principle was not deemed worth of similar attention by the drafters of the Amsterdam Treaty, it has stirred up great controversy in academic writing. Some have characterized it as the most important element of Article 151 EC, establishing the European Union as a cultural community,[60] while others argued

57. *See* Treaty Establishing a Constitution for Europe of 29 October 2004, OJ C 310, 2004, Art. III-280 (5).
58. Commission Communication on a European agenda for culture in a globalizing world, 10 May 2007, COM (2007) 242 final, 12.
59. L. Krämer, *EC Environmental Law* (4th edn, London, Sweet & Maxwell, 2000), p. 14.
60. Bekemans and Ballodimos, 'Le traité de Maastricht', 134; Häberle, *Verfassungslehre als Kulturwissenschaft*, p. 892.

that its value had been largely exaggerated.[61] It is therefore necessary to assess the implications of this principle for Union policy-making.

The culture integration principle is phrased in a non-committal manner if compared to the environmental integration clause since cultural aspects only have to be *taken into account*, whereas under Article 6 EC environmental protection requirements must be *integrated* into the definition and implementation of Union policies.[62] Moreover, Article 151 (4) EC does not prescribe a high level of protection in cultural issues as it is the case with public health, consumer protection and the environment.[63] This can be attributed to the elusive notion of culture, encumbering the definition of a high level of protection, and also to the Union's effort to approach this field in as light-handed a manner as possible.

Article 151 (4) EC does not explain further what are the cultural aspects that need to be taken into account. This term is, however, generally understood as a reference to the 'cultures of the Member States' and to the 'common cultural heritage'. These cultural aspects have to be considered in the entire spectrum of Union powers, not only in the context of measures aimed at the establishment of the internal market.

The open-ended wording of Article 151 (4) EC makes plain that no '*obligation de résultat*' is intended. The phrase added in the Amsterdam Treaty does not make a difference in this respect. A duty to state the reasons for the integration or non-integration of a cultural dimension in a given piece of legislation can exist at most under Article 253 EC. In view of the wide discretion of the legislator as to how to have regard to the cultural aspects of a matter, it is unlikely that the Court would annul a measure on the ground of its non-compliance with the policy integration principle. However, this is not to discount the legally binding character of this principle.[64] So as to increase awareness of the interface between cultural diversity and other Union policies in all its services, the Commission has recently established a new inter-service group. It is hoped that this will strengthen inter-service coordination and help the Commission strike the right balance between the competing public policy objectives involved.[65]

Disagreement exists with regard to the question whether the integration clause only applies to measures whose thrust lies in a policy area other than culture. This is the most commonly held view.[66] Niedobitek argues, however, that this clause also

---

61. Niedobitek, *Cultural Dimension in EC Law*, p. 25.
62. M. Nettesheim, 'Das Kulturverfassungsrecht der Europäischen Union', (2002) 4 JZ 157, 162.
63. *See* Art. 95 (3) EC; R. Lane, 'New Community Competences under the Maastricht Treaty' (1993) 30 CMLRev, 953.
64. Niedobitek, *Cultural Dimension in EC Law*, p. 26; I. Schwartz, 'Subsidiarität und EG-Kompetenzen: Der neue Titel "Kultur": Medienvielfalt und Binnenmarkt' (1993) 1 AfP, 417; contra Berggreen-Merkel, *Die rechtlichen Aspekte der Kulturpolitik*, p. 18; Lane, 'New Community Competences', 957.
65. Commission Communication on a European agenda for culture in a globalizing world, 10 May 2007, COM (2007) 242 final, 13.
66. Schmahl, *Kulturkompetenz der Europäischen Gemeinschaft*, p. 235 *et seq.*; Fechner, 'Kommentar zum Artikel 128', Vorbem., para. 12; T. Stein, 'Die Querschnittsklausel zwischen

applies to measures whose thrust lies in the cultural field, implying that such measures can also be based on provisions of the Treaty other than Article 151 EC.[67] The substantive thrust of functional Union powers such as those granted by Article 95 EC, so the argument goes, always resides in areas different from the 'establishment of the internal market', which is not a substantive area in its own right.

It is submitted that the dispute is more apparent than real. Niedobitek only has the *content* of measures adopted under internal market provisions in mind. Such measures can unquestionably be concerned with the cultural field. The characteristic feature of measures with a 'dual nature', envisaged by Article 151 (4) EC, is that they are inextricably linked with two disparate areas, in our case with both culture and the economy.

The European Court has however ruled that not only the content of a measure but also its *aim* and *effect* are relevant criteria for determining the appropriate legal basis.[68] If, all these factors taken into consideration, the 'centre of gravity' of an act is cultural policy, its adoption under other provisions on the pretext of the policy integration principle would lead to an unacceptable marginalization of Article 151 EC.[69] It is therefore correct to say that a measure whose 'centre of gravity' is in the area of culture has to be adopted under Article 151 EC so that the policy integration principle is of no avail.

The fear has, however, been expressed that Article 151 (4) EC could entice the EU institutions to favour legal bases other than the narrowly circumscribed Article 151 EC.[70] This undesirable development may come about if the policy integration principle is reduced to the statement that a Union measure does not have to be based on Article 151 EC simply because it also pursues cultural objectives.[71] The adoption of the second phase of the Media programme on the basis of Article 157 (3) EC rather than on Article 151 EC exemplifies this approach. The fact that harmonization is excluded under Article 151 (5) EC whereas under Article 157 (2) EC Member States are invited to coordinate their action proves that the debate on classification is not futile.

Also related to the relationship between Article 151 EC and other legal bases in the Treaty is the question whether the policy integration principle leads to an expansion or to a restriction of Union competence. Some have taken the position

---

Maastricht und Karlsruhe' in *Festschrift für Ulrich Everling*, vol. II, O. Due, M. Lutter and J. Schwarze (eds) (Baden-Baden, Nomos, 1995), pp. 1439, 1452.

67. Niedobitek, *Cultural Dimension in EC Law*, p. 28.
68. Case C-300/89, *Commission of the European Communities v. Council of the European Communities* [1991] ECR 2867 para. 10 (*Titanium Dioxide* case); Case C-155/91, *Commission of the European Communities v. Council of the European Communities* [1993] ECR I-939 para. 19.
69. *See* submissions of Council and Commission in the *Titanium Dioxide* case.
70. Schmahl, *Kulturkompetenz der Europäischen Gemeinschaft*, p. 227; R. Wägenbaur, 'Auf dem Wege zur Bildungs- und Kulturgemeinschaft' in *Gedächtnisschrift für Eberhard Grabitz*, A. Randelzhofer, R. Scholz and D. Wilke (eds) (Munich, C. H. Beck, 1995), p. 858.
71. *See* for the area of the environment Case C-300/89, *Commission of the European Communities v. Council of the European Communities* [1991] ECR 2867 para 22; this trend has been reversed in Case C-155/91, *Commission of the European Communities v. Council of the European Communities* [1993] ECR I-939.

that this principle waters down the limitations of Union competence in the area of culture.[72] Others have asserted that Article 151 (4) EC constitutes an immanent barrier to Union action.[73] It could therefore not lead to an expansion into the cultural field through affirmative action, especially in view of the tight wording of Article 151 EC that urges for a restrictive interpretation of Union cultural competence.[74] Both views are based on the misconception that the exclusion of harmonization and the stringent procedural requirements of Article 151 EC have to be respected when action is taken under other provisions of the Treaty. We have already argued that this is not the case.

Consequently, it is not possible to speak either of an expansion or of a restriction of Union powers. The policy integration principle only puts down in black and white what has been Community practice already prior to the enactment of the Maastricht Treaty, namely the adoption of measures with a cultural dimension in pursuance of economic objectives. It emphasizes the need for Union action to be mindful of cultural interests, without, however, giving them priority over other interests. A balanced satisfaction of all demands involved is the desideratum. Its value lies in the recognition that not all aspects of social life can be regulated according to the market model.

Article 151 (4) EC is not designed as a safeguard against Union encroachment upon the competence of the Member States in the field of culture. Nonetheless, it could turn out to act in favour of national spheres of competence, especially if it is interpreted in the light of the principle of national representation that was developed by Ress prior to the Maastricht Treaty. According to this principle, national cultural policy measures that are strictly speaking incompatible with the Treaty requirements can be tolerated if they are indispensable for the protection of the Member States' national identity.[75] The policy integration principle encompasses the principle of national representation.[76] It goes however beyond it in that it allows ancillary cultural measures to be realized at EU level.

Nonetheless, an important distinction has to be made here. Cultural aspects cannot be included in a Union instrument when they lie outside its legal basis. Therefore, the reference to Article 151 (4) EC in the 24th recital to Dir. 97/36/EC

---

72. Bohr and Albert, 'Die Europäische Union', 64; Ross, 'Cultural Protection', p. 243; Stein, 'Querschnittsklausel zwischen Maastricht und Karlsruhe', p. 1442.
73. Eberle, 'Das europäische Recht und die Medien', 426; with a different justification R. Craufurd Smith, 'Community Intervention in the Cultural Field: Continuity or Change?' in *Culture and European Union Law*, R. Craufurd Smith (ed.) (Oxford, Oxford University Press, 2004), p. 19, 50 in view of the clause '*in particular in order to respect and to promote the diversity of its cultures*'.
74. On the concept of affirmative action *see* G. Ress, *Kultur und europäischer Binnenmarkt: Welche rechtlichen Auswirkungen hat der EWGV jetzt und nach der Verwirklichung des Europäischen Binnenmarktes auf die Kulturpolitik der BRD, insbesondere im Bereich der Kulturförderung? Gutachten für das Bundesministerium des Innern* (Stuttgart, Kohlhammer, 1991), p. 37; C. Tomuschat, 'Rechtliche Aspekte des Gemeinschaftshandelns im Bereich der Kultur', in *F.I.D.E. Reports of the 13th Congress*, vol. 1 (Athens, Ant. N. Sakkoulas, 1988), p. 29.
75. Ress, 'Neue Kulturkompetenz', 949.
76. Fechner, 'Kommentar zum Artikel 128', para. 29; contra Schmahl, *Kulturkompetenz der Europäischen Gemeinschaft*, pp. 227 n.1417, 228.

cannot justify the insertion of the European quota provision in the TwF Directive. This will be discussed in greater depth in Chapter 13 where it will be suggested that Articles 47 (2) and 55 EC have not been the proper legal basis for the adoption of the European quota provision. This defect cannot, however, be cured by means of the policy integration principle that cannot justify the *ultra vires* adoption of cultural policy measures.

4. CONCLUSION

Article 151 EC is not a stepping stone to the emergence of the Union as a major cultural actor. Its tight wording reveals the anxiety of the Member States to confine the Union to a complementary role which, for the most part, consists in adding a European dimension to their cultural activities. The exclusion of harmonization in conjunction with the high hurdle of unanimity acts as a deterrent to the use of Article 151 EC as a legal basis. The policy integration principle reinforces the suspicion that whenever cultural policy is enmeshed with trade policy, the regulatory bargains will take place on the terrain of other provisions of the Treaty. The Title on Culture is inevitably condemned to be an inconspicuous site for cultural cooperation projects and unremarkable emblematic actions.

Chapter 11

Television without Frontiers: The Country of Origin Principle

1. INTRODUCTION

The country of origin principle is central to thc objective of the TwF Directive to create an internal market in broadcasting services. Laid down initially in Article 2 (2) of Dir. 89/552/EEC,[1] it was transferred to Article 2a (1) following the adoption of the revised Dir. 97/36/EC.[2] The meaning of the principle remained the same:

---

1. Council Directive 89/552/EEC of 3 October 1989 on the coordination of certain provisions laid down by law, regulation or administrative action in Member States concerning the pursuit of television broadcasting activities OJ L 298/23, 1989.
2. Article 2a of European Parliament and Council Directive 97/36/EC of 30 June 1997 amending Council Directive 89/552/EEC on the coordination of certain provisions laid down by law, regulation and administrative action in Member States concerning the pursuit of television broadcasting activities OJ L 202/60, 1997:
   1. Member States shall ensure freedom of reception and shall not restrict retransmissions on their territory of television broadcasts from other Member States for reasons which fall within the fields coordinated by this Directive.
   2. Member States may, provisionally, derogate from paragraph 1 if the following conditions are fulfilled:
      (a) a television broadcast coming from another Member State manifestly, seriously and gravely infringes Article 22 (1) or (2) and/or Article 22a;
      (b) during the previous 12 months, the broadcaster has infringed the provision(s) referred to in (a) on at least two prior occasions;
      (c) the Member State concerned has notified the broadcaster and the Commission in writing of the alleged infringements and of the measures it intends to take should any such infringement occur again;
      (d) consultations with the transmitting Member State and the Commission have not produced an amicable settlement within 15 days of the notification provided for in (c), and the alleged infringement persists.

Member States are obliged to ensure the unhindered reception of broadcasts lawfully transmitted in their state of origin. They only have a limited possibility to derogate provisionally from the country of origin principle when foreign television broadcasts manifestly, seriously and gravely breach provisions concerning the protection of minors or public order.[3] Observers of the media policies of the European Union have even contended that the country of origin principle, by ruling out the restriction of transfrontier broadcasts, which are in compliance with the laws of the originating state, has signified the end of the broadcasting sovereignty of the Member States.[4]

The country of origin principle is a specific manifestation of the principle of mutual recognition developed by the European Court in its *van Binsbergen* case with regard to services and in its *Cassis de Dijon* case with regard to goods.[5] However, even though the *Cassis de Dijon* line of reasoning comes close to creating a presumption in favour of the free movement of goods and services satisfying the legal requirements of the home state, it does not remove the capacity of the receiving state to impose its laws within the boundaries set by *Cassis*, including proportionality. The country of origin principle goes beyond mutual recognition, in that the grounds of general interest falling within the ambit of the Directive, which can be invoked by the state of destination, are narrowly circumscribed by the legislature. This is due to the fact that the country of origin principle goes hand

---

The Commission shall, within two months following notification of the measures taken by the Member State, take a decision on whether the measures are compatible with Community law. If it decides that they are not, the Member State will be required to put an end to the measures in question as a matter of urgency.

3. Paragraph 2 shall be without prejudice to the application of any procedure, remedy or sanction to the infringements in question in the Member State which has jurisdiction over the broadcaster concerned.

3. Article 22 of Dir. 97/36/EC of 30 June 1997 OJ L 202/60, 1997:

    1. Member States shall take appropriate measures to ensure that television broadcasts by broadcasters under their jurisdiction do not include any programmes which might seriously impair the physical, mental or moral development of minors, in particular programmes that involve pornography or gratuitous violence.
    2. The measures provided for in paragraph 1 shall also extend to other programmes which are likely to impair the physical, mental or moral development of minors, except where it is ensured, by selecting the time of the broadcast or by any technical measure, that minors in the area of transmission will not normally hear or see such broadcasts.
    3. Furthermore, when such programmes are broadcast in unencoded form Member States shall ensure that they are preceded by an acoustic warning or are identified by the presence of a visual symbol throughout their duration.

    Article 22a of Dir. 97/36/EC of 30 June 1997 OJ L 202/60, 1997:

    Member States shall ensure that broadcasts do not contain any incitement to hatred on grounds of race, sex, religion or nationality.

4. P. J. Humphreys, *Mass Media and Media Policy in Western Europe* (Manchester, Manchester University Press, 1996), p. 276.
5. Case 33/74, *van Binsbergen v. Bestuur van de Bedrijsvereniging voor de Metaalnijverheid* [1974] ECR 1299; [1975] 1 CMLR 298; Case, 120/78 *Rewe Zentrale v. Bundesmonopolverwaltung für Branntwein* [1979] ECR 649; [1979] 3 CMLR 494.

in hand with the harmonization of limited areas of the national broadcasting laws, which has been necessary so as to enable Member States partially to renounce their regulatory powers on cross-border television.[6]

Nonetheless, the extent to which Member States' sovereignty in the area of broadcasting has actually been compromised as a result of the country of origin principle is contentious. Article 2a (1) of Dir. 97/36 states that Member States shall not restrict retransmissions on their territory of television broadcasts from other Member States 'for reasons which fall within the fields coordinated by this Directive'. Does this mean that Member States can still invoke interests not covered by the Directive so as to restrict the transmission of foreign broadcasts? If so, one would need to know the scope of the fields coordinated by the TwF Directive with great precision.

These questions are of great cultural significance, since they impinge upon the power of the Member States to apply to foreign broadcasts programme requirements that are laid down in their broadcasting laws.[7] In spite of the increasing trend towards a relaxation of such requirements, the first Part of this book demonstrated that they are still an inalienable feature of the European public broadcasting landscape. Given that the imposition of such requirements on domestic broadcasters would be rendered absurd if foreign broadcasters were not equally obliged to comply with them, certain states simply extend their broadcasting standards to cross-frontier broadcasts. It is questionable whether the Directive countenances such practices.

The unease about the impact of the country of origin principle on the broadcasting sovereignty of the Member States has recently been heightened pending its extension to non-linear audiovisual media services. It was feared that its application to non-linear services would lead to a 'race to the bottom' in the areas of youth or consumer protection.[8] The AVMS Directive responds to the convergence of information and media services by extending its basic rules on advertising and programme content to all audiovisual media services. Linear ('scheduled') services include in particular analogue and digital television, live streaming, webcasting and near-video-on demand, while non-linear ('on-demand') services include video-on-demand.[9]

6. B. de Witte, 'The European Content Requirement in the EC Television Directive – Five Years After' (1995) I YMEL, 101, 105; B. J. Drijber, 'The Revised Television without Frontiers Directive: Is it Fit for the Next Century?' (1999) 36 CMLRev, 87, 92.
7. Niedobitek, *Cultural Dimension in EC Law*, p. 162; *see* E. J. Mestmäcker, C. Engel, K. Gabriel-Bräutigam and M. Hoffmann, *Der Einfluß des europäischen Gemeinschaftsrechts auf die deutsche Rundfunkordnung* (Baden-Baden, Nomos, 1990), p. 30; L. Seidel, ' "Fernsehen ohne Grenzen": Zum Erlaß der EG-Rundfunkrichtlinie' (1991) 2 NVwZ, 122; ARD and ZDF, 'EG-Politik im Bereich des Rundfunks – Auswirkungen auf die Rundfunkordnung in der Bundesrepublik Deutschland' (1991) *MP Dokumentation* II, 75, 79; L. P. Hitchens, 'Identifying European Community Audio-Visual Policy in the Dawn of the Information Society' (1996) II YMEL, 45, 65, 70.
8. K. Faßbender, 'Zu Inhalt und Grenzen des rundfunkrechtlichen Sendestaatsprinzips' (2006) 6 AfP, 505, 511.
9. AVMS Directive, recital 20.

The AVMS Directive defines television broadcasting, i.e. a linear audiovisual media service, in Art. 1 (e) as 'an audiovisual media service provided by a media service provider for simultaneous viewing of programmes on the basis of a programme schedule' in juxtaposition to an 'on-demand service' which is defined in Art. 1 (g) as 'an audiovisual media service provided by a media service provider for the viewing of programmes at the moment chosen by the user and at his individual request on the basis of a catalogue of programmes selected by the media service provider'. Both are subcategories of the broader concept of an 'audiovisual media service' which encompasses in accordance with Art. 1 (a) 'a service as defined by Articles 49 and 50 of the Treaty which is under the editorial responsibility of a media service provider and the principal purpose of which is the provision of programmes in order to inform, entertain or educate, to the general public by electronic communications networks within the meaning of Article 2(a) of Directive 2002/21/EC.

In some cases it might be difficult to work out whether the provision of audiovisual content is the principal purpose of a service or incidental to it. Does a broadcaster's online presence fall within the scope of the Directive when it consists both of programmes and of text-based content accompanying these programmes?[10] Another borderline case, this of online games, has now been settled. Whereas the updated Commission proposal only excluded them from the scope of the Directive as long as the principal purpose of the audiovisual media service was not reached, the final text of the AVMS Directive removes the ambiguity by altogether excluding them from its scope.[11]

The definition of 'broadcaster' has also been revamped in the AVMS Directive. Article 1 (b) of the TwF Directive, which defined the 'broadcaster' as 'the natural or legal person who has editorial responsibility for the composition of schedules of television programmes within the meaning of (a) [i.e. television programmes for reception by the public, including relays] and who transmits them or has them transmitted by third parties', was outdated. It was tailored to the requirements of terrestrial free-to-air broadcasting and was ill-suited for cable and satellite distribution or for the current structure of the media industry.[12] The AVMS Directive uses the generic term 'media service provider' instead. This term is defined in Article 1 (d) of the AVMS Directive as 'the natural or legal person who has editorial responsibility for the choice of the audiovisual content of the

10. W. Schultz, *Zum Vorschlag für eine Richtlinie über audiovisuelle Mediendienste*, Arbeitspapiere des Hans-Bredow-Instituts, no. 17 (Hamburg, Hans-Bredow-Institut, 2006), p. 12.
11. Amended proposal for a Directive of the European Parliament and of the Council amending Council Directive 89/552/EEC on the coordination of certain provisions laid down by law, regulation or administrative action in Member States concerning the pursuit of television broadcasting activities ('Audiovisual media services without frontiers'), 29 March 2007, COM (2007) 170 final, recital 14; AVMS Directive, recital 18.
12. T. Gibbons, 'Jurisdiction over (Television) Broadcasters: Criteria for Defining "Broadcaster" and "Content Service Provider"' in *The Future of the 'Television without Frontiers Directive'*, Schriftenreihe des Instituts für Europäisches Medienrecht, vol. 29 (Baden-Baden, Nomos, 2005), pp. 53, 56.

audiovisual media service and determines the manner in which it is organised.' The term 'broadcaster', defined in Article 1 (f) as 'a media service provider of television broadcasts', is a subcategory of the wider expression 'media service provider'.

Recital 23 to the AVMS Directive specifies that the notion of editorial responsibility is essential for defining both the role of the media service provider and the definition of audiovisual media services. Article 1 (c) defines 'editorial responsibility' as 'the exercise of effective control both over the selection of the programmes and over their organisation either in a chronological schedule, in the case of television broadcasts, or in a catalogue, in the case of on-demand audiovisual media services.' It is left to the Member States to specify further aspects of this definition, notably the notion of 'effective control'.[13]

It is not entirely clear as to whether this definition only covers the 'publisher' or also other intermediaries in the distribution chain such as content aggregators or platform operators.[14] The criterion of 'organizational control' is intended to cover both the selection of substantive content as well as the economic aspects of the creation of a channel or combination of channels.[15] According to Gibbons, the most significant part of the value chain is the compilation and organization of material into channels for the viewer to select.[16] The mere production and supply of content, or even the supply of a compilation of programme material to another company is not caught by this definition as it is still too far removed from the intended audience.[17] Electronic Programme Guides (EPGs) would, however, fall under this definition.

The extension to non-linear services is justified by reference to the principle of technological neutrality and the need to create a level playing field between different platforms delivering similar content.[18] Nonetheless, the AVMS Directive treats non-linear services differently from linear ones. While non-linear services are only subject to a basic set of rules, there are additional rules for linear services. This graduated treatment is meant to take account of the differences between these types of services as regards their impact on society as well as user choice and control.[19] It will, however, lead to the application of a different regime to the same audiovisual content depending on its mode of delivery.[20] For example, a television programme purchased from a pay-per-view channel is linear

13. AVMS Directive, recital 23.
14. Schultz, *Vorschlag für eine Richtlinie*, p. 12; J. W. van den Bos, 'No Frontiers: The New EU Proposal on Audiovisual Media Services' [2006] 4 ENT L R, 111.
15. Gibbons, 'Jurisdiction over (Television) Broadcasters', pp. 53, 56.
16. *Ibid.*, p. 57.
17. *Ibid.*; T. Kleist and A. Scheuer, 'Audiovisuelle Mediendienste ohne Grenzen' (2006) 3 MMR, 127, 131.
18. Explanatory Memorandum to the Proposal for a Directive of the European Parliament and of the Council amending Council Directive 89/552/EEC on the coordination of certain provisions laid down by law, regulation or administrative action in Member States concerning the pursuit of television broadcasting activities, 13 December 2005, COM (2005) 646 final, 3 (hereafter referred to as Explanatory Memorandum); AVMS Directive, recitals 6, 7.
19. AVMS Directive, recital 42.
20. Van den Bos, 'No Frontiers', 109, 111.

since it is shown at the same time to everyone ordering it. The same content would be non-linear if it was downloaded from the internet. It is questionable whether these two services should be regulated differently.

The country of origin principle is applied to all audiovisual media services under the new Directive. In fact, the 2005 Commission proposal stated that its main objective was the subjection of on-demand audiovisual media services under the country of origin principle so that they can fully benefit from the internal market.[21] In view of the extension of this principle to on-demand services, the more general term 'country of origin principle' seems preferable to the previously used term 'transmission state principle'.[22]

This chapter will consider, first, the criteria determining the state having jurisdiction over a broadcaster in the light of the case-law of the European Court. The TwF Directive sought to ensure that 'one Member State and one only has jurisdiction over a broadcaster'.[23] The question as to which Member State can claim the right to regulate the activities of a broadcaster is relevant but complex. The freedom of establishment and the freedom to provide services guaranteed under the EC Treaty and in secondary legislation allow broadcasters to establish themselves in any Member State and to target non-national markets.

Differences in the broadcasting standards of the Member States invite broadcasters to engage in forum shopping so as to find the most congenial environment from which to operate.[24] Jurisdictional problems typically arise if a channel having established itself in a country exclusively targets the audience of another country.[25] Also, if it tailors its programme for the market of the place of establishment, while at the same time capturing the markets of neighbouring countries with advertising or programme windows targeting these additional audiences.[26] A reception state wishing to apply its own laws will have to prove that it has jurisdiction over this channel.

Secondly, the operation of the country of origin principle will be explained. The rules on jurisdiction and the country of origin principle go hand in hand. While the former determine the one country having personal jurisdiction over a broadcaster, the latter entrusts this very country with the sole responsibility of supervising this broadcaster's programmes to the exclusion of all other countries receiving these programmes. The country of origin principle seeks to

---

21. Explanatory Memorandum, 3.
22. *Ibid.*, recital 19.
23. Dir. 97/36/EC, recital 13.
24. S. Nikoltchev, 'Jurisdiction over Broadcasters: EC-Rules, Case Law, and an Ever-Changing Audiovisual Landscape' in *Transfrontier Television in the European Union: Market Impact and Selected Legal Aspects*, background paper prepared by the European Audiovisual Observatory for a Ministerial Conference on Broadcasting by the Irish Presidency of the European Union, Dublin and Drogheda, 1-3 March 2004 <www.obs.coe.int/online_publication/transfrontier_tv.pdf>, 22 April 2004, 28.
25. A. Lange, 'Transfrontier Television in the European Union: Market Impact' in *ibid.*, pp. 6, 10. Examples are RTL-4 and RTL-5 established in Luxembourg but targeting the Netherlands.
26. *Ibid.* German private channels SAT.1, RTL, Pro7 and Kabel1 have Swiss and Austrian windows. SAT1 has obtained a licence from the targeted countries.

ensure that there are no control gaps and, what is crucial for the creation of the internal market in broadcasting services, no double control of broadcasts in the European Union.

This seemingly hard and fast rule is not as clear-cut in reality. There is no doubt that the receiving state cannot be entirely divested of its regulatory responsibilities, yet the Directive does little to clarify the subjects for which this type of control is not pre-empted. The final section therefore assesses the residual powers of receiving Member States to control incoming broadcasts and concludes that the relationship between partial harmonization and the protection of valuable and vulnerable values in the national broadcasting orders has yet to be clearly defined.

2. THE COUNTRY OF ORIGIN

Given that the competence of supervising broadcasts is only bestowed on the country of origin and that no overarching European broadcasting authority exists as yet, it is apparent that the possibility of clearly identifying the Member State having jurisdiction with regard to a particular broadcaster is of paramount importance.

Dir. 89/552 gave rise to legal uncertainty in this respect by choosing not to lay down criteria determining jurisdiction.[27] The revised Dir. 97/36 responded to this unsatisfactory state of affairs by developing elaborate rules of conflict. Before looking at these amendments, it is pertinent to outline the decisions adopted by the Court under the old regime, since they decisively influenced the legislative process leading to Dir. 97/36. Two of these cases concern infringement proceedings initiated by the Commission against the United Kingdom and Belgium on the ground of the incorrect transposition of the Directive into national law. The other cases arose out of preliminary references concerning broadcasters having links with more than one Member State.

2.1 The Case-law of the European Court

2.1.1 The Criterion of Establishment

In the case *Commission v. United Kingdom*[28] the Commission brought infringement proceedings against the United Kingdom for violation of its obligations under

---

27. Art. 2 (1) of Dir. 89/552/EEC of 3 October 1989 OJ L 298/23, 1989:

    Each Member State shall ensure that all television broadcasts transmitted

    - by broadcasters under its jurisdiction, or
    - by broadcasters who, while not being under the jurisdiction of any Member State, make use of a frequency or a satellite capacity granted by, or a satellite up-link situated in, that Member State, comply with the law applicable to broadcasts intended for the public in that Member State.

28. Case C-222/94, *Commission v. United Kingdom* [1996] ECR I-4025.

the Directive. The Broadcasting Act 1990 determined jurisdiction for satellite broadcasts according to their place of transmission, thereby distinguishing between domestic and non-domestic satellite services. As a result, the United Kingdom also supervised broadcasts transmitted by broadcasters falling under the jurisdiction of other Member States.

The European Court held that the interpretation advocated by the United Kingdom could not be reconciled with the wording of Article 2 (1) of Dir. 89/552, since the place from which a broadcast is transmitted is referred to in the second indent of Article 2 (1) as a criterion applicable to broadcasters who are not under the jurisdiction of any Member State. In the Commission's point of view jurisdiction *ratione personae* over a broadcaster could only be founded on the broadcaster's connection to the State's legal system which is tantamount to its establishment as this concept is used in Article 49 (1) EC.[29] The Court agreed with the Commission's opinion, mainly because of the greater efficiency of the criterion based on establishment. The rule adopted by the United Kingdom would entail the risk of conflicting claims of jurisdiction, given that a broadcaster could transmit its programmes via up-links situated in several Member States.[30] The Court conceded that this risk also exists with the criterion of establishment. It could, however, be reduced by construing establishment as 'the place in which a broadcaster has the centre of its activities, in particular the place where decisions concerning programme policy are taken and the programmes to be broadcast are finally put together'.[31] Moreover, the criterion supported by the United Kingdom would enhance the risk of abuse, since it would be easy for broadcasters to move their up-links to another Member State in order to benefit from its legislation.[32]

A noteworthy contribution of this decision to the understanding of Article 2 (1) of Dir. 89/552 is that it made clear that all television broadcasts transmitted by broadcasters coming under the jurisdiction of a Member State should comply with roughly the same rules. These rules are, according to Article 2 (1), 'the law applicable to broadcasts intended for the public in that Member State'. The Court found the United Kingdom to have violated this obligation by applying, in section 43 of the Broadcasting Act 1990, a different regime to non-domestic satellite services (NDSS) than that applicable to domestic satellite services (DSS).[33] More precisely, NDSS were treated more leniently, since they were exempted from the obligation to abide by Articles 4 and 5 of the Directive. It is not surprising that NDSS, in contrast to DSS, could also be received beyond the United Kingdom. Such attempts by Member States to deregulate broadcasts addressed to foreign viewers, attracting thus satellite channels to operate from their territory, are precluded by the Directive.

29. *Ibid.*, paras 35 *et seq.*
30. AG Lenz in Case C-222/94, *Commission v. United Kingdom* [1996] ECR I-4025, para. 68.
31. Case C-222/94, para. 58.
32. *Ibid.*, para. 60.
33. Case C-222/94, paras 70 *et seq.*

2.1.2 The Circumvention Principle

There is, however, a further angle from which the concept of establishment has been highlighted in the case-law of the European Court. These cases have in common the fact that circumvention was pleaded by Member States which thought that their legislation had been evaded by broadcasting organizations directing most of their programmes to their territory, while being established in different Member States.

The first of these cases concerned Vereniging Veronica Omroep Organisatie (Veronica), a non-commercial broadcasting corporation established in the Netherlands.[34] Veronica contributed to the establishment in Luxembourg of a commercial station, RTL-Véronique broadcasting to the Netherlands, by providing *inter alia* capital and guarantees. This conduct brought Veronica into conflict with the *Commissariaat voor de Media*, which alleged that Article 57 (1) of the *Mediawet* had been breached. This provision prohibits public broadcasting organizations from engaging in activities other than those stipulated in the *Mediawet* or authorized by the *Commissariaat voor de Media*. The commercial activities pursued by Veronica were not held to fall thereunder. The national court, to which Veronica appealed against the sanctions imposed on it by the *Commissariaat*, requested a preliminary ruling on their compatibility with Community law.

The Court first considered the question whether the restrictions on the provision of services resulting from Article 57 (1) of the *Mediawet* were justified on grounds of general interest. This justification was available, given that the provision in question only affected national broadcasting bodies and was thus non-discriminatory. The Court found that its aim was to secure that subsidies available to such bodies, so as to maintain pluralism in the Dutch broadcasting system, were not used for purely commercial purposes.[35] The restrictions on Veronica's activity were consequently justified on grounds of cultural policy.

It is, however, a further line of reasoning deployed by the Court, which is interesting for our discussion. The Court recalled its judgment in *van Binsbergen* in which it held that 'a Member State cannot be denied the right to take measures to prevent the exercise by a person providing services, whose activity is entirely or principally directed towards its territory, of the freedom guaranteed by Article 59 for the purpose of avoiding the professional rules of conduct which would be applicable to him if he were established within that State; such a situation may be subject to judicial control under the provisions relating to the right of establishment and not of that on the provision of services.'[36] Since the effect of setting up a commercial broadcasting station in Luxembourg for the purpose of transmitting programmes to the Netherlands would be to evade national legislation prescribing the pluralist and non-commercial character of broadcasts, the Court ruled

34. Case C-148/91, *Vereniging Veronica Omroep Organisatie v. Commissariaat voor de Media* [1993] ECR I-487.
35. *Ibid.*, para. 11.
36. Case 33/74, *van Binsbergen v. Bedrijfsvereniging Metaalnijverheid* [1974] ECR 1299, para. 13.

that Article 57 (1) of the *Mediawet* was compatible with the freedom to provide services.

It is striking that the Court in this judgment did not clarify the conditions for the pleading of circumvention. It only qualified the evasion of the obligations deriving from the national legislation by the requirement that the broadcasting organizations must have acted 'improperly'.[37] As far as the phrase in the operative part of the judgment is concerned, that the prohibitions have to be necessary in order to ensure the pluralistic and non-commercial character of the audio visual system, it is doubtful whether it was thought of as a restriction to the right of the Member States to plead circumvention.[38] It could also be interpreted as a reference to the principle of proportionality, which constitutes an inherent limitation on the right to invoke objectives relating to the public interest so as to restrict the freedom to provide services.

The reticence of the Court with regard to the parameters of the circumvention argument should, however, be seen against the factual background of this case. The creation of RTL-Véronique had been preceded by repeated requests by Veronica to the national broadcasting authorities to change the *Mediawet* to the effect that commercial broadcasting stations could be established in the Netherlands.[39] Given that the ground was not yet fertile for the Dutch law to be changed, it was clear that the participation of Veronica in a Luxembourg-based commercial broadcasting organization was intended to overcome the restraints of Netherlands legislation.

The circumvention argument has also been at issue in three more judgments handed down by the European Court.

The case *TV 10 SA* v *Commissariaat voor de Media*[40] displays many similarities with the previous case, in that it is also about a commercial broadcasting organization established in Luxembourg, but operated by Netherlands nationals mainly, while its programmes were transmitted by cable to the Netherlands in the first place. The *Commissariaat* denied TV 10 access to the Netherlands cable network on the ground that it had established itself in Luxembourg so as to evade national legislation requiring the pluralist and non-commercial character of domestic programmes. The Court observed that the transmission of TV 10 broadcasts from Luxembourg to the Netherlands was covered by the provisions on the free movement of services, even if TV 10 had chosen the former as the springboard for its operations with the intention of circumvention. Nonetheless, it found the restrictions on their transmission to be justified on identical grounds to those presented in the *Veronica* case. The Netherlands could lawfully resist the retransmission of the TV 10 programmes not merely on the ground of cultural policy objectives. It was also entitled to do so on the basis of the *van Binsbergen* doctrine outlined above.

37. Case C-148/91, *Vereniging Veronica Omroep Organisatie v. Commissariaat voor de Media* [1993] ECR I-487, para. 13.
38. *See* note by W. Hins, (1994) 31 CMLRev, 909.
39. *Ibid.*, 902.
40. Case C-23/93, *TV 10* SA *v. Commissariaat voor de Media* [1994] ECR I 4795 *et seq.*

In this case the Court, once again, did not expand on the facts substantiating the circumvention argument, but relied entirely on the assessment of the national court that TV 10, by establishing itself in Luxembourg, but directing its activities 'wholly or principally' towards the Netherlands, was seeking to avoid the *Mediawet.*[41] The only hint it gave as to the necessary conditions for this argument to be successful is that the broadcasting body must have been established in a Member State other than the receiving state, in order to 'wrongfully' avoid the rules of the latter.[42] The word 'wrongfully' is a touch sharper than the word 'improperly' used in the *Veronica* case and suggests that objective factors are not sufficient to assume circumvention. Subjective elements indicating the intention to frustrate national rules are needed in addition.[43] The requirement that this intention must have existed from the very start narrows down considerably the scope of application of the circumvention principle.[44]

Advocate-General Lenz reached the opposite conclusion in his Opinion. He placed emphasis on the fact that legal persons are not capable of having intentions and that no uniform system of ascribing the attitudes of the organs of a corporate body to legal persons exists in the EU.[45] It is true that the use of a subjective test to gauge the legally relevant behaviour of a legal person is bound to be fraught with difficulties. Objective criteria such as the organization of the company's undertakings,[46] the striking difference between the legislation of various Member States or the impossibility of broadcasting a programme in the target state arguably constitute more conclusive evidence for the circumvention of national legislation.[47] In the present case, the fact that TV 10 was precluded from transmitting a commercial programme in the Netherlands in view of the Dutch law seeking to protect interests recognized in the EU legal order must have weighed in the Court's decision to give the *Raad van State* the green light.[48]

On the same day on which the judgment in the case *Commission v. United Kingdom* was handed down, the Court had to deal with the circumvention argument in a further Article 226 action brought by the Commission against the Kingdom of Belgium.[49] This case concerned Belgian legislation subjecting the

41. *Ibid.*, para. 26.
42. *Ibid.*, para. 21.
43. Case C-23/93, *TV 10* SA *v. Commissariaat voor de Media* [1994] ECR I 4795 *et seq.*; *see* note by P. Wattel, (1995) 32 CMLRev, 1260.
44. L. Woods and J. Scholes, 'Broadcasting: the Creation of a European Culture or the Limits of the Internal Market?' (1997) 17 YEL, 56, 57.
45. Opinion of Advocate-General Lenz in Case 23/93, *TV 10 SA v. Commissariaat voor de Media* [1993] ECR I-487, para. 60.
46. *Ibid.*, para. 65.
47. N. Helberger, 'Die Konkretisierung des Sendestaatsprinzips in der Rechtsprechung des EuGH' (1998) 1 ZUM, 55; *see* Case C-212/96, *Centros Ltd v. Erhvervs- og Selskabsstyrelsen* [1999] ECR I-1459 para. 25.
48. *See* Opinion of Advocate-General Lenz in Case 23/93, para. 67.
49. Case C-222/94, *Commission of the European Communities v. United Kingdom of Great Britain and Northern Ireland* [1996] ECR-I 4025; Case C-11/95, *Commission v. Belgium* [1996] ECR I-4117.

retransmission by cable of television broadcasts from other Member States in the French and Flemish community to the prior authorization of the domestic authorities. The authorization for the transmission of commercial advertisements and of teleshopping programmes in particular, which were directed at the viewers in the French community, was made conditional on the promotion of audiovisual production and the maintenance of pluralism in that community's television channels and press. The Commission considered this rule to be in violation of the transmission state principle. The Belgian Government, on the other hand, sought to defend this rule on the basis of the circumvention argument. It claimed that foreign television channels broadcasting advertisements specifically directed at the French community either fell within its jurisdiction or circumvented its legislation.[50] In any event, they could not invoke Article 2 (2) of the Directive.

The Court, on an integrationist impulse, posed for the first time the rhetorical question whether the *van Binsbergen* doctrine was still applicable after the adoption of Dir. 89/552. It evaded it by stating that the pleading of circumvention does not 'in any event authorize a Member State generally to exclude provision of certain services by operators established in other Member States, since that would entail abolition of the freedom to provide services'.[51] This finding echoes the judgment of the Court in a previous action under Article 226 EC brought by the Commission against Belgium.[52] That case revolved around Belgian legislation prohibiting cable operators from transmitting programmes originating from foreign broadcasting stations in a language other than that of the Member State where the stations were established. The Court dismissed the circumvention argument on the same grounds given that the Belgian rule effectively prevented stations established in other Member States from reaching audiences in the Flemish community by means of programmes broadcast in Dutch.[53]

The formula used by the Court to reject the circumvention argument might appear somewhat cryptic at first sight, particularly since in the *TV 10* case the broadcasts from abroad were also generally denied access to the Netherlands cable network. But, what is meant by this formula is that circumvention must actually be demonstrated by the Member State adopting the countervailing measures. The evidence of circumvention must go beyond the mere fact that broadcasts are specifically addressed to the viewers in a certain Member State.[54] This also becomes apparent from the 14th recital to Dir. 89/552, according to which 'in particular those [broadcasts] intended for reception in another Member State, should respect the law of the originating Member State'.

---

50. *Ibid.*, para. 62.
51. *Ibid.*, para. 65.
52. Case C-211/91, *Commission of the European Communities v. Kingdom of Belgium* [1992] ECR I- 6757.
53. *Ibid.*, para. 12.
54. Opinion of Advocate-General Lenz in Case C-11/95, *Commission v. Belgium* [1996] ECR I-4117, para. 73 *et seq.*

This last consideration was also taken up by the Court in the *VT 4* case,[55] which concerned an English company established in London, whose programmes were directed at the Flemish community in Belgium. VT 4 maintained a 'subsidiary' in Flanders, where contact was taken up with advertisers and production companies, and information for the news programmes was gathered. The Flemish Minister for Culture and Brussels Affairs refused VT 4 access to the cable distribution network with the argument that VTM was the only private company licensed to the Flemish community. Moreover, he did not consider VT 4 to be a television broadcaster licensed by another Member State, which would bring it within the scope of the Cable Decree, since it was allegedly established in the United Kingdom so as to evade Flemish community legislation.[56]

The national court suspended this decision and requested a preliminary ruling from the European Court on the question of the influence of the provisional results of negotiations within the Council on the interpretation of Article 2 of Dir. 89/552. Even though the question was phrased in those terms, the Court replied by indicating the criteria determining a Member State's jurisdiction over a broadcaster for the purposes of Article 2 (1) of Dir. 89/552. It did not regard the matter as *acte clair*, presumably because the question had been raised before the Court handed down its ruling in case *Commission v. United Kingdom.*[57] Moreover, VT 4's place of establishment was far from clear, given that it maintained links in the sense of *Factortame* both with the United Kingdom and Belgium.[58]

The Court repeated its findings from *Commission v. United Kingdom* and referred once more to the 'centre of activities' test.[59] It thus left to the national court the task of determining the Member State having jurisdiction over VT 4.[60] As to the pleading of circumvention, it remarked succinctly that the mere fact that VT 4 addressed all its programmes and advertisements to the Flemish public, did not exclude its being established in the United Kingdom. 'The Treaty does not prohibit an undertaking from exercising the freedom to provide services if it does not offer services in the Member State in which it is established.'[61]

What of the relationship between the rulings of the Court in the *VT 4* and *TV 10* cases? Has the Court in *VT 4* overruled *TV 10* by declaring that the destination of television programmes to the territory of a Member State other than the one where

55. Case C-56/96, *VT4 v. Vlaamse Gemeenschap* [1997] ECR I-3143.
56. *Ibid.*, para. 9.
57. *Ibid.*, para. 13; Case C-222/94, *Commission of the European Communities v. United Kingdom of Great Britain and Northern Ireland* [1996] ECR-I 4025.
58. Case C-221/89, *Factortame and Others* [1991] ECR I 3905; Woods and Scholes, 'Broadcasting', 66.
59. Case C-56/96, para. 19.
60. C. Farrar, 'E.C. Broadcasting Law Clarified: The Paul Denuit and VT4 Cases and the New "Television without Frontiers" Directive' (1998) 1 ENT L R, 18.
61. Case C-56/96, para. 22.

the broadcaster is established does not amount to circumvention? Surely not, for two reasons:

First, while in the earlier case the national court had ascertained that TV 10 sought to evade the Netherlands laws, no such submission had been made by the Belgian court in *VT 4*.

Secondly, as stated above, the Dutch rules evaded by TV 10 aimed to protect important values in accordance with EU law, while VTM's monopoly on private television in the Flemish community was struck by the Commission as incompatible with Article 90 (1) EC in connection with Article 52 EC.[62] However, as regards the second argument, it is not entirely clear why the Court was sensitive in the *TV 10* case to the concern of the Netherlands to protect the non-commercial character of its audiovisual system, which in the *Mediawet* cases had to succumb to the creation of the internal market in broadcasting services.[63]

Advocate-General Lenz adduced a further reason for the different outcomes in the *TV 10* and *VT 4* cases, which is, however, not plausible. He pointed out that TV 10 could have operated in the Netherlands on the condition that requirements with regard to the programmes' content would be satisfied. The same could not be said of VT 4, which could not transmit its programme from Belgium in view of VTM's monopoly. He drew the conclusion from these circumstances that VT 4 was not in a position to abuse Flemish law.[64]

On closer inspection, this reasoning seems to be erroneous. Advocate-General Lenz himself said in the *TV 10* case that 'the objective impossibility of broadcasting in the manner chosen by the appellant in the Netherlands' provided evidence to suggest that the Dutch law had been circumvented.[65] One is bound to subscribe to the view that it was just as impossible for TV 10 to operate from the Netherlands as it was for VT 4 to operate from Belgium. The fact that TV 10 could have transmitted a different programme in compliance with Dutch legislation is immaterial. This impossibility is, however, only one factor to be taken into account when assessing whether avoidance of national legislation has taken place. It is, in other words, a necessary but not sufficient condition for circumvention to occur.

---

62. The *Centros* case lends support to the argument that the circumvention doctrine only applies if the national provisions being evaded protect overriding requirements of the general interest that are recognized in Community law. *See* Case C-212/96, *Centros Ltd v. Erhvervs- og Selskabsstyrelsen* [1999] ECR I-1459; J. G. Huglo, 'Droit d'établissement et libre prestation des services' (1992) 28 RTDE, 687; V. Hatzopoulos, 'Recent Developments of the Case Law of the ECJ in the Field of Services' (2000) 37 CMLRev, 63–64.
63. *See* Part 2, Ch. 12 *below*; K. Sevinga, 'Dutch Broadcasting Continued' (1993) 4 ULR 138; T. Trautwein, 'Grenzen der Dienstleistungsfreiheit im Dienstleistungsbereich: Anmerkung zu EuGH, Urteil vom 05.10.1994, Rs C-23/93, TV10 SA/Commissariat voor de Media' (1995) 5 ZUM, 325.
64. Opinion of Advocate-General Lenz in Case C-56/96, para. 38.
65. Opinion of Advocate-General Lenz in Case 23/93, *TV 10 SA v. Commissariaat voor de Media* [1993] ECR I-487, para. 67.

All in all, the *VT 4* judgment is a further twist in the multifaceted case-law of the European Court with respect to the circumvention argument. It does not signify a departure from the previous judgments, *Veronica* and *TV 10*, which were favourably inclined towards national sovereignty in the area of broadcasting.[66] Still, the *VT 4* case lends weight to the argument that evaded national laws are only worthy of protection if overriding requirements of general interest recognized in EU law are at stake. If the condition of proportionality of these laws is added, the circumvention principle becomes nearly congruent with the rule of reason, so that the scope left for the defence of national broadcasting systems against abuse is very limited. Why would a Member State frame its case in terms of abuse of rights if not for fear that its national laws would not be found justifiable under EU law?

The narrow construction of the circumvention principle is not surprising given that this principle is inherently antithetical to the creation of the internal market. However, the mixing of the rule of reason with the circumvention principle does not seem consistent with the *van Binsbergen* judgment. More importantly, if the circumvention principle protects Member State autonomy by preventing individuals from manufacturing a Union element to evade domestic laws, why would these laws need to be evaluated under EU law in the first place?[67]

The argument has been put forward that the case *VT 4* provided an answer to the question which the Court had left open in case C-11/95, *Commission v. Belgium*, namely whether the *van Binsbergen* doctrine is still valid after the adoption of the Television Directive. [68] The ruling has been interpreted in the sense that circumvention cannot be invoked when a broadcaster is established in a Member State according to the 'centre of activities' test, even if his programmes are exclusively transmitted in another Member State.[69] It is, however, reasonable to be at least slightly sceptical about this interpretation. It only makes sense to have recourse to the *van Binsbergen* doctrine if an undertaking is established in another Member State than the one to which its activities are oriented. Given that the destination of television programmes is not a relevant consideration in the 'centre of activities' test, the above-mentioned interpretation would effectively make a clean sweep of the circumvention argument.

The amended Television Directive 97/36 enhanced legal certainty in this respect. Even though the *van Binsbergen* doctrine was not enacted in the body of the Directive, it was inserted in its 14th recital. The competence of the Member States to exercise control over broadcasters established in other Member States, which have lax licensing requirements, has thus been confirmed.

---

66. *See* D. Dörr, 'Die Entwicklung des Medienrechts' (1995) 35 NJW, 2265; contra Helberger, 'Konkretisierung des Sendestaatsprinzips', 60.
67. R. Craufurd Smith, 'The Establishment of Companies in European Community Law: Choice of Law or Abuse of Rights?' [1999] EuroCLY, xii, xv.
68. Case C-11/95, *Commission v. Belgium* [1996] ECR I-4117; C. Durand and S. van Raepenbusch, 'Les pricipaux développements de la jurisprudence de la Cour de Justice et du Tribunal de première instance du 1er août 1996 au 31 juillet 1997' (1998) 34 CDE, 439.
69. *Ibid.*

This is crucial, especially in view of the interest of the Member States to impose stricter rules on broadcasters under their jurisdiction in the areas covered by the Directive, in accordance with Article 3. This provision has been praised as the seal of national regulatory competence in the area of television.[70] However, one should be cautious not to overestimate Article 3, given that it can be a double-edged sword in the absence of other regulatory mechanisms. This is for the simple reason that national broadcasters exposed to virtually unlimited competition from foreign stations which are subjected to looser programming commitments suffer a considerable competitive disadvantage.[71] Member States are faced with the choice of either succumbing to the pressures for deregulation with the aim of preventing discrimination against their national broadcasters or seeing them wander off to foreign broadcasting havens.[72] More often than not, states take the option of lowering their requirements.

The *van Binsbergen* doctrine keeps the driving-down of regulatory standards within bounds by preventing the relocation of broadcasting companies. Nonetheless, as the *VT 4* case demonstrated, circumvention can only be pleaded under strict conditions that remain obscure in many respects. First, the activity must be entirely or principally directed towards the territory of the state taking anti-circumvention measures. Is this the case only when the broadcaster directs all of his programmes to one country or also when he broadcasts them to two or three countries with stricter programme requirements or even when he transmits his programmes on a domestic channel as well?

Secondly, an intention of circumvention may need to be proved. However, there are no uniform rules of ascribing the attitudes of organs to a corporate body in the EU. Should objective criteria be used instead such as the impossibility of broadcasting a programme in the target state? The judgment in *Centros* lends support to this view.[73] The Court held in *Centros* that the motives for choosing to incorporate a company in a Member State with less restrictive rules of company law and to set up branches in other Member States are immaterial so long as the purpose of the right of establishment has been met. More generally, it can be inferred from recent case-law that the reasons for which an EU national or company exercise a fundamental freedom cannot call into question the protection they

70. D. Kugelmann, *Der Rundfunk und die Dienstleistungsfreiheit des EWG-Vertrages*, Schriften zum Europäischen Recht, vol. 10 (Berlin, Duncker & Humblot, 1991), p. 51.
71. J. Betz, 'Die EG-Fernsehrichtlinie – Ein Schritt zum europäischen Fernsehen?' (1989) 11 MP, 679; Seidel, 'Fernsehen ohne Grenzen', 122; P. Keller, 'The New Television Without Frontiers Directive' (1997/98) III YMEL, 194; W. Hoffmann-Riem, 'The Broadcasting Activities of the European Community and Their Implications for National Broadcasting Systems in Europe' (1993) 16 Hastings Int'l&CompLRev., 612–613; Drijber, 'Revised Television Without Frontiers Directive', 94–95; ARD and ZDF, 'EG-Politik im Bereich des Rundfunks', 80; U. Brühann, 'Der Vorschlag einer Gemeinschaftsrichtlinie zum Rundfunkrecht: Notwendigkeit und werberechtlicher Inhalt' in *Europafernsehen und Werbung: Chancen für die deutsche und europäische Medienpolitik*, Arbeitskreis Werbefernsehen der deutschen Wirtschaft (ed.) (Baden-Baden, Nomos, 1987), p. 21.
72. Hoffmann-Riem, 'Broadcasting Activities of the European Community', 612.
73. Case C-212/96, *Centros Ltd v. Erhvervs- og Selskabsstyrelsen* [1999] ECR I-1459 para. 25.

derive from the Treaty unless if objective factors lead to the conclusion that the aims pursued by this fundamental freedom have been frustrated.[74]

Finally, it is unclear whether the broadcaster will be subject to the rules of the reception state only or also to those of the transmission state. The first option is problematic as contrary to the transmission state principle and the case-law on establishment. The second option could give rise to the application of conflicting rules.

So as to clarify the conditions for pleading circumvention, the AVMS Directive includes a provision enabling receiving states to take measures against broadcasters targeting their audience. In the initial Commission proposal, this provision was embedded in Article 2 of the Directive, complementing the jurisdiction criteria.[75] It allowed the receiving state to take appropriate measures against the abusive delocalization of media service providers directing most or all of their activity to its territory. Such measures could only be taken if the receiving state asked the state of origin to take measures; the latter state did not take such measures; the receiving state notified the Commission and the state of origin of its intention to take such measures and the Commission decided that the measures were compatible with Community law.

This provision was considerably altered after the Council and the European Parliament first reading. First of all, it was transferred from Article 2 to Article 3, making clear that a Member State can only take measures under this provision so as to ensure compliance with more detailed or stricter rules in the area covered by this Directive. Certainly, Member States cannot have recourse to this procedure in cases where the country of origin simply fails to enforce the provisions of the Directive. Nor can Member States use this procedure so as to prevent the circumvention of their rules that lie beyond the fields coordinated by the Directive.

As we will see in more detail later on, Member States' capacity to apply rules that lie beyond the fields coordinated by the Directive is not affected by the country of origin principle. However, delineating the Directive's ambit is fraught with uncertainties. Article 3 of the AVMS Directive requires a demarcation between 'more detailed or stricter rules in the areas covered by this Directive' and rules that are an *aliud* compared to the Directive's provisions. While a language quota is arguably a more detailed rule compared to the Directive's European quota, can the same be said of a provision requiring that a certain percentage be devoted to regional programming? The move of the new procedure to Article 3 is consistent with the Directive's internal logic. However, it restricts this procedure's field

74. Case C-167/01, *Kammer van Koophandel en Fabrieken voor Amsterdam v. Inspire Art* [2003] ECR I-10155; Case C-196/04, *Cadbury Schweppes v. Commissioners of Inland Revenue* [2006] ECRI-7995.
75. Proposal for a Directive of the European Parliament and of the Council amending Council Directive 89/552/EEC on the coordination of certain provisions laid down by law, regulation or administrative action in Member States concerning the pursuit of television broadcasting activities, 13 December 2005, COM (2005) 646 final, Art. 2 (7), (8), (9). Only in recital 23 of this proposal was the circumvention procedure associated with the capacity of the Member States to apply stricter rules in the fields coordinated by the Directive.

of application and poses certain interpretative difficulties. Secondly, a voluntary cooperation procedure preceding the circumvention procedure was devised. This voluntary procedure was significantly amended in the political agreement of 24 May 2007 between the European Parliament and the Council.[76] Finally, whereas in the original Commission proposal the circumvention procedure applied to all audiovisual media services providers, in the AVMS Directive both the voluntary and the circumvention procedures only apply to linear audiovisual media services.

However, the fact that the circumvention principle is referred to in recital 57 to the E-Commerce Directive raises the question as to whether this principle also applies to non-linear audiovisual media services.[77] The AVMS Directive includes a much needed clarification on the relationship between this Directive and the E-Commerce Directive. Article 3 (8) states that the latter will apply fully next to the AVMS Directive except as otherwise provided for in this Directive, i.e. the AVMS Directive. In the event of a conflict between the two instruments, the provisions of the AVMS Directive shall prevail, unless otherwise provided for in this Directive. Does the AVMS Directive provide otherwise by restricting Article 3 (2)-(5) to linear audiovisual media services? It is submitted that the circumvention principle, as developed in the case-law of the Court, should still apply to non-linear audiovisual media services. This would be especially important in view of the inherent mobility of such services which is probably intensified as a result of the smaller degree of European harmonization in this area.[78] Only the Article 3 procedures could not be relied on in relation to these services.

In the following, both the voluntary and the circumvention procedure will be outlined as they have been crystallized in the AVMS Directive. In order to enter into the voluntary procedure, the receiving state must have exercised its freedom to adopt more detailed or stricter rules of general public interest. This open-ended formulation has replaced the non-exhaustive enumeration of grounds of general interest in the amended Commission proposal.[79] Further, the receiving state must assess that a broadcaster under the jurisdiction of another Member State provides a

76. Political agreement on common position of 24 May 2007, <www.ec.europa.eu/avpolicy/reg/tvwf/modernisation/proposal_2005/index_en.htm>, 7 January 2008 (hereafter referred to as 'Political agreement of 24 May 2007').
77. European Parliament and Council Directive 2003/31/EC of 8 June 2000 on certain legal aspects of information society services, in particular electronic commerce, in the internal market (Directive on electronic commerce), OJ L 178/1, 2000.
78. J. Hörnle, 'Country of Origin Regulation in Cross-Border Media: One Step Beyond the Freedom to Provide Services?' (2005) 54 ICLQ, 89, 101; EBU Position on Issues Papers for the Liverpool Audiovisual Conference, 'Rules Applicable to Audiovisual Content Services', 5 September 2005, 4.
79. Amended proposal for a Directive of the European Parliament and of the Council amending Council Directive 89/552/EEC on the coordination of certain provisions laid down by law, regulation or administrative action in Member States concerning the pursuit of television broadcasting activities ('Audiovisual media services without frontiers'), 29 March 2007, COM (2007) 170 final, Art. 3 (2) (b) (hereafter referred to as the amended AVMSD proposal): 'reasons of public policy, including the protection of minors or public security or public health or cultural diversity.'

television broadcast which is wholly or mostly directed towards its territory. The uncertainty as to when a broadcast is 'wholly or mostly' directed towards the territory of another Member State remains. By way of clarification, recital 33 states that a Member State 'may refer to indicators such as the origin of the advertising and/or subscription revenues, the main language of the service or the existence of programmes or commercial communications targeted specifically at the public in the Member State where they are received'. Industry representatives were fiercely opposed to the use of 'the main language of the service' as an indicator of territorial competence.[80] This criterion may indeed be misleading in the case of programmes transmitted across countries of the same linguistic area.

While the final text of the AVMS Directive focuses on the exclusive or main direction of a broadcast, the amended Commission proposal required that a broadcaster under the jurisdiction of another Member State have taken advantage of this Directive in abusive or fraudulent manner in order to circumvent the receiving state's rules. The European Parliament was particularly in favour of proof of abuse as a requirement not only of the circumvention but also of the voluntary procedure for fear that the country of origin principle might be inordinately weakened otherwise. The focus of the AVMS Directive on the direction of the broadcast irrespective of a finding of abusive conduct means that the exercise of the freedom to provide services – a perfectly legal undertaking – is sufficient in itself to trigger the voluntary procedure.

Under the two conditions mentioned earlier on, the receiving Member State can contact the Member State having jurisdiction with a view to achieving a mutually satisfactory solution to any problems posed. On receipt of a substantiated request by the first Member State, the Member State having jurisdiction shall request the broadcaster to comply with the rules of general public interest in question and to inform the first Member State of the results obtained within two months of the request. The AVMS Directive also provides that either Member State may invite the Contact Committee established under Article 23a to examine the case.[81]

The circumvention procedure, laid down in Article 3 (3)-(5) of the AVMS Directive, can only be embarked on if following requirements have been met. First, the voluntary procedure must have been completed without satisfactory results. Second, the broadcaster in question must have established itself in the Member State having jurisdiction in order to circumvent the stricter rules, in the fields coordinated by this Directive, which would be applicable to it if it were established within the receiving Member State. Third, the receiving state must have notified the Commission and the Member State having jurisdiction of its intention to take measures against the broadcaster concerned while substantiating the grounds on which it bases its assessment. Finally, the Commission must have decided that the measures are compatible with Community law, and in particular that

80. AVMS Directive, Art. 3 (2).
81. European Commission, Issues Paper for the Liverpool Audiovisual Conference: Rules Applicable to Audiovisual Content Services, July 2005, 6.

assessments made by the Member State taking these measures are correctly founded. The Commission shall decide on the compatibility within three months following notification.

Under these conditions, the receiving Member State may adopt appropriate measures against the broadcaster concerned. Such measures must be objectively necessary, applied in a non-discriminatory manner, suitable for attaining the objectives which they pursue and may not go beyond what is necessary to attain them. The type of measures that can be taken is not specified further. Presumably, the destination state can treat the broadcaster in question as a domestic provider and subject it to its domestic laws.

The circumvention procedure is not just a second stage following the unsuccessful completion of the voluntary procedure. Whereas there is no need to prove illegal conduct under the voluntary procedure, the circumvention procedure requires such proof to be furnished. The broadcaster in question must have behaved illegally by establishing itself in the Member State having jurisdiction so as to circumvent the stricter rules of the receiving state. The reference to 'abuse or fraudulent conduct' made in the updated Commission proposal was removed from the text agreed upon in the political agreement of 24 May 2007. Consequently, circumvention has to be established primarily on the basis of objective factors, not of the intention of the broadcaster concerned.

Also, while the updated Commission proposal required that the broadcaster concerned must have 'established itself in the Member State having jurisdiction in order *solely* to avoid the stricter rules', the word 'solely' has been omitted in the AVMS Directive. This is sensible given that it is very hard to prove that a broadcaster has opted for delocalization with the only aim of circumventing the broadcasting laws of the destination state and not for other reasons such as a more attractive taxation environment and lower operating costs.

The problem of abusive delocalization has been one of the most controversial issues during the negotiations for the Directive's revision. This is understandable in view of the sensitive economic and cultural issues involved. Member States and EU institutions were divided in two camps. The Commission, the European Parliament and a number of Member States, mainly Germany, Italy, Luxembourg, Spain and the United Kingdom, staunchly defended the country of origin principle. A group of 13 countries consisting of Austria, Belgium, the Czech Republic, Estonia, Ireland, Latvia, Lithuania, Malta, the Netherlands, Poland, Portugal, Slovenia and Sweden urged the Commission to make it possible for them to draw up rules for programmes primarily targeted at their territory. Most of these countries have issues with such programmes.[82]

82. Dutch Media Authority, *Regulation of the Dutch Commercial Television Market*, May 2006; J. Botella I Corral and E. Machet, 'Co-ordination and Co-operation between Regulatory Authorities in the Field of Broadcasting' in *Iris Special: Audiovisual Media Services without Frontiers: Implementing the Rules*, European Audiovisual Observatory (ed.) (Strasbourg, European Audiovisual Observatory, 2007), pp. 13, 16.

Commercial broadcasters operating from Germany hold a large percentage of the Austrian advertising market by tailoring certain programme components and advertising windows to the Austrian viewers. This puts the domestic broadcasters at a considerable competitive disadvantage. Ireland is targeted by similar advertising windows from the United Kingdom, which fail to comply with the Irish ban on advertising strong liquor or with the stricter Irish rules relating to the protection of minors. French advertising windows are directed at the Belgian audience. Also, as from 2006, three RTL stations having their centre of broadcasting activities in Brussels have been operating under Luxembourg licences.

Similar problems are encountered by the Netherlands, Sweden, Latvia, Estonia and Poland. The Dutch language programmes RTL4 and RTL5 target the Dutch market from Luxembourg, taking advantage of the latter's more permissive advertising and sponsorship rules. The programmes of the British channel *Kanal* 5 are aimed at Sweden but do not obey the Swedish ban on commercials for children. TV4, the most popular Swedish commercial channel, allegedly suffers yearly losses of 36 million EUR as a result of this unequal competitive position. The UK station 3+ targets Latvia and Estonia without maintaining minimum percentages for original productions in these languages. Finally, many programmes broadcast under a UK licence are specifically aimed at the Polish audience but do not follow Poland's rules on the protection of minors.

It becomes clear from the abovementioned cases that the issues at the heart of the circumvention problem are multifaceted. Advertising windows specifically intended for another country may be inconsistent with its laws for the protection of minors. Or they may, by simply tapping its advertising market, negatively affect media pluralism. This concern is particularly pronounced in small countries or countries with a restricted linguistic area. Programme windows for a particular country may also undermine its youth protection or cultural policies.

The AVMS Directive, by requiring proof of circumvention and by linking this question to the capacity to adopt stricter rules, fails to address all the situations outlined above and falls short of the 13 Member States' core demands. Despite their weaknesses, the new procedures were too much for the European Parliament and for some of the countries belonging to the opposite camp who went so far as to declare the country of origin principle dead. This raises the question as to whether the codification of the circumvention principle in the new Directive really has the potential to cut a hole in the country of origin rule.

The procedure in Article 3 (2) sends a political signal to broadcasters engaging in 'forum-shopping' that they should not stretch the freedom of broadcasting to its limits by ignoring the broadcasting laws of the destination state. It also provides a positive stimulus for communication and cooperation between broadcasting authorities. Obviously, such cooperation depends on the good will of these authorities and of the countries concerned. In the past, voluntary cooperation between regulatory bodies has been rare but not non-existent. An example of far-reaching cooperation between such bodies is provided by the recent FAVTV case. FANTV applied for a broadcasting licence in Latvia with the intention of targeting the Swedish market with its sports programmes. The Latvian National Broadcasting

Council consulted the Swedish Broadcasting Commission on the broadcasting standards pertaining in Sweden and only awarded FANTV a transfrontier broadcasting licence under the condition that it would adhere to these standards.[83]

The circumvention procedure in Article 3 (3)-(5) has more bite. It empowers the Commission to decide on the legality of anti-circumvention measures, obviating perhaps the need to refer such cases to the Court. It also provides a helpful distinction between the question of establishing the Member State having jurisdiction over a broadcaster and the question whether there is a case of abusive delocalization.[84] However, this procedure only captures delocalizations carried out with the intention of circumvention even though legitimate concerns related to public policy objectives may also arise in other cases. Moreover, the burden of proving that the broadcaster concerned established itself in the Member State having jurisdiction so as to circumvent the stricter rules of the state of reception is heavy. Such a U-turn construction is hard to establish given that the mere fact that an undertaking exercises its freedom to provide services without offering services in the Member State of establishment is not sufficient.[85]

Even if the destination state succeeded in proving circumvention, the problem of implementing anti-circumvention measures in practice would have to be solved. While it is possible to restrict the cable retransmission of programmes, blocking the reception of foreign programmes by satellite or via the internet is technically difficult. It might be necessary to resort to indirect measures against service providers such as banning the sale of airtime for advertising or the sale of decoders.[86] The United Kingdom has in numerous occasions in the past blocked reception of hardcore pornographic channels by banning the sale of smartcards.[87]

At the end of the day, one has to be sceptical about the inclusion in the Directive of yet another procedure – next to the already existing Articles 2a and 3a (now Articles 2a and 3j of the AVMS Directive) – aimed at reconciling the protection of public policy objectives with EU law. This scepticism is also justified in view of the failure of similar mechanisms in Articles 16 and 24a of the European Convention of Transfrontier Television to yield results. Perhaps, the most promising way of solving circumvention problems is by means of an increased cooperation between regulatory authorities at an early stage, before licences have been

83. T. McGonagle, 'Workshop Report' in *Iris Special: Audiovisual Media Services without Frontiers: Implementing the Rules*, European Audiovisual Observatory (ed.) (Strasbourg, European Audiovisual Observatory, 2007), pp. 53, 54.
84. A. Scheuer, 'Implementation and Monitoring: Upholding General Interest in View of Commercial Communications' in *Iris Special: Audiovisual Media Services without Frontiers: Implementing the Rules*, European Audiovisual Observatory (ed.) (Strasbourg, European Audiovisual Observatory, 2007), p. 23, 28.
85. Hörnle, 'Country of Origin', 101; Dutch Media Authority, *Regulation of the Dutch Commercial Television*, p. 16.
86. Drijber, 'Revised Television without Frontiers Directive', 104; Hörnle, 'Country of Origin', 103; Scheuer, 'Implementation and Monitoring', p. 28.
87. Harcourt, *Regulation of Media Markets*, p. 171; C. Jones, 'Television without Frontiers' (1999/2000) 19 YEL, 299, 318 *et seq.*

issued to broadcasters targeting a foreign country. The European Broadcasting Union (EBU) has proposed that the regulatory authorities of the state of establishment should always take into account the laws of the state of reception before granting licences to broadcasters targeting the latter.[88] This suggestion has been taken up in recital 47 to the AVMS Directive which states that 'it is desirable that contacts between the respective bodies take place before such licences are granted.' Such cooperation would also help solve problems of supervision, which are particularly acute when a broadcaster transmits in a language other than the one spoken in the Member State of establishment.[89]

2.2 Directive 97/36/EC

The application of Dir. 89/552/EEC revealed the need to clarify the concept of jurisdiction in relation to the audiovisual sector.[90] Hence, detailed criteria have been enshrined in Article 2 of Directive 97/36/EC with the aim of covering all possible constellations in which a Member State is responsible for the activities of a certain broadcaster. In accordance with the case-law of the European Court, the establishment criterion has been made the 'principal criterion determining the jurisdiction of a particular broadcaster'.[91] It is helpful to cite Article 2 of Dir. 97/36/EC in full in this context:

(1) Each Member State shall ensure that all television broadcasts transmitted by broadcasters under its jurisdiction comply with the rules of the system of law applicable to broadcasts intended for the public in that Member State.

(2) For the purposes of this Directive the broadcasters under the jurisdiction of a Member State are:
- those established in that Member State in accordance with paragraph 3;
- those to whom paragraph 4 applies.

(3) For the purposes of this Directive, a broadcaster shall be deemed to be established in a Member State in the following cases:
(a) the broadcaster has its head office in that Member State and the editorial decisions about programme schedules are taken in that Member State;
(b) if a broadcaster has its head office in one Member State but editorial decisions on programme schedules are taken in another Member State, it shall be deemed to be established in the Member State where a significant part of the workforce involved in the pursuit of the television broadcasting activity operates; if a significant part of the workforce involved in the pursuit of the television broadcasting activity

88. McGonagle, 'Workshop Report', p. 54.
89. Botella i Corral, Machet, 'Co-ordination and Co-operation', p. 17.
90. Dir. 97/36/EC, recital 10.
91. *Ibid.*

operates in each of those Member States, the broadcaster shall be deemed to be established in the Member State where it has its head office; if a significant part of the workforce involved in the pursuit of the television broadcasting activity operates in neither of those Member States, the broadcaster shall be deemed to be established in the Member State where it first began broadcasting in accordance with the system of law of that Member State, provided that it maintains a stable and effective link with the economy of that Member State;

(c) if a broadcaster has its head office in a Member State but decisions on programme schedules are taken in a third country, or vice-versa, it shall be deemed to be established in the Member State concerned, provided that a significant part of the workforce involved in the pursuit of the television broadcasting activity operates in that Member State.

(4) Broadcasters to whom the provisions of paragraph 3 are not applicable shall be deemed to be under the jurisdiction of a Member State in the following cases:

(a) they use a frequency granted by that Member State;

(b) although they do not use a frequency granted by a Member State they do use a satellite capacity appertaining to that Member State;

(c) although they use neither a frequency granted by a Member State nor a satellite capacity appertaining to a Member State they do use a satellite up-link situated in that Member State.

(5) If the question as to which Member State has jurisdiction cannot be determined in accordance with paragraphs 3 and 4, the competent Member State shall be that in which the broadcaster is established within the meaning of Articles 52 and following of the Treaty establishing the European Community.

(6) This Directive shall not apply to broadcasts intended exclusively for reception in third countries, and which are not received directly or indirectly by the public in one or more Member States.

The place of establishment is determined in Article 2 (3) according to rules relying on the place where the broadcaster has its head office, where editorial decisions about programme schedules are taken, where a significant part of the workforce involved in the pursuit of the television broadcasting activity operates, and where the broadcaster first began broadcasting. These rules are set out in a hierarchical order.[92] The prototype case is the one where the broadcaster has its head office in the same Member State in which editorial decisions about programme schedules are taken. This coincides as a rule with the State where the programmes are broadcast, since programme policy is commonly designed there.

If the place where the broadcaster has its head office differs from that where editorial decisions on programme schedules are taken, then, according to Article 2 (3) (b), the place of establishment is deemed to be the place where a significant part

92. Drijber, 'Revised Television without Frontiers Directive', 93.

of the workforce involved in the pursuit of the television broadcasting activity operates.[93] The criterion of the place of the head office prevails, however, if a significant part of the workforce is active in each of those Member States. If no decision can be reached on the basis of these rules, because a significant part of the workforce operates neither in the place of the head office nor in the place where editorial decisions about programme schedules are taken, the Directive introduces a rule of last resort. The Member State, where the broadcaster began broadcasting in accordance with its system of law, is considered to be its place of establishment.

When none of the rules of paragraph 3 are applicable to a broadcaster, it is deemed to be under the jurisdiction of the Member State from whose territory its broadcasts have been transmitted. Criteria identical to those laid down in the second indent of the former Article 2 (1) are employed in Article 2 (4), namely the use of a frequency granted by that Member State, of a satellite capacity appertaining to that Member State or of a satellite up-link situated in that Member State. A difference between the two provisions is that, while under the former Article 2 (1) this last category of broadcasters was referred to as 'not being under the jurisdiction of any Member State', under the new Article 2 (4) these broadcasters are deemed to be under the jurisdiction of a Member State.

Finally, in cases where jurisdiction cannot be determined in accordance with paragraphs 3 and 4, Article 2 (5) refers to the concept of establishment within the meaning of Article 52 (now 43) *et seq.* EC so as to avoid the emergence of a vacuum of competence.[94] It is doubtful whether this test can result in a Member State having jurisdiction other than the one where the broadcaster's head office is located.[95]

The most commonly held view in legal writing is that the rules in Article 2 (3), (4) and (5) have increased legal certainty.[96] Moreover, the argument has been put

---

93. In a case concerning the transmission of the RTL 4 and 5 services to the Dutch market the *Commissariaat voor de Media* (CvdM) concluded by decision of 5 February 2002 that the broadcaster Holland Media Group (HMG) was established in the Netherlands according to Art. 2 (3) (b). HMG's head office was located in Luxembourg, but its editorial decisions were taken in the Netherlands and a major part of the company's workforce was located there. The question whether HMG or the Luxembourg licensed satellite broadcaster CLT-Ufa is responsible for the two channels is in contention between the CvdM and the European Commission. *See* Fourth Report on the application of Directive 89/552/EEC 'Television without Frontiers', 6 January 2003, COM (2002) 778 final, 9.
94. Common Position (EC) no. 49/96 adopted by the Council on 8 July 1996 with a view to adopting Dir. 96/ . . . /EC of the European Parliament and of the Council amending Council Dir. 89/552/ EEC on the coordination of certain provisions laid down by law, regulation or administrative action in Member States concerning the pursuit of television broadcasting activities, OJ C 264/ 52, 1996, recital 11.
95. J. Harrison and L. Woods, 'Determining Jurisdiction in the Digital Age' (1999) 5 EPL, 583, 597.
96. C. O. Lenz, 'Das Sendestaatsprinzip als Teil der europäischen Medienordnung' in *Europäisches Medienrecht – Fernsehen und seine gemeinschaftsrechtliche Regelung*, Schriftenreihe des Instituts für Europäisches Medienrecht Saarbrücken, vol. 18 (Munich, Jehle-Rehm, 1998), p. 21; I. Pingel-Lenuzza, 'La nouvelle directive "Tèlèvision sans frontières" ou la lente structuration du droit communautaire de l'audiovisuel' (1999) 2 RAE, 173, 176; A. Meyer-Heine, 'Les apports de la nouvelle directive "Tèlèvision sans frontières" du 30 juin 1997 entrée en vigueur le 31 décembre 1998' (1999) 35 RTDE, 95, 98.

forward that they have raised the hurdles to be cleared by broadcasters who claim to fall under the jurisdiction of a certain Member State with the aim of circumventing another Member State's legislation.[97] It is not sufficient any more to establish that the legal seat of a broadcasting company is located in a certain Member State. In addition, it has to be demonstrated that editorial decisions concerning programme policy are also taken there.

In reality, the rules of the Directive have caused considerable problems of application. In the recent case of *Extasi TV*, the United Kingdom banned this television service on the ground that it manifestly, seriously and gravely infringed Article 22 of the Directive by broadcasting violent pornography. The Commission found the UK measures compatible with Article 2a (2) of the TwF Directive, but admitted that there was uncertainty as to which Member State had jurisdiction over Extasi TV.[98] The service was transmitted via a satellite uplink located in Spain, but the programming as such was assembled and edited by a company established in Italy. It was thus unclear as to whether Spain or Italy had jurisdiction over the service. A similar jurisdictional conundrum arose recently between Belgium and Luxembourg concerning the services RTL-TVi, Club RTL and Plug TV.[99]

In another well-known case, the Netherlands granted itself jurisdiction over the Luxembourg based channels RTL4 and RTL5. The Dutch Media Authority concluded by decision of 5 February 2002 that the broadcaster Holland Media Group (HMG) was established in the Netherlands according to Article 2 (3) (b) of the Television Directive. HMG's head office was located in Luxembourg, but its editorial decisions were taken in the Netherlands and a major part of the company's workforce was located there.

According to the Dutch Media Authority, editorial decisions are taken where programme directors, editors in chief and editors decide daily on programme schedules. This is the place where the heart of the economic activities of the broadcaster is situated, not where shareholders and programme directors take the final responsibility for these schedules. The Dutch Council of State, finally seized with the case, agreed with the *Commissariaat*'s interpretation, but reached a Solomonic decision so as to prevent a situation of dual jurisdiction from coming about. The Commission closed the infringement proceedings against the Netherlands subsequent to this ruling.[100]

97. Farrar, 'E.C. Broadcasting Law Clarified', 16, 19.
98. Fifth Report from the Commission to the Council, the European Parliament, the European Economic and Social Committee and the Committee of the Regions on the application of Directive 89/552/EEC 'Television without Frontiers', 10 February 2006, COM (2006) 49 final, 5; Sixth Report from the Commission to the European Parliament, the Council, the European Economic and Social Committee and the Committee of the Regions on the application of Directive 89/552/EEC 'Television without Frontiers', 24 October 2007, COM (2007) 452 final, 4.
99. *See* Minutes of the 24th Meeting of the Contact Committee established by the Television without Frontiers Directive, 15 November 2006, Doc. CC TVSF (2006) 6 <www.ec.europa.eu/avpolicy/docs/reg/tvwf/contact_comm/24_cc_minutes_en.pdf>, 30 October 2007, 2 *et seq.*
100. *See* also Part 1, Ch. 6.1, p.102 *above*.

The view prevailing in the Commission is that Article 2 has given rise to more problems of interpretation than it has resolved.[101] The question whether editorial decisions are taken where programme policy is established or where the programmes to be broadcast are finally put together remains contentious.[102] While editorial decisions are customarily taken by senior managers, programme scheduling is often made in the receiving state by personnel of a lower rank. The wording used makes the first alternative seem more plausible. However, would this solution be appropriate in cases where significant decisions concerning programme scheduling are taken in branch offices in the receiving states? Also, the 12th recital to Dir. 97/36 refers to the place where the programme to be broadcast to the public is finally mixed and processed.

The precise meaning of 'significant part of the workforce' is equally open to speculation. Arguably, quantitative as well as qualitative aspects have to be taken into account when determining which percentage is 'significant'.[103] A 'significant part of the workforce' is not necessarily the majority.[104] It has been argued that this term should be construed as 'not insignificant' in the sense that a state where hardly any staff is based is precluded from claiming jurisdiction.[105] Ultimately, it is the task of the European Court to draw the exact line.

All in all, one is left with the suspicion that the criterion of establishment, as it has been interpreted in the case-law of the Court, would have made it possible to determine the jurisdiction of a Member State more clearly. Also, the adoption at EU level of criteria determining the place of establishment of television broadcasters means an indirect interference with the organization and operation of broadcasting systems. Member States do not have a free hand any more to lay down in their national legislation conditions under which a broadcaster falls under their jurisdiction. This development is in sharp contrast with the proclamation in the 13th recital of Dir. 89/552 that the responsibility of the Member States and their authorities with regard to the organization of broadcasting, including the systems of licensing, administrative authorization or taxation, will remain unaffected.

In the course of the consultations for the modernization of the TwF Directive, possibilities for clarifying the establishment criteria of Article 2 have been explored. There was no consensus as to whether clarification of these criteria would help combat circumvention. In the end, these criteria were left largely unchanged. However, it is interesting to note that the ranking of the technical criteria in Article 2 (4) has been reversed in the sense that the satellite up-link was placed

101. From interviews at the Commission, DG Internal Market (MARKT) and DG Education and Culture (EAC) conducted for this work in March 2000.
102. European Commission Focus Group 1, 'Regulation of Audiovisual Content', September 2004, 4; Helberger, 'Konkretisierung des Sendestaatsprinzips', 50, 56; McGonagle, van Loon, *Jurisdiction over Broadcasters in Europe*, p. 12.
103. Helberger, 'Konkretisierung des Sendestaatsprinzips', 56; contra McGonagle, van Loon, *Jurisdiction over Broadcasters in Europe*, p. 13.
104. McGonagle, van Loon, *Jurisdiction over Broadcasters in Europe*, p. 13.
105. *Ibid.*

before the satellite capacity. The subsidiary criteria of Article 2 (4) apply if a broadcaster is not established in one of the EU Member States. They hence concern mostly third country programmes. Given that most of these programmes use satellite capacities provided by *Eutelsat* or by *Astra*, the ranking under Article 2 (4) of the TwF Directive means that most third country programmes in Europe fall under the jurisdiction of two Member States: France and Luxembourg.

What is more, it is the uplink-operators, not the satellite operators, who have direct contracts with the broadcasters. Satellite operators are not in the position anymore to close down one specific channel given that digital television channels are no longer carried individually but are grouped together in a multiplex. Shutting down the entire multiplex would not be practicable as it would also affect other channels. The Member State where the uplink is located does have the technical means of closing down a specific channel.[106] Therefore, the reversal of the order of the subsidiary criteria is expected to bring about a more equitable division of responsibility between Member States and a more effective control of third country programmes. This was deemed to be particularly important in the light of the recent experience with the Al Manar and Sahar1 channels, which were prohibited by the French authorities for inciting racial hatred.[107]

3. THE SCOPE OF THE COUNTRY OF ORIGIN PRINCIPLE

The country of origin principle distinguishes between the powers of the transmitting and those of the receiving Member State. Under the TwF Directive, the obligation was incumbent upon the former to ensure that television broadcasts emanating from broadcasters under its jurisdiction complied with the legislation applicable to broadcasts intended for the public in that Member State (Article 2 (1) of Dir. 97/36/EC) including the provisions of the Directive (Article 3 (2) of Dir. 97/36/EC). The latter, on the other hand, was obliged not to restrict retransmissions on its territory of television broadcasts from other Member States for reasons which fell within the fields coordinated by this Directive according to Article 2a (1) of Dir. 97/36/EC. It was thus divested of the power to control EU broadcasts with the sole exception of Article 2a (2). The AVMS Directive upheld this division of responsibilities between the country of origin and the receiving state, but extended it to all audiovisual media services by media service providers under the jurisdiction of the former.[108]

Given that the burden of ascertaining the legality of broadcasts rests entirely on the Member State under whose jurisdiction a broadcaster falls, it is pertinent to consider briefly the nature of the control exercised by that state. Thereafter, the obligation of the receiving state not to restrict retransmissions will be analysed.

---

106. MEMO/06/208; *See, however*, McGonagle, van Loon, *Jurisdiction over Broadcasters in Europe*, p. 8 who criticize the uplink criterion for being oversimplisitic given that uplink operators do not necessarily have a connection with the economy of the state where they are located.
107. IP/05/325 and MEMO 05/98.
108. AVMS Directive, Arts. 2, 2a.

3.1 The Control Exercised by the Country of Origin

The TwF Directive stipulated in Article 2 (1) that the country of origin should exercise control over broadcasts transmitted by broadcasters under its jurisdiction without, however, determining the ways in which this control would be carried out. Consequently, the methods of control, the competent authority, the imposition of penalties in the case of transgression had to be regulated in the domestic legislation of each Member State. A provision proposed by the Commission, according to which Member States should enforce compliance with the Directive by means of effective, proportionate and dissuasive sanctions, was left out during the negotiations in the Council prior to the 1997 Directive revision the ground that it would clash with the independent status of broadcasters.[109]

Article 3 (2) of Dir. 97/36 stipulated that Member States should by appropriate means ensure, within the framework of their legislation, that television broadcasters under their jurisdiction effectively comply with the provisions of this Directive. The question has been posed whether an obligation binding upon the Member States was enshrined in this provision.[110] This question has to be answered in the affirmative. The effective exercise of control by the country of origin is of paramount importance for the creation of the internal market in broadcasting services. This view is also borne out by the 15th recital to Dir. 89/552, which refers to 'the requirement that the originating Member State should verify that broadcasts comply with national law as coordinated by this Directive'. Besides, Article 3 (2) only repeated what was already stated in Article 10 EC and in Article 249 (3) EC.[111] The former states that Member States shall take all appropriate measure to ensure fulfilment of the obligations arising out of the Treaty and out of secondary EU law, while the latter imposes a more specific obligation on Member States to implement Directives.

It is important to note that Dir. 97/36 removed the ambiguity previously existing as to which broadcasting organizations were subject to the supervision of the country of origin. Article 3 (2) referred to broadcasters under the jurisdiction of Member States. The former Article 2 (1) of Dir. 89/552 used to distinguish them, however, from broadcasters who, while not being under the jurisdiction of any Member State, made use of the technical infrastructure of a Member State. This created the impression that Member States do not have a duty to ensure that broadcasters making use of their technical infrastructure comply with the provisions of the Directive. On the other hand, according to Article 2 (1) of Dir. 89/552, these broadcasters also had to comply with the domestic broadcasting legislation of the country of origin. As was seen above, Article 2 (2), (4) of Dir. 97/36 created the fiction that non-EU broadcasters using the technical facilities of a Member

---

109. Drijber, 'Revised Television without Frontiers Directive', 105.
110. E. Saxpekidou, *Eleuthere kykloforia teleoptikon yperesion sten Europaïke Oikonomike Koinoteta* (Thessaloniki, Ekdoseis Sakkoula, 1990), p. 149.
111. Kleist and Scheuer, 'Neue Regelungen', 209.

State were under its jurisdiction. It thus made it clear that these broadcasters fell under Article 3 (2) so that they had to conform to the provisions of the Directive.

The obligation of Member States to ensure 'within the framework of their legislation, that media service providers under their jurisdiction effectively comply with the provisions of this Directive' is laid down in Article 3 (6) of the AVMS Directive. Also, a new provision has been introduced immediately after Article 3 (6). Article 3 (7) states that 'Member States shall encourage co- and/or self-regulatory regimes at national level in the fields coordinated by this Directive to the extent permitted by their legal systems. These regimes shall be such that they are broadly accepted by the main stakeholders in the Member States concerned and provide for effective enforcement.' The E-Commerce Directive and the 1998 Recommendation for the protection of minors and human dignity already encourage alternative methods of regulation, especially the drawing up of codes of conduct.[112] Article 3 (7) of the AVMS Directive encourages co- and/or self-regulatory regimes in the fields coordinated by the Directive. The main areas in question are hence audiovisual commercial communication and the protection or minors. The two conditions for the adoption of such regimes, namely their acceptance by the main stakeholders and their effective enforcement, are congruent with the conditions stipulated in the study on 'Co-Regulation Measures in the Media Sector' carried out by the Hans-Bredow Institute and the Institute of European Media Law.[113] The fact that this provision has been inserted immediately after Article 3 (6) suggests that co-regulatory regimes are considered an acceptable means to implement the Directive.[114] The same cannot be said of self-regulatory regimes, which can only complement but not replace state regulation, especially in sensitive areas such as the protection of minors.[115]

3.2 The Obligation of the Reception State not to Restrict Retransmission

3.2.1 The Meaning of 'Retransmission'

A first point which needs to be clarified with regard to the obligation of the reception state not to restrict retransmission is the meaning of the term 'retransmission'.

112. European Parliament and Council Directive 2003/31/EC of 8 June 2000 on certain legal aspects of information society services, in particular electronic commerce, in the internal market (Directive on electronic commerce), OJ L 178/1, 2000, Art. 16; Council Recommendation 98/560/EC of 24 September 1998 on the protection of minors and human dignity in audiovisual and information services, OJ L 270/48, 1998, II (2) and Annex.
113. Hans-Bredow-Institut, 'Final Report: Study on Co-Regulation Measures in the Media Sector', June 2006 <www.ec.europa.eu/avpolicy/docs/library/studies/coregul/coregul-final-report_en.pdf>, 12 July 2007, 165.
114. *See ibid.*, 177; Kleist and Scheuer, 'Neue Regelungen', 210.
115. Recommendation of the European Parliament and of the Council of 20 December 2006 on the protection of minors and human dignity and on the right of reply in relation to the competitiveness of the European audiovisual and on-line information services industry OJ L 378/72, 2006 recital 12.

Unlike the European Convention on Transfrontier Television that defines retransmission as 'the fact of receiving and simultaneously transmitting, irrespective of the technical means employed, complete and unchanged television programme services, or important parts of such services, transmitted by broadcasters for reception by the general public', the Directive does not contain any definition of this term.[116] The ensuing ambiguities were brought to the attention of the European Court.

A significant question concerning the term 'retransmission' was raised in the case of *Red Hot Television*.[117] This case concerned a channel, which took up broadcasting in July 1992 from a satellite up-link situated in the Netherlands and, from December 1992, from a satellite up-link situated in Denmark, while its broadcasting activities were partially carried out in the United Kingdom. The British authorities decided to put an end to the transmission of the programme from their territory. However, it turned out that the channel did not fall under the jurisdiction of either of the countries involved, given that they applied different criteria linking broadcasters to their legal systems. Denmark and the Netherlands regarded establishment as the relevant criterion, while the United Kingdom attached weight to the place of transmission.

This incident of a conflicting disclaimer of jurisdiction was used to argue that the Directive had to be amended so as to terminate the state of uncertainty reigning under Article 2 (1) of Dir. 89/552. The Court, finally, did not have to pass judgment on this case, since it was removed from the register following the withdrawal of the questions submitted by the national court.[118] Nonetheless, an interesting question was posed in this case: Does retransmission only apply to cable or does it also apply to satellite television? The Commission argued that retransmission should be broadly interpreted so as not to treat satellite and cable television in an unequal manner. Otherwise, retransmission could be provisionally suspended where a cable channel infringed Article 22, while the same would not apply to a satellite channel. This misconception with regard to the bandwidth of the provisional suspension procedure was dispelled in the revised Dir. 97/36, where the phrase 'provisionally suspend retransmissions of television broadcasts' was replaced by the phrase 'derogate from paragraph 1'. It was thus made plain that the defence mechanism of Article 2a (2) applied equally to direct reception and to cable retransmission.

The mirror image of the question raised in *Red Hot Television* has been at issue in *Commission v. Belgium*.[119] In this case the Belgian Government argued that the Directive only applies to primary television broadcasting, and not to secondary forms of broadcasting, such as transmission by cable. The Court refuted

---

116. Council of Europe, European Convention on Transfrontier Television of 5 May 1989, as amended by Protocol ETS Nr. 171 of 1 October 1998, Art. 2 (b).
117. *See* COM (95) 86 final Report on application of Directive 89/552/EEC and Proposal for a European Parliament and Council Directive amending Council Directive 89/552/EEC, 31 May 1995, 19.
118. AG Lenz in Case C-222/94, *Commission v. United Kingdom* [1996] ECR-I 4025, para. 74 n. 49.
119. Case C-11/95, *Commission v. Belgium* [1996] ECR I-4117, paras 15 *et seq.*

this argument, drawing from the preamble to Directives 89/552, 93/83[120] and the European Convention on Transfrontier Television. It reached the conclusion that cable retransmission falls within the scope of the Directive. This finding of the Court clarified some aspects of the term 'retransmission'; others, however, still remain in dark. The question whether programmes have to be retransmitted simultaneously and in their entirety or whether active cable retransmission is also included within Article 2a (1) has not been answered.[121] Admittedly, the Court was not faced with this problem in the present case, since the Belgian legislation in question only concerned the passive retransmission of television programmes. Nevertheless, this is an important issue that is bound to arise in future.

'Television broadcasting' as defined in Article 1 (a) of Dir. 89/552, and presumably also under Article 1(e) of the AVMS Directive, only refers to the initial transmission of television programmes.[122] Even though the communication of programmes between undertakings with a view to their being relayed to the public is included in this definition, no reference is made to their retransmission. This leaves no doubt that Member States do not have a duty to supervise programmes retransmitted by cable network operators in their territory. Nonetheless, the line between primary television broadcasting and active cable retransmission is difficult to draw. Active cable retransmission takes place where foreign programmes are not retransmitted unchanged at the same time, but where cable distributors are empowered to interfere with their content. This interference can range from the simple postponement of a broadcast to the compilation of parts of different broadcasts.

According to the definition of the European Convention, only the simultaneous transmission of broadcasts in their entirety constitutes retransmission, while it is appropriate to speak of initial transmission where the broadcasts are modified. If this analysis is correct, the Member State where the active cable distribution takes place has to be held responsible under Article 2 (1). It may, however, be felt that this result is undesirable in the case where the content of broadcasts stays the same, while their transmission is deferred. Since the cable distributor does not really create a new programme in this case, it seems justified to subject such broadcasts to the jurisdiction of the state of initial transmission only. Uncertainty surrounding these issues may well lead to instances of double jurisdiction, especially in a digital environment offering more broadcasting opportunities.[123] Greater clarity in this area of law is therefore urgently needed.

---

120. Council Directive 93/83/EEC of 27 September 1993 on the coordination of certain rules concerning copyright and rights related to copyright applicable to satellite broadcasting and cable retransmission OJ L 248/15, 1993.
121. J. M.-P. de Nanclares, *Die Bedeutung des Gemeinschaftsrechts für das Fernsehen: Die Fernsehrichtlinie*, Vorträge, Reden und Berichte aus dem Europa-Institut der Universität des Saarlandes, no. 253 (Saarbrücken, Europa-Institut, 1991), p. 104; Saxpekidou, *Eleutheri kykloforia*, p. 127; A. Coulthard, 'Dutch Television – Too Red Hot for UK!' (1993) 14 Media L&P, 116.
122. Case C-11/95, para. 16.
123. McGonagle, van Loon, *Jurisdiction over Broadcasters in Europe*, p. 15.

3.2.2 The Case-Law of the European Court on the Prohibition on Restricting Retransmission

The European Court had the opportunity for the first time to enforce the prohibition on restricting retransmission in the case *Commission v. Belgium.*[124] This case concerned legislation in the French and Flemish community that created a system of prior authorization for the retransmission by cable of television broadcasts from other Member States. The Court struck down one after another the arguments brought forward by the Belgian Government in support of this legislation. The Belgian Government's main argument was that the receiving Member State must have the power to control whether foreign broadcasts comply with the law of the country of origin, including the provisions of the Directive, pursuant to Articles 2 (1) and 3 (2).[125]

The Court objected that this interpretation is not compatible with the division of obligations between the country of origin and the state of reception in Directive 89/552. According to the system of the Directive, it is only for the former to bring its broadcasts into line with its legislation as adapted to the Directive. Apart from the exceptional circumstances under Article 2 (2), in which the receiving Member State may suspend retransmission, its only other weapon is the recourse to Treaty infringement proceedings under Article 227 EC or the instigation of an action by the Commission under Article 226 EC. In view of the ephemeral character of television broadcasts, the receiving state could also request the Court to prescribe interim measures under Article 243 EC.

For the same reasons, the Court also rejected the argument that the Belgian law was justified on cultural grounds since it sought to secure fulfilment of Articles 4 and 5 of the Directive.[126] Furthermore, the Belgian Government invoked the elusive principle of subsidiarity so as to defend the secondary control imposed on foreign broadcasts. The Court preferred not to touch upon the delicate issue as to whether the subject-matter of the Directive falls entirely within the European Union's exclusive powers.[127] It simply stated that a Member State could not go against the letter of the Directive by relying on Article 5 (2) EC, implying that the country of origin principle is in line with the principle of subsidiarity.

An interesting point made by the Belgian Government is that prior authorization of foreign broadcasts is necessary so as to ascertain that they emanate from a Member State and are hence entitled to free circulation in the European Union. The European Court rejected this argument as well. It found that the system of prior authorization was not indispensable for achieving this aim.[128] This finding of the Court cannot, however, be taken as a denial of the power of the Member States to

124. Case C-11/95, *Commission v. Belgium* [1996] ECR I-4117.
125. *Ibid.*, paras 30 *et seq.*; paras 87 *et seq.*
126. *See also* Case C-14/96, *Criminal Proceedings against Paul Denuit* [1997] ECR I- 2785, paras 31 *et seq.* where the European Court equally dismissed this argument.
127. AG Lenz in Case C-11/95, para. 60.
128. *Ibid.*, para. 86.

verify that foreign programmes retransmitted in their territory fall within the scope of the Directive. The outcome would have been different if the legislation in question merely required cable operators to notify the broadcasting authorities of the origin of the programmes relayed by them.

By dismantling the Belgian legislation that raised obstacles to the free retransmission of programmes, the European Court bolstered the country of origin principle significantly. It goes without saying that broadcasts that originate from third countries and that do not fulfil the subsidiary criteria of Article 2 (4) do not need to receive the same treatment. Member States are at liberty to take whatever measures they deem appropriate against such broadcasts as long as they respect EU law and the international obligations of the Community.[129]

The prohibition for the state of reception to interfere with broadcasts retransmitted in its territory also formed the subject matter of three joined cases judged by the European Court (referred to hereinafter as *De Agostini*) as a result of a reference for a preliminary ruling by the *Marknadsdomstol*, the Swedish Market Court.[130] These cases arose from injunctions applied for by the Consumer Ombudsman who is entrusted with the enforcement of the Marketing Practices Law. He ordered De Agostini and TV Shop to cease certain trade practices in relation to a children's magazine (Case-34/95), skin-care products (Case 35/95) and a detergent (Case C-36/95).

More precisely, the first of these cases, Case C-34/95, concerned De Agostini, the publisher of a children's magazine about dinosaurs that was advertised on the television channels TV 3 and TV 4. TV 3 is a broadcasting company established in the United Kingdom whose programmes are transmitted by satellite to Denmark, Sweden and Norway. TV 4 is a Swedish channel. The Consumer Ombudsman considered the publicity for the magazine in question to be infringing Article 11 of the Swedish Broadcasting law, which stipulates that television advertisements must not be designed to attract the attention of children under 12 years of age. He therefore applied for an injunction based on the Marketing Practices Law to restrain De Agostini, subject to penalty payment, from marketing the magazine in this manner or, subsidiarily, to supply additional information in his advertisements.

The Cases C-35/95 and C-36/95 concerned TV Shop, a company specialized in teleshopping that broadcast two 'infomercials' for skin-care products and a detergent on TV 3 and on Homeshopping Channel, a Swedish channel. The Consumer Ombudsman found these television spots to be contrary to the Marketing Practices Law, in that they were unfair towards consumers, mainly by making misleading statements about the products' effectiveness. He asked the *Marknadsdomstol* for an order prohibiting TV-Shop from making such statements in connection with the marketing of these products.

---

129. Dir. 97/36/EC, recital 23.

130. Joined Cases C-34/95, C-35/95 and C-36/95, *Konsumentombudsmannen (KO) v. De Agostini (Svenska) Förlag AB and Konsumentenombudsmannen* (KO) *v. TV-Shop I Sverige AB* [1997] ECR I- 3843.

The *Marknadsdomstol* referred to the European Court questions on the compatibility of such injunctions with Articles 28 and 49 of the Treaty or Dir. 89/552. Only the questions in connection with the Directive are relevant to our examination. It seems helpful to outline the answers of the Court in a reverse order from which they were given, namely by looking first at Case C-34/95.

The Court held that Articles 16 and 22 of the Directive, which afford protection to minors from television programmes in general and television advertising in particular, have totally harmonized national laws dealing with the permissible content of television advertising in relation to minors. As a result, the subject matter of Article 11 of the Broadcasting Law fell within the fields co-ordinated by the Directive and could not be opposed to broadcasts from other Member States by virtue of Article 2a (1). This finding only precluded the application of the provision in question to TV 3. Its application to the domestic channel TV 4 was not contrary to the Directive in view of Article 3 (1), which allows for more stringent rules to be adopted by a Member State *vis-à-vis* broadcasters under its jurisdiction.

With this ruling the Court tied the hands of national authorities to measure programmes from abroad against the standards of their own broadcasting legislation with regard to minors. It showed, however, respect for the legal order of the state of reception by stating that it is still entitled to apply its legislation 'designed to protect consumers or minors *in general*, provided that its application does not prevent retransmission, *as such*, in its territory of broadcasts from another Member State'.[131] The meaning of this distinction will be considered in the next section.

4. RESIDUAL POWERS OF THE MEMBER STATES TO CONTROL EU BROADCASTS

4.1 Express Powers to Derogate From the Country of Origin Principle

The only exception from the country of origin principle in the TwF Directive was stipulated in Article 2a (2), according to which a Member State might derogate from the requirements of the first paragraph under strict conditions.

First of all, a television broadcast coming from another Member State must have manifestly, seriously and gravely infringed Article 22 (1) or (2) and/or Article 22a. These provisions constituted previously two paragraphs of one and the same Article 22. They were split under Dir. 97/36 into two separate Articles, the first dealing with the protection of minors, the second with the prohibition of programmes containing an incitement to hatred on grounds of race, sex, religion or nationality. This rearrangement of Article 22 helped avoid any misunderstanding, as to whether the transmission ban on broadcasts provoking hatred on the above-mentioned grounds only applies in the framework of the protection of minors.

131. *Ibid.*, para. 59.

If this were the case, such broadcasts could be transmitted late at night, when minors would be unlikely to watch them. This interpretation would contradict the attempts of the European Union to combat racism and xenophobia and has now become untenable. This is also manifest in the heading of Chapter V where the phrase 'and public order' has been added to the 'protection of minors'.

Under the AVMS Directive, Article 22a is divorced from Article 22. It becomes Article 3b as part of Chapter IIA, entitled 'Provisions applicable to all audiovisual media services'. This provision applies hence to linear and non-linear services alike despite considerable opposition by the commercial broadcasters against its extension to the latter. The initial Commission proposal proposed a widening of the scope of this Article by adding 'belief, disability, age or sexual orientation' as new grounds for unlawful incitement to hatred. This revision was meant to include in Article 3b all grounds of discrimination under Article 13 of the EC Treaty. Subsequently, this amendment was rejected and Article 3b was slimmed down to its original scope.[132] It is, however, interesting to note a further revision of the wording of Article 22a that did find its way into the AVMS Directive. Article 3b emphasizes that 'audiovisual media services provided by media service providers under their jurisdiction', i.e. under one of the Member States' jurisdiction, are precluded from inciting to hatred. This clarification seems futile. It serves, however, as a reminder that more Member States will be responsible for third country broadcasts than before as a result of the reversal of the technical criteria in Article 2 (4) of the AVMS Directive.

Article 22 of the TwF Directive on the protection of minors has been left unaltered in the AVMS Directive. Only the title of Chapter V has been changed to 'Protection of Minors in Television Broadcasting' to indicate that a different regime applies to non-linear services. As under the TwF Directive, the protection of minors is realized in Article 22 of the AVMS Directive by means of a total transmission ban on programmes 'which might seriously impair the physical, mental or moral development of minors, in particular programmes that involve pornography or gratuitous violence'. These programmes are distinguished in the second paragraph of Article 22 from others 'which are likely to impair the physical, mental or moral development of minors'. This second category of programmes presents less of a danger to minors as becomes apparent from the omission of the adjective 'seriously'. Therefore, they are only prohibited at times when minors normally watch television, whereas their transmission is permitted, 'where it is ensured, by selecting the time of the broadcast or by a technical measure, that minors in the area of transmission will not normally hear or see the broadcasts'. It makes sense to interpret the 'area of transmission' as the area in which programmes

132. The extended grounds have now migrated to Article 3e (1) (c) (ii) according to which 'audiovisual commercial communications shall not include or promote any discrimination based on sex, racial or ethnic origin, nationality, religion or belief, disability, age or sexual orientation'. Conceptually, they fit better in this provision, which concerns the prohibition of discrimination, not of the more diffuse notion of hatred. *See* McGonagle, 'Safeguarding Human Dignity in the European Audiovisual Sector' (2007) 6 *IRIS plus*, 1, 6.

are received directly or are being retransmitted. A different interpretation, placing emphasis on the time of transmission only, would fail to take account of the time difference between Member States, going thus against the *telos* of Article 22.

Article 22 (2) tries to balance the protection of minors with the freedom of expression and information and takes the view that a varied, pluralistic programme cannot be achieved, unless certain broadcasts not suitable for minors are shown. Additional safeguards to ensure that minors will not be exposed to such broadcasts are contained in the third paragraph of Article 22 in form of an acoustic warning preceding them or a visual symbol throughout their duration. However, differences between the transmitting and the receiving state concerning the assessment of the necessity to adopt such precautionary measures do not entitle the latter to derogate from the country of origin principle.[133]

Article 22 is phrased in a general way, given that neither the notions of pornography nor of gratuitous violence are defined nor the kind of programmes which are likely to impair the development of minors. Likewise, the definition of the age group of minors and of the time that is suitable for adult programmes to be transmitted is left to the discretion of the Member States. This is a wise choice of the European Union legislator, since considerable differences exist between national laws, revealing a diversity of opinion on the upbringing and education of young people and, ultimately, of moral standards.[134] These cultural differences also explain why recent suggestions for a common European rating system did not meet with acceptance. It is true that the elbowroom left to the Member States can give rise to obstacles to the free circulation of television services. Yet this is a fair price to pay for upholding the power of the Member States to decide such sensitive issues, especially since the competence of the European Union to regulate them is doubtful.

Less laudable is the subjection of the right of the receiving state to derogate from the country of origin principle to tight requirements limiting its practical value.[135] Not only does Article 2a (2) require that the infringement of the above-mentioned provisions be manifest, serious and grave. What is more, the receiving Member State has to put up with it on at least two occasions before it is entitled to initiate a preliminary procedure by notifying the broadcaster concerned and the Commission in writing of the alleged infringements and of the measures it intends to take should the infringements persist. Also, consultations with the transmitting Member State and the Commission have to take place with a

133. Harrison and Woods, 'Determining Jurisdiction', 591.

134. 2nd Report from the Commission to the Council, the European Parliament and the Economic and Social Committee on the application of Dir. 89/552/EEC 'Television Without Frontiers', 24 October 1997, COM (97) 523 final, para. 4.2; Council Recommendation 98/560/EC of 24 September 1998 on the protection of minors and human dignity in audiovisual and information services, OJ L 270/48, 1998 recital 18; contra Woods and Scholes, 'Broadcasting', 47, 80.

135. *See* ARD and ZDF, 'Joint Comment on the Review of the Television without Frontiers Directive', 14 July 2003 <www.ec.europa.eu/avpolicy/docs/reg/modernisation/2003_review/contributions/wc_ard-zdf_en.pdf>, 25 June 2007: 'In all probability these requirements can hardly be met in practice'.

view to an amicable settlement. Only if these consultations fail to produce an amicable settlement within 15 days of the abovementioned notification, and the alleged infringement persists, may the receiving Member State prevent access to the programme in question by means of the suspension of retransmission or other adequate measures.

These procedural requirements that already existed in Dir. 89/552 have been retained in the revised Dir. 97/36 and in the AVMS Directive. However, Dir. 97/36 and the AVMS Directive regulate the supervision exercised by the Commission of the proportionality of the measures adopted by receiving states by virtue of Article 2a (2) in more detail. They specify that the Commission has to take a decision on the compatibility of such measures with Community law within a period of two months. This amendment is commendable in view of the grave implications of a suspension of retransmission for the broadcaster affected.

The AVMS Directive proposes a bifurcation of Article 2a. In respect of television broadcasting, Member States will still need to follow the abovementioned procedure so as to derogate from the country of origin principle on the limited ground of manifest, serious and grave infringement of Articles 22 (1) or (2) and/or Article 3b. In respect of on-demand services, however, different grounds for derogation and a different procedure apply. Member States may only take measures to derogate from the country of origin principle if such measures are necessary for one of the following reasons: public policy, in particular the prevention, investigation, detection and prosecution of criminal offences, including the protection of minors and the fight against any incitement to hatred on grounds of race, sex, religion or nationality, and violations of human dignity concerning individual persons; the protection of public health; public security, including the safeguarding of national security and defence; the protection of consumers, including investors.

Such measures must be proportionate and they may only be taken against an on-demand service which prejudices any of these objectives or which presents a serious and grave risk of prejudice to those objectives. Prior to taking such measures, the receiving Member State must ask the Member State under whose jurisdiction the service providers falls to take measures. If the latter does not respond, or if the measures taken are inadequate, the receiving state must notify it as well as the Commission of its intention to take measures. In the case of urgency, Member States may, however, derogate from this procedure. They then have to notify the measures taken to the Commission and to the country of origin in the shortest possible time, indicating why they had to act as a matter of urgency. The Commission is asked to examine the compatibility of the notified measures with Community law as soon as possible. If they prove to be incompatible with Community law, the Member State concerned must refrain from taking them or urgently put an end to them.

The grounds for derogation from the country of origin principle and the procedure to be followed replicate Article 3 (4), (5) and (6) of the E-commerce Directive.[136] This solution is attractive in so far as it minimizes problems of

136. European Parliament and Council Directive 2003/31/EC of 8 June 2000 on certain legal aspects of information society services, in particular electronic commerce, in the internal market (Directive on electronic commerce), OJ L178/1, 2000.

delineation between the AVMS and the E-Commerce Directive. Part of the non-linear audiovisual media services which fall under the AVMS Directive are also regulated by the E-Commerce Directive.[137] If Member were able to restrict incoming services to differing extents depending on whether they fell within the scope of the AVMS or of the E-Commerce Directive, delimitation would be indispensable and potentially problematic. In the case of services covered by both instruments a conflict would arise.

Such problems of delimitation were bound to arise under the initial Commission proposal which allowed no derogation from the country of origin principle for on-demand services. Recital 10 stipulated that 'Because of the introduction of a minimum set of harmonized obligations in Articles 3c to 3h and in the areas harmonized in this Directive Member States can no longer derogate from the country of origin principle with regard to protection of minors and fight against any incitement to hatred on grounds of race, sex, religion or nationality, and violation of human dignity concerning individual persons or protection of consumers as provided in Article 3 (4) of Dir. 2000/31/EC of the European Parliament and the Council'. This recital has been rightly criticized for foreclosing certain grounds of derogation from the country of origin principle that would have been available under the E-Commerce Directive without adequately protecting some of the concomitant objectives of general interest, especially human dignity and the consumers.[138]

The Council, in its general approach of November 2006, reinstated the derogation for on-demand services '. . . according to the conditions and procedures set out in Articles 3 (4), (5) and (6) of Dir. 2000/31/EC.'[139] The European Parliament also took the view that Member States should have the power to take measures against on-demand services that put public interest objectives at risk. It extended the derogation procedure under Article 2a (2) to such services, and added a new paragraph, modelled after the emergency procedure of the E-Commerce Directive, allowing a speedy reaction in urgent cases.[140] The Commission accepted these amendments in principle.[141] However, the Common Position between the European Parliament and the Council separated anew the procedures for television broadcasting and for on-demand services, and the Commission modified its proposal accordingly.[142]

Article 2a (4) in its final version is certainly more sensitive towards concerns of the Member States over legitimate public interest objectives than the initial Commission proposal.[143] Nonetheless, this provision is still problematic, but for

---

137. Faßbender, 'Inhalt und Grenzen', 505, 511.
138. *Ibid.*
139. Council general approach of 13 November 2006, doc. 14616/06 <www.register.consilium.europa.eu/pdf/en/06/st14/st14616.en06.pdf>, 12 October 2007.
140. European Parliament, 13 December 2006, doc. P6_TA(2006)0559 <www.europarl.europa.eu/sides/getDoc.do?pubRef=-//EP//TEXT+TA+P6-TA-2006-0559+0+DOC+XML+V0//EN&language=EN>, 12 October 2007.
141. Amended AVMSD proposal, Art. 2a.
142. Political agreement of 24 May 2007, Art. 2a.
143. Herold, 'Country of Origin Principle', 11 *et seq.*

different reasons. Member States only need to derogate from the country of origin principle if they restrict a retransmission on grounds which fall within the fields coordinated by this Directive. As we will see in the following section, they are free to restrict foreign services for reasons not falling within the fields coordinated by this Directive. Does this mean that the grounds listed under Article 2a (4) (a) (i) fall within the field that is coordinated by the Directive? This question has to be answered in the negative given that most of these grounds, notably the prevention, investigation, detection and prosecution of criminal offences, the protection of human dignity, of public health, of public security and the protection of consumers, including investors are covered by the Directive tangentially at the most. This is due to the fact that the AVMS Directive has a much narrower scope than the E-Commerce Directive.

The coordinated field under the E-Commerce Directive covers both requirements of a general nature and such that specifically regulate information society services. In the words of Article 2 (h) of the E-Commerce Directive, the coordinated field consists of 'requirements laid down in Member States' legal systems applicable to information society service providers or information society services, regardless of whether they are of a general nature or specifically designed for them. The coordinated field concerns requirements with which the service provider has to comply in respect of the taking up of the activity of an information society service, such as requirements concerning the behaviour of the service provider, requirements regarding the quality or content of the service including those applicable to advertising and contracts, or requirements concerning the liability of the service provider'.

The grounds of derogation in the E-Commerce Directive are wider than those in the AVMS Directive since they go hand in hand with the much wider scope of the country of origin principle in the former.[144] The AVMS Directive does not contain a neat definition of the 'coordinated field' similar to that provided by the E-Commerce Directive. However, the European Court has interpreted the scope of the coordinated field in the TwF Directive narrowly. We have already seen that it drew a line in the *De Agostini* case between laws for the protection of minors and the consumer in general and those that specifically regulate cross-border broadcasts. This distinction will be elaborated on more fully in the following section. It suffices to note at this point that the coordinated field and the country of origin rule in the AVMS Directive only cover the areas harmonized by this Directive and not further areas as in the E-Commerce Directive.

The fact that the wide definition of the 'coordinated field' in the E-Commerce Directive has not been adopted in the AVMS Directive is commendable. It means that Member States will only be prevented from taking measures against incoming audiovisual media services that offend their national laws if these laws fall within the narrow fields coordinated by the AVMS Directive. Consequently, the

144. Hörnle, 'Country of Origin', 94.

replication of the E-Commerce Directive's grounds for derogation in Article 2 (4) of the AVMS Directive is confusing and otiose. Member States do not need to derogate from the country of origin principle in the first place as far as public policy objectives are concerned that do not fall within the AVMS Directive's coordinated field.

The two grounds for derogation mentioned in Article 2 (4) that do indeed fall within the areas coordinated by the AVMS Directive are the protection of minors and the fight against any incitement to hatred on grounds of race, sex, religion or nationality. These are the very grounds on which a Member State may derogate from the country of origin principle in respect of television broadcasting. The adoption of the E-Commerce Directive's procedure means, however, that it is easier to derogate in respect of on-demand services than of television broadcasting. First, it suffices that the on-demand service against which the measures are taken prejudices these public policy objectives or presents a grave and serious risk of prejudice to these objectives. A manifest, serious and grave infringement of Article 22 (1) or (2) and/or Article 3b on at least two prior occasions is not required. Second, Member States can in cases of urgency derogate from the preliminary procedure under Article 2a (5).

Do these less onerous procedural requirements mean that the level of protection of minors and from audiovisual media services containing incitement to hatred on grounds of race, sex, religion or nationality is higher in respect of on-demand services than of television broadcasting? It is submitted that, at least as far as the protection of minors is concerned, the benefit of a more flexible procedure is offset by the lax requirements applying to non-linear services. Article 3h of the AVMS Directive states that 'Member States shall take appropriate measures to ensure that on-demand audiovisual media services provided by media service providers under their jurisdiction which might seriously impair the physical, mental or moral development of minors are only made available in such a way that ensures that minors will not normally hear or see such on-demand audiovisual media services.'

Whereas linear television broadcasts must not include programmes which might seriously impair the physical, mental or moral development of minors, non-linear services can include such content provided minors will not normally hear or see it. In other words, programmes involving pornography and gratuitous violence can be shown in on-demand services as long as measures are taken to minimize the chances that minors will have access to them.[145] Moreover, recital 45 to the AVMS Directive advises that measures of this sort, such as PIN codes, filtering systems or labelling, must be carefully balanced with the fundamental right to freedom of expression as laid down in the Charter on Fundamental Rights of the European Union. Also, the obligation 'to clearly draw attention to the specific nature of certain programmes before they are transmitted and in accordance both with Article 1 and Art 24 of the Charter of Fundamental Rights of the

145. Only child pornography is explicitly banned according to the provisions of Council Framework Decision 2004/68/JHA of 22 December 2003 on combating the sexual exploitation of children and child pornography, OJ L 13/44, 2004. *See* AVMS Directive, recital 46.

European Union', which was referred to in recital 32 to the amended Commission Proposal has been done away with.[146]

Already in the initial Commission proposal, the protection of minors in respect of non-linear services was pitched at a lower level than the one applying to linear ones. Article 3d stated that 'Member States shall take appropriate measures to ensure that audiovisual media services under their jurisdiction are not made available in such a way that might seriously impair the physical, mental or moral development of minors'.[147] Consequently, no measures would have to be taken in respect of non-linear audiovisual media services likely to 'simply' impair the physical, mental or moral development of minors. Such content would not even have to be identified by means of an acoustic warning or a visual symbol. This deviation from the principles applying to linear services was only explained in recital 32 by stating that: 'The aim of these measures should thus be to ensure an adequate level of protection of minors with regard to non-linear services but not to ban adult content as such.'[148] This explanation did not do justice to the importance of protecting minors and failed to resolve the tension between an 'adequate level of protection' and freedom of expression.

The wording of Article 3h of the AVMS Directive, signifies a further lowering of the level of protection offered to minors from harmful content in a non-linear environment. Not only programmes that are likely to 'simply' impair the physical, mental or moral development of minors but also such that might seriously impair their development can be made available on-demand. This is hardly compatible with the proclamation in recital 67 that the objectives of this Directive consist in creating 'an area without internal frontiers for audiovisual media services whilst ensuring at the same time a high level of protection of objectives of general interest, in particular the protection of minors and human dignity'.[149]

Can the relaxation of the rules for non-linear services be justified on account of their difference from linear services with regard to the choice and control the user can exercise?[150] It has been argued that users are less shocked by programmes they seek out themselves in on-demand platforms.[151] This may not be true of minors who might be confronted with such 'illegal' content despite best endeavours on the part of the audiovisual media service providers concerned. In any event, it does not adequately explain why measures that are only appropriate for 'simply' harmful content in a linear environment would suffice for seriously harmful content provided on-demand. The study on Parental Control of Television Broadcasting

146. Amended AVMSD proposal, recital 32.
147. Proposal for a Directive of the European Parliament and of the Council amending Council Directive 89/552/EEC on the coordination of certain provisions laid down by law, regulation or administrative action in Member States concerning the pursuit of television broadcasting activities, 13 December 2005, COM (2005) 646 final, Art. 3d.
148. *Ibid.*, recital 32.
149. AVMS Directive, recital 67.
150. *Ibid.*, recital 42.
151. Liverpool Audiovisual Conference, 'Between Culture and Commerce', 20–22 September 2005 <www.ec.europa.eu/avpolicy/docs/reg/modernisation/liverpool_2005/uk-conference-report-en.pdf>, 25 June 2007, 27.

concluded that technical measures alone cannot, at least for the foreseeable future, completely substitute for broadcaster responsibility with regard to the protection of minors. It found that this was particularly true with regard to free-to-air television broadcasting, while 'with regard to encrypted services . . . technical devices could make a valuable contribution to ensuring that minors are not exposed to harmful content.'[152] The cautiously worded conclusions of this study suggest that it might well be too early to rely exclusively on technical measures as regards seriously harmful material on non-linear services.[153]

4.2 Power of the Member States to Restrict Retransmission for Reasons not Falling within the Fields Coordinated by the Directive

4.2.1 The Non-exhaustive Character of Article 2a (1) of Directive 2007/65/EC

The wording of Article 2a (1) of the AVMS Directive leaves no doubt that Member States must not restrict retransmissions on their territory of EU audiovisual media services for reasons only which fall within the fields coordinated by the Directive. It follows *a contrario* that Member States are free to impose on foreign audiovisual media services those aspects of their broadcasting legislation, which have not been harmonized by the Directive. This view, which has been widely accepted already prior to the Directives modernization,[154] has led some commentators to the conclusion that the Directive does not constitute the first step towards the adoption of a European Union media policy.[155]

This conclusion has been countered with the argument that the mutual recognition of national rules afforded by the Directive goes beyond the areas harmonized by it.[156] Decisive importance has been attached, in reaching this

152. Communication from the Commission to the Council, the European Parliament and the Economic and Social Committee, Study on Parental Control of Television Broadcasting, 19 July 1999, COM (99) 371 final.
153. Levy, *Europe's Digital Revolution*, p. 148 fn. 8 notes characteristically that 'the weakest link in most parental control systems is frequently the parents themselves, particularly when it is their children who are the most technically adept users in the household.'
154. N. Petersen, *Rundfunkfreiheit und EG-Vertrag: Die Einwirkungen des Europäischen Rechts auf die Ausgestaltung der nationalen Rundfunkordnungen* (Baden-Baden, Nomos, 1994), p. 101; S. Seelmann-Eggebert, *Internationaler Rundfunkhandel: Im Recht der World Trade Organisation und der Europäischen Gemeinschaft* (Baden-Baden, Nomos, 1998), p. 216; E. Steindorff, *Grenzen der EG-Kompetenzen* (Heidelberg, Verlag Recht und Wirtschaft, 1990), p. 101; J. Gulich, *Rechtsfragen grenzüberschreitender Rundfunksendungen: Die deutsche Rundfunkordnung im Konflikt mit der Dienstleistungsfreiheit* (Baden-Baden, Nomos, 1990), p. 86; Lenz, 'Sendestaatsprinzip', p. 26; Kugelmann, *Rundfunk und die Dienstleistungsfreiheit*, pp. 43, 51; *see* M. Kühn, 'Harmonisierung des Rundfunkrechts in Europa: Zum Entwurf der Richtlinie der EG-Kommission' (1986) 11 ZUM, 585 *et seq.*
155. Kugelmann, *Rundfunk und die Dienstleistungsfreiheit*, p. 43.
156. Niedobitek, *Cultural Dimension*, p. 163.

verdict, to the 12th recital in the preamble to Directive 89/552 according to which it is 'necessary and sufficient that all broadcasts comply with the law of the Member State from which they emanate'. Also, the 14th recital stresses that it is the law of the originating Member State that has to be respected by broadcasts intended for reception in another Member State.

This argument is disputable. According to the 15th recital, 'the requirement that the originating Member State should verify that broadcasts comply with national law as coordinated by this Directive is sufficient under Community law to ensure free movement of broadcasts without secondary control *on the same grounds* in the receiving Member States', i.e. on grounds pertaining to areas coordinated by the Directive. This implies that the freedom of transmission in broadcasting is not guaranteed by the Directive in absolute terms, but only in so far as national laws have been harmonized.

Furthermore, a pure recognition principle, which would preclude importing Member States from invoking both harmonized and non-harmonized interests, would hardly be compatible with the European Union legal order.[157] It is true that, by shifting the focus away from harmonization, mutual recognition obviates the need for a cumbersome regulatory European Union mechanism. Furthermore, it is more deferential to the autonomy of the Member States. Nevertheless, mutual recognition entails the risk that the standards of the importing Member State might be lowered. Therefore, a pure recognition principle would have to be based on the assumption that a common core of broadcasting policy standards exists in the Member States. Such an assumption stands out in sharp relief to the variety of programme content requirements to be encountered in the European Union. Completely deprived of the possibility to exclude foreign broadcasts not consistent with their legislation, receiving Member States would be forced to lower their domestic requirements as well. This is a far cry from the high level of protection to be achieved by means of harmonization according to Article 95 (3) EC.[158]

Moreover, the endorsement of the pure recognition principle would signify a departure from the approach consistently taken by the European Court, that the state in which a service is provided is not entitled to undertake supplementary controls if the supplier is already subject to equivalent controls in the state of establishment.[159] Factual equivalence, as required by this approach, would be replaced by fictitious equivalence.[160]

Finally, the pure recognition principle would be inconsistent with the 17th recital, which states that the Directive is without prejudice to future Community acts of harmonization.[161] If a free market in broadcasting services was created as a result of the pure recognition principle, the subsequent harmonization provided

157. Steindorff, *Grenzen der EG-Kompetenzen*, p. 101.
158. *Ibid.*
159. Case 279/80 *Webb* [1981] ECR 3305; [1982] 1 CMLR 406; Case 205/84 *Commission v. Germany* [1986] ECR 3755; [1987] 2 CMLR 69.
160. Steindorff, *Grenzen der EG-Kompetenzen*, p. 102.
161. *Ibid.*, p. 99; contra, AG Jacobs in *De Agostini*, para. 77.

for in this recital would operate as autonomous lawmaking, not serving the elimination of obstacles to the free movement of television broadcasts. The question whether EU competence can be that far-reaching is a matter for speculation. However, the relevant Treaty provisions, namely Articles 3 (h), 47 (2), 94 and 95, only allow harmonization measures to be adopted if they are necessary for the common or internal market to function. Also, the repealed Article 100b (2) provided for mutual recognition as an alternative to harmonization, not in addition to it, in case the internal market programme had not been completed by the end of 1992. It is therefore unlikely that the Directive empowers the European Union to adopt harmonization acts as instruments of autonomous lawmaking.

The technique of mutual recognition *cum* harmonization adopted by the Directive is thus a *via media*. An important conclusion to be drawn from the foregoing is that the country of origin principle is not written in black and white in the Treaty nor does it emanate from the fundamental freedoms in the interpretation given to them by the European Court in *Cassis de Dijon*.[162] It is no more than a method called into play by the European Union legislature, so as to complete the internal market in broadcasting services.[163]

In view of the foregoing considerations, it seems right to conclude that Article 2a (1) is non-exhaustive so that restrictions of EU broadcasts on grounds not coordinated by the Directive are legitimate.

4.2.2 Which Fields are Coordinated by the Directive?

The extent to which Member States are still allowed to restrict retransmission is not clear. A central controversy concerns the meaning of the terms 'the fields coordinated by this Directive' but also the characteristics of the laws affecting retransmission.

The extent of the power of the Member States to subject foreign programmes to national laws not harmonized by the Directive has been at issue in *Commission v. Belgium*[164] and *De Agostini*.[165]

In the first of these cases, one of the justifications adduced by the Belgian Government in support of the system of prior authorization for retransmission by cable of broadcasts from other Member States in the French community was the need to safeguard pluralism in the media. The Court recalled its judgments in the

162. *See* Case C-233/94, *Germany v. European Parliament and Council* [1997] ECR I- 2405, para. 64, noted at (1998) 35 CMLRev, 459; Drijber, 'Revised Television without Frontiers Directive', 87 n. 2.
163. AG Lenz in Case C-222/94, *Commission v. United Kingdom* [1996] ECR I-4025, para. 38.
164. Case C-11/95, *Commission v. Belgium* [1996] ECR I-4117.
165. Joined Cases C-34/95, C-35/95 and C-36/95, *Konsumentombudsmannen (KO) v. De Agostini (Svenska) Förlag AB and Konsumentenombudsmannen* (KO) *v. TV-Shop I Sverige AB* [1997] ECR I-3843.

cases *Gouda*[166] and *Commission v. Netherlands*[167] where it had found a cultural policy aimed at safeguarding pluralism to constitute an overriding requirement relating to the general interest, which justifies a restriction on the freedom to provide services.[168] It considered it superfluous to examine whether the question of preservation of pluralism in the media had been exhaustively regulated by the provisions of Dir. 89/552 on advertising, in particular Articles 10 (1), 11 (1), 17 (1) (a) and 19, as the Commission contended. The Court observed that in any event 'the Belgian Government has not shown adequately in detail that the system of prior authorization was necessary and proportional for protecting pluralism in the audiovisual field or in the media generally'.[169]

The reasoning of the Court is compelling, given that Article 49 EC is the fall-back standard against which rules impeding the transmission of transfrontier broadcasts, which have not yet been harmonized at EU level, have to be measured. Nonetheless, it is regrettable that the Court avoided answering the question whether the Directive completely covers the topic of media pluralism. The Commission's contention relies on the fact that advertising rules concerning 'when, where and how advertisements may be placed'[170] do not only aim to protect the interests of the captive viewer. An equally if not more important purpose served by them is to secure the diversity of opinion in television programmes, in which the advertisements are embedded, but also of the media in general, especially of the written press.[171] However, as Advocate-General Lenz observed, the rules in Articles 10 *et seq*. are technical in nature, are not immediately related to pluralism in the media and cannot, therefore, regulate this matter comprehensively.[172]

The Commission has recently argued that the AVMS Directive also protects media pluralism by promoting European and independent productions and by requiring Member States to guarantee the independence of national regulatory authorities.[173] However, as will be seen in the following chapter, the European quota cannot promote the transmission of more original content representative of European cultures. Further, the Commission proposal to the AVMS Directive asserted that 'Regulators should be independent from national governments as well as from audiovisual media service providers in order to be able to carry out their work impartially and transparently and to contribute to

166. Case C-288/89 *Stichting Collectieve Antennevorziennning Gouda and Others* [1991] ECR I-4007.
167. Case C-353/89 *Commission v. Netherlands* [1991] ECR I-4069.
168. *See* Part 2, Ch. 4.3.2.1 *below*.
169. Case C-11/95 *Commission v. Belgium* [1996] ECR I-4117, para. 55.
170. AG Jacobs in Joined Cases C-34/95, C-35/95 and C-36/95, para. 58.
171. M. Bullinger, 'Werbung und Quotenregelung zwischen nationalem und europäischem Rundfunkrecht' in *Eine Rundfunkordnung für Europa – Chancen und Risiken*, K. Stern *et al.* (eds), Schriftenreihe des Instituts für Rundfunkrecht an der Universität zu Köln, vol. 54 (Munich, C. H. Beck, 1990), pp. 85, 91 *et seq.*; M. Müller, 'Die Revision der EG-Fernsehrichtlinie – EMR-Dialog am 2.12.1993 in Mainz in Zusammenarbeit mit SAT.1' (1994) 1 AfP, 26, 29.
172. AG Lenz in Case C-11/95, para. 63.
173. MEMO/06/208.

pluralism.'[174] This ambitious proclamation was withdrawn later on. However well-intended it may have been, withdrawing this statement was a sensible move given that the European Union is not competent to decide the organization of broadcasting in the Member States.

Recital 65 to the AVMS Directive reads:

> 'According to the duties conferred upon Member States by the Treaty, they are responsible for the transposition and effective implementation of this Directive. They are free to choose the appropriate instruments according to their legal traditions and established structures, and notably the form of their competent independent regulatory bodies, in order to be able to carry out their work in implementing this Directive impartially and transparently. More specifically, the instruments chosen by Member States should contribute to the promotion of media pluralism.'

Also, Article 23b states that

> Member States shall take appropriate measures to provide each other and the Commission with the information necessary for the application of the provisions of this Directive, in particular Articles 2, 2a and 3 hereof, notably through their competent independent regulatory bodies.

These provisions acknowledge the diversity of broadcasting traditions in Europe. Their tone is much more deferential to the power of the Member States to define the structure of their regulatory bodies. Finding ways to promote media pluralism is also left to the Member States. In the light of what has been said so far, it is suggested that national laws on pluralism in the media have not been fully harmonized by the Directive so that restrictions of retransmission are still permitted on these grounds.

The Belgian Government argued further that the authorization required for the cable retransmission of foreign programmes in the Flemish community was justified on grounds of public policy, public morality or public security.[175] The receiving State should have the power to control whether foreign broadcasts violated these objectives, given that no harmonization had taken place at EU level in this respect. The Court did not accept this argument either. It held that matters related to these legitimate interests were not alien to the Directive yet it was cautious enough to add that, in so far as the rules contained therein were not exhaustive, the prior authorization of broadcasts from other Member States was not justified, since it effectively nullified the freedom to provide services.

Once again one is bound to subscribe to the view of Advocate-General Lenz that questions of public policy, good morals and public security are not expressly and, at any rate, not comprehensively dealt with in the Directive.[176] They are only cursorily touched upon in connection with television advertising and with the

---

174. Amended AVMSD proposal, recital 47.
175. AG Lenz in Case C-11/95 para. 91.
176. *Ibid.*, para. 100.

protection of minors under Articles 3e and 22 of the AVMS Directive. Also, Article 3b of the AVMS Directive aims at the protection of public order. These provisions cannot, however, be taken to constitute an exhaustive regulation of the vulnerable values in question. Suffice it to say that no standards have been set with regard to the treatment of subjects such as violence and sex in programmes addressed to adult audiences.[177]

Consequently, the fact that the Directive vests the receiving states with the express power to deviate from the country of origin principle in the case of infringement of Article 22 cannot be taken to imply that all other defence of public policy and morals against broadcasts from other Member States is outlawed.[178] Admittedly, this reasoning strikes a heavy blow to the principle of mutual trust. Nonetheless, a balanced solution cannot be achieved by denying every right of the receiving states to assert their fundamental interests in the protection of their public order. Instead, the proportionality test should be strictly applied so as to ensure that the curbing of foreign programmes is indispensable.

The judgment of the European Court in the case *Commission v. Belgium* has been described as 'the strongest statement of the ECJ to date that the country of origin principle is primary and cannot be overridden by the concerns of the receiving State regarding the content of programming except in limited circumstances involving a grave and serious breach of Article 22'.[179] This reading of the judgment is not convincing, given that the Court did not pronounce the receiving state ineligible to control transfrontier broadcasts for reasons such as the protection of pluralism or of public policy and good morals.[180] It is only on the facts of this case, in view of the far-reaching secondary control imposed on foreign broadcasts in the French and Flemish community, that the Court upheld the Commission's objections.

The validity of this conclusion is born out in the judgment handed down by the Court in the *De Agostini* case.[181] A main difference between Case C-11/95, *Commission v. Belgium* and this case is that, while the former concerned an obstacle to the retransmission as such of foreign programmes, the latter is about national measures restricting the marketing of products in a manner unfair towards consumers, which only indirectly have repercussions on the broadcasting of

177. W. Hoffmann-Riem, 'Defending Vulnerable Values: Regulatory Measures and Enforcement Dilemmas' in *Television and the Public Interest: Vulnerable Values in West European Broadcasting*, J. G. Blumler (ed.) (London, Sage, 1992), pp. 173, 190.
178. Contra AG Lenz in Case C-11/95, para. 101. *See, however*, para. 104 of the same Opinion, where AG Lenz left the option open that, in the case of flagrant offences against public policy, public security or good morals a Member State might be entitled to take action against broadcasts from other Member States.
179. M. Pullen and B. Ris, 'Television without Frontiers: The Saga Continues' (1997) 1 ENT L R, 3.
180. M. Knothe and H. Bashayan, 'Die Revision der EG-Fernsehrichtlinie: Ein europäischer Entscheidungsprozeß im Lichte nationaler Kompetenzen' (1997) 6 AfP, 849.
181. Joined Cases C-34/95, C-35/95 and C-36/95, *Konsumentombudsmannen (KO) v. De Agostini (Svenska) Förlag AB and Konsumentenombudsmannen* (KO) *v. TV-Shop I Sverige AB* [1997] ECR I- 3843.

programmes. As already mentioned, in Cases C-35/95 and C-36/95 the Consumer Ombudsman sought to restrain TV-Shop from making unsubstantiated statements in connection with the marketing of skin-care products and a detergent. The Court distinguished between provisions in the Directive on the content of television advertisements and others on where and how advertisements can be inserted. It came to the conclusion that the Directive only partially coordinates national laws on television advertising.

Once again, the Court did not directly address the question whether misleading advertising falls within the fields coordinated by the Directive.[182] It took a different approach instead by drawing a line between provisions specifically regulating the broadcasting and distribution of programmes and others having the general aim of protecting consumers from misleading advertising.[183] In the Court's opinion, the Directive and hence the country of origin principle are only concerned with the broadcasting and distribution of programmes; they are not applicable to the general advertising legislation of the Member States. Consequently, Member States are not precluded from imposing their legislation on consumer protection on foreign television advertisements.

This power has however been subjected to two somewhat obscure conditions. The measures taken against an advertiser with regard to advertisements transmitted from another Member State should not entail a secondary control of television broadcasts on top of that exercised by the transmitting state.[184] Moreover, they should not restrict retransmission *as such* of foreign television broadcasts.[185] These conditions will be explored in the following.

It has been argued that the Court created a link between two unrelated issues, namely the question whether advertisers can invoke the country of origin principle and the question which fields have been coordinated by the Directive.[186] However, this judgment cannot be interpreted as excluding advertisers from the scope of the Directive. The allegation that the Directive only applies to broadcasters and not to advertisers was made by the claimants and disputed by Advocate-General Jacobs and the defendants on the ground that it would weaken the country of origin principle in its purpose and effect.[187]

The Court took account of this argument in its judgment. Nonetheless, it did not directly answer the question posed, but made a general observation on the relationship between the TwF Directive and the Misleading Advertising Directive.[188] The latter defines misleading advertising and lays down minimum

182. AG Jacobs in Joined Cases C-34/95, C-35/95 and C-36/95, paras 79 *et seq.*
183. Joined Cases C-34/95, C-35/95 and C-36/95, paras 33 *et seq.*
184. *Ibid.*, para. 34.
185. *Ibid.*, para. 38.
186. Drijber, 'Revised Television without Frontiers Directive', 100.
187. AG Jacobs, paras 35 *et seq.*
188. Council Directive 84/450/EEC of 10 September 1984 relating to the approximation of the laws, regulations and administrative provisions of the Member States concerning Misleading Advertising, OJ L 250/17, 1984.

requirements for its control in the interest of consumers. Drawing support from a judgment handed down by the EFTA Court in a case similar to *De Agostini*,[189] the European Court ruled that the Misleading Advertising Directive would become ineffective as regards television advertising if the receiving Member State was not allowed to apply its implementing legislation to foreign broadcasts.

The Court thus confirmed that measures can be taken against advertisers producing commercials contrary to the Misleading Advertising Directive without, however, excluding the category of advertisers *in toto* from the Television Directive. Such a result would have been inconsistent with the Directive, given that advertising is the area most extensively regulated therein.[190] Moreover, it would not have chimed with the second part of the judgment in which De Agostini successfully relied on the country of origin principle so as to prevent the application of Swedish broadcasting law to its advertisements. All in all, the Directive equally applies to the activity of broadcasters and to more ancillary activities such as those of advertisers or sponsors.

What is the reasoning then behind the distinction drawn by the Court between laws regulating television advertising per se, which fall within the ambit of the Directive, and general legislation on the protection of consumers against misleading advertising, which does not? We have already seen that the Court drew an analogous distinction in the second part of this judgment between general legislation on the protection of minors and legislation specifically designed to control the content of television advertising with regard to minors.[191] These distinctions seem justified, given that the Directive only coordinates provisions concerning the pursuit of television broadcasting activities. The reasoning of the Court is based on a pragmatic view of the scope of the Directive. Since the Directive subjects advertising only to limited rules protecting consumers or minors in their capacity as television viewers, it could not be regarded as a comprehensive piece of consumer protection or child welfare legislation.[192] Being obliged to respect the responsibility of Member States for the financing of programmes, the Directive had to weigh advertising restrictions against their repercussions on the funding of television.[193] Consequently, depriving Member States of their right to apply their general laws to EU broadcasts would curtail their power to set consumer or child protection standards.

In the light of these considerations, the reasoning adopted by the Court has to be welcomed. By putting emphasis on the general nature of the provisions at hand instead of their subject matter (unfair advertising), the Court answered the question

189. Joined Cases E-8/94 and E-9/94, *Forbrukerombudet v. Mattel Scandinavia and Lego Norge*, judgment of 16 June 1995; Joined Cases C-34/95, C-35/95 and C-36/95, *Konsumentombudsmannen (KO) v. De Agostini (Svenska) Förlag AB and Konsumentenombudsmannen* (KO) *v. TV-Shop I Sverige AB* [1997] ECR I- 3843, noted at (1997) 34 CMLRev, 1445, 1449.

190. A. Criscuolo, 'The "TV without Frontiers" Directive and the Legal Regulation of Publicity in the European Community' (1998) 23 ELRev, 357, 363.

191. *See* Part 2, Ch. 11.3.22, p.223 *above*.

192. *See* Dir. 89/552, recital 27.

193. *See* Dir. 89/552, recital 13.

as to the extent of coordination in the Directive in an ingenious way. General legislation falls in any case outside the ambit of the Directive.

The Commission's proposition that misleading advertising is not within the fields coordinated by the Directive was dealt with in a more straightforward manner by Advocate-General Jacobs. He disagreed with the Commission on account of the difference between the 'fields coordinated by the Directive' and 'the specific matters regulated by it'.[194] He held that it is the former concept, which is decisive for the application of the country of origin principle. In his view, even though there are no specific rules in the Directive on misleading advertising, it suffices that television advertising in general is one of the areas coordinated by the Directive.

In support of Advocate-General Jacob's approach, an intriguing argument has been derived by Drijber from the comparison of Article 2a (1) with Article 3 (1) and the 44th recital to Dir. 97/36.[195] Article 3 (1) allows Member States to require television broadcasters under their jurisdiction to comply with more detailed or stricter rules *in the areas covered by the Directive*. The 44th recital sets out by way of example stricter rules *in the fields coordinated by this Directive*, which can be applied by Member States to broadcasters under their jurisdiction, with the aim of the achievement of language policy goals, the protection of pluralism etc. Drijber took issue with the judgment of the Court in *Leclerc-Siplec*.[196] In his opinion, this ruling brings out the breadth of Article 3 (1). The Court found a national provision prohibiting the broadcasting of advertisements for the distribution sector with the aim of protecting the written press to be in accordance with Article 3 (1) even though neither rules on advertising by the distribution sector nor on the protection of pluralism are specifically contained in the Directive. The fact that the Directive does not encompass these interests was not considered by the Court to limit the scope of Article 3. Similarly, the rules listed in the 44th recital as falling within the 'fields coordinated by the Directive' pursue interests, which have not particularly been dealt with in the Directive. Notably, instead of referring to the 'areas covered by the Directive' as in Article 3 (1), this recital uses the same phraseology as Article 2a (1). Given that the 44th recital merely elaborates on Article 3, Drijber considered that the terms 'areas covered by the Directive' and 'fields coordinated by the Directive' are applied interchangeably. Therefore, their meaning in Article 2a (1) and in Article 3 (1) is the same. From this he concluded that the subject matter of a rule, not the value protected by it, determine whether it falls within a coordinated field.

It is submitted that this argument, compelling though it might seem at first sight, is not conclusive. In Article 3 (1), the term 'areas covered by this Directive' does not serve to draw an accurate distinction from the areas not covered by the Directive, since the Member States are equally free to adopt stricter or more

194. AG Jacobs, para. 80.
195. Drijber, 'Revised Television without Frontiers Directive', 101.
196. Case C-412/93, *Société d'Importation Édouard Leclerc-Siplec v. TF1 Publicité SA and M6 Publicité SA* [1995] ECR I-179.

detailed rules in the latter areas. If televised advertising for the distribution sector had been found to be outside the scope of the Directive in *Leclerc-Siplec*, France would have been all the more at liberty to outlaw advertising for this sector. Therefore, the definition of the exact boundaries of the fields coordinated by the Directive was not material to assessing the legality of the provision in question. On the contrary, the phrase 'fields coordinated by this Directive' in Article 2a (1) circumscribes the areas in which the country of origin principle applies so that retransmission of broadcasts from other Member States may not be restricted. A stricter interpretation of this phrase in the sense of 'the specific matters regulated by the Directive' seems justified so as not to let sensitive aspects of the Member States' broadcasting policy go by the board.

Having shed some light on the meaning of the phrase 'the fields coordinated by the Directive', it is necessary to consider, lastly, the above-mentioned conditions for the application of general laws to transfrontier broadcasts. What does the requirement mean that national rules should not involve secondary control of television broadcasts nor prevent retransmission as such? A clue given by the Court in paragraph 35 of the judgment is that consumer protection legislation which 'provides for a system of prohibitions and restraining orders to be imposed on advertisers enforceable by financial penalties' satisfies this requirement. First, this passage suggests that measures should not be taken against the broadcaster, but only against the advertiser. Secondly, there should be no control of broadcasts prior to their transmission. The commercials could only be scrutinized by the courts or other state authorities after their airing.[197]

The distinction drawn by the Court between direct measures taken against a broadcaster and indirect measures taken against an advertiser has been criticized in academic writing for being slightly artificial.[198] Injunctions against advertisements broadcast from other Member States also prevent their retransmission. It could be argued in defence of the Court that indirect measures of this sort are less likely to be motivated by the wish to restrict the free circulation of broadcasting services, not least in view of the practical difficulties of enforcing remedies available in the receiving state's legal system against an advertiser established in a different state.[199] Obviously, such practical difficulties would not arise in cases similar to the present ones where the advertisers were established in the Member State imposing the restraining orders in question. What is more, as we have already noted, indirect measures, not least against advertisers, are often the most effective way of blocking the retransmission of a broadcast. The physical restriction of the retransmission of a broadcast is often impracticable, especially in the case of broadcasts transmitted via satellite or the internet. Consequently, the line drawn by the Court between direct and indirect measures is indeed tenuous.

---

197. E. J. Dommering, 'Advertising and Sponsorship Law – Problems of Regulating Partly Liberalised Markets' in *Europäisches Medienrecht – Fernsehen und seine gemeinschaftsrechtliche Regelung*, Schriftenreihe des Instituts für Europäisches Medienrecht Saarbrücken, vol. 18 (Munich, Jehle-Rehm, 1998), p. 49.
198. Hörnle, 'Country of Origin', 103; Jones, 'Television without Frontiers', 315.
199. AG Jacobs, para. 84.

Even though the Court's conditions on national legislation preventing the distribution of foreign broadcasts may be flawed in practice, it is possible to see a parallel in their theoretical conception with the jurisprudence of the Federal Constitutional Court of Germany on freedom of speech. According to Article 5 (2) of the German Constitution (GG), freedom of speech as well as freedom of the press find their limits in the general laws, in the rules on the protection of youth and in the right to personal honour. General laws have been defined by the Federal Constitutional Court rather long-windedly as laws that 'do not prohibit an opinion or the expression of an opinion as such but are directed towards the protection of legal rights which need such protection regardless of any specific opinion',[200] in other words, laws that are directed towards the protection of a community value, that takes precedence over the exercise of free speech.[201] The European Court, by allowing the free movement of broadcasting services to be limited only by laws satisfying requirements analogous to the ones under Article 5 (2) GG, presumably intended to emphasize its constitutional rank. It aimed to ensure that only laws that do not pursue the segregation of the national broadcasting markets behind the cover of general interests are in keeping with the Television Directive. However, by drawing the ill-informed distinction between direct and indirect measures it may have defied itself.

In conclusion, it may appear that the Court in *De Agostini* made two steps forward and one step back in the completion of the internal market in broadcasting services. On the one hand, it precluded the application of the Swedish broadcasting law prohibiting advertisements directed at children under 12, while on the other it sanctioned the application of the consumer protection legislation. The first part of the judgment is surprisingly considerate towards the interest of the Member States to stem the flood of imported broadcasts in contravention of their general legislation. One should bear in mind, however, that it is merely the general legal order of the Member States to which the Court has been deferential. As for the rest, it remains doubtful how far cultural values cherished in the national broadcasting laws qualify to hinder the free movement of services.

5. CONCLUSION

The country of origin principle is the mechanism chosen by the drafters of the TwF Directive so as to distribute regulatory powers over a single event: the transmission of a transfrontier broadcast. This principle is symptomatic of the subjection of broadcasting to the logic of the internal market that requires only one Member State to be responsible for the content of a given broadcast. It is the country of origin that is entrusted with the supervision of broadcasts falling under its jurisdiction while the reception state has the power to intervene in exceptional

200. *Lüth* Case (1958) 7 BVerfG 198, 209.
201. D. P. Kommers, *The Constitutional Jurisprudence of the Federal Republic of Germany* (2nd edn, Durham, NC, Duke University Press, 1997), p. 365.

circumstances only. The obvious drawback is that the state where broadcasts are received and which is therefore primarily affected is restrained from asserting its legitimate interests. The present article has examined the question whether the Directive has succeeded in resolving the tension between transmission and reception state satisfactorily by means of a balanced and legally secure regulatory framework.

The identification of the state having jurisdiction over a certain broadcaster has been fundamental to the Directive's conception. Dir. 89/552 failed to flesh out the link between state and broadcaster, thus giving rise to legal uncertainty. The revised Dir. 97/36 went from the one extreme to the other by aspiring to cover all possible factual constellations through complex rules of conflict. This formalistic approach is misconceived, since it is prone to abuse and to interpretative difficulties. The more open-ended 'centre of activities' test developed by the European Court is the better option.

It has been suggested that the Directive provides three compensatory mechanisms in an effort to rise to the challenge of creating the internal market in broadcasting services, while giving leeway to the reception state to regulate content issues.

First, Article 2a (2) of the Directive permits a derogation from the country of origin principle on the ground of protection of minors. This exception can only be invoked under very strict conditions that are hardly commensurate with the sensitive issues involved. Instead of taking a proactive attitude towards programmes unsuitable for minors, the Directive puts up with their repeated transmission and allows a belated reaction only. The procedure for derogating from the country of origin principle in respect of on-demand services in the AVMS Directive gives Member States greater latitude. However, the protection from seriously harmful content afforded to minors is quite limited.

Second, the retransmission of foreign broadcasts can be restricted on grounds not coordinated by the Directive. Initial doubts about this interpretation have been undeniably cleared by the judgments of the Court in *Commission v. Belgium* and *De Agostini*. In these cases, the Court did not seize the opportunity to define more accurately the area occupied by the Directive. It is therefore open to debate whether cultural considerations of the Member States related to pluralism and morality in the media fall therein. The Court took recourse to the proportionality test and to the distinction between general and broadcasting legislation instead. Understandably so, given that this approach is more flexible and mitigates the impression of a far-reaching deregulation via quasi-regulation of questions of content. Nonetheless, the fact remains that Member States are loaded with an onerous burden of proof that their restrictive measures are proportionate.

We have seen that the last and most contentious arrow in the reception states' quiver is the circumvention principle. The new procedures proposed in the AVMS Directive have somewhat mitigated the uncertainty as to the conditions that have to be satisfied for the substantiation of abuse of EU law. The voluntary and the circumvention procedures differ both in their requirements and in the spirit in which they will be carried out.

The voluntary procedure is meant to take place in a climate of mutual trust and cooperation. It does not require proof of illegal conduct even though it may constitute the first stage in a case of abusive delocalization. It aims to reconcile the conflicting interests of a transmitting state making a perfectly legitimate use of its freedom to provide broadcasting services and of a receiving state that does not want to see its broadcasting standards watered down by foreign programmes complying with a laxer set of rules. Obviously, this procedure is doomed to fail when there is no willingness to cooperate.

If the Member States involved are unable to solve their dispute amicably, the means of last resort is the circumvention procedure. This procedure enables the receiving state to take matters in its own hands and to adopt appropriate measures against the broadcaster concerned. However, proving a U-turn construction is a difficult undertaking. Also, this procedure offers no means of redress when the receiving state's broadcasting standards are threatened by the sheer diversity of national laws and not by an abusive delocalization.

It follows that the balance between transmission and reception state struck by the Directive is precarious to the extent that it neglects legitimate concerns of the latter. Since these concerns are often related to the cultural priorities of national broadcasting systems, they cannot be catered for by a narrow economic outlook. Is the thesis correct then that the country of origin principle has signified the end of the broadcasting sovereignty of the Member States? This rather extreme suggestion contains a grain of truth. Undeniably, the country of origin principle encroaches upon the power of the Member States to shape their broadcasting orders at will. National broadcasting laws that have been coordinated *expressis verbis* by the Directive cannot be applied to transfrontier broadcasts any more. More worryingly, the shadow of the European Court is hanging over the capacity of the Member States to impose broadcasting standards that lie beyond the Directive's coordinated field on foreign transmissions.

Nonetheless, it is suggested that the impact of the transmission state principle has to be seen against the background of fundamental political and technological changes, which have taken place in the last two decades in Europe, putting traditional models of broadcasting regulation into question. The main factors contributing to the decrease of the state's regulatory responsibility are the emergence of private broadcasting companies and of satellite transmission.

As we have seen in Part One of this book, when broadcasting made its appearance in Western Europe in the 1920s, it was not left to the dynamics of the economic market, but was embedded by the state in a narrow regulatory framework known as the public service model. This model is based on the assumption that broadcasting has to be publicly regulated, so as to conform with a cluster of social values such as its general geographic availability, its impartiality and diversity and its cultural vocation.[202]

---

202. K. Dyson and P. Humphreys, 'Regulatory Change in Western Europe: From National Cultural Regulation to International Economic Statecraft' in *Broadcasting and New Media Policies in Western Europe: A Comparative Study of Technological Change and Public Policy*, K. Dyson and P. Humphreys (London, Routledge, 1988), p. 96; J. G. Blumler, 'Public Service

The most widely invoked rationale for the legal regulation of broadcasting has been the scarcity argument.[203] It has been claimed that, due to the limited number of frequencies available for broadcasting, not allowing everyone to have access, the state had to intervene so as to oblige licensees to present a balanced variety of views as well as to hinder signal disturbance.[204]

The scarcity argument has been challenged by the proliferation of broadcasting outlets as a result of the development of cable and satellite technologies. The expansion of spectrum usage removed this justification for the public service paradigm and provided grist to the mill of the proponents of the commercialization of broadcasting.[205] It was argued that a great number of private channels would, as a matter of course, offer a wide range of programmes. This external pluralism would be preferable to the artificial internal pluralism created by public broadcasting institutions. Under the market model of broadcasting, reliance is placed for the satisfaction of the communication needs of the public on free access by various interest groups to the broadcasting profession rather than on government intervention.[206]

Private channels have increasingly been dispensed from traditional programme standards. This deregulatory tendency has in turn left its imprint upon public channels, which under the pressure of competition for advertising revenues and broadcasting rights also had to adapt to the demands of the market.[207] A shift in the aims of broadcasting regulation has occurred concomitant to these developments. Programming requirements that are not in keeping with the market logic, such as impartiality or plurality duties, have been markedly relaxed. Fairness requirements have been diminished to inflexible, decorative norms with regard to informational programming, while content-related regulation in the field of entertainment has become scarce.[208]

This is not to say that a total eclipse of programme requirements has taken place. That this is not the case has been amply demonstrated in Part One of this book. Interests that cannot be adequately protected by market self-regulation, are still within the state's regulatory responsibility. This applies especially to private interests such as personal integrity, copyright and consumer rights. Further vulnerable values that are guarded by supervisory authorities are morality, decency and the protection of minors.[209] These are, however, the very values that are also

---

Broadcasting before the Commercial Deluge' in *Television and the Public Interest: Vulnerable Values in West European Broadcasting*, J. G. Blumler (ed.) (London, Sage, 1992), p. 7 *et seq.*

203. Dyson and Humphreys, 'Regulatory Change', pp. 95–96; Barendt, *Broadcasting Law*, p. 4.
204. *Ibid.*
205. Humphreys, *Mass Media and Media Policy*, p. 161.
206. W. Hoffmann-Riem, *Regulating Media: The Licensing and Supervision of Broadcasting in Six Countries* (New York, Guilford, 1996), p. 283.
207. *Ibid.*, 341; W. Hoffmann-Riem, 'Trends in the Development of Broadcasting Law in Western Europe'(1992) 7 *European Journal of Communication*, 147, 153.
208. Hoffmann-Riem, *Regulating Media*, pp. 340, 345.
209. *Ibid.*, pp. 346, 361.

protected under Article 2a (2) of the TwF Directive. The Directive does not raise obstacles to the safeguarding of private interests either. As has emerged from *De Agostini*, general legislation which is quite appropriate for the protection of such interests will now as ever be applicable to transfrontier broadcasts.

A further factor that has undermined the regulatory authority of the Member States, next to the emergence of commercial broadcasting, is the introduction of direct broadcasting satellites (DBS) providing television direct to home. Neither fortuitous 'overspill' nor intentional satellite transmission to foreign territories can easily be contained.[210] Unless states completely refrain from creating the necessary infrastructure for the reception of satellite signals, have recourse to technical devices restricting such reception, or enter into bilateral agreements to this effect, they are exposed to programmes broadcast from abroad without being able to exercise any influence over their content. The recent cases of satellite broadcasts from third countries inciting racial hatred brought home to the Commission that cooperation of regulatory authorities within Europe is not sufficient and that regulators from third countries would also need to be taken on board.[211]

The immunity of direct broadcasting satellite television from the broadcasting laws of the Member States has been recognized by the courts and legislators at the national level and has influenced the content of these laws.[212] Concomitantly, programme requirements applicable to the cable retransmission of foreign programmes have also long been relaxed at the national level despite the fact that the distribution via cable easily lends itself to regulatory interventions.[213] The general tendency is to dispense cable and satellite broadcasting from programme content requirements, but to impose on them the same restrictions on the transmission of violent and indecent programmes as on terrestrial channels.[214] These are precisely the vital interests of the Member States the European Union also recognizes by allowing them to restrict transfrontier broadcasts in accordance with Articles 2a (2) and 22.

Consequently, the division of powers between the transmitting and the receiving state under Article 2a of the Directive reflects changes in the media systems of the Member States, which have been effectuated through national law. The Directive does not expressly preclude Member States from applying their programme standards to foreign broadcasts. However, their real possibility to do so will be very limited in view of the power of satellite broadcasting to transcend national borders. What is more, the interest in rigorously enforcing these standards will be weak, given that the state's influence on domestic commercial channels has also declined.

---

210. M. Seidel, 'Europa und die Medien' in *Fernsehen ohne Grenzen: Die Errichtung des Gemeinsamen Marktes für den Rundfunk, insbesondere über Satellit und Kabel*, J. Schwarze (ed.) (Baden-Baden, Nomos, 1985), pp. 127, 139. On the significant problems for the enforcement of content regulation posed by the internet, *see* Part 2, Ch. 14, p. 314.
211. IP/05/325.
212. The impossibility of the isolation of national media systems has been insightfully captured by the German Constitutional Court in its *Fourth Broadcasting Case*, 73 BVerfGE 118 (1986).
213. Seidel, 'Europa und die Medien', p. 138.
214. Barendt, *Broadcasting Law*, p. 110.

The situation is not entirely dissimilar to the abolition of the broadcasting monopoly in Italy and of the restrictions to the diffusion of commercial advertising on cable television in Belgium. These developments have not been instigated by the Community. After all, the Court had accepted the national choices in the cases *Sacchi* and *Debauve*.[215] They have been sparked off by the national legislators or interest groups in the respective Member States.[216] Nonetheless, these findings cannot distract from the fact that the failure of the Member States to protect vulnerable values such as the physical, mental and moral development of minors or the editorial integrity of programmes in a more comprehensive way, opting instead for a Directive with a predominantly economic orientation, drastically influences television towards the market model of broadcasting.[217]

---

215. Case 155/73, *Guiseppe Sacchi* [1974] ECR 409; (1974) 2 CMLR 177; Case 52/79, *Procureur du Roi v. Marc J.V.C. Debauve and others* [1980] ECR-I 833.
216. N. Reich, 'Rundfunkrecht und Wettbewerbsrecht vor dem Forum des europäischen Gemeinschaftsrechts' in *Rundfunk im Wettbewerbsrecht: Der öffentlich-rechtliche Rundfunk im Spannungsfeld zwischen Wirtschaftsrecht und Rundfunkrecht*, W. Hoffmann-Riem (ed.), Symposien des Hans-Bredow-Instituts, vol. 10 (Baden-Baden, Nomos, 1988), p. 227; K. Berg, 'Rechtsprobleme des grenzüberschreitenden Fernsehens – Stellungnahme zum Grünbuch der EG-Kommission aus der Sicht der öffentlich-rechtlichen Rundfunkanstalten' in *Fernsehen ohne Grenzen: Die Errichtung des Gemeinsamen Marktes für den Rundfunk, insbesondere über Satellit und Kabel*, J. Schwarze (ed.) (Baden-Baden, Nomos, 1985), p. 200.
217. *See* the discussion about the legalization of product placement in Part 1, ch. 1.1.1, p.5 *et seq above*.

Chapter 12

Free Movement of Television Broadcasts and National Broadcasting Obligations

1. INTRODUCTION

This chapter takes up a question that was touched upon previously and seeks to pursue it further. It is the question in how far foreign broadcasts can be subjected to national broadcasting obligations such as the duty of pluralism and impartiality of programmes. Even though such obligations mostly concern national rather than cross-frontier transmissions, their 'extraterritorial application' cannot be ruled out. From the very early days of broadcasting, governments have been eager to protect their national broadcasting monopolies by suppressing foreign commercial programmes. As the cases in this chapter demonstrate, intriguing questions about the interplay between fiscal and cultural considerations arise in this context. One could argue that if the character of television as a cultural experience is to be preserved, it is necessary to oppose the assault on the few remaining broadcasters, which abide by traditional cultural obligations, by market-minded, international communication conglomerates. Their subjection to the same obligations could be a step in the right direction.

It emerged from the previous chapter that national programme standards have not been fully harmonized by the AVMS Directive so that room remains for the Member States to restrict the retransmission of Community broadcasts on these grounds. In this chapter we will approach this problem from another angle. The question will be posed whether such standards are compatible with the freedom to provide broadcasting services under Article 49 EC. This is the ultimate barrier to be cleared by rules impeding the transmission of transfrontier broadcasts. The provisions of the Treaty on free movement of services revive as far as measures are concerned, which pertain to fields that have not been harmonized by the AVMS Directive. This has been made abundantly clear by the Court in *De Agostini* where general legislation on protection of consumers against misleading advertising was measured against primary Community law after having been found to lie outside the scope of the Directive.[1]

The provisions on free movement of services not only prohibit national rules discriminating on grounds of nationality but also indirectly discriminatory and truly non-discriminatory rules. The legitimacy of national programme standards depends therefore on whether they can be brought under the express exception to the freedom to provide services, Article 46 EC, or under the 'rule of reason' developed by the European Court. The cases discussed in this chapter have in common that the Member States involved sought to justify their programme content requirements, mainly advertising restrictions, on the basis of cultural policy considerations.

Before embarking on the examination of these cases, it is necessary to consider the question whether impediments to the flow of television programmes resulting from national broadcasting arrangements can be justified on the basis of Article 10 of the European Convention on Human Rights (ECHR). This question is particularly pertinent given that the European Commission argued in the Green paper Television without Frontiers that the general interest implicit in Article 49 EC is limited by Article 10 (2) ECHR.[2]

2. THE JUSTIFIABILITY OF BROADCASTING OBLIGATIONS IN THE LIGHT OF ARTICLE 10 OF THE EUROPEAN CONVENTION ON HUMAN RIGHTS

2.1 The Interpretation of the Commission: The ECHR as a Limitation of the 'General Interest' in the Area of Broadcasting

In the Green paper 'Television without Frontiers' the Commission maintained that freedom of broadcasting is closely linked to freedom of expression under Article 10 (1) ECHR. This led the Commission to conclude that freedom of broadcasting has to be interpreted in the light of Article 10 (1) ECHR and cannot have a more narrow scope than freedom of expression.[3] The Commission relied for this interpretation on the *Rutili* judgment of the European Court according to which the limitations on the powers of the Member States to restrict the free movement of workers under Article 39 (3) EC are a specific manifestation of the general

1. Joined Cases C-34/95, 35/95 and 36/95, *Konsumentenombudsmannen (KO) v. De Agostini (Svenska) Förlag AB and Konsumentenombudsmannen (KO) v. TV-Shop I Sverige AB* [1997] ECR I-3843.
2. COM (84) 300 final.
3. I. Schwartz, 'Broadcasting and the EEC Treaty' (1986) 11 ELRev, 43–44.

principle enshrined in Articles 8, 9, 10 and 11 ECHR. These provisions provide 'in identical terms, that no restrictions in the interests of national security or public safety shall be placed on the rights secured by the above-quoted articles other than such that are necessary for the protection of these interests "in a democratic society' ".[4] The Commission substantiated further the relevance of the Convention for the interpretation of the freedom to provide services with the argument that the Member States had already signed it and were bound by it when they concluded the EEC Treaty in 1957.

Next, the Commission went on to examine possible restrictions of the freedom to provide services on grounds of general interest. On the basis of the affinity between freedom of broadcasting and freedom of expression, it argued that only the interests laid down in Article 10 (2) ECHR, which justify restrictions on the free flow of information, can constitute 'grounds of general interest' in Community law. According to this interpretation, non-discriminatory application of national laws to the retransmission of broadcasts from abroad can only be recognized in Community law for the protection of one of the interests listed in Article 10 (2) ECHR: national security, territorial integrity, public safety, prevention of disorder, prevention of crime, protection of health, protection of morals, protection of the reputation or rights of others, prevention of the disclosure of information received in confidence, maintaining the authority and impartiality of the judiciary. Since the protection of the national broadcasting system does not figure in this list, the Member States would be precluded from defending it against the retransmission of Community broadcasts.

Having taken this interventionist approach, the Commission did not make halt before Article 10 (1) 3 ECHR either. The third sentence of Article 10 (1) authorizes states to require the licensing of broadcasting, cinema or television enterprises. In granting a licence, states are permitted to submit radio and television broadcasts to a certain regulatory regime. The Commission argued, however, that Article 10 (1) 3 allows restrictions to the exercise of broadcasting activity only within the limits of Article 10 (2) ECHR. It concluded that the receiving state may not restrict the reception of foreign broadcasts in its territory, unless the conditions laid down in Article 10 (2) are fulfilled. By interpreting Article 10 (1) 3 restrictively, the Commission ensured that no national broadcasting arrangements could be asserted against foreign broadcasts without going through the sieve of Article 10 (2) ECHR.

2.2 Doubts about this Interpretation

The interpretation of the Commission has met with considerable scepticism in legal writing. Before dealing with the more technical arguments raised against it, it can be said immediately that it limits to a great extent the power of the Member States to justify indirectly discriminatory or non-discriminatory measures in the area of

4. Case 36/75, *Rutili v. Minister for the Interior* [1975] ECR 1219, 1232 para. 32.

broadcasting.[5] It has been argued that this restriction of the Member States' powers brings about a corresponding enhancement of the Community's competence at variance with the conception of the ECHR, which is designed to strengthen individual rights, but not to take influence upon the institutional balance in the Community.[6]

This argument is questionable since the narrowing down of the overriding concerns in the public interest, which can be claimed by a Member State, does not necessarily lead to the growth of Community competence.[7] The Commission merely pointed out to inherent limitations ostensibly emanating from the ECHR. These limitations are solely attributable, according to its reasoning, to the accession of the Member States to the European Convention to which the Community is not a party. This statement is not valid anymore. The Treaty on European Union has confirmed what was already laid down in the case-law of the Court, namely that the fundamental rights guaranteed by the Convention and resulting from the constitutional traditions common to the Member States, are also binding on the European Union, even if only as general principles of Community Law.[8] Moreover, the Draft Reform Treaty, if signed and ratified by all Member States, will afford the Charter of Fundamental Rights a legally binding status and provide for the EU to accede to the ECHR.[9]

Nonetheless, the direct transposition of the exceptions provided in Article 10 (2) ECHR into Community law is problematic. It is true that the Court has recognized fundamental human rights as general principles of Community law. In the case of *Nold v. Commission* it held that 'it cannot therefore uphold measures which are incompatible with fundamental rights recognised and protected by the Constitutions of those States'.[10] As far as national measures are concerned, preliminary questions have been posed to the European Court by national courts with regard to their compatibility with fundamental rights.[11] The Court has held that national measures restricting one of the fundamental freedoms have to conform to the fundamental rights, which are protected as part of Community law.[12] This finding of the Court referred to discriminatory measures, which had to be justified under Article 46 EC. The same will presumably apply, when a judicially recognised legitimate public interest is invoked.

---

5. Kugelmann, *Rundfunk und die Dienstleistungsfreiheit*, p. 222.
6. *Ibid.*; B. Börner, 'Kompetenz der EG zur Regelung einer Rundfunkordnung' (1985) 12 ZUM, 586.
7. Gulich, *Rechtsfragen grenzüberschreitender Rundfunksendungen*, p. 98.
8. Treaty on European Union, Art. 6 (2); *see also* Draft Reform Treaty, Art. 6 (3).
9. Draft Reform Treaty, Art. 6 (1), (2).
10. Case 4/73, *Nold v. Commission* [1974] ECR 491, 507; [1974] 2 CMLR 338.
11. Case C-260/89, *Elliniki Radiophonia Tileorassi AE v. Dimotiki Etairia Pliroforissis and Sotirios Kouvelas* [1991] ECR 2925; [1994] 2 CMLR 540; Case C-159/90, *SPUC v. Grogan* [1991] ECR I-4685.
12. *Opinion 2/94 on Accession by the Community to the ECHR* [1996] ECR I-1759 para. 34; Case C-260/89, *Elliniki Radiophonia Tileorassi AE v. Dimotiki Etairia Pliroforissis and Sotirios Kouvelas* [1991] ECR 2925 para. 42.

However, the Court has the power to examine the compatibility of national measures with fundamental rights only in cases where these measures fall 'within the scope of Community law'.[13] In *Cinéthèqe*, the Court refrained from investigating the conformity with fundamental rights of a French law proscribing the simultaneous exploitation of cinematographic works in cinemas and in the form of video-cassettes on the ground that it fell within the jurisdiction of the national legislator.[14] The same applies to the Charter of Fundamental Rights. Even if it becomes legally binding, it will only bind the Member States 'when implementing EU law'.[15] This is a narrower formulation than the phrase 'within the scope of Community law' used by the Court.[16] But in view of the considerable expansion of EU legislative action, the Charter will not necessarily cover a limited range of national measures.[17] It follows from the foregoing that the Court cannot measure national broadcasting standards against the fundamental rights contained in the Convention or the Charter without further ado. It is one thing to say that the Court ensures the observance of fundamental rights in the Community legal order and another that it controls the legal systems of the Member States in general by the standard of these rights.[18]

Furthermore, the way in which the Commission declared the interests laid down in Article 10 (2) ECHR to be the only relevant general interests is arbitrary, since it failed to consider whether the broadcasting standards of the Member States also form part of their constitutional traditions the observance of which has to be ensured in the Community.[19] In fact, the Commission muddled up the distinction between overriding requirements related to the general interest and the reservation under Article 46 EC by equating the former with Article 10 (2) ECHR.[20]

---

13. Case C-260/89, *Elliniki Radiophonia Tileorassi AE v. Dimotiki Etairia Pliroforissis and Sotirios Kouvelas* [1991] ECR 2925 para. 42.
14. Joined Cases 60 and 61/84, *Cinéthèqe SA and Others v. Fédération nationale des cinémas français* [1985] ECR 2605 para. 26.
15. Charter of Fundamental Rights, Art. 51 (1) 1.
16. Note, however, that the Court also used the narrower term 'implementing' in the context of its Common Agricultural Policy in Case C-292/97, *Karlsson* [2000] ECR 2737, para. 37.
17. P. Eeckhout, 'The Proposed EU Charter of Fundamental Rights: Some Reflections on Its Effects in the Legal Systems of the EU and of its Member States' in *The EU Charter of Fundamental Rights: Text and Commentaries*, K. Feus (ed.) (London, Federal Trust, 2000), p. 97, 108; *see* S. Douglass Scott, 'The EU Charter of Rights: A Poor Attempt to Strengthen Democracy and Citizenship?' in *The Treaty of Nice and Beyond: Enlargement and Constitutional Reform*, M. Andenas and J. A. Usher (eds) (Oxford, Hart, 2003), p. 398, 416 *et seq.*
18. *See* J. Sparr, *Kulturhoheit und EWG-Vertrag: Eine Untersuchung zur Einschränkung des gesetzgeberischen Handlungsspielraums der Mitgliedstaaten in kulturellen Angelegenheiten durch den EWG-Vertrag, dargestellt an Hand des freien Waren- und Dienstleistungsverkehrs* (Baden-Baden, Nomos, 1991), p. 57 *et seq.*
19. Treaty on European Union, Art. 6 (2); W. Hoffmann-Riem, 'Europäisierung des Rundfunks – aber ohne Kommunikationsverfassung?' in *Rundfunk im Wettbewerbsrecht: Der öffentlich-rechtliche Rundfunk im Spannungsfeld zwischen Wirtschaftsrecht und Rundfunkrecht*, W. Hoffmann-Riem (ed.), Symposien des Hans-Bredow-Instituts, vol. 10 (Baden-Baden, Nomos, 1988), p. 206; Gulich, *Rechtsfragen grenzüberschreitender Rundfunksendungen*, p. 96.
20. Kugelmann, *Rundfunk und die Dienstleistungsfreiheit*, p. 222.

The public policy exception under Article 46 EC, allowing the protection of fundamental interests of society, is akin to the *ordre public* clause under Article 10 (2) ECHR even if it has a wider scope than this provision. As a result of the Commission's reasoning, non-discriminatory restrictions to the free movement of services can only be justified under the same limited grounds as discriminatory restrictions.

We mentioned earlier that this paradox result has been reached by invoking the Court's judgment in *Rutili*.[21] This decision does not, however, support the interpretation of the general interest in the light of Article 10 (2) ECHR given that it pertains to the narrow public policy exception under Article 39 (3) EC.[22] The *Rutili* case concerned a regulation that was discriminating against foreign nationals so that it could not be of any assistance for the interpretation of public interest grounds. It is by means of such argumentative acrobatics that the Commission attempted to cut down the reasons that can justify restrictions on the free movement of services. Having analysed the shortcomings of the transplantation of the *ordre public* clause of Article 10 (2) ECHR into the general interest exception, it is pertinent to turn now to the conclusion drawn from this construction, namely that national broadcasting standards cannot be justified under this exception.

We saw above that the Commission took a restrictive view of Article 10 (1) 3 ECHR. It argued that regulations limiting the freedom of broadcasting that have been adopted on the basis of this norm have to aim to the protection of one of the values under Article 10 (2) ECHR. This view has not been substantiated by the Commission and has been contradicted by the case-law of the European Court of Human Rights. The scope of Article 10 (1) 3 ECHR has been very contentious in legal writing in the past. No agreement existed as to whether this provision merely legitimated a formal licensing procedure or could also serve as the basis for the imposition of content requirements upon broadcasters. Its relationship with Article 10 (2) ECHR has also been unclear, some authors requiring that the conditions of this provision also be satisfied,[23] others attaching to Article 10 (1) 3 an independent significance.[24]

The European Court of Human Rights addressed these questions in a series of judgments. The details of this case-law need not detain us now; it is sufficient to focus on its main features. In the cases *Groppera*[25] and *Autronic*[26] the Court ruled that Article 10 (1) 3 ECHR had to be interpreted in the light of the requirements of

---

21. Case 36/75, *Rutili v. Minister for the Interior* [1975] ECR 1219.
22. Hoffmann-Riem, 'Europäisierung des Rundfunks', pp. 206–207; Kugelmann, *Rundfunk und die Dienstleistungsfreiheit*, p. 123.
23. C. Engel, *Privater Rundfunk vor der Europäischen Menschenrechtskonvention* (Baden-Baden, Nomos, 1993), p. 54 *et seq.*
24. W. Hoffmann-Riem, *Rundfunkrecht neben Wirtschaftsrecht: Zur Anwendbarkeit des GWB und des EWGV auf das Wettbewerbsverhalten öffentlich-rechtlichen Rundfunks in der dualen Rundfunkordnung*, Beiträge zum Rundfunkrecht, vol. 43 (Baden-Baden, Nomos, 1991), p. 186 *et seq.*
25. *Groppera Radio AG and Others*, Judgment of 28 March 1990, Series A 173, No. 24.
26. *Autronic AG*, Judgment of 22 May 1990, Series A 178, No. 24.

Article 10 (2) ECHR so that restrictions to the freedom of broadcasting had to be measured against both provisions. So as to compensate for the very narrow scope accorded to Article 10 (1) 3, the Court gave a broad interpretation to the reservation under Article 10 (2).[27] It ruled that it not only covers provisions of general law, but also rules designed to protect the well-functioning of the international telecommunications order and 'to ensure pluralism, in particular of information'.[28]

In the case *Informationsverein Lentia* the Court attached greater importance to Article (1) 3 ECHR.[29] It held that a licensing system not only aimed to safeguard the organization of a broadcasting system in its technical aspects, but also to regulate other issues such as the nature and objectives of the proposed station, its potential audience at national, regional or local level, the rights and needs of a specific audience and the obligations deriving from international legal instruments. Moreover, it recognized that Article 10 (1) 3 ECHR has an independent meaning so that it can justify restrictions not corresponding to any of the objectives laid down in the second paragraph of Article 10. Nonetheless, these restrictions would have to be gauged in the light of the other requirements of Article 10 (2), that is, they would have to be prescribed by law and to be necessary in a democratic society.

This judgment leads to the conclusion that the limitation of Article 10 (1) 3 ECHR to the protection of the interests laid down in Article 10 (2) advocated by the Commission is not acceptable. Consequently, requirements related to the content of programmes can be based upon the former provision. It follows from what has been said so far that the imposition of broadcasting obligations on foreign broadcasts can be justified both under Article 10 (1) 3 and under Article 10 (2) ECHR as long as it is 'prescribed by law' and 'necessary in a democratic society'. The necessity of a certain measure in a democratic society depends on whether there is a 'pressing social need' and on the proportionality between the means employed and the interest sought to be safeguarded. The parties to the Convention have a margin of appreciation with regard to these criteria, which is controlled by the European Court of Human Rights.[30]

In conclusion, the interference by the Member States with the free flow of television programmes on broadcasting policy grounds is not outlawed by the ECHR. The interpretation of the Commission is flawed both in its assumptions as well as in its conclusions. What is more, this interpretation stands out in sharp relief against the TwF Directive.[31] The eighth recital to Directive 89/552 seems to chime with the Commission's reasoning by stating that free movement of television programmes has to be ensured in the light of Article 10 (1) ECHR and 'subject only to the limits set by paragraph 2 of that Article and by Article 56 (1) of the

27. Hoffmann-Riem, *Rundfunkrecht neben Wirtschaftsrecht*, pp. 191, 193.
28. *Groppera Radio AG and Others*, Judgment of 28 March1990, Series A 173, No. 24, § 69 *et seq; Autronic AG*, Judgment of 22 May 1990, Series A 178, No. 24, § 52.
29. *Informationsverein Lentia and Others v. Austria*, Judgment of 24 November 1993, Series A 276, No. 14.
30. Protocol No. 11 of 1 November 1998 abolished the European Commission of Human Rights.
31. Hoffmann-Riem, *Rundfunkrecht neben Wirtschaftsrecht*, p. 194.

Treaty'. However, the Directive's rules do not follow this pattern. The European quota rule as well as the rules on advertising constitute broadcasting obligations that cannot be justified under Article 10 (2) ECHR as it has been interpreted by the Commission.

3. THE JUSTIFIABILITY OF BROADCASTING OBLIGATIONS IN THE LIGHT OF ARTICLE 49 EC

3.1 Directly Discriminatory Restrictions on the Freedom of Services in the Area of Broadcasting

This section examines cases adjudicated by the European Court of Justice involving directly discriminatory restrictions in the area of broadcasting. The purpose of this analysis is to assess in how far Member States are allowed to pursue their cultural policy objectives by means of measures discriminating against other EU broadcasts.

3.1.1 The Case-Law of the European Court of Justice

The first case in which the European Court of Justice had the opportunity to deal with a directly discriminatory measure in the area of broadcasting was *Bond van Adverteerders*.[32] This case took place against the backdrop of the unique broadcasting system of the Netherlands, which has also been the subject of further cases.[33] At the time when the case under examination was brought to the attention of the Court, commercial broadcasting had not yet entered the Dutch media market. The Dutch broadcasting system was characterized by the existence of eight broadcasting organizations representing the main religious, political and cultural currents in the Dutch society.

So as to create a pluralistic, non-commercial broadcasting system, the Broadcasting Law 1967 (*Omroepwet*) allocated air time on the two national television channels to these organizations and the Broadcasting Foundation of the Netherlands (NOS). None of these broadcasters was allowed to transmit advertisements. This right was reserved to the Television and Radio Advertising Foundation ('STER'), which managed advertisements produced by third parties and made air time available for their transmission. The STER was obliged to hand over its revenues to the state, which used them to finance the broadcasting organizations and, to a smaller extent, the press.

This sophisticated system was threatened by the emergence of new satellite and cable technologies in the eighties enabling a great number of foreign programmes to be received in the Netherlands. These commercial broadcasters put the Dutch system under pressure by selling air time for commercials at

32. Case 352/85, *Bond van Adverteerders v. The Netherlands State* [1988] ECR 2085.
33. *See* Part 1, Ch. 6.

considerably lower rates than the STER.[34] In response to this challenge the *Kabelregeling*, a ministerial Decree regulating the retransmission of foreign programmes by cable, prohibited the relay of programmes from abroad which contained advertisements intended especially for the Dutch public or subtitles in Dutch. The Court had to rule on these prohibitions of advertising and subtitling contained in the *Kabelregeling* as a result of civil proceedings started by advertisers who wished to have access to the more extensive advertising facilities of foreign commercial programmes. They claimed that the disputed provisions were incompatible with the freedom to provide services.

The Court first established that the distribution of foreign programmes via a cable network falls under the provisions on services. It then went on to examine the restrictions on the freedom of broadcasting resulting from the prohibitions of advertising and subtitling. It held that the prohibition of advertising was discriminatory given that national programmes were allowed to contain advertisements, even if only with STER's intervention. Interestingly, the Court expanded the notion of discrimination. The origin of the service rather than the nationality or residence of the provider of the service became the point of reference.[35]

These discriminatory provisions could only be justified under the express derogation of Article 46 EC. The Court emphasized that economic aims cannot constitute grounds of public policy. The regulation in question could therefore not be justified by the wish to safeguard STER's advertising revenue against foreign competition. The Netherlands Government, however, adduced a further non-economic reason, namely the maintenance of the non-commercial and thereby pluralistic nature of the Netherlands broadcasting system. The subsidies paid by the STER to the broadcasting organizations allowed them to remain non-commercial, which was a necessary precondition for a pluralistic service.

The Court did not examine whether this reason fell within the scope of Article 46 EC.[36] It left this question open and struck down the disputed measures as disproportionate instead. It held that the envisaged objectives could also be reached by means of non-discriminatory restrictions on the transmission of advertising such as the prohibition on advertising certain products or on certain days and limiting the duration and frequency of advertisements.[37] The reasoning of the Court is not very satisfactory, even if the result reached is understandable. Reich put forward the view that it would have been preferable not to strike down the national rules at issue on ground of their disproportionateness, but to interpret the notion of public policy instead and to address the question whether the maintenance of a

34. J. Pelle and K. Sevinga, 'Dutch Broadcasting System: Free Provision of Services within the EC' (1991) 2 ULR, 174–175.
35. *See* opinion of Advocate-General Mancini in Case 352/85, para. 10.
36. H. Konszuseck, 'Freier Dienstleistungsverkehr und nationales Rundfunkrecht: Anmerkung zum Urteil des Gerichtshofs der Europäischen Gemeinschaften vom 26.04.1988 zur niederländischen "Kabelregeling" – Rs. 352/85 – De Vereniging Bond van Adverteerders u.a./Niederländischen Staat' (1989) 12 ZUM, 544.
37. Case 352/85, para. 37.

non-commercial, pluralistic broadcasting system falls within its scope.[38] This view has to be concurred with.

The argument that objective restrictions could also meet the aims pursued by the Netherlands government fails to grasp the whole picture. The prohibitions of advertising and subtitling aimed to secure the economic base of the Dutch broadcasting system by preventing foreign broadcasters from withdrawing part of the advertising revenue. The Netherlands government considered that foreign channels were unfairly competing with the domestic ones given that they did not have to abide by the strict Dutch broadcasting laws.[39] The objective restrictions suggested by the Court would subject foreign broadcasters to an advertising regime comparable to the Dutch one without, however, actually preventing them from having access to the Netherlands advertising market.[40] Therefore, they would not be equally appropriate for the attainment of the intended economic aims.

Obviously, the Court clearly stated that such economic considerations could not justify restrictions on the freedom of broadcasting. This statement alone, correct though it may be, fails to take account of the close connection between economic considerations and the attainment of cultural objectives.[41] The Netherlands government invoked the *Cinéthèque* case to support the argument that cultural aims can justify restrictions even where the economic foundation of such aims is at issue.[42] Similarly, the German government argued that the purpose of the rules in question was to protect the financial means of achieving the cultural policy objectives of the Dutch broadcasting system.[43] These arguments suggest that when economic aims are coupled with cultural ones the cultural element should prevail and redeem the regulation at stake. This view is, however, the other extreme from the approach taken by the Court since it would enable Member States to pursue protectionist objectives under the cloak of cultural policy.

It is submitted that it is the distinction between the primary and secondary aim of a certain measure that decides whether it passes the 'non-economic objective' test. Admittedly, this is a soft criterion that lends itself to many interpretations. In the case of the *Kabelregeling*, however, it would appear that the objectives pursued by its prohibitions were mainly of an economic nature. The view of Advocate-General Mancini that the link between these restrictions and the maintenance of pluralism in broadcasting was tenuous has to be concurred with.[44]

---

38. Reich, 'Rundfunkrecht und Wettbewerbsrecht', p. 236.
39. Case 352/85, para. 5.
40. Gulich, *Rechtsfragen grenzüberschreitender Rundfunksendungen*, p. 135; M. de Blois, 'Note to Case 352/85, *Bond van Adverteerders v. The Netherlands State* [1988] ECR 2085' (1990) 27 CMLRev, 379.
41. Konszuzeck, 'Freier Dienstleistungsverkehr', 547; G. Herrmann, *Rundfunkrecht: Fernsehen und Rundfunk mit neuen Medien* (Munich, C.H. Beck, 1994), p. 216 para. 56.
42. Joined Cases 60 and 61/84, *Cinéthèque and Others v. Fédération nationale des cinémas français* [1985] ECR 2605.
43. *See ibid.*, observations of the Government of the Federal Republic of Germany, 2098.
44. *See* Opinion of Advocate-General Mancini in Case 352/85, para. 10.

It is tempting to argue that the broadcasting of advertisements especially intended for the Dutch public from abroad does not undermine the non-commercial character of the Dutch system as such. After all, advertising revenues would have to be shared between foreign and domestic broadcasters even if the latter were also allowed to include advertisements in their programmes without STER's intervention. This argument does not, however, suffice to prove the absence of a link between the Dutch advertising restrictions and the protection of pluralism. If advertising in the Netherlands had been unregulated, Dutch broadcasters would have been able to compete on equal terms with their foreign counterparts. Moreover, it should be borne in mind that a non-commercial, pluralistic broadcasting system also needs a financial basis, in the same way as a commercial one. The existence of advertising in a non-commercial system does not justify its complete subjection to market forces.

However, as Advocate-General Mancini observed, only about 30 per cent of the Dutch broadcasting organizations' resources came from the advertising proceeds of the STER, while the remaining 70 per cent were covered by licence fees.[45] Consequently, a decline in STER's receipts would arguably not have rendered the Netherlands broadcasting system ineffective. Other ways of financing the system could have been resorted to such as a mild increase in the licence fees charged on viewers. The objection of the Netherlands government that an extra burden on the end-user would be politically unacceptable does not negate the viability of such a solution.

The existence of alternative if less-effective ways to protect the organization of television as a public service in the Netherlands was conceded by the Netherlands government, which repealed the *Kabelregeling* before the ruling in this case was handed down. The *Mediawet*, which came in force on 1 January 1988, replaced the discriminatory rules of the *Kabelregeling* with others modelled after the suggestions of the Court. All in all, the conclusion reached by the Court has to be welcomed even if its argumentative underpinning leaves much to be desired.

A further case in which the Court had to adjudicate once more on a discriminatory restriction on the freedom to provide broadcasting services is the case *Commission v. Belgium*.[46] This case concerned a Flemish law prohibiting cable network operators from relaying programmes from foreign radio or television stations where these programmes were not transmitted in the language or one of the languages of the Member State in which the network was established. The Court pointedly observed that the barrier to the freedom of services raised by this law was discriminatory in two ways: a formal and a more substantive one. It discriminated against foreign stations in a formal way in that broadcasting stations established in Belgium did not have to conform to the law in question. The main problem it presented was, however, that broadcasters established in a Member

45. *Ibid.*
46. Case C-211/91, *Commission of the European Communities v. Kingdom of Belgium* [1992] ECR 6757. For a discussion of this case in connection with the *van Binsbergen* doctrine, *see* Part 2, Ch. 11.2.1.2, p.199 *above*.

State other than the Netherlands were prevented from accessing the Flemish market in Dutch, while national broadcasters by definition had the possibility to do so. It thus discriminated against them in a substantive way.

The Belgian government invoked cultural policy objectives to justify this legislation. It claimed that the restriction in question was necessary for the maintenance of pluralism in the printed press, which was partly sustained from the advertising revenue of the domestic broadcasters, and also for the protection of the artistic heritage and for the survival of the national broadcasting stations. The Court did not accept these arguments for two reasons. First, it found little difficulty in determining that the real purpose of this measure was to 'restrict genuine competition with the national broadcasting stations in order to maintain their advertising revenue'.[47] Once more the Court drew the line between economic and cultural motives at the expense of the latter. The cultural policy argument could be done away with even more light-heartedly here than in *Bond van Adverteerders*, given that the economic considerations behind it were spelled out more clearly in this case. As to the preservation of the artistic heritage, the Court considered that the disputed measure was in fact detrimental to it since it discouraged the production of television programmes in Dutch.

The second and weightier reason adduced by the Court was that 'the justifications put forward by the Belgian government do not come within any of the grounds for exception from the freedom to provide services permitted by Article 56',[48] this being the only provision justifying discriminatory restrictions on the freedom to provide services. We will consider later on whether the Court thereby answered the question which had been left open in *Bond van Adverteerders*, namely whether the protection of pluralism is excluded from the scope of Article 46 EC.

Lastly, the so-called *Fedicine* or *Spanish dubbing licence* case is of interest for our purposes even though it does not directly relate to television but to the film industry in general.[49] This case also confronted the Court with the question whether cultural policy objectives fall under Article 46 EC. It concerned a Spanish law making the grant of licences to dub films from third countries into one of the official languages of Spain, with the purpose of their distribution there, conditional upon the obligation to distribute a Spanish film.

The Court found first of all that the commercial exploitation of a film falls under the provisions on services. It then examined the restriction on the freedom to provide services brought about by the law in question and concluded that it discriminated against producers established in other Member States by putting them at a competitive disadvantage *vis-à-vis* producers of Spanish films. While the latter had the advantage of the compulsory distribution of each of their films for every

47. *Ibid.*, para. 9.
48. *Ibid.*, para. 10.
49. Case C-17/92, *Federación de Distribuidores Cinematográficos (FEDICINE) v. Spanish State* [1993] ECR-I 2239.

dubbing-licence granted and a guarantee of certain levels of takings, the former did not have any security that their films would be distributed in Spain.[50]

The Court inferred from the discriminatory nature of this measure that it could only be justified under Article 46 EC. Economic objectives such as the invigoration of the national film industry do not come under this provision. The Spanish government attempted, however, to present this objective as a cultural one linked to the promotion of films in one of the official languages of Spain. The Court was not convinced by this argument, since 'cultural policy is not one of the justifications set out in Article 56'.[51] This statement of the Court seems to bar any claims to the exception of public policy to justify discriminatory measures pertaining to the area of culture. Furthermore, the Court held the cultural policy justification to be a sham since the law at stake did not place any requirements on the content or quality of the films to be promoted. This reasoning displays a very narrow understanding of culture, which does not leave much room to the Member States to design policies for the protection of their cultural identities.

3.1.2 Do Broadcasting Obligations Qualify for Justification under Article 46 EC?

The statements of the Court in the cases *Commission v. Belgium*[52] and *Fedicine*[53] could lead to the conclusion that broadcasting obligations related to the pluralistic, non-commercial character of broadcasting, the quality and orientation of programmes or the reliability of information do not fall under Article 46 EC since they are elements of the broadcasting policy of a Member State, which is part and parcel of its cultural policy. Case-law concerning non-discriminatory restrictions on the freedom of broadcasting may also lend some support to this view. In these cases, which we will examine in the next section, the Court consistently characterized cultural policy as an overriding requirement relating to the general interest.[54] This might suggest that cultural policy considerations can only justify non-discriminatory or at most indirectly discriminatory measures, not measures which directly disadvantage programmes transmitted from other Member States.

The answer to the question whether Article 46 EC can legitimate discriminatory broadcasting arrangements of the Member States is, however, more

50. *Ibid.*, para. 15.
51. *Ibid.*, para. 20.
52. Case C-211/91, *Commission of the European Communities v. Kingdom of Belgium* [1992] ECR 6757.
53. Case C-17/92, *Federación de Distribuidores Cinematográficos (FEDICINE) v. Spanish State* [1993] ECR-I 2239.
54. Case C-353/89, *Commission of the European Communities v. Kingdom of the Netherlands* [1991] ECR I-4069 para. 30; Case C-288/89, *Stichting Collectieve Antannevorziening Gouda and Others v. Commissariaat voor de Media* [1991] ECR I-4007 para. 23; Case C-148/91, *Vereniging Veronica Omroep Organisatie v. Commissariaat voor de Media* [1993] ECR I-487 para. 10; Case C-11/95, *Commission v. Belgium* [1996] ECR I-4117 para. 4; Case C-23/93, *TV 10 SA v. Commissariaat voor de Media* [1994] ECR I 4795 para. 19.

controversial than it appears at first sight. This question has been answered in the affirmative with the argument that the functioning of national broadcasting organization and the protection of a balanced, comprehensive programme is quintessential for the freedom of opinion in broadcasting and hence for the maintenance of a democratic system.[55] Gulich considered that measures that are necessary for the protection of freedom of broadcasting, the maintenance of pluralism, the prevention of media concentration and the formation of public opinion can be justified by reference to Article 46 EC.[56]

He distinguished them from other measures related to the cultural role of broadcasting and its responsibility to foster national identity. Given that the cultural mission of broadcasting is not indispensable for the existence of the state, cultural requirements imposed on broadcasters could only be justified as overriding requirements related to the general interest, but not under Article 46 EC.[57] In support of his standpoint he drew a parallel with the freedom of movement of goods where the Court excluded cultural reasons from the scope of Article 30 EC, but recognized them as mandatory requirements.[58] Gulich's distinction is questionable given that cultural identity also exercises an integrative function, which is fundamental for the continued existence of state and society.[59] Moreover, our examination of the cultural obligations of public broadcasters in Part One of this book has shown that the protection of cultural identity is as much part of the public service model as duties related to the opinion-forming role of television.

Advocate General Mancini submitted in *Bond van Adverteerders* that public policy under Article 46 (1) EC is 'in principle broad enough to cover safeguarding a pluralistic, non-commercial television system through the financing of broadcasting organizations'. Nonetheless, he held that the *Kabelregeling* could not be justified under this provision in view of its restrictive interpretation by the Court requiring a 'genuine and sufficiently serious threat . . . affecting one of the fundamental interests of society',[60] which is combated with comparable means at domestic level.[61] The Court did not take a clear position in this case concerning the problem under consideration. However, the reference to less restrictive, non-discriminatory ways of achieving the envisaged objectives in

---

55. Börner, 'Kompetenz der EG', 585; H. Jarass, 'EG-Recht und nationales Rundfunkrecht: Zugleich ein Beitrag zur Reichweite der Dienstleistungsfreiheit' (1986) 1 EuR, 75; de Blois, 'Note to Case 352/85', 379; Holznagel, *Rundfunkrecht in Europa*, p. 140 *et seq*; C. Greissinger, *Vorgaben des EG-Vertrags für nationales Rundfunk-und Multimediarecht* (Baden-Baden, Nomos, 2000), p. 64.
56. Gulich, *Rechtsfragen grenzüberschreitender Rundfunksendungen*, p. 118.
57. *Ibid.*, p. 121 *et seq.*
58. Cases 60, 61/84, *Cinéthèque v. Fédération Nationale des Cinémas Françaises* [1985] ECR 2605 para. 22 *et seq*; [1986] 1 CMLR 365; Case 229/83, *Leclerc v. Au Blé Vert* [1985] ECR 1 para. 28 *et seq*; [1985] 2 CMLR 286.
59. *See* Part 2, Ch. 9, p. 168 *above.*
60. Case 30/77, *R v. Bouchereau* [1977] ECR 1999; [1977] 2 CMLR 800.
61. Cases 115, 116/81, *Adoui and Cornouaille v. Belgian State* [1982] ECR 1665; [1982] 3 CMLR 631.

this judgment indicates that the Court only approved of even-handed broadcasting policy measures that could be justified on grounds of overriding requirements.[62]

It is necessary to consider whether the judgments in the cases *Commission v. Belgium* and *Fedicine* also support the view that discriminatory measures for the protection of the national broadcasting system are not justifiable under Article 56 EC. As we saw earlier on, the Court held in *Commission v. Belgium* that the maintenance of pluralism in the printed press, the preservation of the artistic heritage and the viability of the national broadcasting stations do not come within the scope of Article 46 EC.[63]

It has been suggested that no conclusion can be drawn from this passage of the judgment with regard to the question whether cultural policy considerations fall under Article 46 EC since the Court only examined the specific reasons brought forward by the Belgian government without making general statements about the legitimacy of such considerations.[64] The crux of the Court's reasoning was, so the argument goes, that the Flemish law's real objective was to ward off national broadcasting stations from competition. According to the same opinion, this judgment was only concerned with the maintenance of pluralism in the press, not in broadcasting, so that it casts no light on the questions at issue. Therefore, it could only be inferred from it that the Court is not willing to accept every cultural policy justification as a legitimate interest under Article 46 EC.

It is submitted that these arguments cannot withstand close scrutiny. First, there is no apparent reason why pluralism in television should be treated any differently from pluralism in the press with regard to its classification as a ground of public policy under Article 46 EC. Second, the objective of the protection of the national broadcasting stations' viability was linked in the Belgian government's submissions to the cultural responsibilities of these stations.[65] It follows that the protection of the broadcasting system of the Flemish community was the cultural base of the economic argument put forward by the Belgian government. The Commission also recognized this. It considered the Flemish legislation to be disproportionate since it also applied to programmes complying with the programme requirements of the Flemish executive whose retransmission would hence not thwart cultural policy objectives.[66]

It is suggested that the Court, by refusing to consider the justifications presented by the Belgian government under Article 46 EC, indicated that discriminatory broadcasting arrangements of the Member States cannot be excused under this provision. Support for this view can also be derived from *Fedicine*.[67] The finding of the Court in this case that public policy does not cover cultural policy

62. Case 352/85, *Bond van Adverteerders v. The Netherlands State* [1988] ECR 2085, para. 37.
63. Case C-211/91, *Commission of the European Communities v. Kingdom of Belgium* [1992] ECR 6757 para. 9.
64. Holznagel, *Rundfunkrecht in Europa*, p. 142.
65. Case C-211/91, 6766.
66. *Ibid.*, 6764.
67. Case C-17/92, *Federación de Distribuidores Cinematográficos (FEDICINE) v. Spanish State* [1993] ECR-I 2239.

considerations does not leave any scope for Article 56 EC to be invoked in order to justify discriminatory broadcasting regulations. Clearly, this judgment is consistent with the narrow approach of the concept of public policy always taken by the Court.[68]

3.2 Indirect Discriminatory Restrictions on the Freedom to Provide Broadcasting Services

The purpose of this section is to examine the question whether the imposition of domestic programme requirements upon programmes transmitted from other Member States can be justified on grounds of overriding reasons relating to the public interest. The Court has consistently held that a cultural policy may constitute an overriding requirement relating to the general interest which justifies a restriction on the freedom to provide services.[69] This chapter will not look at the case-law concerned with the problem of circumvention given that it has been comprehensively analysed in the previous chapter.[70] While television organizations falling under the *van Binsbergen* doctrine are treated as *domestic* ones, the Court considered the broadcasters involved in the cases under examination to be *foreign* ones, not wrongfully avoiding obligations under the receiving state's law. It scrutinized the obligation imposed on them to conform to the receiving state's requirements as to the structure of the provider of services or the characteristics of the service as such.

3.2.1 The Case-Law of the European Court of Justice

In line with its previous case-law, the Court emphasised in *Debauve* the 'particular nature of certain services such as the broadcasting and transmission of television signals'[71] that justified the imposition of specific requirements upon providers of services on grounds of general interest. Such requirements would have to apply equally to domestic and to foreign providers and there should not be double regulation. The Court did not specify in this case what the particular nature of

68. Case 30/77, *R v. Bouchereau* [1977] ECR 1999; Cases 115, 116/81, *Adoui and Cornouaille v. Belgian State* [1982] ECR 1665.
69. *See* Case C-353/89, *Commission of the European Communities v. Kingdom of the Netherlands* [1991] ECR-I 4069.
70. *See* Part 2, Ch. 11.2.1.2, pp. 197 *et seq above*; Case C-148/91, *Vereniging Veronica Omroep Organisatie v. Commissariaat voor de Media* [1993] ECR I-487; Case C-11/95, *Commission v. Belgium* [1996] ECR I-4117 para. 4; Case C-23/93, *TV 10* SA *v. Commissariaat voor de Media* [1994] ECR I 4795.
71. Case 205/84, *Commission v. Germany* [1986] ECR 3755; [1987] 2 CMLR 69; Case 279/80, *Webb* [1981] ECR 3305; [1982] 1 CMLR 406; Case 110, 111/78, *Ministère Public v. Van Wesemael* [1979] ECR 35; [1979] 3 CMLR 87; Case 427/85, *Commission v. Germany* [1988] ECR 1123; [1989] 2 CMLR 677; Case 52/79, *Procureur du Roi v. Marc J.V.C. Debauve and Others* [1980] ECR I 833 para. 12.

broadcasting services consists in nor did it define the considerations of general interest underlying the Belgian prohibition of commercial advertising.[72] It confined itself to pointing out that 'in the absence of any approximation of national laws and taking into account the considerations of general interest underlying the restrictive rules [*sic*] this area, the application of the laws in question cannot be regarded as a restriction upon freedom to provide services so long as those laws treat all such services identically'.[73] The Court thus paid tribute to the social, political and cultural dimension of broadcasting, which prevented it from becoming fully liberalized, and recognised a residual power of the Member States for the organization of their broadcasting systems.

The general interest at stake was scrutinized more closely in two cases concerned with the Dutch Media Act, the *Mediawet*, which replaced the *Kabelregeling*. The subject-matter of these cases is almost identical. They have, however, been dealt with in separate proceedings since the first case, *Gouda*, was a preliminary reference by the Council of State, while the second case, *Commission v. Netherlands*, was the result of infringement proceedings initiated by the Commission against Netherlands.[74] The only difference between the two cases is that in the second case the Commission also objected to Article 61 of the *Mediawet*, which obliged national broadcasting bodies to utilize the technical facilities of a domestic undertaking, the NOPB, for the production of their television and radio programmes.

As far as this provision is concerned, the Court held that it restricted freedom to provide services in that it precluded Dutch broadcasters from obtaining technical assistance from undertakings in other Member States. The Netherlands government argued that Dutch undertakings were equally disadvantaged as a result of the monopolistic position of the NOPB. The Court rightly considered this argument to be immaterial. It sufficed that one national undertaking was treated more favourably.

Some further reasons that were adduced to explain the preferential treatment given to the NOPB are of interest for our analysis. These reasons were related to the cultural policy pursued by the Netherlands in the audiovisual area. It was claimed that the NOPB contributed to the protection of the pluralist and non-commercial character of the Dutch broadcasting system by providing all its components with the necessary resources. Moreover, it was argued that the NOPB had certain cultural obligations to fulfil such as the management of a sound library.

The Court accepted that 'a cultural policy understood in that sense may indeed constitute an overriding requirement relating to the general interest which justifies a restriction on the freedom to provide services. The maintenance of pluralism which that Dutch policy seeks to safeguard is connected with freedom of

---

72. P. Troberg, 'Mediawet und kein Ende: Dienstleistungsfreiheit und Fernsehrechtsprechung des EuGH' (1994) 2 ZEuP, 105, 109.
73. Case 52/79, para. 13.
74. Case C-288/89, *Stichting Collectieve Antannevorziening Gouda and Others v. Commissariaat voor de Media* [1991] ECR I-4007; Case C-353/89, *Commission of the European Communities v. Kingdom of the Netherlands* [1991] ECR I-4069.

expression, as protected by Article 10 of the European Convention on Human Rights and Fundamental Freedoms, which is one of the fundamental rights guaranteed by the Community legal order.'[75]

However, it found the obligation laid down in Article 61 of the *Mediawet* to be disproportional and even inappropriate for the attainment of this objective, since pluralism would by no means be endangered by the opening of the market to providers of services from other Member States.[76] As to the cultural duties of the NOPB, the Court maintained that they were completely funded by the state, so that its secured position was not essential for their fulfilment.

It has thus been clarified that rules affording a privileged position to national undertakings will be measured strictly against the requirements of the proportionality test. The conclusion reached by the Court has to be concurred with given that the Netherlands government had not convincingly substantiated the necessity of the special rights granted to the NOPB for the maintenance of pluralism. In fact, the removal of the disputed obligation in respect of television programmes implied the opposite.[77]

Nonetheless, it is astonishing that the Court entered into an examination of the cultural policy arguments put forward by the Netherlands Government in the first place. On the one hand, the Court's finding that foreign undertakings were treated less favourably than the NOPB suggests that they were discriminated against. This was also the opinion of Advocate-General Tesauro. On the other hand, if the Court had accepted overt discrimination by reason of nationality, only the express derogation under Article 46 EC would have been available. The fact that the Court embarked on an analysis of overriding requirements relating to the general interest only stands to reason in the case of covert discrimination. A possible explanation is that foreign providers of services were not discriminated on ground of their nationality but on account of the conferment of an exclusive right as such.[78] It will have to be established in subsequent case-law of the Court whether this interpretation is correct.

Further, the Court examined both in *Commission v. Netherlands* and in *Gouda* the compatibility with the freedom to provide services of the conditions contained in Article 66 of the *Mediawet* on the cable retransmission of programmes broadcast by foreign broadcasters. It is important to note that these conditions only applied to programmes that contained advertisements specifically intended for the Dutch public. This was deemed to be so if the advertisements were broadcast during or immediately after a programme containing Dutch subtitles or transmitted at least partly in Dutch.

---

75. *Ibid.*, para. 30.
76. *Ibid.*, para. 31.
77. *See* Opinion of Advocate-General Tesauro in Case C-288/89, para. 8.
78. J. Feenstra, 'Note to Case C-288/89, *Stichting Collectieve Antannevorziening Gouda and Others v. Commissariaat voor de Media*, Judgment of 25 July 1991, [1991] ECR I-4007; Case C-353/89, *Commission of the European Communities v. Kingdom of the Netherlands*, Judgment of 25 July 1991, [1991] ECR I-4069' (1993) 30 CMLRev, 431.

The Court distinguished between conditions related to the structure of foreign broadcasters and others related to advertising as such. As to the structure of foreign broadcasters, the *Mediawet* stipulated that the legal person producing the advertisements must be separate from the producer of the programmes, that the broadcasting organizations must not permit a third party to make a profit and that their revenue shall be reserved for the production of programmes. As to the form of advertisements and the 'when' of their transmission, it provided that they have to be clearly recognizable as such and separate from other parts of the programme, that they shall not be broadcast on Sundays and that they shall not take up more than 5 per cent of the total broadcasting time. These sets of rules applied equally to domestic broadcasters and to broadcasters from other Member States. However, since foreign broadcasters already had to comply with the broadcasting legislation of the transmission state, these rules placed an additional burden on them, and hence discriminated against them in an indirect manner.[79]

The Netherlands government attempted to justify the conditions relating to foreign broadcasting bodies by raising once more cultural policy arguments. More precisely, it claimed that these conditions were necessary so as to keep the effect of advertisers upon the content of programmes within bounds and to protect the pluralistic character of the Dutch audiovisual system. The Court refuted this argument by saying that there was 'no necessary connection between such a cultural policy and the conditions relating to the structure of foreign broadcasting bodies'.[80] It drew a clear line between the broadcasting policy pursued internally and the requirements that could be imposed on the retransmission of foreign programmes. While the Netherlands government was at liberty to regulate the structure of its own broadcasting bodies, it could not expect foreign broadcasters to adhere to the Dutch model too.

It is beyond question that the requirements of the *Mediawet* impeded the free movement of transfrontier broadcasts significantly given that only broadcasters established in Member States with a legal regime comparable to the Dutch one could broadcast their programmes to the Netherlands. Nevertheless, it is regrettable that the Court applied the proportionality test in a rigorous manner, while avoiding legal analysis. The judgment leaves the reader in doubt why the requirements imposed by the *Mediawet* on foreign broadcasters were inappropriate for the maintenance of the pluralistic and non-commercial character of the Dutch broadcasting system. Even though the Dutch Government had invoked the *van Binsbergen* doctrine, the Court did not address the problem of circumvention.[81] The Commission argued that the rationale of Article 66 of the *Mediawet* is different from that of the regulation in *van Binsbergen*, which intended to enforce obligations relating to professional conduct.[82] This argument is, however, not persuasive.

79. *See* opinion of Advocate-General Tesauro in Case C-288/89, paras 16, 19, 22.
80. Case C-288/89, para. 24.
81. C. Degenhart, 'Note to Case C-288/89, *Stichting Collectieve Antannevorziening Gouda and Others v. Commissariaat voor de Media* [1991] ECR I-4007' (1992) 22 JZ, 1127.
82. Case C-288/89, Report for the hearing, 4017.

Subsequent case-law of the Court in *Veronica* and *TV 10* amply demonstrated that it is quite possible to rely on *van Binsbergen* so as to uphold the applicability of legislation prescribing the pluralistic and non-commercial ethos of a broadcasting system.

The Opinion of Advocate-General Tesauro has been rather more illuminating. He maintained that the conditions on the non-profitable character of foreign broadcasters and on the assignment of advertising revenue were not related to the objectives of the Dutch broadcasting system given that they did not have any impact on programme content.[83] The assumption underlying this reasoning appears to be that the non-commercial nature of broadcasting is only an instrument for the protection of pluralism, but not an end in itself. With this caveat, the outcome of the Court's ruling has to be agreed with. Given that the aim of pluralism, which is common to the broadcasting systems in the European Union, can be attained by means of diverse forms of organization, the adoption of a specific broadcasting model is not indispensable. The envisaged objective can also be reached by means of less restrictive measures such as the stipulation of broadcasting standards. It follows that this finding of the Court constitutes a verdict against any regulation related to the structure of foreign broadcasters, not just against the *Mediawet* requirements *in concreto*.[84]

Needless to say, the path chosen by the Court in this case is not value-free. Even though the organization of broadcasting is not within the realms of Community competence nor is it coordinated by the TwF Directive, this judgment paved the way for an externally pluralistic broadcasting order in Europe in the long run.[85] National legislators have the power to draft the statutes of domestic broadcasters in a spirit of pluralism and non-commercialism. The same cannot, however, be imposed on foreign broadcasters targeting the national territory. Given that the increased orientation towards external pluralistic models of broadcasting on account of digital technologies is imminent, Member States wishing to resist this tide will find themselves powerless.

Turning now to the conditions relating to advertising, the Court considered whether they could be justified by overriding requirements relating to the general interest, namely the protection of consumers against unwarranted advertising or the maintenance of programme quality. The Court was not, however, convinced that this was the genuine intention of these provisions. It attached importance to the fact that the restrictions of the *Mediawet* only applied to advertising directed specifically to the Dutch audience and that an exemption could be granted from them in respect of programmes in Dutch broadcast in Belgium for the Dutch-speaking

83. Opinion of Advocate-General Tesauro in Case C-288/89, para. 17.
84. Petersen, *Rundfunkfreiheit und EG-Vertrag*, 155; Sparr, *Kulturhoheit und EWG-Vertrag*, p. 236; contra D. Frey, *Fernsehen und audiovisueller Pluralismus im Binnenmarkt der EG* (Baden-Baden, Nomos, 1999), p. 97.
85. D. Kugelmann, 'Note to Case C-288/89, *Stichting Collectieve Antannevorziening Gouda and Others v. Commissariaat voor de Media* [1991] ECR I-4007' (1992) 1 AfP, 50; Degenhart, 'Note to Case C-288/89', 1127.

public there.[86] Having drawn a comparison with the *Kabelregeling*, the Court came to the conclusion that the *Mediawet* also had a protectionist objective. Even though it did not secure the entire advertising revenue for the STER any more, it restricted the competition from foreign broadcasters to which the STER could be exposed. The Court regarded this as an eminently economic objective that could not justify the restriction on the free flow of broadcasts.

The Court was undoubtedly influenced in forming its opinion not only by the precedent of the *Bond van Adverteerders* case, but also by the provisions on advertising in connection with the transmission state principle in the TwF Directive. The Directive had been adopted at the time of the proceedings, but the time-limit for its implementation had not yet passed. Provisions such as the prohibition on the broadcasting of advertisements on Sundays and the limitation of their duration to 5 per cent of the total airtime could not be imposed on foreign broadcasts given that these matters had been fully harmonized in the Directive. The possibility of prohibiting broadcast advertising on Sundays was included in the proposal for the Directive with regard to domestic broadcasters.[87] It did not find its way into the final version given that it was covered by Article 3 (1) of the Directive that allows Member States to require broadcasters under their jurisdiction to comply with more detailed or stricter rules.

Notwithstanding these developments, some criticism has to be directed against this ruling. The view of the Court that the conditions in question were not adopted in the general interest since they did not apply to advertisements not specifically intended for the Dutch public is contestable. The Dutch government plausibly argued that it was not necessary to extend these conditions to broadcasts not in Dutch or with Dutch subtitles since only a fraction of viewers would watch such programmes.[88] Therefore, the fact that not all foreign programmes were obliged to comply with these restrictions does not exclude the public interest motivation behind them.

This is not to say that the legislation at issue did not affect competition between foreign and Dutch broadcasters. Formally speaking, the equal application of these rules to national and non-national broadcasters imposed a heavier burden on the latter since they alone had to excise parts of their programmes.[89] Nonetheless, one may wonder whether this was such a heavy burden after all given that these broadcasters had oriented themselves towards the demands of the Dutch public and legal system. In any event, it is incontestable that the extension of the advertising restrictions to foreign broadcasters limited the competition to which the STER was exposed. Given that every commercial coming from abroad inevitably diminished the advertising revenue of the STER, it is obvious that the disputed rules prevented channels from other Member States from exploiting advertising niches in the Dutch programmes so as to enhance their profits.

---

86. Case C-288/89, para. 28.
87. COM (86) 146/2 final.
88. *See* Opinion of Advocate-General Tesauro in Case C-288/89, para. 21.
89. *Ibid.*, para. 22.

It is, however, submitted that the advantage enjoyed by the STER as a result of this legislation is not extraneous to the restriction of the free movement of services but constitutes its immediate economic effect.[90] This is also the approach taken by Advocate-General Tesauro in his Opinion. The Court, by refusing to examine further justifications and by condemning the provisions of the *Mediawet* at issue with the argument that they pursued economic aims, effectively came full circle. Its reasoning could be reduced to the statement that the advertising rules were not justified by overriding requirements relating to the general interest because they restricted the broadcasting of advertisements. This is symptomatic of the half-hearted commitment of the Court to the cultural dimension of broadcasting as opposed to its economic aspects. The Court did not recognize in these judgments that the *Mediawet* only created equal conditions of competition in the Dutch broadcasting market. The existence of equal economic opportunities is a necessary precondition for equal broadcasting opportunities and hence for pluralism.[91] The failure to acknowledge these interrelationships considerably vitiated the strength of the Court's arguments.

Lastly, it is interesting to compare the ease with which the Court rejected the cultural policy reasons in the *Mediawet* cases with the self-restraint it exercised in the case *Duphar*, where the state's objective also involved mixed economic and other public policy considerations.[92] This case concerned Dutch legislation, which provided that only the medicaments listed therein were to be included in the national sickness insurance scheme. This measure clearly inhibited the free movement of goods to a great extent since medicinal products not covered by the scheme had very reduced chances of being imported.

Advocate-General Mancini asserted that the main aim of this measure was not the protection of public health but the improvement of the financial situation of social security bodies. Even though the Court shared this view, it regarded the scheme as falling outside the scope of Article 28 EC. It thus refrained from interfering with the organization of social security systems in the Member States by proposing financing methods with a less restrictive effect on trade. The reason for the Court's reserve in this case was presumably that social security was an area falling exclusively within the national sphere at the time of the judgment.[93] One could follow, *a contrario*, that the organization and financing of the national broadcasting systems have for quite some time now been deemed by the Court to be within Community competence notwithstanding the lip-service paid in the Television Directive to the opposite effect.[94]

90. J. G. Huglo, 'Droit d'établissement et libre prestation des services' (1992) 28 RTDE, 706.
91. Degenhart, 'Note to Case C-288/89', 1127.
92. Case 238/82, *Duphar v. Netherlands* [1984] ECR 523.
93. G. de Búrca, 'The Principle of Proportionality and its Application in EC Law' (1993) 13 YEL, 145.
94. Dir. 89/552/EEC, recital 13.

3.2.2 Broadcasting Obligations as Overriding Requirements Relating to the General Interest

Having analysed the jurisprudence of the European Court of Justice in the *Mediawet* cases, it is necessary to consider what conclusions can be drawn from this case-law with regard to the justifiability of the imposition of broadcasting obligations on foreign programmes on grounds of general interest.

The striking down by the Court of the conditions relating to the structure of broadcasting bodies established in other Member States has been interpreted in legal writing as implying that rules on the content of broadcasts could also only be enforced on domestic, not on foreign broadcasters.[95] This would, however, be inconsistent with the finding of the Court that a cultural policy aiming at the maintenance of pluralism may constitute an overriding requirement relating to the general interest. It follows from this finding that Member States should be free to safeguard pluralism by appropriate means. Besides, neither provisions on the pluralistic content of broadcasts nor other measures specific to the preservation of pluralism, such as on control of ownership of the media, have really been at issue in the *Mediawet* cases. The conditions relating to the structure of broadcasting bodies had the preservation of the non-commercial character of broadcasting as their primary aim, not the protection of pluralism. The rules on advertising only indirectly served the end of pluralism by creating a level playing field between domestic and foreign broadcasters.

Consequently, the *Mediawet* cases do not justify the assumption that every barrier to the retransmission of foreign broadcasts raised by broadcasting standards with pluralism as their objective would be unlawful.[96] Such broadcasting standards would, however, have to pass the proportionality test so as to be in accordance with Community law. The judgments under discussion do not provide any criteria for the assessment of the proportionality of non-discriminatory broadcasting standards. The Court did not find fault with the advertising rules because of their disproportionateness, but because they were allegedly protectionist in nature.

The question whether the restrictive effect brought about by the application of broadcasting obligations upon foreign broadcasters can be justified in the light of the principle of proportionality is difficult to answer in the abstract. As the Commission observed in its Green paper on Pluralism and Media Concentration, the assessment of proportionality is a delicate exercise since it leaves scope for subjective criteria and also poses the problem of the distinction from genuine instances of circumvention.[97] The Commission considered these problems to be more accentuated in the case of the application of national anti-concentration rules to a broadcaster from another Member State. This is not to say that the review of proportionality of measures relating to the services themselves is devoid of legal

95. K. Hesse, 'Rundfunk zwischen demokratischer Willensbildung und dem Zugriff der EG' (1993) 11 JZ, 551.
96. COM (92) 480 final, 70.
97. *Ibid.*, 72.

uncertainty. These difficulties notwithstanding, it is useful to provide some general guidelines for the monitoring of the proportionality of such measures.

An idea that can be traced back to the Commission Green Paper on Television without Frontiers, and that has been eagerly endorsed in legal writing, is that the free flow of information, protected by Article 10 ECHR, is a necessary precondition for the political process in the Community.[98] The enjoyment of the rights conferred by the ECHR would not, however, be complete, if European citizens were not able to receive foreign programmes in their original version, unadulterated by the broadcasting standards of the receiving state. Since the interpenetration not only of national economies but also of national cultures is a goal of the European Community, it is difficult to argue that programmes reflecting the plurality of views in another Member State and obeying to a different cluster of values pose a threat to the domestic broadcasting system.[99]

This line of reasoning, which refers to the cultural and political as opposed to the economic justification behind the free movement of broadcasting services in Europe, rightly calls for caution against a too lenient assessment of the proportionality of barriers raised as a result of diverging national programme requirements. However, it fails to pay tribute to the legitimate interest of the Member States to protect the supporting pillars of their communication order from broadcasts that are not carriers of a foreign broadcasting culture but products of the shortfall on control exercised over exported broadcasts in other Member States.

Therefore, a more differentiated approach towards the proportionality of the imposition of domestic programme requirements on foreign, mostly cable relayed programmes needs to be taken. The influence exercised by a programme emanating from another Member State upon the domestic broadcasting order needs to be identified. Programmes that are primarily intended for the public in the transmission state or for the all-European market do not have to be fully subjected to the broadcasting legislation of the receiving state since they only have a marginal impact upon its communication order. Audiences are separated in Europe by cultural and linguistic factors and preference is for domestic programmes rather than for foreign ones.[100] The influence exercised by this category of broadcasts should therefore not be overestimated.

On the contrary, programmes tailored to the public in the receiving country have a greater potential for torpedoing the national broadcasting system's goals. The interruption of their transmission would therefore be more easily justified. It is no coincidence that the disputed provisions of the *Kabelregeling* and of the *Mediawet* concerned only advertisements specifically intended for the Dutch

98. W.-H. Roth, 'Grenzüberschreitender Rundfunk und Dienstleistungsfreiheit' (1985) 149 ZHR, 692; Schwartz, 'Broadcasting and the EEC Treaty', 54.
99. *See* A. Bueckling, *Fernsehen ohne Grenzen – Fernsehen in Grenzen*, Vorträge, Reden und Berichte aus dem Europa-Institut der Universität des Saarlandes, no. 60 (Saarbrücken, Europa-Institut, 1986), p. 25 *et seq.*; Lord Cockfield, Answer given on behalf of the Commission (27 February 1986), OJ C 123/2, 1986.
100. E. Orf, 'Television without Frontiers – Myth or Reality?' (1990) 8 EIPR, 273.

public. In such cases it is even doubtful whether freedom of transmission is restricted given that broadcasters adapting their programmes to the receiving country will also be in the position to observe its broadcasting laws.[101]

Even so, it would probably be excessive to require from a cross-border channel that it should express the variety of opinion in the society of the receiving country unless the existence of circumvention could be proved.[102] On the other hand, a particular programme infringing the laws of the host state, for example a political advertisement regularly broadcast over a lengthy period and targeting a country where it is outlawed, could be the subject of a transmission ban.[103]

Finally, more far-reaching restrictions on the retransmission of foreign broadcasts are justified in the case of their active retransmission.[104] In this case cable distributors do not relay the foreign broadcasts unchanged at the same time, but interfere with their content and integrate them within a programme autonomously created by them. Given that domestic programmes do not have unrestricted access to the cable network either, the subjection of foreign programme elements to the same regime on broadcasting policy grounds should be in accordance with the principle of proportionality.

4. CONCLUSION

In accordance with the system of the Treaty and its previous case-law, the European Court took a differentiated approach in the broadcasting cases according to whether they involved direct or indirect discrimination on grounds of the origin of a broadcast. The overall tendency is towards a deregulation of national broadcasting systems.

As far as measures directly discriminating against foreign broadcasts are concerned, two main themes can be discerned in the jurisprudence of the Court. First, its reluctance to take cultural policy considerations seriously. Such arguments were dismissed as a sham to disguise the economic objective of protecting the national broadcasting or film industry from competition. Secondly, the clear rejection of cultural policy as a permitted derogation under Article 46 EC. These themes cast some light on the overarching question of this chapter, whether national programme requirements can be imposed on transfrontier broadcasts. Given that broadcasting obligations are essentially cultural obligations, it is safe to conclude that they do not qualify for justification under Article 46 EC.

---

101. M. Rudolph, 'Zur Rahmenordnung eines europäischen Binnenmarktes für den Rundfunk: Harmonisierungsbestrebungen der EG-Kommission' (1986) 2 AfP, 109; Jarass, 'EG-Recht und nationales Rundfunkrecht', 88.
102. *See* COM (92) 480 final, 75; Lord Cockfield, [1986] OJ C 123/3.
103. COM (92) 480 final, 75.
104. *See however* Part 2, Ch. 11.3.2.1, p. 220 for the view that active cable retransmission should be equated with initial transmission. The question of proportionality does not arise then since the retransmission state assumes full responsibility according to Art. 2(1) Dir. 2007/65.

The critical issue is whether this jurisprudence deprives Member States of a means of last resort for the attainment of their broadcasting policy objectives. It could be argued that small Member States whose public broadcasting system relies even more heavily on commercials than the Dutch system under the *Kabelregeling* might have a vital interest in subjecting foreign broadcasts to discriminatory advertising restrictions. This argument seems compelling on the assumption that the viability of a national broadcasting system is genuinely at stake. It is, however, generally recognized that the non-commercial and pluralistic nature of a broadcasting system can also be attained by the even-handed imposition of programme requirements upon domestic and foreign programmes.[105] Even though such measures may not be as drastic as discriminatory ones, the exclusion of cultural policy considerations from the public policy exception is not likely to undermine the organization of broadcasting in the Member States.

The extraterritorial application of the Member States' broadcasting legislation in a manner that only indirectly disadvantages foreign broadcasters has also come under strain. The attempt of the Commission to narrow down the rule of reason, which is implicit in the freedom to provide services, to the interests listed in Article 10 (2) ECHR fell through. The argumentative underpinnings of the Commission's interpretation are fraught with inconsistencies and go against the grain of the jurisprudence of the European Court of Human Rights.

Moreover, the narrow view of the 'general interest' has not been endorsed by the European Court of Justice. In the *Mediawet* cases, the Court recognized a cultural policy aiming at the maintenance of pluralism as an exception from the freedom to provide services under the rule of reason. Nevertheless, it was not satisfied that the requirements of proportionality and of the non-economic nature of the pursued objectives were met. By striking down the provisions on the structure of foreign broadcasters as disproportionate, the Court deprived the Member States of the power to maintain the non-commercial, internally pluralistic character of their own broadcasting system in the long run. Moreover, the rejection of the conditions on advertising on account of their protectionist character is indicative of the predominantly economic orientation of the Court's case-law.

These judgments do not justify the conclusion that the extension of domestic broadcasting obligations to programmes from other Member State is in any event incompatible with primary Community law. However, the chances of measures concerning programme content to be able to pass the proportionality test are bound to diminish as new technologies increasingly blur the boundaries between the national broadcasting markets in Europe.

---

105. Petersen, *Rundfunkfreiheit und EG-Vertrag*, p. 133; Gulich, *Rechtsfragen grenzüberschreitender Rundfunksendungen*, p. 130; Jarass, 'EG-Recht und nationales Rundfunkrecht', 133.

Chapter 13

Television without Frontiers: The European Broadcasting Quota

1. INTRODUCTION

Chapter III of the TwF Directive on the promotion of distribution and production of television programmes has proved to be one of the most controversial areas coordinated by the Directive.[1] Two different kinds of quota are laid down in Chapter III: the so-called 'European quota' in Article 4 in connection with Article 6; and the 'independent quota' in Article 5. Article 4 requires the reservation of a majority proportion of the transmission time for European works, while Article 5 orders the reservation of 10 per cent of the transmission time, alternatively of 10 per cent of the broadcasters' programming budget, to independent productions. The European quota is a pure broadcasting quota, while the independent quota is a hybrid between a broadcasting and a production quota. The European quota has been a bone of contention since the adoption of the Directive, not least because it is more difficult to achieve for broadcasters than the independent quota.[2]

The context in which the European quota has been adopted is all too well known: a European broadcasting services market increasingly dependent on imported films and serials, the great majority of which come from the United States.[3] The dominance

1. European Parliament and Council Directive 97/36/EC of 30 June 1997 amending Council Directive 89/552/EEC on the coordination of certain provisions laid down by law, regulation and administrative action in Member States concerning the pursuit of television broadcasting activities OJ L 202/60, 1997.
2. F. Hurard, 'The Production Quota System of the EU-Television Directive' in *Europäisches Medienrecht – Fernsehen und seine gemeinschaftsrechtliche Regelung*, Schriftenreihe des Instituts für Europäisches Medienrecht, vol. 18 (Munich, Jehle-Rehm, 1998), p. 35.
3. R. Frohne, 'Die Quotenregelungen im nationalen und im europäischen Recht' (1989) 8–9 ZUM 390; V. Salvatore, 'Quotas on TV Programmes and EEC Law' (1992) 29 CMLRev, 967, 974;

of the American film industry is attributed in general to the greater acceptance of its programmes by the viewers. Moreover, American programmes can be offered at more competitive prices overseas, given that their costs have already been amortized at home.[4] It has also been predicted that, paradoxically, this situation was likely to be accentuated by the creation of a single broadcasting market, which – in conjunction with the proliferation of channels – would enhance the competition among broadcasters for productions offering better cost/audience relations.[5]

It becomes clear against this backdrop that the European quota emerged as a counterbalance to the expansion of the American programme industry. By promoting 'markets of sufficient size for television productions in the Member States to recover necessary investments'[6] it was hoped to artificially replicate American conditions in Europe. The Commission considered that the main causes for the decline in the market share of European films were the partitioning of national markets and the fragmentation of distribution structures.[7] Only 20 per cent of European films go beyond their national frontiers on account of cultural and linguistic diversity in Europe and the lack of an overall distribution strategy. The European quota was expected to remove barriers between national markets by encouraging the production and distribution of European programmes. This industrial policy objective was backed up by the cultural policy argument, mainly advocated by France, that European identity needed to be protected from American cultural imperialism.

However, a significant number of Member States of the European Community have not been sympathetic to these arguments, the United Kingdom, Germany and Denmark being the fiercest critics, as well as the United States itself. The criticism of the Member States has been directed at the inefficiency of the quota and at the lack of Community competence, while the US claimed its incompatibility with the GATT Agreement. A further issue, which has been extensively discussed in legal literature, is whether the quota unduly interferes with the broadcasters' freedom of expression and is therefore in breach of Article 10 (1) ECHR.[8]

A. von Bogdandy, 'Europäischer Protektionismus im Medienbereich: Zu Inhalt und Rechtmäßigkeit der Quotenregelungen in der Fernsehrichtlinie' (1992) 1 EuZW, 9, 11.

4. D. Graham and Associates Ltd., *Impact Study of Measures (Community and National) concerning the Promotion of Distribution and Production of TV Programmes provided for under Art. 25 (a) of the TV without Frontiers Directive. Final Report*, 24 May 2005, p. 180.
5. De Witte, 'European Content Requirement', 107; Drijber, 'Revised Television without Frontiers Directive', 87, 107.
6. Recital 20 to Directive 89/552/EEC.
7. Commission of the European Communities, Strategy options to strengthen the European programme industry in the context of the audiovisual policy of the European Union, 6 April 1994, COM (94) 96 final, pp. 5 *et seq.*, 21.
8. De Witte, 'European Content Requirement', 128; Drijber, 'Revised Television without Frontiers Directive', 111; Salvatore, 'Quotas on TV Programmes', 984 *et seq.*; M. Dolmans, 'Quotas Without Content: The Questionable Legality of European Content Quotas under the Television without Frontiers Directive' (1995) 8 ENT L R, 332; J. Gundel, 'Nationale Programmquoten im Rundfunk: Vereinbar mit den Grundfreiheiten und der Rundfunkfreiheit des Gemeinschaftsrechts?' (1998) 12 ZUM, 1008 *et seq.*; von Bogdandy, 'Europäischer Protektionismus', 15.

These arguments have been rehearsed all over again in the framework of the 2003 consultation for the review of the TwF Directive. The findings of this consultation process were summarized by the Commission in an issue paper released in July 2005. The Commission held that 'there was no majority trend in favour of changing the present regulations in substance. Whereas producers, scriptwriters and trade unions proposed raising the majority proportion for European works, some Member States and private broadcasters considered broadcast quotas to be an [*sic*] disproportionate restriction of broadcasters scheduling freedom. A majority of Member State were in favour of keeping the status quo.'[9] Accordingly, the quota provisions have been incorporated *in toto* in the AVMS Directive as far as linear services are concerned.

Recent Commission Communications on the application of the quotas indicate that scheduling of European works has risen throughout the EU.[10] The independent impact study, carried out in accordance with Article 25a of the Directive, found that besides their impact on the scheduling of European works, the quotas have contributed to the cultural objective of creating new outlets for creative works and to the strengthening of the European audiovisual industry. Further, it concluded that the average proportion of European works has increased more in Member States that have placed significant additional cultural requirements on broadcasters and that have implemented Articles 4 and 5 in a prescriptive manner than in those that have implemented them flexibly.[11]

However, considerable doubts exist as to whether the increased scheduling of European works can really be attributed to the European quota. It has been argued that it is the preference of national audiences for domestically-produced content and the fact that such content is cheaper in the long run that have led to the increased transmission of European works.[12] The point has also been made that the market has changed since the 1980s when the few existing private broadcasters were forced to cover their programming needs with inexpensive American productions. Producers can now offer their content to a plethora of broadcasters that prefer to broadcast domestic works.[13]

The consultation process, being part of the wider project of extending the TwF Directive to non-linear audiovisual services, also asked the question whether

9. European Commission, Issues Paper for the Liverpool Audiovisual Conference. Cultural Diversity and the Promotion of European and Independent Audiovisual Production, July 2005, 1.
10. Sixth Commission communication on the application of Articles 4 and 5 of Directive 89/552/EEC 'Television without Frontiers', as amended by Directive 97/36/EC, for the period 2001–2002, 28 July 2004, COM (2004) 524 final; Seventh Commission communication on the application of Articles 4 and 5 of Directive 89/552/EEC 'Television without Frontiers', as amended by Directive 97/36/EC, for the period 2003–2004, 14 August 2006, COM (2006) 459 final.
11. Graham *et al.*, *Impact Study*, p. 180.
12. Written contribution of the Federal Republic of Germany <www.ec.europa.eu/avpolicy/reg/tvwf/modernization/consultation_2003/contributions/index_en.htm>, 4 June 2007.
13. Written contribution of the *Verband Privater Rundfunk und Telekommunikation* (VPRT) <www.ec.europa.eu/avpolicy/reg/tvwf/modernisation/consultation_2003/contributions/index_en.htm>, 4 June 2007.

Articles 4 and 5 should cover such services. This extension of the scope of the quotas was seen as a move to create a more level playing field between broadcasters and service providers. While some stakeholders, especially producers, argued that non-linear service providers should also be obliged to transmit a majority proportion of European works, others feared that such a move would harm the development of a nascent sector and encourage delocalization.

The Commission decided to strike a middle path. In its proposal for the AVMS Directive it did not impose a quota on on-demand services but asked Member States to ensure that such services provided by media service providers under their jurisdiction promote, where practicable and by appropriate means, production of and access to European works.[14] This provision has now been moved to Article 3i (1) of the AVMS Directive, which clarifies further that 'Such promotion could relate, *inter alia*, to the financial contribution made by such services to the production and rights acquisition of European works or to the share and/or prominence of European works in the catalogue of programmes offered by the on-demand audiovisual media service.' It is included in a separate Chapter IIB, which is entitled 'Provisions applicable only to on-demand audiovisual media services'.

It is submitted that this is more than just a political signal to the effect that non-linear services will be expected to contribute to the promotion of European works.[15] The comparison with the wording of Articles 4 and 5 of the TwF Directive leaves no doubt that Article 3i is also intended to be binding.[16] The implementation of Article 3i is left to the individual Member States, which is problematic from the point of view of legal certainty.

Extending the obligation to promote European works to the non-linear sector seems like a precipitate move given that the European quota's expediency and legality were already heavily contested as far as the linear sector was concerned. And while the effect of the 1989 quotas on a mature broadcasting industry was foreseeable, the same does not apply to the rapidly growing non-linear sector. The Commission only states by way of explanation that non-linear audiovisual media services have the potential to partially replace linear services.[17] There is no certainty though that this will in fact happen. Moreover, while it is possible to steer viewing behaviour to some extent in traditional television broadcasting, this becomes quite impossible in an environment where there are no capacity constraints.[18]

---

14. Proposal for a Directive of the European Parliament and of the Council amending Council Directive 89/552/EEC on the coordination of certain provisions laid down by law, regulation or administrative action in Member States concerning the pursuit of television broadcasting activities, 13 December 2005, COM (2005) 646 final, Art. 3f.
15. *See* European Commission, Issues Paper for the Liverpool Audiovisual Conference. Cultural Diversity and the Promotion of European and Independent Audiovisual Production, July 2005, 2; contra C. Holtz-Bacha, 'Die Neufassung der europäischen Fernsehregulierung: Von der Fernseh- zur Mediendiensterichtlinie' (2007) 2 MP, 113, 121.
16. *See* Part 2, Ch. 13.6, p. 300 *et seq below*.
17. Amended AVMSD proposal, recital 35.
18. Van den Bos, 'No Frontiers', 109, 111.

The Commission assumes that the increased availability of European works will be of benefit to these new services. No evidence is, however, adduced that on-demand services will benefit from the obligation to promote European content nor that they will be prepared to observe it. It is possible that they, much like the private broadcasting sector in its beginnings, will prefer to transmit cheap, massively available non-European material.[19] The concern that they might even leave the European Union area so as to escape such obligations is more justified in their case than in the case of the traditional broadcasting industry.

The focus of the present analysis will not be so much on the rules applicable to the non-linear services as on the European quota rule. However, some of the criticisms of the quota are also very relevant as far as these rules are concerned. The main question asked in this chapter is whether the European Union, by adopting the provisions on the European quota, has acted *ultra vires*, encroaching thereby upon Member States' competence in the area of broadcasting.[20]

This is a question which has even sparked off a constitutional dispute in Germany between the Federal Government and some of the *Länder*. The object of this dispute was the approval by the Federal Government of the TwF Directive. The *Länder* argued that the Directive infringed their constitutional rights. They not only questioned the Community competence in the area of broadcasting in general, but also took the standpoint that the European quota in particular was not covered by the Community competence under Articles 49 and 50 EC. In a long-awaited judgment handed down in 1995, the Federal Constitutional Court found the *Länder* rights to have been violated in so far as the Federal Government had not consequently represented their shared view of the incompatibility of the European quota with Community law.[21]

This chapter will measure, first, the legitimacy of the European quota against the requirements of Articles 47 (2), 55 EC. Subsequently, it will ask whether Article 151 EC can serve as the legal basis of the quota rule. Lastly, the legal nature of the European quota will be investigated and its compatibility with the WTO legal order will be assessed.

---

19. T. Kleist, 'Fernsehrichtlinie: Konvergenz und Wettbewerb bei audiovisuellen Angeboten' (2006) 2 MMR, 61, 62.
20. This question even sparked off a constitutional dispute in Germany between the Federal Government and some of the *Länder*. *See* (1995) 2 AfP, 483; P. Lerche, 'Konsequenzen aus der Entscheidung des Bundesverfassungsgerichts zur EG-Fernsehrichtlinie' (1995) 4 AfP, 632; H. Kresse and M. Heinze, 'Der Rundfunk: Das "jedenfalls auch kulturelle Phänomen" – Ein Pyrrhus-Sieg der Länder? Eine Kurzanalyse des Urteils des Bundesverfassungsgerichts zur EU-Fernesehrichtlinie' (1995) 6 ZUM, 394; W. Hess, 'Die EG-Rundfunkrichtlinie vor dem Bundesverfassungsgericht: Anmerkungen zum Verfahren 2 BvG 1/89' (1990) 2 AfP, 95; A. Deringer, 'Pyrrhussieg der Länder: Anmerkung zum Urteil des Bundesverfassungsgerichts vom 22. März 1995 in der Rechtssache 2 BvG 1/89 in dem Verfahren Fernsehrichtlinie' (1995) 5 ZUM, 316.
21. (1995) 2 AfP 483.

2. HOW TO DELIMIT MEMBER STATES' AND EUROPEAN UNION POWERS IN THE AREA OF BROADCASTING

In answering the question of how far the European quota infringes on Member States' competence in the area of broadcasting, two lines of reasoning can be followed. The first one is based on the assumption that the European Union can only adopt economic policy measures, given that its competence is restricted to the economic sector.[22] This assumption leads to the conclusion that the provisions on the European quota are void, since they undoubtedly touch upon cultural issues such as the content of programmes. However, the 13th recital to Dir. 89/552/EEC confirms that the responsibility of the Member States and their authorities with regard to the content of programmes is not affected. The argument that the quota requirements do not concern the content but only the origin of television programmes[23] is not convincing. The origin of a programme necessarily affects its content. Besides, it is as much a part of the Member States' cultural policy to lay down requirements with regard to the content of broadcasts as with regard to their origin.

This straitjacketing of Community competence to strictly economic matters is contentious. Article 2 of the EC Treaty suggests that, by integrating the national economies, wider aims than purely economic ones are pursued such as the promotion of solidarity among Member States. In the same vein, its preamble declares that the creation of the European Community shall lay the foundations of an ever closer union among the peoples of Europe. Also, as the transformation of the European Economic Community into the European Community and the insertion of Article 151 EC into the Treaty amply demonstrate, the Community is by no means blind to cultural issues.

Furthermore, it should be pointed out that the power of the Community under Articles 47 (2), 55 EC, upon which the TwF Directive and hence the European quota have been based, is of a functional nature. This follows from the wording of these provisions in conjunction with Article 3 (h) EC.[24] This is not to say that limited powers, in accordance with the principle of the attribution of powers in Articles 5 (1), 7 (1) EC, can be replaced by broad political aims. The functional nature of a legal basis only implies that, if an area is covered by its specific

---

22. *See* A. von Bogdandy, 'Unity in Diversity? The European Single Market in Broadcasting and the Audiovisual, 1982–92' (1994) 32 JCMS, 89, 113; F. Ossenbühl, *Rundfunk zwischen nationalem Verfassungsrecht und Europäischem Gemeinschaftsrecht: Rechtsgutachten erstattet der Regierung des Landes Nordrhein-Westfalen* (Frankfurt am Main, Alfred Metzner, 1986), pp. 13 *et seq.*, 20; Herrmann, *Rundfunkrecht*, p. 224 para. 26; Konszuseck, 'Freier Dienstleistungsverkehr', 541; T. Vormann, *Kulturelle Souveränität und Fernsehen: Rechtsvergleich der Maßnahmen zur Sicherung der kulturellen Identität in Kanada und den Europäischen Gemeinschaften unter besonderer Berücksichtigung der Quotenregelung im Fernsehen* (Rheinfelden, Schäuble, 1993), p. 225.
23. I. Schwartz, 'EG-Rechtsetzunsbefugnis für das Fernsehen' (1989) 2 ZUM, 381.
24. Von Bogdandy, 'Europäischer Protektionismus', 13; contra H. H. Rupp, 'EG-Rundfunkrecht und Gerichtskontrolle des Bundesverfassungsgerichts' in *Eine Rundfunkordnung für Europa – Chancen und Risiken*, K. Stern *et al.* (eds), Schriftenreihe des Instituts für Rundfunkrecht an der Universität zu Köln, vol. 54 (Munich, C. H. Beck, 1990), p. 76 n. 6.

objectives, the Community institutions have the power to regulate this area irrespective of its economic or other character. The delimitation between Member States' and Community powers according to the economic orientation of a measure does not fit well with the Treaty's structure. It also leads to demarcation problems in the case of so-called cross-cutting issues that touch upon different areas.

In the landmark judgment in Case C-376/98 *Federal Republic of Germany v. European Parliament and Council of the European Union* (*Tobacco Advertising* judgment) the Court held that 'provided that the conditions for recourse to Article 100a, 57 (2) and 66 as a legal basis are fulfilled, the Community legislature cannot be prevented from relying on that legal basis on the ground that public health protection is a decisive factor in the choices to be made. On the contrary, the third paragraph of Article 129 (1) EC provides that health requirements are to form a constituent part of the Community's other policies.'[25] Similarly, Article 151 (4) EC requires that that the Community shall take cultural aspects into account in its action under other provisions of this Treaty, in particular in order to respect and to promote the diversity of its cultures. Nonetheless, an important distinction has to be made here. The policy integration principle cannot cure the inclusion in a Community instrument of cultural aspects, which lie outside its legal basis.[26]

It follows from all the foregoing that a second line of reasoning is preferable, according to which the limits of the Community's competence have to be detected within the provisions of the Treaty themselves. This is also the test the Court used in the *Tobacco Advertising* judgment. The Court found that in order to determine whether a measure genuinely has as its object the improvement of the conditions for the establishment and functioning of the internal market, it is necessary to verify whether it 'actually contributes to eliminating obstacles to the free movement of goods and to the freedom to provide services, and to removing distortions of competition'.[27] The limits of the legal basis of Dir. 2007/65/EC – Articles 47 (2) and 55 EC – lie in its function to establish the internal market.[28] The question to be answered with regard to the European quota is, therefore, whether it has the proper functioning of the internal market as its object. Bearing this in mind, the legitimacy of the European quota will first be measured against the requirements of Articles 47 (2) and 55 EC. Subsequently, it will be asked whether Article 151 EC can serve as its legal basis.

3. ARTICLES 47 (2) AND 55 EC AS THE LEGAL BASIS FOR THE EUROPEAN QUOTA

Article 47 (2) EC, which by virtue of Article 55 EC is also applicable in the area of services, allows the Community to coordinate the provisions laid down by law,

25. Case C-376/98, *Federal Republic of Germany v. European Parliament and Council of the European Union* [2000] ECR I-8419; [2000] 3 CMLR 1175.
26. *See* Ch. 10.3, p. 187 *above*.
27. Case C-376/98, paras 84, 95.
28. A. Dashwood, 'The Limits of European Community Powers' (1996) 21 ELRev, 113, 120; Seelmann-Eggebert, *Internationaler Rundfunkhandel*, p. 144.

regulation and administrative action in Member States, 'in order to make it easier for persons to take up and pursue activities as self-employed persons' and as providers of services. In other words, the condition for Articles 47 (2) and 55 EC to be the legal basis of the provisions on the European quota is the existence of national provisions presenting obstacles to the freedom to provide broadcasting services.

The objective of the free circulation of television broadcasts in the Community as the primary objective of the TwF Directive is expressed in recitals 2, 3, 7, 9, 10, 11, 12 and 13 to Dir. 89/552/EEC, in recitals 7 and 16 to Dir. 97/36/EC and in recitals 2, 6, 7, 27 and 67 to Dir. 2007/65/EC. The 24th recital to Dir. 97/36/EC clarifies that the European quota provision also pursues this general objective by eliminating 'the obstacles arising from differences in national legislation on the promotion of European works'. The different national regulations referred to in this recital are programme restrictions, which a number of Member States of the European Union have laid down in their legislation with the aim of the promotion of their national film production or the protection of their language. A distinction can be drawn between national quotas applying language criteria and others applying geographical criteria.

Language quotas have been adopted for instance by France, Greece, the Netherlands, Poland and Spain. We have discussed the French, Greek and Dutch language quotas in Part One of this book.[29] In Poland, broadcasters have to devote at least 33 per cent of their quarterly transmission time, excluding news, advertising, teleshopping, sports events, teletext services and games, to programmes originally produced in the Polish language.[30] Also, they have to reserve at least 33 per cent of their quarterly transmission time devoted to vocal-musical compositions for compositions performed in the Polish language.[31] In Spain, at least 50 per cent of transmission time devoted to European works must consist of programmes in the Spanish language.

On the other hand, programme restrictions connected with the geographical origin of works existed in the past in Italy, Germany and the United Kingdom. Italian law stipulated that 50 per cent of the transmission time allocated for European works had to be reserved for productions of Italian origin. In contrast, Germany and the United Kingdom did not distinguish between national and European works. German law merely provided that a substantial percentage of German and European programmes had to be broadcast, while the Independent Broadcasting Authority required that 86 per cent of programmes had to consist of works of United Kingdom and EC origin.

National quotas involve a twofold restriction on the freedom to supply services. First, they can be imposed on foreign programmes, obstructing thus their

29. *See* Part1, Ch. 2.8.6; Ch. 4.8.1; Ch. 6.8.1 *above.*
30. Broadcasting Act of 29 December 1992, Art. 15 (1).
31. Broadcasting Act of 29 December 1992, Art. 15 (2).
32. M. Frese, *Die Rechtmäßigkeit europäischer Fernsehquoten aus kompetentieller, grundrechtlicher und welthandelsrechtlicher Sicht* (Frankfurt am Main, Peter Lang, 1998), p. 63.

cross-border diffusion by cable.[32] Operators of cable networks can refuse to transmit programmes broadcast by foreign broadcasting bodies, unless they comply with the domestic requirements. Secondly, they favour national programmes or programmes produced in the national language, creating thus an inequality of opportunities for programmes from other Member States.[33] The need for such restrictions to be justifiable under Article 46 EC or on grounds of a mandatory requirement, so as to be compatible with Community law, has been pointed out by the European Court in the cases *Sacchi*[34] and *ERT*.[35]

However, not all Member States had adopted such quotas prior to the enactment of the Directive. The question emerges whether the Community competence to coordinate national laws only relates to measures already existing in the various Member States or whether the Community is empowered to introduce additional restrictions. The wording used in Article 47 (1), (2) EC, that the coordination shall 'make it *easier* for persons to take up and pursue activities', may militate in favour of the first view. If this was the case, the Community would only be allowed to coordinate national provisions on the basis of the most liberal regulation.

This opinion is not convincing. The primary field of application of Article 47 EC is the freedom of establishment, which differs in certain respects from the freedom to provide services. While the latter goes beyond the mere prohibition of discrimination by proscribing also non-discriminatory restrictions, it is very questionable whether the same applies to the former. It would go beyond our purposes to expand on this issue. Suffice is to say that the freedom of establishment has initially been conceived of as a prohibition of discrimination. All equally applicable barriers in this area had to be removed by means of the approximation of laws that came to have a truly liberalizing function. The same cannot be said of the freedom of services, where even non-discriminatory restrictions are done away with by means of primary Community law. Coordination directives only iron out remaining obstacles, which are justified on grounds of public policy. As a result, the need for liberalization is less pronounced in the area of services, so that the Community institutions are not precluded from adopting stricter rules.

The fact that national quotas can hinder the free movement of services is not, however, in itself sufficient to justify the harmonization of national laws. Necessity is an implicit condition for the adoption of harmonization measures under Article 47 (2) EC. Accordingly, the quota has to be, first, an effective means of creating the internal market in broadcasting. Second, it has to be the least restrictive means to this effect. The Community is only entitled to harmonize national barriers to free movement, if they are justified by a public policy goal under Article 46 EC or

33. Gundel, 'Nationale Programmquoten', 1003, 1004.
34. Case 155/73, *Guiseppe Sacchi (preliminary ruling requested by the Tribunale di Biella)* [1974] ECR 409.
35. Case 260/89, *Elliniki Radiophonia Tileorassi (ERT) v. Dimotiki* [1991] ECR I-2925, [1994] 4 CMLR 540.
36. Frese, *Rechtmäßigkeit europäischer Fernsehquoten*, p. 66; Dolmans, 'Quotas without Content', 331; U. Everling, 'Brauchen wir "Solange III"?' 3 (1990) EuR, 218; J. Currall, 'Some Aspects of the Relation between Articles 30–36 and Article 100 of the EEC Treaty, with a Closer Look

by an overriding reason of general interest.[36] If, on the contrary, the challenged legislation cannot be upheld by reference to such reasons, the least restrictive means of creating the internal market is by doing away with the obstructive law.

The Commission first adopted this new approach to harmonization in its White Paper on Completing the Internal Market.[37] Its harmonization approach was based on the principle that a clear distinction needed to be drawn between what is essential to harmonize and what may be left to mutual recognition of national regulations and standards.[38] National regulations that were excessive in relation to the mandatory requirements pursued and, thus, constituted unjustified barriers to trade under the *Cassis* reasoning would not need to be harmonized. Niedobitek's argument that harmonization measures can also be taken with regard to national provisions that are inconsistent with primary Community law, on grounds of legal certainty or so as to avoid lengthy Treaty infringement proceedings, has to be approached with scepticism.[39] The Community competence to harmonize national laws, as every other functional competence, is not an aim in itself, but only a means of establishing the functioning of the common market.

Consequently, the legitimacy of the European quota depends on whether restrictions to the free provision of services arising from national quotas are justified. Only then would their harmonization be permissible. The two requirements of Articles 47 (2) and 55 EC concerning the effectiveness of the European quota and its necessity for the creation of the internal market will be looked at in turn.

3.1 Is the European Quota an Effective Means of Creating the Internal Market in Broadcasting?

First, we must consider whether the European quota contributes to the free movement of broadcasting services in Europe. Broadcasters are now faced with a unified quota system instead of the different quota regimes previously existing on a national level so that the reception and retransmission of programmes across Europe has been made easier *prima facie*. However, the quota in fact introduced additional restrictions to the operation of certain categories of channels. Its programming requirements are burdensome given that imported programmes are cheaper than European commissioned programmes, especially if they are of non-domestic origin.

Public broadcasters sustained by license fees have no difficulty in achieving the majority proportion for European works. They can afford to schedule films and

at Optional Harmonization' (1985) YEL, 182; P. Craig and G. de Búrca, *EU Law: Text, Cases and Materials* (4th edn, Oxford, Oxford University Press, 2008), p. 621; S. Weatherill and P. Beaumont, *EU Law: The Essential Guide to the Legal Workings of the European Union* (3rd edn, London, Penguin, 1999), pp. 597–598.

37. Completing the Internal Market. White Paper from the Commission to the European Council, 28–29 June 1985, COM (85) 310.
38. *Ibid.*, p. 19, para. 65.
39. Niedobitek, *Cultural Dimension in EC Law*, p. 166.

series from other Member States despite the fact that cultural and linguistic barriers prevent them from being popular with the public. The same cannot be said of private channels having to rely on advertising revenue that makes the purchase of attractive, low-priced programmes imperative.[40] The quota is especially onerous for new entrants to the European audiovisual market, providing thus a disincentive for investments in this area.[41] The Commission has taken the special situation of new broadcasters into consideration by allowing them to achieve the quota progressively, without however releasing them from the obligation to attain it in the long run.

What is more, the European quota cements the audiovisual market and shuts it off to technological developments, such as the pay-per-view and near video-on-demand services. Since channels offering such services are totally dependent on subscribers' selection, the obligation to transmit unpopular European films is contrary to free-market logic and obstructive to their commercial establishment. This problem was at issue in the *Mediakabel* case.[42] Mediakabel offered Filmtime, a near-video on-demand (NVOD) service. The *Commissariaat voor de Media* asked Mediakabel to obtain a specific authorization for this service, which, in its view, constituted a television service falling under the TwF Directive. Such an authorization would not have been needed if Filmtime was classified as an information society service as defined in Article 2 (a) of the E-Commerce Directive in conjunction with Article 1 (2) of the Technical Standards and Regulations Directive.[43] Mediakabel challenged the *Commissariaat*'s decision. The Dutch Council of State, finally seized with the case, made a reference for a preliminary ruling to the European Court.

The European Court held that Filmtime was not an information society service as it was not provided at the individual request of the recipients but as part of a service determined by the service provider. The consumers could not watch the films whenever they wanted but only at the broadcast times determined by the provider. These characteristics of NVOD led the Court to conclude that a service such as Filmtime is a television broadcasting service within the meaning of Article 1 (a) of the TwF Directive.

Mediakabel was particularly opposed to the classification of Filmtime as a television service since this would carry with it the heavy financial burden of having to transmit a majority proportion of European works. It did not, however, phrase its argument exactly in these terms. It argued instead that the requirement to reserve a specific percentage of European works was not apposite in the case of

40. Commission, Background Document 6 – List of television channels in the European Union Member States which failed to achieve the majority proportion according to Art. 4, SEC (2006) 1073, 167.
41. Graham *et al.*, *Impact Study*, p. 84.
42. Case C-89/04, *Mediakabel BV v. Commissariaat voor de Media* [2005] ECR I-4891.
43. European Parliament and Council Directive 2003/31/EC of 8 June 2000 on certain legal aspects of information society services, in particular electronic commerce, in the Internal Market (Directive on electronic commerce), OJ L 178/1, 2000; European Parliament and Council Directive 98/34 of 22 June 1998 laying down a procedure for the provision of information in the field of technical standards and regulations, OJ L 204/37, 1998.

NVOD given that the subscribers pay for and view only the films they have selected. The Court ruled that the possible adverse consequences of the obligation to comply with the European quota requirement for Mediakabel could not alter the classification of this service as a television service. The fact that viewers can select the films they want to watch is, in the Court's view, equally immaterial given that the obligation to achieve the quota rests with the broadcasters, not the viewers. Advocate-General Tizzano did not accept Mediakabel's quota argument either. He stressed, however, that a service should be partially or temporarily exempt from the obligation to fill the quota if it was to be rendered financially unsustainable otherwise.[44]

The problems experienced by Mediakabel are also common in the case of thematic channels, such as movie or cartoon channels. These channels often seek to invoke the 'where practicable' exception.[45] According to the Commission, this exception could not be relied on where European works 'exist in sufficient number for the type of channel in question or where the European programme industry is potentially able to produce them in sufficient quantity'.[46] In any event, the thematic orientation of a channel to non-European programmes would not entitle it to a general ex-ante exemption from the obligation to comply with Article 4. It could only be taken into account if particular reasons for non-compliance were given.[47]

Limiting the possibilities for the transmission of non-European works also runs counter to the objectives of the internal market in a different way. According to the model of Article 49 EC in connection with Article 2 EC, the provision of services in the Community shall be free and guided by market-economy principles. The quota, by obstructing the broadcasting of non-European programmes, defies this model. The internal market is affected as a result, since the quota impacts on the use of such programmes by European channels, even though their importation is not impeded.

The need for harmonizing conditions of competition in a liberalized audiovisual market, referred to in the 24th recital to Dir. 97/36/EC, does not support the adoption of the quota either. The creation of a level playing field cannot automatically justify harmonization measures.[48] While equal conditions of competition reign in centralized states with only one legislator laying down the rules, the situation is different in federal states and even more so in a supranational organization like the European Community. Distortions of competition have to

44. Opinion of Advocate-General Tizzano, para. 56 *et seq.*
45. *See* Commission, Background Document 3 – Application of Articles 4 and 5 in each Member State, SEC (2006) 1073, 19.
46. Communication from the Commission to the Council and the European Parliament on the application of Arts. 4 and 5 of Dir. 89/552/ Television without frontiers, 3 March 1994, COM (94) 57 final, 20.
47. Commission Staff Working Document, Background Documents to the Seventh Commission communication of 14 August 2006 on the application of Articles 4 and 5 of Directive 89/552/ EEC 'Television without Frontiers', as amended by Directive 97/36/EC, for the period 2003–2004, SEC (2006) 1073, 20.
48. G. Perau, *Werbeverbote im Gemeinschaftsrecht: Gemeinschaftsrechtliche Grenzen nationaler und gemeinschaftsrechtlicher Werbebeschränkungen* (Baden-Baden, Nomos, 1997), p. 226.

be more than marginal, so as to vindicate the need for harmonization measures.[49] Besides, the European quota does not automatically create a level playing field. The flexible wording used in Article 4 allows for different methods of implementation and degrees of commitment.[50]

In sum, considerable doubts exist as to whether the adoption of the European quota constitutes less of a hindrance to the creation of the internal market in broadcasting services than the pre-existing system based on national quotas.

3.2 Is the European Quota the Least Restrictive Means of Creating the Internal Market in Broadcasting?

Secondly, it is necessary to consider whether the European quota is the least restrictive means of creating the internal market. We noted earlier that this would be the case if the Member States were entitled to derogate from Article 49 EC by adopting laws for the protection of their national film production or language. A distinction has to be drawn between the different ways in which national quotas impede the cross-border supply of broadcasting services, namely by imposing domestic requirements on foreign broadcasts and by favouring the transmission of national works.

The subjection of foreign cable-transmitted programmes to national quotas for the promotion of national language or film production does not constitute direct discrimination. The same quotas apply to domestic and to foreign broadcasters. However, it discriminates indirectly against the latter, since it is more onerous for them to satisfy the requirements of the state of reception in addition to those of the state of transmission. Is this covert discrimination justified under Article 46 EC or by overriding reasons relating to the general interest?

It is established case-law of the Court that economic aims cannot justify restrictions on the freedoms of movement.[51] As far as cultural objectives are concerned, the Court ruled after initial vacillation, that they do not come under Article 46 EC.[52] They may, however, constitute overriding requirements relating to the general interest.[53] Accordingly, the crucial issue seems to be whether

49. Case C-376/98, *Federal Republic of Germany v. European Parliament and Council of the European Union* [2000] ECR I-8419 para. 106; [2000] 3 CMLR 1175; Case C-300/89, *Commission v. Council* [1991] ECRI-2867 para. 23.
50. Second Communication from the Commission to the Council and the European Parliament on the application of Art. 4 and 5 of Dir. 89/552/EEC Television without Frontiers, 15 July 1996, COM (96) 302 final, 75: 'Arts. 4 and 5 provide what amounts to the minimum coordination of the various national rules which is needed to ensure free movement in TV broadcasting, but do not in themselves make it possible to achieve the objective of strengthening European TV broadcasting, to the same extent as a watertight blanket system'.
51. Case 352/85, *Bond van Adverteerders v. Netherlands State*, [1988] ECR 2085, para. 34; [1989] 3 CMLR 113.
52. *Ibid.*, para. 35 *et seq.*; Case C-211/91, *Commission of the European Communities v. Kingdom of Belgium,* [1992] ECR-I 6757, para. 10.
53. Case C-353/89, *Commission of the European Communities v. Kingdom of the Netherlands*, [1991] ECR-I 4069.

national quotas pursue economic or cultural objectives. However, it is almost impossible to answer this question with certainty in view of the tangle of cultural and economic implications of quotas.

Quotas, especially those geared to the national origin of works, undoubtedly encourage national film production. Nevertheless, it is not easy to dispute their cultural motivation either. They arguably contribute to the protection of national culture and language, even if no high artistic quality is catered for. Support for the opposite view, that cultural justifications are not credible in the absence of quality control, could however be derived from the judgment of the Court in the *Spanish dubbing licence* case.[54] In this case Spain sought to justify an advantage granted to producers of Spanish films on the basis of cultural policy considerations. The Court gave this argument short shrift, pointing out that the distribution of national films is promoted regardless of their content or quality.[55]

It is plausible that the approach taken by the Court is informed by a particular understanding of culture. The term 'culture' is used in at least two different ways: in the sense of 'art', of the 'highest intellectual achievements of human beings'[56] in the fields of music, literature and philosophy among others and in a wider anthropological sense encompassing 'the sum total of the material and spiritual activities and products of a given group which distinguishes it from other similar groups'.[57] According to Advocate-General van Gerven, the overriding reason of the protection of the cultural heritage encompasses the preservation of historical and artistic treasures and the dissemination of knowledge related thereto, the preservation of the freedom of pluralistic expression and the protection of the national language.[58] It seems to be situated therefore between high art and culture in the wider sense.

National quotas, on the other hand, are less concerned with quality as with the protection of cultural identity. This is a notion that is by no means alien to broadcasting regulation, since the concern for national identity and culture is a public service standard common to all European countries. Notwithstanding the difficulties of pinning down the elusive phenomenon of culture and cultural identity, it is characterized, in broad terms, by a concern for the promotion of social cohesion and the preservation of the distinctive way of life of each Member State. This objective, however, is not directly dependent on the quality of the transmitted

54. Case C-17/92, *Federación de Distribuidores Cinematográficos (FEDICINE) v. Spanish State* [1993] ECR-I 2239; Frese, *Rechtmäßigkeit europäischer Fernsehquoten*, p. 66; Dolmans, 'Quotas Without Content', 331.
55. Case C-17/92, *Federación de Distribuidores Cinematográficos (FEDICINE) v. Spanish State* [1993] ECR-I 2239, para. 20.
56. L. V. Prott, 'Cultural Rights as Peoples' Rights in International Law' in *The Rights of Peoples*, J. Crawford (ed.) (Oxford, Clarendon, 1988), pp. 93–94; Loman *et al.*, *Culture and Community Law*, p. 2.
57. L. G. Stavenhagen, 'Cultural Rights and Universal Human Rights' in *Economic, Social and Cultural Rights*, A. Eide, C. Krause and A. Rosas (eds) (The Hague, Martinus Nijhoff, 1995), pp. 63, 66.
58. Opinion of Advocate-General van Gerven, para. 26.

works. Nor can the maintenance of national or regional languages as means of expression only be achieved by the transmission of high quality films.

All in all, national quotas pursue cultural policy objectives that can be considered 'overriding requirements relating to the general interest'. The fact that they allow goals of an economic nature to be achieved as well does not divest them of their cultural character.[59]

Consequently, the single question to which our enquiry comes down to is whether it is necessary to make the transmission of foreign audiovisual programmes via the cable network dependent upon the fulfilment of national quotas so as to attain the envisaged cultural policy objectives. It has been argued that domestic programme requirements should be fully applicable to the unchanged and simultaneous transmission of foreign programmes on the ground of their functional comparability with home programmes.[60] The problem with this approach is that the imposition of programme requirements upon cable programmes is of doubtful effectiveness, given that mushrooming satellite programmes escape such control.[61] More importantly, the influence exercised by cable channels on the public is more limited than that exercised by terrestrial channels.[62] These factors plead for the lowering of programme obligations applicable to cable programmes that do not target the public in the receiving country, but are primarily intended for viewers in the transmission state or for the all-European market. Programmes, on the other hand, that are tailored to the public in the receiving country will contain in any event a substantial amount of material from that country in order to be attractive. Quotas are therefore less relevant in their case.

All in all, the imposition of quota requirements upon foreign cable programmes does not satisfy the principle of proportionality and is therefore incompatible with Community law. Admittedly, it is a prerogative of the Community institutions to assess which harmonization measures are due as the process of European integration advances. The European Court concedes to them a great margin of discretion when complex legislative choices are involved affecting diverse economic and other interests.[63] Nonetheless, the Court can find fault with the legislative choice when the resultant disadvantages for certain economic operators are wholly disproportionate to the advantages otherwise offered.[64] This is the case with the quota provision.

Also, the requirements on the necessity of harmonization measures should be all the higher the more the nucleus of the cultural sovereignty of the Member States is affected.[65] The European quota touches upon the very essence of national

59. Case 118/86, *Openbaar Ministerie v. Nertsvoederfabriek Nederland* [1987] ECR 3883 para. 15; Case 72/83, *Campus Oil Limited v. Minister for Industry and Energy* [1984] ECR 2727 para. 36; Opinion of Advocate-General van Gerven in Case C-17/92, paras 17, 26.
60. Brühann, 'Vorschlag einer Gemeinschaftsrichtlinie', pp. 11, 15.
61. *Ibid.*, p. 16.
62. Barendt, *Broadcasting Law*, p. 110.
63. Case C-233/94, *Germany v. Parliament & Council* [1997] ECR I-2405 paras 55–56.
64. *Ibid.*
65. Bullinger, 'Werbung und Quotenregelung', p. 98.

autonomy in the field of broadcasting. Those Member States whose legislation did not include quotas have been obliged to introduce them for the first time. The remaining Member States are precluded from maintaining for their own broadcasters obligations which fall below the Community level and from imposing their own quotas on foreign broadcasts. The subjection of foreign programmes to national quotas is even less acceptable now under Article 2a (1) of Dir. 2007/65/EC given that Chapter III of the Directive has coordinated this field.

Turning now to the application of national quotas to domestic broadcasts, the question is pertinent whether it runs counter to Community law given that an advantage is granted to national works in comparison with works produced in other Member States. Quotas based on the criterion of the origin of the works to be transmitted manifestly discriminate on grounds of nationality. They cannot be justified on public policy grounds under Article 46 EC and are hence at variance with primary Community law. Advocate-General van Gerven's proposal that even overtly discriminatory measures should be justifiable on cultural grounds has not been endorsed by the Court so far.[66] Nor is this likely to happen in future given that an analogous application of the ground of protection of national treasures under Article 30 EC or a broad interpretation of Article 46 EC would considerably restrict the free movement of services. Moreover, there is no need for this manoeuvre given that cultural policy objectives can in general be achieved without recourse to direct discrimination.[67]

Language quotas, on the other hand, cover even-handedly national works and works from other Member States produced in the specified language. They have at most an indirectly discriminatory effect upon foreign productions originating from Member States not belonging to the same linguistic area. They are justified on the grounds of protection of a national or regional language. Their proportionality is born out by Article 8 of Dir. 89/552/EEC, which authorized Member States to impose on broadcasters under their jurisdiction more detailed or stricter rules in particular on the basis of language criteria.[68]

Language quotas are hence the only possible starting point for the adoption of harmonization measures. However, Article 8 of Dir. 89/552/EEC leaves no doubt that Member States have the power, even after the adoption of the Directive, to maintain quotas within the European quota in favour of works produced in their national language. The extent to which the European quota can be reserved for such works is uncertain. Some take the view that it can even be filled entirely with productions in the own language, a view obviously not shared by the Commission.[69] Be that as it may, the European quota cannot be justified by reference to the need to harmonize national language quotas.

---

66. Opinion of Advocate-General van Gerven in the *Spanish dubbing licence case*, para. 27 *et seq.*
67. Gundel, 'Nationale Programmquoten', 1005.
68. The gist of this provision is contained now in recital 44 to Dir. 97/36/EC.
69. *See* de Witte, 'European Content Requirement', 112; Drijber, 'Revised Television without Frontiers Directive', 108; Collins, 'Unity in Diversity', 72.

Our analysis has demonstrated that the adoption of the European quota was not necessary for the creation of the internal market in broadcasting. The Commission also admitted this, when it stated in the 1994 Green Paper that Articles 4 and 5 exceed 'what is legally strictly necessary to secure freedom to provide services in the programme industry'.[70]

3.3 The European Quota as a Countervailing Measure against the Establishment of the Internal Market in Broadcasting

The point has been made that the European quota is linked to the creation of a single market in broadcasting services in a wider sense. It is generally accepted that the single market is even more vulnerable to American expansionist tendencies in the audiovisual sector than the previously divided domestic markets. The reason is that more distribution channels exist, so that greater profit margins can be obtained. The quota requirement is viewed as a counterbalance that gives a competitive advantage to the European programme industry. This argument may be disputed on at least two grounds.

First, it is doubtful whether the European quota is really an effective means of boosting the European programme industry. No safeguards are built in Article 4 to ensure that broadcasters, instead of opting for the most inexpensive forms of programming, will cooperate in creating a programme stock in the long run. As a consequence, broadcasters are free to transmit low-budget productions, which do not even have to be films or series, since it is left to their discretion how to fill up the quota.[71] The impact study found evidence that primary channels have reduced the proportion of European works that are stock programmes and increased the proportion of flow programmes.[72]

The European quota requirement could also be satisfied by means of repetitive transmissions of old programmes.[73] No outlets for new productions would be created then. On the contrary, the European audiovisual industry would be weakened as a result of the deterioration of programme quality. Nor does any guarantee exist that profits gained by the producers as a result of the quota will be reinvested in the creation of quality television productions.

---

70. COM (94) 96 final.
71. Hitchens, 'Identifying European Community Audio-visual Policy', 69; Mestmäcker *et al.*, *Einfluß des europäischen Gemeinschaftsrechts*, p. 20.
72. Graham *et al.*, *Impact Study*, pp. 4, 6, 177. Stock programmes are generally more expensive than flow programmes. They have repeat value and can be shown again at a later date, while flow programmes have little or no further value after the first transmission. A 'primary channel' is defined in the impact study as a channel with audience share equal to or greater than 3 per cent, while 'secondary channels' have an audience share less than 3 per cent.
73. The requirement to earmark an adequate proportion for recent works under Art. 5, second sentence only applies to the independent, not the European quota.

Moreover, the quota could be circumvented by devoting more transmission time to programme elements, which do not come within the scope of Article 4 such as news and sports events. Also, no conditions exist as to the transmission time for European works. As a result, they can be scheduled during off-peak hours, with the prime-time being reserved for American works. Admittedly, the impact study found that primary channels tend to show a higher proportion of European works in peak time than in the rest of the schedule. However, no such observation was made in relation to smaller primary channels or secondary channels, which have been found to transmit a smaller proportion of qualifying European works.[74]

Lastly, if the aim is 'to promote markets of sufficient size for television productions *in the Member States* to recover necessary investments'[75], this aim is blurred through the inclusion of works originating from European third State parties to the European Convention on Transfrontier Television of the Council of Europe within the definition of 'European works'.

The list of objections against the capacity of the quota to breathe life into the audiovisual industry of the Member States could be extended even further. The loopholes in the drafting of Article 4 demonstrate quite clearly, however, that the quota is not a panacea for the lack of creative activity in Europe.

Secondly, Article 47 (2) EC only allows the coordination of national legislation, not the adoption of positive regulatory measures for the promotion of the internal market.[76] Industrial policy measures going beyond the objective of the establishment of freedom of services cannot be based upon Articles 47 (2) and 55 EC, but only upon Article 308 EC.[77] Therefore, the insertion of the quota requirement in the TwF Directive cannot be justified by the need to protect European film production within the wider market.

It follows from what has been said so far that the European quota was not necessary for the creation of the internal market in broadcasting services. Therefore, it has not been correctly adopted on the basis of Articles 47 (2) and 55 EC. In the following section we will examine whether the European quota could have been based on Article 151 EC.

74. Graham *et al.*, *Impact Study*, p. 177.
75. Recital 20 to Dir. 89/552/EEC.
76. *See* Case C-376/98, *Federal Republic of Germany v. European Parliament and Council of the European Union* [2000] ECR I-2247 para. 83: 'the measures referred to in Article 100a (1) of the Treaty are intended to improve the conditions for the establishment and functioning of the internal market. To construe that article as meaning that it vests in the Community legislature a general power to regulate the internal market would not only be contrary to the express wording of the provisions cited above but would also be incompatible with the principle embodied in Article 3b of the EC Treaty (now Article 5 EC) that the powers of the Community are limited to those specifically conferred on it.'; Steindorff, *Grenzen der EG-Kompetenzen*, p. 97.
77. Niedobitek, *Cultural Dimension in EC Law*, p. 153; M. Pechstein, 'Subsidiarität der EG-Medienpolitik?' (1991) 13 DÖV, 540; Dolmans, 'Quotas Without Content', 331; contra Salvatore, 'Quotas on TV Programmes', 990.

4. ARTICLE 151 EC AS THE LEGAL BASIS FOR THE EUROPEAN QUOTA

Given that the audiovisual industry is determined both by economic as well as cultural interests, it is possible to conceive of the European quota as an instrument designed to protect European cultural identity through the improvement of the knowledge and dissemination of European culture. Even though cultural policy objectives played an important role in the legislative history of the European quota, no word was said about them in the preamble to Dir. 89/552/EEC.[78] Recital 20 of the preamble refers only to the need 'to promote markets of sufficient size for television productions in the Member States to recover necessary investments not only by establishing common rules opening up national markets but also by envisaging for European productions where practicable and by appropriate means a majority proportion in television programmes of all Member States'. If the quota provision was indeed based on cultural reasons related to this avowed industrial policy objective, this omission must have violated Article 253 EC. The infringement of the procedural requirement to state reasons was terminated in Dir. 97/36/EC, which mention Article 151 (4) EC in its preamble.[79] Without clearly saying so, the 25th recital suggests that there is a cultural agenda behind the quota. This view is reinforced by the 48th recital to Dir. 2007/65/EC, which states that on-demand audiovisual services 'should, where practicable, promote the production and distribution of European works and thus contribute actively to the promotion of cultural diversity.'

Could Article 151 (5) EC constitute the legal basis of the European quota provision? In order to answer this question, it is necessary to examine first whether the quota contributes to the achievement of the objectives envisaged in this provision. Subsequently, we will consider whether it pertains to one of the areas of Community action listed in Article 151 (2) EC.

4.1 Does the European Quota Affirm European Culture?

In accordance with the programmatic statement in Article 151 (1) EC, the European quota would have to contribute to 'the flowering of the cultures of the Member States, while respecting their national and regional diversity and at the same time bringing the common cultural heritage to the fore'.[80]

78. Explanatory comment to the Commission's original proposal, 6 June 1986, COM (86) 146 final/2, point 30; Communication from the Commission to the Council and the European Parliament on the application of Arts. 4 and 5 of Dir. 89/552/ Television without frontiers, 3 March 1994, COM (94) 57 final, p. 4; K. McDonald, 'How Would You Like Your Television: With or Without Borders and With or Without Culture – A New Approach to Media Regulation in the European Union' (1999) 22 Fordham Int'l L J, 2004.
79. Recital 25 to Dir. 97/36/EC.
80. On this programmatic statement *see* I. Katsirea, *Cultural Diversity and European Integration in Conflict and in Harmony* (Athens, Ant. N. Sakkoulas, 2001), p. 31 *et seq.*

In the following, certain arguments that have been raised against the cultural conception of the quota will be examined. First, the quota has been criticized for placing itself on the side of cultural protectionism without taking a definite stance towards the issue of the cultural implications of media flows. Secondly, small Member States have voiced concerns that the quota might fling the door of their audiovisual markets wide open to productions in one of the big languages. Lastly, the difficulties with the all-inclusive definition of a 'European work' in Article 6 will be highlighted.

4.2 The European Quota as a Means of Cultural Dissociation

The European quota's cultural conception has to be seen against the background of an affected dispute in communication studies concerning the role played by transnational flows of television programmes in the formation and development of cultural identities. While liberal internationalists favour the cross-fertilization of ideas facilitated by means of transnational flows of television programmes, their opponents warn against the resulting erosion of cultural identity.

The latter view, based on theories of media imperialism, was espoused by the UNESCO during the 1970s, when it proclaimed the need to establish a new world information and communication order (NWICO).[81] This new order would replace the present state of domination of the Third World by the developed countries, both in its economy and communications, by a more balanced flow of information. In order for vulnerable cultures to develop self-reliantly, they would need to dissociate themselves from the existing economic and political dependency structures. The theory of media imperialism has been criticized for its failure to grasp the complex process of reception by viewers of a television programme originating in a different culture.[82] It was argued that message reception is not a unidimensional process, that audiences interpret programmes in the light of their own cultural background.

The European quota is designed to slow the stream of US programmes, contributing thus to the dissociation of the European audiovisual industry from American cultural dominance. At first sight, it may appear that the drafters of the quota endorsed the discourse of media imperialism and transposed the NWICO problematic from the developing world to Europe. Hence, criticism was levelled against the Community for not having taken divergent views into account and for not having provided a well-grounded analysis of the relationship of cultural identity to television viewing. A commentator remarked sharply that Article 4 'would appear to be, at best, an intuitive thrust in the direction of a culture policy'.[83]

81. *See* Unesco, *Many Voices, One World: Towards a New, More Just and More Efficient World Information and Communication Order* (London, Kogan Page, 1980); C. J. Hamelink, *Cultural Autonomy in Global Communications: Planning National Information Policy* (London, Centre for the Study of Communications and Culture, 1988).
82. *See* C. Sparks and C. Roach, 'Editorial' (1990) 12 *Media, Culture and Society*, 275; M. Tracey, 'The Poisoned Chalice? International Television and the Idea of Dominance' (1985) (4) *Daedalus*, 17.
83. Keller, 'New Television without Frontiers Directive', 183.

Indeed, analysed along these lines, the European quota raises more questions than it provides answers. It conspicuously fails to answer the question as to why cultural identities in Europe are more affected by American productions than by European ones.[84] The assumption that European cultures share greater affinity is questionable. Europe embraces a multiplicity of very different cultures, which often display stronger ties with their non-European counterparts. Spanish culture is probably more akin to the Latin-American one than to Northern European cultures and Great Britain may find itself to be culturally more related to other Commonwealth countries than to the Balkans.[85]

However, communication scientists have by no means reached definite conclusions about the impact of the exposure to mass-mediated material.[86] The capitulation of science to the intricate problem under discussion is best captured in the following passage: 'It is claimed that this mass of material coming in from outside is both erasing traditional cultures and inhibiting the emergence of authentic cultural changes. There is no clear evidence that this is in fact happening, nor indeed any that it is not'.[87]

In view of these uncertainties, it is understandable that the European Community did not attempt to tackle the problem of the cultural impact of television along these lines. It approached it from a different angle instead, based on the forceful idea that the control of broadcasting by foreign productions has an injurious influence upon indigenous cultural life, an idea that is attractive to both the supporters and the opponents of the cultural domination thesis. It is precisely the atrophy of the European audiovisual industry due to the withdrawal of resources from domestic production that the European quota aims to fight in the first place. This is a cultural as much as an economic objective.

4.3 The European Quota: A Poisoned Chalice for Small European States?

Not surprisingly, the adoption of the European quota brought to the fore the long-standing divide between large and smaller European countries. While large countries with a strong audiovisual industry aspire to the improved distribution of their programmes, small countries fear that the flow of English, French and

84. *See* P. Schlesinger, 'From Cultural Protection to Political Culture? Media Policy and the European Union' in *Constructing Europe's Identity: The External Dimension*, L.-E. Cederman (ed.) (London, Lynne Rienner, 2001), pp. 91, 99.
85. J. D. Donaldson, ' "Television Without Frontiers": The Continuing Tension between Liberal Free Trade and European Cultural Integrity' (1996) 20 Fordham Int'l L J, 150, 155.
86. D. G. Carrie and A. S. C. Ehrenberg, 'Is Television All that Important?' (1992) 20 (4–5) *Intermedia*, 18; M. E. Price, 'Globalization and National Identity on Television' (1992) 20 *Intermedia*, 9.
87. T. Hollins, *Beyond Broadcasting: Into the Cable Age* (London, Broadcasting Research Unit, 1984), cited in Tracey, 'Poisoned Chalice', 38.
88. J. Drijvers, 'Community Broadcasting: A Manifesto for the Media Policy of Small European Countries' (1992) 14 *Media, Culture and Society*, 194; J. C. Burgelman and C. Pauwels,

German programmes into their audiovisual markets will be one-way with no flow in the opposite direction taking place.[88] These fears seem justified at first sight in view of the low audiovisual production capacity of small European countries linked to their restricted cultural or linguistic area. Their markets are confined, so that funding available for domestic production is limited. Their programmes are rarely successful in foreign markets, whereas their viewers are greatly exposed to imported programmes by way of a dense cable network.

Ironically, if the European quota produced the intended result – the increased circulation of programmes between the Member States – larger states would probably be in a better position to reap the benefit. However, monitoring reports have painted a different picture. The Commission has admitted that prime-time viewing is still dominated by domestic and American productions.[89] Highest audience ratings are attained by the transmission of national material. The proportion of non-national material in the European works transmitted has stagnated at a low level. It grew from 10.4 per cent in 1993 to 11.9 per cent in 2002 on primary channels, mainly public ones.[90] However, the share of qualifying transmission time devoted to European works in general has grown at a faster rate during the same period. As a result, non-national material now forms a slightly smaller proportion of the totality of European works broadcast than in 1993.[91]

Admittedly, smaller Member States that share a language with a larger neighbouring Member State, such as Austria, Belgium and Ireland, have larger proportions of imported European works shown on television. Larger Member States, such as France, Germany, Italy, Spain and the United Kingdom, have the smallest proportion. At the one end of the spectrum is Ireland where a majority proportion (53.3 per cent) of non-domestic European works is broadcast. At the other end of the spectrum is the United Kingdom with virtually zero per cent of non-domestic European works. Between 1993 and 2002, the share of non-domestic European works grew in those Member States where the proportion was already high, while it declined in those Member States where it was historically low.[92] Small Member States that do not share the same language with a larger State, such as Greece and Portugal, continue to broadcast only a small proportion of such works. Consequently, the divide between smaller and larger countries as regards the transmission of imported European works cannot be attributed to the European quota but to the linguistic and cultural affinity between some of these countries as well as the lower price and better quality of works from larger neighbouring countries.

As the Commission admitted in its Issues Paper, these trends suggest that 'Article 4 may have reinforced national objectives to protect and encourage the domestic content sector rather than fostering a truly European market in

---

'Audiovisual Policy and Cultural Identity in Small European States: The Challenge of a Unified Market' (1992) 14 *Media, Culture and Society*, 177.

89. COM (94) 96 final, 27.
90. European Commission, Issues Paper for the Liverpool Audiovisual Conference. Cultural Diversity and the Promotion of European and Independent Audiovisual Production, July 2005, 4.
91. Graham *et al.*, *Impact Study*, p. 183.
92. *Ibid.*, 108.

programming and encouraging the exchange/circulation of European TV programmes within Europe.'[93] Findings of a considerable decrease in the programming of domestic films in the early years after the adoption of the Directive do not hold true anymore.[94] The total volume of European works has risen over the period from 1993 to 2002.[95] This growth is mainly attributable to a rise in domestic content. European programming is perceived to be too informed by a specific national culture and taste to appeal beyond its home market, while US programming tends to attract a global audience.[96] The substantial trade deficit between television companies in the European Union and North America remains. The impact study has not been able to prove that, in the absence of the quotas, the trade deficit with the US would have been larger nor that measures to promote the circulation of programmes within the EU have also promoted exports.[97]

So as to improve the exchange of European programmes within Europe, the Commission envisaged the creation of incentives for the increased distribution of European co-productions. It was argued that such incentives would possibly lead to a more integrated and internationally competitive 'European' film industry and foster a deeper understanding of Europe's cultural diversity and a wider acceptance of the European integration process.[98] Only a minority of stakeholders, mainly film producers, were in favour of a sub-quota for non-domestic European works or of a recommendation to encourage the circulation of such works. These proposals found their way into recital 50 of the AVMS Directive, which urges Member States, when implementing Article 4, to make provision for broadcasters to include an adequate share of co-produced European works or of European works of non-domestic origin.

It is submitted that engaging in more European co-productions would not necessarily enhance Europe's cultural diversity. Intervention of this sort would only favour those Member States best able to support co-production due to the size of their broadcasting industries.[99] The proposal that broadcasters should transmit an adequate share of European works of non-domestic origin is entirely consistent with the European quota's rationale. It signifies an effort to stimulate the

93. European Commission, Issues Paper for the Liverpool Audiovisual Conference. Cultural Diversity and the Promotion of European and Independent Audiovisual Production, July 2005, 4.
94. *See* E. de Bens, M. Kelly and M. Bakke (1992) 'Television Content: Dallasification of Culture?' in *Dynamics of Media Politics: Broadcast and Electronic Media in Western Europe*, K. Siune and W. Truetzschler (eds) (London, Sage, 1992), pp. 75, 91, 94.
95. According to the impact study, the average proportion of qualifying transmission hours devoted to European works for the channels covered has risen from 52.1 per cent in 1993 to 57.4 per cent in 2002. An overall increase in the period 1999–2004 is also documented in the Sixth Report from the Commission to the European Parliament, the Council, the European Economic and Social Committee and the Committee of the Regions on the application of Directive 89/552/EEC 'Television without Frontiers', 24 October 2007, COM (2007) 452 final, 6.
96. Graham *et al.*, *Impact Study*, p. 183.
97. *Ibid.*
98. European Commission, Issues Paper, 4.
99. Written contribution of the Department for Culture, Media and Sport <www.ec.europa.eu/avpolicy/reg/tvwf/modernisation/consultation_2003/contributions/index_en.htm>, 6 June 2007.

cross-border movement of programmes, not just the transmission of a majority proportion of European works.

While the increased circulation of European works would also contribute to the filling of the European quota, causality does not work the other way round. Even though the European quota is overfilled in most Member States, viewers are not being exposed to foreign programmes but get to see more of the same home-grown material. The Commission noted in its Issues Paper that national language quotas may have acted as barrier to intra-Community trade.[100] Indeed, the paradoxical coexistence of European and national quotas is the most eloquent admission of defeat in view of cultural segregation in Europe. It also brings the point home that filling the quota has little to do with the exchange of European programmes. The impact study suggests that Member States operating significant additional cultural requirements have attained higher percentages of European works in their schedules and yet such requirements obstruct intra-Community trade.

The Commission's admonition to Member States to bear in mind the quota's industrial policy rationale when implementing the Directive is understandable against this backdrop. However, the fact that this admonition only found its way into the Directive's recitals speaks volumes. Imposing an obligation on private broadcasters to transmit works from other Member States would go against their commercial logic and their need to prioritize audience share over programme choice. The public funding received by public broadcasters would perhaps allow them to carry such a public service obligation. However, this would only exacerbate the inroads made into the broadcasting sovereignty of the Member States by the already existing European quota rule. Obliging them to transmit non-national works would be quite incompatible with the pronouncement in the Amsterdam Protocol that Member States are responsible for conferring, defining and organizing the public service remit.[101]

Given that there is little scope for the adoption of further, more binding measures at Community level to increase the circulation of European works of non-domestic origin, it becomes quite clear that cultural diversity should be protected otherwise. The preference of national audiences for domestically-produced content should be respected and content regulations at the national level should be accepted as the most efficient way of promoting the cultures of the Member States.

It is very doubtful whether the increase in the volume of European works in the last decade can be attributed to the European quota in the first place or rather to domestic measures and the viewers' preference for domestic content. Even if the European quota has had an impact on the European schedule output, it is even more doubtful that it has strengthened the European audiovisual industry. The many loopholes in Article 4 have rendered it powerless to improve the balance of trade with the US and to lessen the reliance on American programmes.

Consequently, even though the European quota is not the harmful device smaller countries have imagined, its potential for contributing to the invigoration

100. European Commission, Issues Paper, 4.
101. Protocol on the System of Public Broadcasting in the Member States, OJ C 340/109, 1997.

of their programme industries and hence to the flowering of their audiovisual cultures is limited.

4.4 WHAT IS A 'EUROPEAN WORK'?

The cultural conception of the European quota is not only marred by the lack of commitment of governments and market players to overcome the entrenched partitioning of national markets. In view of the more and more international character of the television business it is also unlikely that the definition of 'European works' under Article 1(n) of the AVMS Directive (ex Article 6 of the TwF Directive) can guarantee the expression of a European cultural identity.[102]

Article 6 distinguished in a rather complex way between European works per se and other works, which were deemed to be European works. The first category was divided into three sub-categories: works from the Member States, works from European third States party to the European Convention on Transfrontier Television and works from European third countries with which the Community has concluded agreements relating to the audiovisual sector.

So as to determine when a work originates from a certain country, Article 6 (2) stipulated rules of origin. Emphasis was placed on the country of residence of the authors and workers, who made the work, and on the establishment of the producer, who either made the programme or supervised and controlled it or made a preponderant contribution to the total co-production costs. The criterion of the producer's establishment, responsive to industrial policy objectives, did not guarantee the European character of a work, since it could also be fulfilled by American subsidiaries. The criterion of the workers' residence, more sensitive to cultural considerations, was only half-heartedly committed to them, since it could not guarantee a specifically European character of the works either. The workers' nationality would have been more suitable a criterion for this purpose.

The second category, that of fictitious European works, comprised works fulfilling the criterion of the personnel's residence, but none of the conditions related to the producer. These were considered to be European works under Article 6 (5) 'to an extent corresponding to the proportion of the contribution of Community co-producers to the total production costs'. The idea of measuring the Europeaness of a work by financial criteria alone was abstruse.[103] What is more, the said formula could not always account for the source of financing of an audiovisual work, given that co-producers do not always co-finance a production. The source of financing is hence not necessarily apparent from the production budget.[104]

---

102. J. Harrison and L. Woods, 'Television Quotas: Protecting European Culture?' (2001) 1 ENT L R, 11.
103. *Ibid.*, 12.
104. Commission of the European Communities, Commission staff working paper on certain legal aspects relating to cinematographic and other audiovisual works, 11 April 2001, SEC (2001) 619, 10.

The revised Dir. 97/36/EC added a new category of international co-productions with third countries under a newly inserted fourth paragraph. This category differed from the European works per se under Article 6 (1), in that the works did not have to be made with authors and workers residing in the Community or in European third States party to the European Convention on Transfrontier Television.

This short overview of the TwF Directive's requirements on the European origin of works falling under the quota demonstrates that an all-embracing definition was adopted, which tried to determine what is Europe along cultural rather than geo-political lines.[105] Still, the outcome was rather bewildering, given that a work entirely produced in Vladivostock was considered to be European. While, however, the satisfaction of the quota requirement by films from Vladivostock was unlikely to make a difference in practical terms, the same did not apply to the inclusion of international co-productions between Member States and third countries.

This aspect of Article 6 has been fiercely criticized, not only because it diluted the notion of a European identity to be protected by the European quota, but also because it disguised films produced by the major US production and distribution companies as 'European works'.[106] The distinction between audiovisual material embedded in the multinational production and distribution chains and such that is not integrated in this structure is decisive, since only the latter provide a space for genuine, European cultural expression in the film sector. Article 6 dressed the wolf in sheep's clothing by putting more emphasis on the participation of European creative personnel than on European investment. These inconsistencies are indicative of the lack of political will behind the European quota.

The consultation process for the review of the Directive posed the question whether a more detailed definition of 'European works' was needed so as to increase legal certainty for operators given that Member States have implemented this definition in many different ways. The views were sharply divided concerning the need for further harmonization of the definition of 'European works'. Some Member States perceived the current definition as being satisfactory, giving them sufficient flexibility to implement it in relation to their production landscape.[107] Others were in favour of harmonization and

105. R. Collins, *Broadcasting and Audio-Visual Policy in the European Single Market* (London, John Libbey, 1994), p. 71.

106. S. Venturelli, *Liberalizing the European Media: Politics, Regulation and the Public Sphere* (Oxford, Clarendon, 1998), p. 204; *see* speech by J. Dondelinger, 'Broadcasting in the Single Market' in *Regulating the Audiovisual Industry: The Second Phase*, D. Goldberg and R. Wallace (eds), Current EC Legal Development Series (London, Butterworths, 1991), p. 193: 'This so-called "quota system" has become much less controversial than it was at the time of the adoption of the Directive. Our American friends have learned to live with the idea. Indeed, transantlantic co-operation between companies has never been so great.'

107. *See* for instance the written contributions of the Federal Republic of Germany and of the United Kingdom <www.ec.europa.eu/avpolicy/reg/tvwf/modernisation/consultation_2003/contributions/index_en.htm>, 7 June 2007.

proposed following the definition contained in the European Convention on Cinematographic Co-production.[108]

In view of this controversy, the core of the current definition was left untouched. Its place was moved from Article 6 to Article 1 (n) of Chapter I together with all the other definitions. The only two amendments of the 'European works' definition that were already suggested by the Commission in its initial proposal and that were agreed upon in the Common position are the following. First, the third category of European works, namely those originating from other European third countries with which the Community has concluded agreements related to the audiovisual sector, has been modified. Whereas Article 6 (3) also applied to productions made exclusively by producers established in one or more of these European third countries provided that the authors and workers were resident in one or more European States, the new definition only applies to co-productions fulfilling the conditions defined in each of these agreements. Secondly, the last category of fictitious partially European works under Article 6 (5) has been removed, presumably due to their very tenuous characterization as 'European'. However, the category of international co-productions of doubtful European credentials under Article 6 (4) has found its way into the AVMS Directive.

All in all, it is questionable whether Article 1(n) is conducive to the protection of European cultural diversity. Neither this definition nor, for that matter, the European quota rule promote programmes representative of European cultures.[109] The main concern of the Directive is the development of commercial large-scale productions appealing to an international audience.[110] In this context, the introduction of 'cultural' aspects in the 'European works' definition has been contemplated. However, the adoption of cultural criteria would exacerbate the intrusiveness of the quota mechanism without succeeding in refining its coarse nature.

5. DOES THE EUROPEAN QUOTA FALL WITHIN THE SCOPE OF ARTICLE 151 EC?

Having posed some questions rather than provided definitive answers in respect of the quota's capacity to serve as a tool of cultural policy, we will now consider whether the European quota falls within the substantive scope of Article 151 EC.

---

108. *See* Communication from the Commission to the Council, the European Parliament, the European Economic and Social Committee and the Committee of the Regions, The future of European Regulatory Audiovisual Policy, 15 December 2003, COM (2003) 784 final, 13.
109. ARD and ZDF, 'EG-Politik im Bereich des Rundfunks', 91. Compare the cultural quotas of the Australian Content Standard as interpreted in the judgment of the High Court of Australia, *Project Blue Sky v. Australian Broadcasting Authority* (1998) HCA 28, 28 April 1998, S41/1997. The main criterion for Australian content is whether a programme reflects the Australian identity and culture, while the nationality of the actors, authors or producers is less important. *See* C. B. Graber, 'The Stumbling Block of Trade Liberalisation' in *The WTO and Global Convergence in Telecommunications and Audio-Visual Services*, D. Geradin and D. Luff (eds) (Cambridge, Cambridge University Press, 2004), pp. 165, 183.
110. *See* recital 27 to Dir. 97/36/EC.

The audio-visual sector is mentioned in the 4th indent to the second paragraph of this provision. Nevertheless, it is only covered in so far as it is subservient to artistic and literary creation, instead of being open to Community activity in its entirety. It is therefore pertinent to know whether the European quota encompasses artistic works only. This is not the case. Even though certain categories of works such as news, sports events and games are excluded from the ambit of Article 4, the same does not apply to flow programmes such as studio discussions. It follows that the quota provision is not designed to promote artistic and literary creation only. Consequently, it could not be based on the fourth indent of Article 151 (2) EC.

However, even if one took the view that measures in the audiovisual area not pertaining to arts and literature also fall under Article 151 (2) EC, 4th indent, the result would not be different. The quota rule could still not be based on this provision, given that harmonization of the laws and regulations of the Member States is prohibited under Article 151 (5) EC. Even though the scope of the exclusion of harmonization is contentious, there is no doubt that it applies to measures taken on the basis of Article 151 EC.

Article 151 (4) EC could not serve as the legal basis of the European quota either. This provision does not constitute an independent legal basis. It merely confirms the legality of the already established Community practice to regulate cultural issues on the basis of its functional powers and urges the Community institutions to maintain it, perhaps attaching greater weight than hitherto to cultural aspects. This is why Article 151 (4) EC presupposes the existence of a disparate Treaty provision upon which Community action is based.

The foregoing considerations lead to the conclusion that the European quota rule could not have been adopted on the basis of Article 151 EC. Given that there is no other Treaty provision that could serve as the quota's legal basis, it follows that the European quota rule was adopted *ultra vires*.

6. THE LEGAL NATURE OF THE EUROPEAN QUOTA

The European quota rule that was adopted outside the Community's powers can only encroach upon the Member States' competence in the area of broadcasting if it is legally binding upon them, if they are obliged, in other words, to implement it in their national legislation.

Doubts have been expressed in this respect in view of the soft wording utilized in Article 4, the result of a difficult compromise reached between those Member States in favour of and others opposed to the European quota.[111] Article 4 (1) in its first sentence only requires Member States to ensure 'where practicable' and 'by appropriate means' that the majority proportion of the transmission time is attained. The second sentence of the same paragraph makes a concession to the 'broadcasters' informational, educational, cultural and entertainment responsibilities to its

111. Answer given by M. Bangemann on behalf of the Commission to K. Collins, OJ C 97/22, 1990.

viewing public' and gives them a leeway to achieve the quota 'progressively, on the basis of suitable criteria'. This wording represents a departure from the Commission's initial proposal and from a European Parliament recommendation to adopt a stricter formulation.

It is, however, not possible to reach the conclusion, on the basis of this flexible wording alone, that the European quota is legally non-binding. An argument in support of the opposite view has been derived from Article 249 (3) EC according to which '[a] directive shall be binding, as to the result to be achieved, upon each Member State to which it is addressed'.[112] If the Member States regarded the quota provision as legally unenforceable, they could have adopted it in the form of a recommendation or opinion or they could have included an explicit reservation in the text of the Directive.[113] However, this argument is not conclusive since it is the content of a piece of legislation, not its designation, which determines its legal nature.[114]

A closer look at the wording of Article 4 concurs with the view that this provision has binding force. First, Article 4 (2), the so-called non-slipback clause, specifies the average for 1988 in the Member State concerned as an alternative target, where the proportion laid down in Article 4 (1) cannot be attained. This clause is in fact a white elephant, given that the vast majority of channels in 1988 (or in 1990 in respect of the Hellenic Republic and of the Portuguese Republic) were public and transmitted a majority proportion of European works anyhow. Nonetheless, Article 4 (2) reinforces the notion that the quota rule contains a legal obligation.

Secondly, the close monitoring of Article 4 by the Commission suggests that Member States are obliged to achieve the proportion specified therein. How could the Commission ensure the application of the quota rule in accordance with Article 4 (3), if the Member States were not required to cooperate? This supervisory role of the Commission has in fact been designed to offset the flexible wording of Article 4 (1).[115]

Lastly, the comparison between the wording used in Article 4 (1) and that used in Article 3a (1) of Dir. 97/36/EC also pleads for the legally binding nature of the former. While Member States *shall* ensure that broadcasters reserve a majority proportion for European works under Article 4 (1), they *may* take measures to ensure that broadcasters do not broadcast on an exclusive basis events of major importance for society. The stronger wording used in Article 4 (1) supports the view that Member States are under a legal duty to implement the quota provision.

---

112. N. Klute, 'Die Produktionsquote, ein Protokoll und die Sache mit der Rundfunkfreiheit – eine Zusammenführung europäischen und deutschen Rundfunkrechts' (1991) 3 AfP 595, 596; Communication from the Commission to the Council and the European Parliament on the application of Arts. 4 and 5 of Dir. 89/552/EEC 'TwF', 15 July1996, COM (96) 302 final, 75.
113. BVerfG, 22 March 1995 – 2 BvG 1/89, (1995) 2 AfP, 483, 487.
114. M. Pechstein, 'Die Bedeutung von Protokollerklärungen zu Rechtsakten der EG' (1990) 3 EuR, 264; Eberle, 'Das europäische Recht und die Medien', 426.
115. Answer given by M. Bangemann, OJ C 97/22, 1990.

It follows from the textual interpretation of the quota provision that, even though the Member States are endowed with considerable discretion as to the means of reaching the envisaged aim, they are not allowed to decide whether they wish to introduce a quota in their legislation. The 'where practicable' exception, 'indicating that attainment of the objectives can be overridden by technical constraints or economic imperatives'[116], underlines precisely the binding character of the quota rule, since it permits a derogation only in cases where compliance with it would be impossible.

In order to reach a definitive conclusion on the nature of the quota provision, it is however essential to consider also the much-discussed declarations contained in the minutes annexed to the TwF Directive. The most pertinent of these declarations is the fifteenth, a common declaration of the Council and the Commission, stating that 'the Member States agree, from a political standpoint, to be bound by Articles 4 and 5 as regards the achievement of the objectives stipulated therein'. Martin Bangemann, Vice President of the European Commission responsible for DG III, also gave a statement on 11 October 1989 in the European Parliament that the quota rules were only 'politically binding' and not 'juridically binding' and that proceedings could only be initiated in very extreme cases of non-compliance with Article 4 of the Directive.[117] Are these statements capable of depriving the European quota provision of its legal force?

There is a large degree of consensus that declarations, in view of their internal character, do not have legal force.[118] This is also the position taken by the European Court, which held that a legal act 'must be assessed in the light of its terms and therefore cannot be restricted by reservations or statements which might have been made in the course of drawing up the measure concerned'.[119] It is, however, unclear in how far recourse can be had to declarations as interpretative instruments.

With regard to the European quota, some take the view that it should be interpreted in the light of the declarations. This would be consistent with the Council of Europe Convention on Transfrontier Television, which excludes the quota provision contained therein from the arbitration clause.[120] A significant drawback of such an interpretative technique is that declarations are not published. Legal certainty would hence be undermined if they were to be taken into account. This objection has been countered with the argument that procedural rights of third parties could not possibly be affected given that the quota provision, not being directly effective, would have to be implemented into national law first.[121]

---

116. *Ibid.*
117. Collins, *Broadcasting and Audio-Visual Policy*, p. 71; Pechstein, 'Bedeutung von Protokollerklärungen', 263.
118. Pechstein, 'Bedeutung von Protokollerklärungen', 250; von Bogdandy, 'Europäischer Protektionismus', 13.
119. Case 38/69, *Commission of the European Communities v. Italian Republic* [1970] ECR 47.
120. European Convention on Transfrontier Television of 5 May 1989 as amended by Protocol (ETS No. 171) of 1 October 1998, Art. 10 (2) 2.
121. Everling, 'Brauchen wir "Solange III"?', 219.

Member States would not have an obligation to this end if the declarations had legal effect. Consequently, an action raised on the basis of the quota rule would founder on the non-transposition of this rule into national law, not on a procedural consideration of the declarations.[122]

This argument is of theoretical value only given that the quota rule has been transposed in the laws of the Member States. Nonetheless, there are further forceful arguments militating against the use of declarations for the purposes of interpretation of the quota provision.

In European Community law, textual and teleological methods of interpretation are primarily used whereas historical interpretation only plays a marginal role. The Court has ruled that declarations recorded in the Council minutes at the time of the adoption of a legal act can only be used for the purpose of interpreting it if reference is made to the content of the declaration in the wording of the provision in question.[123] Since no such reference was made to the declaration in question in the text of the TwF Directive, it cannot be used for the interpretation of the European quota provision.

Furthermore, it follows from an earlier judgment of the European Court that an interpretation based on a Council declaration cannot be at odds with the actual wording of the directive.[124] The textual interpretation of the quota rule has showed its legally binding character. Given that the declarations are at variance with the legal obligation contained in the quota rule, they cannot be taken into account. The inconsistency between the declarations and the wording of Article 4 also emerges from the fact that the unanimity that would have been required for the amendment of the Directive under Article 149 (2) EEC has never been achieved. This procedural requirement would have been circumvented, if the declarations, which were adopted under Article 57 (2), 66 EC with qualified-majority voting, were to be taken into account.

Accordingly, the legally binding nature of the European quota provision is not affected by the declarations contained in the minutes annexed to the Directive. This is also the reason why the German Constitutional Court reproached the Federal Government for making do with mere declarations instead of insisting that the quota's non-binding character be laid down in the Directive's text.[125]

A different question is whether the European Commission is obliged to exercise self-restraint with regard to the initiation of Treaty infringement proceedings under Article 226 EC against Member States failing to attain the proportion required by Article 4. Mr. Bangemann's statement, at least, suggests this. However, no weight can be attached to the personal opinion of a single member of a Community institution. To hold otherwise, would be to allow a Commissioner's declaration to bring about legal effects, endangering the uniform interpretation of

122. Pechstein, 'Bedeutung von Protokollerklärungen', 265–266.
123. Case C-292/89, *The Queen v. The Immigration Appeal Tribunal, ex parte Gustaff Desiderius Antonissen* [1991] ECR 745, para. 18.
124. Case 429/85, *Commission v. Italy* [1988] ECR 843.
125. BVerfG, 22 March 1995 – 2 BvG 1/89, (1995) 2 AfP 483, 487.

Community law. As far as the declarations contained in the minutes are concerned, they could not be cited in Article 226 proceedings given that Article 226 infringement proceedings are designed to protect the Community legal order and not individual rights of the plaintiff.[126] Therefore, previous Commission actions have no significance and the Member State concerned has no legitimate expectation that it will not be prosecuted.

At most, the Commission might be politically obliged to abstain from bringing the violation of the European quota provision before the European Court. However, the Commission does not seem to recognize such a political obligation. In its first Communication on the application of Articles 4 and 5 of Dir. 89/552 it stated that it would refrain from initiating infringement proceedings against defaulting states at this stage, meaning that this possibility was not excluded for the future.[127] Indeed, proceedings were opened against the United Kingdom for an alleged failure to fulfil its obligations under Articles 4 and 5 with regard to non-domestic satellite services.[128] These proceedings were only suspended owing to the willingness of the United Kingdom to adapt its legislation to the European quota requirement. Therefore, no guarantee exists that the Commission will not enforce Article 4 in future by bringing an infringement to the attention of the Court.[129]

7. THE COMPATIBILITY OF THE EUROPEAN QUOTA WITH THE WTO LEGAL ORDER

Ever since the adoption of the TwF Directive, the United States have contended that the European quota restricts non-European programming in contravention of the General Agreement on Tariffs and Trade (GATT). This final section examines whether the quota provision not only violates principles of the Community legal order but also of the World Trade Organization (WTO) legal order. The Agreement establishing the WTO and other multilateral agreements, including the General Agreement on Trade in Services (GATS), was concluded on 15 April 1994 as the outcome of the Uruguay Round of Negotiations that had begun in 1986.[130]

---

126. Pechstein, 'Bedeutung von Protokollerklärungen', 259; von Bogdandy, 'Europäischer Protektionismus', 13.
127. Communication from the Commission to the Council and the European Parliament on the application of Arts. 4 and 5 of Dir. 89/552/ Television without frontiers. Brussels, 3 March 1994, COM (94) 57 final, 21.
128. Case C-222/94, *Commission v. United Kingdom* [1996] ECRI- 4025, para. 72.
129. *See* Third Communication from the Commission to the Council and the European Parliament on the application of Art. 4 and 5 of Directive 89/552/EEC 'Television without Frontiers' for the period 1995–96, 3 April 1998, COM (98) 199 final, 58: 'The Commission reserves the right to take action against Member States not meeting the objectives of Arts. 4 and 5'.
130. Marrakech Agreement Establishing the World Trade Organization, 15 April 1994, Final Act Embodying the Results of the Uruguay Round of Multilateral Trade Negotiations, (1994) 33 ILM 1140 (hereafter referred to as the WTO Agreement); General Agreement on Trade in Services, 15 April 1994, (1994) 33 ILM 1167 (hereafter referred to as GATS).

The original GATT Agreement of 1947[131] has been incorporated into the new GATT Agreement of 1994.[132] Initially, the European Economic Community was not a Contracting Party of GATT 1947 but was nonetheless considered to be bound by its substantive provisions.[133] The European Community is a Contracting Party to GATT 1994 and an original Member of the WTO.

According to the United States government, the GATT provisions breached by Article 4 of the Directive are the Most Favoured Nation clause (MFN) under Article I of the GATT Agreement, the National Treatment clause under Article III and the Ban on Quantitative Restrictions under Article XI of the same Agreement. Before entering into an examination of these provisions, it is necessary to address the question whether the GATT Agreement which governs trade in *products* is applicable at all to broadcasting *services*. The main arrow in the quiver of the European Community has been that the transmission of television programmes, restricted by the European quota rule, constitutes a service and is hence not covered by the GATT Agreement.

The transmission of television signals has constantly been classified as a service in the case-law of the European Court of Justice.[134] In the case *Sacchi*, it has been distinguished from the 'material, sound recordings, films, apparatus and other products used for the diffusion of television signals', which are subject to the provisions relating to freedom of movement of goods.[135] The US invoke precisely this distinction by claiming that the quota rules not only limit the transmission of US programmes, but also the sale of videotapes on which these are recorded.

In opposition to this argument, one could point to the *Spanish dubbing licence case*, where the European Court held that the distribution of films comes under the freedom to provide services.[136] Advocate-General van Gerven explained that 'the essential feature of the exploitation of a film does not lie in that physical trade in film bands' but 'in the producer's making available the rights to distribution in a specific market together with the temporary transfer of public exhibition in that market'.[137] This is attributable to the fact that cinematographic films are communicated to the public by performances that can be repeated at will, not by the circulation of material objects, as it is the case with books or video-tapes.[138]

131. General Agreement on Tariffs and Trade, 30 October 1947, (1947) 55 UNTS 187 (hereafter referred to as GATT 1947).
132. General Agreement on Tariffs and Trade, 15 April 1994, Marrakech Agreement Establishing the World Trade Organization, Annex 1A, (1994) 33 ILM 1153 (hereafter referred to as GATT 1994).
133. Case C-21-4/72, *International Fruit Company v. Productschap voor Groenten en Fruit* [1972] ECR 1219.
134. Case 155/73, *Guiseppe Sacchi* [1974] ECR 409, 427 para. 6; Case 52/79, *Procureur du Roi v. J.V.C. Debauve* [1980] ECR 833.
135. Case 155/73, *Guiseppe Sacchi* [1974] ECR 409, 427 para. 7.
136. Case C-17/92, *Federación de Distribuidores Cinematográficos (FEDICINE) v. Spanish State* [1993] ECR-I 2239 para. 9 *et seq.*
137. Opinion of Advocate-General van Gerven, paras 8–9.
138. *Ibid.*, para. 8; Case 262/81, *Coditel v. Ciné Vog Films* ('Coditel II') [1982] ECR 3381 para. 11; compare Cases 60 and 61/84, *Cinéthèque SA and Others v. Fédération nationale des cinémas français* [1985] ECR 2605.

According to this reasoning, the quota affects the supply of services from non-European countries, which is not covered by the GATT.

However, it is reasonable to be at least sceptical of the argument that the distinction between goods and services under Community law has to apply in the same way within the GATT. First of all, this distinction is less important in Community law than it might seem at first sight given that the freedoms of movement of goods and services have been largely interpreted in a parallel manner by the European Court. Moreover, the GATT agreement contains an explicit provision, Article IV, which allows contracting parties to maintain screen quotas relating to cinematograph films. In view of the similarity of television programmes with cinema films, it becomes apparent from Article IV, the so-called Cinema Exception, that television programmes may equally be considered to be goods.

Are television programmes to be classified as goods, their compatibility with the GATT Agreement has to be examined. The Most Favoured Nation (MFN) principle requires each Contracting party to grant immediately and unconditionally to all other Contracting parties any advantage granted to any other country. An exception from the MFN principle is allowed within the framework of customs unions, ergo in the case of the Community, under Article XXIV. However, the Community does not only include within the quota regime works originating from the Member States but also works from European third countries. This privileged treatment is not covered by the Article XXIV exception for customs unions. As a result, the European quota is inconsistent with the MFN principle in that it only guarantees the distribution of a majority proportion of European works, not of works of non-European origin.

Furthermore, the European quota is incompatible with the national treatment principle. Article III (4) requires that imported products be treated equally as domestically produced products, once they have crossed the border. The quantity of non-European works which can be broadcast and therefore distributed in the Community is limited, whereas no such limitation exists in respect of European works.

However, it has been argued that the European quota rule might fall under the above-mentioned 'Cinema Exception' in Article IV GATT.[139] This provision only refers to cinematograph films, not to television programmes. It is true that television was in its infancy at the time of the adoption of the GATT so that Article IV could not have regulated screen quotas for television programmes.[140] Nonetheless, the extension of this provision to television programmes by means of its dynamic interpretation is problematic, given that a GATT working party formed in the 1960s was unable to agree on a resolution to this effect.[141]

139. Von Bogdandy, 'Europäischer Protektionismus', 16; Donaldson, 'Television without Frontiers', 121, 134 *et seq.*

140. Salvatore, 'Quotas on TV Programmes', 989; von Bogdandy, 'Europäischer Protektionismus', 16.

141. I. Bernier, 'Content Regulation in the Audio-Visual Sector and the WTO' in *The WTO and Global Convergence in Telecommunications and Audio-Visual Services*, D. Geradin and D. Luff (eds) (Cambridge, Cambridge University Press, 2004), pp. 215, 225.

Moreover, even if Article IV was to be interpreted extensively, the European quota would still not be exempted under this provision since it does not conform to the requirements of Article IV (b). This paragraph is an expression of the MFN principle and provides that screen-time should not be allocated, formally or in effect, among sources of supply. Given that the European quota violates the MFN principle by privileging works from European third countries, it also contravenes Article IV (b).

Finally, the quota cannot be justified on the basis of Article XX (f) either. This provision exempts the adoption or enforcement by any contracting party of measures imposed, *inter alia*, for the protection of national treasures of artistic, historic or archaeological value. European television programmes for the most part cannot be characterized as national treasures of historic value.

Lastly, it is necessary to consider whether the quota rule is also in breach of Article XI (1) GATT, which expressly prohibits quantitative restrictions and hence quotas. This is doubtful. The European quota does not restrict the importation of non-European programmes into the Community but only their use once the border has been crossed. The restriction on their transmission injures non-European audiovisual exports at most indirectly given that Community broadcasters are likely to purchase only as many programmes as they will be allowed to show. Article XI cannot, however, be taken to apply to internal regulations that do not hinder the actual importation but only the commercial exploitation of foreign products.

Alternatively, if trade in television programmes is classified as a service the compatibility of the European quota with the GATS agreement stands to question. The GATS agreement, adopted in the Uruguay Round, comprises audiovisual services with the aim of their progressive liberalization. The dispute between the European Community and the United States as regards the quota provision could not be settled within the framework of GATS. Representatives of the MPA (Motion Picture Association) proposed to Commission officials that there should be no reopening of the status of the TwF Directive in GATS 2000. The MPA suggested that less emphasis should be put on the removal of existing local content quotas in traditional broadcasting and more emphasis should be put on the prohibition of such requirements in digital products. This is precisely the stance that was taken by the United States in the GATS negotiations on services.[142]

In any event, even as things stand, the European quota cannot be regarded as violating the GATS despite the fact that the Community's proposal for the inclusion within the GATS of a general culture exception clause or of one limited to the audiovisual sector was turned down.[143] The MFN principle applies to services by virtue of Article II (1) GATS.[144] The European Community has notified an

142. Bernier, 'Content Regulation', p. 237.

143. Donaldson, 'Television without Frontiers', 139, 141 *et seq.*; Drijber, 'Revised Television without Frontiers Directive', 112; A. Tinel, 'Qu'est-ce que l'exception culturelle?' (2000) 435 RMUE 79.

144. A. Forrest, 'Can Community Support Measures have a Decisive Impact on European Film and Television Production?' (1996) 8 *European Business Journal*, 46.

elaborate exemption as far as this principle is concerned. According to the Annex on Article II Exemptions, this exemption cannot, however, be maintained for a period longer than 10 years. As far as the principle of national treatment is concerned, it does not directly apply to services under the GATS, but only in accordance with specific commitments entered into by the Contracting Parties. Since the Community and the Member States have not agreed to be bound by the national treatment principle in respect of television broadcasting, they are not in breach of this principle.

In sum, the European quota is currently in conformity with the GATS Agreement. However, it might violate the MFN and National Treatment principles of the GATT Agreement, which are fundamental to the WTO legal order. The question of the quota's conformity with the GATT Agreement remained unresolved at the end of the Uruguay Round negotiations and has not been raised again since.[145]

8. CONCLUSION

The European quota provision has been legally underpinned by the need to eliminate obstacles arising from differences in national legislation on the promotion of European works. Besides this free movement objective, the European quota pursues an avowed industrial policy and an implied cultural policy objective. The economic aim of boosting European audiovisual production goes hand in hand with the cultural aim of protecting European cultural identity by ensuring a minimum presence of European broadcasts in television programmes.

This article has shown that the European quota was adopted *ultra vires* since it was not necessary for the creation of the internal market in the programme industry. The European Court has ruled that the main purpose of a Directive determines its legal basis while the presence of accessory elements does not justify the recourse to other provisions from which these elements emanate. However, this case-law is not applicable in the case of the European quota, which cannot be classified as an accessory element of the Directive.[146] Nor does the situation here resemble the *Titanium Dioxide* case where the measure in question pursued a twofold aim and necessitated the choice between two disparate provisions. The European quota rule does not raise this issue given that it is not covered by the Directive's legal basis in the first place. The present case is more akin to the *Tobacco Advertising* case. The Court found that the Tobacco Advertising Directive did not actually contribute to the free movement of goods or services nor to the elimination of distortions of competition. Similarly, the European quota does not

---

145. Bernier, 'Content Regulation', p. 226.
146. Case C-300/89, *Commission v. Council* [1991] ECR 2867 (*Titanium Dioxide* case); Case C-70/88, *Parliament v. Council* [1991] ECR I- 2041; Case C-155/91, *Commission v. Council* [1993] ECR I-939 para. 7; Case C-271/94, *European Parliament v. Council* [1996] ECR I-1689 paras 32–33.

serve its internal market objective. Also, in *Tobacco Advertising*, Article 129 (4) did not constitute an alternative legal basis for the Directive on ground of its exclusion of harmonization measures. The European quota could not have been based on Article 151 EC for the same reason.[147]

Not only is the European quota legally unjustifiable. It is also flawed in terms of how far it is capable of attaining its industrial and cultural policy objectives. The quota is not an effective mechanism to promote the emergence of economically viable secondary markets for European productions since it imposes onerous obligations on certain categories of broadcasters while others can circumvent it in manifold ways. The increasing domination of prime time viewing by domestic and American productions proves that the quota has not succeeded in reversing the trend.

The attempt to construct an exclusionary European identity by projecting the threat of American cultural influence is misconceived. Whether we want it or not, the US is economically Europe's Other, but not culturally.[148] The English language not only serves as a European lingua franca; it also exposes Europe to the American civilization.[149] American programmes draw Europeans together. Viewers' preferences are, however, even more for domestic productions than for American ones. In most Member States, the quota is filled with national material that attracts highest audience ratings. The fact that Article 4 fails to reserve a percentage for non-domestic productions is the most eloquent admission of defeat in view of cultural segregation in Europe.

The odds have been against the European quota in the process of modernization of the TwF Directive. The emergence of new digital services giving rise to the proliferation of thematic and pay-per-view channels means that compliance with the quota and its monitoring on the basis of the concept of a television channel have become increasingly impracticable.[150] Also, Community intervention is harder to justify now that the scarcity of television broadcasting bandwidth has been overcome.

The Commission has finally admitted that monitoring and enforcement of Articles 4 and 5 of the Directive at national level are deficient. These provisions

---

147. This is not to say that the European quota provision alone would have been capable of invalidating the TwF Directive altogether. In the case of the Tobacco Advertising Directive a multiplicity of flaws led to its annulment. The judgment of the Court in Cases C-95-98/99 and Case C-180/99, *Khalil* [2001] ECR I- 7413 suggests that the extension of Community competence to matters not covered by a legal basis will possibly be tolerated by the Court. *See* M. Dougan, 'Vive La Différence? Exploring the Legal Framework for Reflexive Harmonization within the Single European Market' in *Annual of German and European Law*, R. Miller and P. Zumbansen (eds) (Oxford, Berghahn Books, 2003), p. 113.
148. C. Shore, 'Inventing the "Peoples' Europe": Critical Approaches to European Community "Cultural Policy"' (1993) 28 MAN 793.
149. P. Flora, S. Kuhnle and D. Urwin (eds), *State Formation, Nation-Building and Mass Politics in Europe: The Theory of Stein Rokkan* (Oxford, Oxford University Press, 1999), p. 90.
150. *See* Third Communication from the Commission to the Council and European Parliament on the application of Arts. 4 and 5, 3 April 1998, COM (1998) 199 final.

are not systematically monitored and the regulatory authorities do not apply sanctions against channels that fail to comply with them.[151] It has been proposed that in order to improve the monitoring of the application of these provisions at national level, the bi-annual reporting obligation under Article 4 (3) should be replaced with ex-post controls on a sample basis at Community level. Even though the reporting exercise has become a Sisyphus task with a proliferation of channels and a fragmentation of audience shares in now 27 Member States, no agreement could be reached on amending this cumbersome procedure.

Despite all the legal and policy arguments militating against the quota, the majority trend has been in favour of carrying it as an old relic into the new digital era. The obligation to promote access to European works has even been extended to on-demand services, albeit without introducing strict quotas or specifying means of implementation. The introduction of quotas for European content on the internet and other non-linear audiovisual services has been particularly opposed by the United Kingdom. Only few Member States, notably Germany, wanted to see the European quota scraped also from traditional television broadcasting. Overall, the question of whether or not to impose content quotas on broadcasters and other service providers aroused little controversy.

Presumably, most Member States did not have strong feelings regarding this question as they comfortably meet the targets set by Article 4. More importantly, they can live with a decorative European quota as long as they can maintain their own cultural requirements alongside. The fact that these national requirements have a positive impact on Member States' compliance with the European quota, while at the same time undermining its internal market rationale, is symptomatic of the Janus-faced quota, uneasily combining industrial and cultural policy. It is also symptomatic of the all-pervasive tension between global trade liberalization and the pursuit of cultural policies at national level, a tension that can hardly be disguised behind the European quota's brittle cultural facade.

151. European Commission, Issues Paper for the Liverpool Audiovisual Conference. Cultural Diversity and the Promotion of European and Independent Audiovisual Production, July 2005, 3.

Chapter 14
Conclusion

The main grievance that can validly be harboured against the TwF Directive as the primary embodiment of the internal market in television programmes in Europe is one that also applies to the European integration process in general: 'Europe has mostly only been united against something, rarely for something'.[1] The only cultural standard for television broadcasting that could strenuously be agreed upon in the framework of the Directive was the European quota as a defence mechanism against the cornucopia of American programmes saturating the European audiovisual market.

The European quota has, however, been rightly characterized as 'a bit of a shot in the dark',[2] since it imposes burdensome obligations without remedying the underlying problem of a low level of creativity in Europe. By placing emphasis on systems of distribution and consumption instead of the organization and financing of production, the Directive has missed the point.[3] Admittedly, the promotion of the development of audiovisual works through projects in the pre-production stage and in the field of training is the task of the MEDIA programme.[4] However, to say that the European quota is a useful mechanism complementing the MEDIA programme would overestimate its effectiveness. We have seen that the quota is

---

1. K.-R. Korte, 'Das Dilemma des Nationalstaates in Westeuropa: Zur Identitätsproblematik der europäischen Integration' (1993) B14 *Aus Politik und Zeitgeschichte*, 21: 'Europa hat sich meist nur gegen etwas, selten für etwas zusammenschließen können'.
2. H. Shaughnessy and C. F. Cobo, *The Cultural Obligations of Broadcasting: National and Transnational Legislation concerning Cultural Duties of Television Broadcasters in Europe* (Manchester, European Institute for the Media, 1990), p. 193.
3. P. Schlesinger, *Media, State and Nation: Political Violence and Collective Identities* (London, Sage, 1991), p. 306; A. Silj, *The New Television in Europe*, Television Research Monograph Series (London, John Libbey, 1992), p. 37.
4. A. Forrest, 'Can Community Support Measures have a Decisive Impact on European Film and Television Production?' (1996) 8 *European Business Journal*, 38.

not the right instrument to increase the circulation of European productions as it is largely filled with national works. Also, the hostility towards American television expressed by the European quota is somewhat hypocritical. At the end of the day, the Directive, by opting for the country of origin principle, has fallen back on precisely the US broadcasting system with its market-driven logic. A future development of EU broadcasting policy in the direction of financial support of production instead of market regulation would be desirable.

However, by exaggerating the matter of quotas, one risks loosing sight of a more profound failure of the EU audiovisual policy: the glaring absence of agreement on broadcasting standards. The European quota does not guarantee the high quality of programming nor its subordination to public service aims. The only aspect of the public service model of broadcasting that is reflected in the European quota is its nationalist vocation.[5] As for the rest, the Directive only harmonizes programme requirements concerning independent film production, advertising, the protection of minors and public order and the right of reply.

Given that the TwF Directive is a minimum harmonization Directive, these are minimum standards, setting the floor below which national laws cannot fall. Regrettably, in many respects they are also minimal standards reflecting the lowest common denominator established by the Member States. As a result, these standards, 'have not managed to prevent a slide towards commercialism in certain Member States, often at the expense of programme quality.'[6]

We have seen that possibilities for derogation from the country of origin principle on the ground of the protection of minors are severely constrained by the heavy procedural requirements of Article 2a (2). The AVMS Directive extends the country of origin principle to the on-demand sector and boasts of ensuring 'a high level of protection of objectives of general interest, in particular the protection of minors and human dignity'.[7] Protection of minors is, however, pitched at a low level, relying entirely on encryption to ensure that minors will not watch extremely violent or pornographic content. This contrasts with Ofcom's decision to maintain the prohibition of R-18 rated material in its 2005 Code in view of the perceived insufficiency of technical measures to protect minors.

Human dignity has only been a peripheral concern in the TwF Directive, and the AVMS Directive fails to redress this unsatisfactory state of affairs. The only provision of the AVMS Directive that explicitly mentions human dignity is Article 3e (1) (c) (i), replacing Article 12 of Directive 97/36/EC. This provision prescribes rather vaguely that 'audiovisual commercial communications shall not prejudice respect for human dignity'.[8] As for the rest, human dignity is only

5. *See* for a theoretical criticism of the mixture of the public service with the nationalist model S. Venturelli, *Liberalizing the European Media: Politics, Regulation and the Public Sphere* (Oxford, Clarendon, 1998), p. 195.
6. H. Weber, *Report on the application of Articles 4 and 5 of Directive 89/552/EEC (the "TV without Frontiers" Directive), as amended by Directive 97/36/EC, for the period 2001–2002 (2004/2236(INI))*, A6-0202/200521, June 2005, p. 14.
7. AVMS Directive, recital 67.
8. McGonagle, 'Safeguarding Human Dignity', 6.

indirectly safeguarded by means of the provisions on the protection of minors and public order. The view that all broadcasts that offend human dignity also seriously impair the development of minors, and are hence prohibited, cannot be concurred with.[9] Assaults on human dignity would still be possible in the non-linear domain. Even as far as linear services are concerned, the rules on the protection of minors do not seem adequate to stem the flood of offensive reality shows testing the boundaries of the acceptable ever further. The controversial discussions on 'Big Brother' in Germany and other Member States testify this.

No standards are set in the Directive concerning the quality of programming, its informational and educative content, pluralism, the impartiality of news presentation, taste and decency.[10] The liberalization of product placement in the AVMS Directive suggests that the quality and editorial integrity of programming have to succumb to the imperative drive to enhance the competitiveness of the European audiovisual industry. Nor are any measures envisaged to ensure that television promotes artistic creation by means of its cooperation with cultural organizations or that it produces original drama. Such preoccupations with programme quality are alien to the European quota's narrow quantitative outlook.[11]

The importance of public service obligations, especially pluralism, for the democratic, social and cultural well-being of society has been recognized in the Protocol on Public Broadcasting, annexed to the EC Treaty by the Treaty of Amsterdam. Also, the Commission Communication on services of general interest in Europe lists a number of general interest considerations concerning the content of broadcasts that are common to national broadcasting orders such as pluralism, information ethics and the protection of the individual.[12] It adds, however, that these considerations are catered for and financed in very different ways from one country and region to another. Moreover, the Charter of Fundamental Rights of the European Union stipulates in Article 11 (2) that the freedom and pluralism of the media shall be respected.[13] Such abstract proclamations are all that could be agreed on in terms of television's contribution to the democratic process.

The need for a consensus over programme standards on a European level emerges from their general demise. Both national and transfrontier services find themselves in a mutually reinforcing, downward spiral of programme quality that cannot be reversed in an unregulated environment. Transmission states that have the power to enforce cultural obligations lack the interest to do so. Firstly, they are

9. Kleist and Scheuer, 'Neue Regelungen', 209; contra Faβbender, 'Inhalt und Grenzen', 511.
10. W. Hoffmann-Riem, 'Defending Vulnerable Values: Regulatory Measures and Enforcement Dilemmas' in *Television and the Public Interest: Vulnerable Values in West European Broadcasting*, J. G. Blumler (ed.) (London, Sage, 1992), p. 181 *et seq.*
11. It is also questionable whether the independent quota in Article 5 succeeds in expanding cultural plurality and choice for the audience. It has been argued that its 10 per cent threshold is far too low so that this provision is virtually redundant. *See* O. Castendyk, 'Quotas in Favour of Independent Producers: Article 5 of the "Television without Frontiers" Directive' (2006) 11 (3) *Communications Law*, 88.
12. Services of General Interest in Europe, 11 September 1996, COM (96) 443 final, para 51.
13. OJ C 364/01, 2000.

not affected by cross-frontier services that are not received in their territories. Secondly, they profit from the unimpeded expansion of their media industries. The United Kingdom for instance has resorted to the Article 2a (2) procedure more frequently than any other Member State, while at the same time allowing for pornographic content to be regularly exported abroad. Reception states that would have an interest in restricting undesirable programme content, often lack the power to do so. Firstly, satellite services escape their control. Secondly, their room for manoeuvre has been narrowed down by the country of origin principle of the TwF Directive.

The divide between transmission and reception states coincides to a great extent with that between large and small Member States in the European Union. Larger states with strong audiovisual industries such as France and the United Kingdom, but also Italy, Germany and Spain, are net transmission states in a position to benefit from economies of scale. By contrast, smaller Member States are net reception states and hence more wary of the cultural influence of incoming broadcasts.[14] This clash of interests of big and small Member States gives rise to the need for an agreement on cultural obligations in Europe and at the same time is a major obstacle to it. A more far-reaching agreement on broadcasting standards at European level might be the only way to prevent the emergence of broadcasting havens.[15] If broadcasting companies were prompted to move to countries with low programme standards, this could set off a race to the bottom as a result of which the minimum standard set in the Directive might well become the maximum one.

Even more significant problems for the enforcement of content regulation are posed by technical progress and advancing globalization. The internet with its truly global, borderless nature is much harder to contain than satellite footprints. Its control poses great difficulties given that even service providers are often unaware of the content available on their service.[16] Harmful audiovisual content accessible via mobile telephones also has the capacity to escape national restrictions designed to protect minors.[17]

In the face of these common challenges, rendering national borders more and more permeable, the defence and extension of Member States' self-interest should be less of a driving force behind the building of a European audiovisual space.[18] The protection of national sovereignty in the area of broadcasting has greatly informed the negotiations at European Union level. As has astutely been observed, 'Members of the European Union eagerly guard culture as a national concern.

14. Shaughnessy and Cobo, *Cultural Obligations of Broadcasting*, p. 195.
15. Holznagel, *Rundfunkrecht in Europa*, p. 355.
16. I. Bernier, 'Content Regulation in the Audio-Visual Sector and the WTO' in *The WTO and Global Convergence in Telecommunications and Audio-Visual Services*, D. Geradin and D. Luff (eds) (Cambridge, Cambridge University Press, 2004), p. 239.
17. C. Palzer, 'Horizontal Rating of Audiovisual Content in Europe. An Alternative to Multi-level Classification?' (2003) 10 IRISplus 1.
18. *See* R. Negrine and S. Papathanassopoulos, *The Internationalisation of Television* (London, Pinter, 1990), p. 53.

Although there are many good reasons for such a position, one of its consequences may very well be to deprive the EU of the very tools needed for a cultural counterbalance to the present industrially and commercially-oriented regulation of the media sector.'[19]

The defence of national broadcasting sovereignty has also been underpinned by theoretical arguments. Notably, it has been asserted that the European Union is precluded from adopting measures concerning the democratic will-formation and social integration functions of television, such as standards of pluralism, given that a European communication constitution is missing.[20] The absence of a European communication system manifests itself in the lack of European media serving a public that transcends national borders.[21] A European public space is also non-existent, since political parties, interest associations and social movements are entrenched in the national arena.[22]

These commentators have a valid point in arguing that pan-European media are virtually non-existent and that the prospect for Europeanization of the media seems very distant at the moment.[23] However, to regard these obstacles as insurmountable is equivalent to saying that the European integration process is doomed from the start.[24] Even though pan-European media are very underdeveloped, transnational television, especially among countries belonging to the same linguistic region, is a reality. It undoubtedly raises issues that call for regulation at a higher level than that of the nation state. One might argue that bilateral treaties would have sufficed to solve problems posed by cross–frontier broadcasting. This is a purely hypothetical argument though since European rules are here to stay. Their roll-back from the supranational to the intergovernmental level is illusory.[25]

The point has however been made that as long as pan-European media are marginal, 'the strong political, social and cultural concerns of most content regulation dictate that it should be conducted at the national rather than the EU level. The mutual recognition procedures of the TwF Directive should remain

---

19. C. Nissen, *Public Service Media in the Information Society. Report prepared by the Council of Europe's Group of Specialists on Public Service Broadcasting in the Information Society (MS-S-PSB)* (Strassbourg, Council of Europe, 2006), p. 46.
20. W. Hoffmann-Riem, 'Europäisierung des Rundfunks – aber ohne Kommunikationsverfassung?' in *Rundfunk im Wettbewerbsrecht: Der öffentlich-rechtliche Rundfunk im Spannungsfeld zwischen Wirtschaftsrecht und Rundfunkrecht*, W. Hoffmann-Riem (ed.), Symposien des Hans-Bredow-Instituts, vol. 10 (Baden-Baden, Nomos, 1988), p. 204; N. Petersen, *Rundfunkfreiheit und EG-Vertrag: Die Einwirkungen des Europäischen Rechts auf die Ausgestaltung der nationalen Rundfunkordnungen* (Baden-Baden, Nomos, 1994), p. 305.
21. Grimm, 'Does Europe Need a Constitution?', 294.
22. *Ibid.*; *see* Habermas (1995), 301.
23. Levy, *Europe's Digital Revolution*, p. 156.
24. *See* J. Habermas, 'Remarks on Dieter Grimm's "Does Europe Need a Constitution?" ' (1995) 1 ELJ, 306–307; C. O. Lenz, 'Vertrag von Maastricht – Ende demokratischer Staatlichkeit?' (1993) 31 NJW, 1963; J. Schwartze, 'Das Staatsrecht in Europa' (1993) 12 JZ, 589.
25. D. Krebber, *Europeanisation of Regulatory Television Policy: The Decision-making Process of the Television without Frontiers Directives from 1989 & 1997* (Baden-Baden, Nomos, 2002), p. 21.

adequate to cover those cases where services licensed in one country target another.'[26] The first part of this reasoning, that the scope of regulation should be commensurate with the scale of the regulated industry, is compelling.[27] The second is less so.

The Directive's mutual recognition procedures are designed to ensure the free movement of cross-frontier services, but do not always offer adequate safeguards for the protection of the receiving states' priorities in the political, social and cultural spheres. The European Union has already gone down the road of content regulation, and it is too late to reverse this trend. It is therefore imperative to steer intervention in ways that guarantee the social policy objectives of broadcasting. The establishment of common broadcasting standards, set at a higher level than the one opted for in the Directive, could be a first step towards the creation of the missing communicative context.

This is not to say that there is need for further harmonization in all areas of broadcasting law. On the contrary, such an attempt would be counter-productive as it would inhibit flexibility and cultural diversity. The Directive's partial and minimum harmonization approach has merits as it accommodates different national traditions and allows Member States to experiment with new regulatory instruments. Also, one should not loose sight of the fact that European institutions are only equipped to deal with problems associated with cross-border broadcasting and cannot respond to all challenges arising in the context of Member States' broadcasting orders.[28]

Unless Member States agree to cede more sovereignty on matters of content regulation to the European Union – a prospect that seems very unlikely at the moment– attempts at further harmonization will have to take account of the fact that EU powers in the broadcasting field are limited. Article 151 EC covers the audiovisual sector only as far as artistic and literary creation is concerned. More importantly, it does not leave room for the adoption of harmonization measures with a cultural policy motivation. A legally non-binding recommendation, even if it would overcome the unanimity hurdle, would be a weak instrument.

Another option would be to deepen and widen the level of harmonization of broadcasting standards within the already existing framework of the TwF Directive. The obvious downside of harmonizing broadcasting standards by means of an internal market instrument is that cultural values are doomed to get a rough deal. Content regulation is transformed from an end in its own right to a means to an end: the creation of the level playing field necessary for the cross border transmission of broadcasting services. The experience with the European quota has taught us that in order for broadcasting obligations formulated within an internal market Directive to be powerful, they need to be either directly effective or receiving Member States have to be allowed to block programmes that do not

26. Levy, *Europe's Digital Revolution*, p. 156.
27. *See* D. Ward, *The European Union Democratic Deficit and the Public Sphere. An Evaluation of EU Media Policy* (Amsterdam, IOS Press, 2004), p. 127.
28. Holznagel, *Rundfunkrecht in Europa*, p. 356.

comply with them. Also, if such obligations are to be workable and to elicit high rates of compliance, they need to take account of the fiscal pressures of cross-frontier broadcasters and not to place ruinous burdens on them.[29]

A more fundamental problem is the actual effectiveness of positive programme content requirements. Even at the national level, qualitative obligations of pluralism, impartiality, fairness etc. are in the decline. For one, it is hard to reach a consensus on the interpretation of these open-ended concepts and to actually measure compliance with them. The divergence of views in the Member States means that agreeing on a common set of values at the European level would be more cumbersome, but perhaps not altogether impossible. So as to avoid the uncertainties of qualitative standards, some Member States have opted for quantitative obligations such as the French rule of three thirds. However, quantitative obligations are not a panacea. We saw that France recently abandoned this rule that was perceived as burdensome and inefficient, in favour of a hands-off, Ofcom style monitoring of pluralism. Such instances of cross-fertilization between different broadcasting orders are not unusual.

For another, high quality, challenging programmes that cater for minority tastes pose a risk for broadcasters for they are costly, may not appeal to the general public and may even alienate the audience from other material on offer.[30] The strategy of scheduling less popular programmes between more attractive ones, known as 'hammocking', has become less efficient as viewers zap between ever increasing numbers of channels. A different strategy is gaining ground, that of inserting public service type messages within popular programmes.[31] For example, first aid techniques could feature in a medical drama or instances of environmentally conscious behaviour in a soap. This method resembles product placement, and if the integration of socially desirable content within a storyline is instigated by organizations extraneous to the broadcaster, it raises similar concerns as regards editorial integrity. Moreover, it is doubtful as to whether the injection of useful or politically correct messages in a soap is able to turn the frog to a prince. An overdose would certainly risk frustrating viewers' expectations of bland, easily digestible content.[32]

The 'product placement' strategy for putting public service content across to the public is symptomatic of the minimalist view of public broadcasting that is prevalent across Europe. Public broadcasting is not expected to stimulate and challenge viewers, to cultivate their tastes by confronting them with material they would not otherwise choose to watch, to provide diverse, high-quality programming in a way that will influence future viewing choices and through them society at large.[33] It is meant to follow viewers' tastes and to only punctually and

29. Shaughnessy and Cobo, *Cultural Obligations of Broadcasting*, pp. 192, 194.
30. Holznagel, *Rundfunkrecht in Europa*, p. 266.
31. Armstrong and Weeds, 'Public Service Broadcasting', pp. 81, 110.
32. *Ibid.*
33. For the traditional view of public broadcasting, *see* Born and Prosser, 'Culture and Consumerism', 657.

gently manipulate wider currents of public opinion. Great faith is placed in viewer sovereignty and in the capacity of the market to provide what viewers want to watch.[34]

Needless to say, if public broadcasting is reduced to such inserts of socially desirable material, there is no pressing reason why it should be provided by public broadcasters. In its 1997 Convergence Green Paper, the Commission suggested that different organizations, including organizations from outside the traditional sector, should be allowed to bid to undertake public interest obligations.[35] The idea that public service material could be commissioned from any body designated as fulfilling public interest obligations is unworkable. It disregards the fact that quality and innovation cannot grow on thin air but require production practices and cultures long informed by a public service ethos. However, if soaps boosted with public value inserts count as public service broadcasts, the Commission's view has to be concurred with. Such content can indeed be easily produced by any organization.

Quite apart from the increasing mistrust towards many of the traditional understandings of public broadcasting, a further source of challenge to public service type content regulation stems from the arrival of new technologies. As pay-per-view, video-on-demand and personal video recorders make programming less relevant by allowing viewers to schedule programmes on their own, it becomes necessary to reformulate public service objectives, especially pluralism, and to devise new regulatory arrangements to deliver them. The trend goes towards doing away with positive and lowering negative content requirements for commercial channels, while subjecting on demand services to the lightest possible form of regulation.[36]

The deregulation of the commercial sector calls for the assumption of increased responsibilities by the public broadcasters. It has been predicted that in the digital world the market will broadly cover all of viewers' needs, cutting down the uptake of public service content and causing the death of public broadcasting.[37] This prediction seems exaggerated. In many respects, public broadcasting, informed by public service obligations, will be needed and valued in a digital environment more than ever before. It will be needed so as to enhance social integration, to make available free-to-air mixed schedule programming in a landscape increasingly dominated by niche channels and pay-TV, so as to cater for quality and diversity across all genres. It will be valued by viewers searching for beacons of accuracy in a sea of information. It would be a mistake to view such duties as onerous burdens placing public broadcasting at a competitive

34. For a criticism of the traditional view of public broadcasting, *see* Armstrong and Weeds, 'Public Service Broadcasting', p. 81 *et seq.*
35. European Commission, Green Paper on the Convergence of the Telecommunications, Media and Informational Technology Sectors, and the Implications for Regulation: Towards an Information Society Approach, 3 December 1997, COM (97) 623 final.
36. Levy, *Europe's Digital Revolution*, p. 148.
37. *Ibid.*, p. 117.

disadvantage. If properly promoted, they can become a marketing tool that will set public broadcasters apart from the bulk of commercial channels. The special role of public broadcasting in a digital environment will be explored further in Part Three of this book.

It becomes apparent from all the foregoing that complex factors need to be taken into consideration before reaching a more profound accord on European broadcasting obligations. Reconciling the diversity and divisiveness of European reality with an ideal of European unity within a European Union where social, political and legal structures are incomplete and incoherent is immensely difficult. Whatever form the agreement on content regulation will take, it will have to be responsive to the need to afford the cultural and democratic aspects of television a more prominent role in the EU broadcasting policy if its further degradation to a soulless, money-minded industry is to be prevented.

Part 3

Public Service Obligations and State Aids

Chapter 15

Financing of Public Broadcasting and European Union State Aid Law

1. INTRODUCTION

If public television is expected to adhere to a canon of public service values, to be independent, to deliver high quality, innovative content, it needs to be adequately funded. Put the financial foundations of public broadcasting into question, and the whole edifice is bound to collapse sooner or later. Since the beginning of the nineties public broadcasters across Europe have been faced with a cascade of appeals at European Union level against the allegedly anti-competitive nature of the licence fee and other forms of state support received by them. These appeals were launched with the European Commission by commercial operators claiming that the State financing of public broadcasters constitutes unlawful state aid under Article 87 (1) EC.

At first sight, one cannot but marvel at the application of the state aid rules to the 'sacred cow' of public broadcasting. Unlike other economic activities, public broadcasting plays a vital role in the functioning of modern democracy, the development of citizenship, the formation of cultural identity and the strengthening of social cohesion. How is it possible that one of the main pillars of society has been subjected to the rigid and occasionally soulless discipline of competition law? How did its elusive, yet invaluable, culture and citizenship purposes come to be measured against the hard rigour of the state aid rules?

In order to explain this somewhat paradoxical situation, it is necessary to take things from the start. The gradual process of liberalization that set off in the European Union at the end of the eighties deprived public broadcasting of its monopoly position and rendered it one of many players in a competitive market,

1. Council of Europe, Parliamentary Assembly, Report of the Committee on Culture, Science and Education of 12 January 2004, 'Public Service Broadcasting', Doc. 10029, para. 20.

albeit a privileged one. This process of de-monopolization has arguably had a positive effect on public broadcasting, triggering its modernization.[1] It meant, however, that public broadcasters had to compete with commercial undertakings for viewers, programme rights and often advertising.

Public broadcasters are traditionally funded by means of the licence fee that is paid by viewers/listeners. The licence fee exists in most European states with the exception of Spain, Luxembourg and, as far as television is concerned, Portugal.[2] They also enjoy other forms of state assistance such as tax advantages, capital injections, loans, debt-rescheduling. Also, must-carry rules oblige cable and satellite networks to provide public service channels to subscribers, endowing them with a guaranteed access to final consumption markets not enjoyed by commercial channels.[3]

At the same time, most European public broadcasters supplement public funding with commercial revenues from advertising, sponsorship, subscription and concession fees paid by commercial enterprises. Their reliance on commercial revenue is vital given that the number of television households has stopped increasing significantly so that the licence fee has a very limited potential for growth.[4] However, advertising revenue has also fallen dramatically as the number of channels has rocketed with the arrival of multichannel television. Advertisers who could only choose between two or three channels in the past now have a plethora of new niche and general interest channels at their disposal.[5] With personal video recorders allowing viewers to fast-forward through commercial breaks, advertising revenue is bound to shrink further.[6] If the soaring prices for talent and sport rights are also taken into account, it becomes clear that the audiovisual market is a very competitive one.

Commercial broadcasters, envious of the dual funding public broadcasters enjoy, came up with the ingenious idea of challenging the licence fee as a form of illegal state aid. The first complaint was filed in 1992 by two Spanish commercial broadcasters regarding the public funding of regional broadcasting channels and of the national broadcaster TVE. It was followed by numerous other complaints against the public broadcasters of almost all the Member States of the European Union of fifteen.[7] Private broadcasters alleged in a nutshell

---

2. *Ibid.*, para. 15.
3. M. Cave, R. Collins and P. Crowther, 'Regulating the BBC', 6th World Media Economic Conference, Centre d'études sur les médias and Journal of Media Economics, HEC Montréal, Montréal, 12–15 May 2004, 5.
4. Council of Europe, 'Public Service Broadcasting', para. 16; J. Steemers, 'In Search of a Third Way: Balancing Public Purpose and Commerce in German and British Public Service Broadcasting' (2001) 26 (1) *Canadian Journal of Communication*, 1.
5. J. Cowling, 'From Princes to Paupers: The Future of Advertising-Funded Public Service Television' in *From Public Service Broadcasting to Public Service Communications*, D. Tambini and J. Cowling (eds) (London, IPPR, 2004), p. 61.
6. P. Barwise, 'What are the Real Threats to Public Service Broadcasting?' in *From Public Service Broadcasting to Public Service Communications*, D. Tambini and J. Cowling (eds) (London, IPPR, 2004), pp. 16, 22.
7. *See* A. Bartosch, 'The Financing of Public Broadcasting and EC State Aid Law: An Interim Balance' (1999) 4 ECLR, 197; J. MacLennan, 'Facing the Digital Future: Public Service

that the public service remit was not defined in a sufficiently precise manner, that there was no adequate independent supervision, that the licence fee was excessive and that it distorted competition in advertising and other commercial markets.

The Commission, probably due to the political sensitive nature of these cases, did not act for a while. It ruled on the complaint filed against Portugal only four years later. It was condemned by the Court of First Instance in 1998 for its failure to close the preliminary investigation into the public funding received by regional television companies in Spain.[8] In the meantime, public broadcasters backed up by France and the European Parliament pressed at the Intergovernmental Conference that adopted the Amsterdam Treaty for a clearer recognition of the role of public broadcasting in the European Union. The outcome was the Protocol on public broadcasting that was annexed to the Treaty of Amsterdam, and that entered into force in 1999. Together with the largely symbolic Article 16 EC that was also inserted by the Treaty of Amsterdam, it demonstrates an increased awareness of the importance of services of general economic interest in the European Union.

The Amsterdam Protocol is worded in an enough open-ended and imprecise manner so as to keep everybody satisfied. It provides that:

> The provisions of the Treaty establishing the European Community shall be without prejudice to the competence of Member States to provide for the funding of public service broadcasting insofar as such funding is granted to broadcasting organizations for the fulfilment of the public service remit as conferred, defined and organized by each Member State, and insofar as such funding does not affect trading conditions and competition in the Community to an extent which would be contrary to the common interest, while the realization of the remit of that public service shall be taken into account.

Public broadcasters have interpreted the Protocol as an express recognition of the diversity of institutional and regulatory arrangements for organizing and funding public broadcasting in the Member States. They have rejoiced at the fact that 'far from requiring even so much as a minimum standard or level of definition of public broadcasting, the Protocol definitely does not prescribe that there must be "clearly defined public service obligations"'.[9] They have claimed that the Protocol uses not the plural 'obligations' but the singular 'remit' to signify that the whole range of a public broadcaster's programme output constitutes public broadcasting. Also, they have stressed that a distortion of competition contrary to the common interest could not be found to exist without the realization of the public service remit having first been taken into account.[10] Commercial broadcasters, on the other hand, have been less pleased with the European Union's reluctance to establish common rules as to

---

Broadcasters and State Aid Law in the European Union' (1999) 2 *Cambridge Yearbook of European Legal Studies*, 184.

8. Case T-95/96, *Gestevison Telecinco v. Commission* [1998] ECR II-3407.
9. European Broadcasting Union, 'The Public Service Broadcasting Remit: Today and Tomorrow', 29 April 1998.
10. *Ibid.*

the definition and entrustment of public service obligations.[11] They have, however, been relieved that 'as regards the application of the State aid rules (including the exemption in article 86 (2) of the Treaty) to the public funding of public broadcasters, the Protocol does not change anything.'[12]

In effect, the Amsterdam Protocol does nothing more than establish a division of responsibility between the Member States and the Commission.[13] The Member States define the remit and provide the funding of public broadcasting, while the Commission looks at the effect of national arrangements on trade and competition. The Commission gave more guidance as to the application of Article 86 (2) EC and of the proportionality test to public broadcasting in the Broadcasting Communication that was adopted in 2001.[14] The Communication provides that the financing of public broadcasters through licence fees usually constitutes state aid. It requires a clear and precise definition of public broadcasting, the formal entrustment and independent monitoring of the public service mission and the limitation of public funding to what is necessary for the fulfilment of this mission.

Despite these clarifications, the complaints by private broadcasters against the financing of public broadcasting continued with increased vigour. In 2003, the Commission concluded that the financing schemes of the public broadcasters in Italy, France, Portugal and Spain had to be amended so as to ensure their consistency with the conditions of the Broadcasting Communication. In March 2005, formal letters were sent to Ireland, the Netherlands and Italy accusing them of similar breaches of the requirements of clarity of definition, transparent financing and separation of accounts for public service and commercial activities. The Commission's investigation in these cases does not anymore cover traditional television programme activities but the financing of online information services. As the internet becomes an increasingly prominent medium for the distribution of content, the online activities of public broadcasters come more in the limelight. Public broadcasters claim a strong presence for themselves, arguing that the same democratic, social and cultural needs that apply to television are also valid for new media services. Commercial broadcasters contest this and seek to limit them to an online presence that is strictly aligned to their traditional core service. As technology evolves, the need for a modern definition of the public service remit that can best serve the public interest in the information society is becoming paramount.

This chapter will explore the multifaceted and complex relationship between state aid law and public broadcasting. It will consider the ways in which the European Commission and the European Courts have sought to balance its culture

11. ACT, *Safeguarding the Future of the European Audiovisual Market: A White Paper on the Financing and Regulation of Publicly Funded Broadcasters*, March 2004 <www.epceurope.org/presscentre/archive/safeguarding_audiovisual_market_300304.pdf>, 18 July 2007, p. 6.
12. *Ibid.*
13. V. Wiedemann, 'Public Service Broadcasting, State Aid, and the Internet: Emerging EU Law' <www.ebu.ch/en/union/diffusion_on_line/pub_broadcasting/tcm_6-18560.php>, 14 June 2006, p. 1.
14. Communication from the Commission on the application of state aid rules to public service broadcasting, OJ C 320/5, 2001 (hereafter referred to as the Broadcasting Communication).

and citizenship objectives with the requirements of the internal market and of effective competition. First of all, the more general question will be asked as to whether public broadcasting displays special characteristics that distinguish it from commercial television and that justify its privileged funding from the public purse. Secondly, this chapter will examine whether funding for public broadcasting constitutes state aid, and if so, whether it is new or existing aid. Finally, it will analyze whether it is possible to bring the licence fee under the exceptions of Article 87 (3) (d) EC or of Article 86 (2) EC.

2. THE SPECIAL POSITION OF PUBLIC BROADCASTING

The ever increasing scrutiny of the licence fee against the state aid rules brings the question to the fore as to why public broadcasters should benefit of this special, secure form of funding while their commercial counterparts are fully exposed to the vagaries of the marketplace. What are, the unique features of public broadcasting that justify its financing through licence fees? The different philosophies of public and commercial broadcasting can be captured in the following laconic, but telling epigram: 'In a public system, television producers acquire money to make programmes. In a commercial system they make programmes to acquire money.'[15] In other words, the focus of public broadcasting is on programme making while the focus of commercial broadcasting is on profit making. These divergent assumptions on which public and commercial broadcasters rest, guide their performance, inform their output and determine their potential for the future.

Public broadcasting aims to offer what the German Constitutional Court has called the 'basic provision' (*Grundversorgung*) that is essential for the democratic order and for the cultural life of a nation.[16] It offers programmes that are available to the whole population and that provide a comprehensive range of content.[17] It is in the position to offer a wide range of subject matter as it is not dependent in the same way as commercial broadcasters on high viewing figures. The essential characteristics of public broadcasting can be summed up as universality of access, universality of content, independence and quality of services and output.[18]

Universality of access signifies not only geographical availability but also presence on all significant media and platforms in the age of digital convergence, i.e. terrestrial, satellite, cable and broadband networks. Universality of content means the provision of programming that reflects the interests of all social groups and that includes the entire range of programme genres.[19] This way public

15. Tracey, *Decline and Fall of Public Service Broadcasting*, p. 18; to the same effect also E. G. Mahrenholz cited in M. Ruttig, *Der Einfluß des EG-Beihilferechts auf die Gebührenfinanzierung der öffentlichrechtlichen Rundfunkanstalten* (Frankfurt am Main, Peter Lang, 2001), p. 55.
16. *See* Part 1, Ch. 3, s. 4, p. 44 *above.*
17. BVerfGE 73, 118.
18. Council of Europe, 'Public Service Broadcasting', para. 12.
19. G. Born and T. Prosser, 'Culture and Consumerism: Citizenship, Public Service Broadcasting and the BBC's Fair Trading Obligations' (2001) 64 MLR, 657, 676.

broadcasting not only caters for existing tastes but introduces the public to new and unforeseen types of programming.[20] Universality of content means equally that public broadcasters should not only provide generalist channels but also more specialized channels or channels tailored for specific audiences.[21] Independence is understood as the freedom of public broadcasters from any political or commercial bias. Finally, quality of services and output is perhaps the most elusive of all public broadcasting principles. It refers to the commitment of programme-makers to produce individual programmes, schedules and portfolios of services that constitute a benchmark of professionalism and truthfulness, that are new and original.[22]

Some of these principles are more controversial than others. Many of the challenges launched by commercial media against the public funding of public broadcasters contest precisely the right of the latter to expand into the online sector and into digital television or to launch thematic channels. However, if public broadcasting is not given space to develop beyond its established technologies and programme-profiles it will soon become a relict of the past.

Why is it that these ideals justify the licence fee funding of public broadcasters? Funding undoubtedly influences content so that the choice of the funding scheme has a direct impact on the quality of the programming. If public broadcasting is to remain independent of the government and of commercial forces, it cannot rely on advertising revenue or on state allocations. The licence fee reduces such dependencies and allows broadcasters to focus on their actual task, the making of programmes, rather than on the maximization of ratings. What is more, it creates a link between the public broadcasting organizations and their audience, rendering them more accountable to the public.

However, private broadcasters often make the point that many of them also have public service obligations, yet they do not get compensated as such.[23] It is true that commercial operators are subject to minimum conditions of authorization on grounds of public interest. However, these conditions are less stringent as a rule than the ones imposed on their public service counterparts. The German Constitutional Court accepted a more light-handed regulation of private broadcasters only for as long as and in so far as programme range and balanced plurality were effectively guaranteed at least by public broadcasting.[24] The dual order of broadcasting in Germany evolved over time in the direction of market liberalism so that commercial operators are now virtually free even of those scaled-down public service obligations originally envisaged by the German Constitutional Court.[25] The situation in Germany is characteristic of the trend towards deregulation of commercial broadcasting across Europe.

20. *Ibid.*; Tracey, *Decline and Fall of Public Service Broadcasting*, p. 27.
21. Council of Europe, 'Public Service Broadcasting', para. 12.
22. *Ibid.*; Born and Prosser, 'Culture and Consumerism', 679 *et seq.*
23. ACT, *Safeguarding the Future*, p. 11.
24. BVerfGE 73, 118. *See* Part 1, Ch. 3, s. 4, p. 42 *et seq above* for a more detailed examination of the broadcasting case-law of the German Constitutional Court.
25. M. Stock, 'Zum Reformbedarf im dualen Rundfunksystem: Public-Service-Rundfunk und kommerzieller Rundfunk: Wie können sie koexistieren?' (2005) 204 *Arbeitspapiere des Instituts für Rundfunkökonomie an der Universität zu Köln*, 1.

Still, the picture of public broadcasting that has been painted so far is too idealistic. If commercial sources of funding taint programming by prioritizing the interests of advertisers, sponsors and shareholders over those of citizens, this conflict of interest also applies to public broadcasters in mixed funded systems. Are dually funded public broadcasters still able to live up to their public service mission? This depends on the degree of their commercialization. Commercial tendencies may range from a certain popularization of content on the core channels to the offering of some services on subscription in breach of the principle of universal access to the point where public broadcasting is privatized as was intended by the Berlusconi government in Italy.[26] The German Constitutional Court ruled that mixed funding is best suited to counteract one-sided dependencies and to bolster broadcasters' editorial freedom.[27] Commercial revenue is also beneficial insofar as it strengthens the competitiveness of public broadcasting. The BBC Charter Review White Paper encouraged the BBC to continue to relieve pressure on the licence fee by generating commercial income provided that BBC's commercial activity is fit with its public purposes.[28] This is a fine line to tread, and if public broadcasters are not vigilant they risk losing their public service ethos on the way.

Public broadcasters being forced to compete for audiences, programming and advertising revenue often prioritize audience share at the expense of quality and creativity. So as to minimize the risk of losing viewers, they imitate the programming of commercial operators and concentrate on entertainment programmes while serious programming is scheduled outside of prime time. The temptation to dumb down on standards is greater with the arrival of multi-channel television and the resulting fragmentation of audience.[29] As the choice of available programmes extends hugely, very few programmes attract large numbers of viewers. These tendencies are bound to increase with the impending analogue switch-off and the move to digital-only television.

Public broadcasters find themselves caught between a rock and a hard place. If they reduce mainstream programming, they risk being criticized for being unpopular and for providing services that the licence fee payers are not interested in. If they compete with commercial broadcasters to defend their market shares, they are being accused of unfair trading.[30] Does this tightrope public broadcasters have to walk confirm the so-called convergence hypothesis? The convergence theory, first formulated by Wolfgang Schatz and his colleagues in 1989, predicts the gradual convergence of public and commercial broadcasters towards the same programmes

26. Steemers, 'In Search of a Third Way', 5.
27. BVerfGE 83, 238, 310 *et seq.*
28. DCMS, *A Public Service for All: The BBC in the Digital Age*, Cm 6763 (London, TSO, 2006), para. 7.1.2.
29. D. Bergg, 'Taking a Horse to Water? Delivering Public Service Broadcasting in a Digital Universe' in *From Public Service Broadcasting to Public Service Communications*, D. Tambini and J. Cowling (eds) (London, IPPR, 2004), pp. 5, 9 *et seq.*
30. Born and Prosser, 'Culture and Consumerism', 658.

of mass appeal.[31] However, empirical evidence from Germany indicates that the convergence theory sees the state of television in black and white. In reality, German public broadcasters are at pains to combine distinctiveness with market share and to hold on to their informational functions.[32] They enjoy a journalistic infrastructure that their commercial counterparts cannot imitate. Their world-wide network of correspondents allows them to excel in informational genres. They also dominate the area of children's programmes. Commercial television, on the other hand, is shaped by entertainment genres and a greater amount of advertising.[33]

This empirical evidence suggests that public broadcasters try to employ a mixed strategy, to balance entrepreneurialism with merit programming. This is the only way forward to shield off the identity crisis that looms over them. The dilemma between ratings and quality needs to be resolved by finding ways to generate ratings by quality, not only at the margins of the schedule, but in core programmes and in prime time.[34] The rationale for the existence of public television has evolved since its inception, but the need for it in the multi-channel world is as pronounced as ever.

The establishment of heavily regulated monopoly public broadcasters was initially justified with the provision of 'communication welfare' in conditions of spectrum scarcity. This rationale changed with the arrival of commercial broadcasters. In the public private broadcasting duopoly that ensued public broadcasters were entrusted with the provision of quality television that private operators found commercially unviable.[35]

With digitalization public television is asked to contribute to democracy and social cohesion in different ways. Commercial providers will be able to offer an extraordinary range of specialized services and perhaps even to cater for all tastes and needs. However, these programmes will often only be accessible on pay-TV or on thematic satellite channels reaching extremely small audiences. The great mass of viewers, not having any choice but to watch the generally accessible generalist channels, will find it increasingly hard to detect worthy pieces of programming. Growing competition is likely to force private channels to dumb down their standards even further on free TV.[36]

Therein lies the challenge and the opportunity for public broadcasters. Their special contribution will not be measured in terms of distinct programme genres but in terms of high quality television, available to all without additional payment. The universally available public channels will have the opportunity to act as 'social

31. H. Schatz, N. Immer and F. Marcinkowski, 'Der Vielfalt eine Chance? Empirische Befunde zu einem zentralen Argument für die Dualisierung des Rundfunks in der Bundesrepublik Deutschland' (1989) 1 *Rundfunk und Fernsehen*, 5.
32. H. E. Meier, 'Beyond Convergence: Understanding Programming Strategies of Public Broadcasters in Competitive Environments' (2003) 18 *European Journal of Communication*, 337.
33. U. M. Krüger and T. Zapf-Schramm, 'Sparten, Sendungsformen und Inhalte im deutschen Fernsehangebot' (2006) 4 MP, 201.
34. Stock, 'Reformbedarf im dualen Rundfunksystem', 27.
35. Council of Europe, 'Public Service Broadcasting', para. 20.
36. *Ibid.*, para. 21.

glue' and as reference point for the increasingly fragmented audiences.[37] The argument has, however, been raised that in a new media environment viewers will increasingly act as consumers rather than citizens and adopt a more individual 'on demand' user behaviour.[38] Their willingness to collectively fund public television through the licence fee might diminish as a result.

Collective funding currently corresponds to the 'zero marginal cost' of additional viewers, created by high fixed costs. In the long run the marginal costs of digital services are likely to increase in correlation to the number of simultaneous users. Will users still be prepared to pay collectively for the additional costs of individualized services? It is submitted that even if 'pay per view' makes sense in economic terms, it would signify the end of equal access and universality, two inalienable principles of public broadcasting. If public media are not free at the point of delivery, providing education, information and entertainment to those unable to pay for subscription services, they have failed their mission.

In order to meet the challenges of the information society, public broadcasters need to be adequately funded. If their public funding is insufficient or insecure, they will inevitably have to employ more aggressive strategies to survive the competitive battle with the commercial operators. They may win the fight, but the audience will certainly loose out. Against this backdrop, we will now consider the hurdles the licence fee needs to take so as to prove itself compatible with the EU state aid regime.

3. FUNDING FOR PUBLIC BROADCASTING AS STATE AID

3.1 Is Funding for Public Broadcasting Granted 'by a Member State or through State Resources'?

The licence fee constitutes state aid under Article 87 EC only if it is granted 'by a Member State or through State resources'. This has been questioned in academic literature given that the licence fee is paid by viewers.[39] However, the meaning of 'aid granted by a Member State or through State resources' is not straightforward. To start with, it is unclear how the two alternatives relate to each other. According

37. Barwise, 'Threats to Public Service Broadcasting', p. 19.
38. Nissen, *Public Service Media in the Information Society*, p. 43 *et seq.*
39. C. Koenig and A. Haratsch, 'The Licence-Fee-Based Financing of Public Service Broadcasting in Germany after the Altmark Trans Judgment' (2003) 4 EStAL, 569; C. Koenig and J. Kühling, 'EC Control of Aid Granted through State Resources' (2002) 1 EStAL, 7, 16; C. Koenig and J. Kühling, 'How to Cut a Long Story Short: Das Preussen Elektra-Urteil des EuGH und die EG-Beihilfenkontrolle über das deutsche Rundfunkgebührensystem' (2001) 7 ZUM, 537; C. E. Eberle, 'Die Rundfunkgebühr auf dem EU-Prüfstand' in *Regulierung im Bereich von Medien und Kultur: Gestaltungsmöglichkeiten und rechtliche Grenzen*, J. Schwartze and J. Becker (eds) (Baden-Baden, Nomos, 2002), p. 123; R. Craufurd Smith, 'State Support for Public Service Broadcasting: The Position under European Community Law' (2001) 28 (1) LIEI, 3–4.

to one view, taken by Advocate General Jacobs in *Preussen Elektra*, 'aid granted by a Member State' covers aid measures financed from public funds and granted directly by the state.[40] 'Aid granted through state resources' covers aid financed through state resources which is granted not directly by the state but by public bodies designated or established by the state. Under an alternative interpretation, only aid granted through state resources needs to be financed through public funds, while aid granted by a Member State covers all advantages granted by the state, whether financed through state resources or not.[41]

These alternative readings are informed by divergent opinions as to whether financing through state resources should be a constitutive element of state aid. Under a narrow interpretation of Article 87 (1) EC state aid must entail a financial burden for the state, whether it is granted directly by the state or by public or private bodies designated or established by the state.[42] Under a broad interpretation of Article 87 (1) EC any measure supporting specific undertakings, and which is attributable to the state, constitutes state aid regardless of whether it costs the state money.[43] In its jurisprudence, the Court vacillates between the two lines of reasoning. Broadly speaking, the extensive view of state resources was taken by the Court in its case-law up to *Sloman Neptun*, which marked the shift to a narrower, formalistic approach.[44] To complicate things further, a number of judgments rendered after *Sloman Neptun* strike a middle ground between the two opposite views.[45] They dispense with the requirement of a burden on the state budget so long as the state can exercise direct or indirect control over the resources in question.

This position was also taken by the Court in a judgment concerning the financial aid granted to the company Stardust Marine by the bank SBT-Batif, a subsidiary of Altus, which was itself part of the Crédit Lyonnais Group.[46] The Court examined, first, whether the financial resources of Crédit Lyonnais, SBT and Altus were state resources and, secondly, whether the aid granted to Stardust was imputable to the state. As to the first question, the Court found that the above

40. Opinion of Advocate-General Jacobs in Case C-379/98, *Preussen Elektra* [2001] ECR 2099, paras 150 *et seq.*
41. G. Schwendinger, *Deutsche Rundfunkgebühren – staatlich oder aus staatlichen Mitteln gewährt? Zugleich eine kritische Bestandsaufnahme der Rechtsprechung des EuGH zur staatlichen Zurechenbarkeit von Beihilfen gemäß Art. 87 Abs. 1 EGV*, EUI Working Paper Law no. 2003/5 (Florence, European University Institute, 2003).
42. Case 82/77, *Van Tiggele* [1978] ECR 25; Case C-72-73/91, *Sloman Neptun* [1993] ECR 887; Case C-189/91, *Kirsammer/Hack* [1993] ECR I-6185; Case C-52-54/97, *Viscido* [1998] ECR 2629; Case C-200/97, *Ecotrade* [1998] ECR I-7907; Case C-379/98, *Preussen Elektra* [2001] ECR I-2099.
43. Case 290/83, *Commission v. France* [1985] ECR 439; Case 67-68/85 and 70/85, *Van der Kooy* [1988] ECR 219; Case 57/86, *Greece v. Commission* [1988] ECR 2855; Case C-303/88, *Italy v. Commission* [1991] ECR I-1433; Case C-305/89, *Italy v. Commission* [1991] ECR I-1603.
44. Case C-72-73/91, *Sloman Neptun* [1993] ECR 887.
45. Case C-387/92, *Banco Exterior de España* [1994] ECR I-877; Case C-6/97, *Italy v. Commission* [1999] ECRI-2981; Case C-83/98, *Ladbroke Racing* [2000] ECR I-3271.
46. Case C-482/99, *French Republic v. Commission* [2002] ECR I-4397.

mentioned companies were public undertakings within the meaning of the Transparency Directive.[47] Interestingly, the Court noted that 'according to settled case-law, it is not necessary to establish in every case that there has been a transfer of State resources for the advantage granted to one or more undertakings to be capable as being regarded as State aid within the meaning of Article 87 (1) EC'.[48] The Court went on to state that 'Article 87 (1) EC covers all the financial means by which the public authorities may actually support undertakings, irrespective of whether or not those means are permanent assets of the public sector. Therefore, even if the sums corresponding to the measure in question are not permanently held by the Treasury, the fact that they constantly remain under public control, and therefore available to the competent national authorities, is sufficient for them to be categorized as State resources'.[49] As the resources of Crédit Lyonnais and of its subsidiaries fell within the control of the state, they were state resources.

As to the imputability to the state of the financial assistance granted to Stardust, the Court held that it could not simply be inferred from the fact that Altus and SBT were public undertakings. It could only be inferred from a set of indicators arising from the circumstances of the case and the context in which the measure was taken. The Court listed in a non-exhaustive way indicators such as the integration of the public undertaking 'into the structures of the public administration . . . or any other indicator showing, in the particular case, an involvement of the public authorities in the adoption of a measure or the unlikelihood of their not being involved, having regard also to the compass of the measure, its content or the conditions which it contains.'[50] The Court concluded that as the Commission had deduced imputability to the state from the organic criterion only according to which *Crédit Lyonnais*, SBT and Altus, as public undertakings, were under the control of the state, its decision was erroneous. The judgment of the Court in Stardust Marine has subsequently been confirmed in Case *Pearle*.[51]

What conclusions can be drawn then from these decisions as to whether the licence fee is granted by a Member State or through state resources? In the first instance, it is necessary to answer the question whether the licence fee is a state resource within the meaning of Article 87 (1) EC. For this question to be answered in the affirmative it would suffice if the licence fee remained constantly under public control and therefore available to the national authorities.

The Commission has repeatedly held that the funds obtained by the licence fee are state funds. In the case *Kinderkanal/Phoenix* it established the use of state resources as regards the funding of two new special purpose channels by the public broadcasters ARD and ZDF in view of the compulsory legal character of the

47. Commission Directive 2005/81/EC of 28 November 2005 amending Directive 80/723/EEC on the transparency of financial relations between Member States and public undertakings OJ L 312/47, 2005.
48. *Ibid.*, para. 36.
49. *Ibid.*, para. 37.
50. *Ibid.*, para. 56.
51. Case 345/02, *Pearle* [2004] ECR I-7139.

licence fee, which had to be paid by all owners of a television set regardless of whether the public service programmes were actually watched.[52] In its decisions concerning the financing of various BBC services out of the licence fee the Commission reached the same conclusion on the basis of the compulsory legal nature of the licence fee and of the express approval by the Secretary of State for the use of licence fee funds.[53] According to Article 16 (1)(a) of the BBC Charter, the BBC collects the licence fee and receives all funds paid by the Secretary of State out of moneys provided by the Parliament. The Commission adds that 'even if the revenue, after collection by the BBC would stay within the BBC budget the aid character would not change, as the revenue remains under public control, and therefore available to the competent national authorities.'[54]

Similarly, its assessment of the compensation indemnities granted to the Portuguese public broadcaster RTP has been that they are directly provided by the state and allocated from the public budget. They therefore constitute public funds in the meaning of Article 87 (1) EC.[55] These decisions were confirmed in the cases concerning the state financing of the Danish public broadcaster TV2/Danmark and of the public broadcasters France 2 and France 3.[56] Also, in its 2001 Broadcasting Communication, the Commission took the view that the financing of public broadcasters out of the state budget or through a levy on TV-set holders is normally attributable to the public authorities and involves the transfer of state resources.[57]

There is less guidance from the Commission as far as the second criterion of the *Stardust Marine* jurisprudence is concerned, namely the imputability to the state of the financial aid granted to public broadcasters by means of the licence fee. It would have to be established on a case by case basis, taking different indicators into account, in how far public authorities have been involved *in concreto* in the decision to finance a certain service by licence fee funds. Only hints to the imputability to the state can be detected in some of the Commission decisions. In the decision on *BBC News 24* the Commission explains that not only is the obligation to pay the licence fee enforced by the public authorities, but also, the use of licence fee funds in the present case, namely to finance *BBC News 24*, was authorized by the Secretary of State.[58] Also, in the TV2 case the Commission establishes the

52. Case NN 70/98 para. 6.1.1. *Kinderkanal/Phoenix*.
53. Case NN 88/98, 14 December 1999, *BBC 24-Hour News Channel*, SG (99)D/10201, paras 22, 23; Case N 631/2001, 22 May 2002, *Nine Digital Services*, C (2002) 1886 final, para. 20; Case N 37/2003, 1 October 2003, *BBC Digital Curriculum*, C (2003) 3371 final, para. 21.
54. Case N 631/2001, 22 May 2002, *Nine Digital Services*, C (2002) 1886 final, para. 20.
55. Case NN 133/A/01, NN85/A/01 and NN 94/A/99, *Compensation indemnities to public service broadcaster RTP*, OJ C 98/1, 2002.
56. Case C 2/03 (ex NN 22/02), 19 May 2004, *State Financing of TV2/Danmark*, C (2004) 1814 final, paras 57 *et seq*; Case E 10/2005 (ex C 60/1999), 20 April 2005, *Redevance radiodiffusion*, decision C (2005) 1166 final, para. 21.
57. Broadcasting Communication, para. 17.
58. Case NN 88/98, 14 December 1999, *BBC 24-Hour News Channel*, SG (99)D/10201, paras 22, 23; A. Roßnagel and P. Strothmann, *Die duale Rundfunkordnung in Europa: Gemeinschaftsrechtliche Rahmenbedingungen und aktuelle Ansätze zum dualen System in ausgewählten*

presence of state resources, *inter alia*, on the basis that TV2's share of the income from licence fees is determined by the Minister of Culture. The amount of the licence fees to be allocated to TV2 is thus ultimately determined by a public authority.[59]

The imputability to the state of the licence fee system may, however, be questioned, if an independent body of experts is appointed to determine the financial requirements of public broadcasters in a way that ensures their freedom from state control.[60] This is the case in Germany where the Independent Commission for the Assessment of Financial Requirements of German Public Broadcasting (*Kommission zur Überprüfung und Ermittlung des Finanzbedarfs der Rundfunkanstalten*, KEF) fixes licence fees at three stages.[61]

According to one view, taken by Koenig and Kühling, intermediate bodies between the television viewers who ultimately bear the burden of financing the aid and the recipients, i.e. the public broadcasters, need to have a certain degree of organizational independence and need to be able to manage or dispose freely of the funds in question for their behaviour to be imputable to the state.[62] KEF fulfils the first of these criteria, not, however, the second one since it only assesses the financial requirements of public broadcasters, but is not in the position to dispose of the licence fee nor does the fee ever enter its budget.[63] A further such intermediate body is the German centre for collecting radio and television licence fees (*Gebühreneinzugszentrale*, GEZ) that collects and redistributes licence fees according to rules fixed in the Interstate Treaty on Broadcasting Finance. The same authors argue that GEZ cannot be considered an independent body designated by the state as it merely acts as a joint account manager for the public broadcasters whose budget is not burdened by the distribution of the licence fee. Support is drawn from the *Preussen Elektra* case.[64] In the same way in which producers of electricity from renewable energy sources received payment directly from the private electricity supply undertakings in that case, public broadcasters receive the licence fee directly from the viewers without state intervention.

This view has rightly been opposed in academic writing.[65] The constitutional requirement of the freedom of public broadcasters from the state and KEF's

---

Mitgliedstaaten, Schriftenreihe der Rundfunk und Telekom Regulierungs-GmbH (Wien, Rundfunk und Telekom Regulierungs-GmbH, 2004), p. 124.

59. C 2/03, *TV2/Danmark*, para. 59.
60. C.-E. Eberle, 'Aktivitäten der Europäischen Union auf dem Gebiet der Medien und ihre Auswirkungen auf den öffentlich-rechtlichen Rundfunk' (1995) 5 ZUM, 763 *et seq.*; D. Dörr, *Die öffentlich-rechtliche Rundfunkfinanzierung und die Vorgaben des EG-Vertrages*, Arbeitspapiere des Instituts für Rundfunkökonomie an der Universität zu Köln, no. 94 (Köln, Institut für Rundfunkökonomie, 1998) , p. 24 *et seq*.
61. *See* Part I, Ch. 3, s. 3, p. 40 *above*.
62. Koenig and Kühling, 'Preussen Elektra-Urteil', 544.
63. *Ibid.*, 545.
64. Case C-379/98, *Preussen Elektra* [2001] ECR I-2099.
65. Schwendinger, *Deutsche Rundfunkgebühren*, p. 61 *et seq.*; P. Selmer and H. Gersdorf, *Die Finanzierung des Rundfunks in der Bundesrepublik Deutschland auf dem Prüfstand des EG-Beihilferegimes* (Berlin, Duncker & Humblot, 1994), p. 29; A. Damm, *Gebührenprivileg und*

independent character are quite distinct from the question of the imputability of the licence fee to the state. KEF's intervention does not alter the compulsory nature of the licence fee system. Also, KEF's members are appointed by the *Länder* presidents, and its recommendations can be overruled if needed. Besides, the Court has clarified in *Stardust Marine* that the burden of proof of the imputability to the state of actions taken by public authorities should not be too onerous in view of the real risk of circumvention of the rules on state aid.[66] Consequently, the independence from the state of the system for assessing the financial requirements of public broadcasters in Germany does not put into question the character of the licence fee as state aid.

This view was also taken by the Commission in its letter of 3 March 2005 to the German authorities concerning the financing of public broadcasting in Germany, albeit with a different justification.[67] The Commission argued that the licence fee constitutes a parafiscal charge given that it is a compulsory contribution imposed by State legislation and apportioned in accordance with that legislation.[68] Even though public broadcasters are distinct from public authorities, they are organized under public law, they are empowered to levy the licence fee funds and to apply, if needed, enforcement rules under public law. These features distinguish the licence fee system from the system described in *Preussen Elektra*, characterized by a direct private law relationship between the providers and the recipients of the service.[69]

All in all, the licence fee is financed from state funds and is imputable to the state. It fulfils therefore the first criterion of Article 87 (1) EC for its categorization as state aid.

3.2 Is Funding for Public Broadcasting Compensation for Delivering the Remit?

The question whether state measures compensating undertakings for the performance of services of general economic interest constitute state aid has been controversial for a long time. State aid within the meaning of Article 87 (1) EC is *per definitionem* a gratuitous advantage granted by a Member State or through state resources to certain undertakings.[70] Is it, however, possible to regard payment

Beihilferecht: Zur Vereinbarkeit der Finanzierung des öffentlich-rechtlichen Rundfunks in Deutschland mit Art. 92 EGV (Berlin, Springer, 1998), p. 105 *et seq.*

66. Schwendinger, *Deutsche Rundfunkgebühren*, p. 62; Roßnagel and Strothmann, *Duale Rundfunkordnung in Europa*, p. 127.
67. 'Mitteilung der Generaldirektion Wettbewerb der EU-Kommission zur Finanzierung des öffentlich-rechtlichen Rundfunks in Deutschland' (2005) 10 *Funkkorrespondenz*, 1, 9 (hereafter referred to as Article 17 letter).
68. Case 173/73, *Italy v. Commission* [1974] ECR 709, para. 16.
69. Broadcasting Communication, para. 118; N. Tigchelaar, 'State Aid to Public Broadcasting – Revisited: An Overview of the Commission's Practice' (2003) 2 EStAL, 169, 173; Case E 3/2005, 24 April 2007, *Financing of public broadcasters in Germany*, C (2007) 1761 final, para. 151
70. Case 78/76, *Steinike & Weinling v. Germany* [1977] ECR 595, para. 22.

for performing public service obligations as gratuitous when it is only designed to offset additional costs incurred? In the case concerning compensation payments by the Portuguese State to RTP, the Portuguese public broadcaster, such additional costs were alleged to emanate from obligations not undertaken by private television channels, namely the obligation to cover the whole of the continental territory, to broadcast programmes in the autonomous regions of Madeira and the Azores, to maintain audiovisual archives, to cooperate with Portuguese-speaking countries, to broadcast religious programmes, and to operate an international channel.[71] The Commission took the view that the payments to RTP did not constitute state aid as they were only meant to cover the actual cost of its public service obligations.[72] The Court of First Instance disagreed with the Commission's assessment. It held that 'the fact that a financial advantage is granted to an undertaking by the public authorities in order to offset the cost of public service obligations which that undertaking is claimed to have assumed has no bearing on the classification of that measure as aid within the meaning of Article 92 (1) of the Treaty, although that aspect may be taken into account when considering whether the aid in question is compatible with the common market under Article 90 (2) of the Treaty'.[73]

The different views taken by the Commission, on the one hand, and the Court of First Instance, on the other, in the Portuguese case are commonly referred to as 'the compensation approach' and the 'state aid approach'. The position of the Courts and of the Commission on the correct approach has shifted over time. The Court of Justice followed initially, in *ADBHU*, the compensation approach, arguing that indemnities granted to waste oil disposal undertakings did not constitute state aid, but only consideration for the services performed by them.[74] In a later case, *Banco Exterior de España*, it found a Spanish tax exemption for public banks to constitute existing aid without regard to their public service obligations.[75] The Commission has for a long time been in favour of the compensation approach.[76] However, following the decision of the Court of First Instance in *FFSA*,[77] a case concerning the tax concession granted to the French Post to alleviate the additional costs of its public service obligations, it endorsed the state aid approach. In *Kinderkanal/Phoenix* the Commission held that the financing of two new special interest channels by means of licence fee revenues did constitute state aid as the compensation was fixed without any form of open competition.[78] Similarly, in *BBC News 24* the Commission did not accept the argument of the UK authorities that the BBC did not gain any economic advantage from the licence

71. Case T-46/97, *SIC v. Commission* [2000] ECR II-2125, para. 20.
72. Case NN141/95, *Financing of the public Portuguese television.*
73. Case T-46/97, *SIC v. Commission* [2000] ECR II-2125, para. 84.
74. Case 240/83, *ADBHU* [1985] ECR 531.
75. Case C-387/92, *Banco Exterior de España* [1994] ECR I-877.
76. J. A. Winter, 'Re(de)fining the Notion of State Aid in Article 87 (1) of the EC Treaty' (2004) 41 CMLRev, 475, 496; C. Quigley and A. Collins, *EC State Aid Law and Policy* (Oxford, Hart, 2004), p. 45.
77. Case T-106/95, *FFSA v. Commission* [1997] ECR II-229.
78. NN 70/98, *Kinderkanal/Phoenix*, para. 6.1.1.

fee as the funds were merely intended to reimburse BBC's costs in fulfilling its public service obligations.[79] Both in *Kinderkanal/Phoenix* and in *BBC News 24* the Commission found state aid to exist, but accepted that it was justified on Article 86 (2) grounds. The 2001 Broadcasting Communication spells out clearly that 'any transfer of State resources to a certain undertaking – also when covering net costs of public service obligations – has to be regarded as state aid.[80]

The conflict between the compensation and the state aid approach was rekindled with the judgments in *Ferring* and *Altmark*.[81] In *Ferring* the Court held that a tax exemption granted to wholesale distributors of pharmaceutical products in France would not constitute state aid provided it did not exceed the additional costs they had to bear in discharging their public service obligations. The tax on direct sales was levied on sales of medicines by pharmaceutical laboratories, not by wholesale distributors who were under a duty of public service to keep sufficient stock to satisfy the needs of regular customers. The Court reasoned that if the necessary equivalence between the exemption and the additional costs was there – a finding left to the national courts to make – the only effect of the tax would be to restore the balance of competition between distributors and laboratories.

The judgment of the Court in *Ferring* came under attack in the Opinion of Advocate General Léger in *Altmark* on the state aid character of grants to local public transport services in Germany. Advocate General Léger appealed to the Court to reverse its judgment in *Ferring* and to revert to the state aid approach. In his view, the compensation approach posed three areas of difficulty: It confused the characterizing of a measure as state aid and the question of its justification, it deprived Article 86 (2) EC of a substantial part of its effect, and, last but not least, it removed measures for financing public services from the Commission's control.[82]

Indeed, the main advantage of *Ferring*, freeing Member States from notifying measures having no adverse effects to the functioning of the common market, was also its Achilles heel. Would *Ferring* grant Member States the necessary leeway to fulfil their public service tasks or rather give them an incentive to conceal potentially harmful financing measures? Advocate General Jacobs proposed in the *GEMO* case a two tier solution to take the sting out of the compensation approach.[83] A distinction should be made, in his view, between two categories of cases depending on the link between the financing granted and the general interest duties involved and on how clearly these duties are defined. Financing measures intended as a *quid pro quo* for clearly defined public service obligations

79. NN 88/98, *BBC News 24*, paras 25, 26.
80. Broadcasting Communication, para. 19.
81. Case C-53/00, *Ferring v. ACOSS* [2001] ECR I-9067; Case C-280/00, *Altmark Trans GmbH v. Regierungspräsidium Magdeburg* [2003] ECR I-7747.
82. Opinion of Advocate General Léger of 19 March 2002 in Case C-280/00, *Altmark Trans GmbH v. Regierungspräsidium Magdeburg* [2003] ECR I-7747 paras 75–97.
83. Opinion of Advocate General Jacobs of 30 April 2002 in Case C-126/01, *French Minister of Economic, Financial and Industrial Affairs v. GEMO* [2003] ECR I-13769 paras 118 *et seq.*

should be exonerated in accordance with the compensation approach. Cases, on the other hand, where it is not clear from the outset that the state funding is intended as a *quid pro quo* for clearly defined public service obligations should be assessed in accordance with the state aid approach. The most obvious example of a direct and manifest link between state financing and clearly defined obligations was according to Advocate General Jacob the case of public service contracts awarded after public procurement procedures. Such contracts specify the general interest obligations of the undertakings involved and the remuneration they will receive in return. Advocate General Jacobs conceded that the suggested distinction would not always be easy to draw.[84]

The *quid pro quo* approach was criticized by Advocate General Léger in his second opinion to the *Altmark* case for giving rise to legal uncertainty and for relying on criteria of purely formal and procedural nature.[85] Nonetheless, the Court's ruling in the *Altmark* case was informed by Advocate General Jacob's reasoning. The Court clearly endorsed the compensation approach, but at the same time stipulated four qualifying requirements that have to be met for compensation to escape classification as state aid.

First, the recipient undertaking must actually have public service obligations to discharge, and the obligations must be clearly defined. Second, the parameters on the basis of which the compensation is calculated must be established in advance in an objective and transparent manner, to avoid it conferring an economic advantage which may favour the recipient undertaking over competing undertakings. Third, the compensation cannot exceed what is necessary to cover all or part of the costs incurred in the discharge of public service obligations, taking into account the relevant receipts and a reasonable profit for discharging those obligations. Fourth, where the undertaking which is to discharge public service obligations in a specific case is not chosen pursuant to a public procurement procedure, the level of compensation needed must be determined on the basis of an analysis of the costs which a typical undertaking, well run and adequately provided with the appropriate means of production, would have incurred in discharging those obligations, taking into account the relevant receipts and a reasonable profit for discharging the obligations.

The *Altmark* judgment has been commended in academic writing for enhancing legal certainty and for being 'a fine and successful attempt at squaring the circle and at striking a balance between the two views', i.e. the compensation and the state aid approach.[86] If the four abovementioned criteria are satisfied, there is no

84. Opinion of Advocate General Jacobs of 30 April 2002 in Case C-126/01, *French Minister of Economic, Financial and Industrial Affairs v. GEMO* [2003] ECR I-13769 para. 129.
85. Opinion of Advocate General Léger of 14 January 2003 in Case C-280/00, *Altmark Trans GmbH v. Regierungspräsidium Magdeburg* [2003] ECR I-7747 para. 79 *et seq*; A. Bartosch, 'Has the Commission Practice Applied Double Standards?' (2003) 3 EStAL, 345; A. Sinnaeve, 'State Financing of Public Services: The Court's Dilemma in the Altmark Case' (2003) 3 EStAL, 351, 356.
86. S. Santamato and N. Pesaresi, 'Compensation for Services of General Economic Interest: Some Thoughts on the Altmark Ruling' (2004) 1 *Competition Policy Newsletter*, 17; A. Bartosch, 'Die

state aid involved and no role for the European Commission. If, on the contrary, a state measure does not meet these criteria, but fulfils all four conditions under Article 87 (1) EC, it is up to the Commission to examine whether the state aid is justified under Article 87 (2), (3) EC or under Article 86 (2) EC.

What has been the impact of the *Altmark* judgment on the licence-fee-based financing of public broadcasting so far? The European Court has not yet ruled on the legitimacy of the licence fee in the light of the *Altmark* criteria. However, the Commission has investigated the mechanisms in place for financing public broadcasting in numerous cases. Some of these cases were concerned with ad-hoc funding measures granted to public broadcasters such as capital injections, loans, debt-rescheduling and tax exemptions.[87] This type of measures is beyond the scope of this chapter which is only concerned with recurrent public funding.

In the cases concerning the French, Italian, Spanish and Portuguese public broadcasters the Commission closed the investigation following commitments to amend the funding systems in place in these Member States.[88] In the case concerning the Danish public broadcaster TV2 the Commission found overcompensation and required the excess amount to be recovered.[89] The Danish Government and TV2 appealed the Commission Decision before the Court of First Instance, claiming *inter alia* that the licence fee resources transferred to TV2 were not state resources.[90] Nonetheless, TV2 complied with the Decision by setting up a recapitalization plan which was approved by the Commission in its Decision of 6 October 2004.[91] The plan was set up so as to avoid bankruptcy of TV2 and to prepare its sale to a private broadcaster.[92] The Decision of 6 October 2004 was in turn challenged by TV Danmark and Kanal 5 before the Court of First Instance.[93] These cases are still pending.

The system for financing public service broadcasting in Germany was also found wanting. In its Article 17 letter of 3 March 2005, the Commission took the preliminary view that it is incompatible with the common market and proposed appropriate measures. Germany recently proposed concrete measure to remove the Commission's concerns on its funding arrangements for public broadcasting, which will be implemented within two years through a state treaty. These measures

---

Kommissionspraxis nach dem Urteil des EuGH in der Rechtssache Altmark – Worin liegt das Neue?' (2004) 10 EuZW, 295, 300.

87. *See* S. Depypere, J. Broche and N. Tigchelaar, 'State Aid and Broadcasting: State of Play' (2004) 1 *Competition Policy Newsletter*, 71.
88. Case E 10/2005 (ex C 60/1999), 20 April 2005, *Redevance radiodiffusion*, C (2005) 1166 final; Case E3/2005, 20 April 2005, *Canone di abonamento Rai*, C (2005) 1164 final; Case E8/2005, 20 April 2005, *Ayuda estatal en favour del Ente Público Españde Televisión (RTVE)*, C (2005) 1163 final; Commission Press release IP/06/349 on the Portuguese public broadcaster.
89. C 2/03, *TV2/Danmark*, para. 163.
90. Case T-309/04, OJ C 262/43, 2004.
91. Case N313/2004, 6 October 2004, *Recapitalisation of TV2/Danmark A/S*, C (2004) 3632 final.
92. E. Thuesen, 'Court of First Instance: Commission's Decision to Approve Recapitalisation of Danish Broadcaster TV2 Contested' <www.merlin.obs.coe.int/iris/2005/5/article1.en.html>, 18 July 2007.
93. Case T-12/05, OJ C 69/23, 2005.

include a more precise definition and proper entrustment of the public service remit especially as regards new media activities, adequate controls of overcompensation and cross-subsidization, compatibility with commercial principles, financial control and more transparency as regards the sublicensing of sport rights. On this basis the Commission decided to formally close the state aid procedure.[94] Similar investigations are still pending as regards the Irish and Dutch public broadcasters.[95]

The Commission's assessment in these cases followed similar patterns. It found that the conditions of Article 87 (1) were fulfilled and therefore, the financial measures in question constituted state aid. To decide whether these measures conferred an advantage on the beneficiaries, the Commission applied the *Altmark* test. Time after time it reached the conclusion that the second and fourth *Altmark* conditions were not met.

In the German case, the Commission found that the determination of the financial requirements of public broadcasters by KEF did not guarantee separation of accounts distinguishing between public service and other activities in line with the Transparency Directive.[96] Nor did the existing system exclude the takeover of losses from commercial subsidiaries.[97] Consequently, the compensation was not calculated in advance in an objective and transparent manner as required by the second *Altmark* condition. As far as the fourth condition is concerned, the Commission observed that public broadcasters in Germany are not chosen pursuant to a public procurement procedure. Moreover, the KEF method for determining financial requirements is largely based on past expenses. The way in which KEF examines whether the activities of public broadcasters accord with the principles of business efficiency and thrift is not based on an analysis of the costs of a typical well run undertaking.[98] In its submissions following the 'Article 17-letter', Germany argued that the Commission should have provided proof that the financial needs of the German public broadcasters exceed those of a well run undertaking. The Commission disagreed. It explained that the Member States invoking the Altmark exception carry the burden of proof.[99]

Turning now to the case of Denmark, the compensation is determined in a media agreement set for four years. The Commission begrudged that there is no publicly available budget establishing a link between compensation and output and that TV2 receives a number of advantages that are not transparent such as tax exemptions and

94. Case E 3/2005, 24 April 2007, *Financing of public broadcasters in Germany*, C (2007) 1761 final.
95. Commission press releases IP/05/259 and IP/06/349.
96. Commission Directive 2005/81/EC of 28 November 2005 amending Directive 80/723/EEC on the transparency of financial relations between Member States and public undertakings OJ L 312/47, 2005.
97. Article 17 letter, para. 130.
98. *Ibid.*, para. 131.
99. 'Mitteilung der Bundesregierung an die Europäische Kommission: Die Finanzierung der öffentlich-rechtlichen Rundfunkanstalten – Deutschland, 6. Mai 2005' (18 May 2005) 38 *epd medien*, 27 (referred to hereafter as 'Mitteilung der Bundesregierung').

interest waivers. As to the fourth *Altmark* condition, the Commission noted that TV2 has not been chosen on the basis of a tender, nor has any analysis been carried out to ensure that the level of compensation is determined on an analysis of the costs of a typical well run undertaking.[100] The Commission's findings in the French, Italian and Spanish cases were much the same.[101]

The decisions on the recurrent funding mechanisms so far have amply demonstrated that it is nearly impossible for public broadcasters to pass the *Altmark* test. The second *Altmark* criterion requires Member States to prognosticate the cost of their public service tasks. This poses a certain risk that the *ex ante* evaluation by the Member States and the *ex post* control in a Commission investigation may differ.[102] The fourth *Altmark* criterion is particularly problematic in the area of broadcasting given that it is difficult to identify a typical well run private undertaking that provides a wide range of high quality programmes comparable to those offered by public broadcasters.

The question arises whether a comparison should be made with private broadcasters or rather with other public broadcasters.[103] It could be argued that only private broadcasters who are fully subject to competitive pressures are suitable benchmarks. Koenig and Haratsch argue that no typical well run comparable companies exist in the private sector so that the comparison should be made with other public broadcasters.[104]

It is not too far-fetched to imagine a situation in which a hypothetical reference undertaking does not exist at all so that no comparison can be made. The *Altmark* judgment and the Commission's practice so far suggest that there is state aid if a typical well run undertakings does not exist, and no public procurement procedure has taken place.[105] As a result, measures risk being labelled as aid on procedural grounds regardless of whether they favour the recipient.[106] Compensations for public service providers can only be authorized then via Article 86 (2) EC. This practice is arguably inconsistent with the *Chronopost* decision where the European Court took the additional costs of the French Post Office itself as a benchmark given that no appropriate comparison with the public postal network was available.[107]

In its decision in the German case, the Commission left the question open as to whether the findings in *Chronopost* are relevant for the assessment of the financing of

100. C 2/03, *TV2/Danmark*, para. 71.
101. *Redevance radiodiffusion*, paras 24, 25; *Canone di abonamento Rai*, para. 23; *Ayuda estatal en favour del Ente Público Espańde Televisión (RTVE)*, para. 46.
102. A. Bartosch, 'Clarification or Confusion? How to Reconcile the ECJ's Rulings in Altmark and Chronopost' (2003) 3 EStAL, 375, 385.
103. Koenig and Haratsch, 'Licence-Fee-Based Financing', 577.
104. *Ibid.*
105. Sinnaeve, 'State Financing of Public Services', 358; Bartosch, 'Kommissionspraxis', 300.
106. Santamato and Pesaresi, 'Compensation for Services of General Economic Interest', 21.
107. Cases C-83/01 P, C-93/01 P and C-94/01 P, *Chronopost and Others* [2003] ECR I-6993; T. Prosser, *The Limits of Competition Law: Markets and Public Services* (Oxford, Oxford University Press, 2005), p. 143.

public broadcasters under the *Altmark* conditions.[108] It disagreed that it is impossible to establish the costs of an efficient operator as a benchmark. It argued that the costs incurred by private competitors could be used as a benchmark, while taking into account the specific obligations of public broadcasters. Alternatively, if one were to find the comparison with private operators inadequate, one would need to establish a single benchmark on the basis of the costs incurred by public broadcasters. The Commission observed that KEF had not come up with such a benchmark yet.

The intricacies of the fourth condition clearly safeguard the Commission's prerogatives. Member States are obliged to notify their mechanisms for funding public broadcasting for fear that they might fall foul of the *Altmark* test. Public broadcasters who rejoiced at the *Altmark* ruling in the first place, interpreting it as a clear statement in favour of the licence fee, have been disillusioned with its subsequent application. This is a bizarre outcome if one considers that the compensation approach, which was at the core of the *Altmark* ruling, was meant to remove unsuspicious financing measures from the Commission's control.

3.3 Distortion of Competition and Effect on Trade between Member States

The analysis of the Commission's broadcasting decisions after *Altmark* has made clear that the licence fee cannot be taken to constitute compensation for the public service remit without further ado. In the many cases in which public broadcasters fail to meet the requirements of the *Altmark* test, the next question to ask is whether the licence fee distorts or threatens to distort competition and affects trade between Member States.

In order to assess whether distortion of competition takes place it is necessary to identify the relevant product market. One possible product market is the programme market where broadcasters compete for viewers. The existence of such a market in the case of free TV has been questioned in academic writing.[109] It can safely be answered in the affirmative in the case of broadcasters who carry advertisements and hence compete for viewers so as to maximize their advertising revenue. The Commission has also consistently taken the view that there is such a thing as a programme market in free TV.[110]

It could, however, be argued that cross border competition between public and private broadcasters for viewers is negligible given that viewers lack interest in programmes broadcast in a language other than their own language. Programme markets are largely national.[111] Even if this is the case, other markets have an

108. Case E 3/2005, *Financing of public service broadcasters in Germany*, para. 168.
109. Selmer and Gersdorf, *Finanzierung des Rundfunks*, p. 46; T. Oppermann, *Deutsche Rundfunkgebühren und europäisches Beihilferecht* (Berlin, Duncker & Humblot, 1997), p. 60 *et seq.*
110. *Magill TV Guide*, OJ L 78/43, 1989; *VTM*, OJ L 244/18, 1997.
111. Ruttig, *Einfluß des EG-Beihilferechts*, p. 242.

indisputable international dimension. Prime examples according to the Broadcasting Communication are the market for the acquisition and sale of programme rights and the advertising market, especially in the case of homogeneous linguistic areas across national boundaries.[112] Moreover, the ownership structure of commercial broadcasters may extend to more than one Member State.[113]

The Commission has had no difficulty in finding a distortion of competition in its broadcasting decisions.[114] In its decision on *BBC's Digital Curriculum*, concerning BBC's new online service to provide interactive learning materials free to homes and schools, the Commission held that trade between Member States was affected. The fact that the service was intended for students in the UK did not prevent an effect on intra-Community trade given that BBC's competitors in the UK also sold to other Member State markets and had an international ownership structure.[115] Public funding for BBC affected such competitors. It follows that, as a rule, the licence fee distorts competition and affects trade between Member States.

3.4 Existing Aid?

Once the Commission reaches the conclusion that all conditions of Article 87 (1) EC have been met, the next question arising is whether the licence fee constitutes new or existing aid. This is a matter of great practical importance given that existing aid may not be the subject of a recovery order. In accordance with Article 7 (5) of Regulation 659/1999, the Commission can only decide that the aid shall not be put into effect *ex nunc*.[116]

What distinguishes new from existing aid? Article 1 (b) of the same Regulation stipulates that existing aid is all aid which existed in a Member State prior to its accession to the European Union and which is still applicable after the entry into force of the Treaty. 'New aid' is defined in Article 1 (c) as 'all aid, that is to say, aid schemes and individual aid, which is not existing aid, including alterations to existing aid. An alteration to existing aid is according to Article 4 (1) of Regulation 794/2004 'any change, other than modifications of a purely formal or administrative nature which cannot affect the evaluation of the compatibility of the aid measure with the common market'.[117]

The Court of First Instance clarified in the *Gibraltar* case that only the alteration as such is liable to be classified as new aid, not the altered aid in full. Only where the alteration touches upon the actual substance of the original scheme is the

112. Broadcasting Communication, para. 18.
113. *Ibid.*
114. *Nine Digital Services*, paras 21, 22; C 2/03, *TV2/Danmark*, paras 72, 76.
115. *BBC Digital Curriculum*, para. 25.
116. Council Regulation 659/1999 of 22 March 1999 laying down detailed rules for the application of Article 93 of the EC Treaty OJ L 83/1, 1999.
117. Commission Regulation (EC) No. 794/2004 of 21 April 2004 implementing Council Regulation (EC) No. 659/1999 laying down detailed rules for the application of Article 93 of the EC Treaty OJ L 140/1, 2004.

latter transformed into a new aid scheme. Otherwise, where the alteration is severable from the existing aid, only the modifications need to be notified.[118] The Broadcasting Communication explained that a case by case approach is the most appropriate one to verify whether or not the legal framework under which the aid is granted has changed since its introduction. To this end, all the legal and economic elements related to the broadcasting system of a given Member State must be taken into account.[119]

The Commission has classified aid in some cases as new aid, in others as existing one depending on the circumstances of each case. In *BBC Digital Curriculum*, the UK argued that funding for the new online service is existing aid since the licence fee has existed since 1927. The Commission disagreed. Digital Curriculum was provided by the BBC as 'ancillary service' under Article 3 (b) of the 1996 Charter. However, the term ancillary services could not, according to the Commission, give credence to the notion of 'existing aid' in perpetuity.[120] The critical issue was rather the nature of the service and its consistency with the scope of the Charter. In other words, the provision of educational material over the internet would have to remain closely associated with BBC's 'television and radio services'.[121] The Commission concluded that, despite the educational traditions of the BBC, the Digital Curriculum was a digression from the various markets within which the BBC has been active, and hence, did not constitute existing aid.

The Commission failed to provide a convincing explanation in this case as to why the Digital Curriculum was an *aliud* compared to traditional education services. It only noted that the BBC used public funding 'to enter markets that are already developed and where the commercial players have had little or no exposure to the BBC as a competitor'.[122] Indeed, private enterprises were fiercely opposed to the BBC initiative as they had developed a digital learning offer that was educationally appealing and commercially viable. However, their offer was inferior to that of the BBC as it was only concentrating on the core subjects, such as maths and English. Moreover, it was relying on CD-ROM distribution rather than the more expensive broadband distribution.[123] The benefits to the public therefore outweighed the risk of crowding out commercial providers.

In any event, the Commission deployed a criterion that is extraneous to the nature of the service, namely the expectations of competitors in the market of educational services, instead of asking whether the provision of such services over the internet changed the actual substance of the BBC's educational activities.

118. Joined Cases T-195/01and T-207/01, *Government of Gibraltar v. Commission* [2002] ECR II 2309, paras 109–111.
119. Broadcasting Communication, para. 24.
120. *BBC Digital Curriculum*, para. 33.
121. *Ibid.*, para. 36.
122. *Ibid.*
123. S. Barnett, 'Which End of the Telescope: From Market Failure to Cultural Value' in *From Public Service Broadcasting to Public Service Communications*, D. Tambini and J. Cowling (eds) (London, IPPR, 2004), p. 34.

The criterion used by the Commission confuses two distinct questions, the definition of the public service remit and the effect on competition. The participation of public broadcasters on the internet should not change the substance of the public service as long as it serves the same democratic, social and cultural needs of society regardless of the effects on competitors.[124] Subjecting the legitimacy of public broadcasting to market criteria blatantly encroaches upon the prerogative of the Member States to define the remit in accordance with the Amsterdam Protocol.

The Commission's reasoning in *BBC Digital Curriculum* may be contrasted to its decision in the case of the French licence fee.[125] Here the Commission held that even though Law 49-1032 of 30 July 1949 and the legal personality of the fee's beneficiary have changed many a time, these modifications have not been substantial and have left the main principles of the scheme, i.e. its nature, objective, legal foundation, destination and its financial source unaltered. In line with the Court's judgment in *Namur-Les Assurances*, increases in the amount of the licence fee cannot affect its classification as existing aid either.[126]

In the German case the Commission also concluded that changes to the legal framework in which the licence fee was granted have not affected the actual substance of the original scheme. It acknowledged that the extension of the public service remit to cover new services such as the internet did not amount to a substantial change so long as the content transmitted via the new medium was part of the existing remit and the legal foundations of the financing mechanism chosen to provide these services were unaltered. Online services displaying a close link to public broadcasters' traditional mission have not brought about a substantial change of the original scheme.[127] For the same reasons, the Commission assessed that the digital transmission of existing programmes did not affect the original remit either.[128] In its Article 17 letter the Commission refrained from making a definitive statement as to the classification of new digital programmes.[129] In its final decision the Commission held, however, that the additional digital channels offered by the German public broadcasters have not altered the initial public service missions given that they relied extensively on the re-packaging of existing programme material.[130]

---

124. Wiedemann, 'Public Service Broadcasting', p. 5 *et seq.*
125. *Redevance radiodiffusion*, 20 April 2005, decision C (2005) 1166 fin.
126. Case 44/93, *Namur-Les Assurances du credit v. Office national du ducroire and Belgian State* [1994] ECR I-3829.
127. Article 17 letter, para. 162; Case E 3/2005, *Financing of public service broadcasters in Germany*, para. 208.
128. Article 17 letter, para. 164; Case E 3/2005, *Financing of public service broadcasters in Germany*, para. 210.
129. Article 17 letter, para. 165.
130. Case E 3/2005, *Financing of public service broadcasters in Germany*, para. 211.

4. IS THE STATE FINANCING OF PUBLIC BROADCASTING JUSTIFIED?

4.1 JUSTIFICATION UNDER ARTICLE 87 (3) (d) EC

In a few instances Member States have sought to justify their funding of public broadcasting by attempting to bring it under the exception of Article 87 (3) (d) EC. In none of these cases have they been successful. Under this provision the Commission has discretion to exempt 'aid to promote culture and heritage conservation where such aid does not affect trading conditions and competition in the Community to an extent that is contrary to the common interest'. The Commission has stressed that exemptions from the prohibition on state aids must be applied restrictively in accordance with established case-law of the Court.[131]

In its decision in *Kinderkanal/Phoenix* the Commission drew a rather artificial distinction between the educational and democratic needs of a Member State as opposed to its cultural needs.[132] It held that the two thematic channels in question, a children's channel and a channel specializing in politics and society were not concerned with culture and heritage conservation and could hence not benefit from Article 87 (3) (d) EC.[133] Also, in *BBC News 24* the Commission argued that a 24-hour news channel is aimed more at fulfilling the information needs of UK citizens than at promoting culture or national heritage.

The Commission reiterated its view that broadcasting does not constitute a cultural activity in general in the Broadcasting Communication. It noted that state aid to public broadcasters often does not differentiate between the democratic, social and cultural needs of society, and affirmed that 'unless a Member State provides for the separate definition and the separate funding of State aid to promote culture alone, such aid cannot generally be approved under Article 87 (3) (d)'.[134] This narrow criterion was not met in the Commission's view in a case concerning aid for local television stations in the French-speaking Community of Belgium. The local television stations were entrusted with the provision of full-time news, animation, cultural development and education programmes and no separate funding was earmarked for culture alone. The Commission concluded that the activities of these stations were not entirely or specifically directed at the promotion of culture and could therefore not be exempted under Article 87 (3) (d) EC.[135]

131. *Kinderkanal/Phoenix*, para. 6.2.; Case N548/2001, 13 February 2002, *Local Belgium TV stations*, C (2002) 446 final, 6.
132. *See* Part 2, Ch. 9, p. 168, Part 2, Ch. 12.3.1.2, p. 260.
133. *Kinderkanal/Phoenix*, para. 6.2.
134. Broadcasting Communication, para. 27.
135. *Local Belgium TV stations*, 6.

4.2 Justification under Article 86 (2) EC

Given that the licence fee cannot readily be justified on the basis of the cultural derogation, its compatibility with the common market depends on Article 86 (2) EC. According to the 2001 Broadcasting Communication, the following three conditions need to be satisfied in order for the licence fee to benefit from the derogation. First, the service in question must be a service of general economic interest and clearly defined as such by the Member State (definition). Secondly, the undertaking in question must be explicitly entrusted by the Member State with the provision of that service (entrustment). Thirdly, the ban on state aid must obstruct the performance of the particular tasks assigned to the undertaking and the exemption from such rules must not affect the development of trade to an extent that would be contrary to the interests of the Community (proportionality test).[136] In the following, the application of these conditions to the broadcasting sector will be analysed.

4.2.1 Definition of the Public Service Remit

The Broadcasting Communication requires a clear and precise definition of the public service mandate for the Commission to be able to assess with sufficient legal certainty whether Article 86 (2) EC is applicable. In line with the Amsterdam Protocol, which refers to the 'public service remit as conferred, defined and organized by each Member State', the Communication acknowledges that the definition of the public service mandate falls within the competence of the Member States. Taking account of the specific nature of the broadcasting sector, even a wide definition, 'entrusting a given broadcaster with the task of providing balanced and varied programming in accordance with the remit, while preserving a certain level of audience, may be considered . . . legitimate'.[137] The requirements of a 'clear and precise' or of a 'wide' definition of the public service remit are somewhat contradictory. In any event, the role of the Commission is a limited one, namely to check for manifest error in the definition of the remit. Such error would be found to exist if the remit included activities that could not reasonably be considered to meet the democratic, social and cultural needs of each society.[138]

In the German case, the Commission is satisfied that the remit of German public broadcasters is defined in a sufficiently precise manner as far as television broadcasting activities are concerned.[139] It disagreed, however, in its Article 17 letter with the German view that commercial activities to obtain revenue such as the sale of advertising space should be viewed as part of the remit.[140] The Broadcasting Communication already stated that 'the question of the definition

---

136. Broadcasting Communication, para. 29.
137. *Ibid.*, para. 33.
138. *Ibid.*, para. 36.
139. *Financing of public service broadcasters in Germany*, para. 224.
140. Article 17 letter, para. 180.

of the public service remit must not be confused with the question of the financing mechanism chosen to provide these services'. From this it drew the conclusion that 'such activities cannot *normally* be viewed as part of the remit'.[141] The use of the word 'normally' indicates that exceptions may be justified, but it is uncertain under which circumstances this should be the case. In its decisions on *Ad-hoc measures for RAI* and on *Local Belgium TV stations* the Commission also took the view that commercial activities fall outside the remit.[142] Nonetheless, programmes that are partly funded through advertisements and other forms of commercial revenue constitute public service activities.[143]

The Commission also had reservations with regard to other activities such as digital channels and online services. It considered that the requirement in § 19 (4) of the Interstate Treaty on Broadcasting that additional digital channels should have a focus on culture, information and education was not sufficiently precise. It argued that the categories of 'culture, information and education' are so broad that they would cover most programme genres offered by public broadcasters, thus posing a risk that undue weight might be given to certain programme genres, in particular sport, to the detriment of others.[144]

So as to allay the Commission's fears, Germany proposed to include in the Interstate Treaty an illustrative list of programme categories. 'Information' would comprise the sub-categories of news, political information, regional information, but also sports. 'Education' would refer to science and technology, children and youth, religion etc. 'Culture' would include theatre, music, architecture, philosophy etc. Public broadcasters would also be obliged to develop a programme concept further concretizing these programme categories.[145] The Commission approved of these measures that are, in its view, adequate to delineate the scope of digital channels in a sufficiently clear manner and to allow private operators to plan their activities.[146] Moreover, Germany committed itself to broadcasting sports events over digital channels only as a supplement to the main programme. According to the Commission, this should be sufficient to ensure that public broadcasters will not change the focus of digital channels without proper entrustment in order to operate dedicated sports channels.[147]

---

141. Broadcasting Communication, para. 36.
142. *Ad-hoc measures for RAI SpA*, OJ L 119/1, 2004, para. 117; *Local Belgium TV stations*, 7.
143. T. Held and W. Schulz, *Europarechtliche Beurteilung von Online-Angeboten öffentlich-rechtlicher Rundfunkanstalten: Inwieweit beeinflussen die Beihilferegeln die Einbeziehung neuer Dienste in den Funktionsauftrag öffentlich-rechtlichen Rundfunks? Gutachten im Auftrag der Friedrich-Ebert-Stiftung* (Berlin, Friedrich-Ebert-Stiftung, 2004), p. 66; European Broadcasting Union, 'Comments on the Communication from the Commission on the application of State aid rules to public service broadcasting (2001/ C 320/04)', 8 Mai 2002, 6.
144. *Financing of public service broadcasters in Germany*, para. 227.
145. *Ibid.*, para. 336.
146. *Ibid.*, para. 360.
147. *Ibid.*, para. 361.

The Commission was also concerned that a vaguely circumscribed mandate to provide online services could serve as a disincentive for other market participants to develop new media services.[148] This echoes the dictum in the Broadcasting Communication that a 'clear identification of the activities covered by the public service remit is also important for non-public service operators, so that they can plan their activities'.[149] The emphasis on the commercial expectations of competitors, already familiar from the *BBC Digital Curriculum* case, has been criticized in academic writing for implying that private and public broadcasters should develop different activities.[150]

One may have doubts as to whether this is the hidden message behind these statements. If public broadcasters were only to offer online services that are not otherwise being offered by the market, why would they need to notify other market participants? The requirement of advance notice to competitors does not make sense if public broadcasters are required to produce distinctive programming. On the other hand, the Commission, in its final decision in the German case, stressed that online services offered by public broadcasters should display specific features that differentiate them from other services already offered by the market.[151] Plainly, the Commission was not only concerned about the clear articulation of the public service remit, but also about its distinctiveness.

More precisely, the Commission was concerned that § 11 (1) second sentence RStV does not say clearly what kind of online services public broadcasters are allowed to provide. This provision states that public broadcasting can offer print media that accompany its programmes and telemedia with programme related content. The Commission bemoans that the required link of telemedia to the programme is not fleshed out in a way that would allow for a clear determination of which online offerings contribute to the same democratic, social and cultural needs of society as traditional television.[152] Can online games and chatrooms qualify as services of general economic interest when they are not clearly related to the public television programmes and when they do not differ from similar commercial products? In its final decision, the Commission asked for more precise criteria to be developed, which would unequivocally demonstrate the link of online activities to traditional television offers.[153] It is worth noting that in the *TV2/Danmark* case the Commission also drew a similar distinction between TV2's internet pages that are limited to informing the user about its public television programmes and hence fall within its public service programming task and TV2's commercial internet services that do not constitute services of general economic interest.

148. *Ibid.*, paras 229 *et seq.*
149. Broadcasting Communication, para. 38.
150. S. Coppieters, 'The Financing of Public Service Broadcasting' in *The Law of State Aid in the European Union*, A. Biondi, P. Eeckhout, J. Flynn (eds) (Oxford, Oxford University Press, 2004), p. 273; Wiedemann, 'Public Service Broadcasting', p. 5.
151. *Financing of public service broadcasters in Germany*, paras 231 *et seq.*
152. *Ibid.*, para. 234.
153. *Ibid.*, para. 235.

In response to the Commission's criticisms, Germany proposed to establish an illustrative list of online services which shall or shall not be part of the public service remit. It explained that activities such as e-commerce and local reporting would be excluded from the remit, that sponsoring and advertisement would still be prohibited in public broadcasters' online presence, and that there should be no direct links to commercial offers. In addition, Germany proposed to limit the public service mission to editorially arranged offers, i.e. offers where the selection and focus of topics is based on journalistic criteria.[154] Furthermore, it undertook to include in the Interstate Treaty the functions to be performed by public broadcasters' telemedia services: enabling the whole population and also minorities to gain access to the information society, promoting media literacy etc.

Notably, Germany also committed itself to taking into account the scope and quality of already existing offers. All new or modified mobile services or digital offers will need to pass a three-step test. It will be necessary to establish, first, whether an offer is covered by the public service remit and therefore serves the democratic, social and cultural needs of society, secondly, whether it contributes in a qualitative way to 'editorial competition' and, third, the financial impact of the offer.[155] The Commission is satisfied that these additional criteria are adequate to define the public service remit in more exact terms and to ward off possible distortive effects of new media services.[156]

Some of the commitments extracted from Germany by the Commission such as the exclusion of e-commerce from the public service remit and the prohibition of direct links to commercial offers make good sense. Others such as the keeping out of local reporting and the obligation to take into account already existing services are more problematic. The three-step test is on the borderline of what is constitutionally permissible in Germany. By pushing public broadcasters into the mould of competition regulation, it verges on violating the constitutional principles of programme autonomy and freedom from state control. Notably, it also inflicts a great competitive disadvantage on public broadcasters. The lengthy preparations and deliberations needed so as to satisfy this test put planned programme offers in jeopardy, in particular by heightening the risk that information might leak to competitors.[157] The Commission's preoccupation with the protection of the private sector from market distortions is thus turned on its head.

Two of the criteria used by the Commission to decide whether online services fall within the public service remit, namely programme alignment and the lack of similar commercial programmes, are questionable also for other reasons. Different views exist as to the role to be fulfilled by public broadcasters in the internet. Some take the view that the public service remit might only extend to online information services if these constitute a functional equivalent to 'programmes' in the

154. *Ibid.*, para. 362.
155. *Ibid.*, para. 328.
156. *Ibid.*, para. 362.
157. From a telephone interview with a legal adviser for the WDR Köln conducted for this work in October 2007.

traditional sense. This means that viewers' behaviour and expectations would have to be at least partly equivalent to those associated with traditional broadcasting.[158] An independent online presence of public broadcasters would be redundant as pluralism is already guaranteed by the variety of services on offer.

Others argue that functional equivalence to traditional programmes would not sufficiently cover the democratic, social and cultural needs of society given that online offerings act as a special medium in the free formation of public and individual opinion.[159] Commercial online services, so the argument goes, display structural deficits that would need to be made good by public service offerings. At first sight, the Commission requirement of programme alignment comes close to the first view as it tries to secure the closest possible linkage between online services and television programmes. Curiously, however, functional equivalence may militate against programme alignment as will be seen below.

Public service offerings of search-engines and portals, online newspapers and webcasting or even games address the same democratic, social and cultural needs as traditional programmes, especially as far as young persons and other target groups are concerned. In so far as the internet comes to usurp functions, hitherto fulfilled by television programmes, most prominently information, to a lesser extent also education and entertainment, functional equivalence can hardly be questioned. For the time being, programme alignment is not an issue as public broadcasters' online services usually refer to their radio and television programmes, share with them the same resources and lend support to their public service tasks.[160] However, in the long run, the decision whether to supply offerings that are closely linked to the classical television programme or whether to create content especially for the internet will ultimately depend on the function to be fulfilled by the internet. The more traditional television functions wander off to the web, the more it will appear legitimate to offer original content online.[161] Looking at each online service in isolation would disregard the fact that even services that are not strictly aligned with the television programme are linked with it by means of cross-references and corporate design. Also, the internet presence strengthens public broadcasters' brand by tying in users.[162]

The criterion of programme alignment narrows down public broadcasters' online services to a role strictly complementary to that played by traditional broadcasting. In its Broadcasting Communication, the Commission pronounced that 'the public service remit might include certain services that are not 'programmes' in the traditional sense, such as on-line information services, to the extent that while taking into account the development and diversification of activities in the digital age, they

158. C. Degenhart, *Der Funktionsauftrag des öffentlich-rechtlichen Rundfunks in der digitalen Welt* (Heidelberg, Verlag Recht und Wirtschaft, 2001), p. 65.
159. W. Hoffmann-Riem, *Regulierung der dualen Rundfunkordnung* (Baden-Baden, Nomos, 2000), p. 241.
160. Mitteilung der Bundesregierung, para. 323.
161. Held and Schultz, *Europarechtliche Beurteilung von Online-Angeboten*, p. 59.
162. *Ibid.*, pp. 17, 59.

are addressing the same democratic, social and cultural needs of the society in question.' By the use of the phrase 'the same . . . needs' the Commission cannot, however, have intended to limit online services to the same functions as are performed by television. This would freeze opinion formation to the status quo regardless of advances in public communication.[163]

Besides, the Broadcasting Communication in conjunction with the Amsterdam Protocol accord Member States a wide margin of appreciation in assessing whether activities included in the remit meet the democratic, social and cultural needs of society. We have already seen that the Commission cannot substitute their assessment with its own without further ado but would need to prove that a manifest error has been committed in the definition of the remit.[164] In its Article 17 letter to the German authorities the Commission found such a manifest error in the characterization of e-shops and mobile services as services of general economic interest.[165] It argued that both e-shops and mobile services are commercial activities. What is more, mobile services are not directed to the whole population, but only to the owner of a mobile phone or of a personal digital assistant (PDA). They are not part of a balanced, comprehensive programme, but are designed to satisfy the needs of individual users.

In its final decision, the Commission upheld its justified reservations with regard to e-shops and other purely commercial activities, but reversed its position on mobile services. It held that the use of new platforms to deliver content under conditions that are similar to those for traditional television broadcasting does not constitute a 'manifest error'. Only the sale of content to telecom operators constitutes a typical commercial activity that falls outside the public service remit.[166] Indeed, as the Federal Government had already observed correctly, the special treatment of mobile services goes against the principle of technological neutrality enshrined in Article 8 (1) of Directive 2002/21/EC of the European Parliament and the Council.[167] Why should it make a difference whether you receive BBC News on your handheld or on your television set? Also, the category of mobile services is flawed and does not help determine whether a certain activity is covered by the public service remit or not. Mobile services are not directed to specific users only. In fact, more people own a mobile phone than a computer so that the distinction between mobile services and online services is not convincing.[168]

Finally, the Commission's dictum that online services which do not differ from similar commercial products cannot qualify as services of general economic interest is puzzling. It creates the impression that the Commission has endorsed the so-called 'market failure' model of public broadcasting.[169] According to this

163. *Ibid.*, p. 59.
164. Wiedemann, 'Public Service Broadcasting', p. 8.
165. Article 17 letter, para. 192.
166. *Financing of public service broadcasters in Germany*, para. 240.
167. OJ L 108/33, 2002.
168. Mitteilung der Bundesregierung, para. 337.
169. Prosser, *Limits of Competition Law*, p. 209; P. Booth, 'Introduction' in *Public Service Broadcasting without the BBC?*, A. Peacock (ed.) (London, Institute of Economic Affairs, 2004), p. 18; Barwise, 'Threats to Public Service Broadcasting', p. 26.

model public broadcasting is only there to fill gaps left by the market in, for example news, current affairs, cultural programming etc. Underlying this model is the assumption that commercial broadcasting only suffers from certain punctual deficits that can be remedied by public broadcasters.[170] The implication is that public broadcasters need to concentrate on these types of programmes that are not provided by the commercial broadcasting sector. This residual role is constantly under threat as a more segmented market caters for minority interests by means of subscription channels. It forces public broadcasters to go on the defensive whenever they try to expand into new areas, as in this case into online services, which commercial broadcasters also provide.

A radical different view of public broadcasting is taken by the so-called 'cultural model'.[171] According to this model, public broadcasters are there to forge citizenship and social solidarity, to provide a universal service not only in geographical terms but also in social and cultural terms by catering for a wide range of interests, and to provide high-quality programmes. Underlying this model is the assumption that commercial broadcasting suffers not just from punctual but from structural deficits that can only be filled by a comprehensive public service programme.[172] These structural deficits emanate essentially from the reliance of commercial broadcasters on private sources of funding. As a result, they are dependent on high viewing figures and are, therefore, geared towards the satisfaction of mass interests and hence not capable of providing a comprehensive range of content in programmes.

Advertising funded commercial broadcasters focus on a target audience with high disposable incomes, making up only a small percentage of the general audience.[173] Public broadcasters, on the other hand, are not only there to fill in gaps in the market but rather to shape consumer preferences and to attract new audiences by offering a wide span of programmes. The expansion of public broadcasters into a terrain already occupied by their commercial counterparts is not controversial according to this model as market provision is always tainted by the said structural deficits.

The German Federal Constitutional Court has consistently been in favour of the cultural model of public broadcasting.[174] The Commission's position to date has been less clear. In an internal Discussion Paper circulated by the Competition Directorate General in 1998 the idea was put forward that entertainment and sports programmes are not generally in the public interest and could therefore not be funded out of the licence fee where broadcasters also relied on advertising

170. Held and Schultz, *Europarechtliche Beurteilung von Online-Angeboten*, p. 60.
171. Prosser, *Limits of Competition Law*, p. 210; R. Foster, J. Egan and J. Simon, 'Measuring Public Service Broadcasting' in *From Public Service Broadcasting to Public Service Communication*, D. Tambini. J. Cowling (eds) (London, IPPR, 2004), pp. 151–152.
172. Held and Schultz, *Europarechtliche Beurteilung von Online-Angeboten*, p. 60.
173. Barnett, 'Which End of the Telescope', p. 34.
174. BVerfGE 73, 118, 155 *et seq.*; BVerfGE 83, 238, 310 *et seq.*

income.[175] Also, in its decisions on *BBC News 24*[176] and *Kinderkanal/Phoenix*[177] the Commission emphasized that the channels in question had features that could not be found in services provided by private operators such as the lack of advertisements combined with the non-violent character of the children's programme in the case of Kinderkanal.

The criterion of distinctiveness employed in these decisions has rightly been criticized in academic writing as it is tantamount to saying that the licence fee would more easily be characterized as unlawful state aid in the case of dual funded public broadcasters.[178] The Amsterdam Protocol and the 2001 Broadcasting Communication made short shrift of the idea of a narrow remit limited to specific programme categories. Also, both the Communication and recent Commission decisions demonstrate that the Commission is not opposed to dual funding schemes as long as public funds are not used to depress prices in the advertising market.[179] However, the Commission's statements in its Article 17 letter and in its final decision on the financing of German public broadcasting as well as in *TV2/ Danmark* indicate that the criterion of distinctiveness is alive and kicking. The battle between the 'market failure' and the 'cultural model' of broadcasting is set to be fought again on the terrain of online services.

4.2.2 Entrustment

Closely linked with the definition of the public service remit is the question of its entrustment. It is necessary to clarify in this context which body and by means of which type of instrument defines and entrusts the public service. The Broadcasting Communication requires the remit to be entrusted 'to one or more undertakings by means of an official act (for example, by legislation, contract or terms of reference)'.[180] The official act does not therefore necessarily need to be in form of a legislative measure or regulation. In *Nine Digital Services* the Commission accepted the letter of approval of the Secretary of State as a sufficient act of entrustment.[181] Also, the European Court held in the *Almelo* case that the grant of a public service concession governed by public law would be sufficient.[182] In *Commission* v. *France* it stressed that 'this is so a fortiori where such concessions have been granted in order to give effect to the obligations imposed on

175. Craufurd Smith, 'State Support for Public Service Broadcasting', 3, 16; MacLennan, 'Facing the Digital Future', 182.
176. *BBC 24-Hour News Channel*, para. 53.
177. *Kinderkanal/Phoenix*, para 6.3, p. 10.
178. Craufurd Smith, 'State Support for Public Service Broadcasting', 15.
179. Broadcasting Communication, para. 46; C 2/03, *TV2/Danmark*, para. 102; *Ad-hoc measures for RAI SpA*, para. 124.
180. Broadcasting Communication, para. 40.
181. *Nine Digital Services*, para. 35.
182. Case C-393/92, *Municipality of Almelo and Others v. NV Energibedrijf Ijselmij* [1994] ECR 1477 para. 47.

undertakings which, by statute, have been entrusted with the operation of a service of general economic interest'.[183]

We have seen that the Broadcasting Communication requires the public service remit to be defined as precisely as possible. However, this requirement is at odds with the rapidly changing broadcasting environment the remit has to keep pace with so as to take account of technological developments and new consumer behaviour and needs. It follows that a detailed definition of the remit in the broadcasting law itself would be impracticable as the law could not be constantly adjusted.[184] Therefore, Member States often have a two-layer procedure in place to define the public service remit. The statutory law lays down the basic principles of the remit, while more concrete obligations are included in self-regulatory or co-regulatory instruments. In the United Kingdom, for instance, the BBC needed to obtain the approval of the Secretary of State prior to launching a new service such as the Digital Curriculum.[185] The complainants alleged in this case that the conditions imposed by the Secretary of State were too vague and did not clearly define the contents of the new service. Further clarifications were provided in the 'commissioning plan' setting out the subjects to be covered during the first five years of the service. Similarly, in Germany, § 11 of the Ninth Interstate Treaty on Broadcasting (*Rundfunkänderungsstaatsvertrag*, RStV) describes the public service remit in general terms. The remit is then concretized further by means of binding guidelines adopted by the broadcasters on the basis of § 11 (4) RStV.

The Commission explained, however, in the Broadcasting Communication that it is not sufficient that the public broadcaster be formally entrusted with the provision of a well-defined public service. An appropriate authority or appointed body must also monitor its application to ensure that the public service is actually supplied as provided in the official entrustment.[186] It is within the competence of the Member States to choose the mechanism to ensure effective supervision of the public service obligations. However, it is paramount that the elected authority is independent from the entrusted undertaking.[187] In *Nine Digital Services* the Commission considered that the control of the activities of the BBC by the Board of Governors together with an Audit Committee ensured in principle the effective supervision of the fulfilment of public service obligations with regard to the new digital channels.[188] In *TV2* the Commission noted that the National Audit Office and the Public Service Council were the bodies responsible to ensure that TV2 complied with its public service obligations. It was critical, however, of the fact that the Council has never published any reports while the Office had no power to prevent overcompensation of TV2's public service costs.[189]

183. Case C-159/94, *Commission v. France* [1997] ECR I-5815 para. 66.
184. European Broadcasting Union, 'Comments', 6.
185. This power has now been vested in the BBC Trust; *see* Part 1, Ch. 7.2.1, p. 127 *above.*
186. Broadcasting Communication, para. 41.
187. *Ibid.*, para. 43.
188. *Nine Digital Services*, para. 38.
189. C 2/03, *TV2/Danmark*, paras 95, 97.

In its Article 17 letter to the German authorities the Commission was satisfied that the remit was properly entrusted to the public broadcasters in § 11 (1) 1 RStV as far as their traditional functions are concerned. According to this provision, public broadcasting shall serve as a medium and factor of the process of forming free, individual and public opinion by producing and distributing radio and television programmes. The Commission's preliminary view was that the control mechanisms in place were also sufficient to secure the actual supply of the public service. Such mechanisms are the instruction of the *Länder* Parliaments on the financial situation of the broadcasters and on the fulfilment of their remit as well as the control competences of the KEF and of the Auditor General's offices of the *Länder*.[190] Nonetheless, the Commission noted that the consequences of a failure on the part of the public broadcasters to fulfil their mission were uncertain. It did not, however, raise this issue anymore in its final decision.

As far as online-services and digital channels are concerned, the Commission expressed serious reservations as regards their entrustment and the monitoring of their application both in its Article 17 letter and in the final decision. Its main grievance was directed at § 11 (1) 2 RStV that *allows* public broadcasters to offer programme-aligned printed works and online services without obliging them to perform specific tasks. In *BBC News 24* and *Digital Curriculum* where it was equally unclear which services BBC could provide as ancillary services, the Commission found that the lack of a clear definition was compensated by the official entrustment to the BBC by the Secretary of State of the task of providing a specific public service.[191] Also, in *Kinderkanal and Phoenix*, the Commission did not object to the entrustment of these services even though the law did not define their remit given that the broadcasters had developed sufficiently precise programme concepts that had been subsequently approved of by the Prime Ministers of the *Länder* by means of a protocol.[192]

In the Commission's view, no such detailed programme concepts nor the approval of the *Länder* exist in the case of online services and digital channels. Self-commitments drawn up by the public broadcasters, specifying further the envisaged online and digital offers, cannot substitute for a formal act of entrustment.[193] Furthermore, the Commission, in its Article 17 letter, expressed doubts that there was effective supervision of the performance of the public service tasks. The broadcasters failed to supply KEF with data concerning the extent of their public service offer. What is more, KEF did not really have the power to control whether programme decisions were within the scope of the remit. Even when KEF disagreed with the notified financial requirements for online services, broadcasters financed them from their general budget.[194]

190. Article 17 letter, para. 200.
191. *BBC Digital Curriculum*, para. 48; *BBC 24-Hour News Channel*, para. 70.
192. *Kinderkanal/Phoenix*, para. 6.3.
193. Case E 3/2005, *Financing of public service broadcasters in Germany*, para. 248.
194. Article 17 letter, para. 204.

The Federal Government defended the system for entrusting public broadcasting in Germany by referring to the constitutional provision of freedom from state control.[195] The remit must be defined in such a way that the state cannot exert control on programme design. Specifications in the law concerning the content of online services are not compatible with this constitutional imperative. The Government thus eschewed the question of the facultative character of § 11 (1) 2 RStV.

A different interpretation of § 11 (1) 2 RStV has been attempted in academic writing. Public broadcasters are obliged to offer programme-aligned online services as much as traditional radio and television programmes. In view of the fact that the functions of traditional television increasingly wander off to the web, broadcasters would not be able to fulfil their mission otherwise. The word 'may' needs therefore to be read in conjunction with the word 'programme-aligned'. In other words, public broadcasters may only offer programme aligned online services but not independent ones. This interpretation of § 11 (1) 2 RStV seems artificial as it arbitrarily reads the word 'only' into the provision. The legislator would not need to phrase this provision in a facultative way to express that online services have to be programme-aligned.

In its final decision, the Commission made short shrift of the argument that the German constitutional principles of programme autonomy and freedom from state control would debar a more specific form of entrustment. It drew a distinction between entrustment and editorial independence. While the latter dictates that the *content* of individual services should be for the public broadcasters to decide, the former signifies that the *scope* of their activities should be clearly countersigned by the *Länder*.[196] The Commission thus clarified that editorial independence would not need to be sacrificed in the process of circumscribing public broadcasters' activities more closely. This was a compromise to prevent the Commission's requirements from being wholly incompatible with the German Constitution.[197] In response to the Commission's criticisms, Germany announced the adoption of a procedure for the formal entrustment of all new digital or online offers by the *Länder*. The *Länder* will also have the duty to attest that the self-commitments entered into by public broadcasters for a specific offer are in line with legal requirements and hence part of the public service mission.[198]

4.2.3 Proportionality

The final test the licence fee needs to pass so as to benefit from the exemption under Article 86 (2) EC is the proportionality test. In accordance with the Broadcasting Communication, it is necessary to demonstrate that state funding does not exceed

195. *See* Part 1, Ch. 3.4, p. 43 *above*.
196. *Financing of public service broadcasters in Germany*, para. 251.
197. From a telephone interview with a legal adviser for the WDR Köln conducted for this work in October 2007.
198. *Financing of public service broadcasters in Germany*, para. 332.

the net cost of the public service, also taking into account other direct or indirect revenues derived from the public service.[199] Furthermore, the Communication explains that state funding is not proportionate when it gives rise to market distortions that are not necessary for the fulfilment of the public service mission. This is the case when public broadcasters undercut the prices of advertising or other non-public service activities below what is necessary to recover the stand-alone costs that an efficient commercial operator in a similar situation would normally have to recover. The motive for such tactics is to reduce the revenue of competitors. The Commission's assessment of proportionality has therefore two aspects. The first is the calculation of the net cost of the public service mission and the assessment of possible overcompensation. The second is the detection of possible market distortions. These two aspects will be analysed in turn.

4.2.3.1 Net Cost of the Public Service Mission

Broadcasters usually carry out non-public service next to their public service activities. In order to assess whether public financing is actually limited to the net costs of the public service remit and to exclude cross-subsidization, the Broadcasting Communication requires a proper cost and revenue allocation between the two types of activities.[200] The Transparency Directive requires Member States to maintain separate accounts for public service and non-public service activities and to allocate costs and revenues correctly on the basis of clearly established, objective cost accounting principles.[201] The transparency requirements apply to public broadcasters as long as they are beneficiaries of state aid and they are entrusted with the operation of a service of general economic interest. Broadcasters are only exempted if the state aid was fixed following an open, transparent and non-discriminatory procedure, if their activities are limited to the provision of services of general economic interest, or if their total annual net turnover is less than EUR 40 million.[202]

The Commission calculates the net cost of the public service mission by deducting from the gross public service costs all the benefits accruing from the commercial exploitation of the public service activity.[203] In other words, the net advertising revenues generated during the transmission of public service programmes and the net revenues derived from the marketing of such programmes are deducted from the total amount of the public service costs.[204] It makes sense to take revenue derived from, for instance, the sale of advertising space on public

199. Broadcasting Communication, para. 57.
200. *Ibid.*, para. 49.
201. Commission Directive 2000/52/EC of 26 July 2000 amending Directive 80/723/EEC on the transparency of financial relations between Member States and public undertakings, OJ L 193/75, 2000.
202. *Ibid.*, recitals 5, 7, 10, 11 and Art. 4 (2).
203. C 2/03, *TV2/Danmark*, para. 105.
204. *Ad-hoc measures for RAI SpA*, para. 123.

channels into account, as it diminishes the need for public funding for those channels.[205] Also, this method is followed given that no full cost allocation takes place for this type of commercial activities so that they would otherwise generate extra-ordinary profits.[206] This is due to peculiarities in the broadcasting sector posing problems to the separation of accounts on the cost side.

Member States normally attribute the whole programming of the broadcasters to the public service remit, while at the same time allowing for its commercial exploitation. As different activities largely share the same inputs, the Broadcasting Communication allows costs that are completely attributable to public service activities, while benefiting also commercial activities, to be entirely allocated to the public service rather than being apportioned between the two. A full distribution of these costs between the two activities would risk being arbitrary and not meaningful.[207] This is different from the approach generally adopted in other utilities sectors and also in commercial broadcasting. Whereas commercial broadcasters are required to allocate both their direct cost, such as the cost for the advertising sales personnel, and indirect cost, i.e. the cost of programmes, to advertising, public broadcasters only need to allocate the direct cost of advertising to this activity. The cost of programming, which is the biggest part of the cost, is allocated in its entirety to the public service activity.

The argument of overcompensation was raised in a number of cases. In the *RAI* case, the Commission calculated the net cost of the public service entrusted to RAI in comparison to the total financial support granted to it by the state and found that RAI had actually been undercompensated in the period under investigation. In the *TV2* case the Commission found that the financing granted to the Danish public broadcaster exceeded its costs by DKK 628.2 (EUR 84, 3 million). The arguments that were advanced by the Danish Government to justify the surplus funding that has been provided were all turned down by the Commission.[208]

A stumbling block in the case against the German public broadcasters has been the non-implementation of the Transparency Directive vis-à-vis the broadcasting sector in Germany.[209] German public broadcasters do not keep separate accounts for public service and commercial activities. German authorities argue that the Transparency Directive is not applicable to broadcasting in Germany for two reasons. First, commercial activities are considered to be ancillary activities falling under the public service remit.[210] From this starting point German authorities jump to the conclusion that public broadcasters in Germany only provide services of general economic interest. Secondly, the assessment of the financial requirements of the public broadcasters by the KEF is considered to be 'an open, transparent and

205. European Broadcasting Union, 'Comments', 9.
206. Tigchelaar, 'State Aid to Public Broadcasting', 180.
207. Broadcasting Communication, para. 56.
208. C 2/03, *TV2/Danmark*, para. 111 *et seq.*
209. The Transparency Directive has so far only been implemented by the Federal Government, not by the individual *Länder* who are responsible for broadcasting policy.
210. *See* Part 2, Ch. 6.42.1, p. 348 *above*.

non-discriminatory procedure' in line with Article 4 (2) (c) of the Transparency Directive.

These arguments are not convincing. As far as the first of these arguments is concerned, it is very questionable whether in German law commercial activities of public broadcasters such as advertising fall under the public service remit.[211] In any event, such activities cannot be regarded as services of general economic interest.[212] The second argument is based on a literal interpretation of Article 4 (2) (c) of the Transparency Directive, paying no attention to the objective of assuring fair and effective application of the rules on competition in accordance with the 2nd and the 8th recitals to the Directive.

Section 13 (3) RStV requires that a high degree of objectivity be achieved when assessing the financial requirements of public broadcasters. However, the KEF procedure is not concerned with the prevention of market distortions, in particular of cross-subsidizations. As long as the activities of public broadcasters accord with the principles of business efficiency and thrift, it is immaterial whether competitors are disadvantaged. For example, the maintenance of separate accounts for independent subsidiaries of public broadcasters such as production or advertising companies are indispensable from the point of view of competition law, but does not fall within the KEF remit.[213] Also, KEF is entrusted with the prior calculation of the licence fee in an objective and transparent manner, but by no means does it control the use to which the licence fee is actually put. The supervision of the actual use of public funds is, however, a main concern of the Directive as is evident from Article 1 (1) (c).[214]

The Commission objects further to the fact that expenses related to commercial activities are not distinguished from the expenses related to the public service, that commercial proceeds are not necessarily deducted from the costs of the public service remit and that the licence fee is possibly used to compensate losses suffered by commercial subsidiaries.[215] The Commission comes to the conclusion that overcompensation cannot be excluded under these circumstances. The German authorities object that it is not their duty to prove that the licence fee does not spill over to their commercial activities. In their view, the Commission should not take cross-subsidization for granted but should prove that it is actually taking place.[216] Such proof is, however, hard to furnish given that transparency requirements are not obeyed with in the broadcasting sector. The transposition of

211. C. Trzaskalik, *Transparenzpflichten des öffentlich-rechtlichen Rundfunks: Die Rechtsstellung der der deutschen Rundfunkanstalten im Lichte der EG-Richtlinie der Transparenz der finanziellen Beziehungen zwischen den Mitgliedstaaten und den öffentlichen Unternehmen* (Place Berlin, Verband Privater Rundfunk und Telekommunikation Vistas, 2000), p. 22.
212. *Ibid.*; Article 17 letter, para. 212; Case E 3/2005, *Financing of public service broadcasters in Germany*, para. 266.
213. Trzaskalik, *Transparenzpflichten des öffentlich-rechtlichen Rundfunks*, p. 26.
214. *Ibid.*, p. 27.
215. Case E 3/2005, *Financing of public service broadcasters in Germany*, paras 270, 271 *et seq.*
216. Mitteilung der Bundesregierung, para. 381 *et seq.*

the Transparency Directive is therefore indispensable for the Commission to be able to confirm the proportionality of public funding.

Moreover, Germany gave the commitment to structurally separate public broadcasters' public service activities from their commercial activities. While the former will be carried out by the broadcasting corporations, the latter will be carried out by commercial subsidiaries.[217] Structural separation goes beyond the requirements of the Transparency Directive, which is only concerned with separate accounting. The separation of commercial from non-commercial activities is not necessarily straightforward. It has been predicted that the grey zone between the two will grow in the coming years as the same material, e.g. the background research for a news story, will be increasingly packaged in many different ways: as a news site on the internet or on teletext, as a mobile phone service or a podcast.[218] Some of these services will fall within the remit, while others will have to be classified as purely commercial undertakings. Structurally separating such integrated services will not be easy.

4.2.3.2 Market Distortions

The Commission examined the existence of market distortions in commercial markets in the *TV2* case. TvDanmark, TV2's competitor, contended that TV2's pricing practices did not allow commercial competitors to recover stand-alone costs. In view of TV2's unique position as regards coverage and programming budget advertisers would always place part of their advertisements with it so as to obtain maximum impact.[219] The Commission assessed, first, whether TvDanmark could be considered 'an efficient commercial operator in a similar situation' and concluded that this was not the case. TV2 could not be directly compared to TvDanmark as a result of differences in viewer share, share of the advertising market, advertising turnover and coverage.[220] The Commission could not establish whether TvDanmark is an efficient commercial operator either as it could not conclude with certainty whether TvDanmark's losses resulted from TV2's pricing behaviour or by other factors attributable to TvDanmark itself.[221]

The Commission went on to analyse instead whether Tv2 acted with a view to maximizing its advertising revenues in the period under investigation. This would indicate that it was behaving as a rational commercial operator. It examined TV2's pricing behaviour and found that its price cuts have actually brought it higher overall income. It concluded that TV2's pricing behaviour was not one of price undercutting but of revenue maximization.[222] Also, the comparison between television advertising expenditure in Denmark compared to the EU as a whole

217. *Financing of public service broadcasters in Germany*, paras 342, 343.
218. Nissen, *Public Service Media in the Information Society*, p. 45.
219. C 2/03, *TV2/Danmark*, para. 43 *et seq.*
220. *Ibid.*, para. 134.
221. *Ibid.*, para. 136.
222. *Ibid.*, para. 153.

indicated that the Danish television advertising market was not systematically and continuously depressed due to TV2's pricing behaviour.[223]

The method followed by the Commission in the TV2 case differs from the one adopted with regard to the Italian public broadcaster RAI. Given that the audience shares and the structure of RAI and the private broadcaster Mediaset were similar, the Commission held that Mediaset could be considered an efficient commercial operator in a situation similar to that of RAI.[224] It compared the advertising prices of the two operators and found that RAI's prices have been constantly higher than those of Mediaset. From this it followed that RAI did not set prices in the advertising market below the level that would allow an efficient commercial operator in a similar situation to cover its costs. As the claimants were not able to substantiate their allegations of price undercutting either, the Commission concluded that RAI operated in the advertising market as a normal commercial operator.

In its Article 17 letter to the German authorities, the Commission held that the existing legal framework does not provide adequate guarantees that public broadcasters apply market principles vis-à-vis their commercial subsidiaries.[225] The Commission maintained the view in its final decision that existing investment management and control mechanisms were inadequate to prevent a rise in the financial needs of public broadcasters as a result of non market conform behaviour. In particular, it noted, first, that the Interstate Treaty on Broadcasting does not impose an explicit obligation on public broadcasters to respect market principles, and secondly, that KEF had no means of checking compliance with the arm's length principle.[226] So as to remedy these deficiencies, Germany undertook to oblige public broadcasters in a legally binding way to respect market conformity and the arm's length principle as well as the 'private investor test'.[227]

Furthermore, the Commission in its Article 17 letter touched upon the contentious issue of the acquisition of sport rights. It posed the question whether public broadcasters need to obtain pay-TV rights and exclusive rights for the transmission of sport events so as to be able to fulfil their public service remit. It did not rule out that exclusivity is justified, but proposed that public broadcasters should sublicense exclusive rights so as not to prevent other free-or pay-TV operators from entering the market. The Commission held that the costs of the public service have been unnecessarily inflated by the failure of public broadcasters to use fully and to sub-license acquired sport rights. German public broadcasters are not allowed to offer pay-TV programmes.[228] This means, in the Commission's view, that pay-TV rights that are not made available to private broadcasters are unjustifiably left unused. Finally, the Commission argued that public broadcasters possibly distort the market by paying excessively high prices for the acquisition of sport rights.

---

223. *Ibid.*, para. 157.
224. *Ad-hoc measures for RAI SpA*, para. 140.
225. Article 17 letter, para. 230.
226. *Financing of public service broadcasters in Germany*, paras 287, 288.
227. *Ibid.*, paras 342 *et seq.*
228. RStV, § 13.

The German authorities refuted these arguments. They replied that behavioural conditions related to exclusivity and sublicensing could not be imposed in the framework of state aid proceedings in the first place. As regards the substance of the Commission's allegations, they explained that public broadcasters absolutely relied on exclusive rights in order to be able to offer a competitive programme. They denied that any of the acquired sport rights remained unused, at least as far as football and the Olympiad were concerned. Other events were either fully transmitted or were offered to commercial operators as in the case of packaged products including unpopular competitions. Understandably, the prospects for sublicensing such rights were marginal.[229]

The German authorities argued further that the value of sport rights lies in their live transmission and is greatly diminished when programmes are transmitted live on free-TV and pay-TV simultaneously. The accusation of not using pay-TV rights would not stand to reason as public broadcasters were obliged to acquire both free- and pay-TV rights so as to gain exclusivity. There was, in other words, no separate market for pay-TV rights in this context as live transmission on free-TV was addressed to all viewers.[230] As regards the Commission's argument that public broadcasters pay disproportionate prices for sport rights, the German authorities pointed out that KEF only approves limited funds for the purchase of sport rights. Besides, the Commission's reasoning would imply that public broadcasters would not be allowed to outbid their commercial counterparts. They would thus be prevented from effectively competing for the top sporting events.[231]

In its final decision, the Commission held that exclusivity is not per se contrary to Article 86 (2) EC since it is necessary to maximize revenues and to be distinctive from other broadcasters.[232] It did not consider anymore that public broadcasters were consistently and regularly offering disproportionate prices, thus structurally outbidding private competitors.[233] It disagreed, however, with Germany that pay-TV was consumed by the exploitation of free-TV rights. It argued that the current system did not allow a proper assessment of what constitutes a justified non-use of rights nor did it guarantee the sublicensing of unused rights in a predictable way.[234] Germany committed itself *inter alia* to defining in a transparent way under which circumstances sport rights are considered as 'unused' and to offering unused rights to third parties for sub-licensing.[235]

It follows from what has been said so far that the Commission decision on the funding of German public broadcasters is beset with the same problems as other EU interventions in this sensitive area of media regulation. It is beneficial in so far as it sheds more light into the mechanisms for financing public broadcasting,

229. Mitteilung der Bundesregierung, para. 361 *et seq.*
230. *Ibid.*, para. 366.
231. *Ibid.*, para. 369 *et seq.*
232. *Financing of public service broadcasters in Germany*, para. 294.
233. *Ibid.*, para. 298.
234. *Ibid.*, paras 301 et seq.
235. *Ibid.*, para. 355.

rendering it more transparent and accountable, and averting risks of market distortion. However, it is likely to store up great troubles for the future development of public broadcasting in so far as it seeks, under enormous pressure from the commercial media sector, to confine it to a narrow presence in the field of new media, a presence that is strictly aligned to its traditional television programming and strictly residual to what is offered by the market.

5. CONCLUSION

A snowball of appeals at European Union level against the anti-competitive nature of the licence fee and other forms of state support received by public broadcasters has placed a large question mark over their continuous legitimacy. This is a crucial question for the future of public broadcasting, since the licence fee is not only a method of raising revenues, but also a prominent vehicle of its political and creative independence. It has been devised to establish the necessary distance between public service operators and the state as well as the market forces.

Recent judgments of the European Court put an end to the yearlong uncertainty as to whether state funding for public broadcasting constitutes state aid or merely compensation for the discharge of public service obligations. State measures compensating for the net additional costs of providing a public service do not confer a financial advantage on public broadcasters and do not qualify as state aid. Still, it is quite impossible to satisfy the conditions stipulated in the *Altmark* case for escaping such classification. In none of the broadcasting cases decided by the Commission so far has it been concluded that the Member States concerned fulfilled the *Altmark* test.

The last resort for public broadcasters is Article 86 (2) EC. In order for a service to benefit from this derogation, the conditions of definition, entrustment and proportionality need to be fulfilled. In accordance with the Amsterdam Protocol and the Broadcasting Communication Member States can define the remit of public broadcasting in broad terms. However, the more public broadcasters move into new media markets such as the internet, the more the Commission is likely to ask for a precise identification of the public service remit and for a clearer demarcation from their commercial counterparts. The balance between the creation of the internal market and the public service remit cannot be struck once and for all, but needs to be reassessed as economic and technological realities change.

The unceasing stream of complaints made by commercial broadcasters against the licence fee raises fundamental questions about the future of public broadcasting in Europe. The debate about the public funding of television has made abundantly clear that there is little consensus on whether a special regulatory regime really needs to be applied to broadcasting or whether competition law is sufficient to guarantee pluralism as in the case of the print media. Nor is there any agreement as to whether public broadcasting should be allowed to adapt to the requirements of the digital age or should rather be confined to its traditional modes of delivery.

These questions not only go to the heart of what constitutes public broadcasting and what its function should be in the digital age. They also impinge on the ideological underpinnings of society and the role of the state and of public services in catering for the needs of its citizens. The widespread assault on the legitimacy of public broadcasting is only one symptom of the general ideological shift across Europe towards a greater reliance on market-based solutions and an increasing unease with the public sector. This ideological challenge to public broadcasting is probably more threatening than technological shifts and the concomitant changes in audience behaviour that are imminent but highly unpredictable.[236]

In view of the great uncertainty surrounding the future of public broadcasting, it is pertinent to ask whether the Commission decisions on the compatibility of the licence fee with state aid law have paved the way towards increased legal certainty for both public and private operators and have achieved a satisfactory balance between the policy interests involved. What are the main outcomes of the cases which have been brought to the Commission's attention in this area? It is helpful to distinguish between aspects of public broadcasting the European Commission has no problem with and others that have been greatly affected by its decision-making.

First, it has been anticipated in the past that the intricate competition issues surrounding mixed funding could lead states to abandon this system.[237] The discussion of the Commission's decisions has revealed that it is not opposed to dual funding systems as long as public broadcasters do not use the licence fee to undercut prices in the advertising market. Commercial broadcasters continue to press for the departure of publicly funded broadcasters from the advertising market, but they are unlikely to attract the Commission's support.

Second, the 1998 Commission's internal discussion paper on the application of state aid rules in the audiovisual sector aired the idea that entertainment and sports programmes could not be regarded as part of the public service remit. No signs of such splitting between good and popular programming can be detected in the more recent Commission decisions, at least as far as the traditional public service functions are concerned. However, the very problematic criterion of distinctiveness still informs the Commission's approach towards the online presence of public broadcasters.

Which are the main safeguards the Commission wants to introduce into public broadcasting to ensure its compliance with state aid rules? First, a clear and precise definition of the public service remit. Second, the separation of accounts for commercial and public service activities in line with the Transparency Directive. Third, the introduction of mechanisms to prevent over-compensation of public service costs. Fourth, the exclusion of market distortions in commercial markets by charging market prices for commercial activities and by keeping an arm's length relationship between the public broadcaster and its commercial subsidiaries. Are these safeguards to be welcomed?

236. Barwise, 'Threats to Public Service Broadcasting', p. 25.
237. Craufurd Smith, 'State Support for Public Service Broadcasting', 5.

A clear definition of the public service remit would enhance the legitimacy of public broadcasting in the eyes of the public and of the national and European competition authorities. Commission officials are suspicious of broad definitions of public broadcasting as they may lead to a so-called 'mission-creep'.[238] Knowing what is meant by public broadcasting and what it is set to achieve would render it more accountable. Nonetheless, a word of caution is in order here. The requirement for a clear and precise remit should not be used to slow down the development of public broadcasters in ways suited to contemporary realities. An inflexible 'corset' of public broadcasting obligations would interfere with broadcasters' autonomy and prevent them from adjusting to technological change.

This is not to say that public broadcasting is indefinable as has often been argued in the United Kingdom in the past. The Davies panel claimed in 1999 whilst reviewing the funding of the BBC that 'we may not be able to offer a tight new definition of public broadcasting, but we nevertheless each felt we knew it when we saw it'.[239] Another case in point is the observation of the Pilkington Committee in 1962 that 'though its standards exist and are recognisable, broadcasting is more nearly an art than an exact science. It deals in tastes and values and is not exactly definable.'[240] It is necessary to steer a middle path between this extreme hands-off attitude and a state of asphyxiating control. Self-regulatory commitments issued by the broadcasting bodies may be the way forward, allowing the remit to be described more accurately while preserving broadcasters' editorial freedom.[241]

What about the requirements of accounts separation, financial transparency, fair trading and proportionality of funding? It is hardly surprising that the Commission came to impose these constraints on public broadcasters since its focus is an economic one. The dangers of an extreme preoccupation with these more mundane aspects of the broadcasting business have been well described by Born and Prosser. By shifting efforts and expenditure from actual programme-making to the 'tasks of installing quasi-market processes', 'public broadcasting values may become subordinated to the creation of an apparently level playing field with commercial competitors'.[242]

Fair trading is unobjectionable as long as it does not pose such debilitating demands on broadcasting as to render it 'the culture of accountants'.[243] This shift of emphasis from the core values of quality and of serving the audience to the

238. S. Depypere and N. Tigchelaar, 'The Commission's State Aid Policy on Activities of Public Service Broadcasters in Neighbouring Markets' (2004) 2 *Competition Policy Newsletter*, 19.
239. DCMS, *The Future Funding of the BBC: Report of the Independent Review Pannel* July 1999, p. 10.
240. Postmaster-General, *Report of the Committee on Broadcasting (Pilkington report), 1960* (Cmnd 1753, 1962), p. 13, para. 34.
241. B. Holznagel, 'The Mission of Public Service Broadcasting' (2000) 5 IJCLP, 1, 5.
242. Born and Prosser, 'Culture and Consumerism', 667.
243. Tracey, *Decline and Fall of Public Service Broadcasting*, p. 37.

demands of the marketplace needs to be avoided by all means if public broadcasting is not to lose sight of its mission. Member States will no doubt invest much time and effort in restructuring their public broadcasting systems so as to comply with the state aid rules. It is, however, by no means certain that this will curb the appetite of their rivals for further lawsuits. As public broadcasters reinvent themselves to keep up with new technologies, more grounds for challenges undoubtedly loom. The Commission would be well-advised to close the floodgates for further complaints if public broadcasters are to set off the much-desired virtuous circle.

General Conclusion

The analysis of the media policy of the European Union has demonstrated that it has limited in manifold ways the power of the Member States to organize their broadcasting systems as they wish. The question that still awaits an answer is: has this policy contributed to the emergence of a shared consciousness, to the creation of a European demos? Has it enhanced the solidarity of Europeans among themselves and their allegiance to the EU institutions?

Blanke made the optimistic prediction that Europe is on the way to becoming an educational and cultural community.[1] Yet, the European Union is cautious enough to avoid the use of the word 'community' with its heavy axiomatic burdens in this context. It has opted instead for the lighter notion of 'area' and coined the expressions of a 'European audiovisual area'[2] and of a 'European educational area'.[3] The suspicion suggests itself that the word 'area' was chosen so as to sidestep too obvious allusions to identity and belongingness. However, the qualifying adjective 'European' brings us straight back to the question of culture, of 'us' and the 'others'.

The socio-political thrust behind the creation of a European audio-visual area is undeniable. Media policy is entrusted with the protection of cultural diversity, not least from the influx of US television programmes.[4] At the same time, the European area for audiovisual services is intended to strengthen the European programme industry. This duality of cultural and economic objectives is a hallmark of the integration process in the audiovisual fields.

---

1. Blanke, *Europa auf dem Weg*.
2. European Commission, *1998 Audiovisual Policy of the European Union: The New Era of the Picture Industry, Television without Frontiers, Greater Europe in the Year 2000* (Luxembourg, OOPEC, 1997), p. 5.
3. Towards a Europe of Knowledge COM (97) 563 final, 3.
4. European Commission, *1998 Audiovisual Policy*, p. 5.

The expansion of the European Union agenda to the new policy area of broadcasting, which was not included in the 1957 Treaty of Rome, has been convincingly explained by Pollack.[5] Pollack clarified the scope of application of the neofunctionalist theory of 'task expansion'[6] by applying Lowi's classification of policy types as distributive, regulatory and redistributive. In accordance with this typology, the TwF Directive is an instance of regulatory policy.[7] This is policy whereby Member States agree to approximate their regulations on the activities of public and private persons.[8] Pollack argues that the neofunctionalist hypothesis of 'functional spillover' holds true concerning this policy type.[9] Regulatory policy results primarily from a functional or economic spillover from the internal market project.

Understandably, the economically motivated birth of EU audiovisual policy influences its outlook. However, it is important to also keep its cultural dimension in mind. We have seen that the European Parliament was eager to create a pan-European public service channel at the outset so as to instil in European citizens a sense of allegiance to the European Union. This project was short-lived. Subsequently, attention shifted to the commercial television sector in the hope that it could bring Europeans together by means of a shared viewing experience of a different kind: by exposing them to each other's television programmes. More recently, the European Union has placed faith in the capacity of the new media to close the 'communication gap' with its citizens.

This endless search for ways to enlist audiovisual policy in bridging the European Union democratic deficit raises the question as to whether this policy has been conducive to the emergence of a European demos. As already stated, one should best understand a European demos not in ethno-cultural, homogeneous terms but as a social construct, engineered in similar ways to those in which states constituted their nations.[10] The bounded integration perspective suggests that the Europeanization of the areas of the media can only improve the legitimacy of the European Union if national sensitivities are respected and prerogatives of the Member States are not unnecessarily compromised.[11]

---

5. M. A. Pollack, 'Creeping Competence: The Expanding Agenda of the European Community' (1994) 14 *Journal of Public Policy* 95.
6. *Ibid.*, 96; for a different meaning of the concept of 'task expansion' *see* A. Niemann, 'The PHARE Programme and the Concept of Spillover: Neofunctionalism in the Making' (1998) 5 *Journal of European Public Policy* 430.
7. *See* Pollack, 'Creeping Competence', 126.
8. *Ibid.*, 110.
9. Contra Meckel, *Fernsehen ohne Grenzen*, p. 26 *et seq.* with the argument that neo-functionalism cannot explain the Europeanization of television given that no spill-over has taken place into the cultural domain, no European channel has been created.
10. J. H. H. Weiler, 'The State "über alles": Demos, Telos and the German Maastricht Decision' in *Festschrift für Ulrich Everling*, vol. II, O. Due, M. Lutter and J. Schwarze (eds) (Baden-Baden, Nomos, 1995), p. 1672.
11. On the meaning of the term 'Europeanization' *see* Laffan, O'Donnell and Smith, *Europe's Experimental Union*, p. 84.

This is also the essence of the subsidiarity principle that has been elevated to a general principle of the European Union in Article 5 (2) EC. Admittedly, the distinction between functions that can be effectively carried out at the national level and those that require EU intervention is fraught with difficulties. In the case of culture, it stands to reason that responsibility should remain within the purview of the national or regional levels, while the free movement of cultural goods calls for action at the European level.[12] This example shows that subsidiarity cannot provide clear-cut answers as to the proper use of Union competence. However, if the basic idea behind it is that things should be done 'at the lowest level that is efficiently possible', this principle can contribute to the legitimization of the European polity.[13]

The cumbersome formulation of Article 5 (2) EC could be translated into a cost-benefit analysis, not in the strictly economic sense, but in the sense that the profit of further integration has to be balanced against the encroachment upon Member States' powers.[14] Accordingly, no measure should be adopted by the Union that unnecessarily affects the cultural identity of the Member States or their regions. Having this principle as a starting point, we must consider, first, whether integration in the area of broadcasting has enhanced the legitimacy of the European Union despite the fact that the power of the Member States to influence developments in their broadcasting systems has been compromised.

The EC Treaty lacks a specific legal basis for EU intervention in this area.[15] The classification of broadcasting as a service entrusts the Union with a narrow economic mandate which prevents it from taking a more holistic approach to television as an economic and at the same time cultural phenomenon. Not surprisingly, steps towards the establishment of a European communication constitution, as in the form of the European quota, have been misguided and met with criticism. My analysis of the quota requirement showed that it was adopted *ultra vires*, given that it was not necessary for the creation of the internal market in broadcasting services. It has been vigorously opposed by certain Member States, since it needlessly affected their responsibility with regard to programme content.

Is the encroachment of the European quota provision upon the broadcasting sovereignty of the Member States counterbalanced by its potential to bring forth a European identity of sorts? The European quota was adopted under the banner

12. R. Dehousse, 'Community Competences: Are there Limits to Growth?' in *Europe after Maastricht: An Ever Closer Union?*, R. Dehousse (ed.) (Munich, C. H. Beck, 1994), p. 123.
13. T. Wright, 'Reinventing Democracy' in *Reinventing Democracy*, P. Hirst and S. Khilnani (eds) (Oxford, Blackwell, 1996), p. 15; A. Beierwaltes, *Demokratie und Medien: Der Begriff der Öffentlichkeit und seine Bedeutung für die Demokratie in Europa* (Baden-Baden, Nomos, 2000), p. 238.
14. J. Backhaus, 'Integration, Harmonisation and Differentiation of Law' in *The Common Law of Europe and the Future of Legal Education*, B. de Witte and C. Forder (eds) (The Hague, Kluwer, 1990), pp. 501, 520–521; Ress, *Kultur und europäischer Binnenmarkt*, p. 948.
15. F. Beltrame, 'Creating a Directive on Pluralism and Media Concentration: A Case Study of the European Union Legislative Process' in *Lawmaking in the European Union*, P. Craig and C. Harlow (eds) (The Hague, Kluwer, 1998), p. 348.

of safeguarding cultural diversity by way of the development of a predominantly European programme industry. However, the quota is not an effective mechanism to boost European audiovisual production, since it imposes onerous obligations on certain categories of broadcasters while others can circumvent it in manifold ways. The continuing domination of prime time viewing by domestic and American productions indicates that the quota has not succeeded in reversing the trend.

The attempt to construct an exclusionary European identity by projecting the threat of American cultural influence is misconceived. Whether we want it or not, the US is economically Europe's Other, but not culturally.[16] The English language not only serves as a European lingua franca; it also exposes Europe to the American civilization.[17] It is American programmes that draw Europeans together. Viewers are, however, attracted by domestic productions even more than by American ones. Most Member States fill the quota with national material that attracts highest audience ratings. The fact that Article 4 fails to reserve a percentage for non-domestic productions is the most eloquent admission of defeat in view of cultural segregation in Europe. The mere admonition in recital 50 of the AVMS Directive to schedule an adequate share of non-domestic European works is unlikely to make a difference. In sum, the quota stands for the ineffective and at the same time interventionist type of measure that is likely to alienate Europeans from the Union even more.

As far as the country of origin principle is concerned, it is the main instrument for opening up national markets by limiting the power of Member States to restrict the reception of broadcasts lawfully transmitted in their state of origin. It sweeps aside a great deal of public-interest based concerns that pose legal barriers to the cross-frontier circulation of programmes. Consequently, the states where broadcasts are received and which are therefore directly affected are restrained from asserting their legitimate interests. We have seen that three compensatory mechanisms are available to receiving states for the regulation of content issues. These mechanisms fail, however, to strike a balance between the creation of the internal market in audiovisual services and the broadcasting orders of the Member States.

First, the only express derogation from the country of origin principle, laid down in Article 2a (2) of Dir. 2007/65, allows the suspension of retransmission on grounds of the protection of minors. The procedural requirements stipulated in this provision are, however, excessively strict. The AVMS Directive proposes a more flexible procedure for the derogation from the country of origin principle in respect of on-demand services. However, the level of protection afforded to minors is low given that gratuitously violent and pornographic programmes can be scheduled freely in such services as long as technical measures are taken to ensure that minors will not *normally* have access to them.

Second, in the cases *Commission v. Belgium* and *De Agostini*, the Court took, by and large, a sensitive approach towards the broadcasting sovereignty of the

16. C. Shore, 'Inventing the "Peoples' Europe": Critical Approaches to European Community "Cultural Policy"' (1993) 28 MAN 779.
17. Flora, Kuhnle and Urwin, *State Formation*, p. 90.

Member States in that it implicitly confirmed their discretionary power to control incoming broadcasts on grounds not coordinated by the Directive. Even though the exact scope of the Directive has yet to be clarified, this jurisprudence laudably curbs the lowering down of regulatory standards as a result of the competition between different broadcasting systems. Still, programme content regulation is unquestionably in decline in Europe. The failure of the Member States to afford vulnerable values a higher level of protection, opting instead for a Directive with a predominantly economic orientation, drastically influences television towards the market model of broadcasting.

Lastly, the European Court has construed the circumvention principle, the anchor of the Member States' broadcasting policy, narrowly, while leaving many questions unanswered. As a result, the frontiers that have been primarily removed by the TwF Directive so far are those preventing the evasion of national broadcasting laws by undertakings established in one state but targeting the audience of another. The new procedures devised of in the AVMS Directive shed some light into the conditions for pleading circumvention. It is, however, doubtful that these procedures will make much difference in practice. The voluntary procedure relies heavily on the cooperation between regulatory authorities, which will not always be forthcoming. The circumvention procedure has more bite but is framed in narrow terms since it only applies to cases of abusive delocalization, which are hard to prove.

The jurisprudence on the freedom to provide broadcasting services under Article 49 EC restricts further the capacity of the Member States to subject foreign broadcasts to their regulatory standards. What the Court gave with the one hand by recognizing in *Mediawet* a cultural policy as a pressing reason justifying a restriction on the free movement of services, it took with the other by applying the non-economic objective and proportionality tests without adequate regard for the cultural dimension of broadcasting.

Finally, by examining the compatibility of the licence fee with the EC state aid regime, the Commission made great inroads into the competence of the Member States to organize their systems of public broadcasting. The Amsterdam Protocol grants Member States substantial latitude in defining the public service remit and the 2001 Broadcasting Communication only allows the Commission to check for manifest error in the definition of the remit. The Commission recently overstepped these boundaries when examining the online activities of public broadcasters. In doing so, it questioned the right of public broadcasters to offer online services that are not clearly linked to their traditional television programmes and that do not differ from similar commercial programmes.

These criteria are not only unduly intrusive. They also condemn public broadcasting to a fossilized existence, out of touch with technological developments, a residual role dependent on the gaps left by the market. Moreover, the Commission's insistence on an ever clearer definition of the public service remit has brought it in collision course with Germany's constitutional principle of freedom from state control. If the measures Germany has committed itself to taking, so as to remove the Commission's grievances do not prove satisfactory, the German

Constitutional Court might well step in to rescue the German system of public broadcasting, if necessary in defiance of the rigours of EU state aid law.

Are these limitations in the control Member States have over their broadcasting affairs counterbalanced by the 'nation-building' value of an integrated field of communications? The answer is no. Contrary to what the ambitious titles of the present AVMS and of the past TwF Directives evoke, audiovisual markets in Europe remain segregated by language and culture. Admittedly, linguistic barriers have been partly overcome by digital compression technology, enabling viewers to follow the same programme in up to eight different languages.[18] A prominent example of a bilingual programme is Arte that is transmitted both in French and German, albeit with considerable expenditure.[19]

There are, however, more entrenched obstacles to the intra-EU circulation of programmes that are connected with the cultural background of these programmes and the capacity of the public to identify with them.[20] Reconciling national preferences is problematic even when neighbour countries such as France and Germany are involved. Characteristically, an Edith Piaf evening programme transmitted by Arte attracts 1,5 million viewers in France, but only 40,000 in Germany.[21] Viewing habits also differ widely in Europe with the prime time beginning at 11 P.M. in Spain, 9 P.M. in Britain and 7 P.M. to 8 P.M. in Germany.[22] Reaching a pan-European audience is therefore fraught with difficulties.

Neither the EC Treaty nor the Directive has succeeded in enhancing the exposure to other Member States' cultures. They have only encouraged the transmission of nominally foreign programmes by service-providers who establish themselves in Member States with lax access conditions only to broadcast across the border. These programmes are tailor-made for a given national audience, which therefore gets to see more of the same home-grown material.

Other pan-European ventures that have proved to be commercially viable are thematic channels in areas such as sports, music, international and business news. Nonetheless, these channels have low viewer quotas and small development potential in view of the limited interest advertisers take in them.[23] Lastly, a different type of productions that sell both across Europe as well as internationally are entertainment programmes such as 'The Wheel of Fortune' or 'Big Brother'.[24] However, they only generate low-quality, homogeneous programme content, not a true European audiovisual space. The same applies to the bulk of American film productions that have the remarkable knack for surmounting all cultural hurdles.

---

18. Orf, 'Television without Frontiers', 270; COM (94) 96 final, 19.
19. T. Oppermann, 'ARTE – Ein Experiment in Europäischer Kultur' in *Gedächtnisschrift für Eberhard Grabitz*, A. Randelzhofer, R. Scholz and D. Wilke (eds) (Munich, C. H. Beck, 1995), p. 495; Beierwaltes, *Demokratie und Medien*, p. 228.
20. Beierwaltes, *Demokratie und Medien*, p. 229.
21. Oppermann, 'ARTE', p. 494; *see* Meckel, Fernsehen ohne Grenzen, p. 332 *et seq.*
22. Meckel, *Fernsehen ohne Grenzen*, p. 230.
23. *Ibid.*, p. 228.
24. A. Rogalski, 'L'Europe des télévisions entre le rêve et la réalité' (1995/96) 299 *L' Éurope en formation*, 59; Ward, *European Union Democratic Deficit*, p. 22.

The dominance of US broadcasts and also the divide between large and small European countries as regards their potential to export their programmes in the Union are major obstacles to the rapprochement of European cultures in a 'Europe of viewers'.[25] Perhaps, one should abandon the idea of one European public space that is underpinned by a common broadcasting system. Much more realistic is the view that partially overlapping spaces of communication coexist at the European level.[26] This is more and more true even of national contexts where audiences become partitioned in ever smaller fragments as a result of the vast range of specialized programmes on offer and the possibilities opened by interactive television. Europeanizing television is not about the transmission of all-European programmes. Television operators have little incentive to create such programmes in view of the higher costs incurred and the narrow target audience. Nor can it be just about the free circulation of television programmes throughout the Union, as envisaged by the Directive. Viewing the same programmes is no guarantee for the emergence of a European consciousness.[27]

A theoretically more promising path for television to become a vehicle for European unification is by promoting the discourse of political parties about European themes; by reporting on decision-making processes in the European institutions, but not through the lens of domestic politics; by presenting the European Union in a differentiated manner; by articulating cross-border interests and by sensitizing the public to national differences by way of high-quality programmes.[28] However, protests against the European quota have shown that a top-down Europeanization of the media sector is not acceptable. Also, the political will to enlist television in advancing the European cause is largely lacking. This is not surprising if one considers that Europe's leaders are very reluctant to communicate to their electorates the politics of integration and the substance of the European project.[29] For fear not to upset domestic politics, they stick to the 'old language of national interest'.[30] In Grimm's words 'A Europeanised media system ought not to be confused with increased reporting on European topics in national media. These are directed at a national public and remain attached to national viewpoints and communication habits.'[31]

All in all, one should not place too much hope in European audiovisual policies to render Europe a more significant political community. The European Union is not 'a scaled up version of the nation state'.[32] Being deprived of a centre of political authority, it cannot take on all functions performed by the nation state.

---

25. Negrine and Papathanassopoulos, *Internationalisation of Television*, p. 69.
26. Beierwaltes, *Demokratie und Medien*, p. 235.
27. Shore, 'Inventing the "Peoples' Europe"', 790; Harrison and Woods, 'European Citizenship', 486.
28. Beierwaltes, *Demokratie und Medien*, p. 243; Rogalski, 'L'Europe des télévisions', 55; *see also* Part I, Ch. 7.6.1, p. 139 on the BBC's coverage of European issues.
29. Laffan, O'Donnell and Smith, *Europe's Experimental Union*, pp. 204, 206.
30. *Ibid.*, 204.
31. Grimm, 'Does Europe Need a Constitution?', pp. 294, 295.
32. P. Hirst cited in Laffan, O'Donnell and Smith, *Europe's Experimental Union*, p. 196.

Nor would this be desirable. The reservations of the theory of bounded integration concerning the prospects for overcoming nationalism can surely be shared in so far as coordinated intervention on the cultural front has small chances of success. European identity can only be instilled if the emotional attachments associated with nationality are partly eradicated. However, the idea that European integration should be a state-transcending project is not widely nourished beyond the domain of the European Parliament and the Commission.[33]

Cultural integration should be a natural process. A change of attitudes towards the European Union can only occur in the course of time as Europeans 'learn about national interdependencies and the loss of national "fate control"'.[34] Through this process, political actors may gradually embrace the interest of other Member States and even find, in the long run, a common interest that is more than the sum total of national self-interests.[35] Such a rational learning process is more realistic than the artificial Europeanization of television.

A non-negligible source of legitimacy is, finally, the problem-solving effectiveness of the European Union.[36] Legitimacy can flow from the ability of the Union to offer instrumental benefits and to cater for material policy interests, not least by strengthening public broadcasting standards. Exposing minors to risks in the linear or the non-linear environment, relaxing the rules on product placement and keeping public broadcasting on a tight rein may translate as increased revenues for the European audiovisual industry. However, they risk alienating further a powerful constituency: the users of audiovisual media services. Conversely, protecting minors in a proactive and comprehensive way, defending the editorial integrity and quality of programmes and affording public broadcasting the necessary financial support to enable it to keep pace with technological developments are viable avenues for enhancing public support for integration. Treating a diverse continent as though it could become a nation is a *folie de grandeur*.[37]

---

33. Theiler, 'European Union', 333.
34. J. Olsen, *Organising European Institutions of Governance: A Prelude to an Institutional Account of Political Integration*, ARENA Working Papers, no. 00/2 (Oslo, ARENA Norwegian Research Council, 1998), p. 14.
35. *See* P. Allott, 'The European Community is Not the True European Community' (1991) 100 YLJ 2493, 2498.
36. Laffan, O'Donnell and Smith, *Europe's Experimental Union*, p. 197; contra Theiler, 'European Union', 310; Olsen, *Organising European Institutions*, p. 10.
37. Schlesinger, *Media, State and Nation*.

Bibliography

Ader, T., 'Der kulturelle Auftrag und der Aspekt "Regionalität" im Pflichtenprogramm der Rundfunkveranstalter' (2006) 8 *IRIS plus.*

Alivizatos, N., *Kratos kai Radioteleorase* (Athens, Ant. N. Sakkoulas, 1986).

Alivizatos, N., 'E "trite" apofase tou Symvouliou tes Epikrateias gia ten radioteleorase: Sxolio sten StE 930/1990 Ol.' (1990) 16 ΤοΣ.

Allott, P., *Eunomia: New Order for a New World* (Oxford, Oxford University Press, 1990).

Allott, P., 'The European Community Is Not the True European Community' (1991) 100 YLJ.

Ang, I., *Living Room Wars: Rethinking Media Audiences for a Postmodern World* (London, Routledge, 1996).

ARD and ZDF, 'EG-Politik im Bereich des Rundfunks – Auswirkungen auf die Rundfunkordnung in der Bundesrepublik Deutschland' (1991) *MP Dokumentation* II.

Armstrong, K. A., 'New Institutionalism and European Union Legal Studies' in *Lawmaking in the European Union*, P. Craig and C. Harlow (eds) (The Hague, Kluwer, 1998).

Armstrong, M. and H. Weeds, 'Public Service Broadcasting in the Digital World' in *The Economic Regulation of Broadcasting Markets: Evolving Technology and Challenges for Policy*, P. Seabright and J. von Hagen (eds) (Cambridge, Cambridge University Press, 2007).

Arnull, A., *The General Principles of EEC Law and the Individual* (London, Leicester University Press, 1990).

Arnull, A., A. Dashwood, M. Ross and D. Wyatt (eds), *Wyatt & Dashwood's EU Law* (4th edn, London, Sweet & Maxwell, 2000).

Ashiagbor, D., 'Economic and Social Rights in the European Charter of Fundamental Rights' (2004) 1 EHRL.

Astheimer, S. and K. Moosmayer, 'Europäische Rundfunkordnung – Chance oder Risiko?' (1994) 7 ZUM.

Backhaus, J., 'Integration, Harmonisation and Differentiation of Law' in *The Common Law of Europe and the Future of Legal Education*, B. de Witte and C. Forder (eds) (The Hague, Kluwer, 1990).

Bamberger, C., 'Sicherung der Meinungsvielfalt durch die Landesmedienanstalten' (2000) 7 ZUM.

Banchoff, T. and M. P. Smith, 'Introduction: Conceptualizing Legitimacy in a Contested Polity' in *Legitimacy and the European Union: The Contested Polity*, T. Banchoff and M. P. Smith (eds) (London, Routledge, 1999).

Barendt, E. M., 'The Influence of the German and Italian Constitutional Courts on their National Broadcasting Systems' [1991] *Public Law*.

Barendt, E. M., 'Towards a European Media Law?' (1994) 1 MJ.

Barendt, E. M., *Broadcasting Law: A Comparative Study* (Oxford, Clarendon, 1995).

Barendt, E. M., 'Free Speech and Abortion' [2003] *Public Law*.

Barendt, E. M., *Freedom of Speech* (2nd edn, Oxford, Oxford University Press, 2005).

Barendt, E. M. and L. Hitchens, *Media Law: Cases and Materials* (Harlow, Longman, 2000).

Barnett, S., 'Which End of the Telescope: From Market Failure to Cultural Value' in *From Public Service Broadcasting to Public Service Communications*, D. Tambini and J. Cowling (eds) (London, IPPR, 2004).

Bartosch, A., 'The Financing of Public Broadcasting and EC State Aid Law: An Interim Balance' (1999) 4 ECLR.

Bartosch, A., 'Clarification or Confusion? How To Reconcile the ECJ's Rulings in Altmark and Chronopost' (2003) 3 EStAL.

Bartosch, A., 'Has the Commission Practice Applied Double Standards?' (2003) 3 EStAL.

Bartosch, A., 'Die Kommissionspraxis nach dem Urteil des EuGH in der Rechtssache Altmark – Worin liegt das Neue?' (2004) 10 EuZW.

Barwise, P., 'What Are the Real Threats to Public Service Broadcasting?' in *From Public Service Broadcasting to Public Service Communications*, D. Tambini and J. Cowling (eds) (London, IPPR, 2004).

Bausch, H., *Rundfunk in Deutschland: Rundfunkpolitik nach 1945*, vol. I (Munich, Deutscher Taschenbuch Verlag, 1980).

Beetham, D. and C. Lord, 'Legitimacy and the European Union' in *Political Theory and the European Union: Legitimacy, Constitutional Choice and Citizenship*, A. Weale and M. Nentwich (eds) (London, Routledge, 1998).

Behrens, P., 'Mindestharmonisierung im Binnenmarkt – Stellungnahme' in *Mindestharmonisierung im Europäischen Binnenmarkt: Referate des 7. Bonner Europa-Symposions vom 27. April 1996*, U. Everling and W.-H. Roth (eds) (Baden-Baden, Nomos, 1997).

Beierwaltes, A., *Demokratie und Medien: Der Begriff der Öffentlichkeit und seine Bedeutung für die Demokratie in Europa* (Baden-Baden, Nomos, 2000).

Bekemans, L. and A. Ballodimos, 'Le traité de Maastricht et l'education, la formation professionelle et al culture' (1993) 2 RMUE.

Beltrame, F., 'Creating a Directive on Pluralism and Media Concentration: A Case Study of the European Union Legislative Process' in *Lawmaking in the European Union*, P. Craig and C. Harlow (eds) (The Hague, Kluwer, 1998).

Bens, E. de, M. Kelly and M. Bakke 'Television Content: Dallasification of Culture?' in *Dynamics of Media Politics: Broadcast and Electronic Media in Western Europe*, K. Siune and W. Truettzschler (eds) (London, Sage, 1992).

Bens, E. de and H. de Smaele, 'The Inflow of American Television Fiction on European Broadcasting Channels Revisited' (2001) 16 *European Journal of Communication*.

Berekoven, L., 'Europa-Fernsehen – Ein Kommunikationsinstrument des internationalen Marketings' in *Europafernsehen und Werbung: Chancen für die deutsche und europäische Medienpolitik*, Arbeitskreis Werbefernsehen der deutschen Wirtschaft (Baden-Baden, Nomos, 1987).

Berg, K., 'Rechtsprobleme des grenzüberschreitenden Fernsehens – Stellungnahme zum Grünbuch der EG-Kommission aus der Sicht der öffentlich-rechtlichen Rundfunkanstalten' in *Fernsehen ohne Grenzen: Die Errichtung des Gemeinsamen Marktes für den Rundfunk, insbesondere über Satellit und Kabel*, J. Schwarze (ed.) (Baden-Baden, Nomos, 1985).

Bergg, D., 'Taking a Horse to Water? Delivering Public Service Broadcasting in a Digital Universe' in *From Public Service Broadcasting to Public Service Communications*, D. Tambini and J. Cowling (eds) (London, IPPR, 2004).

Berggreen, I. and I. Hochbaum, 'Bildung, Ausbildung und Kultur' in *Die deutschen Länder in Europa: Politische Union und Wirtschafts- und Währungsunion*, H. F. U. Borkenhagen *et al.* (eds) (Baden-Baden, Nomos, 1992).

Berggreen-Merkel, I., *Die rechtlichen Aspekte der Kulturpolitik nach dem Maastrichter Vertrag*, Vorträge, Reden und Berichte aus dem Europa-Institut der Universität des Saarlandes, no. 329 (Saarbrücken, Europa-Institut, 1995).

Bernier, I., 'Content Regulation in the Audio-Visual Sector and the WTO' in *The WTO and Global Convergence in Telecommunications and Audio-Visual Services*, D. Geradin and D. Luff (eds) (Cambridge, Cambridge University Press, 2004).

Betz, J., 'Die EG-Fernsehrichtlinie – Ein Schritt zum europäischen Fernsehen?' (1989) 11 MP.

Beukel, E., 'Reconstructing Integration Theory: The Case of Educational Policy in the EC' (1994) 29 *Cooperation and Conflict*.

Beyme, K. von, *Kulturpolitik und nationale Identität: Studien zur Kulturpolitik zwischen staatlicher Steuerung und gesellschaftlicher Autonomie* (Opladen, Westdeutscher Verlag, 1998).

Birk, H. J., A. Dittmann and M. Erhardt (eds) *Kulturverwaltungsrecht im Wandel: Rechtsfragen der Praxis in Schule und Hochschule*, Festschrift for Thomas Oppermann (Stuttgart, Richard Boorberg, 1981).

Blanke, H.-J. *Europa auf dem Weg zu einer Bildungs- und Kulturgemeinschaft*, Kölner Schriften zum Europarecht, vol. 41 (Cologne, Carl Heymanns, 1994).

Blois, M. de, 'Note to Case 352/85, *Bond van Adverteerders v. The Netherlands State* [1988] ECR 2085' (1990) 27 CMLRev.

Blumler, J. G., 'Public Service Broadcasting before the Commercial Deluge' in *Television and the Public Interest: Vulnerable Values in West European Broadcasting*, J. G. Blumler (ed.) (London, Sage, 1992).

Blumler, J. G. (ed.), *Television and the Public Interest: Vulnerable Values in West European Broadcasting* (London, Sage, 1992).

Blumler, J. G. and W. Hoffmann-Riem, 'New Roles for Public Service Television' in *Television and the Public Interest: Vulnerable Values in West European Broadcasting*, J. G. Blumler (ed.) (London, Sage, 1992).

Bogdandy, A. von, 'Europäischer Protektionismus im Medienbereich: Zu Inhalt und Rechtmäßigkeit der Quotenregelungen in der Fernsehrichtlinie' (1992) 1 EuZW.

Bogdandy, A. von, 'Unity in Diversity? The European Single Market in Broadcasting and the Audiovisual, 1982–92' (1994) 32 JCMS.

Bogdandy, A. von, 'The Contours of Integrated Europe: The Origin, Status and Prospects of European Integration' in *European Legal Cultures*, V. Gessner, A. Hoeland and C. Varga (eds) (Aldershot, Dartmouth, 1996).

Bohr, K. and H. Albert, 'Die Europäische Union – das Ende der eigenständigen Kulturpolitik der deutschen Bundesländer?' (1993) 2 ZRP.

Booth, P., 'Introduction' in *Public Service Broadcasting without the BBC?*, A. Peacock (ed.) (London, Institute of Economic Affairs, 2004).

Borchmann, M., 'Der Artikel 235: Generalklausel für EG – Kompetenzen' in *Die deutschen Länder in Europa: Politische Union und Wirtschafts- und Währungsunion*, H. F. U. Borkenhagen *et al.* (eds) (Baden-Baden, Nomos, 1992).

Born, G., *Uncertain Vision: Birt, Dyke and the Reinvention of the BBC* (London, Vintage, 2005).

Born, G. and T. Prosser, 'Culture and Consumerism: Citizenship, Public Service Broadcasting and the BBC's Fair Trading Obligations' (2001) 64 MLR.

Börner, B., 'Kompetenz der EG zur Regelung einer Rundfunkordnung' (1985) 12 ZUM.

Bos, J. W. van den, 'No Frontiers: The New EU Proposal on Audiovisual Media Services' (2006) 4 ENT L R.

Botella i Corral, J. and E. Machet, 'Co-ordination and Co-operation between Regulatory Authorities in the Field of Broadcasting' in *Iris Special: Audiovisual Media Services without Frontiers: Implementing the Rules* (Strasbourg, European Audiovisual Observatory, 2007).

Bourges, H., 'La télévision publique en Europe' (1998) 111 *La lettre du CSA*.

Bradley, A. W. and K. D. Ewing, *Constitutional and Administrative Law* (14th edn, Harlow, Longman, 2006).

Brems, E., 'Note to Case C-337/97, *C. P. M. Meeusen v. Hofdirectie van de Informatie Beheer Groep* (ECJ, 8 June 1999)' (2000) 6 ColumJEurL.

Brugmans, H., 'Five Starting Points' in *Europe from a Cultural Perspective: Historiography and Perceptions*, A. Rijksbaron, W. H. Roobol and M. Weisglas (eds) (The Hague, Nijgh & Van Ditmar, 1987).

Brühann, U., 'Der Vorschlag einer Gemeinschaftsrichtlinie zum Rundfunkrecht: Notwendigkeit und werberechtlicher Inhalt' in *Europafernsehen und Werbung: Chancen für die deutsche und europäische Medienpolitik*, Arbeitskreis Werbefernsehen der deutschen Wirtschaft (Baden-Baden, Nomos, 1987).

Bueckling, A., *Fernsehen ohne Grenzen – Fernsehen in Grenzen*, Vorträge, Reden und Berichte aus dem Europa-Institut der Universität des Saarlandes, no. 60 (Saarbrücken, Europa-Institut, 1986).

Bullinger, M., 'Werbung und Quotenregelung zwischen nationalem und europäischem Rundfunkrecht' in *Eine Rundfunkordnung für Europa – Chancen und Risiken*, K. Stern *et al.* (eds), Schriftenreihe des Instituts für Rundfunkrecht an der Universität zu Köln, vol. 54 (Munich, C. H. Beck, 1990).

Bullinger, M., *Die Aufgaben des öffentlichen Rundfunks: Wege zu einem Funktionsauftrag* (Gütersloh, Bertelsmann Stiftung, 1999).

Bülow, L., 'Themen-Sponsoring im Fernsehen' (1999) 2 CR.

Búrca, G. de, 'The Principle of Proportionality and Its Application in EC Law' (1993) 13 YEL.

Burgelman, J. C. and C. Pauwels, 'Audiovisual Policy and Cultural Identity in Small European States: The Challenge of a Unified Market' (1992) 14 *Media, Culture and Society*.

Campbell of Alloway, A. and Z. Yaqub, *The European Handbook on Advertising Law* (London, Cavendish, 1999).

Cappello, M. and R. Mastroianni, 'Italy' in *Iris Special: The Public Service Broadcasting Culture* (Strasbourg, European Audiovisual Observatory, 2007).

Carey, P. and J. Sanders, *Media Law* (3rd edn, London, Sweet & Maxwell, 2004).

Carrie, D. G. and A. S. C. Ehrenberg, 'Is Television All That Important?' (1992) 20 (4–5) *Intermedia*.

Castendyk, O., 'Werbeintegration im TV-Programm – wann sind Themen Placements Schleichwerbung oder Sponsoring?' (2005) 12 ZUM.

Castendyk, O., 'Quotas in Favour of Independent Producers: Article 5 of the "Television without Frontiers" Directive' (2006) 11 (3) *Communications Law*.

Cederman, L.-E., *Nationalism and Bounded Integration: What It Would Take to Construct a European Demos*, European Forum Series RSC, no. 2000/34 (Florence, European University Institute, 2000).

Charbit, N., 'Une nouvelle télévision sans frontière: Directive 97/36/CE du 30 juin 1997 modifiant la directive 89/552/CEE' (1997) 7 *Europe*.

Chrysogonos, K., *Mia vevaiotike anatheorese: E anatheorese ton diataxeon tou Syntagmatos gia ta atomika kai koinonika dikaiomata* (2nd edn, Athens, Ant. A. Sakkoulas, 2002).

Closa, C., 'Supranational Citizenship and Democracy: Normative and Empirical Dimensions' in *European Citizenship: An Institutional Challenge*, M. La Torre (ed.) (The Hague, Kluwer, 1998).

Collins, R., 'The Screening of Jaques Tati: Broadcasting and Cultural Identity in the European Community' (1993) 11 CardozoArts&EntLJ.

Collins, R., *Broadcasting and Audio-Visual Policy in the European Single Market* (London, John Libbey, 1994).

Collins, R., 'Unity in Diversity? The European Single Market in Broadcasting and the Audiovisual, 1982–92' (1994) 32 JCMS.

Collins, R., 'Public Service Broadcasting: Too Much of a Good Thing?' in *From Public Service Broadcasting to Public Service Communications*, D. Tambini and J. Cowling (eds) (London, IPPR, 2004).

Commissie Jeugd, Geweld en Media, *Wijzer Kijken: Schadelijkheid, geschiktheid en kennisbevordering bij het gebruik van audiovisuele producten door jeugdigen* (Den Haag, Ministerie van Onderwijs, Cultuur en Wetenschap, 2005).

Coppieters, S., 'The Financing of Public Service Broadcasting' in *The Law of State Aid in the European Union*, A. Biondi, P. Eeckhout and J. Flynn (eds) (Oxford, Oxford University Press, 2004).

Cornu, M., *Compétences culturelles en Europe et principe de subsidiarité* (Brussels, Bruylant, 1993).

Coulthard, A., 'Dutch Television – Too Red Hot for UK!' (1993) 14 Media L&P.

Council of Europe, *Report of the Committee on Culture, Science and Education: Public Service Broadcasting*, Doc. 10029 (Strasbourg, Council of Europe, 2004).

Cowling, J., 'From Princes to Paupers: The Future of Advertising-Funded Public Service Television' in *From Public Service Broadcasting to Public Service Communications*, D. Tambini and J. Cowling (eds) (London, IPPR, 2004).

Cowling, J. and D. Tambini, 'Conclusions and Recommendations' in *From Public Service Broadcasting to Public Service Communications*, D. Tambini and J. Cowling (eds) (London, IPPR, 2004).

Craig, P. and G. de Búrca, *EU Law: Text, Cases and Materials* (4th edn, Oxford, Oxford University Press, 2008).

Craufurd Smith, R., *Broadcasting Law and Fundamental Rights* (Oxford, Clarendon, 1997).

Craufurd Smith, R., 'The Establishment of Companies in European Community Law: Choice of Law or Abuse of Rights?' [1999] *European Current Law*.

Craufurd Smith, R., 'State Support for Public Service Broadcasting: The Position under European Community Law' (2001) 28 (1) LIEI.

Craufurd Smith, R., 'Community Intervention in the Cultural Field: Continuity or Change?' in *Culture and European Union Law*, R. Craufurd Smith (ed.) (Oxford, Oxford University Press, 2004).

Craufurd Smith, R., 'Article 151 EC and European Identity' in *Culture and European Union Law*, R. Craufurd Smith (ed.) (Oxford, Oxford University Press, 2004).

Criscuolo, A., 'The "TV without Frontiers" Directive and the Legal Regulation of Publicity in the European Community' (1998) 23 ELRev.

Crosby, S., 'The Single Market and the Rule of Law' (1991) 16 ELRev.

CSA, *The Protection of Children and Adolescents on French Television* (Paris, CSA, 2005).

CSA, 'Election présidentielle 2007: le CSA publie sa recommandation' (2006) 200 *La lettre du CSA*.

CSA, *Publicité, parrainage, et téléachat à la télévision et á la radio* (Paris, CSA, 2006).

CSA, *La Protection de l'Enfance et de l'Adolescence à la télévision et à la radio: Bilan de l'Action du CSA* (Paris, CSA, 2006).

Currall, J., 'Some Aspects of the Relation between Articles 30–36 and Article 100 of the EEC Treaty, with a Closer Look at Optional Harmonisation' [1985] YEL.

Curall, J., 'Kommentar zum Art. 128' in *Kommentar zum EWG-Vertrag*, vol. 3, H. von der Groeben, J. Thiesing and C. D. Ehlermann (eds) (4th edn, Baden-Baden, Nomos, 1991).

Daalmeijer, J. 'Public Service Broadcasting in the Netherlands' (2004) 12 (1) *Trends in Communication*.

Dagtoglou, P., *Radioteleorase kai Syntagma* (Athens, Ant. N. Sakkoulas, 1989).

Dagtoglou, P., *Atomika dikaiomata*, vol. 2 (2nd edn, Athens, Ant. N. Sakkoulas, 2005).

Damm, A., *Gebührenprivileg und Beihilferecht: Zur Vereinbarkeit der Finanzierung des öffentlich-rechtlichen Rundfunks in Deutschland mit Art. 92 EGV* (Berlin, Springer, 1998).

Dashwood, A., 'The Limits of European Community Powers' (1996) 21 ELRev.

DCMS, *An Agreement Between Her Majesty's Secretary of State for Culture, Media and Sport and the British Broadcasting Corporation*, Cm. 6872 (London, TSO, 2006).

DCMS, *A Public Service for All: The BBC in the Digital Age*, Cm. 6763 (London, TSO, 2006).

DCMS, *Government Response to the Lords Committee Report on Charter Review*, Cm. 6739 (London, TSO, 2006).

Debbasch, C., X. Agostinelli *et al.*, *Droit des médias* (Paris, Dalloz, 2002).

Degenhart, C., 'Note to Case C-288/89, *Stichting Collectieve Antannevorziening Gouda and Others v. Commissariaat voor de Media* [1991] ECR I-4007' (1992) 22 JZ.

Degenhart, C., *Der Funktionsauftrag des öffentlich-rechtlichen Rundfunks in der digitalen Welt* (Heidelberg, Verlag Recht und Wirtschaft, 2001).

Degenhart, C., 'Öffentlich-rechtlicher Rundfunkauftrag und Rundfunkgebühr nach dem siebten und achten Rundfunkänderungsstaatsvertrag' (2005) 7 K&R.

Dehousse, R., 'Community Competences: Are There Limits to Growth?' in *Europe after Maastricht: An Ever Closer Union?*, R. Dehousse (ed.) (Munich, C. H. Beck, 1994).

Dehousse, R., *The European Court of Justice: The Politics of Judicial Integration* (Basingstoke, Macmillan, 1998).

Delikostopoulou, A., 'Note to Case 523/2000 Decided by the Athens Court of First Instance' (2000) 11 ΔΕΕ.

Department of National Heritage, *Royal Charter for the Continuance of the British Broadcasting Corporation*, Cm. 3248 (HMSO, London, 1996).

Depypere, S., J. Broche and N. Tigchelaar, 'State Aid and Broadcasting: State of Play' (2004) 1 *Competition Policy Newsletter.*

Depypere, S. and N. Tigchelaar, 'The Commission's State Aid Policy on Activities of Public Service Broadcasters in Neighbouring Markets' (2004) 2 *Competition Policy Newsletter.*

Deringer, A., 'Pyrrhussieg der Länder: Anmerkung zum Urteil des Bundesverfassungsgerichts vom 22. März 1995 in der Rechtssache 2 BvG 1/89 in dem Verfahren Fernsehrichtlinie' (1995) 5 ZUM.

Deutsch, K. W., *Nationalism and Social Communication: An Inquiry into the Foundations of Nationality* (2nd edn, Cambridge, MA, MIT Press, 1966).

Dicke, K., 'Eine europäische Rundfunkordnung für welches Europa?' (1989) 4 MP.

Dörr, D., 'Der deutsche Föderalismus und die entstehende Medienordnung' (1991) 9 EWS.

Dörr, D., 'Die Entwicklung des Medienrechts' (1995) 35 NJW.

Dörr, D., 'Die Entwicklung des Medienrechts' (1997) 20 NJW.

Dörr, D., *Die öffentlich-rechtliche Rundfunkfinanzierung und die Vorgaben des EG-Vertrages*, Arbeitspapiere des Instituts für Rundfunkökonomie an der Universität zu Köln, no. 94 (Cologne, Institut für Rundfunkökonomie, 1998).

Dörr, D., *Big Brother und die Menschenwürde: Die Menschenwürde und die Programmfreiheit am Beispiel eines neuen Sendeformats* (Frankfurt am Main, Peter Lang, 2000).

Dörr, D., K. Beucher, J. Eisenbeis and E. Jost, *Die Einflüsse europarechtlicher Entwicklungen auf das Bund-Länder-Verhältnis im Rundfunkwesen*, Schriftenreihe des Instituts für Europäisches Medienrecht Saarbrücken, vol. 4 (Munich, Jehle-Rehm, 1993).

Dolmans, M., 'Quotas without Content: The Questionable Legality of European Content Quotas under the Television without Frontiers Directive' (1995) 8 ENT L R.

Dommering, E. J., 'Advertising and Sponsorship Law – Problems of Regulating Partly Liberalised Markets' in *Europäisches Medienrecht – Fernsehen und seine gemeinschaftsrechtliche Regelung*, Schriftenreihe des Instituts für Europäisches Medienrecht Saarbrücken, vol. 18 (Munich, Jehle-Rehm, 1998).

Donaldson, J. D., '"Television without Frontiers": The Continuing Tension between Liberal Free Trade and European Cultural Integrity' (1996) 20 Fordham Int'l L J.

Dondelinger, J., 'Broadcasting in the Single Market' in *Regulating the Audiovisual Industry: The Second Phase*, D. Goldberg and R. Wallace (eds), Current EC Legal Development Series (London, Butterworths, 1991).

Dougan, M., 'Vive La Différence? Exploring the Legal Framework for Reflexive Harmonisation within the Single European Market' in *Annual of German and European Law*, R. Miller and P. Zumbansen (eds) (Oxford, Berghahn Books, 2003).

Douglass Scott, S.,'The EU Charter of Rights: A Poor Attempt to Strengthen Democracy and Citizenship?' in *The Treaty of Nice and Beyond: Enlargement and Constitutional Reform*, M. Andenas and J. A. Usher (eds) (Oxford, Hart, 2003).

Drijber, B. J., 'The Revised Television without Frontiers Directive: Is It Fit for the Next Century?' (1999) 36 CMLRev.

Drijvers, J., 'Community Broadcasting: A Manifesto for the Media Policy of Small European Countries' (1992) 14 *Media, Culture and Society*.

Durand, C. and S. van Raepenbusch, 'Les pricipaux développements de la jurisprudence de la Cour de Justice et du Tribunal de première instance du 1er août 1996 au 31 juillet 1997' (1998) 34 CDE.

Dyson, K. and P. Humphreys, 'Regulatory Change in Western Europe: From National Cultural Regulation to International Economic Statecraft' in *Broadcasting and New Media Policies in Western Europe: A Comparative Study of Technological Change and Public Policy*, K. Dyson and P. Humphreys (London, Routledge, 1988).

Eberle, C. E., 'Das europäische Recht und die Medien am Beispiel des Rundfunkrechts' (1993) 1 AfP.

Eberle, C. E., 'Aktivitäten der Europäischen Union auf dem Gebiet der Medien und ihre Auswirkungen auf den öffentlich-rechtlichen Rundfunk' (1995) 5 ZUM.

Eberle, C. E., 'Die Rundfunkgebühr auf dem EU-Prüfstand' in *Regulierung im Bereich von Medien und Kultur: Gestaltungsmöglichkeiten und rechtliche Grenzen*, J. Schwartze and J. Becker (eds) (Baden-Baden, Nomos, 2002).

Eeckhout, P., 'The Proposed EU Charter of Fundamental Rights: Some Reflections on Its Effects in the Legal Systems of the EU and of Its Member States' in *The EU Charter of Fundamental Rights: Text and Commentaries*, K. Feus (ed.) (London, Federal Trust, 2000).

Eijk, N. van, L. Asscher, N. Helberger and J. Kabel, *De regulering van media in internationaal perspectief* (Amsterdam, Wetenschappelijke Raad voor Regeringsbeleid/Pallas, 2005).

Eijk, N. van, 'The Netherlands' in *Iris Special: The Public Service Broadcasting Culture* (Strasbourg, European Audiovisual Observatory, 2007).

Electoral Commission, *Party Political Broadcasting: Report and Recommendations* (London, The Electoral Commission, 2003).

Engel, C., *Privater Rundfunk vor der Europäischen Menschenrechtskonvention* (Baden-Baden, Nomos, 1993).

EPRA, 'Background Paper – Plenary, Political Advertising: Case Studies and Monitoring', 23rd EPRA Meeting', Elsinore, 17–19 May 2006.

Euromedia Research Group/M. Kelly, G. Mazzoleni and D. McQuail, *The Media in Europe* (London, Sage, 2004).

European Commission, *1998 Audiovisual Policy of the European Union: The New Era of the Picture Industry, Television without Frontiers, Greater Europe in the Year 2000* (Luxembourg, OOPEC, 1997).

Everling, U., 'Brauchen wir "Solange III"?' (1990) 3 EuR.

Farrar, C., 'E.C. Broadcasting Law Clarified: The Paul Denuit and VT4 Cases and the New "Television without Frontiers" Directive' (1998) 1 ENT L R.

Faßbender, K., 'Zu Inhalt und Grenzen des rundfunkrechtlichen Sendestaatsprinzips' (2006) 6 AfP.

Fechner, F., 'Kommentar zum Art. 128' in *Handbuch des Europäischen Rechts: Systematische Sammlung mit Erläuterungen*, 335th instalment, H. von der Groeben, J. Thiesing and C. D. Ehlermann (eds) (Baden-Baden, Nomos, 1995).

Feenstra, J., 'Note to Case C-288/89, *Stichting Collectieve Antannevorziening Gouda and Others v. Commissariaat voor de Media*, Judgment of 25 July 1991, [1991] ECR I-4007; Case C-353/89, *Commission of the European Communities v. Kingdom of the Netherlands*, Judgment of 25 July 1991 [1991] ECR I-4069' (1993) 30 CMLRev.

Feintuck, M. and M. Varney, *Media Regulation, Public Interest and the Law* (Edinburgh, Edinburgh University Press, 2006).

Fenwick, H. and G. Phillipson, *Media Freedom under the Human Rights Act* (Oxford, Oxford University Press, 2006).

Fishman, J., 'The New Linguistic Order' (1988/89) 113 *Foreign Policy.*

Flessner, R., 'The EuroCulture Network: An Interim Report' in *Studying Europe: Challenges and Prospects for European Studies*, H. Lichtenberg and W. Petzold (eds) (Baden-Baden, Nomos, 1999/2000).

Flora, P., S. Kuhnle and D. Urwin (eds), *State Formation, Nation-Building and Mass Politics in Europe: The Theory of Stein Rokkan* (Oxford, Oxford University Press, 1999).

Forrest, A., 'Can Community Support Measures Have a Decisive Impact on European Film and Television Production?' (1996) 8 *European Business Journal.*

Foster, R., J. Egan and J. Simon, 'Measuring Public Service Broadcasting' in *From Public Service Broadcasting to Public Service Communication*, D. Tambini and J. Cowling (eds) (London, IPPR, 2004).

Franceschini, L., *Télévision et Droit de la Communication* (Paris, Ellipses, 2003).

Franzone, D., 'L'économie et la culture dans l'approche communautaire de la radiodiffusion' (1988) 317 RMC.

Frese, M., *Die Rechtmäßigkeit europäischer Fernsehquoten aus kompetentieller, grundrechtlicher und welthandelsrechtlicher Sicht* (Frankfurt am Main, Peter Lang, 1998).

Frey, D., *Fernsehen und audiovisueller Pluralismus im Binnenmarkt der EG* (Baden-Baden, Nomos, 1999).

Frohne, R., 'Die Quotenregelungen im nationalen und im europäischen Recht' (1989) 8–9 ZUM.

Gavin, B., 'Television without Frontiers' in *European Broadcasting Standards in the 1990s*, B. Gavin (ed.) (Manchester, NCC Blackwell, 1991).

Gazzo, E., 'Le culturel dans l'information européenne' in *Acte du Colloque 'Culture et Cultures Européennes' 28–30 mai 1986*, D. Roche (ed.), version provisoire (Florence, European University Institute, 1987).

Gellner, E., *Nations and Nationalism* (Oxford, Blackwell, 1983).

Gibbons, T., *Regulating the Media* (London, Sweet & Maxwell, 1998).

Gibbons, T., 'Jurisdiction over (Television) Broadcasters: Criteria for Defining "Broadcaster" and "Content Service Provider"' in *The Future of the 'Television without Frontiers Directive'*, Schriftenreihe des Instituts für Europäisches Medienrecht, vol. 29 (Baden-Baden, Nomos, 2005).

Gifreu, J., 'Linguistic Order and Spaces of Communication in Post-Maastricht Europe' (1996) 18 *Media, Culture and Society*.

Goerens, P., 'Interplay between Relevant European Legal Instruments: ECTT and TVwF Directive: Competition or Complementarity?' in *Iris Special: Audiovisual Media Services without Frontiers: Implementing the Rules* (Strasbourg, European Audiovisual Observatory, 2007).

Goldberg, D., T. Prosser and S. Verhulst, *EC Media Law and Policy*, European Law Series (Harlow, Longman, 1998).

Graber, C. B., 'The Stumbling Block of Trade Liberalisation' in *The WTO and Global Convergence in Telecommunications and Audio-Visual Services*, D. Geradin and D. Luff (eds) (Cambridge, Cambridge University Press, 2004).

Grant, J., 'Ofcom Buys into Product Placement: Consultation on Issues Related to Product Placement' (2006) 4 ENT L R.

Greaves, R., 'Advertising Restrictions and the Free Movement of Goods and Services' (1998) 23 ELRev.

Green, N., T. C. Hartley and J. A. Usher, *The Legal Foundations of the Single Market* (Oxford, Oxford University Press, 1991).

Greissinger, C. *Vorgaben des EG-Vertrags für nationales Rundfunk- und Multimediarecht* (Baden-Baden, Nomos, 2000).

Grimm, D., 'Does Europe Need a Constitution?' (1995) 1 ELJ.

Gulich, J., *Rechtsfragen grenzüberschreitender Rundfunksendungen: Die deutsche Rundfunkordnung im Konflikt mit der Dienstleistungsfreiheit* (Baden-Baden, Nomos, 1990).

Gundel, J., 'Nationale Programmquoten im Rundfunk: Vereinbar mit den Grundfreiheiten und der Rundfunkfreiheit des Gemeinschaftsrechts?' (1998) 12 ZUM.

Häberle, P., *Verfassungslehre als Kulturwissenschaft* (2nd edn, Berlin, Duncker & Humblot, 1998).

Habermas, J., 'Citizenship and National Identity: Some Reflections on the Future of Europe' (1992/93) 12 *Praxis International*.

Habermas, J., 'Remarks on Dieter Grimm's "Does Europe Need a Constitution?"' (1995) 1 ELJ.

Hailbronner, K. and C. Weber, 'Möglichkeiten zur Förderung der europäischen Kultur in Rundfunk und Fernsehen anhand der Fernsehrichtlinie der Europäischen Gemeinschaft' (1997) 14 DÖV.

Hamelink, C. J., *Cultural Autonomy in Global Communications: Planning National Information Policy* (London, Centre for the Study of Communications and Culture, 1988).

Harcourt, A., *The European Union and the Regulation of Media Markets* (Manchester, Manchester University Press, 2005).

Harrison, J. and L. Woods, 'Determining Jurisdiction in the Digital Age' (1999) 5 EPL.

Harrison, J. and L. Woods, 'European Citizenship: Can Audio-Visual Policy Make a Difference?' (2000) 38 JCMS.

Harrison, J. and L. Woods, 'Television Quotas: Protecting European Culture?' (2001) 1 ENT L R.

Hartstein, R., W.-D. Ring, J. Kreile, D. Dörr and R. Stettner, *Rundfunkstaatsvertrag Kommentar*, vol. I (Munich, Jehle-Rehm, 2003).

Hatzopoulos, V., 'Recent Developments of the Case Law of the ECJ in the Field of Services' (2000) 37 CMLRev.

Hedetoft, U., 'The State of Sovereignty in Europe: Political Concept or Cultural Self-Image' in *National Cultures and European Integration: Exploratory Essays on Cultural Diversity and Common Policies*, S. Zetterholm (ed.) (Oxford, Berg, 1994).

Helberger, N., 'Die Konkretisierung des Sendestaatsprinzips in der Rechtsprechung des EuGH' (1998) 1 ZUM.

Held, T. and W. Schulz, *Europarechtliche Beurteilung von Online-Angeboten öffentlich-rechtlicher Rundfunkanstalten: Inwieweit beeinflussen die Beihilferegeln die Einbeziehung neuer Dienste in den Funktionsauftrag öffentlich-rechtlichen Rundfunks? Gutachten im Auftrag der Friedrich-Ebert-Stiftung* (Berlin, Friedrich-Ebert-Stiftung, 2004).

Hense, A., 'Bundeskulturpolitik als verfassungs- und verwaltungsrechtliches Problem' (2000) 6 DVBl.

Herold, A., 'Country of Origin Principle in the EU Market for Audiovisual Media Services: Consumer's Friend or Foe?', unpublished paper, 3 October 2007.

Herrmann, G. and M. Lausen, *Rundfunkrecht: Fernsehen und Hörfunk mit Neuen Medien* (2nd edn, Munich, C. H. Beck, 2004).

Herzog, R., 'Kommentar zum Artikel 5 I, II' in *Grundgesetz: Kommentar*, vol. I: *GG Text – Artikel 11*, T. Maunz and G. Dürig (eds) (Munich, C. H. Beck, 2002).

Hess, W., 'Die EG-Rundfunkrichtlinie vor dem Bundesverfassungsgericht: Anmerkungen zum Verfahren 2 BvG 1/89' (1990) 2 AfP.

Hesse, K., 'Rundfunk zwischen demokratischer Willensbildung und dem Zugriff der EG' (1993) 11 JZ.

Hins, W., 'Note to Case C-148/91, *Vereniging Veronica Omroep Organisatie v. Commissariaat voor de Media* [1993] ECR I-487' (1994) 31 CMLRev.

Hirsch, V., 'L'audiovisuel européen: État d'urgence' (1988) 317 RMC.

Hitchens, L. P., 'Identifying European Community Audio-Visual Policy in the Dawn of the Information Society' (1996) II YMEL.

Hobsbawm, E. J., *Nations and Nationalism since 1780* (Cambridge, Cambridge University Press, 1990).

Hobsbawm, E. J., 'Nationalism and Ethnicity' (1992) 29 *Intermedia*.

Hochbaum, I., 'Kohäsion und Subsidiarität – Maastricht und die Länderkulturhoheit' (1992) 7 DÖV.

Hoefnagel, F. J. P. M., *Geschiedenis van het Nederlands inhoudelijk mediabeleid* (Amsterdam, Wetenschappelijke Raad voor Regeringsbeleid/ Pallas, 2005).

Hoffmann-Riem, W., 'Europäisierung des Rundfunks – aber ohne Kommunikationsverfassung?' in *Rundfunk im Wettbewerbsrecht: Der öffentlich-rechtliche Rundfunk im Spannungsfeld zwischen Wirtschaftsrecht und Rundfunkrecht*, W. Hoffmann-Riem (ed.), Symposien des Hans-Bredow-Instituts, vol. 10 (Baden-Baden, Nomos, 1988).

Hoffmann-Riem, W., 'International Regulation of Direct Satellite Broadcasting: Illusions and Alternatives' (1988) 3 *European Journal of Communication.*

Hoffmann-Riem, W., *Rundfunkrecht neben Wirtschaftsrecht: Zur Anwendbarkeit des GWB und des EWGV auf das Wettbewerbsverhalten öffentlich-rechtlichen Rundfunks in der dualen Rundfunkordnung*, Beiträge zum Rundfunkrecht, vol. 43 (Baden-Baden, Nomos, 1991).

Hoffmann-Riem, W., 'Defending Vulnerable Values: Regulatory Measures and Enforcement Dilemmas' in *Television and the Public Interest: Vulnerable Values in West European Broadcasting*, J.G. Blumler (ed.) (London, Sage, 1992).

Hoffmann-Riem, W., 'Trends in the Development of Broadcasting Law in Western Europe' (1992) 7 *European Journal of Communication.*

Hoffmann-Riem, W., 'The Broadcasting Activities of the European Community and Their Implications for National Broadcasting Systems in Europe' (1993) 16 Hastings Int'l&CompLRev.

Hoffmann-Riem, W., *Regulating Media: The Licensing and Supervision of Broadcasting in Six Countries* (New York, Guilford, 1996).

Hoffmann-Riem, W., *Regulierung der dualen Rundfunkordnung* (Baden-Baden, Nomos, 2000).

Hoggart, R., 'The Public Service Idea' in *British Broadcasting: Main Principles* (London, Broadcasting Research Unit, 1983).

Holmes, J., 'European Community Law and the Cultural Aspects of Television' in *Culture and European Union Law*, R. Craufurd Smith (ed.) (Oxford, Oxford University Press, 2004).

Holtz-Bacha, C., 'Die Neufassung der europäischen Fernsehregulierung: Von der Fernseh- zur Mediendiensterichtlinie' (2007) 2 MP.

Holznagel, B., *Rundfunkrecht in Europa: Auf dem Weg zu einem Gemeinrecht europäischer Rundfunkordnungen*, Jus publicum, vol. 18 (Tübingen, J. C. B. Mohr, 1996).

Holznagel, B., 'The Mission of Public Service Broadcasting' (2000) 5 IJCLP.

Hondius, F., 'Regulating Transfrontier Television – The Strasbourg Option' (1988) 8 YEL.

Hörnle, J., 'Country of Origin Regulation in Cross-Border Media: One Step beyond the Freedom to Provide Services?' (2005) 54 ICLQ.

House of Commons 4th Standing Committee on Delegated Legislation, *Copy of the Amendment dated 4 December 2003 to the Agreement of 25 January 1996 (as amended) Between Her Majesty's Secretary of State for Culture, Media and Sport and the British Broadcasting Corporation*, Cm. 6075 (London, TSO, 2003).

House of Commons Culture, Media and Sport Committee, *A Public BBC. First Report of Session 2004–05,* vol. I, HC 82-I (London, TSO, 2004).

House of Lords Select Committee on the BBC Charter Review, *The Review of the BBC's Royal Charter, First Report of Session 2005–06*, vol. I, HL 50-1 (London, TSO, 2005).

Huglo, J. G., 'Droit d'établissement et libre prestation des services' (1992) 28 RTDE.

Huglo, J. G., 'Droit d'établissement et libre prestation des services' (1999) 35 RTDE.

Hümmerich, K., 'Nationale Rundfunkordnung oder Europäischer Medienmarkt? Die deutsche Rundfunkordnung unter dem Einfluß des europäischen Gemeinschaftsrechts' (1991) 3 AfP.

Hümmerich, K. and J. Eisenbeis, *Der Einfluß des Europäischen Rechts auf die Tätigkeit der Rundfunk- und Fernsehveranstalter in Deutschland* (Munich, Jehle-Rehm, 1992).

Humphreys, P. J., *Mass Media and Media Policy in Western Europe* (Manchester, Manchester University Press, 1996).

Hurard, F., 'The Production Quota System of the EU-Television Directive' in *Europäisches Medienrecht – Fernsehen und seine gemeinschaftsrechtliche Regelung*, Schriftenreihe des Instituts für Europäisches Medienrecht, vol. 18 (Munich, Jehle-Rehm, 1998).

Hutton, B. Lord, *Report of the Inquiry into the Circumstances Surrounding the Death of Dr David Kelly C.M.G* (London, HMSO, 2004).

IOM, *O Optikoakoustikos Tomeas sten Ellada* (Athens, European Commission Representation in Greece, 2003).

Ipsen, H. P., 'Der Kulturbereich im Zugriff der EG' in *Verfassungsrecht und Völkerrecht: Gedächtnisschrift für Wilhelm Karl Geck*, W. Fiedler and G. Ress (eds) (Cologne, Carl Heymanns, 1989).

Jarass, H., 'EG-Recht und nationales Rundfunkrecht: Zugleich ein Beitrag zur Reichweite der Dienstleistungsfreiheit' (1986) 1 EuR.

Joint Committee on the Draft Communications Bill, *Report of the Joint Committee on the Draft Communications Bill (Puttnam Report)*, HL Paper 169-1: HC 876-1 (London, TSO, 2002).

Jones, C., 'Television without Frontiers' (1999/2000) 19 YEL.

Jorna, K., 'EC Audiovisual Policy in the European Community – Cornerstones and Trends' in *Audiovisual Media and Copyright in Europe*, H. C. Jehoram, P. Keuchenius and J. Seignett (eds) (The Hague, Kluwer, 1994).

Kakabadse, M., 'The External Trade Aspects of European Broadcasting: The Uruguay Round in GATT' in *European Broadcasting Standards in the 1990s*, B. Gavin (ed.) (Manchester, NCC Blackwell, 1991).

Kamtsidou, I., 'E ekthese pepragmenon tou ESR gia to etos 2004: E anexartete arxe se diarke apostase apo te rythmistike apostole tes' (2005) 3 ΔιΜΕΕ.

Karakostas, V., *To Syntagma, Ermeneutika sxolia, Nomologia* (Athens, Nomike Vivliotheke, 2006).

Karakostas, I. K., *To Dikaio ton MME* (Athens, Ant. N. Sakkoulas, 2003).

Karakostas, I. K. and A. D. Tsevas, *E Nomothesia ton MME* (2nd edn, Athens, Ant. N. Sakkoulas, 2003).

Katsirea, I., *Cultural Diversity and European Integration in Conflict and in Harmony* (Athens, Ant. N. Sakkoulas, 2001).

Katsirea, I., 'Why the European Broadcasting Quota Should Be Abolished' (2003) 28 ELRev.

Katsirea, I., 'The Transmission State Principle: The End of the Broadcasting Sovereignty of the Member States?' (2003/04) 6 *Cambridge Yearbook of European Legal Studies*.

Katsirea, I., 'European Citizenship and Post-national Ideal in the Light of the Jurisprudence of the European Court of Justice' (2004) 24 *Revue Hellénique de Droit Européen*.

Katsirea, I., 'The Circumvention Principle: An Effective Defence of National Broadcasting Systems against Abuse?' (2005) 10 *Communications Law*.

Katsirea, I., 'Culture: Cornerstone of the European Union Edifice?' (2006) 13 *Maastricht Journal of European and Comparative Law*.

Keller, P., 'The New Television without Frontiers Directive' (1997/98) III YMEL.

Keller, P., 'Re-thinking Ethnic and Cultural Rights in Europe' (1998) 18 OxJLS.

Kiki, I., 'Greek Broadcasting Law: Past and Present' (1989) 10 (1) *Journal of Media Law and Practice*.

Kiki, I., *E Kalodiake Teleorase* (Athens, Ant. A. Sakkoulas, 1993).

Kiki, I., *E Eleutheria ton Optikoakoustikon Meson (Ypo to prisma tes Syntagmatikes anatheoreses tou 2001)* (Athens, Ekdoseis Sakkoula, 2003).

Kiki, I., 'Bouleutikes Ekloges 2000 kai 2004: Pros exomalynse ton kanonon radioteleoptikes provoles ton kommaton' (2007) 1 *Efemerida Dioiketikou Dikaiou*.

Klein, E. and A. Haratsch, 'Neuere Entwicklungen des Rechts der Europäischen Gemeinschaften – 1. Teil' (1993) 18 DÖV.

Kleist, T., 'Fernsehrichtlinie: Konvergenz und Wettbewerb bei audiovisuellen Angeboten' (2006) 2 MMR.

Kleist, T. and A. Scheuer, 'Audiovisuelle Mediendienste ohne Grenzen' (2006) 3 MMR.

Kleist, T. and A. Scheuer, 'Neue Regelungen für audiovisuelle Mediendienste: Vorschriften zu Werbung und Jugendschutz und ihre Anwendung in den Mitgliedstaaten' (2006) 4 MMR.

Kloepfer, M. and A. Neun, 'Rechtsfragen der europäischen Informationsgesellschaft' (2000) 4 EuR.

Klute, N., 'Die Produktionsquote, ein Protokoll und die Sache mit der Rundfunkfreiheit – eine Zusammenführung europäischen und deutschen Rundfunkrechts' (1991) 3 AfP.

Knothe, M. and H. Bashayan, 'Die Revision der EG-Fernsehrichtlinie: Ein europäischer Entscheidungsprozeß im Lichte nationaler Kompetenzen' (1997) 6 AfP.

Koenig, C. and A. Haratsch, 'The Licence-Fee-Based Financing of Public Service Broadcasting in Germany after the Altmark Trans Judgment' (2003) 4 EStAL.

Koenig, C. and J. Kühling, 'EC Control of Aid Granted through State Resources' (2002) 1 EStAL.

Koenig, C. and J. Kühling, 'How to Cut a Long Story Short: Das Preussen Elektra-Urteil des EuGH und die EG-Beihilfenkontrolle über das deutsche Rundfunkgebührensystem' (2001) 7 ZUM.

Kommers, D. P., *The Constitutional Jurisprudence of the Federal Republic of Germany* (2nd edn, Durham, NC, Duke University Press, 1997).

Konow, G., 'Bildungs- und Kulturpolitik in der Europäischen Gemeinschaft' (1989) 37 RdJB.

Konszuseck, H., 'Freier Dienstleistungsverkehr und nationales Rundfunkrecht: Anmerkung zum Urteil des Gerichtshofs der Europäischen Gemeinschaften vom 26.04.1988 zur niederländischen "Kabelregeling" – Rs. 352/85 – De Vereniging Bond van Adverteerders u.a./Niederländischen Staat' (1989) 12 ZUM.

Korte, K.-R., 'Das Dilemma des Nationalstaates in Westeuropa: Zur Identitätsproblematik der europäischen Integration' (1993) B14 *Aus Politik und Zeitgeschichte*.

Kostakopoulou, T., 'European Union Citizenship as a Model of Citizenship beyond the Nation State: Possibilities and Limits' in *Political Theory and the European Union: Legitimacy, Constitutional Choice and Citizenship*, A. Weale and M. Nentwich (eds) (London, Routledge, 1998).

Krämer, L., *EC Environmental Law* (4th edn, London, Sweet & Maxwell, 2000).

Krebber, D., *Europeanisation of Regulatory Television Policy: The Decision-Making Process of the Television without Frontiers Directives from 1989 & 1997* (Baden-Baden, Nomos, 2002).

Kreile, J. and M. Diesbach, 'Der neue Jugendmedienschutz-Staatsvertrag – was ändert sich für den Rundfunk?' (2002) 12 ZUM.

Kresse, H. and M. Heinze, 'Der Rundfunk: Das "jedenfalls auch kulturelle Phänomen" – Ein Pyrrhus-Sieg der Länder? Eine Kurzanalyse des Urteils des Bundesverfassungsgerichts zur EU-Fernesehrichtlinie' (1995) 6 ZUM.

Krüger, U. M. and T. Zapf-Schramm, 'Sparten, Sendungsformen und Inhalte im deutschen Fernsehangebot' (2006) 4 MP.

Kugelmann, D., *Der Rundfunk und die Dienstleistungsfreiheit des EWG-Vertrages*, Schriften zum Europäischen Recht, vol. 10 (Berlin, Duncker & Humblot, 1991).

Kugelmann, D., 'Note to Case C-288/89, *Stichting Collectieve Antannevorziening Gouda and Others v. Commissariaat voor de Media* [1991] ECR I-4007' (1992) 1 AfP.

Kühn, M., 'Die europarechtliche Einordnung des grenzüberschreitenden Fernsehens aus der Sicht beteiligter privater Unternehmen' in *Fernsehen ohne Grenzen: Die Errichtung des Gemeinsamen Marktes für den Rundfunk, insbesondere über Satellit und Kabel*, J. Schwarze (ed.) (Baden-Baden, Nomos, 1985).

Kühn, M., 'Harmonisierung des Rundfunkrechts in Europa: Zum Entwurf der Richtlinie der EG-Kommission' (1986) 11 ZUM.

Kühn, M., *Meinungsvielfalt im Rundfunk: Die Sicherung von Pluralismus in den Rundfunksystemen Deutschlands und der USA* (Munich, C. H. Beck, 2003).

Ladeur, K. H., 'Towards a Legal Theory of Supranationality – The Viability of the Network Concept' (1997) 3 ELJ.

Laffan, B., 'The Politics of Identity and Political Order in Europe' (1996) 34 JCMS.

Laffan, B., R. O'Donnell and M. Smith, *Europe's Experimental Union: Rethinking Integration* (London, Routledge, 2000).

Lane, R., 'New Community Competences under the Maastricht Treaty' (1993) 30 CMLRev.

Leidinger, A., 'Programmverantwortung im Spannungsfeld von Programmgrundsätzen und Rundfunkfreiheit' [1989] DVBl.

Lenaerts, K., 'Constitutionalism and the Many Faces of Federalism' (1990) 38 Am J Comp L.

Lenaerts, K. and P. van Nuffel, *Constitutional Law of the European Union* (London, Sweet & Maxwell, 1999).

Lenz, C. O., 'Vertrag von Maastricht – Ende demokratischer Staatlichkeit?' (1993) 31 NJW.

Lenz, C. O., 'Das Sendestaatsprinzip als Teil der europäischen Medienordnung' in *Europäisches Medienrecht – Fernsehen und seine gemeinschaftsrechtliche Regelung*, Schriftenreihe des Instituts für Europäisches Medienrecht Saarbrücken, vol. 18 (Munich, Jehle-Rehm, 1998).

Lerche, P., 'Konsequenzen aus der Entscheidung des Bundesverfassungsgerichts zur EG-Fernsehrichtlinie' (1995) 4 AfP.

Levy, D. A. L., *Europe's Digital Revolution. Broadcasting Regulation, the EU and the Nation State* (London, Routledge, 1999).

Liehm, A. J., 'Aider la création pour sauver les identities: La culture, mal-aimée de l'Europe', *Le Monde Diplomatique*, September 1999.

Lodge, J., 'Towards a Political Union?' in *The European Community and the Challenge of the Future*, J. Lodge (ed.) (London, Pinter, 1993).

Loman, J. M. E., K. J. M. Mortelmans, H. H. G. Post and J. S. Watson, *Culture and Community Law before and after Maastricht* (The Hague, Kluwer, 1992).

Lübbe, H., 'Für eine europäische Kulturpolitik' in *Europäische Kultur: Das Zukunftsgut des Kontinents: Vorschläge für eine europäische Kulturpolitik*, W. Weidenfeld, H. Lübbe, W. Maihofer and J. Rovan (Gütersloh, Bertelsmann Stiftung, 1990).

Lupinacci, T., 'The Pursuit of Television Broadcasting Activities in the European Community: Cultural Preservation or Economic Protectionism?' (1991) 24 Vand J Transnat'l L.

MacCormick, N., 'Problems of Democracy and Subsidiarity' (2000) 6 EPL.

Mackenzie, W. J. M., *Political Identity* (Manchester, Manchester University Press, 1978).

MacLennan, J., 'Facing the Digital Future: Public Service Broadcasters and State Aid Law in the European Union' (1999) 2 *Cambridge Yearbook of European Legal Studies*.

Magiera, S., 'Rechtliche Grundfragen einer werdenden europäischen Rundfunkordnung' in *Eine Rundfunkordnung für Europa – Chancen und Risiken*, K. Stern *et al.* (eds) (Munich, C. H. Beck, 1990).

Maihofer, W., 'Culture politique et identité européenne' in *Structure and Dimensions of European Community Policy*, J. Schwartze and H. G. Schermers (eds) (Baden-Baden, Nomos, 1988).

Mangoldt, H. von, F. Klein and C. Starck, *Das Bonner Grundgesetz: Kommentar*, vol. I: *Präambel, Artikel 1 bis 19* (4th edn, Munich, Franz Vahlen, 1999).

Marcangeo-Leos, P., 'France' in *Iris Special: The Public Service Broadcasting Culture* (Strasbourg, European Audiovisual Observatory, 2007).

Margue, T. L., 'L'action culturelle de la Communauté européenne: Bilan et perspectives' (1993) 2 RMUE.

Martín Estebanez, M. A., 'The Protection of National or Ethnic, Religious or Linguistic Minorities' in *The European Union and Human Rights*, N. A. Neuwahl and A. Rosas (eds) (The Hague, Martinus Nijhoff, 1995).

Martín, J. M. F. and S. O'Leary, 'Judicial Exceptions to the Free Provision of Services' (1995) 1 ELJ.

Mauboussin, E., 'Le CSA et les élections: entre lois et jurisprudence, une competence sous haute surveillance' (1997) 143 (2) *Légipresse*.

Mazzoleni, G., 'Medienpluralismus in Italien zwischen Politik und Marktwettbewerb' (2003) 11 MP.

Mazzoleni, G. and G. Vigevani, 'Italy' in *Television across Europe: Regulation, Policy and Independence* (New York, Open Society Institute, 2005).

McColgan, A., 'Editorial: The EU Charter of Fundamental Rights' (2004) 1 EHRL.

McDonald, K., 'How Would You Like Your Television: With or without Borders and with or without Culture – A New Approach to Media Regulation in the European Union' (1999) 22 Fordham Int'l L J.

McGonagle, T. and A. van Loon, *Iris Special: Jurisdiction over Broadcasters in Europe – Report on a Round-Table Discussion and Selection of Background Materials* (Strasbourg, European Audiovisual Observatory, 2002).

McGonagle, T., 'Regulating Minority-Language Use in Broadcasting: International Law and the Dutch National Experience' (2004) 16 *Mediaforum*.

McGonagle, T., 'Workshop Report' in *Iris Special: Audiovisual Media Services without Frontiers: Implementing the Rules*, (Strasbourg, European Audiovisual Observatory, 2007).

McGonagle, T., 'Safeguarding Human Dignity in the European Audiovisual Sector' (2007) 6 *IRIS plus*.

McMahon, J., *Education and Culture in European Community Law* (London, Athlone, 1995).

Meckel, M., *Fernsehen ohne Grenzen? Europas Fernsehen zwischen Integration und Segmentierung*, Studien zur Kommunikationswissenschaft, vol. 3 (Opladen, Westdeutscher Verlag, 1994).

Meier, H. E., 'Beyond Convergence: Understanding Programming Strategies of Public Broadcasters in Competitive Environments' (2003) 18 *European Journal of Communication*.

Meij, J. M. de, *Uitingsvrijheid: De vrije informatiestroom in grondwettelijk perspectief* (Amsterdam, Otto Cramwinckel, 2000).

Mestmäcker, E. J., 'Wege zur Rundfunkfreiheit in Europa' in *Offene Rundfunkordnung: Prinzipien für den Wettbewerb im grenzüberschreitenden Rundfunk*, E. J. Mestmäcker (ed.) (Gütersloh, Bertelsmann Stiftung, 1988).

Mestmäcker, E. J., C. Engel, K. Gabriel-Bräutigam and M. Hoffmann, *Der Einfluß des europäischen Gemeinschaftsrechts auf die deutsche Rundfunkordnung* (Baden-Baden, Nomos, 1990).

Meyer-Heine, A., 'Les apports de la nouvelle directive "Tèlèvision sans frontières" du 30 juin 1997 entrée en vigueur le 31 décembre 1998' (1999) 35 RTDE.

Milner, S., 'Introduction: A Healthy Scepticism?' (2000) 22 *European Integration*.

Mohn, R., 'The Role of the Communications Media in the Cultural Policy of a United Europe' in *Presentation on the Occasion of the Meeting of the Catalan Publishers' Association 'NIT DE L'EDICIO' at Barcelona on 12 June 1991* (Gütersloh, Bertelsmann Stiftung, 1991).

Mohr, I., 'Standards gesetzt: Jugendmedienschutz in der ARD' [2005] *ARD-Jahrbuch*.

Möller, H., 'Die Stellung der "Gesellschaftlich relevanten Gruppen" im öffentlich-rechtlichen Rundfunk' (2001) 4 AfP.

Mourik, M., 'European Cultural Co-operation' in *Europe from a Cultural Perspective*, A. Rijksbaron, W. Roobol and M. Weisglas (eds) (The Hague, Nijgh & Van Ditmar, 1987).

Mouzelis, N., 'Ernest Gellner's Theory of Nationalism: Some Definitional and Methodological Issues' in *The State of the Nation: Ernest Gellner and the Theory of Nationalism*, J. Hall (ed.) (Cambridge, Cambridge University Press, 1998).

Müller, M., 'Die Revision der EG-Fernsehrichtlinie – EMR-Dialog am 2.12.1993 in Mainz in Zusammenarbeit mit SAT.1' (1994) 1 AfP.

Mulgan, G. and R. Patterson (eds), *Hollywood of Europe? The Future of British Film* (London, BFI, 1993).

Nanclares, J. M.-P. de, *Die Bedeutung des Gemeinschaftsrechts für das Fernsehen: Die Fernsehrichtlinie*, Vorträge, Reden und Berichte aus dem

Europa-Institut der Universität des Saarlandes, no. 253 (Saarbrücken, Europa-Institut, 1991).

Negrine, R., *Parliament and the Media: A Study of Britain, Germany and France* (London, Royal Institute of International Affairs, 1998).

Negrine, R. and S. Papathanassopoulos, *The Internationalisation of Television* (London, Pinter, 1990).

Negrine, R. and S. Papathanassopoulos, 'The Internationalization of Television' (1991) 6 *European Journal of Communication*.

Nicoltchev, S., 'European Backing for Public Service Broadcasting: Council of Europe Rules and Standards' in *Iris Special: The Public Service Broadcasting Culture*, European Audiovisual Observatory (Strasbourg, European Audiovisual Observatory, 2007).

Niedobitek, M., 'Die kulturelle Dimension im Vertrag über die Europäische Union' (1995) 4 EuR.

Niedobitek, M., *The Cultural Dimension in EC Law* (The Hague, Kluwer, 1997).

Niemann, A., 'The PHARE Programme and the Concept of Spillover: Neofunctionalism in the Making' (1998) 5 *Journal of European Public Policy*.

Nieuwenhuis, A. J., 'Media Policy in the Netherlands: Beyond the Market?' (1992) 7 *European Journal of Communication*.

Nissen, C., *Public Service Media in the Information Society. Report prepared by the Council of Europe's Group of Specialists on Public Service Broadcasting in the Information Society (MS-S-PSB)* (Strasbourg, Council of Europe, 2006).

Ofcom, *Ofcom Review of Public Service Television Broadcasting: Phase 1: Is Television Special?* (London, Ofcom, 2004).

Ofcom, *Ofcom Rules on Party Political and Referendum Broadcasts* (London, Ofcom, 2004).

Ofcom, *Research into the Effectiveness of PIN Protection Systems in the UK: A Report of the Key Findings of Research among Schoolchildren Aged 11–17, and a Separate Study of Parents* (London, Ofcom, 2005).

Ofcom, *Product Placement: A Consultation on Issues Related to Product Placement* (London, Ofcom, 2005).

Ofcom, *Product Placement: Summary of Responses to Consultation on Issues Related to Product Placement* (London, Ofcom, 2006).

Ofcom, *Outline Procedures for Handling Fairness and Privacy Complaints* (London, Ofcom, 2006).

Ofcom, *Guidance Notes, Section 10: Commercial References and Other Matters* (London, Ofcom, 2006).

Ofcom and BBC Trust, *Memorandum of Understanding between the Office of Communications (Ofcom) and the BBC Trust* (London, Ofcom, 2007).

Oikonomou, A., 'Ethniko Symvoulio Radioteleorases: treis anekplerotes proupotheseis gia ten apotelesmatike leitourgia tou os anexartetes arxes' (2004) 2 ΔιΜΕΕ.

O' Leary, S., 'The Social Dimension of Community Citizenship' in *A Citizens' Europe – In Search of a New Order*, A. Rosas and E. Antola (eds) (London, Sage, 1995).

O'Leary, S., *The Evolving Concept of Community Citizenship: From the Free Movement of Persons to Union Citizenship* (The Hague, Kluwer, 1996).

O'Leary, B., 'Ernest Gellner's Diagnoses of Nationalism: A Critical Overview of What Is Living and What Is Dead in Ernest Gellner's Philosophy of Nationalism?' in *The State of the Nation: Ernest Gellner and the Theory of Nationalism*, J. Hall (ed.) (Cambridge, Cambridge University Press, 1998).

Olsen, J., *Organising European Institutions of Governance: A Prelude to an Institutional Account of Political Integration*, ARENA Working Papers, no. 00/2 (Oslo, ARENA Norwegian Research Council, 1998).

Oppermann, T., 'ARTE – Ein Experiment in Europäischer Kultur' in *Gedächtnisschrift für Eberhard Grabitz*, A. Randelzhofer, R. Scholz and D. Wilke (eds) (Munich, C. H. Beck, 1995).

Oppermann, T., *Deutsche Rundfunkgebühren und europäisches Beihilferecht* (Berlin, Duncker & Humblot, 1997).

Orf, E., 'Television without Frontiers – Myth or Reality?' (1990) 8 EIPR.

Ossenbühl, F., *Rundfunk zwischen nationalem Verfassungsrecht und Europäischem Gemeinschaftsrecht: Rechtsgutachten erstattet der Regierung des Landes Nordrhein-Westfalen* (Frankfurt am Main, Alfred Metzner, 1986).

Ossenbühl, F., 'Spielräume des Gesetzgebers bei der Gebührenfestsetzung' (2004) 3 MP.

Palzer, C., 'Germany' in *Iris Special: The Public Service Broadcasting Culture*, European Audiovisual Observatory (Strasbourg, European Audiovisual Observatory, 2007).

Pantel, M., 'Unity in Diversity: Cultural Policy and EU Legitimacy' in *Legitimacy and the European Union: The Contested Polity*, T. Banchoff and M. P. Smith (eds) (London, Routledge, 1999).

Papatheodorou, F. and D. Machin, 'The Umbilical Cord That Was Never Cut: The Post-dictatorial Intimacy between the Political Elite and the Mass Media in Greece and Spain' (2003) 18 (1) *European Journal of Communication.*

Pechstein, M., 'Die Bedeutung von Protokollerklärungen zu Rechtsakten der EG' (1990) 3 EuR.

Pechstein, M., 'Subsidiarität der EG-Medienpolitik?' (1991) 13 DÖV.

Peifer, N., 'Die neuen Vorschriften für die Rundfunkwerbung in Italien' (1994) GRUR Int.

Peifer, N., *Vielfaltssicherung im bundesweiten Fernsehen: Voraussetzungen und Grenzen einer Prüfung der medienrelevanten verwandten Märkte* (Munich, Reinhard Fischer, 2005).

Pelle, J. and K. Sevinga, 'Dutch Broadcasting System: Free Provision of Services within the EC' (1991) 2 ULR.

Perau, G., *Werbeverbote im Gemeinschaftsrecht: Gemeinschaftsrechtliche Grenzen nationaler und gemeinschaftsrechtlicher Werbebeschränkungen* (Baden-Baden, Nomos, 1997).

Petersen, N., *Rundfunkfreiheit und EG-Vertrag: Die Einwirkungen des Europäischen Rechts auf die Ausgestaltung der nationalen Rundfunkordnungen* (Baden-Baden, Nomos, 1994).

Picht, R., 'Die "Kulturmauer" durchbrechen: Kulturelle Dimensionen politischer und wirtschaftlicher Zusammenarbeit in Europa' (1987) 10 *Europa-Archiv*.

Pingel-Lenuzza, I., 'La nouvelle directive "Tèlèvision sans frontières" ou la lente structuration du droit communautaire de l'audiovisuel' (1999) 2 RAE.

Plumb, H., C. Tongue and F. Wijsenbeek, *Shaping Europe: Reflections of Three MEPs* (London, Federal Trust for Education and Research, 2000).

Pollack, M. A., 'Creeping Competence: The Expanding Agenda of the European Community' (1994) 14 *Journal of Public Policy*.

Pragnell, A. (ed.), *Opening up the Media 1983–1993: Challenges and Responses during the Institute's First Ten Years*, Media Monograph, no. 17 (Manchester, European Institute for the Media, 1993).

Price, M. E., 'Globalisation and National Identity on Television' (1992) 20 *Intermedia*.

Price, M. E., *Television, the Public Sphere and National Identity* (Oxford, Oxford University Press, 1995).

Prima, M. Di, 'Publicità ingannevole e comparative' (2005–2006) 13/14 *Concorrenza e mercato*.

Prosser, T., *The Limits of Competition Law: Markets and Public Services* (Oxford, Oxford University Press, 2005).

Prosser, T., 'United Kingdom' in *Iris Special: The Public Service Broadcasting Culture* (Strasbourg, European Audiovisual Observatory, 2007).

Prott, L. V., 'Cultural Rights as Peoples' Rights in International Law' in *The Rights of Peoples*, J. Crawford (ed.) (Oxford, Clarendon, 1988).

Pullen, M., 'Television without Frontiers: Fact or Fiction?' (1996) 5 ENT L R.

Pullen, M. and B. Ris, 'Television without Frontiers: The Saga Continues' (1997) 1 ENT L R.

Quigley, C. and A. Collins, *EC State Aid Law and Policy* (Oxford, Hart, 2004).

Rasmussen, H., 'Structure and Dimensions of EC Cultural Policy – "L'Europe des bonnes volontés culturelles"' in *Structure and Dimensions of European Community Policy*, J. Schwarze and H. G. Schermers (eds) (Baden-Baden, Nomos, 1987).

Raworth, P., 'A Timid Step Forward: Maastricht and the Democratisation of Europe' (1994) 19 ELRev.

Reich, N., 'Rundfunkrecht und Wettbewerbsrecht vor dem Forum des europäischen Gemeinschaftsrechts' in *Rundfunk im Wettbewerbsrecht: Der öffentlich-rechtliche Rundfunk im Spannungsfeld zwischen Wirtschaftsrecht und Rundfunkrecht*, W. Hoffmann-Riem (ed.), Symposien des Hans-Bredow-Instituts, vol. 10 (Baden-Baden, Nomos, 1988).

Reinemann, S., 'Die Auswirkungen des Legge Gasparri auf die Meinungsmacht von Silvio Berlusconi in Italien' (2004) 12 ZUM.

Ress, G., *Kultur und europäischer Binnenmarkt: Welche rechtlichen Auswirkungen hat der EWGV jetzt und nach der Verwirklichung des Europäischen Binnenmarktes auf die Kulturpolitik der BRD, insbesondere im Bereich der Kulturförderung? Gutachten für das Bundesministerium des Innern* (Stuttgart, Kohlhammer, 1991).

Ress, G., 'Die neue Kulturkompetenz der EG' (1992) 22 DÖV.

Riché-Magnier, M. and J. Metthey, 'Société de l'information: "New Deal" libéral ou nouveau modèle de société?' (1950) 390 RMC.

Roach, C., 'The Movement for a New World Information and Communications Order: A Second Wave?' (1990) 12 *Media, Culture and Society*.

Robillard, S. and J. Libby, *Television in Europe: Regulatory Bodies* (London, European Institute for the Media, 1995).

Robins, K. and D. Morley, 'What Kind of Identity for Europe?' (1992) 20 *Intermedia*.

Rogalski, A., 'L'Europe des télévisions entre le rêve et la réalité' (1995/96) 299 *L' Éurope en formation.*

Ross, M., 'Cultural Protection: A Matter for Union Citizenship or Human Rights?' in *The European Union and Human Rights*, N. A. Neuwahl and A. Rosas (eds) (The Hague, Martinus Nijhoff, 1995).

Roßnagel, A. and P. Strothmann, *Die duale Rundfunkordnung in Europa: Gemeinschaftsrechtliche Rahmenbedingungen und aktuelle Ansätze zum dualen System in ausgewählten Mitgliedstaaten*, Schriftenreihe der Rundfunk und Telekom Regulierungs-GmbH (Vienna, Rundfunk und Telekom Regulierungs-GmbH, 2004).

Roth, W.-H., 'Grenzüberschreitender Rundfunk und Dienstleistungsfreiheit' (1985) 149 ZHR.

Roth, W.-H., 'Note to Case C-233/94, *Federal Republic of Germany v. European Parliament and Council of the European Union* [1997] ECR I- 2405' (1998) 35 CMLRev.

Rudolph, M., 'Zur Rahmenordnung eines europäischen Binnenmarktes für den Rundfunk: Harmonisierungsbestrebungen der EG-Kommission' (1986) 2 AfP.

Rupp, H. H., 'EG-Rundfunkrecht und Gerichtskontrolle des Bundesverfassungsgerichts' in *Eine Rundfunkordnung für Europa – Chancen und Risiken*, K. Stern *et al.* (eds), Schriftenreihe des Instituts für Rundfunkrecht an der Universität zu Köln, vol. 54 (Munich, C. H. Beck, 1990).

Ruttig, M., *Der Einfluß des EG-Beihilferechts auf die Gebührenfinanzierung der öffentlichrechtlichen Rundfunkanstalten* (Frankfurt am Main, Peter Lang, 2001).

Salvatore, V., 'Quotas on TV Programmes and EEC Law' (1992) 29 CMLRev.

Santamato, S. and N. Pesaresi, 'Compensation for Services of General Economic Interest: Some Thoughts on the Altmark Ruling' (2004) 1 *Competition Policy Newsletter*.

Saxpekidou, E., *Eleuthere kykloforia teleoptikon yperesion sten Europaïke Oikonomike Koinoteta* (Thessaloniki, Ekdoseis Sakkoula, 1990).

Schaar, O., *Programmintegrierte Fernsehwerbung in Europa: Zum Stand der kommunikationsrechtlichen Regulierung in Europa* (Baden-Baden, Nomos, 2001).

Scharpf, F., *Governing in Europe: Effective and Democratic?* (Oxford, Oxford University Press, 1999).

Schatz, H., N. Immer and F. Marcinkowski, 'Der Vielfalt eine Chance? Empirische Befunde zu einem zentralen Argument für die Dualisierung des Rundfunks in der Bundesrepublik Deutschland' (1989) 1 *Rundfunk und Fernsehen*.

Schellenberg, M., 'Pluralismus: Zu einem medienrechtlichen Leitmotiv in Deutschland, Frankreich und Italien' (1994) 119 AöR.

Schermers, H. G., 'Comment on Weiler's *The Transformation of Europe*' (1991) 100 YLJ.

Scheuer, A., 'Implementation and Monitoring: Upholding General Interest in View of Commercial Communications' in *Iris Special: Audiovisual Media Services without Frontiers: Implementing the Rules*, European Audiovisual Observatory (Strasbourg, European Audiovisual Observatory, 2007).

Schlesinger, P., *Media, State and Nation: Political Violence and Collective Identities* (London, Sage, 1991).

Schlesinger, P., 'From Cultural Protection to Political Culture? Media Policy and the European Union' in *Constructing Europe's Identity: The External Dimension*, L.-E. Cederman (ed.) (London, Lynne Rienner, 2001).

Schmahl, S., *Die Kulturkompetenz der Europäischen Gemeinschaft* (Baden-Baden, Nomos, 1996).

Schmitt-Vockenhausen, M., 'Revision der EG-Fernsehrichtlinie: Ein weiterer Schritt in eine europäische Medienordnung?' (1998) 5 ZUM.

Schröder, W., 'Zu eingebildeten und realen Gefahren durch kompetenzüberschreitende Rechtsakte der Europäischen Gemeinschaft'(1999) 4 EuR.

Schultz, W., *Zum Vorschlag für eine Richtlinie über audiovisuelle Mediendienste*, Arbeitspapiere des Hans-Bredow-Instituts, no. 17 (Hamburg, Hans-Bredow-Institut, 2006).

Schulze-Fielitz, H., 'Kommentar zum Artikel 5 I, II', in *Grundgesetz: Kommentar*, vol. I: *Präambel, Artikel 1-19*, H. Dreier (ed.) (2nd edn, Tübingen, J. C. B. Mohr, 2004).

Schwartz, I., 'Broadcasting and the EEC Treaty' (1986) 11 ELRev.

Schwartz, I., 'Zur Zuständigkeit der Europäischen Gemeinschaft im Bereich des Rundfunks' in *Europafernsehen und Werbung: Chancen für die deutsche und europäische Medienpolitik*, Arbeitskreis Werbefernsehen der deutschen Wirtschaft (Baden-Baden, Nomos, 1987).

Schwartz, I., 'The Kabelregeling Judgment of the Court of Justice', unpublished paper presented at the symposium of the Vereiniging voor Media- en Communicatierecht, Amsterdam, 16 May 1988.

Schwartz, I., 'EG-Rechtsetzunsbefugnis für das Fernsehen' (1989) 2 ZUM.

Schwartz, I., 'Rundfunk, EG-Kompetenzen und ihre Ausübung' (1991) 4 ZUM.

Schwartz, I., 'Subsidiarität und EG-Kompetenzen: Der neue Titel "Kultur": Medienvielfalt und Binnenmarkt' (1993) 1 AfP.

Schwartze, J., 'Das Staatsrecht in Europa' (1993) 12 JZ.

Schwendinger, G., *Deutsche Rundfunkgebühren – staatlich oder aus staatlichen Mitteln gewährt? Zugleich eine kritische Bestandsaufnahme der Rechtsprechung des EuGH zur staatlichen Zurechenbarkeit von Beihilfen gemäß Art. 87 Abs. 1 EGV*, EUI Working Paper Law no. 2003/5 (Florence, European University Institute, 2003).

Scientific Council for Government Policy (WRR), *Media Policy for the Digital Age* (Amsterdam, Amsterdam University Press, 2005).

Seelmann-Eggebert, S., *Internationaler Rundfunkhandel: Im Recht der World Trade Organisation und der Europäischen Gemeinschaft* (Baden-Baden, Nomos, 1998).

Seidel, L. '"Fernsehen ohne Grenzen": Zum Erlaß der EG Rundfunkrichtlinie' (1991) 2 NVwZ.

Seidel, M., 'Europa und die Medien' in *Fernsehen ohne Grenzen: Die Errichtung des Gemeinsamen Marktes für den Rundfunk, insbesondere über Satellit und Kabel*, J. Schwarze (ed.) (Baden-Baden, Nomos, 1985).

Selekos, P. D., *O Kanonas tou Diaxorismou ton Diafemiseon apo to Programma ste Radioteleorase* (*To zetema tes 'synkekalymmenes' diafemises*) (Athens, Ant. N. Sakkoulas, 1997).

Selmer, P. and H. Gersdorf, *Die Finanzierung des Rundfunks in der Bundesrepublik Deutschland auf dem Prüfstand des EG-Beihilferegimes* (Berlin, Duncker & Humblot, 1994).

Sepstrup, P., *Transnationalization of Television in Western Europe* (London, John Libbey, 1990).

Seri, P., 'Das Mediensystem Griechenlands' in *Internationales Handbuch Medien 2004/2005*, Hans-Bredow Institut (Baden-Baden, Nomos, 2004).

Servaes, J., '"Europe 1992": The Audiovisual Challenge' (1992) 49 *Gazette*.

Sevinga, K., 'Dutch Broadcasting Continued' (1993) 4 ULR.

Shaughnessy, H. and C. F. Cobo, *The Cultural Obligations of Broadcasting: National and Transnational Legislation Concerning Cultural Duties of Television Broadcasters in Europe* (Manchester, European Institute for the Media, 1990).

Shaw, J., and A. Wiener, 'The Paradox of the "European Polity"', Harvard Jean Monnet Chair Working Paper Series, no. 10 (1999) <www.jeanmonnet-program.org/papers/99/991002.html>, 1 November 2007.

Shaw, J., 'Constitutional Settlements and the Citizen after the Treaty of Amsterdam' in *European Integration after Amsterdam: Institutional Dynamics and Prospects for Democracy*, K. Neunreither and A. Wiener (eds) (Oxford, Oxford University Press, 2000).

Shore, C., 'Inventing the "Peoples' Europe": Critical Approaches to European Community "Cultural Policy"' (1993) 28 MAN.

Shore, C., *Building Europe: The Cultural Politics of European Integration* (London, Routledge, 2000).

Silj, A., *The New Television in Europe*, Television Research Monograph Series (London, John Libbey, 1992).

Sinnaeve, A., 'State Financing of Public Services: The Court's Dilemma in the Altmark Case' (2003) 3 EStAL.

Siune, K. and W. Truetzschler (for the Euromedia Research Group), *Dynamics of Media Politics* (London, Sage, 1992).

Smith, A., 'National Identity and the Idea of European Unity' (1992) 68 *International Affairs*.

Smith, A., 'Is There a Global Culture?' (1992) 20 (4–5) *Intermedia*.

Somers, M., 'What's Political or Cultural about Political Culture or the Public Sphere? Toward a Historical Sociology of Concept Formation' (1995) 23 *Sociological Theory*.

Sparks, C. and C. Roach, 'Editorial' (1990) 12 *Media, Culture and Society*.

Sparr, J., *Kulturhoheit und EWG-Vertrag: Eine Untersuchung zur Einschränkung des gesetzgeberischen Handlungsspielraums der Mitgliedstaaten in kulturellen Angelegenheiten durch den EWG-Vertrag, dargestellt an Hand des freien Waren- und Dienstleistungsverkehrs* (Baden-Baden, Nomos, 1991).

Staay, A. van der, 'On the Feasibility of a European Cultural Policy' in *Europe from a Cultural Perspective*, A. Rijksbaron, W. Roobol and M. Weisglas (eds) (The Hague, Nijgh & Van Ditmar, 1987).

Stavenhagen, L. G., 'Cultural Rights and Universal Human Rights' in *Economic, Social and Cultural Rights*, A. Eide, C. Krause and A. Rosas (eds) (The Hague, Martinus Nijhoff, 1995).

Stazi, A., *Mercati emergenti fra convergenza tecnologica e concorrenza: Il caso della televisione in mobilitá* (Milan, Giuffrè, 2006).

Steemers, J., 'In Search of a Third Way: Balancing Public Purpose and Commerce in German and British Public Service Broadcasting' (2001) 26 (1) *Canadian Journal of Communication*.

Stein, T., 'Die Querschnittsklausel zwischen Maastricht und Karlsruhe' in *Festschrift für Ulrich Everling*, vol. II, O. Due, M. Lutter and J. Schwarze (eds) (Baden-Baden, Nomos, 1995).

Steindorff, E., *Grenzen der EG-Kompetenzen* (Heidelberg, Verlag Recht und Wirtschaft, 1990).

Stock, M., 'Eine Grundrechtscharta für die Europäische Union: Wie sollte die Medienfreiheit darin ausgestaltet werden?' (2000) 7 ZUM.

Stock, M., 'Zum Reformbedarf im dualen Rundfunksystem: Public-Service-Rundfunk und kommerzieller Rundfunk: Wie können sie koexistieren?' (2005) 204 *Arbeitspapiere des Instituts für Rundfunkökonomie an der Universität zu Köln*.

Streinz, R., 'Mindestharmonisierung im Binnenmarkt' in *Mindestharmonisierung im Europäischen Binnenmarkt: Referate des 7. Bonner Europa-Symposions vom 27. April 1996*, U. Everling and W.-H. Roth (eds) (Baden-Baden, Nomos, 1997).

Stuyck J., 'Note to Joined Cases C-34/95, C-35/95 and C-36/95, *Konsumentombudsmannen (KO) v. De Agostini (Svenska) Förlag AB and Konsumentenombudsmannen (KO) v. TV-Shop I Sverige AB* [1997] ECR I- 3843' (1997) 34 CMLRev.

Szporluk, R., 'Thoughts about Change: Ernest Gellner and the History of Nationalism' in *The State of the Nation: Ernest Gellner and the Theory of Nationalism*, J. Hall (ed.) (Cambridge, Cambridge University Press, 1998).

Taylor, C., 'Invoking Civil Society' in *Philosophical Arguments*, C. Taylor (Cambridge, MA, Harvard University Press, 1995).

Tettenborn, A., 'Europäische Union: Rechtsrahmen für die Informationsgesellschaft' (1998) 1 MMR.

Theiler, T., 'The European Union and the "European Dimension" in Schools: Theory and Evidence' (1998) 21 *Journal of European Integration.*

Theiler, T., 'Why the European Union Failed to Europeanize Its Audiovisual Policy' in *Constructing Europe's Identity: The External Dimension*, L.-E. Cederman (ed.) (Boulder, CO, Lynne Rienner, 2001).

Thomas, J., 'A British Film Industry for the 1990s: A Proposal' in *Hollywood of Europe? The Future of British Film*, G. Mulgan and R. Patterson (eds) (London, BFI, 1993).

Tigchelaar, N., 'State Aid to Public Broadcasting – Revisited: An Overview of the Commission's Practise' (2003) 2 EStAL.

Tinel, A., 'Qu'est-ce que l'exception culturelle?' (2000) 435 RMUE.

Tomuschat, C., 'Rechtliche Aspekte des Gemeinschaftshandelns im Bereich der Kultur', in *F.I.D.E. Reports of the 13th Congress*, vol. 1 (Athens, Ant. N. Sakkoulas, 1988).

Tracey, M., 'The Poisoned Chalice? International Television and the Idea of Dominance' (1985) 114 (4) *Daedalus.*

Tracey, M., *The Decline and Fall of Public Service Broadcasting* (Oxford, Oxford University Press, 1988).

Trautwein, T., 'Grenzen der Dienstleistungsfreiheit im Dienstleistungsbereich: Anmerkung zu EuGH, Urteil vom 05.10.1994, Rs C-23/93, TV10 SA/ Commissariat voor de Media' (1995) 5 ZUM.

Troberg, P., 'Mediawet und kein Ende: Dienstleistungsfreiheit und Fernsehrechtsprechung des EuGH' (1994) 2 ZEuP.

Troberg, P., 'Kommentar zum Art. 59' in *Handbuch des Europäischen Rechts: Systematische Sammlung mit Erläuterungen*, 334th instalment, H. von der Groeben, J. Thiesing and C. D. Ehlermann (eds) (Baden-Baden, Nomos, 1995).

Trzaskalik, C., *Transparenzpflichten des öffentlich-rechtlichen Rundfunks: Die Rechtsstellung der der deutschen Rundfunkanstalten im Lichte der EG-Richtlinie der Transparenz der finanziellen Beziehungen zwischen den Mitgliedstaaten und den öffentlichen Unternehmen* (Berlin, Verband Privater Rundfunk und Telekommunikation Vistas, 2000).

Tuytschaever, F., *Differentiation in European Union Law* (Oxford, Hart, 1999).

Unesco, *Many Voices, One World: Towards a New, More Just and More Efficient World Information and Communication Order* (London, Kogan Page, 1980).

Vedel, T., 'France' in *Television across Europe: Regulation, Policy and Independence* (New York, Open Society Institute, 2005).
Venizelos, E., 'E radioteleoptike periodos se anazetese kanonistikou plaisiou' (1990) 31 ΕλλΔ.
Venturelli, S., *Liberalizing the European Media: Politics, Regulation and the Public Sphere* (Oxford, Clarendon, 1998).
Verbiest, T. and P. Reynaud, 'Le régime juridique du droit de réponse sur internet' (2006) 236 *Légipresse*.
Vick, D. W., 'Regulatory Convergence ?' (2006) 26 *Legal Studies*.
Vorhoof, D., 'The Netherlands TV10-Case and the Judgment of the European Court of Justice ECJ, 5 October 1994, C-23/93' (1995) 16 Media L&P.
Vormann, T., *Kulturelle Souveränität und Fernsehen: Rechtsvergleich der Maßnahmen zur Sicherung der kulturellen Identität in Kanada und den Europäischen Gemeinschaften unter besonderer Berücksichtigung der Quotenregelung im Fernsehen* (Rheinfelden, Schäuble, 1993).

Wägenbaur, R., 'Auf dem Wege zur Bildungs – und Kulturgemeinschaft' in *Gedächtnisschrift für Eberhard Grabitz*, A. Randelzhofer, R. Scholz and D. Wilke (eds) (Munich, C. H. Beck, 1995).
Wallace, R. and D. Goldberg, 'Television Broadcasting: The Community's Response' (1989) 26 CMLRev.
Wangermée, P., 'The European Institutions and Broadcasting' in *Opening up the Media 1983–1993: Challenges and Responses during the Institute's First Ten Years*, A. Pragnell (ed.), Media Monograph, no. 17 (Manchester, European Institute for the Media, 1993).
Ward, D., *The European Union Democratic Deficit and the Public Sphere. An Evaluation of EU Media Policy* (Amsterdam, IOS Press, 2004).
Ward, D., 'United Kingdom' in *Television across Europe: Regulation, Policy and Independence* (New York, Open Society Institute, 2005).
Ward, I., *The Margins of European Law* (Basingstoke, Macmillan, 1996).
Wattel, P., 'Note to Case C-23/93, *TV 10 SA v. Commissariaat voor de Media* [1994] ECR I 4795' (1995) 32 CMLRev.
Weatherill, S. and P. Beaumont, *EU Law: The Essential Guide to the Legal Workings of the European Union* (3rd edn, London, Penguin, 1999).
Weber, R. H., A. Roßnagel, S. Osterwalder, A. Scheuer and S. Wüst, *Kulturquoten im Rundfunk* (Baden-Baden, Nomos, 2006).
Weiler, J. H. H., 'The State "über alles": Demos, Telos and the German Maastricht Decision' in *Festschrift für Ulrich Everling*, vol. II, O. Due, M. Lutter and J. Schwarze (eds) (Baden-Baden, Nomos, 1995).
Weiler, J. H. H., 'The Transformation of Europe' in J. H. H. Weiler, *The Constitution of Europe: 'Do the New Clothes Have an Emperor?' and Other Essays on European Integration* (Cambridge, Cambridge University Press, 1999).

Wemmer, B., *Die neuen Kulturklauseln des EG-Vertrages: Eine Analyse der Art. 128 EGV und Art. 92 Abs. 3 lit. d) EGV* (Frankfurt am Main, Peter Lang, 1995).
Wenger, K., 'Euro-Fernsehen oder Euro-Flimmern? Zur Debatte um die europäische Medienordnung' (1989) 18 *Europa-Archiv*.
Winter, J. A., 'Re(de)fining the Notion of State Aid in Article 87 (1) of the EC Treaty' (2004) 41 CMLRev.
Wintle, M. (ed.), *Culture and Identity in Europe: Perceptions of Divergence and Unity in Past and Present* (Aldershot, Ashgate, 1996).
Witte, B. de, 'Eléments d'une politique Européenne de la culture' in *Acte du Colloque 'Culture et Cultures Européennes' 28–30 mai 1986*, D. Roche (ed.), version provisoire (Florence, European University Institute, 1987).
Witte, B. de, 'The Scope of Community Powers in Education and Culture in the Light of Subsequent Practice' in *Die Dynamik des Europäischen Gemeinschaftsrechts/The Dynamics of EC-Law: Die Auslegung des Europäischen Gemeinschaftsrechts im Lichte nachfolgender Praxis der Mitgliedstaaten und der EG-Organe*, R. Bieber and G. Ress (eds) (Baden-Baden, Nomos, 1987).
Witte, B. de, 'Cultural Policy: The Complementarity of Negative and Positive Integration' in *Structure and Dimensions of European Community Policy*, J. Schwarze and H. G. Schermers (eds) (Baden-Baden, Nomos, 1987).
Witte, B. de, 'Cultural Linkages' in *The Dynamics of European Integration*, W. Wallace (ed.) (London, Pinter, 1990).
Witte, B. de, 'The European Content Requirement in the EC Television Directive – Five Years after' (1995) I YMEL.
Witte, B. de, 'Public Service Broadcasting, Cultural Diversity and Cultural Integration in EC Law and Policy', unpublished paper presented at workshop 'Public Service Broadcasting and European Law', European University Institute, Florence, 27–28 October 2000.
Woldt, R., 'Germany' in *Television across Europe: Regulation, Policy and Independence* (New York, Open Society Institute, 2005).
Woldt, R., 'Neue Royal Charter für die BBC: Der Wert des öffentlichen Rundfunks in der digitalen Ära' (2006) 12 MP.
Woods, L. and J. Scholes, 'Broadcasting: The Creation of a European Culture or the Limits of the Internal Market?' (1997) 17 YEL.
Wright, T., 'Reinventing Democracy' in *Reinventing Democracy*, P. Hirst and S. Khilnani (eds) (Oxford, Blackwell, 1996).

Zaxaropoulos, T. and M. Parasxos, *Mass Media in Greece* (London, Praeger, 1993).
Zeinstra, H., 'De financiering van de publieke omroep in Europa' [2003–2005] *Mediaforum*.
Zeno Zencovich, V., 'Il "servizio pubblico televisivo" nel nuovo quadro normativo communitario' [2003] *Diritto dell 'informazione e dell' informatica*.
Zeno Zencovich, V., 'La disciplina della radiotelevisione nella società della comunicazione' [2004] *Quaderni Costituzionali*.

Table of Cases

AUSTRALIA

High Court of Australia, *Project Blue Sky v. Australian Broadcasting Authority* (1998) HCA 28, 28 April 1998, S41/1997.

FRANCE

Conseil Constitutionnel

Decision 82-141 of 27 July 1982.
Decision 84-181 of 10–11 October 1984.
Decision 86-217 of 18 September 1986.

GERMANY

Bundesverfassungsgericht

BVerfGE 7, 99 (1958).
BVerfGE 7, 198 (1958).
BVerfGE 12, 205 (1961).
BVerfGE 14, 121 (1962).
BVerfGE 31, 314 (1971).
BVerfGE 47, 198 (1978).
BVerfGE 57, 295 (1981).
BVerfGE 73, 118 (1986).
BVerfGE 74, 297 (1987).
BVerfGE 83, 238 (1991).
BVerfGE 87, 181 (1992).

BVerfGE 90, 60 (1994).
BVerfGE, 22 March 1995 – 2 BvG 1/89, (1995) 2 AfP, 483.
BVerfGE 94, 297, 324 (1996).
BVerfGE of 30 August 2002, (2003) JZ, 365.

Bundesgerichtshof

BGH, judgment of 6 July 1995, (1995) AfP, 966 and (1996) AfP, 63.

Oberverwaltungsgerichte/Verwaltungsgerichte

VG Berlin, judgment of 15 April 1999, (1999) ZUM, 742.
OVG Niedersachsen, judgment of 15 December 1999, (1999) ZUM, 347.

GREECE

Symvoulio tes Epikrateias

Decision 2423/84, [1986] ΤοΣ 77.
Decision 5040/87.
Decision 930/90, [1990] ΤοΣ, 68.
Decision 930/1992.
Decision 944/1999, [1999] ΤοΣ, 614.
Decision 2544/1999.
Decision 656/2000, [2000] ΤοΣ, 192.
Decision 553/2003.
Decision 554/2003.
Decision 152/2004.
Decision 4348/2005, (2006) 1 ΕΔΔΔ, 98.
Decision 926/2006, (2006) 4 ΔιΜΕΕ, 573.
Decision 2631/2006, (2006) 4 ΔιΜΕΕ, 565.
Decision 2647/2006.

Other Courts

Athens Court of First Instance 523/2000.
Athens Court of First Instance 4701/2002.

ITALY

Corte Constitutionale

Decision 59/1960, [1960] *Giur. Cost.* 759.
Decision 225/1974, [1974] *Giur. Cost.* 1775.
Decision 202/1976, [1976] *Giur. Cost.* 1267.
Decision 148/1981, [1981] *Giur. Cost.* 1379.

Decision 153/1987, [1987] *Giur. Cost.* 1141.
Decision 826/1988, [1988] *Giur. Cost.* 3893.
Decision 420/1994, [1995] *Il Foro Italiano*, Part I, 4.
Decision 155/2002, [2002] *Giur. Cost.* 1310.
Decision 284/2002, *Gazzetta Ufficiale* Nr. 26, 3 July 2002.

Other Courts

Controcampo speciale Champions League, PI 4420, Provv. N. 13317/2004, in Boll. 26/2004.
MSC Crociere/Trasmissioni Mediaset, PI 4643B, Provv. N. 14149/2005, in Boll. 11/2005.
Mediaset Premium, PI 4786, Provv N. 14536/2005, in Boll. 29/2005.
Settimanale S.T.A.R. + TV, PI 4833, Provv. N. 14700/2005, in Boll. 35/2005.
MSC Crociere/Trasmissioni Mediaset, PI 4643, Provv. N. 14100/2005, in Boll. 8/2005.

THE NETHERLANDS

Raad van State

Decision of 24 July 2002, LJN AE5780.
Decision of 8 August 2003, LJN AI0788.

Hoge Raad der Nederlanden

Decision of 6 January 1995, NJ 1995, 422.
Decision of 16 April 1996, NJ 1996, 527.
Decision of 14 July 2006, LJN AX5380.

Other Courts

Amsterdam Court of Appeal, 29 October 1988.
Highest Administrative Court of the Netherlands, 10 January 2005, AZ5851, (2007) 2 *Mediaforum*, 49 (summary).

UNITED KINGDOM

Queen's Bench Division

R v. Broadcasting Complaints Commission, ex p. British Broadcasting Corporation, 13 May 1994, [1994] EMLR 497.
R v. Broadcasting Complaints Commission, ex p. British Broadcasting Corporation, 22 February 1995, [1995] EMLR 241.
R v. Broadcasting Complaints Commission, ex p. Channel 4 Television Limited, 19 December 1994, [1995] EMLR 170.

Court of Appeal

R v. British Broadcasting Corporation, ex p. Prolife Alliance [2002] EWCA Civ. 297; [2002] 3 WLR 1080.

House of Lords

R v. British Broadcasting Corporation, ex p. Prolife Alliance [2003] UKHL 23.

EUROPEAN COURT OF JUSTICE

ADBHU, Case 240/83 [1985] ECR 531.
Adoui and Cornouaille v. Belgian State, Cases 115, 116/81 [1982] ECR 1665; [1982] 3 CMLR 631.
Altmark Trans GmbH v. Regierungspräsidium Magdeburg, Case C-280/00 [2003] ECR I-7747.
Banco Exterior de España v. Ayuntamiento de Valencia, Case C-387/92 [1994] ECR I-877.
Cadbury Schweppes v. Commissioners of Inland Revenue, Case C-196/04, [2006] ECR I-7995.
Campus Oil Limited v. Minister for Industry and Energy, Case 72/83 [1984] ECR 2727.
Centros Ltd v. Erhvervs- og Selskabsstyrelsen, Case C-212/96 [1999] ECR I-1459.
Chronopost and Others, Cases C-83/01 P, C-93/01 P and C-94/01 P [2003] ECR I-6993.
Cinéthèque SA and Others v. Fédération nationale des cinémas français, Cases 60 and 61/84 [1985] ECR 2605.
Coditel v. Ciné Vog Films, Case 262/81 [1982] ECR 3381 (*Coditel II* case).
Commission v. Council, Case C-300/89 [1991] ECR 2867 (*Titanium Dioxide* case).
Commission v. Council, Case C-155/91 [1993] ECR I-939.
Commission v. Italian Republic, Case 38/69 [1970] ECR 47.
Commission v. Belgium, Case C-211/91 [1992] ECR I-6757.
Commission v. Netherlands, Case C-353/89 [1991] ECR I-406.
Commission v. United Kingdom, Case C-222/94 [1996] ECR I-4025.
Commission v. Belgium, Case C-211/91 [1992] ECR 6757.
Commission v. Belgium, Case C-11/95 [1996] ECR I-4117.
Commission v. France, Case 290/83 [1985] ECR 439.
Commission v. France, Case C-159/94 [1997] ECR I-5815.
Commission v. Germany, Case 205/84 [1986] ECR 3755; [1987] 2 CMLR 69.
Commission v. Germany, Case 427/85 [1988] ECR 1123; [1989] 2 CMLR 677.
Commission v. Netherlands, Case C-353/89 [1991] ECR I-4069.
Commission v. United Kingdom, Case C-222/94 [1996] ECR I-4025.
Criminal Proceedings against Paul Denuit, Case C-14/96 [1997] ECR I-2785.
Duphar v. Netherlands, Case 238/82 [1984] ECR 523.
Ecotrade, Case C-200/97 [1998] ECR I-7907.

Elliniki Radiophonia Tileorassi (ERT) v. Dimotiki, Case 260/89 [1991] ECR I-2925; [1994] 4 CMLR 540.
European Parliament v. Council, Case C-271/94 [1996] ECR I-1689.
Factortame and Others, Case C-221/89 [1991] ECR I-3905.
Federación de Distribuidores Cinematográficos (FEDICINE) v. Spanish State, Case C-17/92 [1993] ECR I-2239.
Federal Republic of Germany v. European Parliament and Council, Case C-233/94 [1997] ECR I-2405.
Ferring v. ACOSS, Case C-53/00 [2001] ECR I-9067.
French Minister of Economic, Financial and Industrial Affairs v. GEMO, Case C-126/01 [2003] ECR I-13769.
French Republic v. Commission, Case C-482/99 [2002] ECR I-4397.
Greece v. Commission, Case 57/86 [1988] ECR 2855.
Guiseppe Sacchi (preliminary ruling requested by the Tribunale di Biella), Case 155/73 [1974] ECR 409.
International Fruit Company v. Productschap voor Groenten en Fruit, Case C-21-4/72 [1972] ECR 1219; [1975] 2 CMLR 1.
Italy v. Commission, Case 173/73 [1974] ECR 709.
Italy v. Commission, Case C-303/88 [1991] ECR I-1433.
Italy v. Commission, Case C-305/89 [1991] ECR I-1603.
Italy v. Commission, Case C-6/97 [1999] ECR I-2981.
Kammer van Koophandel en Fabrieken voor Amsterdam v. Inspire Art, Case C-167/01 [2003] ECR I-10155.
Karlsson, Case C-292/97 [2000] ECR 2737.
Khalil, Case C-180/99 [2001] ECR I- 7413.
Kirsammer/Hack v. Sidal, Case C-189/91 [1993] ECR I-6185.
Konsumentombudsmannen (KO) v. De Agostini (Svenska) Förlag AB and Konsumentenombudsmannen (KO) v. TV-Shop I Sverige, AB, Joined Cases C-34/95, C-35/95 and C-36/95 [1997] ECR I-3843.
Ladbroke Racing, Case C-83/98 [2000] ECR I-3271.
Mediakabel BV v. Commissariaat voor de Media, Case C-89/04 [2005] ECR I-4891.
Ministère Public v. Van Wesemael, Case 110, 111/78 [1979] ECR 35; [1979] 3 CMLR 87.
Municipality of Almelo and Others v. NV Energibedrijf Ijselmij, Case C-393/92 [1994] ECR 1477.
Namur-Les Assurances du credit v. Office national du ducroire and Belgian State, Case 44/93 [1994] ECR I-3829.
Nold v. Commission, Case 4/73 [1974] ECR 491; [1974] 2 CMLR 338.
Openbaar Ministerie v. Nertsvoederfabriek Nederland, Case 118/86 [1987] ECR 3883.
Opinion 2/94 on the accession of the Community to the European Convention on Human Rights [1996] ECR I-1759.
Procureur du Roi v. Marc J.V.C. Debauve and Others, Case 52/79 [1980] ECR I-833.

Preussen Elektra, Case C-379/98 [2001] ECR 2099.
Rewe-Zentrale v. Bundesmonopolverwaltung für Branntwein, Case 120/78 [1979] ECR 649;[1979] 3 CMLR 494.
Rutili v. Minister for the Interior, Case 36/75 [1975] ECR 1219.
R v. Bouchereau, Case 30/77 [1977] ECR 1999; [1977] 2 CMLR 800.
R v. Secretary of State for Transport ex parte Factortame, Case C-221/89 [1991] ECR I 3905; [1991] 3 CMLR 589.
Sloman Neptun, Case C-72-73/91 [1993] ECR 887.
Société d' Importation Édouard Leclerc-Siplec v. TF1 Publicité SA and M6 Publicité SA, Case C-412/93 [1995] ECR I-179.
SPUC v. Grogan, Case C-155/90 [1991] ECR I-4685.
Steinike & Weinling v. Germany, Case 78/76 [1977] ECR 595.
Stichting Collectieve Antennevorziennning Gouda and Others, Case C-288/89 [1991] ECR I-4007.
The Queen v. The Immigration Appeal Tribunal, ex parte Gustaff Desiderius Antonissen, Case C-292/89 [1991] ECR 745.
TV 10 SA v. Commissariaat voor de Media, Case C-23/93 [1994] ECR I-4794.
Van Binsbergen v. Bestuur van de Bedrifsverniging voor de Metaalnijverheid, Case 33/74 [1974] ECR 1299.
Van der Kooy, Case 67-68/85 and 70/85 [1988] ECR 219
Van Tiggele, Case 82/77 [1978] ECR 25.
Vereniging Veronica Omroep Organisatie v. Commissariaat voor de Media, Case C-148/91 [1993] ECR I-487.
Viscido, Case C-52-54/97 [1998] ECR 2629.
VT4 v. Vlaamse Gemeenschap, Case C-56/96 [1997] ECR I-3143.
Webb, Case 279/80 [1981] ECR 3305; [1982] 1 CMLR 406.

EUROPEAN COURT OF FIRST INSTANCE

Denmark v. Commission, Case T-309/04, OJ C 262/43, 2004, not yet decided.
FFSA v. Commission, Case T-106/95 [1997] ECR II-229.
Gestevison Telecinco v. Commission, Case T-95/96 [1998] ECR II-3407.
Government of Gibraltar v. Commission, Joined Cases T-195/01 and T-207/01 [2002] ECR II-2309.
SIC v. Commission, Case T-46/97 [2000] ECR II-2125.

EFTA COURT

Joined Cases E-8/94 and E-9/94, *Forbrukerombudet v. Mattel Scandinavia and Lego Norge*, Judgment of 16 June 1995 <www.eftacourt.lu>, 26 November 2007.

EUROPEAN COURT OF HUMAN RIGHTS

Autronic AG, Judgment of 22 May 1990, Series A 178, No. 24.
Groppera Radio AG and Others, Judgment of 28 March 1990, Series A 173, No. 24.
Informationsverein Lentia and Others v. Austria, Judgment of 24 November 1993, Ser. A 276, No. 14.

Table of Legislation

FRANCE

1. Constitution

French Constitution of 4 October 1958 <www.assemblee-nationale.fr/english/8ab.asp>, 12 November 2007.

2. Laws

Law 77-808 of 19 July 1977 on the publication and diffusion of opinion polls, JO of 20 July 1977.

Law 82-652 of 29 July 1982 on audiovisual communication <www.csa.fr/upload/dossier/mai2007_loi86-1067.pdf>, 12 November 2007, 98.

Law 86-1067 of 30 September 1986 on freedom of communication <www.csa.fr/upload/dossier/mai2007_loi86-1067.pdf>, 12 November 2007, 1.

Law 99-1174 of 30 December 1999 on the creation of the parliamentary channel, JO Nr. 303 of 30 December 1999.

Law 2004-575 of 21 June 2004 on confidence in the digital economy, JO Nr. 143 of 22 June 2004.

3. Decrees

Decree 90-66 of 17 January 1990 on the diffusion of cinematographic and audiovisual works <www.csa.fr/infos/textes/textes_detail.php?id=5933>, 12 November 2007.

Decree 90-174 of 23 February 1990 on the classification of cinematographic works <www.csa.fr/infos/textes/textes_detail.php?id=9233>, 12 November 2007.

Decree 92-280 of 27 March 1992 on advertising, sponsorship and teleshopping <www.csa.fr/infos/textes/textes_detail.php?id=5934>, 12 November 2007.
Decree 2001-609 of 9 July 2001 on the contribution of analogue terrestrial television services to the development of the production of audiovisual and cinematographic works <www.csa.fr/infos/textes/textes_detail.php?id=8165>, 12 November 2007.
Decree 2007-1527 of 24 October 2007 on the right of reply in online communication services, JO Nr. 249 of 26 October 2007.

4. Decisions

Decision 2003-443 of 17 June 2003 sanctioning measures related to the protection of young viewers on France 2 and France 3, JO of 7 August 2003.

5. Miscellaneous

Electoral Code, modified by Law 2004-575 of 21 June 2004, JO of 22 June 2004.
Recommendation of 7 June 2005 on minimum age marking and programme classification <www.csa.fr/infos/textes/textes_detail.php?id=27943>, 12 November 2007.
Recommendation of 7 November 2006 on the presidential election on 6 May 2007, JO Nr. 262 of 11 November 2006.
Recommendation of 7 June 2006 to editors of television services on advertising practices in connection with the broadcasting of animated and fiction works directed at minors, JO Nr. 151 of 1 July 2006.
Recommendation of 4 July 2006 on the presentation on television of cinematographic or audiovisual works, video games, telephone and telematic services, and internet sites that may not be accessed by minors, JO Nr. 180 of 5 August 2006.

GERMANY

1. Constitution

Constitution for the Federal Republic of Germany of 23 May 1949, last modified on 28 August 2006, BGBl. I 1949, 1; 2006, 2034.

2. Laws

Law on Hessischen Rundfunk (HRG) of 2 October 1948, last modified by Law of 5 June 2007, GVBl. Hessen 1948, 123; 2007, 300.

Law on Parties (Parteiengesetz) of 24 July 1967, last modified by Law of 22 December 2004, BGBl. I 1994, 149; 2004, 3673.

Law on Westdeutschen Rundfunk Köln (WDR-G) of 31 March 1993, last modified by Law of 30 November 2004, GV. NRW of 17 December 2004, 770.

Law on the Interstate Treaty on the establishment of a common broadcaster for the Länder Berlin and Brandenburg (RBB) of 25 June 2002.

Law on the Protection of Minors (JuSchG) of 23 July 2002, last modified by Law of 20 July 2007, BGBl. I 2002, 2730; 2003, 476; 2007, 1595.

Law on Bayerischen Rundfunk (BayRG) of 22 October 2003, last modified on 11 December 2006, GVBl. 2003, 792; 2006, 1008.

Law on Telemedia (TMG) of 26 February 2007, BGBl. I 2007, 179.

3. Interstate Treaties

Interstate Treaty on Broadcasting and Telemedia (Rundfunkstaatsvertrag, RStV) of 31 August 1991, last modified by the 9. RfÄndStV of 1 March 2007, MP Dokumentation I/2007, 2.

Interstate Treaty on Financing (Rundfunkfinanzierungsstaatsvertrag, RFinStV) of 31 August 1991, last modified by the 9. RfÄndStV of 1 March 2007, MP Dokumentation I/2007, 55.

Interstate Treaty on the Licence Fee (Rundfunkgebührenstaatsvertrag, RGebStV) of 31 August 1991, last modified by the 9. RfÄndStV of 1 March 2007, MP Dokumentation I/2007, 49.

Interstate Treaty on the Protection of Human Dignity and of Minors (Jugendmedienschutz-Staatsvertrag, JMStV) of 10–27 September 2002, last modified by the 9. RfÄndStV of 1 March 2007, MP Dokumentation I/2007, 60.

ZDF-Interstate Treaty (ZDF-StV), last modified by the 9. RfÄndStV of 1 March 2007, MP Dokumentation I/2007, 31.

Interstate Treaty on Mitteldeutschen Rundfunk (MDR-StV) of 30 May 1991 <www.mdr.de/presse/unternehmen/114587.html>, 12 November 2007.

Interstate Treaty on Norddeutschen Rundfunk (NDR-StV) of 17–18. December 1991, GVOBl. M-V 1992, 77.

4. Guidelines

ARD Guidelines for the Protection of Minors of 22 June 1988, last modified on 16 June 2003 <www.br-online.de/br-intern/organisation/pdf/ard-richtlinie-jugendschutz.pdf>, 12 November 2007.

ARD Criteria for the Protection of Minors of 4 February 1997, last modified on 9 September 2003 <www.br-online.de/br-intern/organisation/pdf/ard-kriterien-jugendschutz.pdf>, 12 November 2007.

ARD Advertising Guidelines of 6 June 2000 <www.br-online.de/br-intern/organisation/pdf/ard-werberichtlinien.pdf>, 12 November 2007.

GREECE

1. Constitution

Greek Constitution of 1975, last modified in 2001, ΦΕΚ Α' 85/18 April 2001.

2. Laws

Law 1730/87 on ERT-S.A., last modified by Laws 1866/89 and 2173/93, ΦΕΚ Α' 145/18 August 1987.
Law 2251/94 on consumer protection, ΦΕΚ Α'191/16 November 1994.
Law 2328/95 on the legal regime for private television and local radio, and the regulation of matters pertaining to the audiovisual market and other provisions, ΦΕΚ Α' 159/03 August 1995.
Law 2644/98 on the provision of subscription radio and television services and similar provisions, ΦΕΚ Α' 233/13 October 1998.
Law 2863/2000 on the National Council for Radio and Television and other authorities and bodies for the provision of audiovisual services, last modified by Law 3051/2002, ΦΕΚ Α' 262/29 November 2000.
Law 3023/2002 of 21/25 June 2002 on the funding of political parties by the state, (2002) 50 *Kodikas Nomikou Bematos*, 1262.
Law 3051/2002 on the constitutionally anchored independent authorities, on the modification and completion of the system for appointments in the public sector and related provisions, ΦΕΚ Α' 220/20 September 2002.

3. Decrees

Common Ministerial Decree (K.Y.A.) Α.Π. 24/1 of 2 January 1997 on the free transmission of messages of social nature by radio and television stations, ΦΕΚ Β' 11/15 January 1997.
Presidential Decree 100/2000 on the harmonization of the Greek audiovisual legislation with the provisions of European Parliament and Council Directive 97/36/EC of 30 June 1997, ΦΕΚ Α' 98/17 March 2000.
Ministerial Decree 6138/E of 17 March 2000 on the classification and designation of television programmes, ΦΕΚ Β' 345/17 March 2000.
Common Ministerial Decree (K.Y.A.) 6140/1 of 16 March 2000 on the conditions for the allocation of broadcasting time on public and private television to political parties represented in the Hellenic Parliament in the course of the parliamentary elections of 9 April 2000, ΦΕΚ Β' 340/17 March 2000.
Presidential Decree 77/2003, Code of Conduct for News and Other Political Programmes, ΦΕΚ Α' 75/28 March 2003.
Presidential Decree 351 of 29/31 December 2003, (2003) 51 *Kodikas Nomikou Bematos*, 2406.

Common Ministerial Decree (K.Y.A.) 2846/E of 10 February 2004, ΦEK B' 343/12 February 2004.

4. Decisions

NCRTV Decision 205 of 2 April 2002 on 'Big Brother' <www.esr.gr>, 12 November 2007.
NCRTV Decision 7 of 27 January 2004 on political pluralism <www.esr.gr>, 12 November 2007.
NCRTV Decision 229 of 20 July 2004 on surreptitious advertising <www.esr.gr>, 12 November 2007.
NCRTV Decision 92 of 21 February 2006 on 'Big Brother' <www.esr.gr>, 12 November 2007.
NCRTV Decision 144 of 27 March 2006 on 'Big Brother' <www.esr.gr>, 12 November 2007.

5. NCRTV Deontology Codes

NCRTV Reg. 1/1991, Code of Journalistic Deontology, ΦEK B' 421/21 June 1991.
NCRTV Reg. 2/1991, Code for Radio and Television Programmes, ΦEK B' 421/ 21 June 1991.
NCRTV Reg. 3/1991, Deontology Code for Television Advertising, ΦEK B' 538/ 18 July 1991.
NCRTV Reg. 4/1991 on the Submission and Examination of Complaints, ΦEK B' 768/20 September 1991.

6. NCRTV Directives

NCRTV Directive 1/2001 of 20 March 2001 on the protection of minors from harmful audiovisual material in news and current affairs programmes <www.esr.gr/odigies.php>, 12 November 2007.
NCRTV Directive 7/2002 of 3 December 2002 on the transmission of advertisements for childrens' toys in the Christmas period <www.esr.gr/odigies.php>, 12 November 2007.
NCRTV Directive 2/2003 of 14 April 2003 on the protection of underage viewers of or participants in news and current affairs programmes <www.esr.gr/odigies.php>, 12 November 2007.
NCRTV Directive 6 of 16 February 2004 on impartiality and quality in news and current affairs programmes <www.esr.gr/odigies.php>, 12 November 2007.
NCRTV Directive 1 of 21 February 2006 on political pluralism <www.esr.gr/odigies.php>, 12 November 2007.

7. Miscellaneous

NCRTV, internal document 385EΣ of 30 March 2005.

Hellenic Advertising and Communication Code of 24 February 1977, in I. K. Karakostas, A. D. Tsevas, *E Nomothesia ton MME* (2nd edn, Athens, Ant. N. Sakkoulas, 2003), p. 1034.

ITALY

1. Constitution

Italian Constitution of 27 December 1947, *Gazzetta Ufficiale* Nr. 298 of 27 December 1947.

2. Laws

Law 103 of 14 April 1975, New standards for radio and television broadcasting, *Gazzetta Ufficiale* Nr. 102 of 17 April 1975.

Law 10 of 4 February 1985 transposing 'law decree 807' of 6 December 1984 on urgent dispositions in the area of television broadcasting, *Gazzetta Ufficiale* Nr. 30 of 5 February 1985.

Law 223 of 6 August 1990 regulating public and private broadcasting (*Mammì Law*), *Gazzetta Ufficiale* Nr. 185 of 9 August 1990.

Law 203 of 30 May 1995 on the reordering of functions in the field of tourism, spectacles and sport, *Gazzetta Ufficiale* Nr. 124 of 30 May 1995.

Law 249 of 31 July 1997 setting up the Italian Communications Guarantee Authority and introducing regulations of the telecommunications and broadcasting systems (*Maccanico Law*), *Gazzetta Ufficiale* Nr. 177 of 31 July 1997.

Law 28 of 22 February 2000, Provisions about equality of access to the information media during the electoral and referendum campaigns and about political communication (*Par Condicio Law*), *Gazzetta Ufficiale* Nr. 43 of 22 February 2000.

Law 112 of 3 May 2004, Regulations and principles governing the set-up of the broadcasting system and the RAI-Radiotelevisione Italiana Spa, as well as authorizing the government to issue a consolidated Broadcasting Act (*Gasparri Law*), *Gazzetta Ufficiale* Nr. 104 of 5 May 2004.

Law 37 of 6 February 2006 on amendments to Article 10 of Law 112 of 3 May 2004, relating to the protection of minors in television programming, *Gazzetta Ufficiale* Nr. 38 of 15 February 2006.

3. Decrees

Legislative Decree 74 of 25 January 1992 on misleading and comparative advertising, *Gazzetta Ufficiale* Nr. 36 of 13 February 1992.

Presidential Decree of 28 March 1994 approving the licence convention between the State and RAI-Radiotelevisione Italiana S.p.a, *Gazzetta Ufficiale* Nr. 188 of 12 August 1994.
Legislative Decree 259 of 1 August 2003, Code on electronic communications, *Gazzetta Ufficiale* Nr. 214 of 15 September 2003.
Legislative Decree 28 of 22 January 2004 on the reform of the rules relating to cinematographic activity on the basis of Article 10 of Law 137 of 6 July 2002, *Gazzetta Ufficiale* Nr. 29 of 5 February 2004.
Legislative Decree 177 of 31 July 2005, Consolidated broadcasting law, *Gazzetta Ufficiale* Nr. 208 of 7 September 2005.
Legislative Decree 206 of 6 September 2005 on the Consumer Code, *Gazzetta Ufficiale* Nr. 235 of 8 October 2005.

4. Decisions

Parliamentary Commission for the Communication Services, Decision of 21 June 2000, *Political communication and self-managed communication spaces in the programming of the concessionary society for public service broadcasting* <www.camera.it>, 13 November 2007.
AGCOM, Decision 200/00/CSP of 22 June 2000, *Provisions for the implementation of the rules relating to political communication and equal access to the media in non-electoral periods, Gazzetta Ufficiale* Nr. 152 of 1 July 2000.

5. Miscellaneous

Code of advertising self-regulation of 12 May 1966 <www.iap.it/en/codice.htm>, 13 November 2007.
Code TV and Minors of 29 November 2002 <www.comitatotveminori.it>, 13 November 2007.
Licence Convention between the Ministry of Communications and RAI-Radiotelevisione Italiana S.p.a, approved by Presidential Decree of 5 April 2007.

THE NETHERLANDS

1. Constitution

Constitution of 24 August 1815, Stb. 1815, 45.

2. Laws

Media Act of 21 April 1987, last modified on 1 July 2007, Stb. 1987, 249.

3. Decrees

Media Decree of 19 November 1987, last modified on 13 November 2007, Stb. 1987, 573.

4. Miscellaneous

CvdM, Policy Rules for Programme Quotas, 1 December 2006 <www.cvdm.nl/pages/regelgeving.asp?m=r&>, 13 November 2007.

Advertising Code <www.reclamecode.nl/bijlagen/rcc_code.pdf>, 13 November 2007.

Advertising Code for Games of Chance offered by Licensees of 15 February 2006, by virtue of the Games of Chance Act of 15 February 2006 <www.reclamecode.nl/bijlagen/rcc_code.pdf>, 13 November 2007.

Advertising Code for Tobacco Products of 7 November 2002 <www.reclamecode.nl/bijlagen/rcc_code.pdf>, 13 November 2007.

Telemarketing Code of 2 December 2003 <www.reclamecode.nl/bijlagen/rcc_code.pdf>, 13 November 2007.

Advertising Code for Food Products of 2 June 2005 <www.reclamecode.nl/bijlagen/rcc_code.pdf>, 13 November 2007.

Code of Conduct of the Dutch Society of Chief Editors <www.genootschapvan-hoofdredacteuren.nl/>, 13 November 2007.

UNITED KINGDOM

1. Laws

Broadcasting Act of 1990.

Broadcasting Act of 1996.

Communications Act of 2003.

2. Guidelines

BBC Editorial Guidelines, July 2005 <www.bbc.co.uk/guidelines/editorialguidelines/>, 13 November 2007.

BBC Trust, *BBC Protocol: D4-Editorial Standards*, January 2007 <www.bbc.co.uk/bbctrust/>, 13 November 2007.

3. Miscellaneous

Royal Charter for the Continuance of the British Broadcasting Corporation, October 2006, Cm. 6925.

Agreement dated July 2006 between Her Majesty's Secretary of State for Culture, Media and Sport and the British Broadcasting Corporation, Cm. 6872.

Copy of the Amendment dated 4 December 2003 to the Agreement of 25 January 1996 (as amended) between Her Majesty's Secretary of State for Culture, Media and Sport and the British Broadcasting Corporation, Cm. 6075.

Ofcom, Broadcasting Code, 25 July 2005 <www.ofcom.org.uk/tv/ifi/codes/bcode/>, 13 November 2007.

BCAP, Television Advertising Standards Code, 13 March 2007 <www.bcap.org.uk>, 13 November 2007.

BCAP, Rules on Scheduling of Television Advertisements, 13 March 2007 <www.cap.org.uk>, 13 November 2007.

EUROPEAN UNION

1. Treaties

Protocol on the System of Public Broadcasting in the Member States, OJ C 340/109, 1997.

Charter of Fundamental Rights of the European Union of 7 December 2000, OJ C 364/01, 2000.

Treaty on European Union, OJ C325/1, 2002.

Treaty Establishing the European Community, OJ C325/1, 2002.

Treaty Establishing a Constitution for Europe of 29 October 2004, OJ C 310, 2004.

2. Community Acts
Commission

Communications

COM (84) 300 final Television without Frontiers. Green Paper on the establishment of the Common Market for broadcasting, especially by satellite and cable, 14 June 1984.

COM (86) 146/2 final Proposal for a Council Directive on the coordination of certain provisions laid down by law, regulation or administrative action in Member States concerning the pursuit of broadcasting activities (submitted to the Council by the Commission), 29 April 1986.

COM (92) 480 final Green Paper on Pluralism and Media Concentration in the Internal Market. An assessment of the need for Community action, 23 December 1992.

COM (94) 57 final Communication from the Commission to the Council and the European Parliament on the application of Articles 4 and 5 of Directive 89/552/ Television without Frontiers, 3 March 1994.

COM (94) 96 final Green Paper, Strategy Options to Strengthen the European Programme Industry in the Context of the Audiovisual Policy of the European Union, 6 April 1994.

COM (94) 356 final European Community action in support of culture, 27 July 1994.

COM (95) 86 final Report on application of Directive 89/552/EEC and Proposal for a European Parliament and Council Directive amending Council Directive 89/552/EEC on the coordination of certain provisions laid down by law, regulation or administrative action in Member States concerning the pursuit of television broadcasting activities, 31 May 1995.

COM (96) 52 final Cohesion Policy and Culture. A contribution to employment, 20 November 1996.

COM (96) 160 final 1st Report on the Consideration of Cultural Aspects in European Community Action, 17 April 1996.

COM (96) 302 final Communication from the Commission to the Council and the European Parliament on the application of Articles 4 and 5 of Directive 89/552/EEC "TwF", 15 July 1996.

COM (96) 443 final Services of General Interest in Europe, 11 September 1996.

COM (96) 512 final Cohesion Policy and Culture. A contribution to employment, 20 November 1996.

COM (97) 523 final 2nd Report from the Commission to the Council, the European Parliament and the Economic and Social Committee on the application of Directive 89/552/EEC 'Television without Frontiers', 24 October 1997.

COM (97) 563 final Towards a Europe of Knowledge, 12 November 1997.

COM (97) 623 final Green Paper on the Convergence of the Telecommunications, Media and Informational Technology Sectors, and the Implications for Regulation: Towards an Information Society Approach, 3 December 1997.

COM (98) 199 final Third Communication from the Commission to the Council and the European Parliament on the application of Articles 4 and 5 of Directive 89/552/EEC 'Television without Frontiers' for the period 1995–1996, 3 April 1998.

COM (98) 266 final First European Community Framework Programme in Support of Culture (2000–2004), 6 May 1998.

COM (99) 371 final Communication from the Commission to the Council, the European Parliament and the Economic and Social Committee, Study on Parental Control of Television Broadcasting, 19 July 1999.

COM (99) 657 final Principles and guidelines for the Community's audiovisual policy in the digital age, 14 December 1999.

COM (2000) 442 final Fourth Communication from the Commission to the Council and the European Parliament on the application of Articles 4 and 5 of Directive 89/552/EEC 'Television without Frontiers' for the period 1997–1998, 17 July 2000.

Communication from the Commission on the application of state aid rules to public service broadcasting, OJ C320/5, 2001.

COM (2002) 778 final Fourth Report from the Commission to the Council, the European Parliament, thc Economic and Social Committee and the Committee of the Regions on the application of Directive 89/552/EEC 'Television without Frontiers', 6 January 2003.

COM (2003) 784 final Communication from the Commission to the Council, the European Parliament, the European Economic and Social Committee and the Committee of the Regions, The Future of European Regulatory Audiovisual Policy, 15 December 2003.

COM (2004) 469 final Proposal for a Decision of the European Parliament and of the Council establishing the Culture 2007 Programme (2007–2013), 14 July 2004.

COM (2004) 524 final Sixth Commission communication on the application of Articles 4 and 5 of Directive 89/552/EEC 'Television without Frontiers', as amended by Directive 97/36/EC, for the period 2001–2002, 28 July 2004.

COM (2004) 1450 final Interpretative communication on certain aspects of the provisions on televised advertising in the 'Television without Frontiers' Directive, 28 April 2004.

COM (2005) 646 final Explanatory Memorandum to the Proposal for a Directive of the European Parliament and of the Council amending Council Directive 89/552/EEC on the coordination of certain provisions laid down by law, regulation or administrative action in Member States concerning the pursuit of television broadcasting activities, 13 December 2005.

COM (2006) 35 final White Paper on a European Communication Policy, 1 February 2006.

COM (2006) 49 final Fifth Report from the Commission to the Council, the European Parliament, the European Economic and Social Committee and the Committee of the Regions on the application of Directive 89/552/EEC 'Television without Frontiers', 10 February 2006.

COM (2006) 459 final Seventh Commission communication on the application of Articles 4 and 5 of Directive 89/552/EEC 'Television without Frontiers', as amended by Directive 97/36/EC, for the period 2003–2004, 14 August 2006.

COM (2007) 170 final Amended proposal for a Directive of the European Parliament and of the Council amending Council Directive 89/552/EEC on the coordination of certain provisions laid down by law, regulation or administrative action in Member States concerning the pursuit of television broadcasting activities ('Audiovisual media services without frontiers'), 29 March 2007.

COM (2007) 242 final Commission Communication on a European agenda for culture in a globalizing world, 10 May 2007.

COM (2007) 452 final Sixth Report from the Commission to the European Parliament, the Council, the European Economic and Social Committee and the Committee of the Regions on the application of Directive 89/552/EEC 'Television without Frontiers', 24 October 2007.

COM (2007) 639 final Communication from the Commission to the European Parliament pursuant to the second subparagraph of Article 251 (2) of the EC Treaty concerning the Common Position of the Council on the adoption of a proposal for a Directive of the European Parliament and of the Council amending Council Directive 89/552/EEC on the coordination of certain provisions laid down by law, regulation or administrative action in Member States concerning the pursuit of television broadcasting activities ('Audiovisual Media Services Directive'), 18 October 2007.

Regulations

Commission Regulation (EC) No. 794/2004 of 21 April 2004 implementing Council Regulation (EC) No. 659/1999 laying down detailed rules for the application of Article 93 of the EC Treaty, OJ L 140/1, 2004.

Directives

Commission Directive 2005/81/EC of 28 November 2005 amending Directive 80/723/EEC on the transparency of financial relations between Member States and public undertakings, OJ L 312/47, 2005.

Decisions

Case IV/31.851, 21 March 1989, *Magill TV Guide* [1989], OJ L 78/43, 1989.
Case NN141/95, 7 November 1996, *Financing of the Public Portuguese Television*, OJ C 67/7, 1997.
Case 97/606/EC, 6 September 1997, *VTM* [1997], OJ L 244/18, 1997.
Case NN 70/98, 22 March 1999, *Kinderkanal/Phoenix*, OJ C238/3, 1999.
Case NN 88/98, 14 December 1999, *BBC 24-Hour News Channel*, OJ C 78/6, 2000.
Case NN 133/A/01, NN85/A/01 and NN 94/A/99, 23 April 2002, *Compensation Indemnities to Public Service Broadcaster RTP*, OJ C 98/1, 2002.
Case N 631/2001, 22 May 2002, *Nine Digital Services*, OJ C 23/6, 2003.
Case N 548/2001, 13 February 2002, *Local Belgium TV Stations*, OJ C 150/7, 2002.
Case N 37/2003, 1 October 2003, *BBC Digital Curriculum*, OJ C 271/47, 2003.
Case 2004/339/EC, 23 April 2004, *Ad-hoc Measures for RAI SpA*, OJ L 119/1, 2004.
Case C 2/03 (ex NN 22/02), 19 May 2004, *State Financing of TV2/Danmark*, OJ L 85/1, 2006.
Case N 313/2004, 6 October 2004, *Recapitalisation of TV2/Danmark A/S*, OJ C 172/3, 2005.
Case E 3/2005, 24 April 2007, *Financing of public service broadcasters in Germany*, OJ C185/1, 2007.
Case E 8/2005, 20 April 2005, *Ayuda estatal en favour del Ente Público Españde Televisión (RTVE)*, OJ C 239/17, 2006.
Case E 9/2005, 20 April 2005, *Canone di abonamento Rai*, OJ C 235/3, 2005.
Case E 10/2005 (ex C 60/1999), 20 April 2005, *Redevance radiodiffusion*, OJ C 240/20, 2005.

Miscellaneous

A people's Europe: reports from the ad hoc committee, Bulletin of the European Communities, Supplement 7/85.

Commission of the European Communities, Commission staff working paper on certain legal aspects relating to cinematographic and other audiovisual works, 11 April 2001, SEC (2001) 619.

European Commission, Commission Staff Working Paper: Media Pluralism in the Member States of the European Union, SEC (2006), 42.

Commission, Background Document 3 – Application of Articles 4 and 5 in each Member State, SEC (2006) 1073.

Commission, Background Document 6 – List of television channels in the European Union Member States which failed to achieve the majority proportion according to Article 4, SEC (2006) 1073.

Commission Staff Working Document, Background Documents to the Seventh Commission communication of 14 August 2006 on the application of Articles 4 and 5 of Directive 89/552/EEC 'Television without Frontiers', as amended by Directive 97/36/EC, for the period 2003–2004, SEC (2006) 1073.

Modified Commission proposal after political agreement on common position of 24 May 2007 <www.ec.europa.eu/information_society/newsroom/cf/itemlongdetail.cfm?item_id=3430>, 10 July 2007.

COUNCIL

Regulations

Council Regulation 3911/92/EEC of 9 December 1992 on the export of cultural goods, OJ L 395/1, 1992.

Council Regulation 659/1999 of 22 March 1999 laying down detailed rules for the application of Article 93 of the EC Treaty, OJ L 83/1, 1999.

Directives

Council Directive 84/450/EEC of 10 September 1984 relating to the approximation of the laws, regulations and administrative provisions of the Member States concerning misleading advertising, OJ L 250/17, 1984.

Council Directive 89/552/EEC of 3 October 1989 on the coordination of certain provisions laid down by law, regulation or administrative action in Member States concerning the pursuit of television broadcasting activities, OJ L 298/23, 1989.

Council Directive 93/7/EEC of 15 March 1993 on the return of cultural objects unlawfully removed from the territory of a Member State, OJ L 74/74, 1993.

Council Directive 93/83/EEC of 27 September 1993 on the coordination of certain rules concerning copyright and rights related to copyright applicable to satellite broadcasting and cable retransmission, OJ L 248/15, 1993.

European Parliament and Council Directive 97/36/EC of 30 June 1997 amending Council Directive 89/552/EEC on the coordination of certain provisions laid down by law, regulation and administrative action in Member States concerning the pursuit of television broadcasting activities, OJ L 202/60, 1997.

European Parliament and Council Directive 98/34 of 22 June 1998 laying down a procedure for the provision of information in the field of technical standards and regulations, OJ L 204/37, 1998.

European Parliament and Council Directive 2003/31/EC of 8 June 2000 on certain legal aspects of information society services, in particular electronic commerce, in the Internal Market (Directive on electronic commerce), OJ L 178/1, 2000.

European Parliament and Council Directive 2002/21/EC of 7 March 2002 on a common regulatory framework for electronic communications networks and services (Framework Directive), OJ L 108/33, 2002.

Decisions

European Parliament and Council Decision 508/2000/EC of 14 February 2000 establishing the Culture 2000 Programme, OJ L 63/1, 2000.

Council Framework Decision 2004/68/JHA of 22 December 2003 on combating the sexual exploitation of children and child pornography, OJ L13/44, 2004.

European Parliament and Council Decision 1855/2006/EC of 12 December 2006 establishing the Culture Programme (2007–2013), OJ L 372/1, 2006.

Recommendations

Council Recommendation 98/560/EC of 24 September 1998 on the development of the competitiveness of the European audiovisual and information services industry by promoting national frameworks aimed at achieving a comparable and effective level of protection of minors and human dignity, OJ L 270/48, 1998 II.

Recommendation of the European Parliament and of the Council of 20 December 2006 on the protection of minors and human dignity and on the right of reply in relation to the competitiveness of the European audiovisual and on-line information services industry, OJ L 378/72, 2006.

Miscellaneous

Common position (EC) No. 49/96 adopted by the Council on 8 July 1996 with a view to adopting Directive 96/ . . . /EC of the European Parliament and of the Council amending Council Directive 89/552/EEC on the coordination of certain provisions laid down by law, regulation or administrative action in Member States concerning the pursuit of television broadcasting activities, OJ C 264/52, 1996.

Council general approach of 13 November 2006, doc. 14616/06 <www.register.consilium.europa.eu/pdf/en/06/st14/st14616.en06.pdf>, 12 October 2007.

Common position adopted by the Council with a view on 15 October 2007 to the adoption of a Directive of the European Parliament and of the Council amending Council Directive 89/552/EEC on the coordination of certain provisions laid down by law, regulation or administrative action in Member States concerning the pursuit of television broadcasting activities <www.register.consilium.europa.eu/pdf/en/07/st10/st10076-re06.en07.pdf>, 26 November 2007.

European Parliament

Documents

Report on radio and television broadcasting in the European Community, Document 1-1013/81, OJ C 87/110, 1982. (Hahn Report I).

Report by Mr. José Escudero (PPE, E) on culture: consideration of cultural aspects in the European Community action COS/1996/2075.

Resolutions

Resolution of 12 March 1982 on radio and television broadcasting in the European Community, OJ C 87/110, 1982.

Resolution of 30 March 1984 on a policy commensurate with new trends in European television, OJ C 117/201, 1984.

Resolution A3-0139/92 of 15 May 1992 on education and training policy in the run-up to 1993, OJ C 150/366, 1992.

Committee of the Regions

Opinion of the Committee of the Regions on the 'Proposal for a decision of the European Parliament and of the Council establishing the Culture 2007 Programme (2007–2013)', (2005/C 164/08).

Council of Europe

European Convention for the Protection of Human Rights and Fundamental Freedoms of 4 November 1950, ETS Nr. 5, 213.

European Convention on Transfrontier Television of 5 May 1989, 28 ILM 857 (1989).
Protocol amending the European Convention on Transfrontier Television of 1 October 1998, ETS Nr. 171.
Protocol Nr. 11 amending the European Convention for the Protection of Human Rights and Fundamental Freedoms of 1 November 1998, ETS Nr. 155.

World Trade Organization

General Agreement on Tariffs and Trade, 30 October 1947, (1947) 55 UNTS 187.
General Agreement on Tariffs and Trade, 15 April 1994, Marrakech Agreement Establishing the World Trade Organization, Annex 1A, (1994) 33 ILM 1153.
Marrakech Agreement Establishing the World Trade Organization, 15 April 1994, Final Act Embodying the Results of the Uruguay Round of Multilateral Trade Negotiations, (1994) 33 ILM 1140.
General Agreement on Trade in Services, 15 April 1994, (1994) 33 ILM 1167.

Index

Introductory Note

References such as '101–9' indicate (not necessarily continuous) discussion of a topic across a range of pages. Wherever possible, topics with many references have been divided into sub-topics or the most significant references are highlighted in bold. Because the entire volume is about the European Union and broadcasting (especially television), the use of these and certain related terms as entry points has been minimized.

B

D

E

G

H

I

INFORMATION LAW SERIES

1. Egbert J. Dommering (ed.) *Protecting Works of Fact: Copyright, Freedom of Expression and Information Law,* 1991 (ISBN 90-654-4567-6).
2. W.F. Korthals Altes, *Information Law Towards the 21st Century*, 1992 (ISBN 90-654-4627-3).
3. Jacqueline Seignette, *Challenges to Creator Doctrine, Authorship, Copyright Ownership*, 1994 (ISBN 90-654-4876-4).
4. P. Bernt Hugenholtz, *The Future of Copyright in a Digital Environment*, 1996 (ISBN 90-411-0267-1).
5. Julius C.S. Pinckaers, *From Privacy Toward a New Intellectual Property Right in Persona*, 1996 (ISBN 90-411-0355-4).
6. Jan J.C. Kabel & Gerard J.H.M. Mom, *Intellectual Property and Information Law: Essays in Honour of Herman Cohen Jehoram*, 1998 (ISBN 90-411-9702-8).
7. Ysolde Gendreau, Axel Nordemann & Rainer Oesch (eds), *Copyright and Photographs: An International Survey*, 1999 (ISBN 90-411-9722-2).
8. P. Bernt Hugenholtz, *Copyright and Electronic Commerce: Legal Aspects of Electronic Copyright Management*, 2000 (ISBN 90-411-9785-0).
9. Lucie Guibault, *Copyright Limitations and Contracts: An Analysis of the Contractual Overridability of Limitations on Copyright*, 2002 (ISBN 90-411-9867-9).
10. Lee A. Bygrave, *Data Protection Law: Approaching its Rationale, Logic and Limits*, 2002 (ISBN 90-411-9870-9).
11. Niva Elkin-Koren & Neil Weinstock Netanel, *The Commodification of Information*, 2002 (ISBN 90-411-9876-8).
12. Mireille van Eechoud, *Choice of Law in Copyright and Related Rights: Alternatives to the Lex Protectionis*, 2003 (ISBN 90-411-2071-8).
13. Martin Senftleben, *Copyright, Limitations and the Three-Step Test*, 2004 (ISBN 90-411-2267-2).
14. Paul Torremans, *Copyright and Human Rights*, 2004 (ISBN 90-411-2278-8).
15. Natalie Helberger, *Controlling Access to Content: Regulating Conditional Access in Digital Broadcasting*, 2005 (ISBN 90-411-2345-8).
16. Lucie Guibault & P. Bernt Hugenholtz (eds), *The Future of Public Domain: Identifying the Commons in Information Law*, 2006 (ISBN 978-90-411-2435-7).
17. Irini Katsirea, *Public Broadcasting and European Law: A Comparative Examination of Public Service Obligations in Six Member States*, 2008 (ISBN 978-90-411-2500-2).